ARCO GOLD
THE MASTER SERIES LSAT

2005

Thomas H. Martinson

THOMSON
PETERSON'S

Australia • Canada • Mexico • Singapore • Spain • United Kingdom • United States

About The Thomson Corporation and Peterson's
With revenues of US$7.8 billion, The Thomson Corporation (www.thomson.com) is a leading
global provider of integrated information solutions for business, education, and professional
customers. Its Learning businesses and brands (www.thomsonlearning.com) serve the
needs of individuals, learning institutions, and corporations with products and services for
both traditional and distributed learning.

Peterson's, part of The Thomson Corporation, is one of the nation's most respected providers
of lifelong learning online resources, software, reference guides, and books. The Education
Supersite^{SM} at www.petersons.com—the Internet's most heavily traveled education resource—has searchable databases and interactive tools for contacting U.S.-accredited
institutions and programs. In addition, Peterson's serves more than 105 million education
consumers annually.

For more information, contact Peterson's, 2000 Lenox Drive, Lawrenceville, NJ 08648;
800-338-3282; or find us on the World Wide Web at www.petersons.com/about.

Editor: Mandie Rosenberg; Production Editor: Teresina Jonkoski; Manufacturing Manager:
Ray Golaszewski; Composition Manager: Michele Able; Interior and Cover Design: Allison
Sullivan; CD Producer: Carol Aickley; CD Quality Assurance: Jeff Pagano

ISBN (book only): 0-7689-1471-X
ISBN (book with CD-ROM): 0-7689-1470-1

Printed in the United States of America

10 9 8 7 6 5 4 3 2 1   05   04 03

Contents

PART I: LSAT BASICS

Contents

Before You Begin

HOW THIS BOOK WILL HELP YOU

Taking the LSAT is a skill. It shares some things in common with other skills, such as playing basketball or singing opera. These are skills that can be improved by coaching, but ultimately improvement also requires practice. This book gives you both.

- "The Top 10 Ways to Raise Your Score" gives you a preview of some of the critical strategies you'll learn. "Track your Progress" is where you'll record your scores on the Diagnostic and Practice Tests as you work through the book.

- Part I provides essential general information about taking the LSAT. You'll learn how to register for the test, what kinds of questions to expect, and how the test is scored. You'll also find out how to make the most of whatever time you have to study.

- Part II is a full-length Diagnostic Test. It can show you where your skills are strong—and where they need some shoring up. Record your score in "Track Your Progress."

- Part III is the coaching program. The chapters in this part analyze each question type and give you powerful strategies for taking the test on its own terms.

- Part IV contains three full-length practice LSATs. Record your scores in "Track Your Progress." Each test is followed by a detailed analysis of each question. The detailed analysis is very important because it helps you learn from your mistakes.

ABOUT THE AUTHOR

Professor Thomas H. Martinson is widely acknowledged to be America's leading authority on test preparation. A graduate of Harvard Law School and a member of the New York State and Washington, D.C., bars, Professor Martinson has published more than three dozen books on test preparation. He is routinely invited to lecture on test preparation and related topics at top colleges and universities throughout the United States and abroad.

THE TOP 10 WAYS TO RAISE YOUR SCORE

When it comes to taking the LSAT, some test-taking skills will do you more good than others.

There are concepts you can learn, techniques you can follow, and tricks you can use that will give you the biggest "bang for your buck." Here's our pick of the Top 10.

1 **Make a study plan and follow it.** The LSAT study plan will help you get the most out of this book in whatever time you have. See Chapter 1.

2 **Learn the directions in advance.** If you already know the directions, you won't have to waste precious test time reading them. You'll be able to jump right in and start answering questions as soon as the test clock starts. See Chapter 2.

3 **If you don't know the answer, always make a guess.** On the LSAT, it's to your advantage to answer every question. If you can make an educated guess by eliminating one or more answer choices, so much the better. See Chapter 2.

4 **In logical reasoning questions, start by finding the conclusion.** Since the conclusion is the main point of the argument, it's the key to answering every question of this type. See Chapter 5.

5 **In logical reasoning questions, use circle diagrams to define relationships.** When a problem asks you to deduce how certain terms are related, a circle diagram can make the relationship clear. See Chapter 5.

6 **In reading comprehension, read for structure, not details.** When you read LSAT passages, don't let the details bog you down. Most of the questions will ask about the structure of the passage rather than specific facts. If you need the facts, they're always there in the passage. See Chapter 6.

7 **In reading comprehension, there are really only six kinds of questions.** Identify the type of question asked and you're halfway to finding the correct answer. See Chapter 6.

8 **For analytical reasoning questions, set up a "bookkeeping" system to summarize the information.** Use your own notational devices or adapt the ones shown in this book. See Chapter 7.

9 **For analytical reasoning questions, treat each question separately.** In these "puzzle" sets, don't use new information supplied in any question to answer any other question in the set. But see Chapter 7 for "What the Smartest Test-Takers Know—Breaking News on Puzzles."

10 **For the writing sample, don't try to do too much.** It's better to write a short but balanced and structurally complete essay than one that you have to cut off in the middle because you've run out of time. See Chapter 8.

TRACK YOUR PROGRESS

For each exam:

1. Enter the number of questions that you answered correctly in each section in the appropriate row. Experimental sections are NOT scored.

2. Enter the total number of questions that you answered correctly for that exam in the "TOTAL" row.

3. Enter your score for the exam in the "SCORE" row using the chart below.

4. Enter the appropriate data from the top part of the table into the rows in the second part of the table to keep track of your progress in each of the three content areas.

LSAT SCORE TRACKER

	Diagnostic Examination (Number Correct)	Practice Test 1 (Number Correct)	Practice Test 2 (Number Correct)	Practice Test 3 (Number Correct)
Section 1			Experimental	
Section 2	Experimental			
Section 3				
Section 4		Experimental		Experimental
Section 5				
TOTAL				
SCORE				

Content Areas—Raw Subscores
(Enter data from above)

Logical Reasoning	Sec. 3 + Sec. 4 =	Sec. 1+ Sec. 5 =	Sec. 2 + Sec. 5 =	Sec. 3 + Sec. 5 =
Analytical Reasoning	Sec. 1 =	Sec. 2 =	Sec. 3 =	Sec. 2 =
Reading	Sec. 5 =	Sec. 3 =	Sec. 4 =	Sec. 1 =

PART I

LSAT BASICS

Getting Started

OVERVIEW

- Can you prepare for the LSAT?
- What is an LSAT study plan?
- How can you tell if your work is paying off?

CAN YOU PREPARE FOR THE LSAT?

This is the question of the day. Can you indeed prepare for a test that purports to test your aptitude for success in law school rather than your mastery of any particular subject? Of course you can. The LSAT is long, and some of its questions are tough, but it's not unconquerable.

There are many ways to prepare and many tricks and tips to learn. One of the most important things to learn is to think like the test-makers so you can find the answers they have designated as best. Once you learn "LSAT thinking," you'll be more likely to pick the best answer—and up will go your score.

WHAT IS AN LSAT STUDY PLAN?

As you can tell, this book contains a lot of information about the LSAT, and you'll need a plan for getting through it. The right study plan will help you manage your time so that you get the most out of this book whether you have three months, three weeks, or only a few days to prepare. It will help you work efficiently and keep you from getting stressed out.

Choose the Plan That's Right for You

To decide on your study plan, answer these two questions: (1) How long do you have until the test? (2) How much time can you devote to LSAT study?

Here are some suggestions to make your job easier. If you are starting early and the LSAT is two or three months away, go for broke. Complete the book from beginning to end. If the LSAT is a month or less away and you need a more concentrated course, focus on the chapter exercises and Practice Tests.

chapter 1

Start with the tough stuff. To make the most of your study time, study the difficult sections first. If you run out of time later, you can just skim the sections that are easy for you.

HOW CAN YOU TELL IF YOUR WORK IS PAYING OFF?

No matter what plan you choose, you should start by taking the Diagnostic Test. After you score it, you'll be able to see where you need to concentrate your efforts. Note your scores in "Track Your Progress."

The next step is to see how you do with the exercises at the end of each chapter. Compare your scores to your results on the Diagnostic Test. Have you improved? Where do you still need work?

When you're ready, take the Practice Tests. These are just like the test you'll take, and you should try to simulate test conditions as nearly as you can. After you score a Practice Test, again note your scores in "Track Your Progress." Make another comparison to the chapter exercises and to the Diagnostic Test. This will show you how your work is paying off.

All about the LSAT

OVERVIEW
- What is the LSAT?
- How do you register for the LSAT?
- What kinds of questions are on the test?
- How is the test structured?
- What does the answer sheet look like?
- How is the test scored?
- What smart test-takers know

WHAT IS THE LSAT?

The Law School Admission Test (LSAT) is a half-day-long standardized exam that is required for admission by all law schools approved by the American Bar Association as well as by many Canadian law schools. It consists of six separately timed sections, five of which use multiple-choice questions; the sixth presents an essay topic. The essay portion is not scored.

The LSAT is given four times a year—in February, June, September, and December. Scores are reported to law schools by the Law School Data Assembly Service (LSDAS), which also forwards applicants' transcripts and biographical information.

According to the Law School Admission Council (LSAC), the consortium of law schools that owns and controls the LSAT, the test scores are designed to measure an applicant's ability to "read, understand, and reason" at a level required for success in law school. The LSAT is considered to be an "objective" measure, and that is very important to law school admissions officers. A law school's applicant pool is made up of candidates from many different undergraduate institutions, some with advanced degrees and others without, and each with a unique life history, but all have taken the LSAT. LSAT scores are the one objective measure that an admissions officer has.

For this reason, your LSAT score is very important. Simply stated, if your LSAT score is too low, you will be rejected. That is not to say, however, that a high LSAT score guarantees that you will be accepted. On the contrary, every year, top law schools reject a significant number of applicants with perfect or near-perfect LSAT scores. While it is a very important factor in the admissions process, the LSAT score is not the only factor. Law schools also consider grades, extracurricular activities, work experience, and other aspects of your background.

chapter 2

HOW DO YOU REGISTER FOR THE LSAT?

You must register in advance to take the LSAT; you cannot simply walk in on the day of the test. Registration materials for both the LSAT and the Law School Data Assembly Service are available either from your college's prelaw adviser or by writing to the following address:

Law School Admissions Services
Box 2000
Newtown, PA 18940-1001

You can also get information about the LSAT on line:

http://www.lsas.org

Regular registration requests must be postmarked approximately six weeks before the test. Late registration is also available.

Special arrangements can be made for the visually and physically disabled, for persons whose religious beliefs forbid taking the test on a Saturday, and for other persons with special needs. The key to making satisfactory arrangements is time. If you want to make any special arrangements for taking the LSAT, communicate immediately with the Law School Admissions Services at the address given above.

Most law schools require LSAT scores by December for admission the following fall. Because you must allow at least six weeks for your score to be reported, you might not receive September scores in time. Therefore, the June test date is recommended.

WHAT KINDS OF QUESTIONS ARE ON THE TEST?

The LSAT uses three different kinds of multiple-choice questions.

1 Reading Comprehension

Reading Comprehension questions are based on reading passages that are each approximately 450 words long. You will be asked to demonstrate your understanding of the passage by answering questions about the structure, meaning, and implications of the passage. Your Reading Comprehension section will have 26 to 28 questions.

2 Logical Reasoning

Logical Reasoning questions present an argument contained in a short paragraph. You are asked to demonstrate that you understand the argument by choosing an answer that describes the argument, weakens or strengthens it, identifies its premises, or states its conclusions or its implications. Your test will have two Logical Reasoning sections. Each section will have 24 to 26 questions.

3 Analytical Reasoning

Analytical Reasoning questions present a situation and some conditions. You will need to organize the conditions in order to answer the questions. Diagrams of

various sorts are almost sure to be helpful. When you talk to oth[er]
going to take the LSAT, they may refer to this section as the "lo[gic]
"logical puzzles." The number of questions is 22 to 24.

MYSTERY SECTION

Your LSAT will also include a mystery section. The Mystery Section is a
timed section that contains questions that will not be scored. These question[s]
in the experimental or testing phase.

WRITING SAMPLE

The Writing Sample is technically not a part of the LSAT. It is an essay exercise that
was added on. It is not scored, but copies of your essay response are sent to the law
schools.

HOW IS THE TEST STRUCTURED?

The order of sections in an LSAT varies. You might have Analytical Reasoning first and
Reading Comprehension last or vice versa or Reading Comprehension first and the
Mystery Section second or vice versa. Even at the same test administration, different
test booklets will have the sections arranged in different orders. Do not be concerned
about the order in which the question types are presented; just take them as they come.

The following table shows the structure of a typical LSAT.

ANATOMY OF A TYPICAL LSAT

Section	Number of Questions	Time Allowed
Logical Reasoning 1	24–26	35 min.
Reading Comprehension	27–28	35 min.
Analytical Reasoning	24–25	35 min.
Logical Reasoning 2	24–26	35 min.
Mystery Section	??	35 min.
Writing Sample	One Essay	30 min.

(Note: The order of the sections varies from administration to administration, and the Mystery
Section is not necessarily the last section of multiple-choice questions.)

You will not be told which is the Mystery Section, and you will probably not be able to
tell. So do your best on all test sections.

WHAT DOES THE ANSWER SHEET LOOK LIKE?

On the LSAT, your test materials come in two parts: a booklet of 30-odd pages
containing the test questions and an answer sheet covered with rows of lettered spaces

[...] on the
[...]d Wide Web. The
address is http://
www.lsas.org.

for your responses. The space for marking your answers to a section will look something like this:

$$15 \; Ⓐ \; Ⓑ \; Ⓒ \; Ⓓ \; Ⓔ$$

The answer sheet is graded by a machine that "reads" the marks you have made. Therefore, it is important to record your answers properly and neatly, completely filling each answer space with a dark pencil mark. Leave no stray marks on the answer sheet. Enter one, and only one, answer per question. Don't worry if the answer sheet has more blanks than your booklet has questions. Leave the extra spaces blank.

Take a look at these examples of properly and improperly recorded answers.

SECTION 1	SECTION 2
1 Ⓐ ● Ⓒ Ⓓ Ⓔ	1 Ⓐ Ⓑ Ⓒ Ⓓ Ⓔ
2 Ⓐ Ⓑ Ⓒ ● Ⓔ	2 Ⓐ Ⓒ Ⓓ Ⓔ
3 Ⓐ ● Ⓒ Ⓓ Ⓔ	3 Ⓐ Ⓑ ● Ⓓ ●
4 Ⓐ Ⓑ Ⓒ ● Ⓔ	4 Ⓐ Ⓑ Ⓒ Ⓓ Ⓔ
5 Ⓐ Ⓑ Ⓒ Ⓓ ●	5 Ⓐ Ⓑ Ⓒ Ⓓ Ⓔ
6 ● Ⓑ Ⓒ Ⓓ Ⓔ	6 Ⓐ Ⓑ Ⓒ ✗ Ⓔ
7 Ⓐ Ⓑ ● Ⓓ Ⓔ	7 Ⓐ Ⓑ Ⓒ Ⓓ Ⓔ

NOTE

Why does the LSAT use scaled scores?

Scaled scores allow the test-makers to account for differences from one version of the LSAT to another. Using scaled scores ensures that a score of, say, 165 on one LSAT is equivalent to 165 on another.

All of the answers in Section 1 are properly recorded. Each mark is black and completely fills the answer space, so the scoring machine is sure to read it correctly. In Section 2, the answer to question 1 is too light; the machine might not see it. The answer to question 2 is messy and covers two answer spaces; the machine will record this as an incorrect answer. In question 3, two answers are marked correctly, but there can be only one right answer; again, the machine will record this as an incorrect response. Question 4 will be treated in the same way since it has been left blank. Leaving it blank was a mistake. It should have been answered, even with a guess, because there is no penalty on the LSAT for wrong answers. Questions 6 and 7 have been marked with an "X" and a checkmark, respectively. Both answers will register as incorrect because neither mark totally fills the answer space.

The most common error in answer sheet management is misplacing an entire block of answers. This occurs when a test-taker skips a question in the test booklet but fails to skip a corresponding space on the answer sheet. The result is that the intended pattern of response is there, but it is displaced by one or more spaces. Unfortunately, the machine that grades the paper reads what actually is on the answer sheet—not what the test-taker intended.

HOW IS THE TEST SCORED?

The scoring system used by the LSAT is very simple: Each correct answer is worth +1 on the raw score; and, unlike some other exams that you may have taken (such as the SAT), there is no adjustment made for incorrect responses. The scoring system simply ignores wrong answers and omitted questions. *In other words, there is no guessing penalty.*

Because each form of the LSAT contains 100 or so questions (with no penalty for guessing), raw scores range from a theoretical minimum of 0 to a theoretical maximum of slightly more than 100. The bell-curve distribution of raw scores can vary slightly from test administration to test administration, so to keep test results comparable over time, scores are reported to law schools on a scale of 120 (the minimum) to 180 (the maximum). The following table gives you some idea of how many correct answers are needed for selected scaled scores.

SAMPLE SCORING TABLE

Correct/Score	Correct/Score	Correct/Score	Correct/Score
98+/180	77/164	56/152	35/138
97/179	76/163	55/151	34/137
96/178	75/163	54/151	33/137
95/177	74/162	53/150	32/136
94/176	73/162	52/150	31/135
93/175	72/161	51/149	30/134
92/174	71/161	50/148	29/133
91/173	70/160	49/148	28/132
90/173	69/159	48/147	27/132
89/172	68/159	47/146	26/131
88/171	67/158	46/145	25/130
87/170	66/158	45/144	24/129
86/170	65/157	44/144	23/128
85/169	64/157	43/143	22/127
84/168	63/156	42/143	21/126
83/168	62/156	41/142	20/125
82/167	61/155	40/142	19/124
81/167	60/154	39/141	18/123
80/166	59/154	38/141	17/122
79/165	58/153	37/140	16/121
78/164	57/152	36/139	15/120

The Writing Sample is not graded by LSAT and does not affect your LSAT score. Copies of your essay, however, are sent to each law school that you designate to receive an LSAT score report.

The Writing Sample is usually used as a "tie-breaker" or secondary credential of much less importance than the LSAT score. However, a very poor Writing Sample could seriously undermine an otherwise strong application at many schools. While a very strong Writing Sample will not equally redeem an otherwise weak application, it may be the deciding factor when your application is approximately as strong as someone else's.

WHAT SMART TEST-TAKERS KNOW

General Test Smarts

Change is always possible.

Be cautious regarding the test format. Some small adjustments are always possible, and you do not want to be caught off guard. When you are told to begin work on a section, take five or ten seconds to look through the pages of that section. If there are unexpected changes, you can readily adjust your plan of attack.

The LSAT takes concentration.

The LSAT is an arduous task. There is no way that you can maintain your concentration throughout all five of the 35-minute sections. There will be times when your attention begins to flag. Learn to recognize this. For example, if you find that you are reading and rereading the same line without understanding, put down your pencil, close your eyes, take a deep breath or two (or rub your eyes or whatever), and then get back to work.

Obsessing doesn't pay.

You're not going to be able to answer every question with supreme confidence. In fact, you may answer very few questions with confidence. That does not mean, however, that you are not doing well. In fact, answering even 75 percent of the questions correctly will earn you a 160 or so, which is above the 80th percentile.

Pacing

A watch can be an asset.

The proctors in charge of administering the test are supposed to keep you advised of the passing time, for example, by writing on a blackboard how many minutes remain. But you should not rely on their diligence. In the first place, it's easy for a proctor to forget to mark the passing time at exactly the right moment. So when you see the proctor write "5 minutes left," you might have only 4 minutes left or as many as 6 minutes left.

TIP

Set your watch to exam time. At the beginning of each test section, set your watch to 12 o'clock. Then all you have to do is glance quickly at the hands (or the readout of a digital watch) to see how much of the section has passed.

Further, the proctor might mark the correct time at the right moment without your knowledge. When you look up from your work you see "5 minutes left," but when did the proctor write that down? The solution is to have a watch with you. If you have a digital watch with a stopwatch function, you can use that. If your digital watch does not have a stopwatch function, write down the starting time for the section when you begin. Quickly add 35 minutes to that and write down the time you must finish. Circle that number for easy reference.

It's important to find the pace that's right for you.

The scoring mechanism for the LSAT is the simple formula "score = correct answers." No points are awarded for near misses, and no extra points are given for difficult questions. This means you have got to cover as much ground as possible.

On the one hand, you want to respond correctly to as many questions as you can in the 35 minutes; on the other hand, you cannot afford to be so careful that you begin to beat yourself by not answering enough questions to get a good score. There is a trade-off between speed and accuracy, one that only you can find through practice.

To demonstrate the necessity of the trade-off, consider the cases of three hypothetical students: Timmy Toocareful, Carl Careless, and Terry Testwise.

On his exam, Timmy Toocareful attempted only 65 questions, but he was very accurate. Of the 65, Timmy answered 60 correctly, missing only 5. In addition, he guessed at the remaining 35 questions, getting one fifth of those right (as expected) for another 7 points.

Carl Careless used the opposite strategy. He worked very quickly to ensure that he attempted all 100 questions, and he paid the price. Of the 100, he answered only 70 correctly.

Terry Testwise used the proper strategy of working as quickly as possible without unnecessarily sacrificing accuracy. Of the 100 questions, she attempted 85, missing 10. And she guessed at the other 15 questions, hitting one fifth of them (as expected) for another 3 points.

The score reports would show the following:

Timmy Toocareful:	Raw Score 67	Scaled Score 157
Carl Careless:	Raw Score 70	Scaled Score 159
Terry Testwise:	Raw Score 78	Scaled Score 165

Most students are probably prone to err on the side of caution. In this case, Timmy, fearful of answering incorrectly, doesn't attempt enough questions to get his best score. Since there is no penalty for answering incorrectly, don't be overly worried about mistakes. Of course you don't want to be needlessly careless, but it's probably better to go too quickly than too slowly.

ALERT!

Don't spin your wheels. Don't spend too much time on any one question. Give it some thought, take your best shot, and move along.

It pays to keep moving.

All questions are given equal weight. No extra credit is given for a difficult question. So there is no reason to keep working on a question after you have given it your best shot. Instead, once you realize that you are spinning your wheels, make the decision to make a guess and move on to the next question.

If you know the directions in advance, you won't have to waste time reading them.

Your allotted 35 minutes is all the time you get for a section. No additional time is given for reading directions. If you spend 30 seconds reading the directions each time you begin a new section, you could lose a whole question in each section. The solution to this problem is to be thoroughly familiar in advance with the directions for every question type and with the format in which each question type appears. Then, when you get to the exam, you will recognize those formats and already know what is required without having to review any directions.

It's more efficient to code answers in groups.

Most test-takers code their response to each question just after they have answered the question. They work in the rhythm: solve, code, solve, code, solve, code, and so on. It is this rhythm that can trip them up if they skip a question. Instead of coding your responses one by one, try coding them in groups. Work problems for a while (noting your choices). Then find an appropriate moment to enter your responses on your answer sheet. You might wait until you have reached the end of a page. As time for a section draws to a close, you should make sure you are current with your coding, so you will probably want to go to the one by one method. You don't want to run out of time on a section without the opportunity to enter answers to every question that you have worked. Even if you are coding in groups, there is the ever-present danger of an error. If you find that you have made a mistake, what do you do? You erase the wrong responses and enter the correct ones.

Questions you want to return to can be found more quickly if you flag them.

A mark in the margin of your test booklet will quickly identify questions you want to reconsider if you have time. Develop a shorthand marking system to identify skipped questions, doubtful questions, and answer choices that you're sure can be eliminated. Here's one marking system you might try:

Correct Answer: Circle the letter of the choice.
Definitely Eliminated Choice: Put an "X" over the letter.
Changed Choice: Fill in the circle of the first answer, and circle the new choice.
Skipped Question: Put a "?" by the number of the question.
Question to Recheck: Circle the number.

If you find that you have made a mistake, what do you do? You erase the wrong responses and copy the correct ones from your "paper trail."

Guessing Strategies

Because of the multiple-choice format, you have a real advantage over the LSAT. The correct answer is always right there on the page. To be sure, it's surrounded by wrong choices, but it may be possible to eliminate one or more of those other choices as non-answers.

You can toss out dumb answers.

Look at the following Reading Comprehension question:

The author argues that the evidence supporting the new theory is

- **(A)** hypothetical.
- **(B)** biased.
- **(C)** empirical.
- **(D)** speculative.
- **(E)** fragmentary.

You might think that it is impossible to make any progress on a Reading Comprehension question without the reading selection, but you can eliminate three of the five answers in this question as non-answers. Study the question stem. We can infer that the author of the selection has at least implicitly passed judgment on the evidence supporting the new theory. What kind of judgment might someone make about the evidence adduced to support a theory? Choices (A), (C), and (D) all seem extremely unlikely. As for choice (A), while the theory is itself an hypothesis, the evidence supporting the theory would not be hypothetical. As for choice (C), evidence is empirical by definition. So it is unlikely that anyone would argue "This evidence is empirical." And choice (D) can be eliminated for the same reason as choice (A). Admittedly, this leaves you with a choice of (B) or (E), a choice that depends on the content of the reading selection; but at least you have a 50–50 chance of getting the question correct—even without reading the selection.

You absolutely, positively must GUESS.

Because there is no penalty assessed for wrong answers, guessing, even randomly, is necessary to ensure that you get your best score. Two techniques will help you to garner every possible point.

Unlike some other standardized exams you might have taken (such as the SAT), no points are deducted for incorrect answers. Since there is no penalty for taking a guess and since there is always a chance you will hit on the right answer, don't leave any answer space blank. For those questions on which you can eliminate choices, make an educated guess. But even if you don't get to some questions, at least make a random guess on your answer sheet. You can't lose; you can only win.

Strings of three letters are used, but strings of four or more letters are not used.

Although strings of four or more of one letter are theoretically possible, they just don't occur. This is because the test-writers break them up. So you will not find a string of four (A)s in a row. If you do, at least one of your four answers will be wrong. Which one is it? There is no way of knowing for sure without checking your work.

There has been one exception to this rule in nearly twenty-five years, and there appears to be no logical explanation for it; so go with the trend—no strings of fours.

LSAT Questions:
A First Look

OVERVIEW
- **What can you expect on the test?**
- **How does the LSAT test Logical Reasoning?**
- **How does the LSAT test Reading Comprehension?**
- **How does the LSAT test Analytical Reasoning?**
- **What is the Writing Sample?**

WHAT CAN YOU EXPECT ON THE TEST?

The LSAT uses three different types of multiple-choice questions to test your abilities in Logical Reasoning, Reading Comprehension, and Analytical Reasoning. There is also a 30-minute Writing Sample that tests your ability to organize and compose a short essay. This chapter will describe each question type in turn and show you samples. Learning the question types in advance is the best way to prepare for the LSAT. This way, you'll know what to expect, and you won't have any unpleasant surprises on test day.

HOW DOES THE LSAT TEST LOGICAL REASONING?

A typical Logical Reasoning question presents an argument or an explanation that you are asked to analyze. You may be asked to describe the argument, draw further conclusions from it, attack or defend it, or just find the assumptions of the argument. The LSAT contains two Logical Reasoning sections, each with 24 to 26 questions. Here are the directions for this question type and a sample item:

> **Directions:** In this section, the questions ask you to analyze and evaluate the reasoning in short paragraphs or passages. For some questions, all of the answer choices may conceivably be answers to the question asked. You should select the *best* answer to the question; that is, an answer that does not require you to make assumptions that violate commonsense standards by being implausible, redundant, irrelevant, or inconsistent.
>
>   After choosing the best answer, blacken the corresponding space on the answer sheet.

chapter 3

1. Wilfred commented, "Of all the musical instruments I have studied, the trombone is the most difficult instrument to play."

   Which of the following statements, if true, would most seriously weaken Wilfred's conclusion?

   (A) The trombone is relatively easy for trumpet players to learn to play.

   (B) Wilfred has not studied trombone as seriously as he has studied other instruments.

   (C) Wilfred finds he can play the violin and the cello with equal facility.

   (D) The trombone is easier to learn as a second instrument than as a first instrument.

   (E) There are several instruments that Wilfred has not studied and that are very difficult to play.

The correct answer is (B). The question asks you to identify a possible weakness in the argument. The conclusion of the argument is that the trombone is intrinsically more difficult to play than other instruments. The question asks you to find another explanation for Wilfred's impression. Choice (B) suggests the fault is not in the trombone but in Wilfred. The seeming difficulty of the trombone stems from the fact that Wilfred did not study it as diligently as he has studied other instruments.

HOW DOES THE LSAT TEST READING COMPREHENSION?

As the name implies, LSAT Reading Comprehension questions test your ability to understand the substance and logical structure of a written selection. An LSAT Reading Comprehension section contains four reading passages, each approximately 450 words in length. Each passage is followed by 5–8 questions, for a total of 26–28 questions per section. The questions ask about the main point of the passage, about what the author specifically states, about what can be logically inferred from the passage, and about the author's attitude or tone. Here are the directions for LSAT Reading Comprehension questions and an example of a reading passage. (This sample passage is shorter than an actual LSAT passage and is followed by only 2 questions rather than the usual 6 to 8.)

Directions: Below each of the following passages, you will find questions or incomplete statements about the passage. Each statement or question is followed by lettered words or expressions. Select the word or expression that most satisfactorily completes each statement or answers each question in accordance with the meaning of the passage. After you have chosen the best answer, blacken the corresponding space on the answer sheet.

The international software market represents significant business opportunity for U.S. microcomputer software companies, but illegal copying of programs is limiting the growth of sales abroad. If not dealt with quickly, international piracy of software could become one of the
(5) most serious trade problems faced by the United States.

Software piracy is already the biggest barrier to U.S. software companies entering foreign markets. One reason is that software is extremely easy and inexpensive to duplicate compared to the cost of developing and marketing the software. The actual cost of duplicating
(10) a software program, which may have a retail value of $400 or more, can be as little as a dollar or two—the main component being the cost of the CD. The cost of counterfeiting software is substantially less than the cost of duplicating watches, books, or blue jeans. Given that the difference between the true value of the original and the cost of the
(15) counterfeit is so great for software, international piracy has become big business. Unfortunately, many foreign governments view software piracy as an industry in and of itself and look the other way.

U.S. firms stand to lose millions of dollars in new business, and diminished U.S. sales not only harm individual firms but also adversely
(20) affect the entire U.S. economy.

2. In this passage, the author's primary purpose is to

   (A) criticize foreign governments for stealing U.S. computer secrets.

   (B) describe the economic hazards software piracy pose to the United States.

   (C) demand that software pirates immediately cease their illegal operations.

   (D) present a comprehensive proposal to counteract the effects of international software piracy.

   (E) disparage the attempts of the U.S. government to control software piracy.

The correct answer is (B). This question, typical of the LSAT, asks about the main point of the selection. Choice (A) is incorrect. Though the author implies criticism of foreign governments, their mistake, so far as we are told, is not stealing secrets but tacitly allowing the operation of a software black market. Choice (C) is incorrect since this is not the main point of the selection. You can infer that the author would approve of such a demand, but issuing the demand is not the main point of the selection you just read. Choice (D) can be eliminated for a similar reason. Though the author might elsewhere offer a specific proposal, there is no such proposal in the selection you just read. Choice (E) also is wrong since no such attempts are ever discussed. Finally, notice how well choice (B) describes the main issue. The author's concern is to identify a problem and to discuss its causes.

TIP

It's an open-book test. In LSAT Reading Comprehension questions, the answers will always be directly stated or implied in the passage.

3. The author's attitude toward international software piracy can best be described as
    (A) concern.
    (B) rage.
    (C) disinterest.
    (D) pride.
    (E) condescension.

The correct answer is (A). This question asks about the tone of the passage, and *concern* very neatly captures that tone. You can eliminate choice (B) as an overstatement. Though the author condemns the piracy, the tone is not so violent as to qualify as rage. Choice (C) must surely be incorrect since the author does express concern and, therefore, cannot be disinterested.

HOW DOES THE LSAT TEST ANALYTICAL REASONING?

Make the best of it.
Note that these directions ask you to choose the best answer. That's why you should always read all the answer choices before you make your final selection.

LSAT Analytical Reasoning questions involve a situation such as people standing in a row, choosing items from a menu, or scheduling vacations. Based on the conditions described, you are asked to draw logical conclusions about the situation. An LSAT Analytical Reasoning section contains 4 to 5 problem sets, with 5 to 7 questions per set for a total of 22 to 24 questions per section. Here are the directions for this question type and two sample items:

> **Directions:** Each group of questions is based on a set of propositions or conditions. Drawing a rough picture or diagram may help in answering some of the questions. Choose the best answer for each question and blacken the corresponding space on your answer sheet.

Questions 4 and 5

Five people, P, Q, R, S, and T, are standing single file in a ticket line. All are facing the ticket window.

Q is the second person behind P.
P is not the second person in the line.
R is somewhere ahead of S.

4. T could occupy all of the following positions in the line EXCEPT
    (A) 1
    (B) 2
    (C) 3
    (D) 4
    (E) 5

The correct answer is (C). The initial conditions establish that Q is behind P separated by one person, an arrangement that can be shown as P →? → Q. And because P cannot be the second person in line, only two arrangements are possible for Q and P:

	1	2	3	4	5
	P		Q		
or			P		Q

With these as the only two possibilities, either Q or P must be third in line, which means no one else can be third. Therefore, T cannot stand in the third position.

5. If R is the fourth person in line, which of the following must be true?
   (A) T is the second person in line.
   (B) Q is the second person in line.
   (C) P is the third person in line.
   (D) S is the third person in line.
   (E) Q is the fifth person in line.

The correct answer is (A). Here we are given additional information to use in answering this item. Given that R is the fourth in line, since R is ahead of S, S must be fifth in line.

1	2	3	4	5
			R	S

This forces P and Q into positions 1 and 3:

1	2	3	4	5
P		Q	R	S

Finally, T must be second in line:

1	2	3	4	5
P	T	Q	R	S

WHAT IS THE WRITING SAMPLE?

The LSAT Writing Sample is a 30-minute exercise administered at the end of the test. For the Writing Sample, you are given a situation in which a choice must be made between two possible courses of action. You must write an argument in favor of either one of the two given choices. In each case, either course of action can be taken. The idea of the exercise is to support the course you choose with reasoned arguments and a well-written essay, given the time constraints. You are given a page of lined paper on which to write your essay.

NOTE

What other kinds of questions will there be on the LSAT? What you see is what you get. The questions on these pages show you what you'll find.

PART II

DIAGNOSING STRENGTHS AND WEAKNESSES

CHAPTER 4   Diagnostic Test

Diagnostic Test

SECTION I

24 Questions • 35 Minutes

> **Directions:** Each group of questions is based on a set of propositions or conditions. Drawing a rough picture or diagram may help in answering some of the questions. Choose the *best* answer for each question and blacken the corresponding space on your answer sheet.

Questions 1–6

The programming manager of a television station is scheduling movies for the upcoming week. The station has seven films, J, K, L, M, N, O, and P. Exactly one of the films will be shown each day, and no film will be shown more than once. The films must be shown in accordance with the following programming restrictions:

K must be shown either Monday or Saturday.
O must be shown on Thursday.
P must be shown on Sunday.
J and L must be shown on consecutive days.
J and N must not be shown on consecutive days.

1. If M is shown on Tuesday, which of the following must be true?
    (A) N is shown on Monday.
    (B) N is shown on Wednesday.
    (C) L is shown on Friday.
    (D) J is shown on Saturday.
    (E) K is shown on Saturday.

2. If J and K are shown on consecutive days, which of the following must be true?
    (A) J is shown on Wednesday.
    (B) K is shown on Saturday.
    (C) L is shown on Wednesday.
    (D) M is shown on Saturday.
    (E) N is shown on Friday.

3. If N is shown on Tuesday, which of the following must be true?
    (A) K is shown on Saturday.
    (B) L is shown on Friday.
    (C) M is shown on Wednesday.
    (D) J is shown on Friday.
    (E) N is shown on Thursday.

4. If K is shown on Saturday, which of the following must be true?
    (A) M is shown on Monday.
    (B) N is shown on Tuesday.
    (C) If N and L are shown on consecutive days, J is shown on Wednesday.
    (D) If J and M are shown on consecutive days, L is shown on Wednesday.
    (E) If K and M are shown on consecutive days, L is shown on Tuesday.

5. If J is not shown on Monday, Tuesday, or Wednesday, which of the following must be true?

    (A) If J is shown on Saturday, M is shown on Wednesday.

    (B) If L is shown on Friday, N is shown on Tuesday.

    (C) If M is shown on Tuesday, J is shown on Friday.

    (D) If M is shown on Wednesday, L is shown on Saturday.

    (E) If N is shown on Wednesday, M is shown on Tuesday.

6. If L is shown on Tuesday, which of the following must be true?

    (A) If M is shown on Monday, N is shown on Friday.

    (B) If K is shown on Monday, M is shown on Friday.

    (C) If K is shown on Saturday, J is shown on Wednesday.

    (D) If N is shown on Friday, J is shown on Wednesday.

    (E) If N is shown on Friday, M is shown on Saturday.

Questions 7–12

Nine people, G, H, J, K, L, M, N, O, and P, are taking part in a parade. They will ride in three cars, the cars forming a line. Three people will sit in each car.

G and H must ride in the same car.
J must ride in the second car.
N and P must ride in the same car.
K and O must not ride in the same car.
M must ride in the same car with either O or J or both.

7. Which of the following groups of people could ride together in the same car?

    (A) G, J, and N

    (B) J, L, and O

    (C) K, H, and L

    (D) K, N, and O

    (E) O, N, and P

8. Which of the following CANNOT be true?

    (A) K rides in the first car.

    (B) M rides in the first car.

    (C) N rides in the second car.

    (D) O rides in a car two cars behind M's car.

    (E) L rides in a car two cars behind G's car.

9. If P rides in the second car and O rides in the third car, which of the following must be true?

    (A) G rides in the third car.

    (B) L rides in the first car.

    (C) L rides in the third car.

    (D) M rides in the first car.

    (E) M rides in the second car.

10. All of the following people could ride in the same car as G EXCEPT

    (A) J

    (B) K

    (C) L

    (D) N

    (E) O

11. If G and O are riding in the first car, which of the following people must ride in the second car?

    (A) H

    (B) K

    (C) L

    (D) M

    (E) N

12. If P rides in the same car as J, and if M rides in the third car, who must ride in the first car?

    (A) H and O

    (B) K and N

    (C) O and N

    (D) H, K, and G

    (E) H, L, and O

Questions 13–18

Seven children, J, K, L, M, N, O, and P, are students at a certain grammar school with grades 1 through 7.

One of these children is in each of the seven grades.

N is in the first grade, and P is in the seventh grade.

L is in a higher grade than K.

J is in a higher grade than M.

O is in a grade somewhere between K and M.

13. If there are exactly two grades between J and O, which of the following must be true?

    (A) K is in the second grade.

    (B) J is in the sixth grade.

    (C) M is in a higher grade than K.

    (D) L is in a grade between M and O.

    (E) K and L are separated by exactly one grade.

14. If J is in the third grade, which of the following must be true?

    (A) K is in grade 4, and L is in grade 5.

    (B) K is in grade 5, and O is in grade 6.

    (C) L is in grade 4, and M is in grade 6.

    (D) M is in grade 2, and K is in grade 5.

    (E) O is in grade 4, and L is in grade 5.

15. If K is in the second grade, which of the following is a complete and accurate listing of the students who could be in grade 5?

    (A) J

    (B) J and M

    (C) L and M

    (D) L, M, and J

    (E) O, L, M, and J

16. If J and N are separated by exactly one grade, which of the following must be true?

    (A) L is in grade 6.

    (B) L is in grade 3.

    (C) K is in a lower grade than J.

    (D) K is in a lower grade than O.

    (E) O is in a grade between J and N.

17. Which of the following CANNOT be true?

    (A) O is in the third grade.

    (B) O is in the fourth grade.

    (C) O is in the fifth grade.

    (D) M is in the fourth grade.

    (E) M is in the fifth grade.

18. If L is in the grade immediately ahead of J, the number of logically possible orderings of all seven children, from the lowest grade to the highest grade, is

    (A) 1

    (B) 2

    (C) 3

    (D) 4

    (E) 5

Questions 19–24

Ten sports car enthusiasts, J, K, L, M, N, O, P, Q, R, and T, participate in a sports car rally in which a series of races are held. Five cars participate in each race, finishing first through fifth, with no ties. Exactly two people ride in each car.

P and M always ride together and never finish last.
L and Q never ride in the same car.
N and O always ride in the same car.
R's car always finishes exactly one place ahead of L's.

19. All of the following lists of pairs of participants, in order of finish from first to last, are possible EXCEPT

    (A) J, T; R, Q; K, L; M, P; O, N
    (B) P, M; R, T; L, K; J, Q; O, N
    (C) K, T; R, Q; J, L; P, M; N, O
    (D) O, N; P, M; R, J; L, Q; K, T
    (E) O, N; P, M; R, Q; L, T; K, J

20. If the car in which L is riding finishes somewhere ahead of the car in which M is riding and somewhere behind the car in which O is riding, which of the following must be true?

    (A) R rides in the first-place car.
    (B) J rides in the first-place car.
    (C) R rides in the second-place car.
    (D) Q rides in the second-place car.
    (E) Q rides in the fifth-place car.

21. If N's car finishes second and R's car finishes third, which of the following must be true?

    (A) M's car finishes first.
    (B) Q's car finishes second.
    (C) Q's car finishes fourth.
    (D) J's car finishes ahead of K's car.
    (E) O's car finishes exactly two places ahead of Q's car.

22. If J and T ride together in a car, and if L's car finishes fourth, which of the following must be true?

    (A) P's car finishes first.
    (B) N's car finishes second.
    (C) Q's car finishes third.
    (D) M's car finishes fourth.
    (E) N's car finishes fifth.

23. If L, O, and T ride in cars finishing second, third, and last, respectively, and if J and R ride in the same car, which of the following must be true?

    (A) P's car finishes first.
    (B) L's car finishes first.
    (C) N's car finishes second.
    (D) P's car finishes third.
    (E) Q's car finishes last.

24. If P's car finishes third and K and T ride in the same car, Q could be riding in a car that finishes either

    (A) first or second.
    (B) first or fourth.
    (C) first or last.
    (D) second or fourth.
    (E) second or last.

STOP

END OF SECTION 1. IF YOU HAVE ANY TIME LEFT, GO OVER YOUR WORK IN THIS SECTION ONLY. DO NOT WORK IN ANY OTHER SECTION OF THE TEST.

SECTION 2

28 Questions • 35 Minutes

> **Directions:** Below each of the following passages, you will find questions or incomplete statements about the passage. Each statement or question is followed by lettered words or expressions. Select the word or expression that most satisfactorily completes each statement or answers each question in accordance with the meaning of the passage. After you have chosen the *best* answer, blacken the corresponding space on the answer sheet.

Reverse discrimination, minority recruitment, racial quotas and, more generally, affirmative action are phrases that carry powerful emotional charges.
(5) But why should affirmative action, of all government policies, be so controversial? In a sense, affirmative action is like other governmental programs, such as defense, conservation and public schools.
(10) Affirmative action programs are designed to achieve legitimate government objectives such as improved economic efficiency, reduced social tension and general betterment of the public wel-
(15) fare. While it cannot be denied that there is no guarantee that affirmative action will achieve these results, neither can it be denied that there are plausible, even powerful, sociological and economic
(20) arguments pointing to its likely success.

Government programs, however, entail a cost, that is, the expenditure of social or economic resources. Setting aside cases in which the specific user is
(25) charged a fee for service (toll roads and tuition at state institutions), the burdens and benefits of publicly funded or mandated programs are widely shared. When an individual benefits personally
(30) from a government program, it is only because of membership in a larger beneficiary class, for example, a farmer; and most government revenue is obtained through a scheme of general taxation to
(35) which all are subject. Affirmative action programs are exceptions to this general rule, though not, as might at first seem, because the beneficiaries of the programs

are specific individuals. It is still the
(40) case that those who ultimately benefit from affirmative action do so only by virtue of their status as a member of a larger group, a particular minority. Rather, the difference is the location of
(45) the burden. In affirmative action, the burden of "funding" the program is not shared universally, and that is inherent in the nature of the case, as can be seen clearly in the case of affirmative action
(50) in employment. Often job promotions are allocated along a single dimension, seniority; and when an employer promotes a less senior worker from a minority group, the person disadvantaged by
(55) the move is easily identified: the worker with greatest seniority on a combined minority–non-minority list passed over for promotion.

Now we are confronted with two
(60) competing moral sentiments. On the one hand, there is the idea that those who have been unfairly disadvantaged by past discriminatory practices are entitled to some kind of assistance. On the
(65) other, there is the feeling that people ought not to be deprived of what is rightfully theirs, even for the worthwhile service of other humans. In this respect, disability due to past racial discrimina-
(70) tion, at least insofar as there is no connection to the passed-over worker, is like a natural evil. When a villainous person willfully and without provocation strikes and injures another, there is
(75) not only the feeling that the injured person ought to be compensated but

there is consensus that the appropriate party to bear the cost is the one who inflicted the injury. Yet, if the same (80) innocent person stumbled and was injured, it would be surprising to hear someone argue that the villainous person ought to be taxed for the injury simply because the villainous person (85) might have tripped the victim had there been the opportunity. There may very well be agreement that the injured person should be aided with money and personal assistance, and many will give (90) willingly; but there is also agreement that no one individual ought to be singled out and forced to do what must ultimately be considered an act of charity.

1. The passage is primarily concerned with

    (A) comparing affirmative action programs to other government programs.

    (B) arguing that affirmative action programs are morally justified.

    (C) analyzing the basis for moral judgments about affirmative action programs.

    (D) introducing the reader to the importance of affirmative action as a social issue.

    (E) describing the benefits that can be obtained through affirmative action programs.

2. The author mentions toll roads and tuition at state institutions (lines 25–26) in order to

    (A) anticipate a possible objection on counterexamples.

    (B) avoid a contradiction between moral sentiments.

    (C) provide illustrations of common government programs.

    (D) voice doubts about the social and economic value of affirmative action.

    (E) offer examples of government programs that are too costly.

3. With which of the following statements would the author most likely agree?

    (A) Affirmative action programs should be discontinued because they place an unfair burden on non-minority persons who bear the cost of the programs.

    (B) Affirmative action programs may be able to achieve legitimate social and economic goals such as improved efficiency.

    (C) Affirmative action programs are justified because they are the only way of correcting injustices created by past discrimination.

    (D) Affirmative action programs must be redesigned so that society as a whole rather than particular individuals bears the cost of the programs.

    (E) Affirmative action programs should be abandoned because they serve no useful social function and place unfair burdens on particular individuals.

4. The author most likely places the word "funding" in quotation marks (line 46) in order to remind the reader that

    (A) affirmative action programs are costly in terms of government revenues.

    (B) particular individuals may bear a disproportionate share of the burden of affirmative action.

    (C) the cost of most government programs is shared by society at large.

    (D) the beneficiaries of affirmative action are members of larger groups.

    (E) the cost of affirmative action is not only a monetary expenditure.

5. The "villainous person" discussed in lines 72–73 functions primarily as

   (A) an illustration.

   (B) a counterexample.

   (C) an authority.

   (D) an analogy.

   (E) a disclaimer.

6. According to the passage, affirmative action programs are different from most other government programs in the

   (A) legitimacy of the goals the programs are designed to achieve.

   (B) ways in which costs of the programs are distributed.

   (C) methods for allocating the benefits of the programs.

   (D) legal structures that are enacted to achieve the objectives.

   (E) discretion granted to the executive for implementing the programs.

7. It can be inferred that the author believes the reader will regard affirmative action programs as

   (A) posing a moral dilemma.

   (B) based on unsound premises.

   (C) containing self-contradictions.

   (D) creating needless suffering.

   (E) offering a panacea.

8. The primary purpose of the passage is to

   (A) reconcile two conflicting points of view.

   (B) describe and refute a point of view.

   (C) provide a historical context for a problem.

   (D) suggest a new method for studying social problems.

   (E) analyze the structure of an institution.

The number of aged in Sweden is one of the largest in the world, close to 14 percent of the total population, and the need for health and social support for
(5) them has been intensified by improvements in the standard of living. Life expectancy has increased and at the same time there is a greater unwillingness on the part of adult offspring to care
(10) for aged parents living in their households. The percentage of aged persons living with their children a decade ago was approximately 10 in Sweden (3 in Stockholm), contrasted with 20 in Den-
(15) mark, 30 in the United States, 40 in England, 70 in Poland, and 90 in Russia. Sweden placed a moratorium on the construction of new acute beds in favor of long-term beds, but that has foun-
(20) dered because care in a long-stay facility, if done correctly, while less costly than an acute facility, may still be prohibitively expensive.

Payroll is the single most important budgetary component in all
(25) branches of hospital service, accounting for over 60 percent of total costs; and the staff-bed ratio requirements for the chronic aged are higher than for acute
(30) patients, especially with respect to nursing and rehabilitation personnel. Payroll expenditures have grown sizably as the result of advancing standards of industrial justice which challenge the
(35) validity of the traditional idea that health workers other than doctors should work for lower wages than persons doing comparable work elsewhere in the economy because of the eleemosynary and hu-
(40) manitarian ethic of patient care. The progress of women in securing greater parity with men in income and employment opportunities are especially notable in the health field where women
(45) who comprise roughly three-fourths of the labor force have been concentrated disproportionately in low-paying and low-status jobs.

In nearly all highly developed coun-
(50) tries recently the policy has been to bring the wages of low-income hospital workers into line with those in industry

and manufacturing. Even so, the conditions of employment are unattractive
(55) and staffing remains a problem, especially during off hours, weekends, and summers when people prefer to be with their families or on vacation. The magnitude of these problems is greater in
(60) long-stay than in short-stay facilities, because of the differences in prestige and responsiveness of patients to intervention.

Paradoxically, the cutbacks in
(65) long-term care spending in Sweden may have contributed to an improvement in treatment outcomes. Patients have been required to take maximum responsibility for their own care, and this has
(70) lessened dependency and fostered rehabilitation. A similar principle of self-care applies to the treatment of the mentally retarded and the aged. In addition to the patient care benefits, significant econo-
(75) mies can be obtained, demonstrating that the two objectives are not necessarily incompatible. The medical director of a large-sized long-term care facility has found that in the case of the aged over
(80) 80, multiple-patient rooms are better than single-patient rooms. Older and mentally disoriented patients are much quieter when they have roommates, and because of the tendency of people to help
(85) one another, they require less staff time. Staff time per patient is directly correlated to the number of beds in the room, decreasing from 217 minutes for single room to 99 minutes for four-bed rooms.
(90) Many new long-term hospitals for the psychogeriatrics of advanced age are being designed for four to five beds per room. The reaction to resource scarcity has resulted in unexpected contribu-
(95) tions to patient welfare.

9. It can be inferred from the passage that the increasing number of aged requiring care prompted Sweden to

  (A) shift funds from construction of facilities for care of the acutely ill to projects to build facilities for long-term care.

  (B) restructure its tax laws to penalize families who refused to provide in-house care for their aging relatives.

  (C) attempt to reduce long-term care costs by depressing salaries of hospital workers and delaying wage increases.

  (D) crowd four or five patients into a room designed for only one patient in order to reduce payroll costs.

  (E) discontinue construction of long-term hospitals for the psychogeriatrics of the aged.

10. All of the following are mentioned in the passage as difficulties in staffing long-stay facilities EXCEPT

  (A) the low prestige of such jobs.

  (B) the relatively low rate of pay.

  (C) the character of the patient population.

  (D) the inconvenient work schedules.

  (E) the large number of weekly hours.

11. It can be inferred from the passage that pay rates in the health field have historically been lower than those for manufacturing and industry because

  (A) jobs in the health field have a lower status.

  (B) service in the health field was considered charitable work.

  (C) doctors insisted on receiving higher salaries than other workers.

  (D) labor costs are the greatest category of expenditures for hospitals.

  (E) aged people are not able to pay high fees for long-term care.

12. It can be inferred from the passage that the staff/bed cost of long-stay care in Sweden is

(A) greater than that for acute care.

(B) increasing less rapidly than that for acute care.

(C) unrelated to the number of persons being cared for.

(D) borne primarily by the individual patient.

(E) less than in other countries such as England and the United States.

13. The author refers to the results of cutbacks in long-term care spending as "paradoxical" because

(A) cutbacks in expenditures ordinarily result in worse care.

(B) the longer a patient lives, the greater is the need for care.

(C) fewer adult offspring are willing to care for aged parents in their own homes.

(D) reduced staffing needs mean fewer positions for hospital workers.

(E) reductions in spending placed a moratorium on new construction.

14. Which of the following, if true, would most strengthen the author's contention that improvements in the standard of living increase the reluctance of adults to care for aged parents?

(A) The United States has a higher standard of living than Sweden.

(B) Stockholm has a substantially higher standard of living than the rest of Sweden.

(C) The number of long-term care beds in England has not increased appreciably in the past five years.

(D) Sweden has fewer aged persons than Denmark.

(E) Sweden has a higher acute to long-term beds ratio than Russia.

Can computers reason? Reasoning requires the individual to take a given set of facts and draw correct conclusions. Unfortunately, errors frequently occur,
(5) and we are not talking about simple carelessness as occurs when two numbers are incorrectly added, nor do we mean errors resulting from simple forgetfulness. Rather, we have in mind
(10) errors of a logical nature—those resulting from faulty reasoning. Now, or at least soon, computers will be capable of error-free logical reasoning in a variety of areas. The key to avoiding errors is to
(15) use a computer program that relies on the last two decades' research in the field of automated theorem proving. AURA (Automated Reasoning Assistant) is the program that best exemplifies this
(20) use of the computer.

AURA solves a problem by drawing conclusions from a given set of facts about the problem. The program does not learn, nor is it self-analytical, but it
(25) reaches logical conclusions flawlessly. It uses various types of reasoning and, more important, has access to very powerful and sophisticated logical strategies. AURA seldom relies on brute force
(30) to find solutions. Instead it solves almost all problems by using sophisticated techniques to find a contradiction. One generally starts with a set of assumptions and adds a statement that
(35) the goal is unreachable. For example, if the problem is to test a safety system that automatically shuts down a nuclear reactor when instruments indicate a problem, AURA is told that the system
(40) will not shut the reactor down under those circumstances. If AURA finds a contradiction between the statement and the system's design assumptions, then this aspect of the reactor's design has
(45) been proved satisfactory. This strategy, known as the set of support strategy, lets AURA concentrate on the problem at hand and avoid the many fruitless steps required to explore the entire
(50) theory underlying the problem. Almost never does the program proceed by carrying out an exhaustive search. The chief

use for AURA at this time is for electronic circuit design validation, but a
(55) number of other uses will arise. For example, there already exist "expert systems" that include a component for reasoning. An expert system is a special-purpose program designed to au-
(60) tomate reasoning in a specific area such as medical diagnosis. These expert programs, unlike human experts, do not die. Such systems continue to improve and have an indefinite life span. More-
(65) over, they can be replicated for pennies. A human who can expertly predict where to drill for oil is in great demand. A program that can predict equally well would be invaluable and could be dupli-
(70) cated any number of times.

Will the computer replace the human being? Certainly not. It seems likely that computer programs will reproduce—that is, design more clever
(75) computer programs and more efficient, more useful components. Reasoning programs will also analyze their own progress, learn from their attempts to solve a problem, and redirect their at-
(80) tack on a problem. Such programs will assist, rather than replace, humans. Their impact will be felt in design, manufacturing, law, medicine, and other areas. Reasoning assistants will enable
(85) human minds to turn to deeper and far more complex ideas. These ideas will be partially formulated and then checked for reasoning flaws by a reasoning program. Many errors will be avoided.

15. According to the passage, the primary purpose of AURA is to
   (A) design new and easily replicated programs.
   (B) function as a safety mechanism in nuclear reactors.
   (C) detect contradictions and other faults in computer programs.
   (D) develop expert human programs for technical fields.
   (E) check human reasoning for possible errors.

16. Which of the following titles best describes the content of the passage?
   (A) "Scientific Applications of Computers"
   (B) "Theories of Artificial Intelligence"
   (C) "Some Suggested Applications for AURA"
   (D) "Using Computers to Assist Human Reasoning"
   (E) "The Dangers of Automated Reasoning Assistants"

17. According to the passage, all of the following are advantages of expert programs EXCEPT
   (A) they have an indefinite life span.
   (B) they cost little to reproduce.
   (C) many copies can be made available.
   (D) they are self-analytical.
   (E) more knowledge can be added to them.

18. The author mentions all of the following as areas for applying AURA EXCEPT
   (A) electronic engineering.
   (B) nuclear engineering.
   (C) mathematic and formal logic.
   (D) medical diagnosis.
   (E) petroleum exploration.

19. If the design of an electronic circuit were tested by AURA, and the conclusion that under certain circumstances a switching device would remain open generated a contradiction, this would lead to the conclusion that
   (A) the circuit was properly designed.
   (B) the switch would remain closed under the circumstances.
   (C) the switch would remain open under the circumstances.
   (D) an error in human reasoning invalidated the design.
   (E) the circuit was incorrectly designed.

20. The author's attitude toward the developments he describes can best be described as

(A) enthusiastic.

(B) reluctant.

(C) cautious.

(D) skeptical.

(E) worried.

21. The author is primarily concerned to

(A) discuss recent developments.

(B) correct a misconception.

(C) propose a theory.

(D) refute an objection.

(E) recommend a solution.

Until Josquin des Prez, 1440–1521, Western music was liturgical, designed as an accompaniment to worship. Like the intricately carved gargoyles perched
(5) atop medieval cathedrals beyond sight of any human, music was composed to please God before anybody else; its dominant theme was reverence. Emotion was there, but it was the grief of Mary stand-
(10) ing at the foot of the Cross, the joy of the faithful hailing Christ's resurrection. Even the secular music of the Middle Ages was tied to predetermined patterns that sometimes seemed to stand in
(15) the way of individual expression.

While keeping one foot firmly planted in the divine world, Josquin stepped with the other into the human. He scored magnificent masses, but also
(20) newly expressive motets such as the lament of David over his son Absalom or the "Deploration d' Ockeghem," a dirge on the death of Ockeghem, the greatest master before Josquin, a motet written
(25) all in black notes, and one of the most profoundly moving scores of the Renaissance. Josquin was the first composer to set psalms to music. But alongside *Benedicite omnia opera Domini Domino*
(30) ("Bless the Lord, all ye works of the Lord") he put *El Grillo* ("The cricket is a good singer who manages long poems") and *Allegez moi* ("Solace me, sweet pleas-

ant brunette"). Josquin was praised by
(35) Martin Luther, for his music blends respect for tradition with a rebel's willingness to risk the horizon. What Galileo was to science, Josquin was to music. While preserving their allegiance to God,
(40) both asserted a new importance for man.

Why then should Josquin languish in relative obscurity? The answer has to do with the separation of concept from performance in music. In fine art, con-
(45) cept and performance are one; both the art lover and the art historian have thousands of years of paintings, drawings and sculptures to study and enjoy. Similarly with literature: Poetry, fic-
(50) tion, drama, and criticism survive on the printed page or in manuscript for judgment and admiration by succeeding generations. But musical notation on a page is not art, no matter how lofty or excel-
(55) lent the composer's conception; it is, crudely put, a set of directions for producing art. Being highly symbolic, musical notation requires training before it can even be read, let alone performed.
(60) Moreover, because the musical conventions of other days are not ours, translation of a Renaissance score into modern notation brings difficulties of its own. For example, the Renaissance notation
(65) of Josquin's day did not designate the tempo at which the music should be played or sung. It did not indicate all flats or sharps; these were sounded in accordance with musicianly rules, which
(70) were capable of transforming major to minor, minor to major, diatonic to chromatic sound, and thus affect melody, harmony, and musical expression. A Renaissance composition might include
(75) several parts—but it did not indicate which were to be sung, which to be played, nor even whether instruments were to be used at all.

Thus, Renaissance notation per-
(80) mits of several interpretations and an imaginative musician may give an interpretation that is a revelation. But no matter how imaginative, few modern musicians can offer any interpretation
(85) of Renaissance music. The public for it is

small, limiting the number of musicians who can afford to learn, rehearse, and perform it. Most of those who attempt it at all are students organized in *collegia* (90) *musica* whose memberships have a distressing habit of changing every semester, thus preventing directors from maintaining the year-in, year-out continuity required to achieve excellence (95) of performance. Finally, the instruments used in Renaissance times—drummhorns, recorders, rauschpfeifen, shawms, sackbuts, organettos—must be specially procured.

22. The primary purpose of the passage is to

    (A) introduce the reader to Josquin and account for his relative obscurity.

    (B) describe the main features of medieval music and show how Josquin changed them.

    (C) place Josquin's music in an historical context and show its influence on later composers.

    (D) enumerate the features of Josquin's music and supply critical commentary.

    (E) praise the music of Josquin and interest the reader in further study of medieval music.

23. The passage contains information that would help answer all of the questions EXCEPT which of the following?

    (A) What are the titles of some of Josquin's secular compositions?

    (B) What are the names of some Renaissance musical instruments?

    (C) Who was the greatest composer before Josquin?

    (D) Where might it be possible to hear Renaissance music performed?

    (E) What are the names of some of Josquin's most famous students?

24. The passage implies that all of the following are characteristics of modern musical notation EXCEPT which of the following?

    (A) The tempo at which a composition is to be played is indicated in the notation.

    (B) Whether a note is sharp or flat is indicated in the notation.

    (C) The notation indicates which parts of the music are to be played by which instruments.

    (D) Whether a piece is in a major or minor key is clearly indicated.

    (E) The notion leaves no room for interpretation by the musician.

25. The author would most likely agree with which of the following statements?

    (A) Music is a more perfect art form than painting or sculpture.

    (B) Music can be said to exist only when it is being performed.

    (C) Josquin was the greatest composer of the Middle Ages.

    (D) Renaissance music is superior to music produced in modern times.

    (E) Most people dislike Josquin because they do not understand his music.

26. The passage leads most logically to a proposal to

    (A) establish more *collegia musica*.

    (B) study Josquin's compositional techniques in greater detail.

    (C) include Renaissance music in college studies.

    (D) provide funds for musicians to study and play Josquin.

    (E) translate Josquin's music into modern notation.

27. The author cites all of the following as reasons for Josquin's relative obscurity EXCEPT

(A) the difficulty one encounters in attempting to read his musical notation.

(B) the inability of modern musicians to play instruments of the Renaissance.

(C) the difficulty of procuring unusual instruments needed to play the music.

(D) the lack of public interest in Renaissance music.

(E) problems in finding funding for the study of Renaissance music.

28. The author's attitude toward Galileo can best be described as

(A) admiring.

(B) critical.

(C) accepting.

(D) analytical.

(E) noncommittal.

STOP

END OF SECTION 2. IF YOU HAVE ANY TIME LEFT, GO OVER YOUR WORK IN THIS SECTION ONLY. DO NOT WORK IN ANY OTHER SECTION OF THE TEST.

diagnostic test

SECTION 3

25 Questions • 35 Minutes

> **Directions:** In this section, the questions ask you to analyze and evaluate the reasoning in short paragraphs or passages. For some questions, all of the answer choices may conceivably be answers to the question asked. You should select the *best* answer to the question; that is, an answer that does not require you to make assumptions that violate commonsense standards by being implausible, redundant, irrelevant, or inconsistent. After you have chosen the *best* answer, blacken the corresponding space on the answer sheet.

1. All of the following conclusions are based upon accurate expense vouchers submitted by employees to department heads of a certain corporation in 2003. Which of them is LEAST likely to be weakened by the discovery of additional 2003 expense vouchers?

    (A) The accounting department had only 15 employees and claimed expenses of at least $500.

    (B) The sales department had at least 25 employees and claimed expenses of at least $35,000.

    (C) The legal department had at least 2 employees and claimed no more than $3,000 in expenses.

    (D) The public relations department had no more than 1 employee and claimed no more than $200 in expenses.

    (E) The production department had no more than 500 employees and claimed no more than $350 in expenses.

2. Mr. Mayor, when is the city government going to stop discriminating against its Hispanic residents in the delivery of critical municipal services?

    The form of the question above is most nearly paralleled by which of the following?

    (A) Mr. Congressman, when is the Congress finally going to realize that defense spending is out of hand?

    (B) Madam Chairperson, do you anticipate the committee will take luncheon recess?

    (C) Dr. Greentree, what do you expect to be the impact of the Governor's proposals on the economically disadvantaged counties of our state?

    (D) Gladys, since you're going to the grocery store anyway, would you mind picking up a quart of milk for me?

    (E) Counselor, does the company you represent find that its affirmative action program is successful in recruiting qualified minority employees?

3. The main ingredient in this bottle of Dr. John's Milk of Magnesia is used by nine out of ten hospitals across the country as an antacid and laxative.

   If this advertising claim is true, which of the following statements must also be true?

   (A) Nine out of ten hospitals across the country use Dr. John's Milk of Magnesia for some ailments.

   (B) Only one out of ten hospitals in the country does not treat acid indigestion and constipation.

   (C) Only one out of ten hospitals across the country does not recommend Dr. John's Milk of Magnesia for patients who need a milk of magnesia.

   (D) Only one of ten hospitals across the country uses a patent medicine other than Dr. John's Milk of Magnesia as an antacid and laxative.

   (E) Nine out of ten hospitals across the country use the main ingredient in Dr. John's Milk of Magnesia as an antacid and laxative.

Questions 4 and 5

   (1) All wheeled conveyances that travel on the highway are polluters.

   (2) Bicycles are not polluters.

   (3) Whenever I drive my car on the highway, it rains.

   (4) It is raining.

4. If the above statements are all true, which of the following statements must also be true?

   (A) Bicycles do not travel on the highway.

   (B) Bicycles travel on the highway only if it is raining.

   (C) If my car is not polluting, then it is not raining.

   (D) I am now driving on the highway.

   (E) My car is not a polluter.

5. The conclusion "my car is not polluting" could be logically deduced from statements (1)–(4) if statement

   (A) (1) were changed to "Bicycles are polluters."

   (B) (2) were changed to "My car is a polluter."

   (C) (3) were changed to "If bicycles were polluters, I would be driving my car on the highway."

   (D) (4) were changed to "Rainwater is polluted."

   (E) (4) were changed to "It is not raining."

6. Statistics published by the U.S. Department of Transportation show that nearly 80 percent of all traffic fatalities occur at speeds of under 50 miles per hour and within 25 miles of home. Therefore, you are safer in a car if you are driving at a speed over 50 miles per hour and not within a 25-mile radius of your home.

   Which of the following, if true, most weakens the conclusion of the argument above?

   (A) Teenage drivers are involved in 75 percent of all traffic accidents resulting in fatalities.

   (B) Eighty percent of all persons arrested for driving at a speed over the posted speed limit are intoxicated.

   (C) Fifty percent of the nation's annual traffic fatalities occur on six weekends that are considered high-risk weekends because they contain holidays.

   (D) The Department of Transportation statistics were based on police reports compiled by the 50 states.

   (E) Ninety percent of all driving time is registered within a 25-mile radius of the driver's home and at speeds less than 50 miles per hour.

7. Usually when we have had an inch or more of rain in a single day, my backyard immediately has mushrooms and other forms of fungus growing in it. There are no mushrooms or fungus growing in my backyard.

Which of the following would logically complete an argument with the premises given above?

(A) Therefore, there has been no rain here in the past day.

(B) Therefore, there probably has been no rain here in the past day.

(C) Therefore, we have not had more than an inch of rain here in the past day.

(D) Therefore, we probably have not had more than an inch of rain here in the past day.

(E) Therefore, mushroom and fungus will be growing in my backyard tomorrow.

Questions 8 and 9

Can you really have that body you want without a monotonous program of daily exercise? Is there really an exercise routine that will help you to shed that fat quickly and painlessly? Now, a university study shows that this is possible. Surely, you would not want to miss a chance to find out whether you can have that body once again. Try the new Jack Remain's twice-a-week workout—and judge for yourself.

8. Which of the following conclusions can be completely justified assuming that the statements made are true?

(A) Only Jack Remain's program offers the possibility for effortless weight loss.

(B) Exercise experts have developed a program to help people of all ages lose weight.

(C) Following Jack Remain's twice-a-week workout program might help you to lose weight.

(D) If you follow Jack Remain's twice-a-week workout program, you will lose weight.

(E) Most people must exercise in order to lose weight.

9. The method of persuasion used by the advertisement can be described as

(A) providing evidence and allowing the listener to arrive at his or her own conclusions.

(B) presenting the reader with a logical set of premises and inviting the reader to draw a further conclusion.

(C) presenting both sides of an issue while carefully avoiding influencing the reader's decision.

(D) asking that the reader provide evidence to test the truth of the claims made in the advertisement.

(E) attempting to convince the reader that similar claims made by others are false.

10. I recently read a book by an author who insists that everything a person does is economically motivated. Leaders launch wars of conquest in order to capture the wealth of other nations. Scientists do research in order to receive grants or find marketable processes. Students go to college to get better jobs. The author even maintains that people go to museums to become better informed on the off-chance that some day they will be able to turn that knowledge to their advantage. So persuaded was I by the author's evidence that, applying the theory on my own, I was able to conclude that the author had written the book _____ .

Which of the following provides the most logical completion of the above paragraph?

(A) as a labor of love

(B) in order to make money

(C) as a means of reforming the world

(D) as an exercise in scientific research

(E) in response to a creative urge to be a novelist

11. In our investigation of this murder, we are guided by our previous experience with the East End Killer. You will recall that in that case, the victims were also carrying a great deal of money when they were killed but the money was not taken. As in this case, the murder weapon was a pistol. Finally, in that case also, the murders were committed between six in the evening and twelve midnight. So we are probably after someone who looks very much like the East End Killer, who was finally tried, convicted, and executed: 5'11" tall, a mustache, short brown hair, walks with a slight limp.

The author makes which of the following assumptions?

(A) Crimes similar in detail are likely to be committed by perpetrators who are similar in physical appearance.

(B) The East End Killer has apparently escaped from prison and has resumed his criminal activities.

(C) The man first convicted as the East End Killer was actually innocent, and the real East End Killer is still loose.

(D) Serial killers usually do not take money or personal property from their victims.

(E) Serial killers are more likely to use a firearm than a knife or a blunt instrument.

12. (1) Everyone who has not read the report either has no opinion in the matter or holds a wrong opinion about it.

    (2) Everyone who holds no opinion in the matter has not read the report.

Which of the following best describes the relationship between the two above propositions?

(A) If (2) is true, (1) may be either false or true.

(B) If (2) is true, (1) must also be true.

(C) If (2) is true, (1) is likely to be true.

(D) If (1) is true, (2) must also be true.

(E) If (1) is false, (2) must also be false.

13. The idea that women should be police officers is absurd. After all, women are on the average three to five inches shorter than men and weigh 20 to 50 pounds less. It is clear that a woman would be less effective than a man in a situation requiring force.

Which of the following, if true, would most weaken the above argument?

(A) Some of the female applicants for the police force are larger than some of the male officers presently on the force.

(B) Police officers are required to go through an intensive eighteen-month training program.

(C) Police officers are required to carry pistols and are trained in the use of their weapons.

(D) There are a significant number of desk jobs in the police force that women could fill.

(E) Many criminals are women.

14. No sophomores were selected for Rho Rho Phi. Some sophomores are members of the Debating Society. Therefore, some members of the Debating Society were not selected for Rho Rho Phi.

Which of the following is logically most similar to the argument given above?

(A) Everyone who exercises in the heat will get ill. I never exercise in the heat, so I will probably never be ill.

(B) Drivers who wish to avoid expensive automobile repairs will have their cars tuned up regularly. My uncle refuses to have his car tuned up regularly. Therefore, he enjoys paying for major repairs.

(C) Some books that are beautiful were written in French, and French literature is well respected. Therefore, any book that is beautiful is well respected.

(D) All pets are excluded from this apartment complex. But many pets are valuable. Therefore, some valuable animals are excluded from this apartment complex.

(E) St. Paul is a long way from London. Minneapolis is a long way from London. Therefore, St. Paul is a long, long way from Minneapolis.

15. All Burrahobbits are Trollbeaters, and some Burrahobbits are Greeblegrabbers.

If these statements are true, which of the following must also be true?

(A) If something is neither a Trollbeater nor a Greeblegrabber, it cannot be a Burrahobbit.

(B) It is not possible to be a Trollbeater without being a Greeblegrabber.

(C) An elf must be either a Trollbeater or a Greeblegrabber.

(D) No Greeblegrabbers are Trollbeaters.

(E) No Burrahobbits are Trollbeaters.

16. If the batteries in my electric razor are dead, the razor will not function. My razor is not functioning. Therefore, the batteries must be dead.

    Which of the following arguments is most similar to that presented above?

    (A) If Elroy attends the meeting, Ms. Barker will be elected club president. Ms. Barker was not elected club president; therefore, Elroy did not attend the meeting.

    (B) All evidence is admissible unless it is tainted. This evidence is inadmissible. Therefore, it is tainted.

    (C) If John committed the crime, his fingerprints will be found at the scene. John's fingerprints were found at the scene; therefore, John committed the crime.

    (D) Grant is my uncle. Sophie is Grant's niece. Therefore, Sophie is my sister.

    (E) Jonathan will wear his dark glasses if the coast is clear. The coast is clear. Therefore, Jonathan will wear his dark glasses.

17. All general statements are based solely on observed instances of a phenomenon. That the statement has held true up to a certain point in time is no guarantee that it will remain unexceptionless. Therefore, no generalization can be considered free from possible exception.

    The logic of the above argument can best be described as

    (A) self-defeating.

    (B) circular.

    (C) ill defined.

    (D) valid.

    (E) inductive.

Questions 18 and 19

The films of Gonzalez have had a lasting impact on motion pictures in this country. By showing what a Mexican-American woman could accomplish as a director, she paved the way for other, more commercially acceptable movie makers of similar backgrounds. Furthermore, by firmly resisting pressure to abandon the political and social themes that are central to her work, she _____ .

18. Which of the following best completes the paragraph above?

    (A) demonstrated the remarkable popularity that politically engaged films can have

    (B) set an example of integrity for younger, socially conscious filmmakers

    (C) revealed the underlying ethnic and social bias so pervasive in the film industry

    (D) weakened the chances for later filmmakers to develop similar themes

    (E) overcame the obstacles she faced as a member of an oppressed minority group

19. The passage implies that the films of Gonzalez

    (A) deal mainly with feminist issues.

    (B) have become widely popular.

    (C) are generally regarded with favor by film critics and historians.

    (D) portray Mexican Americans in a positive light.

    (E) were not extremely profitable.

20. Hospital administrators and medical officials often say that bringing spiralling health-care costs under control will require a reduction in the levels of care expected by many groups in our society, particularly the elderly and the chronically ill. And it is true that recent increases in health-care costs have been caused partly by improved levels of care for these groups. But the basic causes of the uncontrolled growth of health-care costs lie elsewhere. Duplication of the most costly services within regions, inefficient allocation of medical expertise and resources, and excessive salaries for some groups of health-care professionals—these are some of the more fundamental problems that must be addressed.

Which of the following conclusions is most strongly supported by the paragraph above?

(A) Controlling the growth of health-care costs need not involve a significant reduction in the level of services for the elderly and chronically ill.

(B) Duplication and inefficient allocation of medical resources are important factors contributing to the increasing cost of health-care services for the elderly and chronically ill.

(C) To control costs in the health-care sector, it will be necessary to reduce the levels of services provided to certain groups.

(D) People who are elderly and/or chronically ill are forced to pay higher prices in order to receive the same quality of health-care services once purchased at a lower price.

(E) Unless immediate action is taken to slow the rate of inflation in the health-care sector, health-care services will be beyond the means of most elderly and chronically ill people.

21. A recent study ranked American cities according to ten different criteria, including among others, the incidence of crime, cost of living, ease of transportation, and cultural amenities. Since San Francisco ranked third overall and Detroit sixth, we can conclude that Detroit has a more serious crime problem than San Francisco.

Which of the following, if true, most weakens the argument above?

(A) The cost of living is higher in Detroit than in San Francisco.

(B) San Francisco ranked higher than Detroit on seven of the ten criteria.

(C) Both Atlanta and Houston, which have more serious crime problems than Detroit, ranked higher than Detroit on the overall index.

(D) Seattle, which has a more serious crime problem than Boston, also ranked below Boston in seven other categories.

(E) San Francisco and Detroit both have more serious crime problems than Washington, D.C., which ranked first in overall desirability.

22. Adults often assume that the emotional lives of children are radically different from those of adults, while their thinking is basically the same (though less accurate and skillful). In fact, psychologists who have studied children carefully know that the very opposite is true.

Which of the following conclusions can be most reliably drawn from the statements above?

(A) Children react to the world around them in ways that clearly prefigure the adult personalities they will develop.

(B) Children's feelings are much like those of adults, but their ways of reasoning are often very different.

(C) Differences between individuals of the same age are more important than differences between groups of different ages.

(D) Emotional responses and thought patterns are established at a very early age and continue into adulthood.

(E) The reactions of children are the mirror images of those that would be expected of adults in the same situation.

23. Whenever it is sunny, Hector either goes fishing or goes swimming. When Hector goes swimming, Sharon plays tennis. On Saturday, Sharon did not play tennis.

If the statements above are true, then which of the following must also be true?

(A) Hector did not go swimming on Saturday.

(B) It was not sunny on Saturday.

(C) Hector did not go fishing on Saturday.

(D) Sharon did not go fishing on Saturday.

(E) Sharon does not play tennis when it is cloudy.

24. JOHN: I oppose spending more money on the space program. Those tax dollars should be spent right here on Earth rather than being used to construct satellites and spaceships to be sent to the heavens.

JOAN: Well, then you should support the space program, for those dollars are spent right here on Earth, creating jobs for thousands of scientific and technical workers in the aerospace and other industries.

Which of the following best describes Joan's response to John?

(A) It points out that John's position is inherently contradictory.

(B) It attempts to force John into choosing between two horns of a dilemma.

(C) It exploits an ambiguity in a key phrase in John's statement of his position.

(D) It tries to refute John's position by attacking John personally rather than by analyzing the merits of John's claim.

(E) It uncovers a hidden assumption in John's position that is highly questionable.

25. I am perfectly capable of driving home safely from this party. I drank only wine and scrupulously avoided all hard liquor.

The statement above presupposes that

(A) someone who has been drinking hard liquor is drunk.

(B) drinking hard liquor impairs driving more than drinking wine.

(C) the police are less likely to arrest someone who has been drinking wine than someone who has been drinking hard liquor.

(D) only someone who has had no alcohol to drink is fit to drive.

(E) drinking wine will impair driving ability only if the person has also been drinking hard liquor.

STOP

END OF SECTION 3. IF YOU HAVE ANY TIME LEFT, GO OVER YOUR WORK IN THIS SECTION ONLY. DO NOT WORK IN ANY OTHER SECTION OF THE TEST.

SECTION 4

24 Questions • 35 Minutes

Directions: In this section, the questions ask you to analyze and evaluate the reasoning in short paragraphs or passages. For some questions, all of the answer choices may conceivably be answers to the question asked. You should select the *best* answer to the question; that is, an answer that does not require you to make assumptions that violate commonsense standards by being implausible, redundant, irrelevant, or inconsistent. After you have chosen the *best* answer, blacken the corresponding space on the answer sheet.

1. Which of the following activities would depend upon an assumption that is inconsistent with the judgment that you cannot argue with taste?

   (A) A special exhibition at a museum

   (B) A beauty contest

   (C) A system of garbage collection and disposal

   (D) A cookbook filled with old New England recipes

   (E) A movie festival

2. If George graduated from the University after 1974, he was required to take Introductory World History.

   The statement above can be logically deduced from which of the following?

   (A) Before 1974, Introductory World History was not a required course at the University.

   (B) Every student who took Introductory World History at the University graduated after 1974.

   (C) No student who graduated from the University before 1974 took Introductory World History.

   (D) All students graduating from the University after 1974 were required to take Introductory World History.

   (E) Before 1974, no student was permitted to graduate from the University without having taken Introductory World History.

3. Largemouth bass are usually found living in shallow waters near the lake banks wherever minnows are found. There are no largemouth bass living on this side of the lake.

   Which of the following would logically complete an argument with the preceding premises given?

   (A) Therefore, there are no minnows on this side of the lake.

   (B) Therefore, there are probably no minnows on this side of the lake.

   (C) Therefore, there will never be any minnows on this side of the lake.

   (D) Largemouth bass are not found in the shallow water of rivers unless minnows are also present.

   (E) Lakes that contain minnows are the only habitat where largemouth bass are found.

4. TOMMY: That telephone always rings when I am in the shower and can't hear it.

   JUANITA: But you must be able to hear it; otherwise you couldn't know that it was ringing.

   Juanita's response shows that she presupposes that

   (A) the telephone does not ring when Tommy is in the shower.

   (B) Tommy's callers never telephone except when he is in the shower.

   (C) Tommy's callers sometimes hang up, thinking he is not at home.

   (D) Tommy cannot tell that the telephone has rung unless he actually heard it.

   (E) the telephone does not always function properly.

5. ADVERTISEMENT: You cannot buy a more potent pain-reliever than RELIEF without a prescription.

   Which of the following statements is inconsistent with the claim made by the advertisement?

   (A) RELIEF is not the least expensive non-prescription pain-reliever one can buy.

   (B) Another non-prescription pain-reliever, TOBINE, is just as powerful as RELIEF.

   (C) Some prescription pain-relievers are not as powerful as RELIEF.

   (D) An experimental pain-reliever more powerful than RELIEF is available to subjects in a study free of charge.

   (E) A non-prescription pain-reliever more powerful than any other, including RELIEF, is available for purchase without a prescription.

Questions 6 and 7

A behavioral psychologist interested in animal behavior noticed that dogs who are never physically disciplined (e.g., with a blow from a rolled-up newspaper) never bark at strangers. He concluded that the best way to keep a dog from barking at strange visitors is not to punish the dog physically.

6. The psychologist's conclusion is based on which of the following assumptions?

   (A) Striking a dog with a newspaper or other object is an inappropriate method for conditioning canine behavior.

   (B) Dogs that are never physically disciplined grow up better adjusted than dogs that have been subjected to such discipline.

   (C) There were no instances of an unpunished dog barking at a stranger that had not been observed.

   (D) Dogs normally bark only at strangers who have previously been physically abusive or threatening.

   (E) Human children who are physically disciplined are more likely to react negatively to strangers than those who are not.

7. Suppose the psychologist decides to pursue his project further, and he studies 25 dogs that are known to bark at strangers. Which of the following possible findings would undermine his original conclusion?

(A) Some of the owners of the dogs studied did not physically punish the dog when it barked at a stranger.

(B) Some of the dogs studied were never physically punished.

(C) The owners of some of the dogs studied believe that a dog that barks at strangers is a good watchdog.

(D) Some of the dogs barked at people who were not strangers.

(E) None of the dogs was disciplined by the method of a rolled-up newspaper.

8. Everything a child does is the consequence of some experience he has had before. Therefore, a child psychologist must study the personal history of his patient.

The author's conclusion logically depends upon the premise that

(A) everything that a child is doing he has already done before.

(B) every effect is causally generated by some previous effect.

(C) the study of a child's personal history is the best way of learning about that child's parents.

(D) a child will learn progressively more about the world because experience is cumulative.

(E) it is possible to ensure that a child will grow up to be a mature, responsible adult.

9. It is sometimes argued that we are reaching the limits of the earth's capacity to supply our energy needs with fossil fuels. In the past ten years, however, as a result of technological progress making it possible to extract resources from even marginal wells and mines, yields from oil and coal fields have increased tremendously. There is no reason to believe that there is a limit to the earth's capacity to supply our energy needs.

Which of the following statements most directly contradicts the conclusion drawn above?

(A) Even if we exhaust our supplies of fossil fuel, the earth can still be mined for uranium for nuclear fuel.

(B) The technology needed to extract fossil fuels from marginal sources is very expensive.

(C) Even given the improvements in technology, oil and coal are not renewable resources; so we will eventually exhaust our supplies of them.

(D) Most of the land under which marginal oil and coal supplies lie is more suitable to cultivation or pasturing than to production of fossil fuels.

(E) The fuels that are yielded by marginal sources tend to be high in sulphur and other undesirable elements that aggravate the air pollution problem.

Questions 10–12 refer to the following arguments.

(A) The Bible must be accepted as the revealed word of God, for it is stated several times in the Bible that it is the one, true word of God. And since the Bible is the true word of God, we must accept what it says as true.

(B) It must be possible to do something about the deteriorating condition of the nation's interstate highway system. But the repairs will cost money. Therefore, it is foolish to reduce federal appropriations for highway repair.

(C) The Learner Commission's Report on Pornography concluded that there is a definite link between pornography and sex crimes. But no one should accept that conclusion because the Learner Commission was funded by the Citizens' Committee Against Obscenity, which obviously wanted the report to condemn pornography.

(D) People should give up drinking coffee. Of ten people who died last year at City Hospital from cancer of the pancreas, eight of them drank three or more cups of coffee a day.

(E) Guns are not themselves the cause of crime. Even without firearms, crimes would be committed. Criminals would use knives or other weapons.

10. Which of the above arguments contains circular reasoning?

11. Which of the above arguments contains a generalization that is based on a sample?

12. Which of the above arguments addresses itself to the source of the claim rather than to the merits of the claim itself?

13. Some sociologists believe that religious sects such as the California-based Waiters—who believe the end of the world is imminent and seek to purify their souls by, among other things, abstaining completely from sexual relations—are a product of growing disaffection with modern, industrialized, and urbanized living. As evidence, they cite the fact that there are no other active organizations of the same type that are more than 50 or 60 years old. The evidence, however, fails to support the conclusion for_____ .

Which of the following is the most logical completion of the passage?

(A) the restrictions on sexual relations are such that the only source of new members is outside recruitment, so such sects tend to die out after a generation or two

(B) it is simply not possible to gauge the intensity of religious fervor by the length of time the religious sect remains viable

(C) the Waiters group may actually survive beyond the second generation of its existence

(D) there are other religious sects that emphasize group sexual activity that currently have several hundred members

(E) the Waiters are a California-based organization and have no members in the Northeast, which is even more heavily urban and industrialized than California

14. Any truthful auto mechanic will tell you that your standard 5,000-mile checkup can detect only one fifth of the problems that are likely to go wrong with your car. Therefore, such a checkup is virtually worthless and a waste of time and money.

Which of the following statements, if true, would strengthen the above conclusion?

(A) Those problems that the 5,000-mile checkup will turn up are the ten leading causes of major engine failure.

(B) For a new car, a 5,000-mile checkup is required to protect the owner's warranty.

(C) During a 5,000-mile checkup, the mechanic also performs routine maintenance that is necessary to the proper functioning of the car.

(D) During a 5,000-mile checkup of a vehicle, a mechanic can detect incipient problems that might later lead to major difficulties.

(E) A manufacturer's review of reports based on 5,000-mile checkups shows that the checkups found problems in less than 1/10 of 1 percent of the cars checked.

Questions 15 and 16

In recent years, unions have begun to include in their demands at the collective bargaining table requests for contract provisions that give labor an active voice in determining the goals of a corporation. Although it cannot be denied that labor leaders are highly skilled administrators, it must be recognized that their primary loyalty is and must remain to their membership, not to the corporation. Thus, labor participation in corporate management decisions makes about as much sense as _____ .

15. Which of the following represents the best continuation of the passage?

(A) allowing inmates to make decisions about prison security

(B) a senior field officer asking the advice of a junior officer on a question of tactics

(C) a university's asking the opinion of the student body on the scheduling of courses

(D) Chicago's mayor inviting the state legislators for a ride on the city's subway system

(E) the members of a church congregation discussing theology with the minister

16. The author's reasoning leads to the further conclusion that

(A) the authority of corporate managers would be symbolically undermined if labor leaders were allowed to participate in corporate planning.

(B) workers have virtually no idea of how to run a large corporation.

(C) workers would not derive any benefit from hearing the goals of corporate management explained to them at semiannual meetings.

(D) the efficiency of workers would be lowered if they were to divide their time between production line duties and management responsibilities.

(E) allowing labor a voice in corporate decisions would involve labor representatives in a conflict of interest.

17. DRUGGIST: Seventy percent of the people questioned stated that they would use Myrdal for relief of occasional headache pain. Only 30 percent of those questioned indicated that they would take Blufferin for such pain.

CUSTOMER: Oh, then more than twice as many people preferred Myrdal to Blufferin.

DRUGGIST: No, 25 percent of those questioned stated they never took any medication.

In what manner may the seeming inconsistency in the druggist's statements be explained?

(A) The 30 percent who indicated they would take Blufferin are contained within the 70 percent of those who indicated they would take Myrdal.

(B) The questioner asked more than 100 people.

(C) The questioner did not accurately record the answers of at least 25 percent of those questioned.

(D) The sampling population was too small to yield results that were statistically significant.

(E) Some of those questioned indicated that they would take both brands of pain relievers.

18. (1) No student who commutes from home to a university dates a student who resides at a university.

(2) Every student who lives at home commutes to his university, and no commuter student ever dates a resident student.

Which of the following best describes the relationship between the two preceding sentences?

(A) If (2) is true, (1) must also be true.

(B) If (2) is true, (1) must be false.

(C) If (2) is true, (1) may be either true or false.

(D) If (1) is true, (2) is unlikely to be false.

(E) If (2) is false, (1) must also be false.

19. All books from the Buckner collection are kept in the Reserve Room.

All books kept in the Reserve Room are priceless.

No book by Hemingway is kept in the Reserve Room.

Every book kept in the Reserve Room is listed in the card catalogue.

If all of the statements given are true, which of the following must also be true?

(A) All priceless books are kept in the Reserve Room.

(B) Every book from the Buckner collection that is listed in the card catalogue is not valuable.

(C) No book by Hemingway is priceless.

(D) The Buckner collection contains no books by Hemingway.

(E) Every book listed in the card catalogue is kept in the Reserve Room.

20. The new car to buy this year is the Goblin. We had 100 randomly selected motorists drive the Goblin and the other two leading subcompact cars. Seventy-five drivers ranked the Goblin first in handling. Sixty-nine rated the Goblin first in styling. From the responses of these 100 drivers, we can show you that they ranked Goblin first overall in our composite category of style, performance, comfort, and drivability.

The persuasive appeal of the advertisement's claim is most weakened by its use of the undefined word

(A) randomly.

(B) handling.

(C) first.

(D) responses.

(E) composite.

21. Recently, the newspaper published the obituary notice of a novelist and poet that had been written by the deceased in anticipation of the event. The last line of the verse advised the reader that the author had expired a day earlier and gave as the cause of death "a deprivation of time."

The explanation of the cause of the author's death is

(A) circular.

(B) speculative.

(C) self-serving.

(D) medically sound.

(E) self-authenticating.

22. Since Ronnie's range is so narrow, he will never be an outstanding vocalist.

The statement above is based on which of the following assumptions?

(A) A person's range is an important indicator of his probable success or failure as a professional musician.

(B) Vocalizing requires a range of at least two and one half octaves.

(C) It is possible for a singer, through study and practice, to expand the vocal range.

(D) Physical characteristics can affect how well one sings.

(E) Very few people have vocal ranges sufficiently broad enough to permit them to be successful vocalists.

Questions 23 and 24

During the 1970s, the number of clandestine CIA agents posted to foreign countries increased 25 percent and the number of CIA employees not assigned to field work increased by 21 percent. In the same period, the number of FBI agents assigned to case investigation rose by 18 percent, but the number of non-case-working agents rose by only 3 percent.

23. The statistics best support which of the following claims?

(A) More agents are needed to administer the CIA than are needed for the FBI.

(B) The CIA needs more people to accomplish its mission than does the FBI.

(C) The proportion of field agents tends to increase more rapidly than the number of non-field agents in both the CIA and the FBI.

(D) The rate of change in the number of supervisory agents in an intelligence gathering agency or a law-enforcement agency is proportional to the percentage change in the results produced by the agency.

(E) At the end of the 1960s, the CIA was more efficiently administered than the FBI.

24. In response to the allegation that it was more overstaffed with support and supervisory personnel than the FBI, the CIA could best argue that

(A) the FBI is less useful than the CIA in gathering intelligence against foreign powers.

(B) the rate of pay for a CIA non-field agent is less than the rate of pay for a non-investigating FBI agent.

(C) the number of FBI agents should not rise so rapidly as the number of CIA agents given the longer tenure of an FBI agent.

(D) a CIA field agent working in a foreign country requires more backup support than does an FBI investigator working domestically.

(E) the number of CIA agents is determined by the Congress each year when they appropriate funds for the agency, and the Congress is very sensitive to changes in the international political climate.

STOP

END OF SECTION 4. IF YOU HAVE ANY TIME LEFT, GO OVER YOUR WORK IN THIS SECTION ONLY. DO NOT WORK IN ANY OTHER SECTION OF THE TEST.

SECTION 5

28 Questions • 35 Minutes

Directions: Below each of the following passages, you will find questions or incomplete statements about the passage. Each statement or question is followed by lettered words or expressions. Select the word or expression that most satisfactorily completes each statement or answers each question in accordance with the meaning of the passage. After you have chosen the *best* answer, blacken the corresponding space on the answer sheet.

There is extraordinary exposure in the United States to the risks of injury and death from motor vehicle accidents. More than 80 percent of all households own
(5) passenger cars or light trucks, and each of these is driven an average of more than 11,000 miles each year. Almost one-half of fatally injured drivers have a blood alcohol concentration (BAC) of 0.1
(10) percent or higher. For the average adult, over five ounces of 80 proof spirits would have to be consumed over a short period of time to attain these levels. A third of drivers who have been drinking, but
(15) fewer than 4 percent of all drivers, demonstrate these levels. Although less than 1 percent of drivers with BACs of 0.1 percent or more are involved in fatal crashes, the probability of their involve-
(20) ment is 27 times higher than for those without alcohol in their blood.

There are a number of different approaches to reducing injuries in which intoxication plays a role. Based on the
(25) observation that excessive consumption correlates with the total alcohol consumption of a country's population, it has been suggested that higher taxes on alcohol would reduce both. While the
(30) heaviest drinkers would be taxed the most, anyone who drinks at all would be penalized by this approach.

To make drinking and driving a criminal offense is an approach directed
(35) only at intoxicated drivers. In some states, the law empowers police to request breath tests of drivers cited for any traffic offense and elevated BAC can

be the basis for arrest. The National
(40) Highway Traffic Safety Administration estimates, however, that even with increased arrests, there are about 700 violations for every arrest. At this level there is little evidence that laws serve as
(45) deterrents to driving while intoxicated. In Britain, motor vehicle fatalities fell 25 percent immediately following implementation of the Road Safety Act in 1967. As Britishers increasingly recog-
(50) nized that they could drink and not be stopped, the effectiveness declined, although in the ensuing three years the fatality rate seldom reached that observed in the seven years prior to the
(55) Act.

Whether penalties for driving with a high BAC or excessive taxation on consumption of alcoholic beverages will deter the excessive drinker responsible
(60) for most fatalities is unclear. In part, the answer depends on the extent to which those with high BACs involved in crashes are capable of controlling their intake in response to economic or penal threat.
(65) Therapeutic programs which range from individual and group counseling and psychotherapy to chemotherapy constitute another approach, but they have not diminished the proportion of acci-
(70) dents in which alcohol was a factor. In the few controlled trials that have been reported there is little evidence that rehabilitation programs for those repeatedly arrested for drunken behavior
(75) have reduced either the recidivism or crash rates. Thus far, there is no firm

evidence that Alcohol Safety Action Project supported programs, in which rehabilitation measures are requested
(80) by the court, have decreased recidivism or crash involvement for clients exposed to them, although knowledge and attitudes have improved. One thing is clear, however; unless we deal with automo-
(85) bile and highway safety and reduce accidents in which alcoholic intoxication plays a role, many will continue to die.

1. The author is primarily concerned with

(A) interpreting the results of surveys on traffic fatalities.

(B) reviewing the effectiveness of attempts to curb drunk driving.

(C) suggesting reasons for the prevalence of drunk driving in the United States.

(D) analyzing the causes of the large number of annual traffic fatalities.

(E) making an international comparison of experience with drunk driving.

2. It can be inferred that the 1967 Road Safety Act in Britain

(A) changed an existing law to lower the BAC level defining driving while intoxicated.

(B) made it illegal to drive while intoxicated.

(C) increased drunk driving arrests.

(D) placed a tax on the sale of alcoholic drinks.

(E) required drivers convicted under the law to undergo rehabilitation therapy.

3. The author implies that a BAC of 0.1 percent

(A) is unreasonably high as a definition of intoxication for purposes of driving.

(B) penalizes moderate drinkers but allows heavy drinkers to consume without limit.

(C) will effectively deter more than 90 percent of the people who might drink and drive.

(D) is well below the BAC of most drivers who are involved in fatal collisions.

(E) proves a driver has consumed five ounces of 80 proof spirits over a short time.

4. With which of the following statements about making driving while intoxicated a criminal offense versus increasing taxes on alcohol consumption would the author most likely agree?

   (A) Making driving while intoxicated a criminal offense is preferable to increased taxes on alcohol because the former is aimed only at those who abuse alcohol by driving while intoxicated.

   (B) Increased taxation on alcohol consumption is likely to be more effective in reducing traffic fatalities because taxation covers all consumers and not just those who drive.

   (C) Increased taxation on alcohol will constitute less of an interference with personal liberty because of the necessity of blood alcohol tests to determine BACs in drivers suspected of intoxication.

   (D) Since neither increased taxation nor enforcement of criminal laws against drunk drivers is likely to have any significant impact, neither measure is warranted.

   (E) Because arrests of intoxicated drivers have proved to be expensive and administratively cumbersome, increased taxation on alcohol is the most promising means of reducing traffic fatalities.

5. The author cites the British example in order to

   (A) show that the problem of drunk driving is worse in Britain than in the U.S.

   (B) prove that stricter enforcement of laws against intoxicated drivers would reduce traffic deaths.

   (C) prove that a slight increase in the number of arrests of intoxicated drivers will not deter drunk driving.

   (D) suggest that taxation of alcohol consumption may be more effective than criminal laws.

   (E) demonstrate the need to lower BAC levels in states that have laws against drunk driving.

6. Which of the following, if true, most WEAKENS the author's statement that the effectiveness of proposals to stop the intoxicated driver depends, in part, on the extent to which the high-BAC driver can control his intake?

   (A) Even if the heavy drinkers cannot control intake, criminal laws against driving while intoxicated can deter them from driving while intoxicated.

   (B) Rehabilitation programs aimed at drivers convicted of driving while intoxicated have not significantly reduced traffic fatalities.

   (C) Many traffic fatalities are caused by factors unrelated to the excessive consumption of alcohol of the driver.

   (D) Even though severe penalties may not deter the intoxicated driver, these laws will punish that driver for the harm caused by driving while intoxicated.

   (E) Some sort of therapy may be effective in helping the problem drinker to control his intake of alcohol, thereby keeping him off the road.

7. The author's closing remarks can best be described as

    (A) ironic.

    (B) indifferent.

    (C) admonitory.

    (D) indecisive.

    (E) indignant.

At the present time, 98 percent of the world energy consumption comes from stored sources, such as fossil fuels or nuclear fuel. Only hydroelectric and wood
(5) energy represent completely renewable sources on ordinary time scales. Discovery of large additional fossil fuel reserves, solution of the nuclear safety and waste disposal problems, or the de-
(10) velopment of controlled thermonuclear fusion will provide only a short-term solution to the world's energy crisis. Within about 100 years, the thermal pollution resulting from our increased
(15) energy consumption will make solar energy a necessity at any cost.

Total energy consumption is currently about one part in ten thousand that of the energy we receive from the
(20) sun. However, it is growing at a 5 percent rate, of which about 2 percent represents a population growth and 3 percent a per capita energy increase. If this growth continues, within 100 years
(25) our energy consumption will be about 1 percent of the absorbed solar energy, enough to increase the average temperature of the earth by about one degree centigrade if stored energy contin-
(30) ues to be our predominant source. This will be the point at which there will be significant effects in our climate, including the melting of the polar ice caps, a phenomenon which will raise the level of
(35) the oceans and flood parts of our major cities. There is positive feedback associated with this process, since the polar ice cap contributes to the partial reflectivity of the energy arriving from
(40) the sun: As the ice caps begin to melt, the reflectivity will decrease, thus heating the earth still further.

It is often stated that the growth rate will decline or that energy conser-
(45) vation measures will preclude any long-range problem. Instead, this only postpones the problem by a few years. Conservation by a factor of two together with a maintenance of the 5 percent
(50) growth rate delays the problem by only 14 years. Reduction of the growth rate to 4 percent postpones the problem by only 25 years; in addition, the inequities in standards of living throughout
(55) the world will provide pressure toward an increase in growth rate, particularly if cheap energy is available. The problem of a changing climate will not be evident until perhaps ten years before it
(60) becomes critical due to the nature of an exponential growth rate together with the normal annual weather variations. This may be too short a period to circumvent the problem by converting to
(65) other energy sources, so advance planning is a necessity.

The only practical means of avoiding the problem of thermal pollution appears to be the use of solar energy.
(70) (Schemes to "air-condition" the earth do not appear to be feasible before the twenty-second century.) Using the solar energy before it is dissipated to heat does not increase the earth's energy bal-
(75) ance. The cost of solar energy is extremely favorable now; particularly when compared to the cost of relocating many of our major cities.

8. The author is primarily concerned with

    (A) describing a phenomenon and explaining its causes.

    (B) outlining a position and supporting it with statistics.

    (C) isolating an ambiguity and clarifying it by definition.

    (D) presenting a problem and advocating a solution for it.

    (E) citing a counterargument and refuting it.

9. According to the passage, all of the following are factors that will tend to increase thermal pollution EXCEPT

(A) Earth's increasing population.

(B) melting of the polar ice caps.

(C) increase in per capita energy consumption.

(D) pressure to redress standard of living inequities by increasing energy consumption.

(E) expected anomalies in weather patterns.

10. The positive feedback mentioned in line 36 means that the melting of the polar ice caps will

(A) reduce per capita energy consumption.

(B) accelerate the transition to solar energy.

(C) intensify the effects of thermal pollution.

(D) necessitate a shift to alternative energy sources.

(E) result in the inundations of major cities.

11. The author mentions the possibility of energy conservation (lines 43–51) in order to

(A) preempt and refute a possible objection to the argument.

(B) directly support the central thesis of the passage.

(C) minimize the significance of a contradiction in the passage.

(D) prove that such measures are ineffective and counterproductive.

(E) supply the reader with additional background information.

12. It can be inferred that the "air-condition" of the earth (line 70) refers to proposals to

(A) distribute frigid air from the polar ice caps to coastal cities as the temperature increases due to thermal pollution.

(B) dissipate the surplus of the release of stored solar energy over absorbed solar energy into space.

(C) conserve completely renewable energy sources by requiring that industry replace these resources.

(D) avoid further thermal pollution by converting to solar energy as opposed to conventional and nuclear sources.

(E) utilize hydroelectric and wood energy to replace non-conventional energy sources such as nuclear energy.

13. The tone of the passage is best described as one of

(A) unmitigated outrage.

(B) cautious optimism.

(C) reckless abandon.

(D) smug self-assurance.

(E) pronounced alarm.

14. Which of the following would be the most logical topic for the author to address in a succeeding paragraph?

(A) The problems of nuclear safety and waste disposal

(B) A history of the development of solar energy

(C) The availability and cost of solar energy technology

(D) The practical effects of flooding of coastal cities

(E) The feasibility of geothermal energy

It would be enormously convenient to have a single, generally accepted index of the economic and social welfare of the people of the United States. A glance at

(5) it would tell us how much better or worse off we had become each year, and we would judge the desirability of any proposed action by asking whether it would raise or lower this index. Some

(10) recent discussion implies that such an index could be constructed. Articles in the popular press even criticize the Gross Domestic Production (GDP) because it is not such a complete index of welfare,

(15) ignoring, on the one hand, that it was never intended to be, and suggesting, on the other, that with appropriate changes it could be converted into one.

The output available to satisfy our

(20) wants and needs is one important determinant of welfare. Whatever want, need, or social problem engages our attention, we ordinarily can more easily find resources to deal with it when output is

(25) large and growing than when it is not. GDP measures output fairly well, but to evaluate welfare we would need additional measures which would be far more difficult to construct. We would need an

(30) index of real costs incurred in production, because we are better off if we get the same output at less cost. Use of just hours-worked for welfare evaluation would unreasonably imply that to in-

(35) crease total hours by raising the hours of eight women from 60 to 65 a week imposes no more burden then raising the hours of eight men from 40 to 45 a week, or even than hiring one involuntarily

(40) unemployed person for 40 hours a week. A measure of real costs of labor would also have to consider working conditions. Most of us spend almost half our waking hours on the job and our welfare

(45) is vitally affected by the circumstances in which we spend those hours.

To measure welfare we would need a measure of changes in the need our output must satisfy. One aspect, popu-

(50) lation change, is now handled by converting output to a per capita basis on the assumption that, other things equal,

twice as many people need twice as many goods and services to be equally well off.

(55) But an index of needs would also account for differences in the requirements for living as the population becomes more urbanized and suburbanized; for the changes in national defense require-

(60) ments; and for changes in the effect of weather in our needs. The index would have to tell us the cost of meeting our needs in a base year compared with the cost of meeting them equally well under

(65) the circumstances prevailing in every other year.

Measures of "needs" shade into measure of the human and physical environment in which we live. We all are

(70) enormously affected by the people around us. Can we go where we like without fear of attack? We are also affected by the physical environment—purity of water and air, accessibility of park land and

(75) other conditions. To measure this requires accurate data, but such data are generally deficient. Moreover, weighting is required: to combine robberies and murders in a crime index; to com-

(80) bine pollution of the Potomac and pollution of Lake Erie into a water pollution index; and then to combine crime and water pollution into some general index. But there is no basis for weighting these

(85) beyond individual preference.

There are further problems. To measure welfare we would need an index of the "goodness" of the distribution of income. There is surely consensus

(90) that given the same total income and output, a distribution with fewer families in poverty would be the better, but what is the ideal distribution? Even if we could construct indexes of output,

(95) real costs, needs, state of the environment, we could not compute a welfare index because we have no system of weights to combine them.

15. The author is primarily concerned with
    (A) refuting arguments for a position.
    (B) making a proposal and defending it.
    (C) attacking the sincerity of an opponent.
    (D) showing defects in a proposal.
    (E) reviewing literature relevant to a problem.

16. The author implies that hours-worked is not an appropriate measure of real cost because it
    (A) ignores the conditions under which the output is generated.
    (B) fails to take into consideration the environmental costs of production.
    (C) overemphasizes the output of real goods as opposed to services.
    (D) is not an effective method for reducing unemployment.
    (E) was never intended to be a general measure of welfare.

17. It can be inferred from the passage that the most important reason a single index of welfare cannot be designed is
    (A) the cost associated with producing the index would be prohibitive.
    (B) considerable empirical research would have to be done regarding output and needs.
    (C) any weighting of various measures into a general index would be inherently subjective and arbitrary.
    (D) production of the relevant data would require time; thus, the index would be only a reflection of past welfare.
    (E) accurate statistics on crime and pollution are not yet available.

18. The author regards the idea of a general index of welfare as
    (A) an unrealistic dream.
    (B) a scientific reality.
    (C) an important contribution.
    (D) a future necessity.
    (E) a desirable change.

19. According to the passage, the GDP is
    (A) a fairly accurate measure of output.
    (B) a reliable estimate of needs.
    (C) an accurate forecaster of welfare.
    (D) a precise measure of welfare.
    (E) a potential measure of general welfare.

20. According to the passage, an adequate measure of need must take into account all of the following EXCEPT
    (A) changing size of the population.
    (B) changing effects on people of the weather.
    (C) differences in needs of urban and suburban populations.
    (D) changing requirements for governmental programs such as defense.
    (E) accessibility of park land and other amenities.

21. The passage is most likely
    (A) an address to a symposium on public policy decisions.
    (B) a chapter in a general introduction to statistics.
    (C) a pamphlet on government programs to aid the poor.
    (D) the introduction to a treatise on the foundations of government.
    (E) a speech by a university president to a graduating class.

Our current system of unemployment compensation has increased nearly all sources of adult unemployment; seasonal and cyclical variations in the demand
(5) for labor, weak labor force attachment, and unnecessarily long durations of unemployment. First, for those who are already unemployed, the system greatly reduces the cost of extending the period
(10) of unemployment. Second, for all types of unsteady work—seasonal, cyclical, and casual—it raises the net wage to the employee, relative to the cost of the employer.

(15)   As for the first, consider a worker who earns $500 per month or $6,000 per year if she experiences no unemployment. If she is unemployed for one month, she loses $500 in gross earnings but only
(20) $116 in net income. How does this occur? A reduction of $500 in annual earnings reduces her federal, payroll and state tax liability by $134. Unemployment compensation consists of 50 percent of
(25) her wage or $250. Her net income therefore falls from $366 if she is employed, to $250 paid as unemployment compensation. Moreover, part of the higher income from employment is offset by the
(30) cost of transportation to work and other expenses associated with employment; and in some industries, the cost of unemployment is reduced further or even made negative by the supplementary
(35) unemployment benefits paid by employers under collective bargaining agreements. The overall effect is to increase the duration of a typical spell of unemployment and to increase the frequency
(40) with which individuals lose jobs and become unemployed.

The more general effect of unemployment compensation is to increase the seasonal and cyclical fluctuations in
(45) the demand for labor and the relative number of short-lived casual jobs. A worker who accepts such work knows she will be laid off when the season ends. If there were no unemployment compen-
(50) sation, workers could be induced to accept such unstable jobs only if the wage rate were sufficiently higher in those

jobs than in the more stable alternative. The higher cost of labor, then, would
(55) induce employers to reduce the instability of employment by smoothing production through increased variation in inventories and delivery lags, by additional development of off-season work
(60) and by the introduction of new production techniques, e.g., new methods of outdoor work in bad weather.

Employers contribute to the state unemployment compensation fund on
(65) the basis of the unemployment experience of their own previous employees. Within limits, the more benefits that those former employees draw, the higher is the employer's tax rate. The theory of
(70) experience rating is clear. If an employer paid the full cost of the unemployment benefits that his former employees received, unemployment compensation would provide no incentive to an excess
(75) use of unstable employment. In practice, however, experience rating is limited by a maximum rate of employer contribution. For any firm which pays the maximum rate, there is no cost for
(80) additional unemployment and no gain from a small reduction in unemployment.

The challenge at this time is to restructure the unemployment system
(85) in a way that strengthens its good features while reducing the harmful disincentive effects. Some gains can be achieved by removing the ceiling on the employer's rate of contribution and by
(90) lowering the minimum rate to zero. Employers would then pay the full price of unemployment insurance benefits and this would encourage employers to stabilize employment and production. Fur-
(95) ther improvement could be achieved if unemployment insurance benefits were taxed in the same way as other earnings. This would eliminate the anomalous situations in which a worker's net
(100) income is actually reduced when he returns to work.

22. The author's primary concern is to

    (A) defend the system of unemployment compensation against criticism.

    (B) advocate expanding the benefits and scope of coverage of unemployment compensation.

    (C) point to weaknesses inherent in government programs that subsidize individuals.

    (D) suggest reforms to eliminate inefficiencies in unemployment compensation.

    (E) propose methods of increasing the effectiveness of government programs to reduce unemployment.

23. The author cites the example of a worker earning $500 per month in order to

    (A) show the disincentive created by unemployment compensation for that worker to return to work.

    (B) demonstrate that employers do not bear the full cost of worker compensation.

    (C) prove that unemployed workers would not be able to survive without unemployment compensation.

    (D) explain why employers prefer to hire seasonal workers instead of permanent workers for short-term jobs.

    (E) condemn workers who prefer to live on unemployment compensation to taking a job.

24. The author recommends which of the following changes be made to the unemployment compensation system?

    (A) Eliminating taxes on benefits paid to workers

    (B) Shortening the time during which a worker can draw benefits

    (C) Removing any cap on the maximum rate of employer contribution

    (D) Providing workers with job retraining as a condition of benefits

    (E) Requiring unemployed workers to accept public works positions

25. The author mentions all of the following as ways by which employers might reduce seasonal and cyclical unemployment EXCEPT

    (A) developing new techniques of production not affected by weather.

    (B) slowing delivery schedules to provide work during slow seasons.

    (C) adopting a system of supplementary benefits for workers laid off in slow periods.

    (D) manipulating inventory supplies to require year-round rather than short-term employment.

    (E) finding new jobs to be done by workers during the off-season.

26. With which of the following statements about experience rating would the author most likely agree?

    (A) Experience rating is theoretically sound, but its effectiveness in practice is undermined by maximum contribution ceilings.

    (B) Experience rating is an inefficient method of computing employer contribution because an employer has no control over the length of an employee's unemployment.

    (C) Experience rating is theoretically invalid and should be replaced by a system in which the employee contributes the full amount of benefits he will later receive.

    (D) Experience rating is basically fair, but its performance could be improved by requiring large firms to pay more than small firms.

    (E) Experience rating requires an employer to pay a contribution that is completely unrelated to the amount his employees draw in unemployment compensation benefits.

27. The author makes which of the following criticisms of the unemployment compensation system?

    (A) It places an unfair burden on firms whose production is cyclical or seasonal.

    (B) It encourages out-of-work employees to extend the length of time they are unemployed.

    (C) It constitutes a drain on state treasuries that must subsidize unemployment compensation funds.

    (D) It provides a source of income for employees who have no income or only reduced income from employment.

    (E) The experience rating system means that employers responsible for higher-than-average turnover in staff pay higher-than-average premiums.

28. It can be inferred that the author regards the unemployment compensation system as

    (A) socially necessary.

    (B) economically efficient.

    (C) inherently wasteful.

    (D) completely unnecessary.

    (E) seriously outdated.

STOP

END OF SECTION 5. IF YOU HAVE ANY TIME LEFT, GO OVER YOUR WORK IN THIS SECTION ONLY. DO NOT WORK IN ANY OTHER SECTION OF THE TEST.

WRITING SAMPLE

Time—30 Minutes

ASHLEY REEVE has just inherited $50,000. Ashley wants to invest the $50,000 in a business that she can operate herself. She is considering two possibilities, a fast-food franchise and a clothing store. Write an argument in favor of one of the two proposals. The following criteria should be considered:

—Ashley recently received her M.B.A. and wants a business that will give her an opportunity to apply her theoretical knowledge in a practical setting.

—Ashley has considerable student loans and no substantial assets, so the $50,000 must cover the start-up costs of the business.

Ashley is considering buying a Hearty Burger franchise. Hearty Burger is a regional company with 5 company-owned stores and 20 franchise stores. The cost of the franchise is $10,000, and the estimated cost of the physical plant is another $25,000, depending on whether the franchisee buys or leases a building and on the extent of renovation required. A franchisee must attend a two-week "Hearty Burger Orientation" and is required to purchase all supplies from the company's commissary. The main company does regional advertising and special promotional campaigns and supplies franchisees with everything they need to run their restaurants, including cooking equipment, employee time sheets, tax forms, cooking procedure booklets, and technical assistance. Ashley is also considering purchasing an existing clothing store. The owner of the store, which has been in operation for more than fifty years, is retiring and is willing to sell the store with all its fixtures and stock for $40,000. In recent years, the store has not been very profitable, but the current owner apparently failed to keep abreast of style changes. Ashley anticipates that there is a large student market in the area that has not yet been tapped. She is concerned, however, about the terms of the lease on the store. The current lease will expire in eight months. The owner intends to co-op the building. Ashley will be given the opportunity to buy the commercial space, provided she has the funds available. Otherwise, she will be forced to relocate.

ANSWER KEY AND EXPLANATIONS

Section 1

1. B	6. A	11. D	16. A	21. A
2. C	7. E	12. D	17. C	22. C
3. C	8. D	13. B	18. B	23. E
4. E	9. C	14. D	19. D	24. B
5. E	10. D	15. D	20. C	

Section 2

1. C	7. A	13. A	19. B	25. B
2. A	8. E	14. B	20. A	26. D
3. B	9. A	15. E	21. A	27. B
4. E	10. E	16. D	22. A	28. A
5. D	11. B	17. D	23. E	
6. B	12. A	18. C	24. E	

Section 3

1. B	6. E	11. A	16. C	21. C
2. A	7. D	12. A	17. A	22. B
3. E	8. C	13. A	18. B	23. A
4. A	9. D	14. D	19. E	24. C
5. E	10. B	15. A	20. A	25. B

Section 4

1. B	6. C	11. D	16. E	21. A
2. D	7. B	12. C	17. E	22. D
3. B	8. B	13. A	18. A	23. C
4. D	9. C	14. E	19. D	24. D
5. E	10. A	15. A	20. E	

Section 5

1. B	7. C	13. B	19. A	25. C
2. B	8. D	14. C	20. E	26. A
3. A	9. E	15. D	21. A	27. B
4. A	10. C	16. A	22. D	28. A
5. C	11. A	17. C	23. A	
6. A	12. B	18. A	24. C	

Section 1

Questions 1–6

Here we have a linear ordering set. Even though the ordering is temporal, it can be represented spatially like a calendar. We begin by summarizing the given information:

K = (Mon. or Sat.)

O = Th.

P = Sun.

J = L

J ≠ N

1. **The correct answer is (B).** We begin by entering the additional information:

Mon. Tu. Wed. Th. Fri. Sat. Sun.

K   M   N   O   J/L   J/L   P

The only open question, as shown by the diagram, is of J or L, which is shown on Friday and Saturday. With M shown on Tuesday and O and P on Thursday and Sunday, J and L must be shown on Friday and Saturday, though not necessarily respectively. Then, K must be shown on Monday, which means N must be shown on Wednesday. As the diagram shows, only choice (B) is necessarily true. Choices (C) and (D) are possibly, though not necessarily, true. Choices (A) and (E) are definitely untrue.

2. **The correct answer is (C).** We begin by processing the additional stipulations:

Mon. Tu. Wed. Th. Fri. Sat. Sun.

K   J   L   O   M/N   M/N   P

If J and K are shown on consecutive days, then to respect the requirement that J and L also be shown on consecutive days, we have a group of either KJL or LJK. With Thursday and Sunday already scheduled, however, this group must be aired on Monday through Wednesday.

This means K must be Monday, J Tuesday, and L Wednesday. As a result, M and N will be scheduled Friday and Saturday, though we cannot establish which one will be shown on which day. Thus, choices (D) and (E) are only possible, not necessary. Choices (A) and (B) are both impossible. Choice (C), however, makes a necessarily true statement.

3. **The correct answer is (C).** We begin by processing the additional information:

Mon. Tu. Wed. Th. Fri. Sat. Sun.

K   N   M   O   J/L   J/L   P

With N scheduled for Tuesday, this forces the programming manager to air J and L on Friday and Saturday, though which is shown on which day is not established. Then, K must be aired on Monday, which means that M is aired on Wednesday.

4. **The correct answer is (E).** We begin by processing the additional information:

Mon. Tu. Wed. Th. Fri. Sat. Sun.

          O   K   P

This is not sufficient to establish either choices (A) or (B). We must then look to the remaining answer choices and process the extra information supplied therein. As for choice (C), knowing that N and L are aired on consecutive days establishes only that N, L, and J are aired consecutively: NLJ or JLN; but this does not determine which film is shown on Wednesday. As for choice (D), knowing that J is aired either immediately before or immediately after M sets up a LJM or a JLM sequence. Choice (E) is the correct answer. If K and M are shown on consecutive days, then M is shown on Friday. We are left with J and L, which must be shown on consecutive days, and

N, which must not be shown on a day before or after J. There are only two possible schedules for this three-film sequence that must be aired Monday, Tuesday, and Wednesday: JLN or NLJ. Either way we schedule the films, L is scheduled on Tuesday.

5. **The correct answer is (E).** For this question, we must use not only the additional stipulation provided in the stem of the question but also the additional information provided in the answer choices as well. If J is not shown on Monday, Tuesday, or Wednesday, we know:

    Mon. Tu. Wed. Th. Fri. Sat. Sun.

    K   O   J/L J/L   P

    because K must be shown on either Monday or Saturday. Tuesday and Wednesday must be dedicated to M and N, though not necessarily in that order. As for choices (A) and (B), fixing the JL combination for Friday and Saturday is not going to affect the showing of films on Tuesday and Wednesday. As for choices (C) and (D), scheduling M and N will not affect the order of J and L. Choice (E), however, is correct. If N is shown on Wednesday, then M must be scheduled for Tuesday.

6. **The correct answer is (A).** Here we have a similar problem. We must test each statement using all the information available. The stem establishes:

    Mon. Tu. Wed. Th. Fri. Sat. Sun.

         L   O   P

    As for choice (A), knowing that M is shown on Monday allows us to determine that L is shown on Tuesday, K on Saturday, and N on Friday:

    Mon. Tu. Wed. Th. Fri. Sat. Sun.

    M   L   J   O   N   K   P

    So choice (A) is correct. As for choice (B),

if K is shown on Monday, we deduce:

Mon. Tu. Wed. Th. Fri. Sat. Sun.

K   L   J   O   P

And we know that M and N must be shown on Friday and Saturday, but we do not know their order. So choice (B) is not necessarily true. As for choice (C), if K is shown on Saturday, this leaves both Monday and Wednesday open for J, so choice (C) is not necessarily true. So the correct answer is choice (A) only.

Finally, test choices (D) and (E):

Mon. Tu. Wed. Th. Fri. Sat. Sun.

     L   O   N   P

Since K could be shown on either Monday or Saturday, J could be shown on either Monday or Wednesday, and M could be shown on Monday, Wednesday, or Saturday.

Questions 7–12

Here we have a selection problem. The three-cars aspect introduces what seems to be an element of spatial ordering, but in actuality, this aspect does nothing more than specify that three groups will be selected. We could as easily have dispensed with spatial ordering in favor of another device, say, three tables at a banquet, the blue table, the green table, and the red table. We begin by summarizing the information for ready reference:

$$G = H$$
$$J = 2$$
$$N = P$$
$$K \neq O$$
$$M = (J) \text{ v } (O) \text{ v } (J \& O)$$

7. **The correct answer is (E).** With this question we just check each answer choice against the restrictions given in the initial conditions. Using the requirement

that G = H, we eliminate both choices (A) and (C). Then, using the requirement that N = P, we eliminate choice (D). Choice (B) can be eliminated because we have both J and O together with L, but that means M cannot be riding with J or O, as required. Finally, choice (E) is consistent with all the restrictions. We can show this by example: First (GHL), second (JMK), and third (ONP). But as a matter of test practice, we would not do so. Once we have eliminated choice (A) through choice (D) for good reasons, we would assume that the test-writers had correctly drafted the problem and that choice (E) could be proved correct by example. Trying to construct such an example will not further the issue of the correct answer: It must, by elimination, be choice (E).

8. **The correct answer is (D).** For this question, we must again check our choices against the restrictions given, but here we will have to dig a little deeper. As a matter of tactics, we would look at choices (A), (B), and (C) first, since they are simpler than choices (D) and (E). On the surface, there appears no good reason why those three could not be true. This is not to say that they are possible; rather, since there is no obvious reason for them to be impossible, we look for another, obvious answer. We find it in choice (D). This asserts that O and M ride in cars 1 and 3, in that order. But this is not possible, for this places M in a car without O or J. (Remember that J must ride in car 2.) Choice (E) is possible, for L is under no such restriction. So, as a matter of tactics, we preview the choices, looking for a good reason to select one. The point is, there might be some exotic reason why choice (B) or choice (A) is impossible, such as when K is in the first car, and M is in the third, G cannot be in the

second. But for a train of reasoning of this sort to be the key to the correct answer would make a very difficult problem indeed. With a set such as this, we do not expect to see such a difficult problem. So we look for a more obvious answer.

9. **The correct answer is (C).** We begin by using the additional information. With O in the third car and P in the second, we deduce:

1	2	3
G	J	O
H	P	M
K	N	L

for P requires N in the second car.

This means M must go with O in the third. Now, for G and H to go together, they must be in the first car. And K must go in the first car as well—not with O in the third car. This means that L will ride in the third car. Our diagram shows that choice (C) is necessarily true, while choices (A), (B), (D), and (E) are all false.

10. **The correct answer is (D).** Here we are looking for a reason to disqualify one of the individuals listed from riding with G. We know that G and H must go together, so what might disqualify another individual from riding in the same car? Again, rather than look for very subtle tricks, we look for an obvious disqualification. N and P must ride together, so N cannot ride with G, for that would put a total of four persons in the same car. Thus, choice (D) is correct. As for choice (A), we could have J, G, and H in the second car. As for choice (B), we could have G, K, and H in the first or third cars. Similarly with L, since L is under no restriction at all. Finally, choice (E) is also possible; with G, O, and H together, we can put M into the second car, so that M rides with J.

11. The correct answer is (D). We begin by processing the additional information. With G and O in the first car, we have H in the first car as well, so choice (A) is incorrect. With that first car full, M must ride in the second car with J, proving choice (D) is the correct answer. As for choice (E), this is false, since N and P together would preclude us from placing M with J. Finally, either K or L could ride with J and M in the second car, but that is only possibly and not necessarily true.

12. The correct answer is (D). Processing the additional information, we have:

1	2	3
G	J	M
H	N	O
K	P	L

With P in the second car, N must also ride in the second car. And this means that O must accompany M in the third car. This requires that G and H go in the first car, and that they be accompanied by K, who must not ride with O. So L must ride in the remaining spot in the third car. This proves that the correct answer is (D).

Questions 13–18

Here we have a linear ordering problem, a type now very familiar. We begin by summarizing the information:

N = 1 and P = 7
L > K
J > M
K > O > M or K < O < M

13. The correct answer is (B). We begin by processing the additional information. For J and O to be separated by exactly two grades, it must be that they

are in grades 2 and 5 or grades 3 and 6, though not necessarily in that order:

1	2	3	4	5	6	7
N	J			O		P
N	O			J		P
N		O			J	P
N		J			O	P

We can eliminate all but the third possibility. The first arrangement is not possible because we cannot honor the requirement J > M. The second is not possible because we cannot place O between K and M. The fourth is not possible for the same reason. Using only the third possibility, we know further:

	1	2	3	4	5	6	7
	N	K	O	M	L	J	P
or:	N	K	O	L	M	J	P
or:	N	M	O	K	L	J	P

This proves choice (B) is necessarily true. The diagram further shows that choices (A), (C), (D), and (E) are only possibly, though not necessarily, true.

14. The correct answer is (D). We begin by processing the additional information:

1	2	3	4	5	6	7
N	M	J	O	K	L	P

With J in grade 3, M must be in grade 2. And we know that L must be higher than K and, further, that O must go between K and M. This means that O, K, and L must be in grades 4, 5, and 6, respectively. The diagram shows that choice (D) is necessarily true and that each of the remaining choices is necessarily false.

15. The correct answer is (D). Enter the new information on a diagram:

1	2	3	4	5	6	7
N	K					P

Next, since K is in grade 2, the three students, O, M, and J, must be arranged in that order. So the only question is where to put L:

1	2	3	4	5	6	7
N	K	L	O	M	J	P
N	K	O	L	M	J	P
N	K	O	M	L	J	P
N	K	O	M	J	L	P

So L, M, or J could be in the fifth grade—but not O.

16. **The correct answer is (A).** We begin by processing the additional information:

1	2	3	4	5	6	7
N	M	J	O	K	L	P

We separate J from M by one grade by placing J in grade 3, which means that M, to be in a lower grade, must be in grade 2. Next, we reason that for L to be in a grade higher than K's and yet allowing that O must be between K and M, we have O, K, and L in grades 4 through 6, respectively. The diagram, therefore, proves that choice (A) is correct, while each of the other choices is necessarily false.

17. **The correct answer is (C).** Looking back over the work we have already done, we learned in our discussion of question 13 that O can be in grade 3 and that M can be in grade 4 or grade 5. Our discussion of question 14 shows that O can be in grade 4. So choices (A), (B), (D), and (E) are all possible. Choice (C), however, is not possible. If O is in the fifth grade, we cannot place either K or M above O without violating one or the other restriction that L > K and that J > M.

18. **The correct answer is (B).** We begin by processing the additional information:

1	2	3	4	5	6	7
N	K/M	O	K/M	J	L	P

For L to be in the grade ahead of J, they must be in grades 6 and 5, respectively; otherwise, it will not be possible to get O between K and M, since both K and M must be in grades lower than those of L and J, respectively. Then, we must put O between K and M, but there is no reason to place K in grade 2 and M in grade 4, as opposed to K in 4 and M in 2. So there are two possible arrangements, as shown by the diagram.

Questions 19–24

This is an ordering problem in which individuals are aligned two by two. We begin by summarizing the information:

$$\text{(P \& M)} \neq \text{last}$$
$$\text{L} \neq \text{Q}$$
$$\text{N} = \text{O}$$
$$\text{R} \rightarrow \text{L}$$

19. **The correct answer is (D).** With this question, we simply apply the initial conditions to each choice. All choices meet the requirement regarding P and M. Further, all choices meet the requirement on N and O. Finally, all choices meet the requirement on R and L. Choice (D), however, fails to meet the requirement that L and Q never ride together. The remaining choices respect this requirement. Choice (D), therefore, is not a possible order.

20. **The correct answer is (C).** We begin by processing the additional information. We know that R and L finish so that R is one place ahead of L. This means

that the order for this question must be O, R, and L. But with M following L, this means our O, R, L, and M order must be 1 through 4, respectively, for M never finishes last:

1	2	3	4	5
ON	R	L	MP	

There do not appear to be any further deductions of an obvious nature, so we check our choices against the diagram. We can see that choice (A) is definitely false, that choice (B) is definitely false, that choice (D) is only possibly true, and that choice (E) is only possibly true. Choice (C), however, is necessarily true, as shown by the diagram.

21. **The correct answer is (A).** We begin by processing the additional information:

1	2	3	4	5
PM	NO	R	L	

If N finishes second, then O must also finish second. And if R finishes third, then L must finish fourth. Since P and M must finish together in any place but fifth, P and M must finish first. This seems to be as far as we can go, so we look to the choices. Choice (A) is confirmed by our diagram. Choice (B) is shown by the diagram to be false. Choices (C) and (E) are incorrect for similar reasons. Q does not ride with L, so Q cannot finish in fourth place. Finally, choice (D) is possibly, though not necessarily, true.

22. **The correct answer is (C).** We begin by processing the additional information:

1	2	3	4	5
			R	L

We have three pairs of participants who must ride together: P and M, N and O, and, by stipulation, J and T. Of course, P and M cannot finish last, but they may

finish first or second. This means there are several ways of distributing our pairs. There is, however, one further deduction. Since our pairs, in whatever order they finish, occupy cars 1, 2, and 5 and since Q cannot ride with L, Q must ride in the third-place car and K in the fourth-place car.

23. **The correct answer is (E).** We begin by processing the additional information:

1	2	3	4	5
JR	KL	NO	MP	QT

With L in second place, R must finish first. This leaves only place 4 for the pair P and M. Then we know further that N finishes with O in place 3 and by stipulation that J rides with R and finishes first. Q cannot ride with L, so Q rides with T and finishes last, and K rides with L in the second-place car. Thus, the diagram confirms that choice (E) is correct and that the other choices are incorrect.

24. **The correct answer is (B).** For the final time, we begin by processing the additional information:

1	2	3	4	5
		MP		
or: R	L		R	L

We see that R and L must finish first and second or fourth and fifth, respectively. Since Q cannot ride with L and since the non-L car not occupied by a pair of participants is the R car, Q must ride with R. This means that Q finishes either first or fourth.

Section 2

1. **The correct answer is (C).** This is a main idea question. The author begins by posing the question: Why are affirmative action programs so controversial? The author then argues that affirmative

action is unlike ordinary government programs in the way it allocates the burden of the program. Because of this, the passage concludes, we are torn between supporting the programs (because they have legitimate goals) and condemning the programs (because of the way the cost is allocated). Choice (C) neatly describes this development. The author analyzes the structure of the moral dilemma. Choice (A) is incorrect since the comparison is but a subpart of the overall development and is used in the service of the larger analysis. Choice (B) is incorrect since the author reaches no such clear-cut decision. Rather, we are left with the question posed by the dilemma. Choice (D) is incorrect since the author presupposes in the presentation that the reader already understands the importance of the issue. Finally, choice (E) is incorrect since the advantages of the programs are mentioned only in passing.

2. **The correct answer is (A).** This is a logical structure question. In the second paragraph, the author will describe the general structure of government programs in order to set up the contrast with affirmative action. The discussion begins with "Setting aside...," indicating the author recognizes such cases and does not wish to discuss them in detail. Tolls and tuition are exceptions to the general rule, so the author explicitly sets them aside in order to preempt a possible objection to his analysis based on claimed counterexamples. Choice (B) is incorrect since the overall point of the passage is to discuss this dilemma, but the main point of the passage will not answer the question about the logical substructure of the argument. Choice (C) is incorrect since tolls and tuition are not ordinary government programs. Choice (D) is incorrect since the author never raises such doubts.

Finally, choice (E) misses the point of the examples. The point is not that they are costly but rather that the cost is borne by the specific user.

3. **The correct answer is (B).** This is an application question. In the first paragraph, the author states affirmative action is designed to achieve social and economic objectives. Although the claim is qualified, the author seems to believe that those arguments are in favor of affirmative action. So choice (B) is clearly supported by the text. Choice (A) is not supported by the text since the author leaves us with a question; the issue is not resolved. Choice (C) can be eliminated on the same ground. The author neither embraces nor rejects affirmative action. Choice (D) goes beyond the scope of the argument. While the author might wish that this were possible, nothing in the passage indicates such restructuring is possible. Indeed, in paragraph 3, the author remarks that the "funding" problem seems to be inherent. Finally, choice (E) can be eliminated on the same ground as choice (A). Though the author recognizes the unfairness of affirmative action, he also believes that the programs are valuable.

4. **The correct answer is (E).** In paragraph 2, the author mentions that government programs entail both social and economic costs. Then, the cost of the specific example, the passed-over worker, is not a government expenditure in the sense that money is laid out to purchase something. So the author is using the term "funding" in a non-standard way and wishes to call readers' attention to this. Choice (E) parallels this explanation. Choice (A) is incorrect since it is inconsistent with the reasoning just provided. Choice (B) is incorrect, for though the

author may believe that individuals bear a disproportionate share of the burden, this is not a response to the question asked. Choice (C) is incorrect for the same reason: It is a true but non-responsive statement. Finally, choice (D) fails for the same reason. Though the author notes that affirmative action programs are similar to other government programs in this respect, this is not an explanation for the author's placing "funding" in quotation marks.

5. **The correct answer is (D).** This is a logical structure question. In the final paragraph, the author analyzes a similar situation. This technique is called arguing from analogy. The strength of the argument depends on our seeing the similarity and accepting the conclusion of the one argument (the "villainous person") as applicable to the other argument (affirmative action). Choice (A) is perhaps the second-best response, but the author is not offering an illustration (e.g., an example of affirmative action). To be sure, the author is attempting to prove a point, but attempting to prove a conclusion is not equivalent to illustrating a contention. Choice (B) is incorrect since the author adduces the situation to support his contention. Choice (C) is incorrect since the author cites no authority. Finally, choice (E) can be eliminated since the author uses the case of the villainous person to support, not to weaken, the case.

6. **The correct answer is (B).** This is an explicit idea question. In paragraph 1, the author mentions that affirmative action is like other government programs in that it is designed to achieve certain social and economic goals. So choice (A) cites a similarity rather than a difference. Choice (C) can also be eliminated.

In paragraph 3, the author states that the relevant difference is not the method of allocating benefits. The salient difference is set forth in the same paragraph, and it is the difference described by choice (B). Choices (D) and (E) are simply not mentioned anywhere in the selection.

7. **The correct answer is (A).** This is an inference question. In the first paragraph, the author asks why affirmative action is so controversial. In the final paragraph, the answer is revealed: the moral dilemma. The wording of the passage, for example, "we are confronted with...," indicates that the author expects his reader will share this tension. So the passage is addressed to those who think affirmative action has value but who also believe it is unfair to non-minority persons. As for choice (B), the author believes that affirmative action is based on sound premises, achieving a legitimate social goal, but that the world is built so that we encounter this conflict. As for choice (C), it is not the programs themselves that contain contradictions. Rather, it is our value structure that creates the conflict. As for choice (D), the author believes the reader will regard the programs as creating suffering but not that the suffering is needless. It may very well be the cost that must be paid. Choice (E) is easily eliminated since the author expresses reservations about the programs.

8. **The correct answer is (E).** This is a main idea question but one that asks about the main idea in the abstract. The discussion thus far makes clear the justification for choice (E). The author has a sense of this moral dilemma—which, it is expected, will be shared by readers—and wants to explain why we experience this as conflict. As for choice (A), though the author develops a dilemma, the text does

not suggest that it is possible to slip between the horns of the dilemma. As for choice (B), the author offers no refutation, so we will eliminate this as incorrect. As for choice (C), any historical references are purely incidental to the overall development of the thesis. And as for choice (D), though the analysis of affirmative action may suggest to the reader a method of analyzing other social problems, the focus of the passage is a particular problem—not methodology.

9. **The correct answer is (A).** This is an inference question. The material we need is in the first paragraph. There the author discusses the high percentage of aged persons living in Sweden and notes that relatively few live with family. The author then states that Sweden placed a moratorium on the construction of acute beds in favor of long-term beds. From the order of presentation, we may infer that the one caused the other. So choice (A) is inferable from the text. Choice (B) is incorrect since no mention is made of tax laws. Choice (C) is incorrect and represents a confused reading of the second paragraph. Wages in the health field are depressed because of historical circumstances, not government policy. Choice (D) is incorrect and is a confused reading of the final paragraph. The text states that rooms are now designed to accommodate more patients, not that more patients are being crowded into small rooms. Choice (E) is incorrect and is a misreading of the first paragraph. The moratorium halted the building of acute-care beds, not long-term beds.

10. **The correct answer is (E).** This is an explicit idea question. Choices (A), (B), (C), and (D) are all mentioned in paragraph 3 as contributing to staffing problems. Choice (E), however, is not

mentioned. Though the author cites irregular hours as a problem, long hours are never mentioned as contributing to the staffing problem.

11. **The correct answer is (B).** This is an inference question. In the second paragraph, the author notes that wages in the health sector (aside from those of doctors) have traditionally been lower than those for comparable work in non-health-care sectors because of a traditional presumption that health care is eleemosynary, or charitable, work. Choice (B) nicely captures this idea. Choice (A) is incorrect since it fails to make this connection. Moreover, it will not do to argue that, generally speaking, low-paying jobs have a lower status. In the first place, that does not respond to the question, which asks about the health field. In the second, that low status and low pay are correlated does not mean that one necessarily causes the other. As for choice (C), though the passage states that doctors earned acceptable salaries, the passage does not suggest that other workers were paid low wages because of this. It was traditional bias against health-care workers other than doctors, who are professionals, which accounted for the low compensation. Choice (D) is incorrect, for while it makes a true statement, the statement is not responsive to the question. Finally, choice (E) is not suggested by the text.

12. **The correct answer is (A).** This is an inference question. At the beginning of paragraph 2, the author notes that staff costs are the most important budgetary component of health care and, further, that this is higher for chronic aged than for acute patients. Since the author uses long-term care and care for the chronic aged almost interchangeably, we may

infer that most long-term care is for the aged. So we conclude that the staff cost for long-term care generally is greater than for acute care. This is stated by choice (A). Every other answer choice can be eliminated. Choice (B) must be incorrect, for to the extent that staffing requirements are greater for long-term than for acute care, the general inflationary trend in labor costs will cause the cost of long-term care to rise more rapidly than that of acute care. Choice (C) can be eliminated because the last paragraph establishes that there is a connection. Choice (D) cannot be inferred since no mention is ever made of methods of payment. Finally, choice (E) is not supported by the passage. Though we have information about relative numbers of aged living with family, that will not generate a conclusion about relative cost.

13. **The correct answer is (A).** This is an inference question. The author states in the final paragraph that cutbacks in funding actually lead to better care. This is labelled paradoxical. This can only be paradoxical if cutbacks in funding ordinarily result in a decline in the quality of care and increases improve quality. This is answer choice (A). As for choice (B), though this may be true (and that is a question we need not answer), this will not answer the question posed. As for choice (C), though this is clearly stated in the passage, it does not explain why the cutback in funding led, paradoxically, to an improvement in care. Choice (D) can be eliminated for it, too, does not explain the paradox. Finally, choice (E) is a confused reading of the first paragraph. The moratorium was placed on construction of acute-care beds; then, later, there was a cutback in funding for long-term care.

14. **The correct answer is (B).** This is an application question of some difficulty. The author states that rising standards of living have decreased the willingness of young adults to care for aging parents in their own homes. The percentage in Sweden is 10 percent as compared with 20 to 30 and even higher percentages in other countries. There is also the intriguing note that it is only 3 percent in Stockholm. Why the large difference between Sweden as a whole and Stockholm? If it were the case that the standard of living is higher in Stockholm than in Sweden as a country, this would add support to the author's explanation. This is articulated in choice (B). As for choice (A), if the U.S. has a higher standard of living, this would undermine the author's point. That would suggest a higher percentage of aged not cared for in homes, yet the numbers show a higher percentage of aged living with family in the U.S. Choice (C) is incorrect for it is only remotely connected, if at all, with the cause for the percentages under consideration. Choice (D) will not do the trick, for we are interested in percentage of aged living with family, not in the absolute number of aged. Finally, choice (E) must fail for the same reason that choice (C) fails: it is only remotely, if at all, connected to the question of why aged parents are not cared for in family homes.

15. **The correct answer is (E).** This is an explicit idea question. According to the passage, automated theorem proving, of which AURA is the best example, is used to check human reasoning. So choice (E) is the best response to the question. Choice (A) is incorrect, since though this is a feature of programs such as "expert" programs, it is not the primary purpose of a system such as AURA. Choice (B)

fails for the same reason; this is one of many possible applications. Choice (C) is incorrect since the function of AURA is to check human reasoning. To the extent that it can be used to analyze other computer programs, an issue we need not resolve, that is not the ultimate or primary purpose. The passage is quite clear on this score. The purpose of AURA is to aid human beings in solving problems by checking logic. Finally, choice (D) is just one of several possible applications.

16. **The correct answer is (D).** This is a main idea question, cast in the form of a "best title" question. The best title will be neither too broad nor too narrow—that is, just right. Choice (A) is too broad. The author is discussing one limited aspect of computer use. Choice (B) too is wide of the mark. Though AURA programs may have some implications for theories of artificial intelligence, the author does not discuss them. Choice (C) is surely the second best answer, but it is too narrow on two counts. First, AURA is just an example of how computers might be used to assist human reasoning. So choice (D) is better in this respect. Second, even allowing that AURA is the best example of this possibility, the discussion of AURA is broader than just possible applications. The author sketches some basic theoretical concepts of AURA as well. Choice (E) is wide of the mark since the author seems to endorse the use of AURA.

17. **The correct answer is (D).** This is an explicit idea question. Choices (A), (B), (C), and (E) are all mentioned as advantages of expert programs in paragraph 3. The only reference to self-analytical programs is in paragraph 2. There the author states that AURA is not self-analytical.

18. **The correct answer is (C).** This is an explicit idea question. Choices (A) and (E)

are mentioned in paragraph 3. Choices (B) and (D) are mentioned in paragraph 2.

19. **The correct answer is (B).** This is a fairly interesting application question. In the second paragraph, the author describes the theory of the AURA program. The computer is given the design of the system and then told that the goal cannot be reached given the design. Then, if the computer finds a contradiction in that information, this means the goal will be achieved by the design. In other words, we have a sort of indirect proof. We take the set of premises and the negation of the conclusion we hope to prove. If a contradiction can be found in the premises and negation of the conclusion, then the conclusion itself is proved. Applying this to our question, if the assertion that the switch remains open generates a contradiction, then the opposite conclusion is proved: The switch should be closed. And that answer is choice (B). Choice (A) is too broad a conclusion. The contradiction does not prove the system was well designed, only that the result described by choice (B) will occur. That may or may not be the desired result. Choice (C) is incorrect for it is contradicted by our analysis. Choices (D) and (E) make the same error as choice (A), just in the opposite direction.

20. **The correct answer is (A).** This is a tone question. The author obviously thinks very highly of the development he is describing. The only adjective in the array of choices consistent with this attitude is choice (A). Every other choice has certain negative connotations. But no reservations are expressed by the author.

21. **The correct answer is (A).** This is a main idea question. Choice (A) nicely describes the approach of the author. He

describes recent developments in computer applications. Choice (B) is incorrect since there is no misconception mentioned. To be sure, the author answers the second question (Will computers replace humans?) in the negative. But that is not the same thing as correcting a misconception. Choice (C) is incorrect since the author describes, but does not propose, a theory. Choice (D) is incorrect, for no objections are raised. Finally, choice (E) is incorrect since the author does not focus on any particular problem and propose a solution. In general, it is possible to argue that there are elements of choices (B), (C), (D), or (E) in the passage, but it cannot be said that any one of those is the main point of the passage.

22. **The correct answer is (A).** This is a main idea question. The passage actually makes two points: Who is Josquin, and why have we never heard of him? Choice (A) correctly mentions both of these. Choice (B) is incorrect since the main focus is not to describe medieval music at all. Rather, the author focuses on Josquin, a man of the Renaissance. Choice (C) is incorrect because the author is more concerned to introduce the reader to Josquin than to place Josquin into a context. And in any event, though the author mentions some ways in which Josquin broke with his predecessors, this is not a discussion of his "influence on later composers." Choice (D) is incorrect, for the enumeration of features of Josquin's music is incidental to the task of introducing the reader to Josquin. Moreover, the author does not offer critical commentary. The mere fact that the passage praises Josquin's music does not constitute critical analysis. Finally, choice (E) is incorrect because it fails to refer to

the second major aspect of the passage: Why is Josquin not better known?

23. **The correct answer is (E).** This is an explicit idea question. Choice (A) is answered in paragraph two ("Solace me, . . ."). Choice (B) is answered in the final paragraph (sackbut). Choice (C) is answered in the second paragraph (Ockeghem). An answer to choice (D) is suggested in the final paragraph. Choice (E) must be the correct answer, since the author never makes reference to any students.

24. **The correct answer is (E).** This is an inference question. In the third paragraph, the author lists certain difficulties in reading a Renaissance score: no tempo specified, missing flats and sharps, no instrument/voice indication, and no instruction as to whether a piece is written in a major or a minor key. Since these are regarded as deficiencies of Renaissance scoring, we may infer that modern music notation contains all of these. But choice (E) overstates the case. Although modern notation provides more guidance, the author does not say that it leaves literally no room for individual interpretation.

25. **The correct answer is (B).** This is an application question. The support for choice (B) is found in paragraph 3, where the author discusses the distinction between concept and performance. The author states that music does not exist as printed notes. The notation is just a set of instructions for producing music. So the author would agree with choice (B). As for choice (A), it is conceivable that the author might endorse this statement—though it is also possible that the author would reject it. It is clear, however, that as between the statement in choice (B) and that in choice (A), we can be sure that

the author would endorse choice (B). So choice (B), rather than choice (A), must be correct. Choice (C) is incorrect because Josquin belongs to the Renaissance, not the Middle Ages. Choice (D) fails for the same reason that choice (A) fails. Finally, there is no support for the statement in choice (E).

26. **The correct answer is (D).** Here, too, we have an application question. There is some merit to each of the choices, but we are looking for the one answer that is most closely connected with the text. Since the author discusses the lack of funding as one important reason for Josquin's obscurity, an obscurity the author deplores, the argument might be used to support a proposal for funds to promote Josquin's music. That is choice (D). Choice (A) is less clearly supported by the text. To the extent that it is read as a device to promote Josquin's music, it would be less effective than choice (D) since the author states that *collegia musica* have a high turnover of students. Establishing yet another one would not do as much to bring Josquin's music to more people as choice (D). As for choices (B) and (E), these do not tie in with the idea of publicizing Josquin's music. Finally, choice (C) has some plausibility, but choice (D) has a connection with the passage that choice (C) lacks.

27. **The correct answer is (B).** This is an explicit idea question. Choices (C), (D), and (E) are mentioned in the final paragraph. Choice (A) is mentioned in the third paragraph. Choice (B) is never mentioned. The author states that musicians who read modern notation have difficulty reading Renaissance notation—not that these musicians lack talent.

28. **The correct answer is (A).** This is a tone question. The author compares Josquin to Galileo in order to praise Josquin. This must mean that the author has a very high opinion of Galileo. So choices (D) and (E) can be eliminated because they are merely neutral. Choice (B) can be eliminated because of its negative connotations. And choice (C) can be eliminated as being lukewarm, when the author is clearly enthusiastic about Josquin and therefore Galileo as well.

Section 3

1. **The correct answer is (B).** This question requires careful attention to the quantifiers in each claim. An additional expense voucher might indicate additional expenses for an already identified employee or expenses incurred by an additional employee. A claim that states only that there are "at least so many employees" and that they incurred "at least this in expenses" cannot be contradicted by a revision upward in any number. A claim that states "there were exactly so many employees" or which states "there were at most so many employees" is contradicted by the discovery of another employee. The same reasoning applies to expenses. An "at least" claim is not contradicted by an upward revision, but the other claims are. Choice (A) can be contradicted by an upward revision in the number of employees. Choice (C) can be contradicted by an upward revision in the amount of expenses claimed. Choices (D) and (E) can be contradicted on both grounds. Choice (B) cannot be contradicted by any new finding.

2. **The correct answer is (A).** The question stem contains a hidden assumption: It is a loaded question. It presupposes that the person questioned agrees that

the city is discriminating against its Hispanic residents. Choice (A) is a pretty nice parallel. The questioner assumes that the Congressman agrees that defense spending is out of hand, which may or may not be true. Choice (B) makes no such assumption. It can be answered with a simple "yes" if the chairperson plans to take a luncheon recess; otherwise a "no" will do the job. Choice (C) requires more than a "yes" or "no" answer, but it still contains no presuppositions. Since the question asks "what," the speaker may respond by saying much, little, or none at all. Choice (D) may be said to make a presupposition—Gladys is going to the store—but here the presupposition is not concealed. It is made an explicit condition of the answer. Finally, choice (E) is a little like choice (B) in that a simple "yes" or "no" can communicate the counselor's opinion. It might be objected that choice (E) presupposes that the company has an affirmative action program and that this makes it similar to the question stem. Two responses can be made. First, choice (E) is in this way like choice (D): The assumption—if there is one—is fairly explicit. Second, choice (E) does not have the same loaded tone as choice (A) does, so by comparison, choice (A) is a better choice.

3. **The correct answer is (E).** The ad is a little deceptive. It tries to create the impression that if hospitals are using Dr. John's Milk of Magnesia, people will believe it is a good product. But what the ad actually says is that Dr. John uses the same *ingredient* that hospitals use (milk of magnesia is a simple suspension of magnesium hydroxide in water). The ad is something like an ad for John's Vinegar that claims it has "acetic acid," which is vinegar. Choices (A), (B), (C), and (D), in various ways, fall into the trap of the

inviting wording, and those statements are not conclusions that can be logically inferred. Choice (E), however, is logically inferable: from 9 of 10 X use Y, you can infer that it is true that Y is used by 9 out of 10 X.

4. **The correct answer is (A).** Statements (1) and (4) combine to give us choice (A). If all wheeled conveyances that travel on the highway are polluters, and a bicycle does not travel on the highway, then a bicycle cannot be a polluter. If choice (A) is then correct, choice (B) must be incorrect because bicycles do not travel on the highways at all. Choices (C) and (D) make the same mistake. (3) must be read to say, "If I am driving, it is raining," not "If it is raining, I am driving." Choice (E) is clearly false since my car is driven on the highway. Don't make the problem harder than it is.

5. **The correct answer is (E).** Picking up on our discussion of choices (C) and (D) in the previous question, (3) must read, "If I am driving, then it is raining." Let that be: "If P, then Q." If we then had not-Q, we could deduce not-P. Choice (E) gives us not-Q by changing (4) to "It is not raining." Changing (1) or (2) or even both is not going to do the trick, for they don't touch the relationship between my driving my car and rain—they deal only with pollution and we need the car to be connected. Similarly, if we change (3) to make it deal with pollution, we have not adjusted the connection between my driving and rain, so choice (C) must be wrong. Choice (D) is the worst of all the answers. Whether or not rainwater is polluted has nothing to do with the connection between my driving and rain. Granted, there is the unstated assumption that my car only pollutes when I drive it, but this is OK.

6. **The correct answer is (E).** The reasoning in the argument is representative of the fallacy of false cause. Common sense tells you that you are not necessarily safer driving at higher speeds. Moreover, the distance you are from your home does not necessarily make you more or less safe. And it will not do to engage in wild speculation, e.g., people suddenly become more attentive at speeds over 45 miles per hour. The exam is just not that subtle. Rather we should look for a fairly obvious alternative explanation, and we find it in choice (E). The real reason there are fewer fatalities at speeds over 50 miles per hour and at a distance greater than 25 miles from home is that less driving time is logged under such conditions. Most driving originates at home and proceeds at speeds set for residential areas. Choices (A), (B), and (C) all seem to make plausible statements, but they are irrelevant to the claim made in the stem paragraph. It is difficult to see how they could either weaken or strengthen the argument. Choice (D) has the merit of addressing the statistics used to support the argument, but without further information choice (D) does not weaken the argument—it merely makes an observation. To be sure, if we knew that states were notoriously bad at gathering statistics, choice (D) could weaken the argument. But that requires speculation, and we always prefer an obvious answer such as choice (E).

7. **The correct answer is (D).** The author states that a certain amount of rain in a given time *usually* results in mushrooms growing in his backyard. Both choices (A) and (B) are wrong for the same reason. From the fact that there has not been the requisite minimum rainfall required for mushrooms, we would not want to conclude that there has been *no* rain at all. Choice (C) overstates the author's case and is for that reason wrong. The author specifically qualifies his claim by saying it "usually" happens this way. Thus, we would not want to say that the absence of mushrooms and fungus definitely means that the requisite amount of rain has not fallen—only that it seems likely or probable that there has not been enough rain. And choice (E) would not be supportable without some further premise about rain now. Notice that choice (D) is a safe conclusion: "probably" and "not more."

8. **The correct answer is (C).** Given the fairly "soft" information provided in the paragraph, any conclusion that is to be "completely justified" on the basis of that information will have to be a fairly minimal claim. We can eliminate choice (A) since the paragraph asserts something about the effect of Jack Remain's program but never claims that the Jack Remain program is unique in this respect. Choice (B) goes beyond the scope of the argument by asserting the program is effective for all ages. The paragraph actually makes only a minimal claim, namely, this is possible. Even if the program is effective only for persons 20 to 25, the claim is not false—it is true though only for that limited age group. Choice (D) overstates the case. The paragraph claims that weight loss is possible—not that it is certain. Choice (E) cannot be justified since that would be to move from the premise "weight loss is possible" to the conclusion "most people need exercise to lose weight." But the conclusion does not follow from the premise. Choice (C), however, can be justified. If it is true, as the stem asks us to assume, that a

study shows weight loss is possible, then it must be true that the program is effective for some—even if only for one person. This is all choice (C) claims: You might be one of the lucky ones.

9. **The correct answer is (D).** In essence, the advertisement attempts to shift the burden of proof to the reader. It is possible—you try it and find out whether it is possible for you. Choice (E) is incorrect since no other claims are cited. Choice (C) is incorrect since the ad is clearly an attempt to influence the reader's decision. Choice (B) should be eliminated in favor of choice (A) since the paragraph is not a logical set of premises. This leaves choice (A) as the second-best answer. And it can be argued that the paragraph does provide evidence (the study) and, further, that it does allow the reader to reach a conclusion. But what would that conclusion be? If the conclusion mentioned in choice (A) is to try or not to try the product, then choice (A) is incorrect since the ad reaches the conclusion that the reader should try it. But if the conclusion is whether or not the product works, then choice (D) is better because it more accurately describes the attempt to shift the burden of proof.

10. **The correct answer is (B).** The author's claim is self-referential—it refers to itself or includes itself in its own description. The author says that *every* action is economically motivated; therefore, we may conclude that the motivation in making such a claim and in writing a book about it is also economically motivated. The speaker in our passage says it is possible to apply the author's theory to the author's own actions. This is why choice (B) is correct. Neither choice (A)

nor choice (E) can be correct inasmuch as the author of the book claims that there are no such motivations. Ultimately, the author says, all motivations can be reduced to one, economics. Choice (C) has to be wrong, since the author of the book claims that everything done is economically motivated. The examples make it clear that even a reformer with some seemingly non-economic motive would be "pure" only on the surface, with a deeper, economic motivation for reforming. Finally, choice (D) can be rejected since it conflicts with one of the examples given by the author of the book.

11. **The correct answer is (A).** The argument makes the rather outlandish assumption that the physical characteristics of the criminal dictate the kind of crime that will be committed. But as unreasonable as that may seem in light of common sense, it *is* an assumption made by the speaker. (We did not make the assumption, the speaker did.) Choice (B) is not an assumption of the argument, since the paragraph specifically states that the killer was executed—the speaker cannot have escaped. Choice (C) does not commit the blatant error committed by choice (B), but it is still wrong. Although choice (C) might be a better explanation for the crimes now being committed than that proposed by our speaker, our speaker advances the explanation supported by choice (A), not choice (C). In fact, the speaker uses phrases such as "looks very much like" that tell us that he assumes there are two killers. As for choices (D) and (E), these may or may not be true in the real world, but they are not assumptions of the speaker's argument.

12. **The correct answer is (A).** The form of
the argument can be represented using
letters as follows:

(1) All R are either O or W. (All
non-Readers are non-Opinion holders or Wrong.)

(2) All O are R.

If (2) is true, (1) might be either false or
true, since it is possible that there are
some who have not read the report who
hold right opinions. That is, even if (2) is
true and all O are R, that does not tell us
anything about all the Rs, only about all
the Os. The rest of the Rs might be Ws
(wrong-opinion holders) or something else
altogether (right-opinion holders). By this
reasoning, we see that we cannot conclude that (1) is definitely true, so choice
(B) must be wrong. Moreover, we have no
ground for believing (1) to be more or less
likely true, so choice (C) can be rejected.
As for choice (D), even if we assume that
all the Rs are either O or W, we are not
entitled to conclude that all Os are Rs.
There may be someone without an opinion who has not read the report. Finally
choice (E), if it is false that all the Os
(non-opinion holders) are not Rs, this
tells us nothing about all Rs and their
distribution among O and W.

13. **The correct answer is (A).** The fallacy
in the author's argument is that he takes
a group term ("the average size of women")
and applies it to the individual. Choice
(A) calls attention to this fallacy. The
average size of women is irrelevant in the
case of those women who are of sufficient
size. Choice (D) concedes too much to the
author. We do not have to settle for the
conclusion that some women may be suitable for desk jobs. We can win the larger
claim that some women may be suitable
to be police officers—or at least as suitable as their male counterparts. Choices

(B), (C), and (E) are possible arguments
to be used against the author's general
position. We might want to claim, for
example, that training or weapons will
compensate for want of size, but again
there is no reason even to grant the
author that much. We do not even have to
concede that the average size is relevant.
Finally, choice (E) also gives away too
much. Although the use of pistols is sometimes called "deadly force," the author's
linkage of size to force specifies force as
being a strength or size idea.

14. **The correct answer is (D).** We can use
our capital letters to see why choice (D) is
the correct answer. The structure of the
stem argument is as follows:

No S are R.

Some S are D.

Therefore, some D are not R.

Choice (D) shares this form:

All pets are excluded: No P are A.

(A = allowed)

Some P are V.

(Many = Some)

Therefore, some V are not A.

Choice (A) has a very different form since
it is presented as a probabilistic, not a
deductive or logical, argument. Choice
(B)'s conclusion goes beyond the information given in the premises. We cannot
conclude that the uncle enjoys paying the
bills, even though he may incur them.
Choice (C) has the following form:

Some BB are F.

All F is WR.

Therefore, all BB are WR.

This does not parallel our question stem
for two reasons. First, our stem argument is valid, while the argument in
choice (C) is not. Second, choice (D) is

more nearly parallel to the stem argument than choice (C); for even if we rearrange the assumptions in choice (C) to put the "all" proposition first and the "some" proposition second, the "all's" and the "some's" of choice (C) do not parallel those of the question stem. Choice (E) does not share the stem form. First, it is not the same argument form (all, some, etc.). Second, choice (E) is clearly not a proper logical argument.

15. **The correct answer is (A).** Perhaps a little diagram is the easiest way to show this problem.

We will show all B are T by eliminating that portion of the diagram where some area of B is not also inside T:

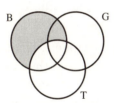

Now, let us put an x to show the existence of those Bs that are Gs:

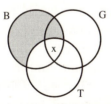

The diagram shows us that (1) is true. Since the only areas left for Bs are within the T circle, the G condition is unimportant. (2) is not inferable. Although there is some overlap of the G and T circles, there is also some non-overlap. This shows that it may be possible to be a T without

also being a G. (3) is not inferable since our diagrams are restricted to the three categories B, G, and T and say nothing about things outside of those categories. The "x" on the diagram shows that choices (D) and (E) are necessarily false.

16. **The correct answer is (C).** The stem argument has the form "If P, then Q. Q. Therefore, P." The argument is invalid. There may be other reasons that the razor is not functioning, e.g., the switch is not on, it is broken, etc. Choice (C) has this form also. John's fingerprints might have been found at the scene, yet he may not have committed the crime. Choice (A) has the form: "If P, then Q. Not Q. Therefore, not P," which not only is not parallel to the question stem, but also is valid and thus a poor parallel to the invalid original argument as well. Choice (B) has the form: "P or Q. Not P. Therefore, Q." This, too, does not parallel the stem argument, and, like choice (B), is valid. Choice (D) is invalid, but the fallacy is not the same as what we find in the stem argument. The stem argument is set up using "if, then" statements. Choice (D) does not parallel this form. Choice (E) does use "if, then" statements, but its form is: "If P, then Q. P. Therefore, P." This argument is clearly valid.

17. **The correct answer is (A).** The author's statement is self-contradictory or paradoxical. It says, in effect, "No statement is always correct," but then that statement itself must be false—since it attempts to make a claim about "always." The author's statement is inductive, that is, a generalization; but choice (E) is not as good an answer as choice (A) because it fails to pick up on the fact that the statement is internally contradictory. The statement cannot be valid, choice (D), since the author tries to pass it off as a

generalization. Generalizations can be strong or weak, well founded or ill founded, but they cannot be valid or invalid. Choice (C) is incorrect since there is nothing ambiguous or poorly defined in the argument. Finally, the argument is not circular, choice (B), because the author does not seek to establish his conclusion by assuming it. As we have noted, the statement is self-contradictory, so it could not possibly be circular.

18. **The correct answer is (B).** This item asks you to draw a conclusion from the paragraph. The best answer will be one that is well supported by the text, and this is choice (B). The initial paragraph sets up a contrast between political commitment and financial reward and indicates that Gonzalez chose political commitment over financial reward. The conclusion of the paragraph should be some consequence of this decision. Choice (B) describes a possible consequence of this decision.

Choice (A) is wrong because the paragraph implies that she did not enjoy popular acclaim. Choice (C) is incorrect because it goes beyond the scope of the selection. Although choice (C) describes an idea that is generally related to the subject matter of the paragraph, it does not flow as a conclusion from the distinction drawn in the paragraph. Choice (D) must surely be wrong, for Gonzalez's resistance to certain inducements would not be calculated to compromise the chances of those who came later. And finally, choice (E) makes the same mistake as choice (C). To be sure, this is an idea that is generally related to the subject of the initial paragraph, but this idea does not follow as a conclusion from the paragraph.

19. **The correct answer is (E).** Again, we are looking for a choice that is strongly supported by the text, and this time it is choice (E). The paragraph clearly implies a distinction between economic reward and political commitment and that the latter was the course chosen by Gonzalez. As for choices (A) and (D), these are topics that conceivably were treated by Gonzalez's films, but nothing in the paragraph requires such a conclusion. Choice (C), though possible, is not supported by the text.

20. **The correct answer is (A).** Analyze the argument into its various premises.

   1 Some experts maintain reductions will hurt care of the elderly and chronically ill.

   2 Part of recent increases in costs have helped provide service to these groups.

   3 But the real causes of high costs are duplication, inefficiency, inflated salaries.

Once the argument is analyzed in this way, you can see that the most likely conclusion is that contained in choice (A): Efforts to control costs will necessarily hurt the elderly and chronically ill that much.

Choice (B) is probably the second best response, but a careful reading of choice (B) shows that it is fatally flawed. Choice (B) asserts that duplication and inefficiency contribute to the rising cost of care for the elderly and the chronically ill. But the passage says (1) that recent increases in the cost of care for those groups reflect improvements in service and (2) that the factors cited inflate health-care costs in general, not just those specifically incurred by the elderly or chronically ill.

Choice (C), of course, is contradicted by the passage. Choice (D), too, is at least in tension with the passage, for the author implies that some of the increase in health-care costs for the elderly and chronically ill have come as the result of improvements in services. Finally, choice (E) goes beyond the scope of the passage. In the first place, you would need to know whether elderly and chronically ill pay their own expenses (as opposed to having them paid by the government or a third-party carrier), and the passage is silent on that question. In addition, you would need a lot more to support the conclusion that rising costs will make health care unaffordable for those groups, as opposed to just burdensome.

21. **The correct answer is (C).** The logical flaw in the argument is not that difficult to find. The argument assumes that a city that ranks below another city in any one category (in particular the crime category) cannot rank above that city in the overall category. Now the question becomes which of the choices attacks this assumption.

The best available attack is provided by choice (C). Although this choice does not state directly that the assumption just isolated is erroneous, it does provide two counterexamples to the assumption. Choices (A), (B), and (E) make assertions not inconsistent with the information provided in the paragraph about Detroit and San Francisco, and they don't attack the hidden premise we have isolated. Finally, choice (D) is somewhat like the correct answer, but it does not attack the hidden assumption in the way that choice (C) does. Notice that choice (D) describes a situation in which the city that ranks lower in the overall standings also ranks lower in other categories as well.

22. **The correct answer is (B).** This item serves as a good reminder of the importance of reading the answer choices carefully, for some of the choices here are very close. The speaker says that adults often assume that a child feels like a child but thinks like an adult. But, according to the speaker, this is wrong—the opposite is true. But what is the opposite? Children feel not like children but like adults, and children think not like adults but like children. This is the conclusion provided by Choice (B).

As for choice (A), while the speaker apparently believes that there is some connection between the emotional and mental functions of a child and those of an adult, nothing in the passage supports the conclusion that the one prefigures the other. Choice (C), too, goes beyond the scope of the paragraph. The speaker claims that there are some similarities and some differences between children and adults, but that premise will not support the conclusion that the differences are more important than the similarities. The suggestion in choice (D) seems to be contradicted by the selection, for the speaker clearly says that thought patterns change. Finally, choice (E) is surely the second best answer, for it at least has the merit of suggesting a reversal of a position. But when the speaker asserts "the opposite is true," the speaker means the opposite of the contention of many adults (specifically, that children think like adults but feel like children). The speaker does not mean that children and adults have opposite reactions to the same situations.

23. **The correct answer is (A).** Here you can use the same devices you use in solving analytical reasoning items to keep track of this information. The statements

in the initial paragraph can be summarized as follows:

SY → (FG or SG)   (Sunny implies Fishing or Swimming)

SG → TS   (Swimming implies Tennis)

~TS   (Not tennis)

From this you can infer ~SG. (Hector did not go swimming.) But you cannot infer from the fact that Hector did not go swimming that he did or did not go fishing; and since he might have gone fishing, it is possible that Saturday was sunny. No information is provided about Sharon's behavior when she is not playing tennis or what anyone does when it is cloudy, so neither choice (D) nor choice (E) can be deduced.

24. **The correct answer is (C).** This is a fun little item. John says the dollars should be spent right here on Earth, meaning, of course, they should be spent on practical projects rather than projects such as space exploration. Joan turned John's language around on him by pointing out that—literally—this money is spent right here on Earth (even if it is for space exploration). Notice how the question stem here guides you. It doesn't just ask you to comment on the exchange. It informs you that the exchange is characterized by a shift in meaning and then asks you to identify the critical term.

25. **The correct answer is (B).** The conclusion of the argument is "I am not impaired." The premise is "I drank wine, but I did not drink liquor." One possible assumption that could underwrite the conclusion is "It is impossible to become impaired drinking wine." This, however, is not a possible choice. But choice (B) does articulate a possible hidden assumption. The speaker means to say "I can't be drunk, I have only been drinking wine and not liquor." (An obviously fallacious argument but for reasons not presently relevant.) This claim depends on the assumption that hard liquor impairs more than wine.

Section 4

1. **The correct answer is (B).** The proposition that you cannot argue with taste says that taste is relative. Since we are looking for an answer choice inconsistent with that proposition, we seek an answer choice that argues that taste, or aesthetic value, is absolute, or at least not relative—that there are standards of taste. Choice (B) is precisely that.

Choices (C) and (D) are just distractions, playing on the notion of taste in the physical sense and the further idea of the distasteful; but these superficial connections are not strong enough.

Choices (A), (B), and (E) are all activities in which there is some element of aesthetic judgment or appreciation. In choice (A), the holding of an exhibition, while implying some selection principle and thus some idea of a standard of taste, does not truly purport to judge aesthetics in the way that choice (B), precisely a beauty contest, does. The exhibition may be of historical or biographical interest, for example. Choice (E) also stresses more of the exhibition aspect than the judging aspect. You should not infer that all movie festivals are contests, since the word "festival" does not require this interpretation and, in fact, there are festivals at which the judging aspect is minimal or non-existent. The Cannes Film Festival, while perhaps the best known, is not the only type of movie festival there is. The questions are not tests of your knowledge of the movie industry.

2. **The correct answer is (D).** Note the question stem very carefully: We are to find the answer choice from which we can deduce the sample argument. You must pay very careful attention to the question stem in every problem. Choice (D) works very nicely as it gives us the argument structure: "All post-1974 students are required…. George is a post-1974 student. Therefore, George is required…." Actually, the middle premise is phrased in the conditional (with an "if"), but our explanation is close enough, even if it is a bit oversimplified. Choice (A) will not suffice, for while it describes the situation before 1974, it just does not address itself to the post-1974 situation. And George is a post-1974 student. Choice (B) also fails. From the fact that all of those who took the course graduated after 1974, we cannot conclude that George was one of them (any more than we can conclude from the proposition that all airline flight attendants lived after 1900 and that Richard Nixon, who lived after 1900, was one of them). Choice (C) fails for the same reason that choice (A) fails. Choice (E) is a bit tricky because of the double negative. It makes the sentence awkward. The easiest way to handle such a sentence is to treat the double negative as an affirmative. The negative cancels the negative, just as in arithmetic a negative number times a negative number yields a positive number. So choice (E) actually says that before 1974, the course was not required. That is equivalent to choice (A) and must be wrong for the same reason.

3. **The correct answer is (B).** Choice (B) is the only one of the three that is completely supported by the argument. Choice (C) is easily dismissed. That there

are no minnows on this side of the lake now surely does not mean that there will never be any, any more than the fact that there are no children in the park now means that there never will be any children in the park. Choice (A) is very close to choice (B) and differs only in the qualification introduced by the word "probably," but that is an important qualification. The author states specifically that bass are usually found wherever there are minnows. So where there are no bass, he expects to find no minnows. But, of course, he cannot be certain. Perhaps there are other reasons for the absence of bass: The water is too cold or too shallow or too muddy for bass, though not for minnows. So choice (A) overstates the case. The author apparently allows that you may find minnows without bass—but not usually. Choice (D) cannot be deduced from the premises since no information is provided about rivers (as opposed to lakes). And choice (E) is not inferable since the information about lakes does not preclude the possibility that largemouths are found elsewhere.

4. **The correct answer is (D).** Juanita wonders how Tommy knows the phone has rung if he couldn't hear it because of the shower. She overlooks the possibility that he learned the phone had rung without actually hearing it himself. Perhaps someone else lives with him who heard it; perhaps Tommy has an answering machine and later learned that the phone rang while he was in the shower; maybe the caller calls back and tells Tommy he called earlier and Tommy says "Oh, I must have been in the shower and didn't hear it." Juanita overlooks these possibilities. Choice (A) is incorrect because Juanita apparently assumes the phone

does ring and that Tommy can hear it ringing. Choices (C) and (E) may or may not be true, but they do not address themselves to Juanita's statement. Choice (B) could only underlie Juanita's objection to Tommy's remarks if hearing calls were the only possible way in which Tommy could learn of the call. But as we show, there are other possibilities.

5. **The correct answer is (E).** Choice (A) is not inconsistent with the advertisement since the ad is touting the strength of the pain-reliever, not its price. Choice (C), too, can easily be seen not to be inconsistent. The ad speaks of non-prescription pain-relievers, but choice (C) brings up the irrelevant matter of prescription pain-relievers. Choice (B) is not inconsistent because RELIEF does not claim to be the one strongest pain-reliever, only that no other non-prescription pain-reliever is stronger. Choice (D) is not inconsistent because it does not talk about sales but medicine given "free of charge" in a study. Choice (E), however, directly contradicts the ad.

6. **The correct answer is (C).** Choice (C) is an assumption of the psychologist. He observed the dogs for a certain period of time and found that each time a stranger approached, they kept silent. From those observed instances, he concluded that the dogs never barked at strangers. Obviously his theory would be disproved (or at least it would have to be seriously qualified) if, when he was not watching, the dogs barked their heads off at strangers. Choice (A) is not an assumption because the speaker makes no value judgment about how dogs ought to be treated. Choice (B) is similar in that no such broad conclusion about "better adjusted" is implied. Choices (D) and (E) are simply confused readings of the speaker's thinking.

7. **The correct answer is (B).** Choice (B) would undermine the psychologist's thesis that "only a beaten dog barks." It cites instances in which the dog was not beaten and still barked at strangers. This would force the psychologist to reconsider his conclusion about the connection between beating and barking. Choice (A) is not like choice (B). It does not state the dogs were never beaten; it states only that the dogs were not beaten when they barked at strangers. It is conceivable that they were beaten at other times. If they were, then even though they might bark at strangers (and not be beaten at that moment), they would not be counter-examples to the psychologist's theory. Choice (C) is not an assumption of the psychologist, as we saw in the preceding question, so denying it does not affect the strength of his argument. The psychologist is concerned with the factual connection between beating a dog and its barking; information about the owners' feelings can hardly be relevant to the factual issue. Choice (D) is an interesting choice, but the fact that some of the dogs also barked at non-strangers doesn't address the connection between discipline and barking at strangers: so they also barked at non-strangers, so what? And choice (E) is wrong because the analysis depends not on the particular object used but rather on the notion of physical discipline.

8. **The correct answer is (B).** Here the author must assume that every effect that is part of the child's experience has been generated by a cause that was also a part of the child's experience, but that is possible only on the assumption that the cause, which is an effect itself, is the result of some previous cause. In other words, every effect flows from some ear-

lier effect. Now, admittedly, that seems to lead to a pretty absurd conclusion: Therefore, there could be no beginning of experience for the child—it must stretch back infinitely. But the question stem does not ask us to critique the argument, only to analyze it and uncover its premises. Choice (A) is wrong because the author does not say all experiences are alike, only that the one today has its roots in the one yesterday. For example, sometimes the presence of moisture in the atmosphere causes rain, sometimes snow. Choice (C) oversimplifies matters in two respects. One, while the author may agree that a child's experiences may tell us something about the parents (assuming the child is in intimate contact with them), we surely would not want to conclude that is the best way to learn about the parents. Two, the parents are not the only source of experience the child has, so the later effects would be the result of non-parental causes as well. Choice (D) is incorrect because the author need not assume that experience is cumulative. In some cases, the cause-and-effect sequence may only reiterate itself so that experience is circular rather than cumulative. Finally, choice (E) is another example of going too far—of extending a simple factual statement beyond the scope the author originally gave it. Here the author says that experience causes experience, but he never suggests that we are in a position to use this principle practically, to manipulate the input to mold the child.

9. **The correct answer is (C).** The author's claim is that we have unbounded resources, and he tries to prove this by showing that we are getting better and better at extracting those resources from the ground. But that is like saying, "I

have found a way to get the last little bit of toothpaste out of the tube; therefore, the tube will never run out." Choice (C) calls our attention to this oversight. Choice (A) does not contradict the author's claim. In fact, it seems to support it. He might suggest, "Even if we run out of fossil fuels, we still have uranium for nuclear power." Now, this is not to suggest that he would. The point is only to show that choice (A) supports rather than undermines the author's contention. Choice (B) is an attack on the author's general stance, but it does not really contradict the particular conclusion he draws. The author says, "We have enough." Choice (B) says, "It is expensive." Both could very well be true, so they cannot contradict one another. Choice (D) is similar to choice (B). Yes, you may be correct, the technology is expensive, or in this case wasteful, but it will still get us the fuel we need. Finally, choice (E) is incorrect for pretty much these same reasons. Yes, the energy will have unwanted side effects, but the author claimed only that we could get the energy. The difficulty with choices (B), (D), and (E) is that though they attack the author's general position, though they undermine his general suggestion, they do not contradict his conclusion.

Questions 10–12

10. **The correct answer is (A).**

11. **The correct answer is (D).**

12. **The correct answer is (C).** Choice (A) is circular. It is like saying, "I never tell a lie; and you must believe that because, as I have just told you, I never tell a lie." So choice (A) is the answer to question 10. Choice (E) might seem circular: Guns do not cause crimes, people do. But it is not. The author's point is that these crimes

would be committed anyway, and he explains how they would be committed. Choice (C) is an *ad hominem* attack. It rejects the conclusion of the argument not because the argument is illogical but because it comes from a particular source. Remember, as we learned in the Test Busters section, not all *ad hominem* are illegitimate. It is perfectly all right to inquire into possible biases of the source, and that is just what occurs here. So choice (C) is the answer to question 12. Choice (D) is a fairly weak argument. It takes a handful of observed instances and generalizes to a strong conclusion. But even though it may be weak, it does fit the description "generalization," so choice (D) is the answer to question 11. Choice (B) is just left over and fits none of the descriptions.

13. **The correct answer is (A).** The author places himself in opposition to the sociologists whom he cites. He claims an alternative interpretation of the evidence. In other words, the most logical continuation of the passage will be the one that explains why such sects are not a recent phenomenon even though there are no old ones around. Choice (A) does this neatly. Since the members abstain from sexual relations, they will not reproduce members and the sect will tend to die out. This explains why there are none more than 50 or 60 years old. Choice (C), if anything, supports the position of the sociologists, for it implicitly gives up trying to explain the evidence differently and also undercuts the explanation the author might have given. Choice (B) is irrelevant because intensity of religious fervor is irrelevant to the length of the sect's existence; it cannot possibly help the author explain away the evidence of the sociologists. Choice (D) is irrelevant

for another reason. The author needs to explain why the sects are all relatively young without having recourse to the thesis of the sociologists that they are a recent phenomenon. That there are other organizations that encourage sexual relations of whatever kind cannot help the author explain a phenomenon such as the Waiters. Finally, choice (E) is a distraction, picking up as it does on a minor detail. The author needs to explain the short-livedness of groups of which the Waiters is only an example.

14. **The correct answer is (E).** The conclusion of the speaker is that the checkup has no value, so anything that suggests the checkup does have value will undermine the conclusion. Choice (A) shows a possible advantage of having the checkup. It says, in effect, while the checkup is not foolproof and will not catch everything, it does catch some fairly important things. Choice (B) also gives us a possible reason for visiting our mechanic for a 5,000-mile checkup. Even if it won't keep our car in running order, it is necessary if we want to take advantage of our warranty. Finally, choice (C) also gives us a good reason to have a checkup: The mechanic will make some routine adjustments. All three of these propositions, then, mention possible advantages of having a checkup. Choice (D) weakens the argument on the theory that "A ounce of prevention is worth a pound of cure." Choice (E), however, actually seems to strengthen the argument: the policy prevents very few problems.

15. **The correct answer is (A).** Here we are looking for the most perfect analogy. Keep in mind, first, that the author opposes the move, and second, all of the features of the union-management situation, in particular that they are adversaries.

Choice (A) captures both elements. The relationship between prison administrators and inmates is adversarial, and the suggestion that inmates make decisions on security is outrageous enough that it captures also the first element. Choice (B) fails on both counts. First, the two are not on opposites of the fence; second, the senior officer is asking for advice—not deferring to the opinion of his junior officer. Choice (C) is very similar. First, the administration of the university and the student body are not necessarily adversaries; at least, although they may disagree on the best means for advancing the goals of the university, there is often agreement about those goals. Second, the administration is, as with choice (B), asking advice, not abdicating responsibility for the decision. In choice (D), we lack both elements; the mayor need not be an adversary of the state legislators (he may be seeking their assistance), nor is he giving them his authority to make decisions. Finally, choice (E) lacks both elements as well; the minister is a leader, not an adversary, who is discussing questions, not delegating authority.

16. **The correct answer is (E).** The author's reason for rejecting the notion of labor participation in management decisions is that the labor leaders first have a responsibility to the people they represent and that the responsibility would color their thinking about the needs of the corporation. His thinking is reflected in the adage (and this could easily have been worked into an LSAT-type question): No man can serve two masters. Choice (B) is incorrect since the author is referring to the labor leaders, not the rank-and-file; and he specifically mentions that the leaders are skilled administrators. Choice (D) is incorrect because

it, too, fails to respect the distinction between union leader and union member. Choice (A) is a distraction. The notion that the authority would be "symbolically undermined" is edifying but finds no support in the paragraph. In any event, it entirely misses the main point of the paragraph as we have explained it. Choice (C) also fails to observe the distinction between leader and worker, not to mention also that it is only remotely connected with the discussion.

17. **The correct answer is (E).** The question stem advises us that the inconsistency is only "seeming." Choice (E) explains it away. Of the total population, 70 percent take X and 30 percent take Y, yet only 75 percent of the population take anything at all. This means that some people took both X and Y. Choice (A) is close, but it gets no cigar. While we can infer that there must be some overlap, we cannot conclude that the 30 percent is totally contained within the 70 percent. It is possible that only 25 percent of the population take both. In that case, we would have 5 percent who take Y only, 45 percent who take X only, and 25 percent who take both X and Y. This still leaves 25 percent of the population who take neither. Choice (B) seems totally unrelated to the logic of the argument. As for choices (C) and (D), while these are possible weaknesses in any statistical argument, there is nothing to indicate that they operate here specifically.

18. **The correct answer is (A).** If (2) is true, then both independent clauses of (2) must be true. This is because a sentence that has the form "P and Q" (Eddie is tall and John is short) can be true only if both subparts are true. If either is false (Eddie is not tall or John is not short) or if both are false, then the entire sentence

makes a false claim. If the second clause of (2) is true, then (1) must also be true, for (1) is actually equivalent to the second clause in (2). That is, if "P and Q" is true, then Q must itself be true. On this basis, choices (B) and (C) can be seen to be incorrect. Choice (D) is wrong, for we can actually define the interrelationship of (1) and (2) as a matter of logic: We do not have to have recourse to a probabilistic statement; that is, it is unlikely. Choice (E) is incorrect since a statement of the form "P and Q" might be false and Q could still be true—if P is false, "P and Q" is false even though Q is true.

19. **The correct answer is (D).** Again, let us resort to the use of capital letters to make it easier to talk about the propositions. Incidentally, you may or may not find this technique useful under test conditions. Some people do, but others do not. We use it here because it makes explanation easier. Let us render the four premises as follows:

(1) All B are R.   (All Buckner are Reserve)

(2) All R are P.   (All Reserve are Priceless)

(3) No H is R.   (No Hemingway is Reserve)

(4) All R are C.   (All Reserve are Catalogue)

From this we can deduce

(5) All B are P.   (using 1 and 2)

and

(6) No H is B.   (using 1 and 3)

Since "no B is H" is equivalent to "no H is B" (there is no overlap between the two categories), choice (D) must be our correct answer. From (2), we would not want to conclude "all P are R," any more than we would go from "all station wagons are cars" to "all cars are station wagons"; so choice (A) is not a proper inference and cannot be our answer. As for choice (B), we can show that "all B are C" (using 1 and 4) and also "all B are P" (5), so we would be wrong in concluding that "no B are not P." As for choice (C), while we know that "no H is R," we would not want to conclude that "no H is P." After all, books by Hemingway may be priceless, but the Buckner collection and the Reserve Room may just not contain any. Finally, choice (E) is not deducible from our four propositions. We cannot deduce "all C is R" from "all R is C."

20. **The correct answer is (E).** Now, it must be admitted that a liar can abuse just about any word in the English language, and so it is true that each of the five answer choices is conceivably correct. But it is important to keep in mind that you are looking for the BEST answer, which will be the one word that, more than all the others, is likely to be abused. As for choice (A), while there may be different ways of doing a random selection, we should be able to decide whether a sample was, in fact, selected fairly. Although the ad may be lying about the selection of participants in the study, we should be able to determine whether they are lying. In other words, though they may not have selected the sample randomly, they cannot escape by saying, "Oh, by random, we meant anyone who liked the Goblin." The same is true of choice (C), first. That is a fairly clear term. You add up the answers you got, and one will be at the top of the list. The same is true of choice (D), a "response" is an answer. Now, choice (B) is open to manipulation. By asking our question correctly, that is, by finagling a bit with what we mean by "handling," we

can influence the answers we get. For example, compare: "Did you find the Goblin handled well?" "Did you find the Goblin had a nice steering wheel?" "Did you find the wheel was easy to turn?" We could keep it up until we found a question that worked out to give a set of "responses" from "randomly" selected drivers who would rank the Goblin "first." Now, if the one category itself is susceptible to manipulation, imagine how much easier it will be to manipulate a "composite" category. We have only to take those individual categories in which the Goblin scored well, construct from them a "composite" category, and announce the Goblin "first" in the overall category. There is also the question of how the composite was constructed, weighted, added, averaged, etc.

21. **The correct answer is (A).** The explanation given is no explanation at all. It is like a mechanic saying to a motorist, "Your car did not get over this steep hill because it did not have enough grade climbing power." While the author may have speculated about when and how his death would occur, it cannot be said that his explanation was speculative. So choice (A) is correct, not choice (B). Of course, since the explanation is merely circular, it cannot be considered medically sound, any more than our hypothetical mechanic's answer is sound as a matter of automotive engineering, so choice (D) must be wrong. As for choice (C), while the author's announcement may be self-serving, designed to aggrandize his reputation, the explanation he gives in the announcement is not. Finally, the explanation is not self-authenticating, that is, it does not provide that standard by which its own validity is to be measured. So choice (E) can be overruled.

22. **The correct answer is (D).** It is important not to attribute more to an author than he actually says or implies. Here the author states only that Ronnie's range is narrow so he will not be an outstanding vocalist. Vocalizing is only one kind of music career, so choice (A), which speaks of professional musicians, takes us far beyond the claim the author actually makes. Choice (B) also goes beyond what the author says. He never specifies what range an outstanding vocalist needs, much less what range is required to vocalize without being outstanding. Choice (C) must be incorrect since the argument depends upon the opposite assumption. The conclusion that Ronnie will *never* be an outstanding vocalist would not follow if it were possible to expand the range. Finally, as for choice (E), the speaker makes a range one condition of success but not necessarily the only or even most important condition. It could be that most people have nice ranges but fail for other reasons—so long as those few with narrow ranges also fail. Choice (D) is an assumption since the author moves from a physical characteristic to a conclusion regarding ability.

23. **The correct answer is (C).** You should remember that there is a very important distinction between "numbers" and "percentages." For example, an increase from one murder per year to two murders per year can be described as a "whopping big 100 percent increase." The argument speaks only of percentages, so we would not want to conclude anything about the numbers underlying those percentages. Therefore, both choices (A) and (B) are incorrect. They speak of "more agents" and "more people," and those are numbers rather than percentages. Furthermore, if we would not want to draw a

conclusion about numbers from data given in percentage terms, we surely would not want to base on percentages a conclusion about efficiency or work accomplished. Thus, choices (D) and (E) are incorrect. What makes choice (C) the best answer of the five is the possibility of making percentage comparisons within each agency. Within both agencies, the number of field agents increased by a greater percentage or proportion than the non-field agents.

24. **The correct answer is (D).** Keeping in mind our comments about choices (D) and (E) in the preceding question, choice (A) must be wrong. We do not want to conclude from sheer number of employees anything about the actual work accomplished. Choices (B) and (E) are incorrect for pretty much the same reason. The question stem asks us to give an argument defending the CIA against the claim that it is overstaffed. Neither rate of pay nor appropriations has anything to do with whether or not there are too many people on the payroll. Choice (C) is the second-best answer, but it fails because it does not keep in mind the ratio of non-field agents to field agents. Our concern is not with the number of agents generally, but rather with the number of support and supervisory workers (reread the question stem). Choice (D) focuses on this nicely by explaining why the CIA should experience a faster increase (which is to say, a greater percentage increase) in the number of its supervisory personnel than the FBI.

Section 5

1. **The correct answer is (B).** This is a main idea question. The author begins by stating that a large number of auto traffic fatalities can be attributed to drivers who are intoxicated. He then reviews two approaches to controlling this problem, taxation and drunk driving laws. Neither is very successful. The author finally notes that therapy may be useful, though the extent of its value has not yet been proved. Choice (B) fairly well describes this development. Choice (A) can be eliminated since any conclusions drawn by the author from studies on drunk driving are used for the larger objective described in choice (B). Choice (C) is incorrect since, aside from suggesting possible ways to reduce the extent of the problem, the author never treats the causes of drunk driving. Choice (D) is incorrect for the same reason. Finally, choice (E) is incorrect, because the comparison between the U.S. and Britain is only a small part of the passage.

2. **The correct answer is (B).** This is an inference question. In the third paragraph, the author discusses the effect of drunk driving laws. He states that after the implementation of the Road Safety Act in Britain, motor vehicle fatalities fell considerably. On this basis, we infer that the RSA was a law aimed at drunk driving. We can eliminate choices (D) and (E) on this ground. Choice (C) can be eliminated as not warranted on the basis of this information. It is not clear whether the number of arrests increased. Equally consistent with the passage is the conclusion that the number of arrests dropped because people were no longer driving while intoxicated. Choice (C) is incorrect for a further reason, the justification for choice (B). Choices (B) and (A) are fairly close since both describe the RSA as a law aimed at drunk driving. But the last sentence of the third paragraph calls for choice (B) over choice (A). As people learned that they would not get caught for drunk driving, the law became less

effective. This suggests that the RSA made drunk driving illegal, not that it lowered the BAC required for conviction. This makes sense of the sentence "… they could drink and not be stopped." If choice (A) were correct, this sentence would have to read, "… they could drink the same amount and not be convicted."

3. **The correct answer is (A).** This is an inference question. In the first paragraph, the author states that for a person to attain a BAC of 0.1 percent, he would need to drink over five ounces of 80 proof spirits over a short period of time. The author is trying to impress on us that that is a considerable quantity of alcohol for most people to drink. Choice (A) explains why the author makes this comment. Choice (B) is incorrect and confuses the first paragraph with the second paragraph. Choice (C) is incorrect since the point of the example is that the BAC is so high that most people will not exceed it. This is not to say, however, that people will not drink and drive because of laws establishing maximum BAC levels. Rather, they can continue to drink and drive because the law allows them a considerable margin in the level of BAC. Choice (D) is a misreading of that first paragraph. Of all the very drunk drivers (BAC in excess of 0.1), only 1 percent are involved in accidents. But this does not say that most drivers involved in fatal collisions have BAC levels in excess of 0.1 percent, and that is what choice (D) says. As for choice (E), the author never states that the only way to attain a BAC of 0.1 percent is to drink five ounces of 80 proof spirits in a short time—there may be other ways of becoming intoxicated.

4. **The correct answer is (A).** This is an application question. In the second paragraph, the author states that increased taxation on alcohol would tax the heaviest drinkers most, but he notes that this would also penalize the moderate and light drinker. In other words, the remedy is not sufficiently focused on the problem. Then, in the third paragraph, the author notes that drunk driving laws are aimed at the specific problem drivers. We can infer from this discussion that the author would likely advocate drunk driving laws over taxation for the reasons just given. This reasoning is presented in answer choice (A). Choice (B) is incorrect for the reasons just given and for the further reason that the passage never suggests that taxation is likely to be more effective in solving the problem. The author never really evaluates the effectiveness of taxation in reducing drunk driving. Choice (C) is incorrect for the reason given in support of choice (A) and for the further reason that the author never raises the issue of personal liberty in conjunction with the BAC test. Choice (D) can be eliminated because the author does not discount the effectiveness of anti-drunk driving measures entirely. Even the British example gives some support to the conclusion that such laws have an effect. Choice (E) is incorrect for the author never mentions the expense or administrative feasibility of BAC tests.

5. **The correct answer is (C).** This is a question about the logical structure of the passage. In paragraph 3, the author notes that stricter enforcement of laws against drunk driving may result in a few more arrests, but a few more arrests is not likely to have much impact on the problem because the number of arrests is small compared to those who do not get caught. As a consequence, people will continue to drink and drive. The author

supports this with the British experience. Once people realize that the chances of being caught are relatively small, they will drink and drive. This is the conclusion of answer choice (C). Choice (A) is incorrect since the passage does not support the conclusion that the problem is any worse or any better in one country or the other. Choice (B) is incorrect since this is the conclusion the author is arguing against. Choice (D) is wrong because the author is not discussing the effectiveness of taxation in paragraph 3. Choice (E) is a statement the author would likely accept, but that is not the reason for introducing the British example. So answer choice (E) is true but non-responsive.

6. **The correct answer is (A).** This is an application question that asks us to examine the logical structure of the argument. In the fourth paragraph, the author argues that the effectiveness of deterrents to drunk driving will depend upon the ability of the drinker to control his consumption. But drunk driving has two aspects: drunk and driving. The author assumes that drunk driving is a function of drinking only. Otherwise, he would not suggest that control on consumption is necessary as opposed to helpful. Choice (A) attacks this assumption by pointing out that it is possible to drink to excess without driving. It is possible that stiff penalties could be effective deterrents to drunk driving if not to drinking to excess. Choice (B) is incorrect because the author himself makes this point, so this choice does not weaken the argument. Choice (C) is incorrect since the author is concerned only with the problem of fatalities caused by drunk driving. It is hardly an attack on his argument to contend that he has not solved all of the world's ills. Then choice (D) can be elimi-

nated since the author is concerned to eliminate fatalities caused by drunk driving. He takes no position on whether the drunk driver ought to be punished, only that he ought to be deterred from driving while intoxicated. Choice (E) is not a strong attack on the argument since the author does leave open the question of the value of therapy in combating drunk driving.

7. **The correct answer is (C).** This is a tone question that focuses on the final sentence of the paragraph. There the author states again that the problem is a serious one and that we must find a solution. Since he admonishes us to look for a solution, choice (C) is an excellent description. Choice (A) can be eliminated since there is no irony in the passage. Choice (B) can be eliminated since the author is concerned to find a solution. Choice (E), however, overstates the case. Concern is not indignation. Finally, choice (D) may seem plausible. The author does leave us with a project. But to acknowledge that a problem exists and that a clear solution has not yet been found is not to be indecisive. The author is decisive in his assessment of the problem.

8. **The correct answer is (D).** This is a main idea question. The author does two things in the passage: He describes the problem of increasing thermal pollution and he suggests that solar energy will solve the problem. Choice (D) neatly describes this double development. Choice (A) is incorrect, for though the author does describe the phenomenon of thermal pollution and its causes, he also proposes a solution. Choice (B) is incorrect since it fails to make reference to the fact that an important part of the passage is the description of a problem. It must be admitted that it can be argued

that choice (B) does make an attempt to describe the development of the passage, but it does not do as nicely as choice (D) does. Choice (C) is easily eliminated since no ambiguity is mentioned. Finally, choice (E) is incorrect since whatever objection the author may implicitly try to refute (opponents of solar energy), he never cites and then refutes a counterargument.

9. **The correct answer is (E).** This is an explicit idea question. Choices (A), (B), and (C) are mentioned in the second paragraph as factors contributing to thermal pollution. Choice (D) is mentioned in the third paragraph as a pressure increasing thermal pollution. Choice (E) is mentioned in the third paragraph—but not as a factor contributing to thermal pollution. Unpredictable weather patterns make it difficult to predict when the thermal pollution problem will reach the critical stage, but the patterns do not contribute to thermal pollution.

10. **The correct answer is (C).** This is an inference question. In discussing the melting of the polar ice caps, the author notes that there is a positive feedback mechanism: Since the ice caps reflect sunlight and therefore dissipate solar energy that would otherwise be absorbed by the earth, the melting of the ice caps increases the amount of energy captured by the earth, which in turn contributes to the melting of the ice caps, and so on. Choice (C) correctly describes this as intensifying the effects of thermal pollution. Choice (A) is easily eliminated since this feedback mechanism has nothing to do with a possible reduction in per capita energy consumption. Choice (B) is incorrect, for though this feedback loop increases the problem and thereby the urgency for the changeover to solar energy, the loop itself will not cause a change

in policy. Choice (D) is incorrect for the same reason. Finally, though the melting of the polar ice caps will result in flooding, this flooding is not an explanation of the feedback loop. Rather, it is the result of the general phenomenon of the melting of the ice caps.

11. **The correct answer is (A).** This is a logical detail question. Why does the author discuss energy conservation? Conservation may appear as a possible alternative to solar energy. The author argues, however, that a closer examination shows that conservation cannot avert but only postpone the crisis. In terms of tactics, the author's move is to raise a possible objection and give an answer to it—as stated in choice (A). Choice (B) is incorrect, for the refutation of a possible objection does not support the central thesis directly, only indirectly by eliminating a possible counterargument. Choice (C) is incorrect since the author never acknowledges he has fallen into any contradiction. Choice (D) is incorrect since it overstates the case. The author admits that conservation has a beneficial effect, but he denies that conservation obviates the need for solar energy. Finally, choice (E) is incorrect since the point is argumentative and not merely informational.

12. **The correct answer is (B).** This is an inference question. In the final paragraph, the author makes references to the possibility of "air-conditioning" the earth, a word placed in quotation marks, which indicates that he is using it in a non-standard way. Ordinarily, we use the word "air-condition" to mean to cool, say, a room or an entire building. Obviously, the author is not referring to some gigantic Carrier air-conditioning unit mounted, say, on top of the earth. But the general idea of removing heat seems to

be what the term means in this context. This is consonant with the passage as well. Thermal pollution is the build-up of energy, and we are showing a positive build-up because fossil fuel and other sources of energy release energy that was only stored. So this, coupled with the sun's energy that comes in each moment, gives us a positive (though not desirable) balance of energy retention over loss. The idea of air-conditioning the earth, though not feasible according to the passage, must refer to schemes to get rid of this energy, say, into outer space. This is the idea presented in choice (B). As for choice (A), redistribution of thermal energy within the earth's energy system will not solve the problem of accumulated energy, so that cannot be what proponents of "air-conditioning" have in mind. Choice (C) is a good definition of conservation but not "air-conditioning." Choice (D) is the recommendation given by the author, but that is not a response to this question. Finally, choice (E) is incorrect for the reason that burning wood is not going to cool the earth.

13. **The correct answer is (B).** This is a tone question. The author describes a very dangerous situation, but he also shows the way to solve the problem. The author does not necessarily believe that the battle for solar energy has been won; otherwise, he would not be advocating a shift to solar energy. On balance, the tone of the passage is hope or optimism, qualified by the realization that solar energy is not yet a high priority. This qualified hope is best described by choice (B). Choice (A) is incorrect since this is not the tone of the passage. Though the author may be distressed at what he perceives to be the short-sightedness of policy makers, this distress does not color

the writing in the passage. Choice (C) is totally inappropriate since the author is analytical. Choice (D) is inconsistent with the author's concern. Finally, choice (E) overstates the case. Though the author is concerned, he is not in a panic.

14. **The correct answer is (C).** This is an application question. We are looking for the most logical continuation. Since the author has urged us to adopt solar energy, an appropriate continuation would be a discussion of how to implement solar energy. And choice (C) would be a part of this discussion. Choice (B) can be eliminated since the proposal depends upon the cost and feasibility of solar energy, not on its history. Choices (A) and (E) can be eliminated since the author has explicitly asserted that only solar energy will solve the problem of thermal pollution. Finally, choice (D) is incorrect since the author need not regale us with the gory details of this situation. He has already made the point. As readers, we will want to see the practical details of his plan to avoid disaster.

15. **The correct answer is (D).** This is a main idea question. The author begins by stating that it would be useful to have a general index to measure welfare and notes that some have even suggested the GNP might be adapted for that purpose. He then proceeds to demonstrate why such an index cannot be constructed. Generally, then, the author shows the defects in a proposal for a general index of welfare, and choice (D) nicely describes this devel-opment. Choice (A) is incorrect since the author never produces any arguments for the position he is attacking. And even when the author raises points such as the suggestion that hours worked might be a measure of cost of production, he is not citing arguments

for that position; he is only mentioning the position to attack it. Choice (B) is incorrect since the author is attacking and not defending the proposal discussed. Choice (C) is easily eliminated because the author never attacks the sincerity of those he opposes. Finally, choice (E) is wrong, for the author never reviews any literature on the subject he is discussing.

16. **The correct answer is (A).** This is an inference question. We turn to the second paragraph. There the author mentions that a general index of welfare would have to include some measure of the cost of producing the output. He suggests that someone might think hours worked would do the trick. He rejects that position by noting that hours worked, as a statistic, does not take account of the quality of the worktime (e.g., long-hours versus short-hours, working conditions, satisfaction of workers). Choice (A) best describes this argument. Choice (B) is incorrect, for the author discusses environmental costs in connection with another aspect of a general index. Choice (C) is incorrect since this distinction is never used by the author. Choice (D) is incorrect since this is not mentioned as a goal of such a measure. Finally, choice (E) confuses the GNP, mentioned in the first part of the paragraph, with the index to measure real costs.

17. **The correct answer is (C).** This is an inference question that asks about the main point of the passage. The author adduces several objections to the idea of a general index of welfare. Then the final blow is delivered in the last paragraph: Even if you could devise measures for these various components of a general index, any combination or weighting of the individual measures would reflect only the judgment (personal preference)

of the weighter. For this reason alone, argues the author, the entire idea is unworkable. Choice (C) makes this point. Choices (A) and (D) can be eliminated since the author never uses cost or time as arguments against the index. Choice (B) can be eliminated on similar grounds. The author may recognize that considerable research would be needed to attempt such measures, yet he does not bother to use that as an objection. Choice (E) can be eliminated for a similar reason. The author may have some arguments against the way such statistics are gathered now, but he does not bother to make them. His argument has the structure: Even assuming there are such data, we cannot combine these statistics to get a general measure of the quality of the environment.

18. **The correct answer is (A).** This is a tone question, and the justification for choice (A) is already implicit in the discussion thus far. The author sees fatal theoretical weaknesses inherent in the idea of an index of welfare. So we might say that he regards such a notion as an unrealistic, that is, unachievable, dream. Choice (B) is incorrect because the author does not believe the idea can ever be implemented. Choices (C), (D), and (E) can be eliminated on substantially the same grounds.

19. **The correct answer is (A).** This is an explicit idea question. In the second paragraph, the author acknowledges that the GNP is a fairly accurate measure of output. He never suggests that the GNP can estimate needs, predict welfare, or measure welfare generally. So we can eliminate the remaining choices.

20. **The correct answer is (E).** This is an explicit idea question, with a thought reverser. Choices (A), (B), (C), and (D)

are all mentioned in the third paragraph as aspects of a needs index. The fourth paragraph does not treat the idea of a needs index but rather the idea of a physical environment index. That is where the author discusses the items mentioned in choice (E). So the author does mention the items covered by choice (E) but not as part of a needs index.

21. **The correct answer is (A).** This is an application question. We are looking for the most likely place for the passage. To be sure, it is possible that the passage might appear in any of the five suggested locations, but the most likely place is that suggested by choice (A). This could easily be one of a series of papers addressed to a group meeting to discuss public policy decisions. As for choice (B), it is not likely that the passage would be an introduction to a general text on statistics. It is too firmly dedicated to a particular idea, and the use of statistics is in a way subordinate to the theoretical discussion. Choice (C) is inappropriate since the discussion bears only remotely on programs to aid the poor. Choice (D) is even less likely since the passage does not discuss the foundations of government. Finally, choice (E) is to a certain extent plausible, but choice (A) is more closely connected to the content of the passage.

22. **The correct answer is (D).** This is a main idea question. The main idea of the passage is fairly clear: suggest reforms to correct the problems discussed. Choice (D) is a very good description of this development. Choice (A) is incorrect since the author himself criticizes the system. Choice (B) is incorrect since no recommendation for expanding benefits and scope is made by the author. Choice (C) overstates the case. The author limits his

indictment to unemployment compensation, even then he believes that the shortcomings of the system can be remedied. Choice (E) is incorrect because the author is discussing unemployment compensation, not government programs designed to achieve full employment generally. We may infer from the passage that unemployment compensation is not a program designed to achieve full employment, but rather a program designed to alleviate the hardship of unemployment. On balance, choice (D) is the most precise description given of the development of the passage.

23. **The correct answer is (A).** This is a logical detail question. In the second paragraph, the author introduces the example of a worker who loses surprisingly little by being unemployed. The author does this to show that unemployment encourages people to remain unemployed by reducing the net cost of unemployment. Choice (A) makes this point. Choice (B) is incorrect, for the author does not discuss the problem of employer contribution until the fourth paragraph. Choice (C) is incorrect, for this is not the reason that the author introduces the point. Choice (D) is incorrect because this topic is not taken up until the third paragraph. Finally, choice (E) is incorrect since the author analyzes the situation in a neutral fashion; there is no hint of condemnation.

24. **The correct answer is (C).** This is an explicit idea or specific detail question. Choice (C) is a recommendation made by the author in the final paragraph. Choice (A) is actually inconsistent with statements made in that paragraph, for the author proposes taxing benefits in the same way as wages. Choices (B), (D), and (E) are interesting ideas, but they are

nowhere mentioned in the passage—so they cannot possibly be answers to an explicit idea question.

25. **The correct answer is (C).** Here, too, we have an explicit idea question. Choices (A), (B), (D), and (E) are all mentioned in the third paragraph as ways by which an employer might reduce seasonal and cyclical fluctuations in labor needs. Choice (C), however, was not mentioned as a way to minimize unemployment. Indeed, we may infer from other information supplied by the passage that supplementary benefits actually increase unemployment.

26. **The correct answer is (A).** This is an application question. We are asked to apply the author's analysis of the rating system to conclusions given in the answer choices. The author is critical of the rating system because it does not place the full burden of unemployment on the employer. This is because there is a maximum contribution limit, and in the final paragraph, the author recommends the ceiling be eliminated. From these remarks, we may infer that the author believes the rating system is, in theory, sound, but that practically it needs to be adjusted. Choice (A) neatly describes this judgment. Choice (B) can be eliminated since the author implies that the system is, in principle, sound. Moreover, the author implies that the employer does have some control over the time his former employees remain out of work. The maximum limit on employer contribution allows the employer to exploit this control. As for choice (C), this is contradicted by our analysis thus far and for the further reason that the passage never suggests employee contribution should replace employer contribution. Indeed, the author implies that he regards the system as serving a useful and necessary social func-

tion. Choice (D) can be eliminated because the author never draws a distinction between contributions by large firms and contributions by small firms. Finally, choice (E) is incorrect since the experience rating system is theoretically tied to the amount drawn by employees. The difficulty is not with the theory of the system, but rather with its implementation.

27. **The correct answer is (B).** This is an explicit detail question. We are looking for criticisms that are made in the passage. Choice (B) is such a criticism, and it can be found in the very opening sentence. As for choice (A), the author actually states the opposite: The system allows firms of this sort to use the unemployment compensation system as a subsidy for their employees, reducing their own costs of production. As for choice (C), the author only states that employers contribute to the fund from which benefits are paid. No mention is ever made of a state contribution. Choice (D) is certainly a goal of the system, but it is not mentioned as a weakness of the system by the author. Finally, choice (E) is true—as mentioned in the final paragraph. But this is not a criticism of the system. In fact, the author views it in a positive light and as a basis for a recommendation for reform.

28. **The correct answer is (A).** This is a tone question. In the final paragraph, as he makes his recommendations, the author states that we must reform the system, preserving its good aspects and correcting its bad effects. Choice (A) describes this judgment. Choice (B) is incorrect since much of the discussion in the passage is an indictment of the system's economic inefficiency. Choice (C) is wrong because the author makes recommendations that, he states, will

correct the wasteful effects. Choice (D) is incorrect, for the author implies that the system has usefulness. Finally, though the author criticizes the system, the objection is that the system is inefficient, not that it is outdated.

WRITING SAMPLE

Following are two responses to the Writing Sample prompt, one in favor of the first option and the other in favor of the second option. Of course, there is no "right" or "wrong" answer to a Writing Sample prompt. Rather, responses are "better" or "worse," and you'll find a discussion of how to write a good response in Chapter 8. For now, just note that the two responses below are serviceable: they are not great works of prose; they are not brilliant pieces of writing, but they are acceptable. And, as you'll learn in Chapter 8, that's really all you should be going for.

Sample Response for the First Option

Ashley should invest her money in a Hearty Burger franchise. A fast-food franchise would provide her with the opportunity for "hands-on" management, and the investment required would be within her reach.

First, a Hearty Burger franchise would give Ashley the opportunity to apply what she's learned in school to a real business. A fast-food restaurant is a small enough operation to permit her to supervise all aspects of the business instead of having responsibility for a narrowly defined set of duties in a large company. Additionally, even though the franchise includes advertising and other support, she would presumably be left free to make choices about hours, labor, community relations, and other exclusively local concerns. Finally, although Ashley may not have had any formal business-school training in operating a fast-food franchise, the company's orientation and technical support should be sufficient to fill in the gaps in her knowledge.

Second, the Hearty Burger franchise is within Ashley's budget, though it would be a tight squeeze. Perhaps she could use some of the money as a down payment on the real estate she'll need and borrow additional funds from a bank. Also, the company will supply many of her restaurant needs, and that can help her cash flow during the start-up period. And the fast-food business is such that her efforts in the store can offset some of her labor costs.

The Hearty Burger franchise seems to answer the two primary concerns that Ashley has and would be the better choice.

Sample Response for the Second Option

Ashley should purchase the clothing store. A clothing store would give her a lot of opportunity to make individual decisions, and the terms of the offer of sale are attractive.

One, the clothing store offers Ashley the opportunity she's looking for to manage a business. With changing styles and tastes, clothing will present her with special challenges as she tries to anticipate shifting patterns of demand and respond to them. Additionally, Ashley still has the student perspective and so should be able to respond effectively to the tastes of the student population in the area. Essentially all of the important decisions will remain under her control.

Two, the clothing store is financially attractive. The store has been in business for 50 years, so Ashley can expect to see sales from loyal customers, money that will help her during the start-up period. Moreover, the store is already stocked, though she will probably want and need to start buying new inventory almost immediately. Of course, the plans of the building owner are a potential stumbling block, but Ashley should be able to work out an arrangement that will permit her to continue in the existing location. Perhaps she can borrow money from the bank for the purchase of the commercial co-op space, or maybe the owner will be willing to finance her purchase of the store space.

So the clothing store will be financially practical, and it will provide Ashley with the opportunity to do those things she's trained to do.

answers

PART III

LSAT QUESTION TYPES

Logical Reasoning

OVERVIEW
- **What is Logical Reasoning?**
- **How do you answer Logical Reasoning questions?**
- **What smart test-takers know**

WHAT IS LOGICAL REASONING?

As the name implies, Logical Reasoning tests your ability to think logically, and you will learn a lot about thinking logically in this chapter. The LSAT, however, does not test technical points that are taught in the typical "Introduction to Logic" college course. You would not, for example, be asked to define categorical syllogism or *petitio principii,* but you might be asked to recognize the following:

All whales are mammals.

All mammals are warm-blooded creatures.

Therefore, all whales are warm-blooded creatures.

This, which technically speaking is a categorical syllogism, is a valid argument form. And you might be asked to show that you understand the following:

Shakespeare was a better playwright than Shaw. Clearly, Shakespeare's plays are better, so the conclusion that Shakespeare was a better playwright than Shaw is unavoidable.

This, which technically speaking is a *petitio principii,* is a specious argument because it simply begs the question.

LSAT Logical Reasoning Questions

The scored portion of the LSAT contains two Logical Reasoning sections, each with 24 to 26 questions. The Logical Reasoning sections can appear as any of the exam's sections. You may receive a test form that includes more than two Logical Reasoning sections, in which case only two of the Logical Reasoning sections will be scored. The other will contain trial questions that are being tested for use in future exams. There will be no way to tell which section is the trial one, so it's important to do your best on every section.

chapter 5

What are the three "building blocks" of logical reasoning?
1. Stimulus material
2. Question stem
3. Answer choices
And each has its role to play.

Logical Reasoning questions are constructed from three elements:

Stimulus Material

Stimulus material is the "content" of the item. Stimulus material is an initial paragraph or statement that presents an argument or otherwise states a position. The stimulus material can be about almost anything, including a medical breakthrough, a moral dilemma, a scientific theory, a philosophical problem, a marketing phenomenon, and even, though very rarely, a legal issue. But you don't need any special knowledge. Everything you need to know in terms of item content is right there in the stimulus material.

Question Stem

This stem is the "question." It may come in the form of a question, or it may come in the form of an instruction. Either way, the stem tells you what to do with the stimulus material. It may ask you to do any one of the following:

- Identify the conclusion of an argument
- Point out a premise of an argument
- Identify strengths or weaknesses in an argument
- Recognize parallel reasoning
- Evaluate evidence
- Draw conclusions and make inferences

Answer Choices

The answer choices are the possible "responses" to the stem. One of them is the "credited" response or right answer. The wrong answers are known as "distractors" because they are carefully written to distract your attention away from the right answer. In essence, they provide the camouflage in which the test-writers hide the right response.

Here are the directions for LSAT Logical Reasoning questions, together with a sample question and its explanation.

Anatomy of a Logical Reasoning Item

Directions: In this section, the questions ask you to analyze and evaluate the reasoning in short paragraphs or passages. For some questions, all of the answer choices may conceivably be answers to the question asked. You should select the *best* answer to the question; that is, an answer that does not require you to make assumptions that violate commonsense standards by being implausible, redundant, irrelevant, or inconsistent. After choosing the best answer, blacken the corresponding space on the answer sheet.

Stimulus Material

Officials of the State Industrial Safety Board notified the management of A-1 Ironworks that several employees of the plant had complained about discomfort experienced as a result of the high levels of noise of the factory operations. A-1's management responded by pointing out that the complaints came from the newest employee at the plant and that more experienced workers did not find the factory noise to be excessive. Based on this finding, management concluded that the noise was not a problem and declined to take any remedial action.

You should notice that management overlooked something: Is there another possible explanation for why complaints came from new employees and not from experienced employees?

Question Stem

Which of the following, if true, indicates a flaw in A-1's decision not to take remedial action at the plant?

The stem tells you that management has made a mistake and asks that you identify the error.

Answer Choices

(A) Because A-1 is located in an industrial park, no residences are located close enough to the plant to be affected by the noise.

A distractor. The issue is the effect of noise on employees inside the plant.

(B) The noise level at the plant varies with activity and is at the highest when the greatest number of employees are on the job.

A distractor. While this is probably true, it does not address the new employee/experienced employee distinction.

(C) The experienced employees do not feel discomfort because of significant hearing loss attributable to the high noise level.	*The credited response. Management overlooked this: Experienced employees do not complain because deafness prevents them from hearing the noise.*
(D) Issuing protective earplugs to all employees would not significantly increase the cost to A-1 of doing business.	*A distractor. If earplugs would be an effective but inexpensive remedial step, then it would make sense to issue them to employees.*
(E) The State Industrial Safety Board has no independent authority to enforce a recommendation regarding safety procedures.	*A distractor. Irrelevant to the issue at hand.*

HOW DO YOU ANSWER LOGICAL REASONING QUESTIONS?

Here's a simple, four-step plan that can help you solve Logical Reasoning questions.

Logical Reasoning: Getting It Right

❶ Preview the question stem.

❷ Read the stimulus material.

❸ Prephrase your answer.

❹ Identify the correct answer.

Let's look at these steps in more detail.

❶ **Preview the question stem.** You could do a number of things with the stimulus material. You could attack the conclusion, you could defend the conclusion, you could analyze its structure, you could draw further inferences from it, you could even invent a similar argument, and there are still more things to do. You will be asked to do only one (or, occasionally, two) of these things by the stem. So previewing the stem will help you to focus your thinking.

❷ **Read the stimulus material.** This is not as easy as it seems. You are going to have to read more carefully than usual. And this makes sense, since words are the tools of the lawyer's trade. The following advertisement will help to make the point. Read it carefully, because there *will* be a test.

> **Advertisement:** Lite Cigarettes have 50 percent less nicotine and tar than regular cigarettes. Seventy-five percent of the doctors surveyed said that they would, if asked by patients, recommend a reduced tar and nicotine cigarette for patients who cannot stop smoking.

Pop Quiz

1. Does the ad say that some doctors are encouraging people to start to smoke?

2. Does the ad say that some doctors recommend Lite Cigarettes for patients who cannot stop smoking?

3. Does the ad say that most doctors would, if asked by a patient, recommend a low tar and nicotine cigarette for patients who cannot stop smoking?

Answers

1. Does the ad say that some doctors are encouraging people to start to smoke?

   No. The ad specifically says that the doctors surveyed would recommend a low tar and nicotine cigarette "for patients who cannot stop smoking." That clearly applies only to people who are already smokers.

2. Does the ad say that some doctors recommend Lite Cigarettes for patients who cannot stop smoking?

   No again. The ad specifically says that the doctors surveyed would recommend "a reduced tar and nicotine cigarette." To be sure, Lite Cigarettes apparently fall into that category, but the ad does not say that the doctors surveyed would recommend Lite Cigarettes as opposed to some other reduced tar and nicotine cigarette.

3. Does the ad say that most doctors would, if asked by patients, recommend a low tar and nicotine cigarette for patients who cannot stop smoking?

   No once again. The claim is restricted to "doctors surveyed." No information is given about how many doctors were included in the survey—perhaps only four. Nor does the ad disclose how many surveys were done. Even if the market experts had to conduct ten surveys before they found a group of four doctors to back up their claim, the ad would still be true—though, of course, potentially misleading.

The important point is this: Read carefully and pay attention to detail. This does not mean that you need to tie yourself up in paranoid knots. The LSAT is not out to get you personally. The LSAT is, however, a test that is, in part, designed to separate those who can read carefully and pay attention to detail from those who cannot. So read carefully.

3 **Prephrase your answer.** Many LSAT problems have answers that go "click" when you find them. They fit in the same way that a well-made key fits a good lock. After you have previewed the stem and then read carefully the stimulus material, try to anticipate what the correct answer will look like. This is particularly true of

questions that ask you to attack or defend an argument. (This technique does not work for questions that ask you to identify a parallel line of thinking.)

4 **Identify the correct answer.** If you have effectively prephrased an answer, then you should be able to identify fairly readily the correct answer. Otherwise, you will have to study the choices carefully. And, again, careful reading means very careful reading. In Logical Reasoning, each word in the answer choices counts.

Now let's look at some sample LSAT Logical Reasoning questions. As you read the explanations, think about how the solution process applies.

The governor claims that the state faces a drought and has implemented new water-use restrictions; but that's just a move to get some free publicity for his reelection campaign. So far this year, we have had 3.5 inches of rain, slightly more than the average amount of rain for the same period over the last three years.

Which of the following, if true, would most weaken the conclusion of the argument above?

(A) The governor did not declare drought emergencies in the previous three years.

(B) City officials who have the authority to mandate water-use restrictions have not done so.

(C) The snow melt that usually contributes significantly to the state's reservoirs is several inches below normal.

(D) The amount of water the state can draw from rivers that cross state boundaries is limited by federal law.

(E) Water-use restrictions are short-term measures and do little to reduce long-term water consumption.

The correct answer is (C). This question stem asks you to attack the stimulus material. The argument is weak because it depends upon an invalid hidden assumption: Rainfall is the only source of water for the reservoirs. So, your prephrased answer might be "there is another source of water for the reservoirs." Choice (C) fits neatly into this prephrase.

"Channel One" is a 12-minute school news show that includes 2 minutes of commercials. The show's producers offer high schools $50,000 worth of television equipment to air the program. Many parents and teachers oppose the use of commercial television in schools, arguing that advertisements are tantamount to indoctrination. But students are already familiar with television commercials and know how to distinguish programming from advertising.

The argument assumes that

(A) the effects of an advertisement viewed in a classroom would be similar to those of the same advertisement viewed at home.

(B) many educators would be willing to allow the indoctrination of students in exchange for new equipment for their schools.

(C) television advertising is a more effective way of promoting a product to high school students than print advertising.

(D) high school students are sufficiently interested in world affairs to learn from a television news program.

(E) a television news program produced especially for high school students is an effective teaching tool.

The correct answer is (A). This question stem asks you to identify a hidden assumption of the stimulus material. The argument makes the assumption that television's effect on children in the classroom will be similar to its effect on them at home. This is a questionable assumption since the teacher/pupil relationship is an authoritative one. So your prephrase might be something like "the two situations are similar," and choice (A) is a hidden assumption of the argument.

> The spate of terrorist acts against airlines and their passengers raises a new question: Should government officials be forced to disclose the fact that they have received warning of an impending terrorist attack? The answer is "yes." The government currently releases information about the health hazards of smoking, the ecological dangers of pesticides, and the health consequences of food.

The argument given relies primarily on

(A) circular reasoning.

(B) generalization.

(C) authority.

(D) analogy.

(E) causal analysis.

The correct answer is (D). This question stem asks you to describe the reasoning in the stimulus material. The argument draws an analogy between two situations. So your prephrase would almost surely be "analogy."

ALERT!

Watch out for the common logical fallacies:

- Wrong cause
- False analogy
- Weak generalization
- Ambiguous terms
- Irrelevant evidence
- Circular argument
- Ad hominem attack

"Parallel" questions can be tricky. The stimulus for a "parallel" question will probably contain an error. Don't fall into the trap of correcting the error. Just find an answer with a similar mistake.

When it rains, my car gets wet. Since it hasn't rained recently, my car can't be wet.

Which of the following is logically most similar to the argument above?

(A) Whenever critics give a play a favorable review, people go to see it; Pinter's new play did not receive favorable reviews, so I doubt that anyone will go to see it.

(B) Whenever people go to see a play, critics give it a favorable review; people did go to see Pinter's new play, so it did get a favorable review.

(C) Whenever critics give a play a favorable review, people go to see it; Pinter's new play got favorable reviews, so people will probably go to see it.

(D) Whenever a play is given favorable reviews by the critics, people go to see it; since people are going to see Pinter's new play, it will probably get favorable reviews.

(E) Whenever critics give a play a favorable review, people go to see it; people are not going to see Pinter's new play, so it did not get favorable reviews.

The correct answer is (A). This question stem asks you to parallel the stimulus material. The fallacy in the argument is confusion over necessary and sufficient causes. A sufficient cause is an event that is sufficient to guarantee some effect; a necessary cause is one that is required for some event. Choice (A) exhibits this same fallacy. (Remember that a prephrase will not be possible with this type of question.)

WHAT SMART TEST-TAKERS KNOW

Thinking Logically

Logical Reasoning stimulus material has a logical structure.

Logical Reasoning stimulus material is almost always an argument—even if it is just a single sentence. An argument is one or more statements or assertions, one of which, the conclusion, is supposed to follow from the others, the premises. Some arguments are very short and simple:

> Premise: No fish are mammals.
> Conclusion: No mammals are fish.

Others are extremely lengthy and complex, taking up entire volumes. Some arguments are good, some are bad. Scientists use arguments to justify a conclusion regarding the cause of some natural phenomenon; politicians use arguments to reach conclusions about the desirability of government policies. But even given this wide variety of structures and uses, arguments fall into one of two general categories—deductive and inductive.

A deductive argument is one in which the inference depends solely on the meanings of the terms used:

Premises:	All bats are mammals.
	All mammals are warm-blooded.
Conclusion:	Therefore, all bats are warm-blooded.

You know that this argument has to be correct just by looking at it. No research is necessary to show that the conclusion follows automatically from the premises.

All other arguments are termed inductive or probabilistic:

| Premises: | My car will not start; and the fuel gauge reads "empty." |
| Conclusion: | Therefore, the car is probably out of gas. |

Notice that here, unlike the deductive argument, the conclusion does not follow with certainty; it is not guaranteed. The conclusion does seem to be likely or probable, but there are some gaps in the argument. It is possible, for example, that the fuel gauge is broken, or that there is fuel in the tank and the car will not start because something else is wrong.

Locating the conclusion is the first step in evaluating an argument.

The conclusion is the main point of an argument, and locating the conclusion is the first step in evaluating the strength of any argument. In fact, some Logical Reasoning questions simply ask that you identify the conclusion or main point:

> Which of the following is the speaker's conclusion?
>
> Which of the following best summarizes the main point of the argument?
>
> The speaker is attempting to prove that . . .
>
> The speaker is leading to the conclusion that . . .

So, developing techniques for identifying the conclusion of the argument would be important in any case.

Conclusions, however, are important for yet another reason: You cannot begin to look for fallacies or other weaknesses in a line of reasoning, or even find the line of reasoning, until you have clearly identified the point the author wishes to prove. Any attempt to skip over this important step can only result in misunderstanding and confusion. You have surely had the experience of discussing a point for some length of time only to say finally, "Oh, now I see what you were saying, and I agree with you."

Locating the main point of an argument sometimes entails a bit of work because the logical structure of an argument is not necessarily dependent on the order in which sentences appear. To be sure, sometimes the main point of an argument is fairly easy to find. It is the last statement in the paragraph:

> Since this watch was manufactured in Switzerland, and all Swiss watches are reliable, this watch must be reliable.

NOTE

How important is Logical Reasoning?
It is the most important topic on the LSAT. Although many students "obsess" about Analytical Reasoning, Logical Reasoning is the "meat and potatoes" of the LSAT—accounting for just about half of all the questions.

Here the conclusion or the point of the line of reasoning is the part that is underlined. The argument also contains two premises: "this watch was manufactured in Switzerland" and "all Swiss watches are reliable." The same argument could be made, however, with the statements presented in a different order:

> <u>This watch must be reliable</u> since it was manufactured in Switzerland and all Swiss watches are reliable.

or

> <u>This watch must be reliable</u> since all Swiss watches are reliable and this watch was manufactured in Switzerland.

or

> Because this watch was manufactured in Switzerland, <u>it must be reliable</u> because all Swiss watches are reliable.

So you cannot always count on the conclusion of the argument being the last sentence of the paragraph even though sometimes it is. Therefore, it is important to know some techniques for finding the conclusion of an argument.

The conclusion of an argument can be the first sentence.

It is true that speakers often lead up to the conclusion and make it the grand finale. Sometimes, however, speakers announce in advance where they are going and then proceed to develop arguments in support of their position. So the second most common position for the conclusion of an argument is the first sentence of the stimulus material.

Key words often signal a conclusion.

The stimulus material often uses transitional words or phrases to signal a conclusion, for example, "Ms. Slote has a Masters in Education, and she has 20 years of teaching experience; <u>therefore</u>, she is a good teacher." Other words and phrases to watch include *hence, thus, so, it follows that, as a result,* and *consequently.*

Key words often signal an important premise.

In some arguments, the premises rather than the conclusion are signaled. Words that signal premises include *since, because,* and *if.*

TIP

Signal words can help
you find conclusions:
therefore
hence
thus
consequently
accordingly
so

> <u>Since</u> Rex has been with the company 20 years and does such a good job, he will probably receive a promotion.

or

> Rex will probably receive a promotion <u>because</u> he has been with the company 20 years and he does such a good job.

or

> <u>If</u> Rex has been with the company 20 years and has done a good job, he will probably receive a promotion.

In each of the three examples just presented, the conclusion is "Rex will probably receive a promotion" and the premise is that "he has been with the company 20 years and does a good job." Of course, many other words can signal premises.

The conclusion is the main point of an argument.

Ask what the author wants to prove. Not all arguments are broken down by the numbers. In such a case, you must use your judgment to answer the question "What is the speaker trying to prove?" For example:

> We must reduce the amount of money we spend on space exploration. Right now, the enemy is launching a massive military buildup, and we need the additional money to purchase military equipment to match the anticipated increase in the enemy's strength.

In this argument, there are no key words to announce the conclusion or the premises. Instead, you must ask yourself a series of questions:

> Is the speaker trying to prove that the enemy is beginning a military buildup?

No, because that statement is the larger argument, so it cannot be the conclusion.

> Is the main point that we must match the enemy buildup?

Again the answer is "no" because that, too, is an intermediate step on the way to some other conclusion.

> Is the speaker trying to prove that we must cut back on the budget for space exploration?

Now the answer is "yes," and that is the author's point.

Things get more complicated when an argument contains arguments within the main argument. The argument about the need for military expenditures might have included this subargument:

> We must reduce the amount of money we spend on space exploration. The enemy is now stockpiling titanium, a metal that is used in building airplanes. And each time the enemy has stockpiled titanium, it has launched a massive military buildup. So right now, the enemy is launching a massive military buildup, and we need the additional money to purchase military equipment to match the anticipated increase in the enemy's strength.

Notice that now one of the premises of the earlier argument is the conclusion of a subargument. The conclusion of the subargument is "the enemy is launching a massive military buildup," which has two explicit premises: "The enemy is now stockpiling titanium" and "a stockpiling of titanium means a military buildup."

No matter how complicated an argument gets, you can always break it down into subarguments. And if it is really complex, those subarguments can be broken down into smaller parts. Of course, the stimulus material on the LSAT cannot be overly complicated because the initial argument will not be much more than 100 or so words in length. So just keep asking yourself "What is the author trying to prove?"

LSAT conclusions are carefully worded.

Defining precisely the main point is also an essential step in evaluating an argument. Once the main point of the argument has been isolated, you must take the second step of exactly defining that point. In particular, you should be looking for three things:

1. Quantifiers *"Many, several, a lot of"*
2. Qualifiers — *Word that restricts the meaning of another*
3. The author's intention

LSAT conclusions are carefully quantified.

Quantifiers are words such as *some, none, never, always, everywhere,* and *sometimes.* For example, there is a big difference in the claims:

> All mammals live on land.
>
> Most mammals live on land.

The first is false; the second is true. Compare also the following:

> Women in the United States have always had the right to vote.
>
> Since 1920, women in the United States have had the right to vote.

Again, the first statement is false and the second is true. And compare the following:

> It is raining, and the temperature is predicted to drop below 32°F; therefore, it will surely snow.
>
> It is raining, and the temperature is predicted to drop below 32°F; therefore, it will probably snow.

The first is a much less cautious claim than the second, and if it failed to snow, the first claim would have been proved false, though not the second. The second statement claims only that it is probable that snow will follow, not that it definitely will. So someone could make the second claim and defend it when the snow failed to materialize by saying, "Well, I allowed for that in my original statement."

LSAT conclusions are carefully qualified.

Qualifiers play a role similar to that of quantifiers, but they are descriptive rather than numerical. As such, they are more concrete and difficult to enumerate. Just make sure that you stay alert for distinctions like this:

> In nations that have a bicameral legislature, the speed with which legislation is passed is largely a function of the strength of executive leadership.

Notice here that the author makes a claim about "nations," so it would be wrong to apply the author's reasoning to states. Further, you should not conclude that the author believes that bicameral legislatures pass different laws from those passed by unicameral legislatures. The author mentions only the "speed" with which the laws are passed, not their content.

> All passenger automobiles manufactured by Detroit auto-makers since 1975 have been equipped with seat belts.

You should not conclude from this statement that all trucks have also been equipped with seat belts since the author makes a claim only about "passenger automobiles," nor should you conclude that imported cars have seat belts, for the author mentions Detroit-made cars only.

> No other major department store offers you a low price and a 75-day warranty on parts and labor on this special edition of the XL 30 color television.

The tone of the ad is designed to create a very large impression on the hearer, but the precise claim made is fairly limited. First, the ad's claim is specifically restricted to a comparison of "department" stores, and "major" department stores at that. It is possible that some non-major department store offers a similar warranty and price; also it may be that another type of retail store, say, an electronics store, makes a similar offer. Second, other stores, department or otherwise, may offer a better deal on the product, say, a low price with a three-month warranty, and still the claim would stand so long as no one else offered exactly a "75-day" warranty. Finally, the ad is restricted to a "special edition" of the television, so depending on what that means, the ad may be even more restrictive in its claim.

On the LSAT, the author's intention may be crucial.

The author's intention may also be important. You must be careful to distinguish between claims of fact and proposals of change. Do not assume that an author's claim to have found a problem means the author knows how to solve it. An author can make a claim about the cause of some event without believing that the event can be prevented or even that it ought to be prevented. For example, consider this argument:

> Because the fifth ward vote is crucial to Gordon's campaign, if Gordon fails to win over the ward leaders, he will be defeated in the election.

TIP

The conclusion is the most important part of the argument. For every Logical Reasoning question, find the conclusion and read it carefully. The logical structure of the argument should then be clear.

TIP

Find the missing link.
When an LSAT
question stem asks
about a premise or an
assumption (the words
mean the same
thing), it is asking
about a hidden,
suppressed, or implicit
(the words all mean
the same thing)
assumption. So look
for the missing link.

You cannot conclude that the author believes Gordon should or should not be elected. The author gives only a factual analysis without endorsing or condemning either possible outcome. Also, consider this argument:

> Each year, the rotation of the Earth slows a few tenths of a second. In several million years, it will have stopped altogether, and life as we know it will no longer be able to survive on Earth.

You cannot conclude that the author wants to find a solution for the slowing of the Earth's rotation. For all we know, the author thinks the process is inevitable, or even desirable.

Premises support the conclusion.

A premise is the logical support for a conclusion. The LSAT usually refers to premises as *assumptions*, but the terminology is not important. It is important not to misunderstand the word *assumption*. Although it is related to the word *assume*, an assumption, as that term is used in logic, does not have the connotation of *surmise or guess*. Consider this argument:

> All humans are mortal.
> Socrates is a human.
> Therefore, Socrates is mortal.

The first two statements are assumptions—even though they are obviously true. You can use the words *assumption* and *premise* interchangeably.

Explicit premises are specifically stated.

In the detective novel *A Study in Scarlet* by Sir Arthur Conan Doyle, Sherlock Holmes explains to Dr. Watson that it is possible logically to deduce the existence of rivers and oceans from a single drop of water, though such a deduction would require many intermediate steps. While this may be an exaggeration, it is true that arguments can contain several links. For example:

> Because there is snow on the ground, it must have snowed last night. If it snowed last night, then the temperature must have dropped below 32°F. The temperature drops below 32°F only in the winter. So, since there is snow on the ground, it must be winter here.

TIP

**Signal words can help
you find premises:**
since
because
given that
inasmuch as

It is easy to imagine a Holmesian chain of reasoning that strings additional links in either direction. Instead of starting with "there is snow on the ground," you could have started with "there is a snowman on the front lawn"; and instead of stopping with "it must be winter here," you could have gone on to "so it is summer in Australia." In other words, you could reason from "there is a snowman on the front lawn" to "it is summer in Australia."

Implicit premises are not stated.

In practice, arguments do not extend indefinitely in either direction. We begin reasoning at what seems to be a convenient point and stop with the conclusion we had hoped to prove: It must have snowed last night because there is snow on the ground this morning. Now, it should be obvious to you that the strength of an argument depends in a very important way on the legitimacy of its assumptions. And one of the LSAT's favorite tools for building a Logical Reasoning item is to focus upon an assumption of a special kind: the implicit premise.

Consider some sample arguments:

> Premise: My car's fuel tank is full.
> Conclusion: Therefore, my car will start.

A very effective attack on this argument can be aimed at a hidden premise—as anyone who has ever had a car fail to start can attest. The battery might be dead or a hundred other things might be wrong. This shows that the argument is not very strong. In logical terms, the argument depends upon an implicit premise:

> Premises: My car's fuel tank is full.
>   (The only reason my car might not start is lack of fuel.)
> Conclusion: Therefore, my car will start.

The statement in parentheses is a necessary part of the argument. Otherwise, the conclusion does not follow.

Implicit premises are also called *suppressed premises* (or assumptions) or *hidden premises* (or assumptions). You do not have to worry about terminology; you just have to know one when you see it:

> Premise: Edward has fewer than ten years of experience.
> Conclusion: Therefore, Edward is not qualified.
> Suppressed Premise: Only people with at least ten years of experience are qualified.

> Premise: This is Tuesday.
> Conclusion: Therefore, the luncheon special is pasta.
> Suppressed Premise: Every Tuesday, the luncheon special is pasta.

> Premise: The committee did not announce its choice by 3:00.
> Conclusion: Therefore, Radu did not get the job.
> Suppressed Premise: Radu gets the job only if the announcement is made by 3:00.

Many Logical Reasoning questions test fallacies.

A *fallacy* is a mistake in reasoning. Many LSAT questions ask you to demonstrate that you know a mistake when you see one. Of course, there are many different ways to make mistakes, so it is not possible to create an exhaustive list of fallacies. However, certain

TIP

Look for the alternative causal linkage. In many items, the stimulus material is an explanation of an event or phenomenon. You are then asked to weaken the explanation. Most often, the correct answer will be an alternative causal explanation.

fallacies come up on the LSAT fairly often. If you know what they look like, then they will be easier to spot.

Remember, however, that you do not get points for memorizing this list of fallacies. You get points for being able to apply it. So use the list as a guide as you do the practice tests in this book, but keep in mind that you will not be tested on the list itself.

Explanations often identify the wrong cause.

The mistake in reasoning that is tested most often by the LSAT is the fallacy of the false cause. An argument that commits this error attributes a causal relationship between two events where none exists or at least the relationship is misidentified. For example:

> Every time the doorbell rings, I find there is someone at the door. Therefore, it must be the case that the doorbell calls these people to my door.

Obviously, the causal link suggested here is backward. It is the presence of the person at the door that then leads to the ringing of the bell, not vice versa. A more serious example of the fallacy of the false cause is as follows:

> There were more air traffic fatalities in 1979 than there were in 1969; therefore, the airplanes used in 1979 were more dangerous than those used in 1969.

The difficulty with this argument is that it attributes the increase to a lack of safety when, in fact, it is probably attributable to an increase in air travel generally. A typical question stem and correct answer for this type of problem might be as follows:

> Which of the following, if true, most undermines the speaker's argument?
>
> (✓)   Total air miles traveled doubled from 1969 to 1979.

Analogies are often false.

A second fallacy that might appear on the LSAT is that of false analogy. This error occurs when a conclusion drawn from one situation is applied to another situation—but the two situations are not very similar. For example:

> People should have to be licensed before they are allowed to have children. After all, we require people who operate automobiles to be licensed.

In this case, the two situations—driving and having children—are so dissimilar that we would probably want to say they are not analogous at all. Having children has nothing to do with driving. An LSAT problem based upon a faulty analogy is likely to be more subtle. For example:

> The government should pay more to its diplomats who work in countries that are considered potential enemies. This is very similar to paying soldiers combat premiums if they are stationed in a war zone.

The argument here relies on an analogy between diplomats in a potentially dangerous country and soldiers in combat areas. Of course, the analogy is not perfect. No analogy can be more than an analogy. So a typical question stem and right answer for this type of problem might be as follows:

> Which of the following, if true, most weakens the argument above?
>
> (✓) Diplomats are almost always evacuated before hostilities begin.

A generalization may be weak.

A common weakness in an inductive argument is the hasty generalization, that is, basing a large conclusion on too little data. For example:

> All four times I have visited Chicago, it has rained; therefore, Chicago probably gets very little sunshine.

The rather obvious difficulty with the argument is that it moves from a small sample—four visits—to a very broad conclusion: Chicago gets little sunshine. Of course, generalizing on the basis of a sample or limited experience can be legitimate:

> All five of the buses manufactured by Gutmann that we inspected have defective wheel mounts; therefore, some other buses manufactured by Gutmann probably have similar defects.

Admittedly, this argument is not airtight. Perhaps the other uninspected buses do not have the same defect, but this second argument is much stronger than the first. So a typical LSAT stem and correct answer might be as follows:

> Which of the following, if true, would most weaken the argument above?
>
> (✓) The five inspected buses were prototypes built before design specifications were finalized.

Some arguments use terms ambiguously.

A fourth fallacy that the LSAT uses is that of ambiguity. Anytime there is a shifting in the meaning of terms used in an argument, the argument has committed a fallacy of ambiguity. For example:

> The shark has been around for millions of years. The City Aquarium has a shark. Therefore, the City Aquarium has at least one animal that is millions of years old.

The error of the argument is that it uses the word *shark* in two different ways. In the first occurrence, *shark* is used to mean sharks in general. In the second, *shark* refers to one individual animal. Here's another, less playful, example:

> Sin occurs only when a person fails to follow the will of God. But since God is all-powerful, what God wills must actually be. Therefore, it is impossible to deviate from the will of God, so there can be no sin in the world.

www.petersons.com/arco

NOTE

Why do I need to know about fallacies? If you know what to look for, you're more likely to find it. This section is a checklist of common fallacies used by the LSAT.

The equivocation here is in the word *will*. The first time it is used, the author intends that the will of God is God's wish and implies that it is possible to fail to comply with those wishes. In the second instance, the author uses the word *will* in a way that implies that such deviation is not possible. The argument reaches the conclusion that there is no sin in the world only by playing on these two senses of "the will of God." So a representative question stem and correct answer might be as follows:

> The argument above uses which of the following terms in an ambiguous way?
>
> (✓)   Will

Some arguments use irrelevant evidence.

Another fallacy you might encounter in a Logical Reasoning section is an appeal to irrelevant considerations. For example, an argument that appeals to the popularity of a position to prove the position is fallacious:

> Frederick must be the best choice for chair because most people believe that he is the best person for the job.

That many people hold an opinion obviously does not guarantee its correctness. After all, many people once thought airplanes couldn't fly. A question stem for the argument above plus the correct answer might look like this:

> Which of the following, if true, most weakens the speaker's argument?
>
> (✓)   Most people erroneously believe that Frederick holds a Ph.D.

Some arguments are circular.

A circular argument (begging the question) is an argument in which the conclusion to be proved appears also as a premise. For example:

> Beethoven was the greatest composer of all time because he wrote the greatest music of any composer, and the one who composes the greatest music must be the greatest composer.

The conclusion of this argument is that Beethoven was the greatest composer of all time, but one of the premises of the argument is that he composed the greatest music, and the other premise states that that is the measure of greatness. The argument is fallacious, for there is really no argument for the conclusion at all, just a restatement of the conclusion. A typical LSAT stem and correct answer are as follows:

> The argument above is weak because
>
> (✓)   it assumes what it hopes to prove.

Ad hominem arguments attack someone personally.

Yes, *ad hominem* is a Latin phrase, and Latin is not tested on the LSAT. This phrase is just a useful shorthand for this fallacy. Any argument that is directed against the source of the claim rather than the claim itself is an *ad hominem* attack:

> Professor Peters' analysis of the economic impact of the proposed sports arena for the Blue Birds should be rejected because Professor Peters is a Red Birds fan—the most fierce rivals of the Blue Birds.

The suggestion is obviously farfetched. And a representative LSAT stem plus correct answer might look like this:

> The speaker's argument is weak because it
>
> (✓) confuses a person's loyalty to a sports team with the person's ability to offer an expert economic opinion.

Making Deductions

In the previous section, we discussed some common inductive fallacies; in this section, we turn our attention to deductive reasoning. You will recall that a deductive argument is one in which the inference depends solely on the meanings of the terms used. The argument form most often associated with deductive reasoning is the *syllogism*, a term that will be familiar to anyone who has studied basic logic:

All trees are plants.
All redwoods are trees.
Therefore, all redwoods are plants.

Deductive arguments like this one hinge on the validity of positive or negative claims about all or some of a group. On the LSAT, deductive arguments come into play in questions like this:

Some lizards are carnivorous.
Some carnivores are intelligent.
Some intelligent creatures are not lizards.

If the statements above are true, which of the following could also be true?

(A) No carnivores are intelligent.

(B) No lizards are carnivores.

(C) No intelligent creatures are carnivores.

(D) No carnivores are lizards.

(E) All lizards are intelligent.

Three useful techniques for determining the validity of deductive arguments are knowing the square of opposition, using circle diagrams, and developing a logic shorthand.

Variations on direct inferences can lay out all the possibilities.

By *direct inference,* we mean a conclusion that follows from a single premise. For example, from the statement "no birds are mammals," we can conclude "no mammals are birds," since there is no individual that is a member of both the group bird and the group mammal. From "no birds are mammals," we could also reach the conclusion that "all birds are not mammals," but this is really nothing more than a grammatical restructuring of the original form, whereas the statement "no mammals are birds" is actually an inference (it is a totally new claim).

Setting aside possible variations in grammatical structure ("no B are M" = "all B are not M"; "some B are M" = "some B are not non-M"; and so on), we may organize such assertions into four groups, depending on whether they make a claim about "some" on the one hand or, on the other hand, either "all" or "no" members of groups and whether they are "affirmative" or "negative." In order to save space and also to show that our techniques are generally applicable—that is, not dependent on any particular content— we will find it convenient to use capital letters as substitutes for terms. Thus, "all birds are mammals" becomes "all B are M," which could also stand for "all bats are myopic," but nothing is lost in the translation since we are concerned with the formal relations and not the actual substantive or content relations between sentences. Using capital letters, we set up the scheme on the following page so that we have sentences that make affirmative claims about all of a group, negative claims about all of a group, affirmative claims about part of a group, and negative claims about part of a group.

(1) All S is P.
(2) No S is P.
(3) Some S is P.
(4) Some S is not P.

If **(1)** is true, then

    (2) is false.

    (3) is true.

    (4) is false.

If **(1)** is false, then

    (2) is undetermined.

    (3) is undetermined.

    (4) is true.

If **(2)** is true, then

    (1) is false.

    (3) is false.

    (4) is true.

If **(2)** is false, then

    (1) is undetermined.

    (3) is true.

    (4) is undetermined.

If **(3)** is true, then

    (1) is undetermined.

    (2) is false.

    (4) is undetermined.

If **(3)** is false, then

    (1) is false.

    (2) is true.

    (4) is true.

If **(4)** is true, then

    (1) is false.

    (2) is undetermined.

    (3) is undetermined.

If **(4)** is false, then

    (1) is true.

    (2) is false.

    (3) is true.

Circle diagrams show relationships.

It is also apparent that there are interrelationships among all the statement forms. For example, if "all A are B" is true, then both "no A are B" and "some A are not B" must be false. One way of exhibiting these relationships is through the use of circle or <u>Venn</u>-type diagrams. (These are also used in Analytical Reasoning problems.)

Diagramming two terms. We can use a circle to mark off a "logical area." So a circle that we label "A" separates the field of the page into two spaces, A and not-A. The interior of the circle is the space where all As are located, and anything located outside the circle is not an A (it is a non-A):

Diagram 1:

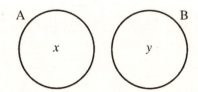

In Diagram 1, *x* is an A, but *y* is not an A; that is to say *y* is a non-A. Now, if we draw two overlapping circles, we can represent not only two groups, A and B, but also the intersection of those groups:

Diagram 2:

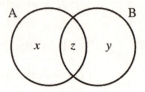

In Diagram 2, *x* is an A that is not, however, a B; *y* is a B that is not, however, an A; and *z* is something that is both A and B.

If it is true that "all A are B," then it is not possible for something to be an "A but not also a B," so we blot out that portion of our circle diagram that contains the area "A but not also B":

Diagram 3:

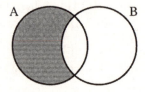

Now if it is true that "all A are B," then

"no A are B" is false. (All the A are B.)

"some A are B" is true. (All the A are within the B circle.)

"some A are not B" is false. (That area is eliminated.)

If it is false that "all A are B," that might be because "no A are B":

Diagram 4:

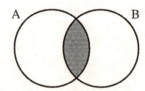

However, it might also be because "some, though not all, A are not B":

Diagram 5:

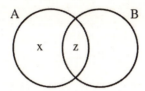

Both situations are consistent with "all A are B" being a false statement. So, if it is false that "all A are B," then

"no A are B" might be true or false. (We cannot choose between Diagram 4 and Diagram 5.)

"some A are B" might be true or false. (We have no basis for choice.)

"some A are not B" is true. (This is the case with both Diagram 4 and Diagram 5.)

If it is true that "no A are B," then there is no overlap between the two:

Diagram 6:

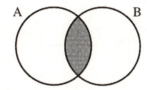

Therefore,

"all A are B" is false. (There is no overlap.)

"some A are B" is false. (There is no overlap.)

"some A are not B" is true. (That part is left open.)

But if "no A are B" is false, that might be because "all A are B":

Diagram 7:

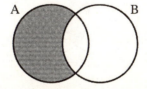

But it might equally well be because "some, though not all, A are B":

Diagram 8:

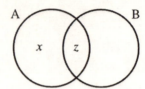

Therefore,

"all A are B" might be true or false. (There is no basis for choice.)

"some A are B" is true. (See Diagrams 7 and 8.)

"some A are not B" might be true or false. (There is no basis for choice between diagrams.)

If it is true that "some A are B,"

Diagram 9:

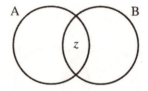

then

"all A are B" might be true or false.

"no A are B" is false. (See Diagram 9.)

"some A are not B" might be true or false.

If it is false that "some A are B," this can only be because there is no overlap between the two circles:

Diagram 10:

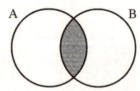

Therefore,

"all A are B" is false. (There is no overlap at all.)

"no A are B" is true. (as shown by Diagram 10)

"some A are not B" is true. (That area is left open.)

If it is true that "some A are not B,"

Diagram 11:

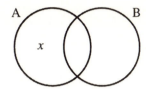

then

"all A are B" is false. (shown by the *x* in Diagram 11)

"no A are B" might be true or false. (The *x* does not close off the overlap of A and B, but, then again, we do not know that there are individuals with the characteristic A and B.)

"some A are B" might be true or false. (See the reasoning just given for "no A are B.")

If it is false that "some A are not B,"

Diagram 12:

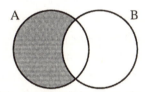

then the area of the A circle that does not overlap the B circle is empty, as shown by Diagram 12. Therefore,

"all A are B" is true. (The one is contained in the other.)

"no A are B" is false. (The one is contained in the other.)

"some A are B" is true. (In fact, all are, but see our discussion of some.)

Diagramming three terms. Technically, a syllogism is supposed to be constructed from three statements, two of which are assumptions and the third the conclusion. However, LSAT arguments of this type often include multiple statements, creating numerous possibilities for relationships. Here is an example:

All trees are plants.
All redwoods are trees.
This tree is a redwood.
Therefore, this tree is a plant.

If we analyzed this argument in a technical way, we would say it includes not one but two syllogisms—the conclusion of the first forming a premise of the second:

> All trees are plants.
> All redwoods are trees.
> Therefore, all redwoods are plants.

> All redwoods are plants.
> This tree is a redwood.
> Therefore, this tree is a plant.

Of course, a syllogism can be constructed using negative statements as well. Depending on the statements, what forms are used, and how the terms are arranged, we can construct many different syllogisms. Not all of these, however, would be valid. For example, the following syllogism is valid:

> All A are B.
> No B are C.
> Therefore, no A are C.

We can show its validity by using a variation on our circle diagrams. Because now we have three terms rather than two terms, we will use three circles to define the possible relationships. Remember that two terms or groups might be related in three ways: an A that is not a B, a B that is not an A, and something that is both A and B. When we add our third term, C, we have to allow for something that is a C but not an A or B; something that is a C and B but not an A; something that is a C and A but not a B; and something that is C, B, and A. In other words, there are seven possible combinations.

1 an A but not a B or C
2 a B but not an A or C
3 an A and B but not a C
4 a C but not an A or B
5 an A and C but not a B
6 a B and C but not an A
7 an A, B, and C

These seven possibilities can be shown on a three-circle diagram:

Diagram 13:

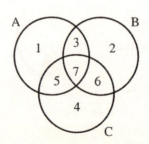

Using our three-circle diagrams, we can show the validity of the original syllogism:

> All A are B.
> No B are C.
> Therefore, no A are C.

Since our first premise states that "all A are B," we can eliminate the areas of the diagram that are within the A circle but not within the B circle. This corresponds to areas 1 and 5 in Diagram 13.

Diagram 14:

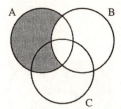

Our second premise states that "no B are C," so we must eliminate those areas, corresponding to 6 and 7 on Diagram 13, that allow that something might be a B and a C. (Notice that something that is an A, B, and C—area 7—is automatically something that is a B and a C.)

Diagram 15:

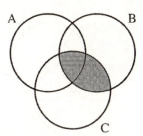

Now if we enter both premises 1 and 2 on the same diagram, we have the following:

Diagram 16:

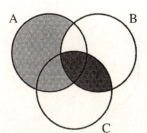

NOTE

Do you need to know "logic" to do well on this part?

No. The LSAT does not test the concepts of formal logic. (And formal language in this chapter is used just for ease of reference and will be explained.) However, an informal course in "practical reasoning" might be useful if you have not yet graduated and can fit it into your curriculum.

The conclusion of our syllogism asserts that "no A are C," and our diagram confirms this. The only area of A left open is within the B circle; all A but non-B areas have been erased.

Another example of a valid three-term syllogism is as follows:

> All A are B.
> Some C are A.
> Therefore, some C are B.

In a syllogism in which one of the propositions uses "some" and the other proposition uses "all" or "no," it is a good idea to enter the "all" or "no" information first. So we enter first "all A are B":

Diagram 17:

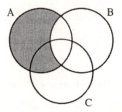

Then we enter "some C are A" by putting an x in the area of C and A. Since there is only one such area left, the x must be placed so:

Diagram 18:

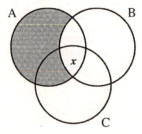

Now the diagram shows the validity of our syllogism: There is at least one C that is also a B.

An example of an invalid deductive argument is the syllogism that has the following form:

No A are B.
No B are C.
Therefore, no A are C.

We can use a circle diagram to show why this syllogism is invalid. We enter the first and second premises:

Diagram 19:

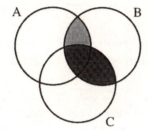

But then we observe that the overlap of A and C is still open, so our conclusion that "no A are C" is not warranted; that is, it does not definitely follow from our premises. So, too, is the following argument invalid:

Some A are B.
Some B are not C.
Therefore, some A are not C.

Since there is no premise that begins with "all" or "no," we are forced to start with a premise that begins with "some." We take premise number one first—"some A are B"—but we have no way of determining whether or not the As that are Bs are also Cs. So we will leave open those possibilities:

Diagram 20:

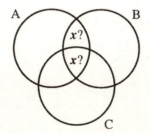

Now we add the information "some B are not C," again keeping open the possibility that something might be a B and an A or a B but not an A:

Diagram 21:

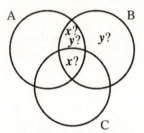

Diagram 21 shows that the conclusion, "some A are not C," does not follow from our premises because we do not definitely know the locations of our xs or ys, as indicated by the question marks.

Of course, you cannot expect that every Logical Reasoning problem on the LSAT with a form similar to the syllogism will fit this form exactly. To be sure, in the past, we have seen problems that fit the technical definition of the syllogism, but more often, LSAT problems involve more terms and more statements. Still, it is possible to adapt our circle diagram technique for use with nonstandard syllogisms:

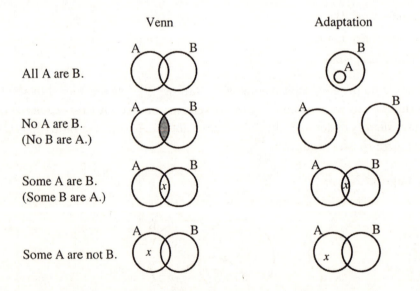

We can apply these adaptations to a nonstandard syllogism of the sort that could appear on the LSAT:

> All admirals are officers.
> No officer is not an honorable person.
> Some gentlemen are officers.
> No rogues are honorable persons.

Which of the following conclusions can be drawn from the statements above?

(A) All honorable persons are officers.

(B) No rogues are admirals.

(C) Some gentlemen are rogues.

(D) Some gentlemen are admirals.

(E) All officers are admirals.

The correct answer is (B). This can be demonstrated using diagrams.

We diagram our first statement using the adaptation:

Then we add our second statement (which is equivalent to saying "All officers are honorable persons"):

Then we add the third statement:

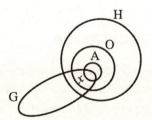

NOTE

Academic training is hazardous to your test-taking health. Look at a page of Logical Reasoning items (any such page in this book, for example). What percentage of the ink on the page is devoted to stimulus material, and what percentage is de- voted to answer choices? It is at least equal, and in many cases, more space is taken up by the choices. You are used to thinking of the question as the important part of the test. For the LSAT, the answers are equally important.

Notice that in adding this statement, we leave open the question of whether all gentlemen are officers or even admirals. We know only that some gentlemen are officers, and that is the reason for the *x* entered in the space as shown. (Each spatial area is a "logical" space.) Finally, we add the fourth statement:

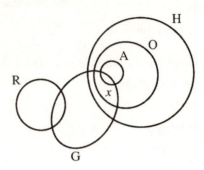

Notice that we leave open the question of whether a rogue might be a gentleman in the same way we have left open the question of whether all gentlemen are honorable.

From the diagram, we see that choices (A) and (E) commit the same error. We cannot conclude from a statement such as "all A are B" that "all B are A." The "admiral" circle is within the "officer" circle, and the "officer" circle is within the "honorable" circle. Then choices (C) and (D) commit the same error. It is possible that some gentlemen are rogues, for that is an area left open on the diagram. It is also possible that some gentlemen are admirals, but that is not necessarily true. It is true, however, as the diagram shows, that no rogues are admirals. The logical space for rogues, represented by the "R" circle, is completely outside the logical space for admirals, the "A" circle, which is completely contained within the "honorable," or "H," circle.

Let us conclude our discussion of circle diagrams by emphasizing that this is just one of many ways of solving Logical Reasoning problems. Some students remark that they find it easier to solve these problems "verbally"; that is, without the assistance of any diagram. That is fine. These diagrams are merely a suggestion. If you find them useful, then you have yet another way of attacking such problems on the exam. If you do not find them helpful, then after at least making an effort to understand how they work, you may rely on some other strategy.

Logical shorthand makes implications easy to see.

Thus far, we have treated deductive inferences that involved relationships among terms. Now we treat a group of deductive arguments, which we will call *implications*, that are based on the connections of sentences as opposed to terms. An example of an implication argument is as follows:

If John is elected president, Mary is elected vice president, and if Mary is elected vice president, Paul is elected secretary. Therefore, if John is elected president, Paul is elected secretary.

If we employ a system of logical shorthand, we can make a capital letter stand for each clause (or sentence). This shows that our argument has the following form:

> If J, then M.
> If M, then P.
> Therefore, if J, then P.

Notice that our entire argument is phrased in the conditional. Our conclusion does not state that "Paul is elected secretary." It states rather that "*if* J, *then* P," and that entire conditional statement is the conclusion of the argument.

Another common form of implication is illustrated by the following argument:

> If John is elected president, Mary is elected vice president. John is elected president. Therefore, Mary is elected vice president.

The form of the argument is as follows:

> If J, then M.
> J.
> Therefore, M.

Notice that this argument differs from the preceding conditional argument because the second premise definitely asserts, "John is elected president." Now, since the validity of an argument is dependent only upon its form, it is clear that any argument that has this form is valid. This form of argument must not, however, be confused with the following superficially similar but invalid form:

> If A, then B.
> B.
> Therefore, A.

The first premise asserts only that A is followed by B; it does not assert that an occurrence of situation B is necessarily preceded by an occurrence of situation A. For example, the following argument is not valid:

> If an object is made of clay, it will not burn. This object will not burn. Therefore, this object is made of clay.

There are many objects that will not burn and that are not made of clay—those made of steel, for example. So any argument that has this form is invalid.

Another common form of implication that is valid is illustrated by the following argument:

> If John is elected president, then Mary is elected vice president. Mary is not elected vice president. Therefore, John is not elected president.

It has the following form:

> If J, then M.
> Not M.
> Therefore, not J.

Because the first premise states that an occurrence of situation J will be followed by an occurrence of situation M and since the second premise tells us that situation M did not occur, we can logically conclude that situation J did not occur, for if J had occurred, so, too, would M have occurred. A similar but invalid argument form is illustrated by the following argument:

> If John is elected president, then Mary is elected vice president. John is not elected president. Therefore, Mary is not elected vice president.

That this argument is invalid is demonstrated by the consideration that the first premise states only that an occurrence of J is followed by an occurrence of M. The premises do not establish that M can occur *only* if J also occurs. The first premise says, "if J, then M," not "M only if J." So any argument of the form "If A, then B. Not A. Therefore, not B" is invalid.

Not all valid implicational forms have been shown; our illustrations are intended to show the technique of substituting capital letters for sentences. This allows us to isolate the general *form* of an argument, which makes analyzing or comparing that form easier.

Devising Attack Strategies

Even though LSAT Logical Reasoning questions are worded in a wide variety of ways, there are several specific attack strategies that you can apply.

The question stem is the best starting place.

The first step in attacking a Logical Reasoning item is to read the question stem (the part to which the question mark is attached). Do this even before you read the paragraph or argument on which the question is based. The reason for this suggestion is simple. There are many different questions that could be asked about an argument: "How can it be strengthened?" "How can it be weakened?" "What are its assumptions?" "How is the argument developed?" and so on. If you read the stem first, it will guide you in what to look for as you read the argument.

The answer choices are your clues.

The differences among the answer choices can help you isolate the issues in the problem. With this in mind, here is a good plan of attack.

1 Always read every choice.

2 If possible, eliminate obviously incorrect choices.

3 Examine the remaining choices and focus on their differences.

4 Choose the best answer. Remember that the best is often not perfect and the less-than-best (incorrect) answers often have some merit.

Answering Special Question Types

Many Logical Reasoning questions are straightforward questions about how to attack and defend arguments. Some questions, however, involve special twists of thinking.

For a logical similarity question, reproduce the error.

For a question that asks, "Which of the following arguments is most similar?" remember that you are not supposed to correct the argument. You are supposed to find an answer choice with a similar structure—even if the original argument contains a fallacy. Also, be careful to notice exactly what is to be paralleled—all of an argument, one speaker, or whatever.

For a completion question, pick a conclusion.

For a question that requires you to complete a paragraph, keep in mind that you must complete the structure of the argument as a whole as well as the particular sentence. This means that an answer choice that repeats something already said is not correct. The correct answer must be the *completion* of the thought.

For an assumption question, pick a hidden premise.

When the question stem asks for the identification of assumptions, it is seeking implicit or unstated premises that—like all premises—are necessary to the argument.

For a weakening question, attack a hidden premise.

When the question stem asks for weakening ideas, it is usually a matter of attacking implicit assumptions that justify the application of the evidence to the conclusion.

ALERT!

For a parallel thinking question, a similar topic is likely to be a wrong answer. Parallel thinking questions ask you to select a line of reasoning that is similar to that in the stimulus material—warts and all. If the stimulus material is fallacious, then the correct answer choice makes the same mistake. A favorite wrong answer strategy is to toss in a choice with a similar topic, e.g., autos in the stimulus material and trucks in the choices.

EXERCISES: LOGICAL REASONING

Exercise 1

25 Questions • 35 Minutes

Directions: The following questions ask you to analyze and evaluate the reasoning in short paragraphs or passages. For some questions, all of the answer choices may conceivably be answers to the question asked. You should select the *best* answer to the question; that is, an answer that does not require you to make assumptions that violate commonsense standards by being implausible, redundant, irrelevant, or inconsistent. After choosing the best answer, circle the letter of your choice.

Example

In an extensive study of the reading habits of magazine subscribers, it was found than an average of between four and five people actually read each copy of the most popular weekly news magazine. On this basis, we estimate that the 12,000 copies of *Poets and Poetry* that are sold each month are actually read by 48,000 to 60,000 people.

The estimate above assumes that

(A) individual magazine readers generally enjoy more than one type of magazine.

(B) most of the readers of *Poets and Poetry* subscribe to the magazine.

(C) the ratio of readers to copies is the same for *Poets and Poetry* as for the weekly news magazine.

(D) the number of readers of the weekly news magazine is similar to the number of readers of *Poets and Poetry*.

(E) most readers enjoy sharing copies of their favorite magazines with friends and family members.

The correct answer is (C).

1. I. Whenever some of the runners are leading off and all of the infielders are playing in, all of the batters attempt to bunt.

   II. Some of the runners are leading off, but some of the batters are not attempting to bunt.

   Which of the following conclusions can be deduced from the two statements given?

   (A) Some of the runners are not leading off.

   (B) Some of the batters are attempting to bunt.

   (C) None of the infielders is playing in.

   (D) All of the infielders are playing in.

   (E) Some of the infielders are not playing in.

2. The federal bankruptcy laws illustrate the folly of do-good protectionism at its most extreme. At the debtor's own request, the judge will list all of his debts; take what money the debtor has, which will be very little; and divide that small amount among his creditors. Then the judge declares that those debts are thereby satisfied, and the debtor is free from those creditors. Why, a person could take his credit card and buy a car, a stereo, and a new wardrobe and then declare himself bankrupt! In effect, he will have conned his creditors into giving him all those things for nothing.

   Which of the following adages best describes the author's attitude about a bankrupt debtor?

   (A) "A penny saved is a penny earned."

   (B) "You've made your bed, now lie in it."

   (C) "Absolute power corrupts absolutely."

   (D) "He that governs least governs best."

   (E) "Millions for defense, but not one cent for tribute."

3. MARY: All of the graduates from Midland High School go to State College.

   ANN: I don't know. Some of the students at State College come from North Hills High School.

   Ann's response shows that she has interpreted Mary's remark to mean that

   (A) most of the students from North Hills High School attend State College.

   (B) none of the students at State College are from Midland High School.

   (C) only students from Midland High School attend State College.

   (D) Midland High School is a better school than North Hills High School.

   (E) some Midland High School graduates do not attend college.

4. Total contributions by individuals to political parties were up 25 percent in this most recent presidential election over those of four years earlier. Hence, it is obvious that people are no longer as apathetic as they were, but they are taking a greater interest in politics.

   Which of the following, if true, would considerably weaken the preceding argument?

   (A) The average contribution per individual actually declined during the same four-year period.

   (B) Per capita income of the population increased by 15 percent during the four years in question.

   (C) Public leaders continue to warn citizens against the dangers of political apathy.

   (D) Contributions made by large corporations to political parties declined during the four-year period.

   (E) Fewer people voted in the most recent presidential election than in the one 4 years earlier.

5. We must do something about the rising cost of our state prisons. It now costs an average of $225 per day to maintain a prisoner in a double-occupancy cell in a state prison. Yet, in the most expensive cities in the world, one can find rooms in the finest hotels that rent for less than $175 per night.

The argument above might be criticized in all of the following ways EXCEPT

(A) it introduces an inappropriate analogy.

(B) it relies on an unwarranted appeal to authority.

(C) it fails to take account of costs that prisons have but hotels do not have.

(D) it misuses numerical data.

(E) it draws a faulty comparison.

6. Antibacterial hand soaps have been available since the 1920s, but only recently have they been mass marketed to consumers in containers bearing labels identifying them as containing an antibacterial agent. None of the antibacterial hand soaps presently available for over-the-counter use, however, truly sterilizes in the way that germ-killing scrubs used by hospitals do. So consumers wind up paying more for an enhancement that really is ineffective.

Which of the following, if true, would most weaken the argument above?

(A) Antibacterial agents are also used extensively in other products such as home cleaners for fabrics, rugs, kitchen counters, and toilet bowls.

(B) Experts generally agree that one of the most effective ways of preventing the spread of disease by personal contact or food handling is by the practice of thoroughly washing one's hands.

(C) Studies show that the agents in antibacterial hand soaps are effective in killing most germs and stopping the growth of common bacteria for as long as 6 hours.

(D) The first germ-killing body and hand soaps, which were introduced in the 1970s, did not include mention on their labels of the antibacterial agents they contained.

(E) Overuse of antibacterial agents in widely used products such as hand soaps may cause bacteria to produce strains that are resistant to the antibacterial agents.

7. The Consumer Price Index is a statistic that measures changes in prices of goods and services purchased by consumers. It is based on a "basket of goods and services" divided into seven categories such as housing, food, and transportation with each category weighted according to its relative impact on a typical budget. Although the Consumer Price Index is a useful measure of inflation, consumers themselves almost always imagine that prices are rising faster than this statistical measure.

Which of the following would help to explain the phenomenon described above?

(A) The typical consumer purchases large ticket items such as a house or a car so infrequently that even given a low rate of inflation, the price of the new purchase will be noticeably higher than that of the previous one.

(B) In recent years, advances in technology have caused the price of electronics such as computers and stereo equipment to decline even as new products are introduced that have more extensive capabilities.

(C) Because of long-term pressures in the health-care sector such as the push for higher wages for the lowest paid health-care workers, the cost of medical care has risen faster than the Consumer Price Index.

(D) The Consumer Price Index is compiled by the Bureau of Labor Statistics and is intended primarily as a measure of the effect of rising prices on a typical urban family.

(E) The prices paid for commodities such a gasoline that depend upon international market conditions are usually more volatile than those determined largely by domestic factors and tend to rise and fall sharply in the short run.

8. If college students are distracted in class, it is because they are bored. If professors are boring lecturers, it is because they are trained as researching scholars rather than as teachers. So the best way to ensure that college students will be attentive in class is to assign them professors who have been trained as teachers instead of researching scholars.

Which of the following would most weaken the argument above?

(A) Some college professors are not trained as researching scholars.

(B) College students may be bored by a subject rather than by the professor.

(C) Professors who are trained as lecturers are not distracted in class.

(D) Colleges have an obligation to ensure that students are not bored.

(E) Teachers not trained in research are almost always interesting lecturers.

9. Zora Neale Hurston, who wrote four novels, a folk opera, and nearly 100 short stories, loved a good lie. When her late-model car aroused suspicion among poor country folk whose lives she was researching, she pretended to be a bootlegger. She lied on official documents like marriage licenses, giving her age at the time of her second marriage as 31 rather than 48. Her letters sometimes seem written by different people, and her autobiography, in which she claims to have been born in Eatonville, Florida, rather than Notasulga, Alabama, is full of misinformation. So, Hurston's own statements and writings are not likely to settle any of the debates over the details of her life.

Which of the following principles best justifies the conclusion of the reasoning above?

(A) Personal details of a writer's life can best be uncovered by studying texts produced by the author herself.

(B) Biographical data on famous people must be confirmed by independent sources such as family and friends.

(C) Statements made by a person who is known to tell falsehoods are not a reliable source of information.

(D) Writers who primarily produce works of fiction cannot be trusted to portray themselves accurately.

(E) Official documents are more authoritative sources for biographical information than personal letters.

10. Is the provincial government really as corrupt as people say? Well, I know one woman who, when her husband got his first driver's license, said that she would not permit him to drive the family car until he actually learned how to drive.

Which of the following is the point the speaker wants to make?

(A) The provincial government is very corrupt.

(B) It is not difficult to learn to drive.

(C) Governments everywhere are more or less corrupt.

(D) A license should not be required to drive a family car.

(E) Governmental corruption should not be tolerated.

11. The success of the new television series *Backroom* has surprised almost all the experts and critics. Unlike the main character of most other successful series, Randall is neither a good guy nor a bad guy with good qualities. Instead, he is an immature and insensitive boor concerned only with his own problems, and audiences howl with laughter as he berates and takes advantage of minor characters such as the store clerk in the first episode who is merely trying to be helpful but comes off like a total loser. Apparently, the key to the success of *Backroom* is that people had rather identify with a successful character with no redeeming social traits than any of the losers who surround him.

Which of the following can be most reliably inferred from the speaker's comments?

(A) Most successful television series feature a main character with relatively few good qualities with which the audience is able to identify.

(B) The Randall character on *Backroom* is someone whom most television viewers would like to know in real life.

(C) *Backroom's* success is likely to inspire other series that feature main characters without commendable personality traits.

(D) The greater the gap between a viewer's expectations and a television program's script, the more likely the program is to succeed.

(E) The Randall character would probably not appeal to audiences if he were featured in a series alongside other characters with admirable personality traits.

12. The Theater Arts Group plans to buy the Odeon Theater, a two-balcony house that has been boarded up for nearly fifteen years, renovate it, and offer it for rent to production companies for plays. But these old two-balcony houses have limited seating capacity, and many people do not want to sit in the second balcony. The Odeon itself can accommodate a maximum of 650 people, and a seating capacity of at least 1,500 is needed to make a production of a musical play profitable. So it seems unlikely that the plan will be successful.

Which of the following, if true, would most weaken the speaker's reasoning?

(A) Larger theaters have about 1,600 seats and only one balcony.

(B) The Odeon Theater is protected by landmark preservation laws.

(C) Musical productions that employ a full orchestra usually require removal of several rows of seats to accommodate the musicians.

(D) The current economic boom that has fueled tourism in general and theater-going in particular is coming to an end.

(E) Straight drama productions, which are less costly because they do not require an orchestra, are becoming increasingly popular with audiences.

13. Recently, a major conservationist organization announced that the spread of exotic species is the second-greatest threat to biodiversity, just behind loss of habitat, and called for the Federal government to take action to ban trade in a lengthy list of exotic plants. The group explained that exotic plants cause nearly $125 billion in damage each year. But what constitutes a disaster in one ecosystem may be a mere nuisance in another or even a positive boon in a third. Lantana, for example, is a terrible pest in Hawaii but a great bedding plant in Pennsylvania.

    Which of the following is most probably the conclusion that the speaker is leading up to?

    (A) An annual cost of $125 billion is a small price to pay to ensure the availability of a wide array of exotic plant species.

    (B) Federal legislation is generally ineffective in controlling traffic in outlawed plants.

    (C) The spread of exotic plant species is unlikely to become a more serious threat to biodiversity than habitat loss.

    (D) A national ban on exotic plants would prevent the sale of some species in areas where they might be valuable.

    (E) Hawaii, as an ecosystem, is not typical of the conditions found in most of the other states.

14. If students find their course work too easy, then they become bored and so achieve less than their abilities would allow them to achieve. But when students find their course work too difficult, they become frustrated and give up too soon and so achieve less than their abilities would allow. Therefore, it is impossible for a teacher to assign course work in such a way that the assignment will enable students to work up to their true abilities.

    Which of the following points out an error in the reasoning above?

    (A) It overlooks the possibility of a third alternative.

    (B) It generalizes on a limited sample of a population.

    (C) It confuses an effect with a causal factor.

    (D) It unfairly questions the credibility of the source.

    (E) It uses a key term in an ambiguous fashion.

15. This season, 14 of the 31 teams in the National Football League will be using some variant of the West Coast offense originated by Bill Walsh. The West Coast, built around a passing attack that features precision throwing and crisp, clear passing routes, can be contrasted with the older-style "Bloody Nose" offense, originated by the Chicago Bears, that relies heavily on grinding out four or five yards per down on the ground. The reason for the popularity of the newer West Coast offense is not hard to explain. Fourteen of the 31 head coaches in the league are former assistants to Bill Walsh or former assistants to head coaches who had previously worked for Walsh.

The speaker assumes that

(A) the West Coast offense is the most effective offense ever used in the National Football League.

(B) the older-style "Bloody Nose" offense will one day be completely supplanted by the West Coast offense.

(C) a style of coaching is something that can be passed along from more experienced coaches to younger ones.

(D) a passing offense is more exciting to watch than an offense that relies primarily on gaining yards by running.

(E) younger football coaches study under Bill Walsh in order to learn a style of offense that they will later use as head coaches.

16. The outbreak of E. coli poisoning that has been traced to contaminated well water used by food vendors at the county fair has already made more than 700 people ill, and health officials expect to add another 50 or so to the list today. The virulence of this particular strain is obvious since the fair closed more than two weeks ago; yet, the number of victims continues to grow.

Which of the following, if true, would most weaken the argument?

(A) The contaminated water was used by food vendors to make frozen drinks that are consumed mainly by children.

(B) The incubation period for the disease is two to nine days, but doctor reports to health officials may be delayed by two to three weeks.

(C) The well water became contaminated when a heavy run washed manure from a cattle exhibition barn into the water supply.

(D) Many people who are infected with E. Coli and experience symptoms may not realize that they have contracted the illness and so do not see a doctor.

(E) Sixty-five of the victims of the outbreak have been hospitalized, and two have died from the poisoning.

Questions 17 and 18

The single greatest weakness of American parties is their inability to achieve cohesion in the legislature. Although there is some measure of party unity, it is not uncommon for the majority party to be unable to implement important legislation. The unity is strongest during election campaigns; after the primary elections, the losing candidates all promise their support to the party nominee. By the time Congress convenes, the unity has dissipated. This phenomenon is attributable to the fragmented nature of party politics. The national committees are no more than feudal lords who receive nominal fealty from their vassals. A member of Congress builds power upon a local base. Consequently, a member is likely to be responsive to local special interest groups. Evidence of this is seen in the differences in voting patterns between the upper and lower houses. In the Senate, where terms are longer, there is more party unity.

17. Which of the following, if true, would most <u>strengthen</u> the author's argument?

    (A) On 30 key issues, 18 of the 67 majority party members in the Senate voted against the party leaders.

    (B) On 30 key issues, 70 of the 305 majority party members in the House voted against the party leaders.

    (C) On 30 key issues, more than half the members of the minority party in both houses voted with the majority party against the leaders of the minority party.

    (D) Of 30 key legislative proposals introduced by the president, only 8 passed both houses.

    (E) Of 30 key legislative proposals introduced by a president whose party controlled a majority in both houses, only 4 passed both houses.

18. Which of the following, if true, would most weaken the author's argument?

    (A) Members of Congress receive funds from the national party committee.

    (B) Senators vote against the party leaders only two thirds as often as House members.

    (C) The primary duty of an officeholder is to be responsive to a local constituency rather than party leaders.

    (D) There is more unity among minority party members than among majority party members.

    (E) Much legislation is passed each session, despite party disunity.

19. ADVERTISEMENT: When you enroll with Future Careers Business Institute (FCBI), you will have access to our placement counseling service. Last year, 92 percent of our graduates who asked us to help them find jobs found them. So go to FCBI for your future!

    The answer to which of the following questions is potentially the <u>LEAST</u> damaging to the claim of the advertising?

    (A) How many of your graduates asked FCBI for assistance?

    (B) How many people graduated from FCBI last year?

    (C) Did those people who asked for jobs find ones in the areas for which they were trained?

    (D) Was FCBI responsible for finding the jobs, or did graduates find them independently?

    (E) Was the person reading the advertisement a paid, professional actor?

20. Either you severely punish a child who is bad or the child will grow up to be a criminal. Your child has just been bad. Therefore, you should punish the child severely.

    All EXCEPT which of the following would be an appropriate objection to the argument?

    (A) What do you consider to be a severe punishment?

    (B) What do you mean by the term "bad"?

    (C) Isn't your "either–or" premise an oversimplification?

    (D) Don't your first and second premises contradict one another?

    (E) In what way has this child been bad?

21. Studies recently published in the *Journal of the American Medical Association* say that despite the widespread belief to the contrary, girls are just as likely as boys to have the reading impairment dyslexia. The new studies examined 450 children over a four-year period, from kindergarten through third grade. The research teams found that fewer than half the students referred to them for reading problems actually had them; and although the schools identified four times as many boys as girls as being dyslexic, independent testing by the research teams revealed that the impairment appeared in both sexes with equal frequency. Yet, over the past decades, elaborate research programs have been set up to find the biological basis for the presumed gender difference in developing dyslexia.

Which of the following, if true, best explains the seeming contradiction outlined above between the new research and the conventional sex-linked view of dyslexia?

(A) Many boys who have dyslexia are not identified as suffering any learning disability.

(B) Many girls who do not have any learning impairment are incorrectly identified as having dyslexia.

(C) Earlier research was based entirely on subjects who were diagnosed by teachers as having reading problems.

(D) For years, the incidence of dyslexia has been underreported in school children of both genders.

(E) Learning disabilities are not likely to become evident until a child has reached the fourth grade.

Questions 22 and 23

We should abolish the public education system and allow schools to operate as autonomous units competing for students. Students will receive government funds in the form of vouchers that they can then "spend" at the school of their choice. This will force schools to compete for students by offering better and more varied educational services. As in private industry, only the schools that provide customer satisfaction will survive. Since schools that cannot attract students will close, we will see an overall improvement in the quality of education.

22. The argument above rests on which of the following unsupported assumptions?

(A) Maximizing student and parent satisfaction also maximizes student learning.

(B) In order to attract students, all schools will eventually have to offer essentially the same curriculum.

(C) Giving students direct financial aid encourages them to study harder.

(D) Schools should provide only educational services and not additional cocurricular or extracurricular activities.

(E) All education, both public and private, should be funded either directly or indirectly by government expenditures.

23. Which of the following, if true, would most undermine the argument above?

(A) Schools will make sure that all parents and students are thoroughly informed about the programs offered.

(B) Most students and parents will select a school based upon the convenience of its location.

(C) Students have different interests and different needs that can best be met by a variety of programs.

(D) By forcing schools to operate on a cost-effective basis, a voucher program would actually reduce total educational expenditures.

(E) Financial barriers currently limit the educational choices of students from poorer families.

24. Though I am an <u>amateur athlete</u>—a long-distance runner—I have no love of the Olympic Games. The original purpose was noble, but the games have become a vehicle for <u>politics and money</u>. For example, when the media mention the 1980 winter games at Lake Placid, they invariably show footage of a hockey game. The real story of the 1980 games—Eric Heiden's winning five gold medals in speedskating—is all but forgotten.

The speaker above implies that

(A) Eric Heiden was a better hockey player than speedskater.

(B) most people would prefer to watch speedskating over hockey.

(C) hockey produces money while speedskating does not.

(D) only professional athletes compete in the Olympic Games.

(E) amateur athletes are more exciting to watch than professional athletes.

25. Some judges are members of the bar. No member of the bar is a convicted felon. Therefore, some judges are not convicted felons.

Which of the following is logically most similar to the argument developed above?

(A) Anyone who jogs in the heat will be sick. I do not jog in the heat and will therefore likely never be sick.

(B) People who want to avoid jury duty will not register to vote. A person may not vote until age 18. Therefore, persons under 18 are not called for jury duty.

(C) All businesses file a tax return, but many businesses do not make enough money to pay taxes. Therefore, some businesses do not make a profit.

(D) All non-students were excluded from the meeting, but some non-students were interested in the issues discussed. Therefore, some non-students interested in the issues are not allowed in the meeting.

(E) The Grand Canyon is large. The Grand Canyon is in Arizona. Therefore, Arizona is large.

Exercise 2

15 Questions • 22 Minutes

Directions: The following questions ask you to analyze and evaluate the reasoning in short paragraphs or passages. For some questions, all of the answer choices may conceivably be answers to the question asked. You should select the *best* answer to the question; that is, an answer that does not require you to make assumptions that violate commonsense standards by being implausible, redundant, irrelevant, or inconsistent. After choosing the best answer, circle the letter of your choice.

Example

In an extensive study of the reading habits of magazine subscribers, it was found than an average of between four and five people actually read each copy of the most popular weekly news magazine. On this basis, we estimate that the 12,000 copies of *Poets and Poetry* that are sold each month are actually read by 48,000 to 60,000 people.

The estimate above assumes that

(A) individual magazine readers generally enjoy more than one type of magazine.

(B) most of the readers of *Poets and Poetry* subscribe to the magazine.

(C) the ratio of readers to copies is the same for *Poets and Poetry* as for the weekly news magazine.

(D) the number of readers of the weekly news magazine is similar to the number of readers of *Poets and Poetry*.

(E) most readers enjoy sharing copies of their favorite magazines with friends and family members.

The correct answer is (C).

1. The Supreme Court's recent decision is unfair. It treats non-resident aliens as a special group when it denies them some rights ordinary citizens have. This treatment is discriminatory, and we all know that discrimination is unfair.

Which of the following arguments is most nearly similar in its reasoning to the above argument?

(A) Doing good would be our highest duty under the moral law, and that duty would be irrational unless we had the ability to discharge it; but since a finite, sensuous creature could never discharge that duty in his lifetime, we must conclude that if there is moral law, the soul is immortal.

(B) Required core courses are a good idea because students just entering college do not have as good an idea about what constitutes a good education as do the professional educators; therefore, students should not be left complete freedom to select course work.

(C) This country is the most free nation on Earth, largely as a result of the fact that the founding fathers had the foresight to include a Bill of Rights in the Constitution.

(D) Whiskey and beer do not mix well; every evening that I have drunk both whiskey and beer together, the following morning I have had a hangover.

(E) I know that this is a beautiful painting because Picasso created only beautiful works of art, and this painting was done by Picasso.

2. Creativity must be cultivated. Artists, musicians, and writers all practice, consciously or unconsciously, interpreting the world from new and interesting viewpoints. A teacher can encourage his pupils to be creative by showing them different perspectives for viewing the significance of events in their daily lives.

Which of the following, if true, would most undermine the author's claim?

(A) In a well-ordered society, it is important to have some people who are not artists, musicians, or writers.

(B) A teacher's efforts to show a pupil different perspectives may actually inhibit development of the student's own creative process.

(C) Public education should stress practical skills, which will help a person get a good job, instead of creative thinking.

(D) Not all pupils have the same capacity for creative thought.

(E) Some artists, musicians, and writers "burn themselves out" at a very early age, producing a flurry of great works and then nothing after that.

3. Opponents to the mayor's plan for express bus lanes on the city's major commuter arteries objected that people could not be lured out of their automobiles in that way. The opponents were proved wrong; following implementation of the plan, bus ridership rose dramatically, and there was a corresponding drop in automobile traffic. Nonetheless, the plan failed to achieve its stated objective of reducing average commuting time.

Which of the following sentences would be the most logical continuation of this argument?

(A) The plan's opponents failed to realize that many people would take advantage of improved bus transportation.

(B) Unfortunately, politically attractive solutions do not always get results.

(C) The number of people a vehicle can transport varies directly with the size of the passenger compartment of the vehicle.

(D) Opponents cited an independent survey of city commuters showing that before the plan's adoption, only one out of every seven used commuter bus lines.

(E) With the express lanes closed to private automobile traffic, the remaining cars were forced to use too few lanes, and this created gigantic traffic tie-ups.

4. Last year, Gambia received $2.5 billion in loans from the International Third World Banking Fund, and its Gross Domestic Product grew by 5 percent. This year, Gambia has requested twice as much money from the ITWBF, and its leaders expect that Gambia's GNP will rise by a full 10 percent.

Which of the following, if true, would LEAST weaken the expectations of Gambia's leaders?

(A) The large 5 percent increase of last year is attributable to extraordinary harvests due to unusually good weather conditions.

(B) Gambia's economy is not strong enough to absorb more than $3 billion in outside capital each year.

(C) Gambia does not have sufficient heavy industry to fuel an increase in its GDP of more than 6 percent per year.

(D) A provision of the charter of the International Third World Banking Fund prohibits the fund from increasing loans to a country by more than 50 percent in a single year.

(E) A neighboring country experienced an increase of 5 percent in its Gross Domestic Product two years ago but an increase of only 3 percent in the most recent year.

5. Efficiency experts will attempt to improve the productivity of an office by analyzing production procedures into discrete work tasks. They then study the organization of those tasks and advise managers on techniques to speed production, such as rescheduling of employee breaks or relocating various equipment such as the copying machines. I have found a way to accomplish increases in efficiency with much less to do. Office workers grow increasingly productive as the temperature drops, so long as it does not fall below 68°F.

The passage leads most naturally to which of the following conclusions?

(A) Some efficiency gains will be short-term gains only.

(B) To maintain peak efficiency, an office manager must occasionally restructure office tasks.

(C) Employees are most efficient when the temperature is at 68°F.

(D) The temperature-efficiency formula is applicable to all kinds of work.

(E) Office workers will be equally efficient at 67°F and 69°F.

Questions 6–8

SPEAKER 1: Those who oppose abortion upon demand make the foundation of their arguments the sanctity of human life, but this seeming bedrock assumption is actually as weak as shifting sand. And it is not necessary to invoke the red herring that many abortion opponents would allow that human life must sometimes be sacrificed for a great good, as in the fighting of a just war. There are counterexamples to the principle of sanctity of life that are even more embarrassing to abor-

tion opponents. It would be possible to reduce the annual number of traffic fatalities to virtually zero by passing federal legislation mandating a nationwide 15-mile-per-hour speed limit on all roads. You see, implicitly we have always been willing to trade off quantity of human life for quality.

SPEAKER 2: The analogy my opponent draws between abortion and traffic fatalities is weak. No one would propose such a speed limit. Imagine people trying to get to and from work under such a law, or imagine them trying to visit a friend or relatives outside their own neighborhoods, or taking in a sports event or a movie. Obviously such a law would be a disaster.

6. Which of the following best characterizes Speaker 2's response to Speaker 1?

(A) His analysis of the traffic fatalities case actually supports the argument of Speaker 1.

(B) His analysis of the traffic fatalities case is an effective rebuttal of Speaker 1's argument.

(C) His response provides a strong affirmative statement of his own position.

(D) His response is totally irrelevant to the issue raised by Speaker 1.

(E) His counterargument attacks the character of Speaker 1 instead of the merits of Speaker 1's argument.

7. Which of the following represents the most logical continuation of the reasoning contained in Speaker 1's argument?

   (A) Therefore, we should not have any laws on the books to protect human life.

   (B) We can only conclude that Speaker 2 is also in favor of strengthening enforcement of existing traffic regulations as a means to reducing the number of traffic fatalities each year.

   (C) So the strongest attack on Speaker 2's position is that he contradicts himself when he agrees that we should fight a just war even at the risk of considerable loss of human life.

   (D) Even the laws against contraception are good examples of this tendency.

   (E) The abortion question just makes explicit that which for so long has remained hidden from view.

8. Which of the following assumptions are made in the argument of Speaker 1?

   (A) The protection of human life is not a justifiable goal of society.

   (B) A human fetus should not be considered a "life" for purposes of government protections.

   (C) Speed limits and other minor restrictions are an impermissible intrusion by government on human freedom.

   (D) An appropriate societal decision is made in the balancing of individual lives and the quality of life.

   (E) Government may legitimately protect the interests of individuals but have no authority to act on behalf of families or groups.

9. Which of the following conclusions can be deduced from the two statements below?

   Some Alphas are not Gammas.

   All Betas are Gammas.

   (A) Some Alphas are not Betas.

   (B) No Gammas are Alphas.

   (C) All Gammas are Betas.

   (D) All Alphas are Gammas.

   (E) Some Alphas are Gammas.

10. I saw Barbara at the racetrack, and she told me that on the same horse race, she made two win bets. She said she bet $10 on Boofer Bear to win at even money and $5 on Copper Cane to win at odds of 10 to 1. After the race, she went back to the parimutuel window. So one or the other of those two horses must have won the race.

    Which of the following is NOT an unstated premise of the reasoning above?

    (A) The only bets Barbara made on the race were her win bets on Boofer Bear and Copper Cane.

    (B) In the race in question, Boofer Bear and Copper Cane did not finish in a dead heat.

    (C) Barbara did not return to the parimutuel window after the race for some reason other than cashing a winning ticket.

    (D) Barbara's representation about the bets that she had placed was accurate.

    (E) Barbara believed that it was more likely that Boofer Bear would win than Copper Cane.

11. Juana is dining at a Chinese restaurant. She will order either combination platter #2 or combination platter #5 but not both. If she orders combination platter #2, she will eat fried rice. If she orders combination platter #5, she will eat an egg roll. Given the statements above, which of the following must be true?

    (A) Juana will eat either fried rice or an egg roll but not both.

    (B) If Juana eats an egg roll, then she ordered combination platter #5.

    (C) If Juana does not eat an egg roll, then she ordered combination platter #2.

    (D) If Juana eats fried rice, then she ordered combination platter #2.

    (E) Anyone who orders combination platter #2 eats fried rice.

12. The harmful effects of marijuana and other drugs have been considerably over-stated. Although parents and teachers have expressed much concern over the dangers that widespread usage of marijuana and other drugs pose for high school and junior high school students, a national survey of 5,000 students of ages 13 to 17 showed that fewer than 15 percent of those students thought such drug use was likely to be harmful.

    Which of the following is the strongest criticism of the author's reasoning?

    (A) The opinions of students in the age group surveyed are likely to vary with age.

    (B) Alcohol use among students of ages 13 to 17 is on the rise and is now considered by many to present greater dangers than marijuana usage.

    (C) Marijuana and other drugs may be harmful to users even though the users are not themselves aware of the danger.

    (D) A distinction must be drawn between victimless crimes and crimes in which an innocent person is likely to be involved.

    (E) The fact that a student does not think a drug is harmful does not necessarily mean he will use it.

13. AL: If an alien species ever visited Earth, it would surely be because they were looking for other intelligent species with whom they could communicate. Since we have not been contacted by aliens, we may conclude that none have ever visited this planet.

    AMY: Or, perhaps, they did not think human beings intelligent.

    How is Amy's response related to Al's argument?

    (A) She misses Al's point entirely.

    (B) She attacks Al personally rather than his reasoning.

    (C) She points out that Al made an unwarranted assumption.

    (D) She ignores the detailed internal development of Al's logic.

    (E) She introduces a false analogy.

14. I maintain that the best way to solve our company's present financial crisis is to bring out a new line of goods. I challenge anyone who disagrees with this proposed course of action to show that it will not work.

    A flaw in the preceding argument is that it

    (A) employs group classifications without regard to individuals.

    (B) introduces an analogy that is weak.

    (C) attempts to shift the burden of proof to those who would object to the plan.

    (D) fails to provide statistical evidence to show that the plan will actually succeed.

    (E) relies upon a discredited economic theory.

15. If quarks are the smallest subatomic particles in the universe, then gluons are needed to hold quarks together. Since gluons are needed to hold quarks together, it follows that quarks are the smallest subatomic particles in the universe.

    The logic of the above argument is most nearly paralleled by which of the following?

    (A) If this library has a good French literature collection, it will contain a copy of *Les Conquerants* by Malraux. The collection does contain a copy of *Les Conquerants*; therefore, the library has a good French literature collection.

    (B) If there is a man-in-the-moon, the moon must be made of green cheese for him to eat. There is a man-in-the-moon, so the moon is made of green cheese.

    (C) Either helium or hydrogen is the lightest element of the periodic table. Helium is not the lightest element of the periodic table, so hydrogen must be the lightest element of the periodic table.

    (D) If Susan is taller than Bob and if Bob is taller than Elaine, then if Susan is taller than Bob, Susan is also taller than Elaine.

    (E) Whenever it rains, the streets get wet. The streets are not wet. Therefore, it has not rained.

EXERCISE 1: ANSWER KEY AND EXPLANATIONS

1. E	6. C	11. E	16. B	21. C
2. B	7. A	12. E	17. E	22. A
3. C	8. B	13. D	18. C	23. B
4. E	9. C	14. A	19. E	24. C
5. B	10. A	15. C	20. D	25. D

1. **The correct answer is (E).** This item tests logical deduction. Statement I establishes that all batters bunt whenever two conditions are met: Some runners lead off and all infielders play in. Statement II establishes that one of the two conditions is met (some runners are leading off) but denies that all batters are bunting. This can only be because the other condition is not met: It is false that "All infielders are playing in." Recalling our discussion of direct inferences in the instructional overview, we know that this means "Some infielders are not playing in," or choice (E). We cannot conclude choice (C), that none of the infielders are playing in, only that some are not. Nor can we deduce choice (D), that all are playing in—for that is logically impossible. Then, recalling our discussion of the meaning of *some* in the instructional overview, we eliminate both choices (A) and (B). Some means "at least one" without regard to the remaining population. That some runners are leading off does not imply that some are not leading off, choice (B). And that some batters are not bunting does not imply that some are bunting.

2. **The correct answer is (B).** The author's attitude toward the bankruptcy law is expressed by his choice of the terms "folly," "protectionism," and "conned." The author apparently believes that the debtor who has incurred these debts ought to bear the responsibility for them and that the government should not help the debtor get off the hook. Choice (B) properly expresses this attitude: You have created for yourself a situation by your own actions; now you must accept it. The author may share choice (A) as well, but it is not a judgment the author would make about the bankrupt, that is, a person who does not have a penny to save. Choice (C) is completely unrelated to the question at hand; the bankrupt has no power to wield. The author may believe choice (D), but the question stem asks for the author's attitude about the bankrupt debtor, not the government. Choice (D) would be appropriate to the latter, but it has no bearing on the question at hand. Finally, choice (E) would be applicable if the government were giving money to pay a ransom to terrorists or some similar situation. The assistance it provides to the bankrupt debtor is not such a program. It does not pay tribute to the debtor.

3. **The correct answer is (C).** Ann's response would be appropriate only if Mary had said, "All of the students at State College come from Midland High." That is why choice (C) is correct. Choice (D) is wrong, because they are talking about the background of the students, not the reputations of the schools. Choice (E) is

wrong, for the question is from where the students at State College come. Choice (B) is superficially relevant to the exchange, but it, too, is incorrect. Ann would not reply to this statement, had Mary made it, in the way she did reply. Rather, she would have said, "No, there are some Midland students at State College." Finally, Ann would have correctly said choice (A) only if Mary had said, "None of the students from North Hills attend State College" or "Most of the students from North Hills do not attend State College." But Ann makes neither of these responses, so we know that choice (A) cannot have been what she thought she heard Mary say.

4. **The correct answer is (E).** If you wanted to determine how politically active people are, what kind of test would you devise? You might do a survey to test political awareness; you might do a survey to find out how many hours people devote to political campaigning each week or how many hours they spend writing letters, etc.; or you might get a rough estimate by studying the voting statistics. The paragraph takes contributions as a measure of political activity. Choice (E) is correct for two reasons. First, the paragraph says nothing about individual activity. It says total contributions were up, not average or per person contributions. Second, choice (E) cites voting patterns that seem as good as or better an indicator of political activity than giving money. This second reason explains why choice (A) is wrong. Choice (A) may weaken the argument, but a stronger attack would use voting patterns. Choice (D) confuses individual and corporate contributions, so even if campaign giving were a strong indicator of activity, choice (D) would still be irrelevant. Choice (B) does not even explain why contributions

in toto rose during the four years, nor does it tell us anything about the pattern of giving by individual persons. Finally, choice (C) seems the worst of all the answers, for it hardly constitutes an attack on the author's reasoning. It seems likely that even in the face of increased political activity, public leaders would continue to warn against the dangers of political apathy.

5. **The correct answer is (B).** The chief failing of the argument is that it draws a false analogy. Since prisons are required to feed and maintain as well as house prisoners (not to mention the necessity for security), the analogy to a hotel room is weak at best. Choice (C) focuses on this specific shortcoming. Remember, in evaluating the strength of an argument from analogy it is important to look for dissimilarities that might make the analogy inappropriate. Thus, choices (A) and (E) are also good criticisms of the argument. They voice the general objection of which choice (C) is the specification. Choice (D) is also a specific objection— the argument compares two numbers that are not at all similar. So the numerical comparison is a false one. Choice (B) is not a way in which the argument can be criticized, for the author never cites any authority.

6. **The correct answer is (C).** This is a "weaken the argument" question, so the correct answer is probably a statement that attacks a hidden premise of the argument. The speaker apparently assumes that, in order to be worthwhile, an antibacterial agent must be as effective as a surgical scrub. But, of course, a hand soap could be less effective than a heavy-duty, industrial strength disinfectant and still have some value—and this is what choice (C) points out. Choice (A) is wide of

the mark, for whether the agents are or are not used in other products doesn't address the central issue, which is "effectiveness." Choice (B) too is wide of the mark. To be sure, this statement helps to prove that washing is effective, but this doesn't prove that washing with an antibacterial soap is better than washing with an ordinary soap. Choice (D) is irrelevant since effectiveness and not labeling is the issue. Finally, choice (E) is a very interesting choice; but, if anything, it is an argument against the soaps. In this case, you're looking for an argument in favor of the soaps.

7. **The correct answer is (A).** The speaker says that the CPI is a fairly accurate measure but that most people still think that prices are rising faster. That's what you have to explain: the timing of purchases gives consumers an inaccurate impression. Choices (B), (C), and (E) do point to various quirks in any general measure of prices, but none of them provides an explanation of the specific phenomenon cited by the speaker. Choice (D) is an interesting choice because it seems to suggest a possible weakness in the CPI and might be leveraged into an argument: well, if the CPI is urban-oriented, then maybe it doesn't do quite such a good job in the other regions, and maybe this creates the wrong impression. There is absolutely nothing wrong with this thinking as a matter of mental exercise, but it's wrong as a matter of test-taking strategy because it is overly speculative. After all, if those outside the urban areas get a wrong impression, it is a mistaken impression of low inflation or high inflation. You should prefer a choice like (A), which, by its terms, takes on the issue directly by giving a reason why prices seem higher than they actually are.

8. **The correct answer is (B).** The speaker's argument rests upon a hidden assumption (suppressed premise): the only reason that students would be bored is because the professor is a poor lecturer. So a good way of attacking the reasoning would be to point out that there are other reasons that students might not pay attention in class; for example, they find the subject uninteresting. As for the other choices, choice (A) implies that some professors might not be boring, but this is not an attack on the proposal advanced by the speaker: Only professors trained as teachers should be used. In other words, choice (A) does not come to grips with the logic of the reasoning; and, as a matter of test-taking tactics, the answer to a "weakening" question is almost always going to be an attack on the logic of the argument and often the denial of a hidden assumption. Choice (C) simply misses the point of the speaker's argument. The question is why students are distracted—not professors. As for choice (D), this choice, if anything, strengthens the speaker's reasoning because it seems to make necessary some kind of proposal. And finally, choice (E) also seems to strengthen the argument by suggesting that non-researchers would be interesting teachers.

9. **The correct answer is (C).** The speaker's point is that Hurston is known to have been untruthful. The problem becomes, then, how to determine which statements about her life, if any, are reliable. The speaker here concludes that this is an impossible task. Choice (A), if anything, contradicts the reasoning of the argument by stating that autobiographical writings do have a privileged status. Choice (B) is an interesting idea, but it is not relevant to the speaker's

point; that is, it doesn't help to explain why the speaker won't rely on Hurston's own statements. Choice (D) is interesting but it misses the point. The problem the speaker sees with Hurston's own statements is that she tells falsehoods when she might otherwise be expected to tell the truth. The speaker is not faulting her for writing fiction that is known by the reader to be fiction but for making false statements that might be taken to be true. And choice (E) simply picks up on a couple of details of the reasoning but doesn't address the underlying issue.

10. **The correct answer is (A).** This is one of those test problems that involves a little logical twist. The speaker is making the somewhat humorous point that the husband was able to secure a driver's license even without knowing how to drive, so the implication is that the government is corrupt.

11. **The correct answer is (E).** This is an inference question, and the correct answer to such a question may not literally be a logical inference but neither will it be wildly speculative. And that's the problem with choices (B) and (C). They may or may not be true, but there is nothing in the text of the argument to support such a deduction. Choice (E), however, is strongly implied by the text because the Randall character works only because it is set in the context of a host of minor characters who are "losers" and with whom audiences apparently will not identify, preferring the successful Randall character even though Randall is not particularly admirable. Choice (A), if anything, seems in tension with the text, for it seems more likely, given the wording, that most programs rely on a "good guy" as opposed to a "bad guy with redeeming features." And choice (D), while edifying,

just really doesn't say anything directly relevant to the issue discussed by the speaker.

12. **The correct answer is (E).** The correct answer to a "weakening" question is usually an attack on a hidden assumption of the argument. In this case, the speaker tacitly assumes that the appropriate use of a theater is the production of musicals, and choice (E) attacks this hidden premise: no, straight drama is becoming increasingly popular. Choices (A) and (B) make interesting points, but the ideas are irrelevant to the speaker's argument. Choice (C), if anything, would strengthen the speaker's argument: not only that, but when you remove the seats to accommodate the orchestra, you further reduce your gross. And so too choice (D) would be a reason for not renovating the theater.

13. **The correct answer is (D).** The stem asks you to draw a further conclusion. The speaker begins by citing the proposed ban and then uses a "But" to introduce the idea that one state's disaster is another state's boon. That suggests that the speaker is opposed to a total ban, not because such bans are ineffective but rather because they have undesirable consequences. And then the speaker gives a "for instance": lantana. So the speaker is arguing against the ban on the ground that it is too broad and would make unavailable some plants that have useful applications. Choice (A) does sound like opposition to the ban, but it doesn't take account of the particular reason the speaker gives. Choice (B) is wrong because there is nothing that suggests the speaker believes the ban would be ineffective; in fact, if anything, the speaker probably believes it would be effective, and that is why the speaker opposes it. Choice (C) is interesting in that it uses

some of the fancy language from the paragraph, but there is absolutely nothing in the paragraph to support the conclusion that the speaker believes that the spread of exotic plants is more or less dangerous than loss of habitat. As for choice (E), this is surely something the speaker would accept, but this seems to be a premise of the argument (a given) as opposed to a further conclusion.

14. **The correct answer is (A).** The speaker creates a false dilemma: either this or that. But there is a happy middle ground: just the right amount of homework.

15. **The correct answer is (C).** One important thing to remember about hidden assumption questions is that the premises you're looking for is a logical part of the argument. Usually, this means that it's going to be a fairly limited claim. So, you need to avoid the temptation to look for some very large and grand conclusion that you might like to draw from the paragraph and focus narrowly on what it said. That's why choice (C) is correct. It is not an earth-shattering revelation; it's really sort of mundane. But it is something the speaker implicitly assumes; otherwise, the argument that the West Coast offense has spread through the mentor relationship doesn't fly. Choices (A) and (B) are exactly the kind of grandiose conclusions that you need to avoid. Choice (D) may be true, but it's not logically supported by the speaker's argument. Finally, choice (E) is interesting, but you should eliminate it if you're reading carefully: "in order to." The fact that the younger coaches picked up the West Coast offense through their employment does not imply that they necessarily took those jobs "in order to" learn how to coach that offense.

16. **The correct answer is (B).** The hidden assumption of the speaker is that the residual cases that keep coming in are due to the virulence of the disease. Choice (B) attacks this assumption by suggesting another explanation: reporting lags behind the diagnosis of the illness. Choice (A) is interesting, because you might want to argue that the immune system of children is not so strong as that of adults, and thus, the sheer number of victims is not necessarily due to the virulence of the strain. The problem with choice (A) is while that is not an unintelligent argument, choice (B) is just a more powerful attack because it aims at a hidden assumption. That's the pattern that you should be looking for. Choice (C) is irrelevant, and it is difficult to see whether choice (D) would weaken or strengthen the argument. Finally, choice (E) seems to strengthen the argument.

17. **The correct answer is (E).** The author is arguing that political parties in America are weak because there is no party unity. Because of this lack of unity, the party is unable to pass legislation. Choice (E) would strengthen this contention. It provides an example of a government dominated by a single party (control of the presidency and both houses), yet the party is unable to pass its own legislation. Choice (A) provides little, if any, support for the argument. If there are only 18 defectors out of a total of 67 party members, that does not show tremendous fragmentation. Choice (B) is even weaker by the same analysis: 70 defectors out of a total of 305 party members. Choice (C) is weak because it focuses on the minority party. Choice (D) strengthens the argument less clearly than choice (E) because there are many possible explanations for the failure; for example, a different party controlled the legislature.

18. **The correct answer is (C).** Here we are looking for the argument that will undermine the position taken by the paragraph. Remember that the ultimate conclusion of the paragraph is that this disunity is a weakness and that this prevents legislation from being passed. One very good way of attacking this argument is to attack the value judgment upon which the conclusion is based: Is it good to pass the legislation? The author assumes that it would be better to pass the legislation. We could argue, as in choice (C), that members of the Congress should not pass legislation simply because it is proposed by the party leadership. Rather, the members should represent the views of their constituents. Then, if the legislation fails, it must be the people who did not want it. In that case, it is better not to pass the legislation. Choice (A) does not undermine the argument. That members receive funding proves nothing about unity after elections. As for choice (B), this seems to strengthen rather than weaken the argument. The author's thesis argues that there is greater unity in the Senate than in the House. Choice (D) would undermine the argument only if we had some additional information to make it relevant. Finally, choice (E) does not weaken the argument greatly. That some legislation is passed is not a denial of the argument that more should be passed.

19. **The correct answer is (E).** This advertisement is simply rife with ambiguity. The wording obviously seeks to create the impression that FCBI found jobs for its many graduates and generally does a lot of good for them. But first we should ask how many graduates FCBI had— one, two, three, a dozen, or a hundred. If it had only 12 or so, finding them jobs might have been easy; but if many people enroll at FCBI, they may not have the same success. Further, we might want to know how many people graduated compared to how many enrolled. Do people finish the program, or does FCBI just take their money and then force them out of the program? So choice (B) is certainly something we need to know in order to assess the validity of the claim. Now, how many of those who graduated came in looking for help in finding a job? Maybe most people had jobs waiting for them (only a few needed help), in which case the job placement assistance of FCBI is not so impressive. Or, perhaps the graduates were so disgusted they did not even seek assistance. So choice (A) is relevant. Choice (C) is also important. Perhaps FCBI found them jobs sweeping streets— not in business. The ad does not say what jobs FCBI helped its people find. Finally, maybe the ad is truthful—FCBI graduates found jobs—but maybe they did it on their own. So choice (D) also is a question worth asking. Choice (E), however, is the least problematic. Even if it turns out that the ad was done by a paid, professional actor, so what? That's what you'd expect for an ad.

20. **The correct answer is (D).** The argument commits several errors. One obvious point is that the first premise is very much an oversimplification. Complicated questions about punishment and child rearing are hardly ever easily reduced to "either–or" propositions. Thus, choice (C) is a good objection. Beyond that, the terms "severely punish" and "bad" are highly ambiguous. It would be legitimate to ask the speaker just what he considered to be bad behavior, choice (B), and

severe punishment, choice (A). Also, since the speaker has alleged the child has been "bad" and since the term is ambiguous, we can also demand clarification on that score, choice (E). The one objection it makes no sense to raise is choice (D). The premises have the very simple logical structure: If a child is bad and not punished, then the child becomes a criminal. Child X is bad. There is absolutely no inconsistency between those two statements.

21. **The correct answer is (C).** Notice that the question gives you some extra guidance here: There is a seeming inconsistency in the reports. On the one hand, much research suggests that dyslexia is a sex-linked problem. On the other hand, the new research suggests it is not. Of course, it is possible that the earlier research was just poorly done, but that wouldn't make a very interesting test answer, e.g., the earlier researchers just added incorrectly. Choice (C) is more representative of the kind of answer you would find on the test: The earlier research was based on data that was biased, and no one suspected that fact until now. As for the remaining choices, they hint at various weaknesses in the data on dyslexia, but they do not address the seeming contradiction that is the focus of the question stem.

22. **The correct answer is (A).** Examine each statement. Choice (A) is a hidden assumption of the argument. Under the proposed system, according to the speaker, schools will have to make the customers happy, and he concludes that this will result in improved education. Thus, a hidden assumption of the argument is the equation between "happy customers" and "improved education."

Choice (B) is not an assumption of the argument. Indeed, the speaker implies that in an effort to attract students, schools will try to differentiate themselves from each other. And as for choice (C), the speaker does not assume that there is any causal connection between "aid" and "study." The speaker expects to see a positive result because schools are doing a better job. That may prompt students to study harder, but the motivating factor then is not "direct financial aid." Choice (D) is apparently a misreading of the paragraph. While the speaker says that schools will compete in terms of "educational services," that may be broad enough to include other activities but in any event certainly does not preclude offering other activities in the mix. And as for choice (E), the speaker does not say that there should be no privately funded schools at all—only that the public schools should be funded on a different model.

23. **The correct answer is (B).** The speaker assumes that students and parents will be educated consumers. (Pardon the play on words.) If it turns out that students and parents select a school because it is nearby, then schools don't have any incentive to offer creative educational programs in order to attract students; a fundamental premise of the plan is proved incorrect. As for choice (A), this idea actually strengthens the argument for the plan: Schools will make sure that students and parents are educated consumers. Choice (C) too is consistent with the speaker's analysis: Schools will create new programs to attract customers. As for choice (D), though this idea of cost is not discussed by the speaker, reducing costs would hardly be a disadvantage of a program. Finally, choice (E) seems to

cut in favor of the program, for then the voucher plan seems calculated to ensure that everyone gets a fair opportunity to get an education.

24. **The correct answer is (C).** The speaker contrasts the Olympic sport of hockey, which gets media coverage because it generates revenues, with speedskating, which does not get media coverage. The implication here is that speedskating does not generate revenue. As for choice (A), it confuses the distinction drawn by the speaker. The speaker is contrasting two sports, not an individual's performance in two sports. Choice (B) misconstrues the logical function of the example of speedskating in the argument. Speedskating is offered as an example of a sport that receives little attention even though it produces exciting amateur performances. (In fact, the speaker implies that hockey is more popular than speedskating, at least if one uses media coverage as a standard.) Choice (D) is an interesting response because it seems at least consistent with the sentiment expressed in the paragraph: Olympic games are really not entirely amateur sports. But choice (D) overstates the case: All Olympians are professionals. (What about Heiden, whom the author mentions favorably?) Finally, choice (E) goes even further beyond the text. The speaker may or may not hold this opinion.

25. **The correct answer is (D).** Let us use our technique of substituting capital letters for categories. The sample argument can be rendered as follows:

Some J are B. (Some Judges are Bar members.)

No B are F. (No Bar members are Felons.)

Therefore, some J are not F. (Some Judges are not Felons.)

This is a perfectly valid (logical) argument. Choice (D) shares its form and validity:

Some N are I. (Some Non-students are Interested.)

No N are M. (No Non-students are Meeting-attenders.)

Therefore, some I are not M. (Some Interested Non-students are not Meeting-attenders.)

Choice (E) has the invalid argument form:

G is L.

G is A.

Therefore, A is L.

Choices (B) and (C) are both set up using more than three categories; therefore, they cannot possibly have the structure of the sample argument that uses only three categories:

Choice (B)—people, people who want to avoid jury duty, people who do not register to vote, persons under 18

Choice (C)—business, entities filing tax returns, business making enough money to pay taxes, business making a profit.

Finally, choice (A) does not parallel the sample argument since it contains the qualification "likely."

EXERCISE 2: ANSWER KEY AND EXPLANATIONS

1.	E	4.	E	7.	E	10.	E	13.	C
2.	B	5.	C	8.	D	11.	C	14.	C
3.	E	6.	A	9.	A	12.	C	15.	A

1. **The correct answer is (E).** The argument given in the question stem is circular; that is, it begs the question. It tries to prove that the decision is unfair by claiming that it singles out a group, which is the same thing as discriminating, and then concludes that *since* all discrimination is unfair, so, too, is the court's decision unfair. Of course, the real issue is whether singling out this particular group is unfair. After all, we do make distinctions, e.g., adults are treated differently than children, businesses differently than persons, soldiers differently than executives. The question of fairness cannot be solved by simply noting that the decision singles out some persons. Choice (E) also is circular: It tries to prove this is a beautiful painting because all paintings of this sort are beautiful. Choice (A) is perhaps the second-best answer, but notice that it is purely hypothetical in its form: *If* this were true, *then* that would be true. As a consequence, it is not as similar to the question stem as choice (E), which is phrased in categorical assertions rather than hypothetical statements. Choice (B) moves from the premise that students are not good judges of their needs to a conclusion about the responsibility for planning course work. The conclusion and the premise are not the same, so the argument is not circular. Choice (C) is not, technically speaking, even an argument. Remember from our instructional material at the beginning of the book, an argument has premises and a conclusion. These are separate state-

ments. Choice (C) is one long statement, not two short ones. It reads "A because B," not "A; therefore B." For example, the statement "I am late because the car broke down" is not an inference but a causal statement. In choice (D), since the premise (everything after the semicolon) is not the same as the conclusion (the statement before the semicolon), the argument is not a circular argument and so does not parallel the stem argument.

2. **The correct answer is (B).** The author's claim depends in a very important way on the assumption that the assistance he advocates will be successful. After all, any proposed course of action that just won't work clearly ought to be rejected. Choice (B) is just this kind of argument: Whatever else you say, your proposed plan will not work; therefore, we must reject it. Choice (A) opens an entirely new line of argument. The author has said only that there is a certain connection between guidance and creativity; he never claims that everyone can or should be a professional artist. Thus, choice (A) is wrong, as is choice (E) for the same reason. Choice (C) is wrong for a similar reason. The author never suggests that all students should be professional artists; and, in fact, he may want to encourage students to be creative no matter which practical careers they may choose. Choice (E) is probably the second-best answer; it does, to a certain extent, try to attack the workability of the proposal. Unfortunately, it does not address the general connection the author says

exists between training and creativity. In other words, choice (E) does not say the proposal will not work at all; it merely says it may work too well. Further, choice (E) is wrong because it does not attribute the "burnout" to the training of the sort proposed by the author.

3. **The correct answer is (E).** What we are looking for here is an intervening causal link that caused the plan to be unsuccessful. The projected train of events was (1) adopt express lanes, (2) fewer cars, and (3) faster traffic flow. Between the first and the third steps, however, something went wrong. Choice (E) alone supplies that unforeseen side effect. Since the cars backed up on too few lanes, total flow of traffic was actually slowed, not speeded up. Choice (A) is irrelevant since it does not explain what went wrong *after* the plan was adopted. Choice (B) does not even attempt to address the sequence of events that we have just outlined. Although choice (C) is probably true and was something the planners likely considered in their projections, it does not explain the plan's failure. Finally, choice (D) might have been relevant in deciding whether or not to adopt the plan, but given that the plan was adopted, choice (D) cannot explain why it then failed.

4. **The correct answer is (E).** We have all seen arguments of this sort in our daily lives, and perhaps if we have not been very careful, we have even made the same mistakes made by the leaders of Gambia. For example, last semester, which was fall, I made a lot of money selling peanuts at football games. Therefore, this spring semester, I will make even more money. Choices (A), (B), (C), and (D) point out weaknesses in the projections made by Gambia's leaders. Choice

(A): Of course, if the tremendous increase in GDP is due to some unique event (my personal income increased last semester when I inherited $2,000 from my aunt), it would be foolish to project a similar increase for a time period during which that event cannot repeat itself. Choice (B): This is a bit less obvious, but the projection is based on the assumption that Gambia will receive additional aid and will be able to put that aid to use. If they are not in a position to use that aid (I cannot work twice as many hours in the spring), they cannot expect the aid to generate increases in GDP. Finally, choice (C) also is a weakness in the leaders' projections. If there are physical limitations on the possible increases, then the leaders have made an error. Their projections are premised on the existence of physical resources that are greater than those they actually have. And choice (D) would also undermine the expectation of additional growth: Gambia won't get the whole loan. Choice (E), however, without more, won't weaken the argument, because there is no reason to believe that the experience of a neighbor is applicable to Gambia.

5. **The correct answer is (C).** The conclusion of the paragraph is so obvious that it is almost difficult to find. The author says office workers work better the cooler the temperature—provided the temperature does not drop below 68°. Therefore, we can conclude, the temperature at which workers will be most efficient will be precisely 68°. Notice that the author does not say what happens once the temperature drops below 68°, except that workers are no longer as efficient. For all we know, efficiency may drop off slowly or quickly compared with improvements in efficiency as the temperature drops to

68°. So choice (E) goes beyond the information supplied in the passage. Choice (D) also goes far beyond the scope of the author's claim. His formula is specifically applicable to *office* workers. We have no reason to believe the author would extend his formula to non-office workers. Choice (B) is probably not a conclusion the author would endorse since he claims to have found a way of achieving improvements in efficiency in a different and seemingly permanent way. Finally, choice (A) is not a conclusion the author seems likely to reach since nothing indicates that his formula yields only short-term gains that last as long as the temperature is kept constant. To be sure, the gains will not be repeatable, but then they will not be short run either.

6. **The correct answer is (A).** Speaker 2 unwittingly plays right into the hands of Speaker 1. Speaker 1 tries to show that there are many decisions regarding human life in which we allow that an increase in the quality of life justifies an increase in the danger to human life. All that Speaker 2 does is to help prove this point. He says the quality of life would suffer if we lowered the speed limits to protect human life. Given this analysis, choice (B) must be incorrect, for Speaker 2's position is completely ineffective as a rebuttal. Moreover, choice (C) must be incorrect, for his response is not a strong statement of his position. Choice (D) is incorrect, for while his response is of no value to the position he seeks to defend, it cannot be said that it is irrelevant. In fact, as we have just shown, his position is very relevant to that of Speaker 1 because it supports that position. Finally, choice (E) is not an appropriate characterization of Speaker 2's position,

for he tries, however ineptly, to attack the merits of Speaker 1's position, not the character of Speaker 1.

7. **The correct answer is (E).** Speaker 1 uses the example of traffic fatalities to show that society has always traded the quality of life for the quantity of life. Of course, he says, we do not always acknowledge that is what we are doing, but if we were honest, we would have to admit that we were making a trade-off. Thus, choice (E) is the best conclusion of the passage. Speaker 1's statement amounts to the claim that abortion is just another case in which we trade off one life to make the lives of others better. The only difference is that the life being sacrificed is specifiable and highly visible in the case of abortion, whereas in the case of highway fatalities, no one knows in advance on whom the ax will fall. Choice (A) certainly goes far beyond what Speaker 1 is advocating. If anything, he probably recognizes that sometimes the trade-off will be drawn in favor of protecting lives, and thus we need some such laws. Choice (B) must be wrong, first, because Speaker 2 claims this is not his position, and second, because Speaker 1 would prefer to show that the logical consequence of Speaker 2's response is an argument in favor of abortion. Choice (C) is not an appropriate continuation because Speaker 1 has already said this is a weak counterexample and that he has even stronger points to make. Finally, Speaker 1 might be willing to accept contraception, choice (D), as yet another example of the trade-off, but his conclusion can be much stronger than that; the conclusion of his speech ought to be that abortion is an acceptable practice—not that contraception is an acceptable practice.

8. **The correct answer is (D).** This is a very difficult question. That choice (D) is an assumption Speaker 1 makes requires careful reading. Speaker 1's attitude about the just war tips us off. He implies that this is an appropriate function of government and, further, that there are even clearer cases. Implicit in his statement is that a trade-off must be made and that it is appropriately a collective decision. Choice (A) is not an assumption of the argument. Indeed, Speaker 1 seems to assume, as we have just maintained, that the trade-off is an appropriate goal of society. Speaker 1 does not assume choice (B); if anything, he almost states that he accepts that the fetus is a life but that it may be traded off in exchange for an increase in the quality of the lives of others. Choices (C) and (E) use language related to the examples used by Speaker 1 but don't address the logical structure of the argument.

9. **The correct answer is (A).** You might attack this item using a circle diagram. To show the possible relationships of three categories, use three overlapping circles:

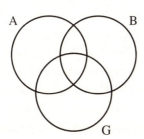

Now enter the information provided by the second statement:

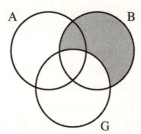

The area that is not logically possible given the second statement is shaded. Now enter the information provided by the first statement:

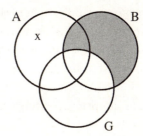

The "x" shows that there is at least one individual that is an Alpha but not a Gamma.

The diagram shows that choice (A) must be true. There is at least one individual that is an Alpha but not a Beta. Choice (B), however, is not necessarily true. The overlap between the Alpha-circle and the Gamma-circle, which represents the possibility that an individual might have both characteristics Alpha and Gamma, is left open. Choice (C) is not necessarily true for a similar reason. There is a portion of the Gamma-circle not contained in the Beta-circle, and this part represents the logical possibility that some individuals could have characteristic Gamma but not characteristic Beta. Choice (D) is shown by the diagram to be false; choice (E) is shown to be possibly but not necessarily true.

10. **The correct answer is (E).** This question asks you to identify hidden assumptions embedded in the speaker's argument. Examine each statement. Choice (A) is an assumption of the argument. Barbara told the speaker about two bets, and the speaker assumes those were the only two she made. (She could have made additional wagers.) Choice (B) is also an assumption of the argument. The speaker concludes that one or the other horse must have won, but that conclusion depends on the assumption that they did not both win. Choice (C) is also an assumption of the argument. The speaker implicitly assumes that the only reason Barbara would return to the parimutuel window is to cash a winning ticket, as opposed to placing another bet. And choice (D) is also a hidden assumption similar to choice (A). Choice (E), however, is not an assumption. Barbara could very well have believed that Copper Cane was more likely to win—indeed, she stood to win more money with that result even though her bet was smaller because of the longer odds.

11. **The correct answer is (C).** It is very important to distinguish what are called necessary conditions from what are called sufficient conditions. A necessary condition is one that must occur for a particular event to take place, e.g., oxygen is a necessary condition for a fire. A sufficient condition is one that is by itself sufficient to ensure that a certain event occurs; for example, failing the final exam of a course may be sufficient to guarantee a failing mark for the course. This distinction is the key to this item. A statement of the sort "If X, then Y" (as used here) sets up a sufficient but not a necessary connection. For example, ordering combination #2 guarantees that Juana will eat fried rice, but that may not be the only condition on which she will eat fried rice. For all we know, combination #5 also includes fried rice. Thus, choices (A), (B), and (D) are wrong. As for choice (E), the statements that set up the problem talk specifically about Juana, not about people in general.

12. **The correct answer is (C).** If you want to determine whether or not drug use is harmful to high school students, you surely would not conduct a survey of the students themselves. This is why choice (C) is correct. That a student does not *think* a drug is harmful does not mean that it *is not* actually harmful. Choice (E) misses the point of the argument. The author is not attempting to prove that drug use is not widespread but rather that it is not dangerous. Choice (D) is part of an argument often used in debates over legalization of drugs by proponents of legalization. Here, however, it is out of place. The question is whether the drugs are harmless, that is, whether they are, in fact, victimless. Choice (D) belongs to some other part of the debate. Choice (A) sounds like the start of an argument. One might suggest that students change their minds as they get older, and eventually many acknowledge the danger of such drugs. But choice (A) does not get that far; and, even if it did, choice (C) would be stronger, for it gives us the final statement up to which that argument would only be leading. Finally, choice (B) is irrelevant. The question here is the harm of drugs, and that issue can be resolved independently of whether or not other things are harmful, such as alcohol or drag racing.

13. **The correct answer is (C).** Amy points out that Al assumes that extraterrestrial visitors to Earth, seeking intelligent life,

would regard human beings here on Earth as intelligent and therefore contact us. Amy hints that we might not be intelligent enough to interest them in contacting us. This is why choice (C) is the best answer. Choice (A) is wrong. Amy does not miss Al's point: She understands it very well and criticizes it. Choice (B) is wrong since Amy is not suggesting that Al is any less intelligent than any other human being, just that the aliens might regard us all as below the level of intelligence that they are seeking. Choice (D) is more nearly correct than any other choice, save choice (C). The difficulties with it are threefold: One, there really is not all that much internal development of Al's argument, so choice (D) does not seem on target; two, in a way she does examine what internal structure there is—she notes there is a suppressed assumption that is unsound; finally, even assuming that what choice (D) says is correct, it really does not describe the point of Amy's remark nearly so well as choice (C) does. Finally, choice (E) is incorrect because Amy does not offer an analogy of any sort.

14. **The correct answer is (C).** The problem with this argument is that it contains no argument at all. Nothing is more frustrating than trying to discuss an issue with someone who will not even make an attempt to prove his case, whose only constructive argument is: "Well, that is my position; if I am wrong, you prove I am wrong." This is an illegitimate attempt to shift the burden of proof. The person who advances the argument naturally has the burden of giving some argument for it. Choice (C) points out this problem. Choice (A) is incorrect because the author uses no group classifications. Choice (B) is incorrect because the au-

thor does not introduce any analogy. Choice (D) is a weak version of choice (C). It is true that the author does not provide statistical evidence to prove the claim, but then again, no kind of argument at all is offered to prove the claim. So if choice (D) is a legitimate objection to the paragraph (and it is), then choice (C) must be an even stronger objection. So any argument for choice (D)'s being the correct choice ultimately supports choice (C) even more strongly. The statement contained in choice (E) may or may not be correct, but the information in the passage is not sufficient to allow us to isolate the theory upon which the speaker is operating. Therefore, we cannot conclude that it is or is not discredited.

15. **The correct answer is (A).** Let us assign letters to represent the complete clauses of the sentence from which the argument is built. "If quarks . . . universe" will be represented by the letter P, the rest of the sentence by Q. The structure of the argument is therefore "If P then Q. Q. Therefore, P." The argument is obviously not logically valid. If it were, it would work for any substitutions of clauses for the letters, but we can easily think up a case in which the argument will not work: "If this truck is a fire engine, it will be painted red. This truck is painted red; therefore, it is a fire engine." Obviously, many trucks that are not fire engines could also be painted red. The argument's invalidity is not the critical point. Your task was to find the answer choice that paralleled it—and since the argument first presented was incorrect, you should have looked for the argument in the answer choice that makes the same mistake: choice (A). It has the form: "If P, then Q. Q. Therefore, P."

Choice (B) has the form: "If P, then Q. P. Therefore, Q," which is both different from our original form and valid to boot. Choice (C) has the form: "P or Q. Not P. Therefore, Q." Choice (D) has the form: "If P, then Q. If Q, then R. Therefore, if P, then R." Finally, choice (E) has the form: "If P, then Q. Not Q. Therefore, not P."

Reading
Comprehension

OVERVIEW

- **What is Reading Comprehension?**
- **How do you answer Reading Comprehension questions?**
- **What smart test-takers know**

WHAT IS READING COMPREHENSION?

LSAT Reading Comprehension is a test of your ability to read and understand unfamiliar materials and to answer questions about them. You will be presented with passages drawn from a variety of subject areas, including humanities, ethics, philosophy, social sciences, physical sciences, and the law. The questions will ask you to analyze what is stated in the passage and to identify underlying assumptions and implications.

Reading Comprehension Questions

The scored portion of the LSAT contains one Reading Comprehension section with four reading passages, each approximately 450 words long. Each passage is followed by 5 to 8 questions for a total of 26 to 28 questions per section.

Question Format

Reading Comprehension questions follow the standard multiple-choice format with five answer choices each. All of the questions fall into one of the following six categories:

1. The main idea of the passage
2. Specific details mentioned in the passage
3. The author's attitude or tone
4. The logical structure of the passage
5. Further inferences that might be drawn from the text
6. Application of the ideas in the text to new situations

Here are the directions for LSAT Reading Comprehension, along with some sample questions and explanations.

chapter 6

Anatomy of a Reading Comprehension Passage

Directions: Below each of the following passages, you will find questions or incomplete statements about the passage. Each statement or question is followed by lettered words or expressions. Select the word or expression that most satisfactorily completes each statement or answers each question in accordance with the meaning of the passage. After you have chosen the best answer, blacken the corresponding space on the answer sheet.

Instead of casting aside traditional values, the Meiji Restoration of 1868 dismantled feudalism and modernized the country while preserving
(5) certain traditions as the foundations for a modern Japan. The oldest tradition and basis of the entire Japanese value system was respect for and even worship of the Emperor.
(10) During the early centuries of Japanese history, the Shinto cult in which the imperial family traced its ancestry to the Sun Goddess became the people's sustaining faith. Although
(15) later subordinated to imported Buddhism and Confucianism, Shintoism was perpetuated in Ise and Izumo until the Meiji modernizers established it as a quasi-state religion.
(20)   Another enduring tradition was the hierarchical system of social relations based on feudalism and reinforced by Neo-Confucianism that had been the official ideology of the pre-
(25) modern world. Confucianism prescribed a pattern of ethical conduct between groups of people within a fixed hierarchy. Four of the five Confucian relationships were vertical,
(30) requiring loyalty and obedience from the inferior toward the superior. Only the relationship between friend and friend was horizontal, and even there the emphasis was on reciprocal
(35) duties.

(This is a much abbreviated Reading Comprehension passage, but it exhibits all of the important features that you can expect to find on the passages on your LSAT.

Summary: *The passage has a main theme that is developed with supporting arguments:*

> *The Meiji Restoration modernized Japan without repudiating traditional values. It did dismantle feudalism. But it preserved important traditions. This kind of organization is typical of LSAT reading passages.*

Note the point of the second paragraph: An important feature of Japanese society that was preserved was a hierarchical system of social relations.)

1. The author is primarily concerned with

   (A) providing a history of the rise of feudalism in Japan.

   (B) identifying the influences of Confucianism on Japanese society.

   (C) speculating on the probable development of Japanese society.

   (D) developing a history of religion in Japan.

   (E) describing some important features of the Meiji Restoration.

The correct answer is (E). *This question asks about the main idea or theme of the passage.*

2. The passage mentions all of the following as being elements of Japanese society EXCEPT

   (A) obedience to authority.

   (B) sense of duty.

   (C) respect for the Emperor.

   (D) concern for education.

   (E) loyalty to one's superior.

The correct answer is (D). *This question asks about details mentioned in the passage. The author does not mention education.*

3. It can be inferred from the passage that those who led Japan into the modern age were concerned primarily with

   (A) maintaining a stable society.

   (B) building a new industrial base.

   (C) expanding the nation's territory.

   (D) gaining new adherents of Confucianism.

The correct answer is (A). *This question asks about an idea that can be inferred from the passage.*

HOW DO YOU ANSWER READING COMPREHENSION QUESTIONS?

To answer Reading Comprehension questions, follow these steps:

READING COMPREHENSION: GETTING IT RIGHT

1   Preview key sentences.

2   Read for structure; ignore details.

3   Do a mental wrap-up.

4   Start with the main idea question.

5   Next, tackle specific detail and attitude/tone questions.

6   Then do logical structure questions.

7   Save inference and application questions for last.

Now let's look at this process in more detail.

1 Preview key sentences. The first sentence of a paragraph is often the topic sentence. It will give you an overview of the paragraph. Previewing the first sentence of each paragraph will give you a general sense of the logical structure of the passage. You should also preview the very last sentence of the passage because it often contains the main conclusion of the passage.

2 Read for structure; ignore details. This is an open-book test, so you do not have to memorize anything. In addition, most of the questions ask about the structure of the passage rather than specific facts. As you read, consciously ask yourself "What is the main point of the passage?" and "Why is the author introducing this idea?"

Your academic training has taught you to read for details because you know that you will be tested on them. Do not dwell on the particulars. In the first place, there are only 5 to 8 questions, so there are not likely to be many questions about details. And in the second place, this is an open-book test, so you can refer to the passage.

3 Do a mental wrap-up. Before moving on to the questions, pause for just a few seconds and review in your mind what you have just read. Try to summarize in your own words the main point of the selection (think up a title for the passage) and to see in your mind's eye an outline of the passage.

4 Start with the main idea question. Each question set usually includes one such as

> Which of the following best summarizes the main point of the passage?
>
> The author's primary concern is to . . .
>
> Which of the following is the best title for the passage?

Regardless of form, this question asks about the overall theme or main point of the selection. Answering this question first will help you to solidify your understanding of the passage.

⑤ Next, tackle specific detail and attitude/tone questions. Most passages are followed by at least one question about a specific detail. Detail questions are easy to recognize:

> According to the passage, . . .
>
> According to the author, . . .
>
> The author mentions all of the following EXCEPT
>
> In line ##, the author says that . . .

Questions with this form are just asking about concrete details. You do not have to have a theory to answer them.

Author's attitude or tone questions look like this:

> The author's attitude can best be described as . . .
>
> Which of the following best describes the tone of the passage?

Attitude/tone questions are usually fairly easy, so it makes perfect sense to do them before moving to the difficult questions.

⑥ Then do logical structure questions. Some questions ask about the overall development of the passage or about why the author introduces a specific point:

> The author develops the passage primarily by which of the following means?
>
> The author introduces the point at line ## in order to . . .

These questions focus on the logical development of the passage. If you understand the main organizing theme, then you should be able to answer them.

⑦ Save inference and application questions for last. Some questions ask you to go beyond what is explicitly stated in the passage. They often are phrased like this:

> The author implies that . . .
>
> It can be inferred that . . .
>
> The author would most likely agree with which of the following statements?

These questions are the most difficult, so save them for last.

Now let's look at a sample Reading Comprehension passage and questions about it. As you read the explanations, think about how the solution process applies.

TIP

The LSAT uses six— and only six— Reading Comprehension questions:

1. What is the main idea?
2. What did the author say?
3. Why did the author say it?
4. How does the author feel about it?
5. What is written between the lines?
6. How could you use it somewhere else?

Directions: The passage below is followed by questions based upon its content. After reading the passage, choose the best answer to each question. Answer all of the questions on the basis of what is stated or implied in the passage.

A fundamental principle of pharmacology is that all drugs have multiple actions. Actions that are desirable in the treatment of disease are considered
(5) therapeutic, while those that are undesirable or pose risks to the patient are called "effects." Adverse drug effects range from the trivial, e.g., nausea or dry mouth, to the serious, e.g., massive
(10) gastrointestinal bleeding or thromboembolism; and some drugs can be lethal. Therefore, an effective system for the detection of adverse drug effects is an important component of the health-care
(15) system of any advanced nation. Much of the research conducted on new drugs aims at identifying the conditions of use that maximize beneficial effects and minimize the risk of adverse effects. The
(20) intent of drug labeling is to reflect this body of knowledge accurately so that physicians can properly prescribe the drug; or, if it is to be sold without prescription, so that consumers can prop-
(25) erly use the drug.

The current system of drug investigation in the United States has proved very useful and accurate in identifying the common side effects associated with
(30) new prescription drugs. By the time a new drug is approved by the Food and Drug Administration, its side effects are usually well described in the package insert for physicians. The investigational
(35) process, however, cannot be counted on to detect all adverse effects because of the relatively small number of patients involved in premarketing studies and the relatively short duration of the stud-
(40) ies. Animal toxicology studies are, of course, done prior to marketing in an attempt to identify any potential for toxicity, but negative results do not guarantee the safety of a drug in humans, as

(In this passage, the author announces a "fundamental principle" of pharmacology. The paragraph then goes on to contrast "desirable" and "adverse" drug effects. The author emphasizes the need for an effective system of making this information available to doctors.)

(In this next paragraph, the author says that the current system of drug investigation is useful and accurate. But then the author goes on to identify some weaknesses in the system.)

(45) evidenced by such well known examples as the birth deformities due to thalidomide.

This recognition prompted the establishment in many countries of pro-
(50) grams to which physicians report adverse drug effects. The United States and other countries also send reports to an international program operated by the World Health Organization. These programs,
(55) however, are voluntary reporting programs and are intended to serve a limited goal: alerting a government or private agency to adverse drug effects detected by physicians in the course of
(60) practice. Other approaches must be used to confirm suspected drug reactions and to estimate incidence rates. These other approaches include conducting retrospective control studies; for example,
(65) the studies associating endometrial cancer with estrogen use, and systematic monitoring of hospitalized patients to determine the incidence of acute common side effects, as typified by the Bos-
(70) ton Collaborative Drug Surveillance Program.

Thus, the overall drug surveillance system of the United States is composed of a set of information bases, special
(75) studies, and monitoring programs, each contributing in its own way to our knowledge of marketed drugs. The system is decentralized among a number of governmental units and is not adminis-
(80) tered as a coordinated function. Still, it would be inappropriate at this time to attempt to unite all of the disparate elements into a comprehensive surveillance program. Instead, the challenge is
(85) to improve each segment of the system and to take advantage of new computer strategies to improve coordination and communication.

(In the next paragraph, the author claims that the system has been improved by establishing programs that keep records of reports by doctors of adverse drug consequences. But, the author notes, these reporting programs are not perfect.)

(In the final paragraph, the author summarizes by saying that the system is a composite one with many different aspects. And the last sentence summarizes the conclusion of the passage.)

1. The author is primarily concerned with discussing

    (A) methods for testing the effects of new drugs on humans.

    (B) the importance of having accurate information about the effects of drugs.

    (C) procedures for determining the long-term effects of new drugs.

    (D) attempts to curb the abuse of prescription drugs.

    (E) the difference between the therapeutic and nontherapeutic actions of drugs.

The correct answer is (B). This is a main idea question. Choice (B) correctly describes the overall point of the passage. The author starts by stating that all drugs have both good and bad effects and that correct use of a drug requires balancing the effects. For such a balancing to take place, it is essential to have good information about how the drugs work. Some of this can be obtained prior to approval of the drug, but some information will not become available until after years of use.

Choice (A) is incorrect, for the different methods for testing drugs are mentioned only as a part of the development just described. The author is not concerned with talking about how drugs are tested but rather about why it is important that they be tested. Choice (C) is incorrect for the same reason. As for choice (E), this is the starting point for the discussion—not the main point of the discussion. Finally, as for choice (D), the idea of drug abuse is not part of the passage at all.

2. The author implies that a drug with adverse side effects

    (A) will not be approved for use by consumers without a doctor's prescription.

    (B) must wait for approval until lengthy studies prove the effects are not permanent.

    (C) should be used only if its therapeutic value outweighs its adverse effects.

    (D) should be withdrawn from the marketplace pending a government investigation.

    (E) could be used in foreign countries even though it is not approved for use in the United States.

The correct answer is (C). This is an inference question. In the first paragraph, the author states that all drugs have effects and that these effects range from the unimportant to the very important. One purpose of drug labeling is to ensure that physicians (and ultimately consumers) are aware of these effects. We can infer, therefore, that drugs with side effects are used—provided the gain is worth the risks. And this is what choice (C) says.

Choice (A) seems to be contradicted by the passage. One purpose of labeling, according to the author, is to let consumers of nonprescription drugs know of possible side effects of those drugs. As for choices (B) and (D), the analysis in the preceding paragraph clearly shows that drugs are approved for use and used even though they have unwanted side effects. Finally, there is nothing in the passage to support the conclusion expressed in choice (E).

3. Which of the following can be inferred from the passage?

(A) Drugs with serious side effects are never approved for distribution.

(B) A centralized drug oversight function would improve public health.

(C) Most physicians are not aware that prescription drugs have side effects.

(D) Some rare adverse drug effects are not discovered during the limited testing.

(E) Consumers are seldom unable to understand directions for proper use of a drug.

The correct answer is (D). This is an inference question. Although this conclusion is not stated in so many words, the author does say that some effects are not uncovered because of the short duration of the studies. We may therefore infer that some effects do not manifest themselves for a long period.

4. The author introduces the example of thalidomide (line 46–47) to show that some

(A) drugs do not have the same actions in humans that they do in animals.

(B) drug testing procedures are ignored by careless laboratory workers.

(C) drugs have no therapeutic value for humans.

(D) drugs have adverse side effects as well as beneficial actions.

(E) drugs are prescribed by physicians who have not read the manufacturer's recommendations.

The correct answer is (A). This is a logical structure question. The example is introduced in line 40 where the author is discussing animal studies. The author says that the fact that a drug shows no dangerous effects in animals does not necessarily mean that it will not adversely affect humans and then gives the example. Thus, the example proves that a drug does not necessarily work in humans the same way it does in animals.

5. The author of the passage regards current drug investigation procedures as

(A) important but generally ineffectual.

(B) lackadaisical and generally in need of improvement.

(C) necessary and generally effective.

(D) comprehensive but generally unnecessary.

(E) superfluous but generally harmless.

The correct answer is (C). This is an author's attitude question. We have already determined that the author regards drug investigation procedures as necessary, so we can eliminate choices (D) and (E). And at various points in the passage, the author speaks of the current mechanism for gathering information as effective. For example, the author states that unwanted side effects are usually described in detail in the pamphlets distributed to physicians and also mentions that there is an entire discipline devoted to this area, so you can eliminate choices (A) and (B).

TIP

Most details are irrelevant.

A passage can be up to 450 words in length and can include a lot of details. However, with all the different types of questions that are asked, there can't be many devoted solely to details. Therefore, most of the details are not important.

6. It can be inferred that the estrogen studies mentioned in lines 64–66

    (A) uncovered long-term side effects of a drug that had already been approved for sale by the Food and Drug Administration.

    (B) discovered potential side effects of a drug that was still awaiting approval for sale by the Food and Drug Administration.

    (C) revealed possible new applications of a drug that had previously been approved for a different treatment.

    (D) are examples of studies that could be more efficiently conducted by a centralized authority than by volunteer reporting.

    (E) proved that the use of the drug estrogen was not associated with side effects such as thromboembolism.

The correct answer is (A). This is an inference question. The key to this question is the word *retrospective*. This tells you that the control study mentioned was done after the drug was already in use. Choice (B) is incorrect because although the study uncovered harmful side effects, according to the passage, the drug was already in use. Choice (C) is incorrect because the paragraph in which this study is mentioned deals with methods of reporting adverse drug effects, not new applications for drugs. Choice (D) is incorrect first because the author does not mention the efficiency of the study and second because the author is not in favor of a centralized authority. In fact, in the last paragraph, the author says that it would be inappropriate at this time to attempt to unite all of the disparate elements into a comprehensive surveillance program. Finally, choice (E) is incorrect because although thromboembolism is mentioned in the passage as one of the possible harmful side effects of drugs, it is not mentioned in connection with estrogen. The use of estrogen is mentioned in connection with endometrial cancer.

7. The author is most probably leading up to a discussion of some suggestions about how to

    (A) centralize authority for drug surveillance in the United States.

    (B) centralize authority for drug surveillance among international agencies.

    (C) better coordinate the sharing of information among the drug surveillance agencies.

    (D) eliminate the availability and sale of certain drugs now on the market.

    (E) improve drug testing procedures to detect dangerous effects before drugs are approved.

The correct answer is (C). This is an application question. In the last paragraph, the author suggests that uniting disparate elements into a comprehensive surveillance program is inappropriate at this time. This eliminates choices (A) and (B). The author suggests, however, that improvements are possible in each segment of the system and urges reliance on computers to improve coordination and communication, so choice (C) is the correct answer. Choice (D) is wrong because although the author might advocate the elimination of the availability of certain drugs, that is not what the passage is leading up to. As for choice (E), although the author acknowledges that preapproval studies are not infallible, this notion is too narrow in scope to be the next logical topic for discussion.

8. The author relies on which of the following in developing the passage?
   (A) Statistics
   (B) Analogy
   (C) Examples
   (D) Authority
   (E) Rhetorical questions

The correct answer is (C). This is a logical structure question. The author frequently illustrates the argument's points with examples. In the first paragraph, there are examples of side effects; in the second, an example of side effects not detected by animal studies; and in the third, the Boston Collaborative Drug Surveillance Program. The author does not, however, use statistics (no numbers in this passage), analogies (no "this is like that"), authority (citing an example is not the same as appealing to an authority), or rhetorical questions.

WHAT SMART TEST–TAKERS KNOW

THE DIFFICULTY FACTOR IS MOSTLY "SMOKE AND MIRRORS."

Three features of LSAT reading passages work like "smoke and mirrors" to make the readings seem more difficult than they really are.

First, the passages will usually be on topics that are unfamiliar to you. This choice of subject matter is deliberate. The test-writers go out of their way to find material that you will not have seen before, since they want to avoid giving anyone an advantage over other candidates. If you do encounter a topic you have studied before, that is an unusual stroke of luck. Rest assured, however, that everything you need to answer the questions is included in the passage itself.

Second, LSAT reading passages always start abruptly in the middle of a passage. You're given no advance warning of the topic discussed, so the passage seems to begin in the middle of nowhere. Imagine that you encounter the following as the opening sentence of a Reading Comprehension selection on your LSAT:

> Of the wide variety of opinions on which evolutionary factors were responsible for the growth of hominid intelligence, a theory currently receiving consideration is that intraspecific warfare played an important role by encouraging strategy sessions requiring a sort of verbal competition.

An appropriate reaction to this might be "What the . . . !" But in reality, the topic introduced by the sentence above is not that bizarre. Let's give the sentence a context, say a scholarly journal.

PRIMITIVE BATTLE PLANS: A NEW THEORY ABOUT THE GROWTH OF HUMAN INTELLIGENCE

Of the wide variety of opinions on which evolutionary factors were responsible for the growth of hominid intelligence, a theory currently receiving consideration is that intraspecific warfare played an important role by encouraging strategy sessions requiring a sort of verbal competition.

The title summarizes the main point of the article and alerts you to the topic that will be introduced in the opening sentence. Unfortunately, on the LSAT, you will not be shown this courtesy. The selections will start rather abruptly, in the middle of nowhere.

Third, the style of LSAT Reading Comprehension passages is dry, compact, and often tedious. To be suitable for the LSAT, the passage must not be too long or too short. So the passages, which are taken from previously published material, are carefully edited. Even when the topic of the passage is itself interesting, the selection that emerges from the editing can be deadly boring.

These three features—unusual topic, abrupt beginning, and dense style—all work to create problems for you. Many students are simply overawed by the reading selections. They begin to think "I've never even heard of this; I'll never be able to answer any questions." And when you start thinking like that, you're already beaten. Keep in mind that the passages are chosen so that you will be surprised, but remember that the selections are written so that they contain everything you need to answer the questions.

PASSAGES THAT INTEREST YOU ARE EASIER TO WORK ON.

LSAT Reading Comprehension passages are drawn from many different content areas. Although all of the information needed to answer the questions will be found in the passage, you may find one content area more comfortable to work in than another. If that is the case, start with the passage that deals with that subject. You should be able to answer the accompanying questions more quickly and easily, thus saving time for the passages you find more difficult.

DETAILS CAN BOG YOU DOWN.

If a part of a passage gets too detailed, just skip it. Bracket it mentally or draw a box around it. You do not need to have a full understanding of every single detail to appreciate the organization of the passage and to answer most of the questions.

YOU ONLY WANT TO READ THIS ONCE.

Reading the passages is very time-consuming. If you skip questions and move on to another passage, when you return to the first passage, you'll have to spend time rereading it. Since you don't want to waste these precious minutes, answer all the questions in a set before moving on. If necessary, make educated guesses.

READING COMPREHENSION QUESTIONS CALL FOR DIFFERENT LEVELS OF UNDERSTANDING.

According to the test writers, good reading involves three levels of understanding and evaluation. First, you must be able to grasp the overall idea or main point of the selection along with its general organization. Second, you must be able to subject the specific details to greater scrutiny and explain what something means and why it was introduced. Finally, you should be able to evaluate what the author has written, determining what further conclusions might be drawn and judging whether the argument is good or bad. This sequence dictates the strategy you should follow in reading the selection.

THE LSAT USES SIX—AND ONLY SIX—READING COMPREHENSION QUESTIONS.

Identify the type of question asked, and you are halfway to finding the correct answer.

1. Main idea questions ask about the central theme or main point of the passage.
2. Specific detail questions ask about details included by the author to support or to develop the main theme.
3. Inference questions ask about ideas that are not explicitly stated in the selection but are strongly implied.
4. Logical structure questions ask about the organization or the overall development of the passage.
5. Application questions ask you to take what you have learned from the passage and apply it to a new situation.
6. Attitude or tone questions ask you to identify the overall tone of the passage or the author's attitude toward something discussed in the passage.

For each of the six question types, there are special clues in the answer choices that help you tell right ones from wrong ones.

IN MAIN IDEA QUESTIONS, THE "GOLDILOCKS PRINCIPLE" APPLIES.

On a main idea question, choose an answer that refers to all of the important elements of the passage without going beyond the scope of the passage. The correct answer to a main idea question will summarize the main point of the passage. The wrong answers are too broad or too narrow. Some will be too broad and attribute too much to the author. Others will be too narrow and focus on one small element of the selection, thereby ignoring the overall point.

ALERT!

Your academic training is hazardous to your test-taking health. In college, you are rewarded for memorizing details. The LSAT penalizes for this. This is an open-book test. Do not waste time trying to understand insignificant points.

IN SOME MAIN IDEA QUESTIONS, THE ANSWER LIES IN THE FIRST WORD OF EACH CHOICE.

Some main idea questions are phrased as sentence completions. With a main idea question in sentence completion form, the first word of each choice may be all you need to pick the answer. Here's an example:

> The author's primary purpose is to
> **(A)** argue for ...
> **(B)** criticize ...
> **(C)** describe ...
> **(D)** persuade ...
> **(E)** denounce ...

Note that the first word in each choice describes the passage differently. If the selection were neutral in tone, providing nothing more than a description of some phenomenon, you could safely eliminate choices (A), (B), (D), and (E).

IN SPECIFIC DETAIL QUESTIONS, LOCATOR WORDS POINT THE WAY.

A detail question basically asks "What did the author say?" So, the correct answer to a detail question will be found right there in the passage. And there will be a word or phrase in the question stem to direct you to the appropriate part of the passage. Just find the relevant information and answer the question.

IN SPECIFIC DETAIL QUESTIONS, "SO WHAT" ANSWERS ARE WRONG.

Often wrong answer choices look like right ones because they refer to specific points in the passage. The point is right there in the passage, but it is not an answer to the question asked. So your reaction to such answer choices should be "Yes, this is mentioned, but so what?"

IN SPECIFIC DETAIL QUESTIONS, "WAY OUT" ANSWERS ARE WRONG.

Wrong answers can also refer to things never mentioned in the selection. On a detail question, eliminate answer choices referring to something not mentioned in the passage or anything going beyond the scope of the passage. One way the test-writers have of preparing wrong answers is to mention things related to the general topic of the selection but not specifically discussed there. An answer to an explicit question will appear in the selection.

IN SPECIFIC DETAIL QUESTIONS, THOUGHT-REVERSERS TURN A QUESTION INSIDE-OUT.

Sometimes the test-writer will use a thought-reverser. For example:

The author mentions all of the following EXCEPT

Sometimes a detail question uses a thought-reverser. In that case, it is <u>asking for what</u> is *not* mentioned in the selection. Out of the five choices, four will actually appear in the selection. The fifth, and wrong, choice will not.

INFERENCE QUESTIONS CALL FOR A FURTHER CONCLUSION.

An inference question should not require a long chain of deductive reasoning. It is usually a one-step inference. For example, the selection might make a statement to the effect that "X only occurs in the presence of Y." The question might ask, "In the absence of Y, what result should be expected?" The correct answer would be "X does not occur."

LOGICAL STRUCTURE QUESTIONS ARE ALL ABOUT ORGANIZATION.

Some logical structure questions ask about the overall structure of the passage. The correct answer to this kind of question should describe in general terms the overall development of the selection.

Another kind of logical structure question asks about the logical function of specific details. For this kind of question, find the appropriate reference and determine why the author introduced the detail at just that point.

APPLICATION QUESTIONS ARE THE TOUGHEST, AND YOU MAY JUST HAVE TO GUESS.

Application questions are the most abstract and therefore the most difficult kind of question. There is no "silver bullet" for this type of question, and you may find that it is better to make a guess and just move on.

TIP

What are the topics of LSAT reading passages?
LSAT Reading Comprehension passages cover a wide variety of subjects. Your test may include passages from the humanities, physical sciences, social sciences, philosophy, ethics, or the law.

FOR ATTITUDE/TONE QUESTIONS, THE ANSWER CHOICES RUN A GAMUT.

Attitude or tone questions often have answer choices that run a gamut of judgments or emotions, from negative to positive. On this kind of question, try to create a continuum of the answer choices and locate the author's attitude or tone on that continuum. Here's an example:

The tone of the passage is best described as one of

(A) outrage.

(B) approval.

(C) objectivity.

(D) alarm.

(E) enthusiasm.

Arrange these attitudes in a line, from the most negative to the most positive:

(-) .. outrage .. alarm .. objectivity .. approval .. enthusiasm .. (+)

EXERCISES: READING COMPREHENSION

Exercise 1

24 Questions • 35 Minutes

> **Directions:** Below each of the following passages you will find questions or incomplete statements about the passage. Each statement or question is followed by lettered words or expressions. Select the word or expression that most satisfactorily completes each statement or answers each question in accordance with the meaning of the passage. After you have chosen the best answer, circle the letter of your choice.

Questions 1–6

Since 1994, the International Monetary Fund (IMF) has functioned as a quasi lender of last resort to developing nations. The principles for operating as a
(5) lender of last resort were systematically expounded by Henry Thornton in 1802 and reformulated independently by Walter Bagehot in 1873: lend liberally, on good collateral, to the market, for a
(10) short term, and at a penalty rate of interest. These recommendations ensure that panic is quelled while the central bank discourages borrowing except by fundamentally solvent parties willing to
(15) pay a premium. It is generally accepted that a financial institution other than an aid institution should avoid lending at subsidized (below-market) rates of interest.
(20)   It has been a matter of debate whether the IMF honors this important principle. Contributor nations to the IMF do earn interest and can withdraw funds at any time, features that suggest the
(25) IMF is like a savings bank, but this ignores the risk involved in IMF loans. Because defaults have been rare, the IMF has not imposed costs in the sense of a nominal operating loss that would
(30) reduce the value of the contributions of the members, but a single default by a large borrower would show clearly that the IMF's status does not exclude it from the kinds of risks the private sector faces

(35) when lending to governments. Even in the absence of serious defaults, the U.S. and other contributors have, from time to time, found it necessary to make supplemental contributions to the fund.
(40)   Additionally, contributors pay an "opportunity cost." Suppose the IMF pays interest of 2 percent a year for funds it lends to other countries, but a contributor country could earn 6 percent a year
(45) lending the funds directly to the same countries. The opportunity cost of the contribution to the IMF is the difference, which amounts to 4 percent a year. Indeed, if participation in the IMF cost
(50) nothing at all, contributors would not need to supplement their positions from time to time; the IMF could instead borrow from international financial markets and lend the funds at a suitable
(55) mark-up, as banks do.
     It has been suggested that conditions imposed on loans by the IMF justify lower rates. Typically, the IMF will require that borrowing governments
(60) reduce their budget deficits and rate of money growth (inflation); eliminate monopolies, price controls, interest-rate ceilings, and subsidies; and in some cases, devalue their currencies. Often
(65) these conditions are unpopular, but setting aside the wisdom of the content of conditionality, the important question is the effect of the conditions on the

(70) prospects of repayment. Banks, for example, require mortgage loans to be collateralized by houses. This type of conditionality improves the prospects of repayment and enables banks to make a profit charging lower interest rates than
(75) they otherwise could. The IMF does not require collateral. IMF conditionality therefore does not significantly improve the prospects for repayment, and conditionality does not reduce the element of
(80) subsidy.

Giving a subsidy is undesirable because instead of making borrowers pay penalty rates of interest when they make mistakes, the IMF allows borrow-
(85) ers to pay lower interest rates during crises than they pay to borrow from the private sector in normal, noncrisis periods. Local taxpayers rather than taxpayers in countries that are net lenders
(90) to the IMF pay most of the cost of a crisis, so the possibility of obtaining loans from the IMF at subsidized rates of interest is not a positive inducement for a crisis; but other things being equal, subsidized
(95) interest rates reduce the incentive to take politically painful measures that may prevent a crisis. Subsidized rates also make countries more inclined to turn to the IMF rather than the private
(100) sector for financing. In this sense, the IMF's subsidized loans create "moral hazard" (reduced vigilance against imprudent behavior because one does not pay its full costs).

1. Which of the following best describes the development of the passage?

   (A) The author reviews two different interpretations of a set of facts and rejects one while accepting the other.

   (B) The author reviews two different interpretations of a set of facts and concludes that neither is valid.

   (C) The author outlines a list of principles and then demonstrates that the principles are outdated.

   (D) The author proposes a new economic theory and argues its advantages over the accepted theory.

   (E) The author sketches a theory and offers various objections to it without endorsing them.

2. According to the passage, opportunity cost is the difference between the

   (A) value received and the cost of pursuing a foregone opportunity.

   (B) value received and savings realized by not pursuing a foregone opportunity.

   (C) value received and the value that would have been received from the foregone opportunity.

   (D) cost of pursuing one option and cost of pursuing a foregone alternative.

   (E) cost of pursuing one option and the value that would have been received from a foregone opportunity.

3. According to the passage, the IMF sometimes uses conditionality for the same purpose that a private bank requires

   (A) payment of interest.

   (B) pledge of collateral.

   (C) deposits from investors.

   (D) proof of solvency.

   (E) repayment of loans.

4. The author mentions the possibility of precipitating a financial crisis in order to obtain loans on favorable terms (paragraph 5) in order to

(A) dispose of a weak argument that might otherwise cloud the analysis.

(B) isolate one of the hidden assumptions of a possible counter-argument.

(C) uncover a hidden contradiction in a competing line of analysis.

(D) clarify the meaning of a key term used in more than one sense.

(E) demonstrate that a line of reasoning leads to an absurd conclusion.

5. With which of the following statements would the author of the passage most likely agree?

(A) The IMF could reduce the moral hazard attached to lending at below-market interest by exacting promises from borrowers to improve the efficiency of markets.

(B) The IMF should lend freely at below-market interest rates because any losses incurred through default can be offset by supplemental contributions from depositor nations.

(C) The IMF could minimize the danger of default of loans by requiring debtor nations to pledge collateral sufficient to secure the value of the loan.

(D) For the IMF to function as a sound financial institution, it must reform its lending practices so that it charges interest that reflects the risk attendant on its loans.

(E) It is immoral for any institution to lend funds to a borrower at interest rates below market because the subsidy encourages the borrower to assume excessive risk.

6. The passage suggests that if the IMF charged interest rates commensurable with the risks of its loans, then

(A) more borrowers would wish to obtain loans from the IMF.

(B) borrowers would be more receptive to conditionality.

(C) rates of default on outstanding loans would decline.

(D) private lenders would relax conditions imposed on loans.

(E) contributors would no longer need to make supplement contributions.

Questions 7–12

Integrating defense technology with commercial technology can reduce fixed costs and result in other significant economic efficiencies by the use of common pro-
(5) cesses, labor, equipment, material, and facilities. This includes cooperation between government and private facilities in research and development, manufacturing, and maintenance operations;
(10) combined production of similar military and commercial items, including components and subsystems, side-by-side on a single production line or within a single firm or facility; and use of commercial
(15) off-the-shelf items directly within military systems. However, several factors determine the extent to which such integration is possible and the ease with which it can be accomplished. It is useful
(20) to compare the experience of the United States with its clear separation of the commercial and defense sectors with that of the People's Republic of China (PRC).
(25)   In the United States, one of the biggest obstacles to integrating civil and military procurement is the body of laws governing military procurement. In large part due to past accounting and acquisi-
(30) tions scandals, myriad reporting requirements frequently deter commercially successful firms from bidding on military contracts. Additionally, the Department of Defense (DOD) demands

(35) extensive rights to technical data to ensure that production of a system continues even in the event of a serious business disruption such as bankruptcy. DOD
(40) may request not only data about the system itself but also information on proprietary manufacturing processes that commercial firms are anxious to protect. The private-public dichotomy that gives rise to these barriers has no
(45) parallel in the PRC because the state owns the bulk of the means of production in the first place.

Additionally, the American military emphasizes high performance, even
(50) marginal improvements, regardless of cost. Not only is this additional performance not necessarily sought in commercial products (e.g., commercial jetliners have little need for an after-
(55) burner), it usually is not cost-effective. In the PRC, although operational parameters are set by the People's Liberation Army (PLA), the standards involved in actual production are set by central
(60) managers. The latter are far more versed in engineering, whereas the former have generally been capable only of setting out operational requirements without necessarily understanding the indus-
(65) trial demands involved. Thus, production standards have been the responsibility of the producers rather than the users. Consequently, in the PRC little effort is made to acquire or
(70) develop the very latest state-of-the art weapons technologies.

Yet another obstacle to commercial-military integration involves militarily unique technologies (e.g., ballistic mis-
(75) siles and electronic warfare programming have no civilian applications). In the PRC military technologies have tended to be rendered "unique" only because certain resources have been in
(80) limited supply. That is, the PLA has priority for receiving many of the more advanced and expensive technologies and facilities, but these are in relatively short supply. It is likely, for example,
(85) that the Chinese air-defense network has a more advanced set of air-traffic

control capabilities than does the Chinese civilian air-traffic network simply because of the scarcity of such equip-
(90) ment.

In general, the PRC appears to have been more successful in integrating military and commercial technology, but it is difficult to assess the extent
(95) to which this success is due to the relatively primitive state of technology or to political and economic conditions. It is likely a combination of both. Certainly, replicating in the United States the full
(100) degree of integration in the PRC would entail unacceptable political and economic costs. In particular, it is unlikely that the American political system would accept the ambiguity inherent in the
(105) commercial use of public facilities and, perhaps more importantly, the conflict of public appropriation of private resources.

7. The primary purpose of the passage is to

   (A) compare the integration of military and commercial technology in the United States and the People's Republic of China.

   (B) use the Chinese political system as the basis for critiquing policies in the United States.

   (C) criticize the United States for failing to completely integrate military and commercial technology.

   (D) assess the extent to which military procurement procedures in the People's Republic of China would be useful in the United States.

   (E) analyze the causes of the failure of the United States to achieve a complete integration of technology between the military and commercial sectors.

8. According to the passage, proprietary rights do not present a barrier to integration of commercial and military technology in the People's Republic of China because

    (A) the state controls the means of production.

    (B) commercial and military sectors rely on similar technology.

    (C) military weapons are not permitted in the commercial sector.

    (D) the PRC does not pursue state-of-the-art weapons systems.

    (E) the army of the People's Republic of China does not control defense manufacturing.

9. It can be inferred that an increase in the availability of high technology air traffic control equipment in the People's Republic of China would result in

    (A) considerable simplification of the procurement policies for both the civilian and military components of air-traffic control.

    (B) less effective performance on the part of air-traffic controllers because of unfamiliarity with new technology.

    (C) increased waste and redundancy as the civilian and military sectors competed for the rights to develop new equipment.

    (D) cost savings that would be achieved by shifting technicians into lower paying positions.

    (E) greater disparity between the capabilities of the civilian air-traffic control system and its military counterpart.

10. The passage mentions all of the following as economic efficiencies that could be achieved by the integration of commercial and military technology EXCEPT

    (A) production lines creating parts for both the commercial and military sectors.

    (B) manufacturing facilities producing subsystems with civilian and military uses.

    (C) research and development facilities working on problems of both commercial and military significance.

    (D) storehoused items originally manufactured for commercial use that also have military applications.

    (E) defense control of commercial manufacturing facilities that produce military components.

11. The experience of the People's Republic of China when compared with that of the United States most strongly supports which of the following conclusions?

    (A) Advanced technologies for weapons systems are adopted more rapidly in countries with planned economies than in nations with capitalistic systems.

    (B) Uniquely military applications of advanced technology are less likely to be developed by military forces that are under the close supervision of civilian authorities.

    (C) Costs of technologically advanced acquisitions tend to be lower when procurement decisions are made by managers with engineering backgrounds.

    (D) Private firms that operate with little or no government oversight prefer to bid on government contracts rather than to produce commercial products for the private sector.

    (E) Economies that are controlled by central planners operate less efficiently than economies in which decision-making authority is widely dispersed.

12. Which of the following best states the conclusion of the passage?

    (A) Attempts at integrating commercial and military technology in the People's Republic of China have been more successful than those in the United States.

    (B) Economic and political differences would make it difficult for the United States to achieve the same integration of commercial and military technology as the People's Republic of China.

    (C) Political factors are more important determinants of a nation's ability to integrate its military and commercial technology sectors than economic considerations.

    (D) Close integration of technological breakthroughs in the civilian and military sectors frequently results in important economic advantages.

    (E) The strength of a country's military posture is in large part determined by the ability of the country's military to incorporate cutting-edge technology into its weapons systems.

Questions 13–18

Helplessness and passivity are central themes in describing human depression. Laboratory experiments with animals have uncovered a phenomenon desig-
(5) nated "learned helplessness." Dogs given inescapable shock initially show intense emotionality, but later become passive in the same situation. When the situation is changed from inescapable to es-
(10) capable shock, the dogs fail to escape even though escape is possible. Neuro-chemical changes resulting from learned helplessness produce an avoidance-escape deficit in laboratory animals.
(15)   Is the avoidance deficit caused by prior exposure to inescapable shock learned helplessness or is it simply stress-induced noradrenergic deficiency leading to a deficit in motor activation?

exercises

(20) Avoidance-escape deficit can be produced in rats by stress alone, i.e., by a brief swim in cold water. But a deficit produced by exposure to extremely traumatic events must be produced by a very

(25) different mechanism than the deficit produced by exposure to the less traumatic uncontrollable aversive events in the learned-helplessness experiments. A nonaversive parallel to the learned

(30) helplessness induced by uncontrollable shock, e.g., induced by uncontrollable food delivery, produces similar results. Moreover, studies have shown the importance of prior experience in learned

(35) helplessness. Dogs can be "immunized" against learned helplessness by prior experience with controllable shock. Rats also show a "mastery effect" after extended experience with escapable shock.

(40) They work far longer trying to escape from inescapable shock than do rats lacking this prior mastery experience. Conversely, weanling rats given inescapable shock fail to escape shock as

(45) adults. These adult rats are also poor at nonaversive discrimination learning. Certain similarities have been noted between conditions produced in animals by the learned-helplessness procedure

(50) and by the experimental neurosis paradigm. In the latter, animals are first trained on a discrimination task and are then tested with discriminative stimuli of increasing similarity. Eventually, as

(55) the discrimination becomes very difficult, animals fail to respond and begin displaying abnormal behaviors: first agitation, then lethargy.

It has been suggested that both

(60) learned helplessness and experimental neurosis involve inhibition of motivation centers and pathways by limbic forebrain inhibitory centers, especially in the septal area. The main function of

(65) this inhibition is compensatory, providing relief from anxiety or distress. In rats subjected to the learned-helplessness and experimental-neurosis paradigms, stimulation of the septum

(70) produces behavioral arrest, lack of behavioral initiation and lethargy, while rats with septal lesions do not show learned helplessness.

How analogous the model of learned

(75) helplessness and the paradigm of stress-induced neurosis are to human depression is not entirely clear. Inescapable noise or unsolvable problems have been shown to result in conditions in humans

(80) similar to those induced in laboratory animals, but an adequate model of human depression must also be able to account for the cognitive complexity of human depression.

13. The primary purpose of the passage is to

(A) propose a cure for depression in human beings.

(B) discuss research possibly relevant to depression in human beings.

(C) criticize the result of experiments that induce depression in laboratory animals.

(D) raise some questions about the propriety of using laboratory animals for research.

(E) suggest some ways in which depression in animals differs from depression in humans.

14. The author raises the question at the beginning of the second paragraph in order to

(A) prove that learned helplessness is caused by neurochemical changes.

(B) demonstrate that learned helplessness is also caused by nonaversive discrimination learning.

(C) suggest that further research is needed to determine the exact causes of learned helplessness.

(D) refute a possible objection based on an alternative explanation of the cause of learned helplessness.

(E) express doubts about the structure of the experiments that created learned helplessness in dogs.

15. It can be inferred from the passage that rats with septal lesions (line 72) do not show learned helplessness because

    (A) such rats were immunized against learned helplessness by prior training.

    (B) the lesions blocked communication between the limbic forebrain inhibitory centers and motivation centers.

    (C) the lesions prevented the rats from understanding the inescapability of the helplessness situation.

    (D) a lack of stimulation of the septal area does not necessarily result in excited behavior.

    (E) lethargy and other behavior associated with learned helplessness can be induced by the neurosis paradigm.

16. It can be inferred that the most important difference between experiments inducing learned helplessness by inescapable shock and the nonaversive parallel mentioned in line 29 is that the nonaversive parallel

    (A) did not use pain as a stimuli to be avoided.

    (B) failed to induce learned helplessness in subject animals.

    (C) reduced the extent of learned helplessness.

    (D) caused a more traumatic reaction in the animals.

    (E) used only rats rather than dogs as subjects.

17. The author cites the "mastery effect" primarily in order to

    (A) prove the avoidance deficit caused by exposure to inescapable shock is not caused by shock per se but by the inescapability.

    (B) cast doubts on the validity of models of animal depression when applied to depression in human beings.

    (C) explain the neurochemical changes in the brain that cause learned helplessness.

    (D) suggest that the experimental-neurosis paradigm and the learned-helplessness procedure produce similar behavior in animals.

    (E) argue that learned helplessness is simply a stress-induced noradrenergic deficiency.

18. Which of the following would be the most logical continuation of the passage?

    (A) An explanation of the connection between the septum and the motivation centers of the brains of rats

    (B) An examination of techniques used to cure animals of learned helplessness

    (C) A review of experiments designed to created stress-induced noradrenergic deficiencies in humans

    (D) A proposal for an experiment to produce learned helplessness and experimental neurosis in humans

    (E) An elaboration of the differences between human depression and similar animal behavior

Questions 19–24

Depletion is a natural phenomenon that characterizes the development of all non-renewable resources and oil in particular. Broadly speaking, depletion is a
(5)   progressive reduction of the overall stock of a resource as the resource is produced; narrowly, the term refers to the decline of production associated with a particular field, reservoir, or well. Typically,
(10) production from a given well increases to a peak and then declines over time until some economic limit is reached and the well is shut in. If it were not for changes in prices, costs, and technology,
(15) depletion of the world's resources would resemble the simple decline curve of a single well.

Estimates of oil resources by field are routinely made by geologists and
(20) engineers, but the estimates are a "best guess" given the available data and are revised as more knowledge becomes available. There is no time frame or probability associated with estimates of
(25) total resources in place. In contrast, proved reserves of crude oil are the estimated quantities that, on a particular date, are demonstrated with reasonable certainty to be recoverable in the future
(30) from known reservoirs under existing economic and operating conditions. Generally, there is at least a 90 percent probability that, at a minimum, the estimated volume of proved reserves in
(35) the reservoir can be recovered under existing economic and operating conditions.

Each year, production is taken from proved reserves, reducing both proved
(40) reserves and the total resource. Innovative production techniques such as well recompletions, secondary and tertiary enhanced recovery techniques, and expanded production of unconventional
(45) resources have reduced net depletion rates at the well and field levels. Advanced exploration and drilling techniques, such as 3-D seismic imaging, directional drilling, and multiple wells
(50) from single boreholes, have reduced the cost of finding new pools, reduced the

risk of dry holes and dry hole costs, and allowed new pools to be developed and produced more quickly. Lower explora-
(55) tion, drilling, and dry hole costs increase the return on capital by lowering costs. More rapid production of resources from a field increases the return on capital because earnings are realized sooner in
(60) the project's life, and therefore, discounted less.

Higher returns make some fields that are too expensive to develop under "normal" circumstances economically
(65) feasible, because reduced costs allow firms to make profits where they could not before. On the other hand, more rapid development and production of a field by definition increases the rate of
(70) depletion. If an operator produces a field more quickly, the rate of depletion must rise. While the rate of depletion increases with technological progress, the adverse effects of depletion are diminished, and
(75) higher levels of production can be maintained for longer periods of time. As depletion leads producers to abandon older fields and develop new ones, the process of developing domestic oil re-
(80) sources leads producers to find and develop the larger, more economical fields first. Later fields tend to be less desirable because they are farther away from existing infrastructure or smaller in size.
(85) Thus, as time progresses more effort is required to produce the same level of the resource from the same exploration area.

While the frontier for new resources is diminishing, increased innovation has,
(90) thus far, served to offset depletion at least partially, keeping production stronger than it would have been in the absence of the innovations. Technological progress is expected to continue to en-
(95) hance exploration, reduce costs, and improve production technology. But eventually, as field sizes decrease, the ultimate recovery from discovered fields will shrink. Thus, despite technological
(100) improvements, ultimate recovery from the average field of the future will be smaller than from the average field today.

19. The passage is primarily intended to

    (A) sketch a plan to prolong production of existing oil resources.

    (B) warn of the consequences of overexploiting oil resources.

    (C) discuss economic factors influencing oil production and depletion.

    (D) describe methods of extracting oil resources more efficiently.

    (E) propose alternative energy sources to replace dependence on oil.

20. According to the passage, the most important difference between total oil resources and proved reserves is that proved reserves

    (A) are determined by geological principles probably to be present beneath the surface.

    (B) require the use of advanced production techniques for recovery.

    (C) cannot be known with certainty to exist until their existence has been verified by experts.

    (D) can be produced at a cost comparable to that required for resources currently being recovered.

    (E) do not presuppose the existence of advanced technologies for their extraction from the ground.

21. Which of the following best explains why the author puts the word *normal* in quotation marks (paragraph 4)?

    (A) Base line conditions are not natural but are artificially defined by economic factors.

    (B) Reduced costs make oil production operations more profitable than other economic activities.

    (C) Oil is strictly a nonrenewable energy resource in spite of technological advances.

    (D) Existing oil production infrastructure eventually wears out and needs to be replaced.

    (E) Oil reserves are gradually being depleted, which makes it more and more difficult to find proved reserves.

22. The passage implies that an oil well is removed from production when

    (A) the supply of oil it produces is completely exhausted.

    (B) the cost of operating the well exceeds the return.

    (C) new wells have been bored to replace the capacity of the existing well.

    (D) the cost of capital required to open the well has been recovered.

    (E) it is no longer possible to accelerate oil production by the well.

23. According to the passage, technological innovation offsets natural depletion because it

    (A) makes it profitable to locate and extract more oil resources.

    (B) reduces the ratio of proved reserves to actual oil resources.

    (C) replenishes oil resources even as it extracts them from the ground.

    (D) permits the exploitation of more expansive oil fields with large resources.

    (E) minimizes the need to invest in capital expenditures in order to produce oil.

24. Which of the following would be most likely to result in an increase in proved reserves in the United States?

    (A) Increased oil production by foreign sources

    (B) A significant rise in the price of crude oil

    (C) A reduction in estimates of total oil resources

    (D) New federal regulations requiring cleaner engines

    (E) Discovery of a large field of clean-burning coal

Exercise 2

14 Questions • 18 Minutes

Directions: Below each of the following passages, you will find questions or incomplete statements about the passage. Each statement or question is followed by lettered words or expressions. Select the word or expression that most satisfactorily completes each statement or answers each question in accordance with the meaning of the passage. After you have chosen the best answer, circle the letter of your choice.

Questions 1–7

Like our political society, the university is under severe attack today and perhaps for the same reason; namely, that we have accomplished much of what we (5) have set out to do in this generation, that we have done so imperfectly, and while we have been doing so, we have said a lot of things that simply are not true. For example, we have earnestly (10) declared that full equality of opportunity in universities exists for everyone, regardless of economic circumstance, race or religion. This has never been true. When it was least true, the asser- (15) tion was not attacked. Now that it is nearly true, not only the assertion but the university itself is locked in mortal combat with the seekers of perfection. In another sense the university has failed. (20) It has stored great quantities of knowledge; it teaches more people; and despite its failures, it teaches them better. It is in the application of this knowledge that the failure has come. Of the great (25) branches of knowledge—the sciences, the social sciences and humanities—the sciences are applied, sometimes almost as soon as they are learned. Strenuous and occasionally successful efforts are (30) made to apply the social sciences, but almost never are the humanities well applied. We do not use philosophy in defining our conduct. We do not use literature as a source of real and vicari- (35) ous experience to save us the trouble of living every life again in our own. The great tasks of the university in the next

generation are to search the past to form the future, to begin an earnest search for (40) a new and relevant set of values, and to learn to use the knowledge we have for the questions that come before us. The university should use one-fourth of a student's time in his undergraduate (45) years and organize it into courses which might be called history, and literature and philosophy, and anything else appropriate and organize these around primary problems. The difference between (50) a primary problem and a secondary or even tertiary problem is that primary problems tend to be around for a long time, whereas the less important ones get solved. One primary problem is that (55) of interfering with what some call human destiny and others call biological development, which is partly the result of genetic circumstance and partly the result of accidental environmental con- (60) ditions. It is anticipated that the next generation, and perhaps this one, will be able to interfere chemically with the actual development of an individual and perhaps biologically by interfering with (65) his genes. Obviously, there are benefits both to individuals and to society from eliminating, or at least improving, mentally and physically deformed persons. On the other hand, there could be very (70) serious consequences if this knowledge were used with premeditation to produce superior and subordinate classes, each genetically prepared to carry out a predetermined mission. This can be done, (75) but what happens to free will and the

rights of the individual? Here we have a primary problem that will still exist when we are all dead. Of course, the tradi-tional faculty members would say, "But
(80) the students won't learn enough to go to graduate school." And certainly they would not learn everything we are in the habit of making them learn, but they would learn some other things. Surely,
(85) in the other three-quarters of their time, they would learn what they usually do, and they might even learn to think about it by carrying new habits into their more conventional courses. The advantages
(90) would be overwhelmingly greater than the disadvantages. After all, the pur-pose of education is not only to impart knowledge but to teach students to use the knowledge that they either have or
(95) will find, to teach them to ask and seek answers for important questions.

1. The author suggests that the university's greatest shortcoming is its failure to

   (A) attempt to provide equal opportunity for all.

   (B) offer courses in philosophy and the humanities.

   (C) prepare students adequately for pro-fessional studies.

   (D) help students see the relevance of the humanities to real problems.

   (E) require students to include in their curricula liberal arts courses.

2. It can be inferred that the author presup-poses that the reader will regard a course in literature as a course

   (A) with little or no practical value.

   (B) of interest only to academic scholars.

   (C) required by most universities for graduation.

   (D) uniquely relevant to today's primary problems.

   (E) used to teach students good writing skills.

3. Which of the following questions does the author answer in the passage?

   (A) What are some of the secondary prob-lems faced by the past generation?

   (B) How can we improve the performance of our political society?

   (C) Has any particular educational insti-tution tried the proposal introduced by the author?

   (D) What is a possible objection to the proposal offered in the passage?

   (E) Why is the university of today a bet-ter imparter of knowledge than the university of the past?

4. Which of the following questions would the author most likely consider a primary question?

   (A) Should Congress increase the level of social security benefits?

   (B) Is it appropriate for the state to use capital punishment?

   (C) Who is the best candidate for presi-dent in the next presidential elec-tion?

   (D) At what month can the fetus be con-sidered medically viable outside the mother's womb?

   (E) What measures should be taken to solve the problem of world hunger?

exercises

5. With which of the following statements about the use of scientific techniques to change an individual's genetic makeup would the author LEAST likely agree?

(A) Society has no right to use such techniques without the informed consent of the individual.

(B) Such techniques can have a positive benefit for the individual in some cases.

(C) Use of such techniques may be appropriate even though society, but not the individual, benefits.

(D) The question of the use of such techniques must be placed in a philosophical as well as a scientific context.

(E) The answers to questions about the use of such techniques will have important implications for the structure of our society.

6. The primary purpose of the passage is to

(A) discuss a problem and propose a solution.

(B) analyze a system and defend it.

(C) present both sides of an issue and allow the reader to draw a conclusion.

(D) outline a new idea and criticize it.

(E) raise several questions and provide answers to them.

7. The development discussed in the passage is primarily a problem of

(A) political philosophy.

(B) educational philosophy.

(C) scientific philosophy.

(D) practical science.

(E) practical politics.

Questions 8–14

The high unemployment rates of the early 1960's occasioned a spirited debate within the economics profession.
(5) One group found the primary cause of unemployment in slow growth and the solution in economic expansion. The other found the major explanation in changes that had occurred in the supply and demand for labor and stressed mea-
(10) sures for matching demand with supply.

The expansionist school of thought, with the Council of Economic Advisers as its leading advocates, attributed the persistently high unemployment level
(15) to a slow rate of economic growth resulting from a deficiency of aggregate demand for goods and services. The majority of this school endorsed the position of the Council that tax reduction
(20) would eventually reduce the unemployment level to 4 percent of the labor force with no other assistance. At 4 percent, bottlenecks in skilled labor, middle-level manpower and professional personnel
(25) were expected to retard growth and generate wage-price pressures. To go beyond 4 percent, the interim goal of the Council, it was recognized that improved education, training and retraining and
(30) other structural measures would be required. Some expansionists insisted that the demand for goods and services was nearly satiated and that it was impossible for the private sector to absorb a
(35) significant increase in output. In their estimate, only the lower-income fifth of the population and the public sector offered sufficient outlets for the productive efforts of the potential labor force.
(40) The fact that the needs of the poor and the many unmet demands for public services held higher priority than the demands of the marketplace in the value structure of this group no doubt influ-
(45) enced their economic judgments. Those who found the major cause of unemployment in structural features were primarily labor economists, concerned professionally with efficient functioning
(50) of labor markets through programs to

develop skills and place individual workers. They maintained that increased
aggregate demand was a necessary but
not sufficient condition for reaching ei-
(55) ther the CEA's 4 percent target or their
own preferred 3 percent. This pessimism
was based, in part, on the conclusion
that unemployment among the young,
the unskilled, minority groups and de-
(60) pressed geographical areas is not easily
attacked by increasing general demand.
Further, their estimate of the numbers
of potential members of the labor force
who had withdrawn or not entered be-
(65) cause of lack of employment opportunity
was substantially higher than that of
the CEA. They also projected that increased demand would put added pressure on skills already in short supply
(70) rather than employ the unemployed,
and that because of technological change,
which was replacing manpower, much
higher levels of demand would be necessary to create the same number of jobs.
(75) The structural school, too, had its hyperenthusiasts: fiscal conservatives who,
as an alternative to expansionary policies, argued the not very plausible position that a job was available for every
(80) person, provided only that he or she had
the requisite skills or would relocate.
Such extremist positions aside, there
was actually considerable agreement
between two main groups, though this
(85) was not recognized at the time. Both
realized the advisability of a tax cut to
increase demand, and both needed to
reduce unemployment below a point
around 4 percent. In either case, the
(90) policy implications differed in emphasis
and not in content.

8. The primary purpose of the passage is to

(A) suggest some ways in which tools to
manipulate aggregate demand and
eliminate structural deficiencies can
be used to reduce the level of unemployment.

(B) demonstrate that there was a good
deal of agreement between the expansionist and structuralist theories
on how to reduce unemployment in
the 1960s.

(C) explain the way in which structural
inefficiencies prevent the achievement
of a low rate of unemployment without wage-price pressures.

(D) discuss the disunity within the expansionist and structuralist schools
to show its relationship to the inability of the government to reduce unemployment to 4 percent.

(E) describe the role of the Council of
Economic Advisers in advocating expansionist policies to reduce unemployment to 4 percent.

9. Which of the following is NOT mentioned in the passage as a possible barrier to achieving a 4 percent unemployment rate through increased aggregate demand?

   (A) Technological innovation reduces the need for workers, so larger increases in demand are needed to employ the same number of workers.

   (B) The increase in output necessary to meet an increase in aggregate demand requires skilled labor, which is already in short supply, rather than unskilled labor, which is available.

   (C) An increase in aggregate demand will not create jobs for certain subgroups of unemployed persons, such as minority groups and young and unskilled workers.

   (D) Even if the tax reduction increases aggregate demand, many unemployed workers will be unwilling to relocate to jobs located in areas where there is a shortage of labor.

   (E) An increase in the number of available jobs will encourage people not in the labor market to enter it, which in turn will keep the unemployment rate high.

10. The author's treatment of the "hyperenthusiasts" (lines 75–76) can best be described as one of

    (A) strong approval.

    (B) lighthearted appreciation.

    (C) summary dismissal.

    (D) contemptuous sarcasm.

    (E) malicious rebuke.

11. Which of the following best describes the difference between the position taken by the Council of Economic Advisers and that taken by dissenting expansionists (Paragraph 2)?

    (A) Whereas the Council of Economic Advisers emphasized the need for a tax cut to stimulate general demand, the dissenters stressed the importance of structural measures such as education and training.

    (B) Although the dissenters agreed that an increase in demand was necessary to reduce unemployment, they argued government spending to increase demand should fund programs for lower income groups and public services.

    (C) The Council of Economic Advisers set a 4 percent unemployment rate as its goal, and dissenting expansionists advocated a goal of 3 percent.

    (D) The Council of Economic Advisers rejected the contention, advanced by the dissenting expansionists, that a tax cut would help to create increased demand.

    (E) The dissenting expansionists were critical of the Council of Economic Advisers because members of the Council advocated politically conservative policies.

12. The passage contains information that helps to explain which of the following?

  (A) The fact that the economy did not expand rapidly in the early 1960s

  (B) The start of wage-price pressures as the employment rate approaches 4 percent

  (C) The harmful effects of unemployment on an individual worker

  (D) The domination of the Council of Economics by expansionists

  (E) The lack of education and training among workers in some sectors

13. Which of the following best describes the author's attitude toward the expansionists mentioned in line 31?

  (A) The author doubts the validity of their conclusions because they were not trained economists.

  (B) The author discounts the value of their judgment because it was colored by their political viewpoint.

  (C) The author refuses to evaluate the value of their contention because he lacks sufficient information.

  (D) The author accepts their viewpoint until it can be demonstrated that it is incorrect.

  (E) The author endorses the principles on which their conclusions are based but believes their proposal to be impractical.

14. It can be inferred from the passage that the hyperenthusiasts (lines 75–76) contended that

  (A) the problem of unemployment could be solved without government retraining and education programs.

  (B) the number of persons unemployed was greatly overestimated by the Council of Economic Advisers.

  (C) a goal of 3 percent unemployment could not be reached unless the government enacted retraining and education programs.

  (D) the poor had a greater need for expanded government services than the more affluent portion of the population.

  (E) fiscal policies alone were powerful enough to reduce the unemployment rate to 4 percent of the workforce.

EXERCISE 1: ANSWER KEY AND EXPLANATIONS

1.	A	6.	E	11.	C	16.	A	21. A
2.	C	7.	A	12.	B	17.	A	22. B
3.	B	8.	A	13.	B	18.	E	23. A
4.	A	9.	E	14.	D	19.	C	24. B
5.	D	10.	E	15.	B	20.	D	

1. **The correct answer is (A).** This is a main idea question in the form of a question about the overall logical development of the selection. The author says that whether or not the IMF follows the accepted principles for a lender of last resort is a matter of debate. The author looks at arguments on both sides and eventually concludes that the IMF is encouraging moral hazard by lending at subsidized rates. For this reason, choices (B) and (E) have to be wrong—the author does defend one interpretation. Choice (C) is wrong because the author does not conclude that the principles are outdated, and choice (D) is wrong because the author is not proposing a new theory (rather, the author is trying to determine whether the IMF follows a long-established one).

2. **The correct answer is (C).** As the phrase "according to" signals, this is an explicit idea question. "Opportunity cost," as that phrase is used here, means the difference between value received and the value one would have received by doing something else. So if you invest $100 in bananas and make a $25 profit but could have invested the same $100 in apples and made a $30 profit, you've lost a $5 opportunity and, in this context, that is a cost you have to absorb.

3. **The correct answer is (B).** As the phrase "according to" signals, this is an explicit idea question. In paragraph four

the author notes that the IMF sometimes imposes conditions on loans in the hopes of increasing the likelihood that the loan will ultimately be repaid. This is analogous to a private institution's requiring collateral. Now, ultimately, the author concludes, the practice of imposing conditions doesn't really do much good, despite the theory of the IMF. The remaining choices are all notions mentioned in other parts of the selection but not offered as analogies to collateral.

4. **The correct answer is (A).** This is a logical structure question, so you need to figure out "why" the author raises this point. The author mentions the suggestion that countries might precipitate a financial crisis in order to qualify for IMF loans on favorable terms and then quickly dismisses that idea. The strategy is to raise the possible objection and then point out that it would be foolish for the local taxpayers (people who pay taxes in the borrowing nation) to do this because of the other costs involved.

5. **The correct answer is (D).** This is a further application question. After sifting through the facts used by both sides in the debate, the author concludes that the lending practices of the IMF are not sound because loans are made at subsidized rates. The rates are lower than they would otherwise be because they do not reflect fully the risk of the loans. And

this is bad policy—like a parent who's ready to bail out a child every time the child makes a money-management mistake. Choice (A) is wrong because the author says in paragraph four that conditionality has little effect on the prospects for repayment. As for choice (B), it is true that the IMF will ask for additional funds, but this is bad policy according to the author. The IMF should be lending at rates that reflect the risk involved. As for choice (C), the author never suggests that nations could offer collateral. (What would it be? The borrowing country pledges as collateral its executive mansion and state house along with 600 miles of navigable riverway and 20 tanks.) Finally, choice (E) overstates the case. The author would allow that it is okay for an aid institution to make such loans, but then it is understood that the loan is a form of aid and not a loan the terms of which fully reflect the risk.

6. **The correct answer is (E).** This is an implied idea question. In paragraph three, the author points out that if the IMF were on a sound footing, like a well-run local bank, then the IMF would be able to cover all of its expenses and bad loans from repayments plus the appropriate interest charged. The author reasons that the fact that contributor nations keep having to make deposits shows that there is a leak somewhere—the interest charged by the IMF isn't sufficient to cover all expenses. You can infer, therefore, that if the interest rates charged by the IMF were high enough, contributor countries would not have to put more money into the system. As for the other choices, these are not supported by the selection. As for choice (A), with interest rates higher, there would likely be fewer borrowers, not more. And a similar analy-

sis applies to choice (B): high interest rates would make the loan more difficult and give another reason to object to the conditions. As for choice (C), a higher rate would mean a greater cost for the borrower, and that could translate into defaults, but higher rates could also mean fewer bad loans in the first place. So there is just not enough information for choice (C). And as for (D), the passage says that private lenders do not, as a rule, use conditions.

7. **The correct answer is (A).** This is a main idea question, so the trick is to find the answer choice—of those that are presented—that gives the best overall description of the development of the selection. On the basis of the first word, it is possible to eliminate choice (C) because the author is not throwing stones. While there are certain criticisms implicit in the passage, it cannot be said that the main theme of the passage is criticism. Then, you'll want to eliminate choices that are too narrow, that is, that refer to part of the development but fail to capture the overall purpose of the passage. Choice (E) fails on this count. Yes, one element of the passage is to present reasons why the U.S. has not been able to integrate completely the two sectors, but that description leaves out a lot, e.g., the PRC experience. And you should eliminate choices that go beyond the scope of the selection, as choice (B) does. "Political system" is much too broad for the specific topic addressed here. And finally, you can exclude any choice that contains a misdescription, like choice (D). The author does not attempt to show that the procedures used in the PRC could be used in the U.S.; and, in fact, the passage implies that profound differences in political structures would preclude that.

And this leaves choice (A), which is a good description of the development. There is a comparison, and the comparison is the technology in the two sectors of the two countries.

8. **The correct answer is (A).** This is an explicit idea question, so the correct answer is specifically stated in the passage. In paragraph two, the author notes that the "proprietary" rights barrier has no parallel in the PRC because there is no analogous concept of proprietary rights; that is, the firms that will produce the technology are also under the control of the government. Typically, some of the wrong answers to an explicit idea question will be ideas mentioned in the passage (somewhere) that are not responsive to the question asked. Choice (C) and choice (D) are good examples. These are ideas mentioned in the passage, but they don't answer the question asked. Choice (E) is similar though perhaps more subtle. You might argue that this is one reason that technological integration has been more fully accomplished in the PRC than in the U.S., and the passage supports that idea. The problem is that choice (E) refers to a different aspect of the situation: demand for high performance weapons. Finally, choice (B) seems to be trivially true in some respects but does not respond to the question.

9. **The correct answer (E).** This is an implied idea question. We learn from the passage (in paragraph four) that even though the military is first in line for new equipment, the disparity between the technological capabilities of the civilian and the military air-traffic controllers is not so much due to the priority accorded the military as the simple lack of advanced equipment. In other words, it is not so much a conscious decision to feed the military and starve the civilian sector as it is a choice of allocating what little there is to the military. As for the wrong answers, some are more plausible than others, but all ultimately fail because there is not enough in the passage to support their conclusions. As for choice (A), what reason is there to believe that matters would be "simplified?" As for choice (B), what support is there for the idea that the technicians would not be familiar with the new equipment or trained quickly in its use? As for choice (C), this must surely be wrong because the passage implies that such competition does not take place. Finally, as for choice (D), what is there in the passage that mentions employment practices or such that would support this conclusion?

10. **The correct answer is (E).** This is an explicit idea question—with a thought-reverser. So four of the five ideas are mentioned in the selection, and you will find choice (A) through choice (D) in the first paragraph. Choice (E), however, is not mentioned. The passage does not mention defense control of production as an example of an economic efficiency.

11. **The correct answer is (C).** This is an application question (signaled by the "most strongly supports"). Remember that with such a question the credited response is not likely to be obviously right in the way that a correct answer to a specific detail item is right. Rather, the credited response to an application question is correct because, all things considered, it is the one most strongly supported by the selection. In this case, in paragraph three we learn that in the PRC military planners have responsibility for operational matters, but central planners, who tend to be engineers, have the authority for setting production

standards. And in the PRC, the engineers, with their understanding of the engineering challenges presented by advanced technologies, tend to de-emphasize cutting-edge technology. And it is this type of "gee-willy-whiz-bang" technology that tends to drive up the cost of weapons systems in the U.S. Or at least you can make a pretty good argument for that interpretation. Now look at the other choices. As for choice (A), this conclusion, if anything, seems to be contradicted by the selection since the PRC is said to lag behind the U.S. in adopting new technologies for weapons. As for choice (B), the passage never offers a comparison as to which of the two countries produces more "uniquely military" applications. As for choice (D), this seems to be inconsistent with the analysis given in paragraph two: some firms don't bid on defense contracts because of the strict oversight. And as for choice (E), while the author compares the two countries in terms of technology, there is no comparison of a bottom line such as efficiency.

12. **The correct choice is (B).** This is a main idea question, and the information you need is in the final paragraph. There the passage states that although the PRC appears to have been more successful than the U.S. at achieving integration, various political and economic factors will likely prevent the U.S. from emulating the PRC model. Choice (A) is incorrect because it gives only a part of the author's findings. The passage sets out not just to compare the two countries but to determine whether the experience of the PRC is applicable to the U.S. Choice (B) is also an element of the passage, but only an element. Choice (D) is really a given so far as the argument is concerned and not a point to be proved. And choice

(E) is not supported by the selection.

13. **The correct answer is (B).** This is obviously a main idea question. The main purpose of the passage is to review the findings of some research on animal behavior and suggest that this may have implications for the study of depression in humans. Choice (B) neatly restates this. Choice (A) can be overruled since the author proposes no such cure and even notes that there are complex issues remaining to be solved. Choice (C) is incorrect since the author does not criticize any experiments. It is important to recognize that in the second paragraph, the author is not being critical of any study in which rats were immersed in cold water but rather is anticipating a possible interpretation of those results and moving to block it. So, the author's criticism is of a possible interpretation of the experiment, not the experiment itself or the results. In any event, that can in no way be interpreted as the main theme of the passage. Choice (D) is way off the mark. Though one might object to the use of animals for experimentation, that is not a burden the author has elected to carry. Finally, choice (E) is incorrect because the author mentions this only in closing, almost as a qualification on the main theme of the passage.

14. **The correct answer is (D).** This is a logical detail question. As we have just noted, the author introduces the question in the second paragraph to anticipate a possible objection: Perhaps the animal's inability to act was caused by the trauma of the shock rather than the fact that it could not escape the shock. The author then lists some experiments whose conclusions refute this alternative explanation. Choice (A) is incorrect since the question represents an inter-

ruption of the flow of argument, not a continuation of the first paragraph. Choice (B) is incorrect and might be just a confusion of answer and question. Choice (C) can be eliminated since that is not the reason for raising the question, though it may be the overall theme of the passage. Here we cannot answer a question about a specific logical detail by referring to the main point of the text. Finally, choice (E) is incorrect since the author does not criticize the experiments but rather defends them.

15. **The correct answer is (B).** This is an inference question. We are referred by the question stem to line 72. There we find that stimulation of the septal region inhibits behavior "while rats with septal lesions do not show learned helplessness." We infer that the septum somehow sends "messages" that tell the action centers not to act. If ordinary rats learn helplessness and rats with septal lesions do not, this suggests that the communication between the two areas of the brain has been interrupted. This idea is captured by choice (B). Choice (A) is incorrect and confuses the indicated reference with the discussion of "immunized" dogs at line 35. Choice (C) seems to offer an explanation, but the text never suggests that rats have "understanding." Choice (D) is incorrect since it does not offer an explanation: Why don't rats with septal lesions learn helplessness? Finally, choice (E) is irrelevant to the question asked.

16. **The correct answer is (A).** This is an inferred idea question. The author contrasts the inescapable shock experiment with a "nonaversive parallel" in order to demonstrate that inescapability rather than trauma caused inaction in the animals. So the critical difference must be the trauma—it is present in the shock

experiments and not in the nonaversive parallels. This is further supported by the example of a nonaversive parallel, the uncontrollable delivery of food. So the relevant difference is articulated by choice (A). Choice (B) is incorrect since the author specifically states that the nonaversive parallels did succeed in inducing learned helplessness. Choice (C) is incorrect for the same reason. Choice (D) is incorrect since the value of the nonaversive parallel to the logical structure of the argument is that it was not traumatic at all. Finally, choice (E) is incorrect because even if one experiment used rats and the other dogs, that is not the defining difference between the shock experiments and the nonaversive-parallel experiments.

17. **The correct answer is (A).** This is a logical detail question, and it is related to the matters discussed above. The author raises the question in paragraph two in order to anticipate a possible objection; namely, that the shock, not the unavoidability, caused inaction. The author then offers a refutation of this position by arguing that we get the same results using similar experiments with non-aversive stimuli. Moreover, if trauma of shock caused the inaction, then we would expect to find learned helplessness induced in rats by the shock, regardless of prior experience with shock. The "mastery effect," however, contradicts this expectation. This is essentially the explanation provided in choice (A). Choice (B) is incorrect since the author does not mention this until the end of the passage. Choice (C) can be eliminated since the "mastery effect" reference is not included to support the conclusion that neurochemical changes cause the learned helplessness. Choice (D) is incorrect, for though the

author makes such an assertion, the "mastery effect" data is not adduced to support that particular assertion. Finally, choice (E) is the point against which the author is arguing when mentioning the "mastery effect" experiments.

18. **The correct answer is (E).** This is a further application question. The author closes with a disclaimer that the human cognitive makeup is more complex than that of laboratory animals, and that for this reason, the findings regarding learned helplessness and induced neurosis may or may not be applicable to humans. The author does not, however, explain what the differences are between the experimental subjects and humans. A logical continuation would be to supply the reader with this elaboration. By comparison, the other answer choices are less likely. Choice (B) is unlikely since the author begins and ends with references to human depression, and that is evidently the motivation for writing the article. Choice (C) is not supported by the text since it is nowhere indicated that any such experiments have been undertaken. Choice (D) fails for a similar reason. We cannot conclude that the author would want to test humans by similar experimentation. Finally, choice (A) is perhaps the second-best answer. Its value is that it suggests the mechanism should be studied further. But the most important question is not how the mechanism works in rats but whether that mechanism also works in humans.

19. **The correct answer is (C).** This is a main idea question. The author begins by defining "depletion." Then, in the second paragraph, the passage distinguishes two senses of reserves—the total amount remaining versus the amount recoverable given reasonable investments. In the third paragraph, the author goes on to show how technology affects production and reserves and in the fourth paragraph points out that technological innovation has the paradoxical effect of extending reserves (because more oil can be extracted) even while using up resources faster. In the final paragraph, the author points to the obvious: continued extraction will depend on further technological innovation. So the best description is choice (C). Choice (A) is wrong because the author does not advance a plan, even though the passage does mention some technological innovations. Choice (B) is wrong because there is no "warning" tone in the passage. Choice (D) is wrong because the mention of various innovations is in the service of the larger discussion; that is, the details found in paragraph three are not the main point. And finally, choice (E) is wrong for the same reasons that (A) and (B) are wrong.

20. **The correct answer is (D).** This is an explicit idea question. According to the passage, total resources is the quantity of oil that actually exists. It's not possible to know exactly how much there is, but experts can make pretty good guesses about the amount. Some of that oil, however, is in places that are hard to get to, so it would be very expensive—though theoretically possible—to produce it. Proved reserves are that subpart of the resources that can be obtained without extraordinary effort, just by using existing technology at a comparable cost. Choice (A) represents a confused reading of paragraph two. The "probability" associated with proved reserves is the likelihood that the oil can be extracted at a reasonable cost. Choice (B) is wrong because, while proved reserves depend

on available technology (that's part of the definition of whether the oil can be recovered at a reasonable cost), the fact that advanced technology makes the oil more accessible is not part of the definition of proved reserves. Choice (C) is attractive because it sounds like "proved," but "proved" in this context has a specialized meaning, as developed in the passage. And choice (E) is wrong because advanced technologies will help to define the quantity of proved reserves; for example, a break-through that reduces the cost of producing oil in otherwise inaccessible spaces increases proved reserves.

21. **The correct answer is (A).** This is a logical structure question. The author places "normal" in quotes because it doesn't have its usual meaning. Ordinarily, we take "normal" to mean "natural" or something like that. In this context, however, "normal" conditions are defined in part by cost considerations. For example, a technological innovation can reduce the cost of recovery, making it profitable to extract a deposit that is otherwise inaccessible because unprofitable. Choice (B) is wrong because it offers a comparison between oil production and other kinds of activities, none of which are mentioned here. Choice (C) is wrong because, while true, the nonrenewability of the resource is not part of the definition of normal or baseline conditions. Choices (D) and (E) are obviously true, but they don't answer the question asked.

22. **The correct answer is (B).** This is an implied idea question. The passage states that during the normal life of a well, production will increase and then gradually fall off until it reaches "some economic limit" at which the well is closed. Later, the author talks about prolonging the life of a well using advanced technol-

ogy, but only when the cost of the technology is acceptable. This implies that the well will be kept in production so long as it is profitable. Choice (A) is wrong because there may be oil remaining in a well or field and yet production is discontinued because it is no longer profitable. Choice (C) simply has no support in the passage; it's a nice idea (make sure you are always building new to replace the old), but the idea just isn't found in this selection about oil. Choice (D) sounds nice, too, but what it really says is that the well should be kept open even if it becomes unprofitable, and that is not what the passage implies. Finally, choice (E) uses some of the language from the passage, but it really doesn't make a statement that is meaningful in this context.

23. **The correct answer is (A).** This is a specific detail question. The last paragraph tells us that, even though total resources are declining (because oil is nonrenewable), technology makes up for the declining base by permitting the faster extraction of oil and by allowing exploitation of deposits that might otherwise be unprofitable. Choice (B) is actually an incorrect statement because innovation would increase proved reserves. Choice (C) also is incorrect since oil is not renewable—period. Choice (D) is wrong because larger fields would be the first discovered and exploited in any case; the passage makes it clear that technology is important in going after the smaller finds. And choice (E) is wrong because technology requires capital investment.

24. **The correct answer is (B).** This is an application question. The analysis of the third and fourth paragraphs shows that an increase in profitability results in an increase in proved reserves because oil

that once would not be extracted because it was unprofitable to do so becomes an economically viable product. Choice (A) would likely have the opposite result: increased production would drive down prices, making production of marginal resources less attractive. Choice (C) might

not affect proved reserves at all; or, if the revision were large enough, might result in a lowering of proved reserve calculations. Choices (D) and (E) could have the effect of making extraction of some oil unprofitable, thereby removing it from the "proved" category.

EXERCISE 2: ANSWER KEY AND EXPLANATIONS

1.	D	4.	B	7.	B	10.	C	13.	B
2.	A	5.	A	8.	B	11.	B	14.	A
3.	D	6.	A	9.	D	12.	B		

1. **The correct answer is (D).** This is a fairly easy inference question. We are asked to determine which of the problems mentioned by the author is the most important. Choice (B) can be eliminated because the author's criticism is not that such courses are not offered, nor even that such courses are not required. So we eliminate choice (E) as well. The most important shortcoming, according to the author, is that students have not been encouraged to apply the principles learned in the humanities. The support for this conclusion is to be found at the end of the second paragraph. As for choice (C), this is not mentioned by the author as a weakness in the present curriculum structure. Rather, the author anticipates that this is a possible objection to the proposal to require students to devote part of their time to the study of primary problems. Choice (A) is indeed a weakness of the university, and the author does admit that the university has not yet achieved equal opportunity for all. But this is discussed in the first paragraph, where the university's successes are outlined. Only in the second paragraph does the discussion of the

university's failure begin. This indicates that the author does not regard the university's failure to achieve complete equality of opportunity as a serious problem.

2. **The correct answer is (A).** This is an inference question as well, though of a greater degree of difficulty. It seems possible to eliminate choices (C) and (E) as fairly implausible. The author's remarks about literature (at the end of the second paragraph), addressed to us as readers, do not suggest that we believe literature is required, nor that it is used to teach writing. As for choice (D), the author apparently presupposes that we, the readers, do not see the relevance of literature to real problems, for that it is relevant is at least part of the burden of his argument. Choice (B) is perhaps the second-best answer. It may very well be that most people regard literature as something scholarly, but that does not prove that choice (B) is a presupposition of the argument. The author states that literature is a source of real and vicarious experience. What is the value of that? According to the author, it relieves us of the necessity of living everyone else's

life. The author is trying to show that literature has a real, practical value. The crucial question, then, is why the author is attempting to prove that literature has real value. The answer is, because the author presupposes that we disagree with this conclusion. There is a subtle but important difference between a presupposition that literature is scholarly and a presupposition that literature has no practical value. After all, there are many nonscholarly undertakings that may lack practical value.

3. **The correct answer is (D).** This is an explicit idea question. It is important to keep in mind that an explicit idea question is almost always answerable on the basis of information actually stated in the text. With a format of this sort, this means that the question should be readily answerable without speculation, and that this answer should be fairly complete. Choice (D) is correct because the author raises a possible objection in the final paragraph. Choice (A) is incorrect because the author never gives any such examples. Choice (B) is incorrect because the author never addresses the issue of political society. That is mentioned only as a point of reference in the introductory remarks. Choice (C) is not answered since no university is ever named. And choice (E) is incorrect since the author makes the assertion, without elaborating, that the university is a better teacher today than in the past. There is a further point to be made. It is possible to argue that choice (B) is partially answered. After all, if we improve our students' ability to pose and answer questions, is this not also a way to improve the performance of our political society? But that is clearly more attenuated than the answer we find in the question in choice (D). The

same reasoning may be applied to other incorrect answers as well. It may be possible to construct arguments in their favor, but this is a standardized exam. And there is a clear, easy answer to choice (D) in the text, indicating that this is the answer the test writer intends that you choose.

4. **The correct answer is (B).** This is an application question. The author uses the term "primary problems" to refer to questions of grave importance that are not susceptible to an easy answer. Each of the incorrect answers poses a question that can be answered with a short answer. Choice (A) can be answered with a yes or no. Choice (C) can be answered with a name. Choice (D) can be answered with a date. Choice (E) can be answered with a series of proposals. And even if the answers are not absolutely indisputable, the questions will soon become dead issues. The only problem that is likely to still be around after "we are all dead" is the one of capital punishment.

5. **The correct answer is (A).** This is an application question—with a thought-reverser. The question asks us to identify the statement with which the author would be least likely to agree. In the fourth paragraph, the author introduces an example of a primary problem. What makes this a primary problem is that there are competing arguments on both sides of the issue: There are benefits to the individual and to society, but there are dangers as well. Choice (A) is not likely to get the author's agreement since the author acknowledges that the question is an open one. The author implies that society may have such a right but points out also that the use of such measures must be studied very carefully. That same paragraph strongly suggests

that the author would accept choices (B) and (C). As for choices (D) and (E), these are strands that are woven into the text at several points.

6. **The correct answer is (A).** This is a main idea question. The author describes a problem and proposes a solution. Choice (B) is incorrect since the analysis of the system leads the author to propose a reform. Choice (C) is incorrect since the author makes a definite recommendation. Choice (D) is incorrect since the new idea the author outlines is defended in the text, not criticized. Choice (E) is incorrect since the author does not develop the passage by raising questions.

7. **The correct answer is (B).** This too is a main idea question in that the question asks, what is the general topic? Choice (B) is the best answer since the author is speaking about the university and is addressing fundamental questions of educational philosophy. Choices (A) and (C) are incorrect since politics and science are only tangentially related to the argument. Choices (D) and (E) can be eliminated on the same ground and on the additional ground that though the author wants to make education practical, the decision to do that will be a decision based on philosophical concerns.

8. **The correct answer is (B).** This is a main idea question presented in the format of a sentence completion. We are looking for the answer choice that, when added to the question stem, produces a sentence that summarizes the main thesis of the passage. Insofar as the verbs are concerned, that is, the first words of each choice, each choice seems acceptable. One could say that the author is concerned with "suggesting," "demonstrating," "explaining," "discussing," or "describing." So we must look at the

fuller content of each choice. The author begins the passage by noting that there were two schools of thought on how to reduce unemployment and then proceeds to describe the main ideas of both schools of thought. Finally, the author concludes by noting that, for all of their avowed differences, both schools share considerable common ground. This development is captured very well by choice (B). Choice (A) is perhaps the second-best choice. It is true that the author does mention some economic tools that can be used to control unemployment, but the main thesis is not that such ways exist. Rather, the main thesis, as pointed out by choice (B), is that the two groups, during the 1960s, had seemingly different yet ultimately similar views on how the tools could best be used. Choice (C) is incorrect since the discussion of structural inefficiencies is only a minor part of the development. Choice (D) is incorrect because the discussion of disunity is included simply to give a more complete picture of the debate and not to show that this prevented the achievement of full employment. Finally, the CEA is mentioned as a matter of historical interest, but its role is not the central focus of the passage.

9. **The correct answer is (D).** This is an explicit idea question. Each of the incorrect answers is mentioned as a possible barrier to achieving 4 percent unemployment in the discussion of structural inefficiencies of the third paragraph. The reference is made to the effect of technological innovation, the shortage of skilled labor, the problem of minority and unskilled labor, and the reserve of workers not yet counted as being in the labor force. There is no mention, however, of the need to relocate workers to areas of

labor shortage. The only reference to relocation is in the final paragraph. Since choice (D) is never mentioned as a possible barrier to achieving the 4 percent goal, it is the correct answer.

10. **The correct answer is (C).** This is an attitude or tone question. The author refers to the position of the hyperenthusiasts as "not very plausible," which indicates the author does not endorse the position. On this ground, we can eliminate choice (A). Choice (B) can be eliminated on the same ground and on the further ground that "lighthearted" is not a good description of the tone of the passage. Choices (D) and (E), however, are overstatements. Though the author obviously rejects the position of the hyperenthusiasts, there is no evidence of so negative an attitude as those suggested by choices (D) and (E). Choice (C) describes well what the author means by mentioning the position and then not even bothering to discuss it.

11. **The correct answer is (B).** This is an explicit idea question. The needed reference is found in the second paragraph. The difference between the CEA and the dissenting expansionists grew out of the question of where to spend the money that would be used to stimulate the economy. The dissenting faction wanted to target the expansionary spending for public services and low-income groups. Choice (B) presents this difference very well. Choice (A) is incorrect and conflates the dissenting expansionists (paragraph 2) and the structuralists (paragraph 3). Choice (C) commits the same error. Choice (D) represents a misreading of the second paragraph: The CEA were expansionists. Choice (E) is incorrect since the passage does not state that the CEA were conservatives.

12. **The correct answer is (B).** This is an explicit idea question. Information that would bear on the issue raised by choice (B) is included in the third paragraph. As for choice (A), there is no such information in the passage. In the first paragraph, the author mentions that the economy failed to expand rapidly in the early 1960s but offers no explanation for that phenomenon. And choice (C) is never mentioned at any point in the text. Choice (D) is a political question that is not addressed by the passage, and choice (E) is a historical one that is not answered.

13. **The correct answer is (B).** The author mentions a dissenting group of expansionists in the closing lines of paragraph 2. The author remarks of their arguments that their commitment to certain political ideals likely interfered with their economic judgments. For this reason, the author places very little faith in their arguments. Choice (B) nicely brings out this point. Choice (A) is incorrect. The author does discount the value of their conclusions, but it is not because they were not trained as economists. As for choice (C), there is nothing that suggests that the author lacks information. Rather, it seems from the passage that the author has sufficient information to discount the position. Choice (D) is clearly in contradiction to this analysis and must be incorrect, and choice (E) can be eliminated on the same ground.

14. **The correct answer is (A).** Here we have a relatively easy inference question. The hyperenthusiasts used structuralist-type arguments to contend that jobs were already available. That being the case, the hyperenthusiasts dissented from both the positions of the expansionists and the structuralists who believed

unemployment to be a problem. We may infer, then, that the essence of the hyperenthusiasts' position was that no government action was needed at all—at least no government action of the sort being discussed by the main camps described by the author. As for choice (B), nowhere in the passage does the author state or even hint that anyone overestimated the number of people out of work.

As for choice (C), this represents a reading that confuses the hyperenthusiasts (paragraph 4) with the main-line structuralists (paragraph 3). Choice (D) is incorrect and conflates the hyperenthusiasts of the expansionary school of thought with those of the structuralist school. Finally, choice (E) is incorrect since it describes the position of the main group of expansionists.

answers

Analytical Reasoning

OVERVIEW
- **What is Analytical Reasoning?**
- **How do you answer Analytical Reasoning questions?**
- **What smart test-takers know**
- **What the smartest test-takers know**

WHAT IS ANALYTICAL REASONING?

Analytical Reasoning problems are just logic games. For example:

> Three musicians—J, K, and L—each play exactly one instrument: the piano, the bass, or the sax—though not necessarily in that order. J, whose sister is the sax player, does not play the piano; and L is an only child.

You have to use the clues to deduce who plays which instrument.

> L does not play the sax because L is an only child (the sax player is J's sister). J cannot be the sax player because J's sister plays the sax. Since the sax player is not J or L, K plays the sax.
>
> If J does not play the sax (K plays the sax) or the piano (as we are told), then J must play the bass.
>
> Finally, since J plays the bass and K plays the sax, you can deduce that L plays the piano.

Thus, you can figure out which musician plays which instrument: J on bass, K on sax, L on piano. You have probably seen similar problems in logic books or in the entertainment section of a newspaper or a magazine.

In this book, you will see a variety of logical puzzles, but initial conditions and questions have some very important characteristics in common. The initial conditions establish the structure of the logical game and introduce you to the individuals involved in the puzzle as well as to the logical connections between and among those individuals.

chapter 7

NOTE

Should I try to do all of the Analytical Reasoning puzzles?
Probably not. Some students should attempt all four or five of the problem sets; some students should try to do only two. The majority of students should attempt at least three of the sets.

The individuals involved in an Analytical Reasoning set are usually designated by letters or names, e.g., 8 people, J, K, L, M, N, O, P, and Q, are sitting around a table. Sometimes, the individuals in the problem may be designated by some physical characteristic, e.g., six flags are displayed in a horizontal row, two red, two blue, one yellow, and one green. Further, the initial conditions always give some information about the logical relations that join the individuals to one another, e.g., J is sitting next to K, and M is not sitting next to P, or the red flags are hanging next to each other and the yellow flag is not next to the green flag.

LSAT Analytical Reasoning Questions

The scored portion of the LSAT typically includes a single Analytical Reasoning section with 4 to 5 problem sets. Each set consists of a list of conditions followed by 5 to 7 questions, for a total of 22 to 24 questions in the section.

Read over these directions for LSAT Analytical Reasoning, and examine a sample question set and explanations.

Anatomy of an Analytical Reasoning Question Set

Directions: Each group of questions is based on a set of propositions or conditions. Drawing a rough picture or diagram may help in answering some of the questions. Choose the best answer for each question and blacken the corresponding space on your answer sheet.

Six runners—J, K, L, M, N, and O—participated in a series of races with the following results:

   J always finished ahead of N but behind O.

   K always finished ahead of L but behind O.

   M always finished ahead of L but behind J.

There were no ties.

Linear ordering sets are the most common type of game used on the test. Notice that the order of finish is not completely determined, though it is possible to deduce that O always finished first.

---

1. Which of the following could be the order of finish of a race from first to last?

   (A) O, J, K, L, M, N

   (B) O, J, K, M, L, N

   (C) O, J, M, N, L, K

   (D) O, M, J, N, K, L

   (E) M, L, J, O, K, N

   The correct answer is (B). Each of the other choices contradicts one or more of the initial conditions.

2. Which of the following must be true of the order of finish for all of the races?

   (A) O finished first.

   (B) J finished second.

   (C) K finished third.

   (D) N finished last.

   (E) L finished last.

   The correct answer is (A). The first two conditions establish that O finished ahead of J, K, L, and N. Then, since O finished ahead of J, O also finished ahead of M.

3. For any race, which of the following is a complete and accurate listing of the runners who could have finished ahead of M?

   (A) J

   (B) J, O

   (C) J, O, K

   (D) J, O, K, N

   (E) J, O, K, N, L

   The correct answer is (D). The third condition states that M finished ahead of L. So the other four runners could have finished ahead of M.

HOW DO YOU ANSWER ANALYTICAL REASONING QUESTIONS?

Here's a simple, four-step plan that can help you solve Analytical Reasoning questions.

ANALYTICAL REASONING: GETTING IT RIGHT

1 Summarize the initial conditions in a "bookkeeping" system.

2 Look for further conclusions.

3 Treat each question separately.

4 Use the answer choices to create a "feedback loop."

Now let's look at these steps in greater detail.

1 Summarize the initial conditions in a "bookkeeping" system. This system will include notational devices and diagramming techniques that you invent for yourself or that you adapt from those suggested in this book. You should not regard the "bookkeeping" system used in this book as the only possible system. Rather, you should regard it as a suggested system. Once you understand the system, you can take some parts of it for your own personal system, leaving behind those devices you find cumbersome or otherwise not useful.

Use these or other symbols to summarize the initial conditions:

LOGICAL CONNECTIVE	SYMBOL
and	+
or	v
not	~
if, then	⊃
same as, next to	=
not same as, not next to	≠
greater than, older, before	>
if and only if	≡
less than, younger, after	<

Be sure to double-check your summary. A mistake at this stage could be very, very costly.

Take a look at this illustration:

A chef is experimenting with eight ingredients to discover new dishes. The ingredients are J, K, L, M, N, O, P, and Q. The ingredients must be used in accordance with the following conditions:

If M is used in a dish, P and Q must also be used in that dish.

If P is used in a dish, then exactly two of the three ingredients, L, M, and N, must also be used in that dish.

L cannot be used in a dish with P.

N can be used in a dish if and only if J is also used in that dish.

K, L, and M cannot all be used in the same dish.

The information could be summarized as follows:

(1) $M \supset (P \, \& \, Q)$

(2) $P \supset (L \, \& \, M) \lor (L \, \& \, N) \lor (M \, \& \, N)$

(3) $L \neq P$

(4) $N \equiv J$

(5) $\sim (K \, \& \, L \, \& \, M)$

The "horseshoe" is used for the first statement, but the arrow could also be used. Notice also that parentheses are used as punctuation marks. If you do not set P & Q off in parentheses, the statement $M \supset P \, \& \, Q$ could be misinterpreted to read "If M is used, then P must be used; and Q must be used."

The second statement shows the logical structure of the second condition. If P is used, then either L and M must be used or L and N must be used or M and N must be used. Again, you should note the parentheses as punctuation marks.

Statement 3 uses the $\neq$, which has many other uses, to assert that L and P cannot be used together. Similarly, statement 4 uses the $\equiv$ to assert that N and J, if used, must be used together. Of course, the $\equiv$ can have many other meanings. Depending on the context in which the symbol is used, the statement "$N \equiv J$" could mean any of the following: N and J are the same age; N and J are of the same sex; N and J must ride in the same car; N and J must sit next to one another. The value of the symbol depends on the context in which it appears.

Finally, statement 5 can be read to say that it is not the case that K and L and M are used in the same dish. Of course, these are just suggestions; there are many other ways to summarize the information. Later, in the answer explanations, you will find different notational devices that will be explained as they are introduced. Remember, however, only adopt those symbols you find convenient and find substitutes for those that do not work for you.

➋ Look for further conclusions. The initial conditions may permit you to draw a further conclusion, and a further conclusion is often the key to one or even more questions. Here is an example:

Six students—T, U, V, X, Y, and Z—are being considered for a field trip. The final selection depends on the following restrictions:

If X is selected, then neither Y nor Z can be selected.

If T is selected, then U cannot be selected.

If U is selected, then Z must also be selected.

NOTE

What are point killers?

Point killers are Analytical Reasoning questions that will definitely take too much time. For example:

Which of the following must be true?

(A) If J is selected, then K must be selected.

(B) If J is selected, then L must be selected.

(C) If K is selected, then J must be selected.

(D) If M is selected, then N must be selected.

(E) If N is selected, then Q must be selected.

Since each answer choice includes an "if" statement, this is like five questions rolled into one. Punt.

You can deduce that certain pairs are not acceptable. For example, X and Z cannot both be selected.

3 **Treat each question separately.** Some questions provide, by stipulation, information that supplements the initial conditions, e.g., "If the traveler visits Paris on Thursday, then which city will she visit on Friday?"

Additional information provided in a question stem is to be used for that question only. In fact, different questions may ask you to make contradictory assumptions. The second question in a set may ask you to assume that the traveler visits Rome on Thursday while the third question asks you to assume that she visits Rome on Monday.

4 **Use the answer choices to create a "feedback loop."** This is a multiple-choice examination in which one and only one of the options can be correct. And an option in this section will be correct or incorrect as a matter of logic. (In this respect, this section is similar to a math test.) Thus, if your analysis of a question yields one and only one correct answer, this indicates that you have probably done the problem correctly. If your analysis produces no correct choice, then you have obviously overlooked something. On the other hand, if your analysis produces more than one seemingly correct choice, then you have made an error somewhere.

Now let's look at some sample Analytical Reasoning puzzles. As you read the explanations, think about how the solution process applies.

Linear Ordering

Over the nearly twenty years since Analytical Reasoning was introduced, the most commonly used type of problem has been the linear ordering problem. This kind of problem sets up a situation like the following:

Seven people standing in a line.

A dozen students in school in grades 1 through 12.

A musical scale consisting of six notes.

Now let's solve a typical linear ordering puzzle.

Six people, J, K, L, M, N, and O, are sitting in one row of six seats at a concert. The seats all face the stage and are numbered, facing the stage from left to right, 1 through 6, consecutively. Exactly one person is sitting in each seat.

J is sitting neither in seat 1 nor in seat 6.

N is not sitting next to L.

N is not sitting next to K.

O is sitting to the immediate left of N.

You would begin your attack by summarizing the initial conditions:

$J \neq (1 \text{ or } 6)$

$N \neq L$

$N \neq K$

$O–N$

Are there any further conclusions to be drawn? Yes and no. Yes, it would be possible to determine every possible seating arrangement given these initial conditions, but that obviously would take a lot of time. Therefore, no, there don't appear to be any further obvious conclusions, so go to the questions.

1. Which of the following seating arrangements, given in order from seat 1 to seat 6, is acceptable?

   (A) L, M, K, O, N, J

   (B) L, J, M, O, N, K

   (C) L, N, O, J, M, K

   (D) K, J, L, O, M, N

   (E) M, K, O, N, J, L

Notice that this question provides no additional information, so it must be answerable just on the basis of the initial conditions. When this is the case, use the initial conditions to eliminate choices.

The correct answer is (E). The first condition states that J is seated neither in seat 1 nor in seat 6. Eliminate choice (A) because that arrangement is inconsistent with the first of the initial conditions. The second condition requires that N not sit next to L, and on that score, we can eliminate choice (C). According to the third condition, N does not sit next to K, and we eliminate choice (B). Finally, the fourth condition states that O is seated immediately to N's left, and we can eliminate choice (D). We have eliminated four of the five choices, so choice (E) must be the only arrangement that respects all of the initial conditions.

2. All of the following seating arrangements, given in order from 1 to 6, are acceptable EXCEPT

   (A) M, J, L, K, O, N

   (B) K, J, O, N, M, L

   (C) K, O, N, J, M, L

   (D) L, O, N, J, K, M

   (E) K, J, O, N, L, M

The correct answer is (E). This question is the mirror image of the first, but you should use the same strategy. Each choice is consistent with the requirement that J not be seated in position 1 or 6. And choices (A) through (D) respect the second condition that N not sit next to L. In choice (E), however, N is seated next to L. Choice (E), therefore, must be the choice we are looking for, as it is NOT an acceptable arrangement.

NOTE

Are some games easier than others?
Yes. Generally speaking, linear ordering problems are the easiest. "Hybrid" sets that combine elements from different types are the most difficult. If you can see that a game has so many variables or rules that it is very difficult, save that one for last or skip it entirely.

3. If L is in seat 1 and K is in seat 5, which of the following must be true?
    (A) J is in seat 2.
    (B) M is in seat 3.
    (C) N is in seat 4.
    (D) O is in seat 4.
    (E) M is in seat 6.

The correct answer is (E). This question provides additional information. When this is the case, begin by determining whether or not further conclusions can be drawn.

A diagram would be helpful. The question stem stipulates that L is in seat 1 and K in seat 5:

1	2	3	4	5	6
L				K	

Now return to the initial conditions. The first doesn't help very much, though you can conclude that J is in seat 2, 3, or 4. The second and third conditions by themselves don't operate to place any person on the diagram, but both together tell you that N must be in seat 3:

1	2	3	4	5	6
L		N		K	

And since O must be seated to N's left:

1	2	3	4	5	6
L	O	N		K	

And since J cannot sit in seat 6, you have a complete order:

1	2	3	4	5	6
L	O	N	J	K	M

4. If M and O are in seats 2 and 3, respectively, which of the following must be true?
    (A) J is in seat 5.
    (B) K is in seat 3.
    (C) L is in seat 1.
    (D) L is in seat 6.
    (E) N is in seat 5.

The correct answer is (A). Begin by processing the initial information:

1	2	3	4	5	6
	M	O			

Since O is seated immediately to N's left:

1	2	3	4	5	6
	M	O	N		

Since neither K nor L can sit next to N, neither can be in seat 5. This means K and L are in seats 1 and 6, though not necessarily respectively:

1	2	3	4	5	6
K/L	M	O	N		K/L

And, of course, J is in seat 5:

1	2	3	4	5	6
K/L	M	O	N	J	K/L

5. If K and L are separated by exactly three seats, what is the maximum number of different arrangements in which the six people could be seated?

   (A) 1
   (B) 2
   (C) 3
   (D) 4
   (E) 5

The correct answer is (D). This question really asks "What could be true?" What are the possible arrangements given the additional information?

1	2	3	4	5	6
K				L	
L				K	
	K				L
	L				K

And since N cannot be seated next to either L or K, but O and N must be seated together:

1	2	3	4	5	6
K	O	N		L	
L	O	N		K	
	K	O	N		L
	L	O	N		K

TIP

There are four—and only four—Analytical Reasoning questions.

1. What must be true as a matter of logic?
2. What must be false as a matter of logic?
3. What can be true or false as a matter of logic?
4. What cannot be true or false as a matter of logic?

And J cannot sit in seats 1 or 6:

1	2	3	4	5	6
K	O	N	J	L	M
L	O	N	J	K	M
M	K	O	N	J	L
M	L	O	N	J	K

The correct answer is (D). So there are only four possible arrangements given the stipulation that K and L are separated by exactly three seats.

6. If K is in seat 2, which of the following is a complete and accurate listing of the seats that O could occupy?

   (A) 1
   (B) 3
   (C) 3 and 4
   (D) 1, 3, and 4
   (E) 3, 4, and 5

The correct answer is (E). As in the previous question, this question asks about logical possibilities. If K is in seat 2, then there are three possible placements for the O N pair:

1	2	3	4	5	6
	K	O	N		
	K		O	N	
	K			O	N

Are each of these possible? Yes, as you can prove to yourself by completing the three diagrams. So O could be seated in seat 3, 4, or 5. So the correct answer is (E).

Distributed Order

Another common problem type is the distributed order game. In a linear ordering problem, only one individual can occupy a position in the order. In some problem sets, however, a position in the order can accommodate more than one individual.

Six individuals, P, Q, R, S, T, and U, live in a five-story apartment building. Each person lives on one of the floors in the building.

Exactly one of the six lives on the first floor, exactly one of them lives on the fourth floor, and at least two of them live on the second floor.

Of the six people, P lives on the highest floor, and no one lives on the same floor as P.

Q does not live on the first floor or on the second floor.

Neither R nor S lives on the second floor.

When an ordering problem contains distributional restrictions, determine what consequences flow from those restrictions.

The initial conditions establish the following:

5

4 Exactly one

3

2 At least two, not Q, not R, not S

1 Exactly one, not Q

And, of course, P cannot live on floor two. (P must live on either floor four or floor five.) Since it is a requirement of the distribution that at least two persons live on floor two, we can deduce that T and U (and of the six only T and U) live on floor two:

5

4 Exactly one

3

2 Exactly two: T and U

1 Exactly one, not Q

1. All of the following must be true EXCEPT
    (A) exactly two persons live on floor two.
    (B) at most, one person lives on floor five.
    (C) at least one person lives on floor five.
    (D) at least one person lives on floor three.
    (E) P does not live on floor two.

The correct answer is (C). The diagram shows that choice (A) is necessarily true. And it has already been determined that P must be on floor four or five, so choice (E) is necessarily true. As for choice (B), this must be true: either P lives on floor five or P lives on floor four (and none of the other five lives above P). As for choice (D), either P lives on floor five, in which case the distribution of individuals is 1, 2, 1, 1, and 1 (from first to fifth) or P lives on floor four, in which case the distribution is 1, 2, 2, 1, 0 (from first to fifth). Choice (C), however, is not necessarily true, for P could live on the fourth floor.

> **TIP**
>
> **The initial conditions are crucial.** Be sure to double check your understanding of the initial conditions. A mistake at the very outset could be fatal. And, if you find that you cannot recognize answers to particular questions (the problem set is falling apart for you), go back to the initial conditions. That is probably where you took a misstep.

2. Which of the following could be true?

   (A) Either Q or R lives on the third floor.

   (B) T and U do not live on the second floor.

   (C) T and U live on the third floor.

   (D) T lives on the first floor.

   (E) U lives on the fourth floor.

   The correct answer is (A). The analysis above shows that choice (A) could be true. The remaining choices must be false since T and U live on the second floor.

3. If P lives on a floor directly above the floor on which R lives, which of the following must be true?

   (A) R lives on a higher floor than Q.

   (B) R and Q live on the same floor.

   (C) T and U live on different floors.

   (D) Q lives on the third floor.

   (E) S lives on the second floor.

   The correct answer is (D). If R is directly beneath P, then since Q cannot be on the first floor, S must be on the first floor. This means there are two possible arrangements:

5	P	
4	R	P
3	Q	R,Q
2	T,U	T,U
1	S	S

   But Q is on the third floor in both arrangements.

Selection Sets

Selection sets are also a common game. Selection sets involve choosing a subset of individuals from a larger collection.

> From a group of three faculty members, P, S, and R, four administrators, T, U, V, and W, and three students, X, Y, and Z, the president of a college must choose an <u>ad hoc</u> committee.
>
> The committee will have exactly seven members.
>
> There must be at least as many faculty members on the committee as there are students, though the number of students may be zero.
>
> P and Z cannot both serve on the committee.

If either T or U serves on the committee, the other must also serve on the committee.

If V serves on the committee, then W must serve on the committee.

With a set like this, you begin by summarizing the information using the notational devices suggested above:

Fac. > or = Stu.

P ≠ Z

T = U

V → W

1. Which of the following must be true of the committee?
    (A) It cannot include more students than administrators.
    (B) It cannot include both T and W.
    (C) It cannot include all three faculty members.
    (D) It must include T and U.
    (E) It must include V and W.

The correct answer is (A). Since P and Z cannot both be on the committee and since there must be at least as many faculty members on the committee as students, the maximum number of students who could serve on the committee is two. And the maximum number of faculty members who could serve is three. This means a minimum of at least two administrators is required. Thus, choice (A) correctly notes that it is impossible to have more students than administrators on the committee. As for choices (B) and (C), the committee of seven could include all three faculty memers and all four administrators with no students. As for choices (D) and (E), a committee might consist of three faculty members and two students plus either T and U or V and W. Thus, it is not the case that either T and U or V and W must be included.

2. If the committee is to include exactly two faculty members and exactly two students, which of the following must be true?
    (A) Z is not included on the committee.
    (B) W is included on the committee.
    (C) X is included on the committee.
    (D) Y is included on the committee.
    (E) S is included on the committee.

The correct answer is (B). If four members of the committee are drawn from faculty and student body, then three must be drawn from the administration. Since T and U cannot be split up, these three must include T and U and either V or W but not both V and W. Since including V requires including W, V cannot be included; therefore, W must be included. As for choice (A), it is possible to include Z by using faculty members S and R (instead of P). As for choices (C) and (D), either X or Y could serve (with Z) or both X and Y could serve together. Finally, as for choice (E), any two of the three faculty members could be included on the committee.

3. If both V and Z are chosen for the committee, then which of the following must be true?
    (A) Neither X nor W is chosen.
    (B) Neither X nor Y is chosen.
    (C) Both X and T are chosen.
    (D) Both Y and U are chosen.
    (E) V and either X or Y is chosen.

The correct answer is (B). If V is chosen, then W must also be chosen. And since Z is chosen, you need at least one faculty member. This gives a total of four people, and you need three more. If you choose another student, this requires another faculty member (for a total of six), but it isn't possible to choose only T or U. Therefore, you cannot include another student. So you must include the other faculty member and T and U. So the committee consists of V, Z, W, S, R, T, and U.

Sleepers

One of the most dangerous things that you can do is to try to guess where the LSAT will be going on the very next administration. As with clothes, Analytical Reasoning puzzles come into fashion and then go out of fashion. There are some that were very popular five years ago but that are not currently the rage. Should you ignore them? Only at your own peril. You never know when they will make a reappearance. These examples that follow fall into this group.

Greater Than, Less Than

Some problem sets rely heavily on the notions of "greater than" and "less than." In the problems, you will often be given a list of people, each of whom has more or less of a certain quality, and asked to determine how each one compares to the others in terms of that quality.

The following information is known about a group of five children:

> Alice is taller than Bob and heavier than Charles.
>
> Ed is heavier than both Diane and Alice and is shorter than Bob.
>
> Diane is not taller than Bob and is heavier than Charles.
>
> Charles is taller than Diane and heavier than Bob.

Use relational lines to organize clues for a "greater than/less than" set. In this case, set up two lines, one of which will represent height and the other weight:

Height ⟶   Weight ⟶

Enter each clue on the diagram. First, Alice is taller than Bob and heavier than Charles:

Height ———— B A ————→   Weight ———— C A ————→

Next, Ed is shorter than Bob and heavier than both Diane and Alice:

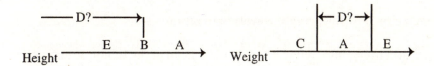

Height ———— E B A ————→   Weight ———— C A E ————→

Next, Diane is not taller than Bob and is heavier than Charles:

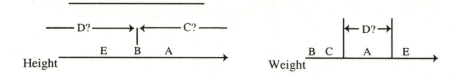

Finally, Charles is taller than Diane and heavier than Bob:

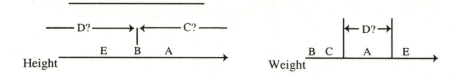

1. Which of the following CANNOT be true?

    (A) Ed is taller than Diane.

    (B) Charles is taller than Alice.

    (C) Bob is taller than Diane.

    (D) Bob weighs more than Diane.

    (E) Ed weighs more than Diane.

The correct answer is (D). Our diagrams show that choices (C) and (E) are true and that choices (A) and (B) might be true. Only choice (D) cannot be true.

2. Which of the following could be true?

    (A) The tallest child is also the heaviest child.

    (B) The shortest child is also the heaviest child.

    (C) The lightest child is also the tallest child.

    (D) Charles is both taller and heavier than Alice.

    (E) Bob is both shorter and lighter than Diane.

The correct answer is (B). You can read the information directly from the completed diagrams.

Seating Arrangements

In some problem sets, individuals are seated around a circular table.

> Eight people, F, G, H, J, K, L, M, and N, are seated in eight equally spaced chairs around a circular table.
>
>> K is sitting directly opposite M.
>>
>> M is sitting immediately to F's left.
>>
>> G is sitting next to L.
>>
>> H is sitting opposite J.

For a set based on a circular table, create a seating diagram.

The seats are not distinguishable (that is, there is not a head of the table), so enter the first clue:

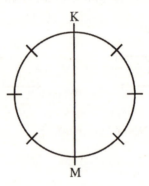

And the second clue:

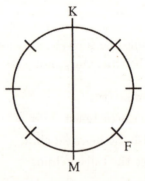

We can't enter the rest of the information without doing a little thinking. H and J are sitting opposite each other, which suggests there are the following possibilities:

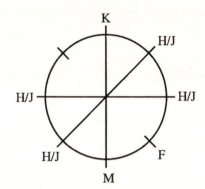

But if either H or J is seated next to F, it isn't possible to place L and G together. Therefore, either H or J is seated next to M:

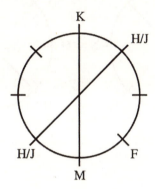

And finally:

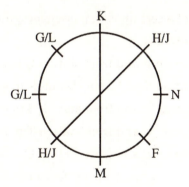

1. Which of the following must be true?

   (A) N is seated next to F.

   (B) N is seated next to H.

   (C) N is seated across from G.

   (D) F is seated across from L.

   (E) G is seated across from F.

The correct answer is (A). As the diagram shows, only choice (A) makes a necessarily true statement.

NOTE

How are "circle" problems different from "line" problems?
A circle seating arrangement is a linear ordering set with an extra feature. Not only are individuals seated next to each other, but they are also seated across from one another.

2. Only one seating arrangement is possible under which of the following conditions?

   (A) G is seated next to J.

   (B) H is seated next to N.

   (C) G is seated opposite N.

   (D) G is seated opposite F.

   (E) H is seated next to K.

The correct answer is (A). If G is next to J, L is next to K, and H is next to N. So only one order is possible.

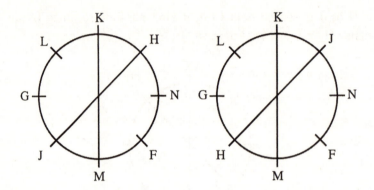

Networks

Some problem sets involve spatial or temporal connections between individuals.

   In the subway system of a certain city, passengers can go as follows:

     From station P to station Q.

     From station Q to station R and from station Q to station S.

     From station R to station S and from station R to station T.

     From station S to station U and from station S to station P.

     From station T to station U and from station T to station R.

     From station U to station P and from station U to station S.

     A passenger at one station can transfer for another station.

The correct approach to any network problem is to sketch the network.

From station P to station Q.

$$P \longrightarrow Q$$

From station Q to station R and from station Q to station S.

$$P \longrightarrow Q \begin{smallmatrix} \nearrow R \\ \searrow S \end{smallmatrix}$$

From station R to station S and from station R to station T.

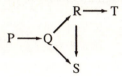

From station S to station U and from station S to station P.

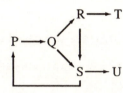

From station T to station U and from station T to station R.

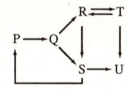

From station U to station P and from station U to station S.

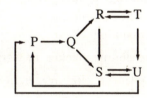

ALERT!

Diagram-mania.
Diagrams are like tools. In some situations, a wrench is the right tool; in other situations, the hammer is the right tool. And in some situations, no tool is needed. While diagrams are useful tools, they cannot substitute for careful reading and hard thinking. Do not succumb to diagram-mania.

1. A passenger at station T who wishes to travel to station Q must pass through a minimum of how many other stations before finally arriving at Q?

   (A) 1
   (B) 2
   (C) 3
   (D) 4
   (E) 5

The correct answer is (B). Consult the network diagram. The shortest route is U to P and then on to Q.

2. A passenger at station U who wishes to travel through the system and return to station U before passing through any other subway station twice can choose from how many different routes?

    (A) 2

    (B) 3

    (C) 4

    (D) 5

    (E) 6

The correct answer is (C). Simply trace the possibilities with your finger:

> U to P to Q to S to U
>
> U to P to Q to R to S to U
>
> U to P to Q to R to T to U
>
> U to S to P to Q to R to T to U

Matrix Problems

Sometimes a problem will refer to individuals who have or lack certain characteristics, and some questions may ask which characteristics are in turn shared by which individuals.

> Five people, George, Howard, Ingrid, Jean, and Kathy, work in a factory. On any given shift, a person can be assigned to one of five jobs: mechanic, truck driver, packer, weigher, or dispatcher.
>
> > George can function as mechanic, packer, or weigher.
> >
> > Howard can function as either packer or weigher.
> >
> > Ingrid can function as mechanic, truck driver, or dispatcher.
> >
> > Jean can function as truck driver or dispatcher.
> >
> > Kathy can function as truck driver or weigher.
> >
> > The five workers can fill only these jobs, and only these five workers can fill these jobs.

For a problem set in which individuals do or do not share certain characteristics (and those characteristics are or are not shared by the individuals), use a matrix or table.

	M	TD	P	W	D
G					
H					
I					
J					
K					

George can function as mechanic, packer, or weigher.

	M	TD	P	W	D
G	✓		✓	✓	
H					
I					
J					
K					

Howard can function as either packer or weigher.

	M	TD	P	W	D
G	✓		✓	✓	
H			✓	✓	
I					
J					
K					

Ingrid can function as mechanic, truck driver, or dispatcher.

ALERT!

Black holes. Scientists believe that there may be black holes in the universe, places where giant stars have collapsed and the gravitational pull is so great that light cannot escape and time is completely warped. Some Analytical Reasoning games are black holes. They will suck you in, completely warp your sense of time, and you will never again see the light of day. Do not get overly committed to a particular game.

	M	TD	P	W	D
G	✓		✓	✓	
H			✓	✓	
I	✓	✓			✓
J					
K					

Jean can function as truck driver or dispatcher.

	M	TD	P	W	D
G	✓		✓	✓	
H			✓	✓	
I	✓	✓			✓
J		✓			✓
K					

Kathy can function as truck driver or weigher.

	M	TD	P	W	D
G	✓		✓	✓	
H			✓	✓	
I	✓	✓			✓
J		✓			✓
K		✓		✓	

1. If Jean is NOT assigned to function as dispatcher, all of the following must be true EXCEPT

   (A) George is the mechanic.

   (B) Howard is the dispatcher.

   (C) the truck driver is Jean.

   (D) the packer is Howard.

   (E) the weigher is Kathy.

The correct answer is (B). Ingrid, not Howard, would be the dispatcher. Just enter the new information into the table, and use the grid to draw further conclusions.

2. If George is assigned as mechanic, which of the following must be true?

(A) Howard is assigned as packer.

(B) Kathy is assigned as weigher.

(C) Ingrid is assigned as truck driver.

(D) Jean is assigned as dispatcher.

(E) Howard is assigned as weigher.

The correct answer is (A). If George is assigned as mechanic, then he is not available to be packer or weigher. There is only one other person who can be the packer, and that is Howard.

Family Relationships

Barbara, an only child, is married, and she and her husband have two children, Ned and Sally.

> Ned is Paula's nephew by blood and Victor's grandson.
>
> Victor and his wife had only two children, Frank and his sister, plus four grandchildren, two boys and two girls.
>
> Wilma is Sally's grandmother.

Use the information to create a family tree.

Barbara, an only child, is married, and she and her husband have two children, Ned and Sally:

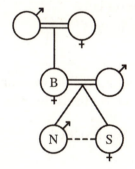

Ned is Paula's nephew by blood and Victor's grandson.

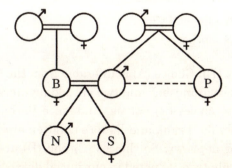

(Since Barbara is an only child, an aunt could be related by blood only by being Ned's father's sister. We don't know, however, whether Victor is Ned's paternal or maternal grandfather.)

Victor and his wife had only two children, Frank and his sister, plus four grandchildren, two boys and two girls.

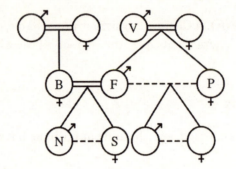

(Since Victor had two children, he could not have been Barbara's father because Barbara is an only child. So in order to be Ned's grandfather, Victor must be Ned's father's father.) It is not possible to enter the last piece of information for it is not clear whether Wilma is Barbara's mother or the mother of Frank and Paula.

1. All of the following must be true EXCEPT
    (A) Wilma is Victor's wife.
    (B) Victor is Sally's grandfather.
    (C) Victor is Barbara's father-in-law.
    (D) Paula is Barbara's sister-in-law.
    (E) Frank is Sally's father.

The correct answer is (A). As we just noted, we cannot definitely place Wilma in the family tree. The diagram, however, confirms that the other statements are true.

2. All of the following must be true EXCEPT
    (A) Sally is Ned's sister.
    (B) Ned has exactly two cousins.
    (C) Paula has one son and one daughter.
    (D) Barbara has only one nephew.
    (E) Wilma is Frank's mother.

The correct answer is (E). Choice (A) is inferable from the first bit of information. Then, since Victor has two grandsons and two granddaughters, Paula must have one son and one daughter, so choice (B) is true. And since Barbara has no siblings and Frank's only sibling is Paula, Frank and Paula's children are Ned's only cousins and Barbara's only nieces or nephews. So choices (C) and (D) are also true. Choice (E), however, is not necessarily true, as noted in our initial discussion of the set.

WHAT SMART TEST-TAKERS KNOW

Accept the situation at face value.

Most of the situations described by the initial conditions are common ones with which you should be familiar.

> Six people, J, K, L, M, N, and O, are standing in a single file line at a movie theater.

> Seven corporations, H, I, J, K, L, M, and N, have offices on four floors in the same building.

> Eight office workers, M, N, O, P, Q, R, S, and T, are deciding in which of three restaurants—X, Y, or Z—to eat lunch.

One reason for using familiar situations is that there is less potential for misunderstanding because there is much information implicit in a situation such as a single-file line: Each person is a separate person, each letter designates a different individual, one individual is immediately ahead of or behind another individual, and so on. Since the situations are selected for this feature, you should be careful not to "fight" with the setup. For example, there is no point in arguing that J could be standing on L's shoulders. The test-writers will add an explicit clarifying note if there is any danger of a legitimate misunderstanding, e.g., each corporation has its own office.

Read the clues carefully.

Although you must accept the general situation with a fairly uncritical reading, you must be very careful in reading the particular information given about the individuals. Pay particular attention to words such as the following:

> *only, exactly, never, always, must be/can be/cannot be, some, all, no, none, entire, each, every, except, but, unless, if, more/less, before/after, immediately (before, after, etc.), possible/impossible, different/same, at least, at most.*

Be careful of asymmetrical clues.

You should be especially careful not to misinterpret conditions that are asymmetrical, e.g., if P goes on the trip, Q must also go; or S cannot eat at X restaurant unless T also eats there. In both of these examples, the dependency operates in only one direction. In the first, P depends on Q but not vice versa (Q can go on the trip without P). Similarly, in the second, S depends on T but not vice versa (S cannot eat at X restaurant without T, but T can eat there without S).

The situation will be fluid.

Often, it will be possible to draw some further inference from the initial conditions, but rarely will it be possible to determine the entire situation using just the information in the initial conditions. For example, a problem set might tell you that X must be standing third in line and that Z is two positions behind X. From this, you can deduce that Z is standing fifth in line. But the initial conditions may not fix the position of any other person in the line.

The open-ended nature of Analytical Reasoning problems will probably be very annoying. Because you will not be able to deduce a definite sequence or some similar conclusions, you will feel that you have overlooked something in the initial conditions. You haven't. The fluidity of the situation is part of the test design.

It's all a matter of logic.

Since the problem sets in this section are logical puzzles, the correct answers are determined by logical inference. And the logical status of a statement must fall into one of three categories:

1 The statement is logically deducible from the information given.

2 The statement is logically inconsistent with (contradicts) the information given.

3 The statement is neither logically deducible from the information given nor logically inconsistent with it.

The questions that can be asked fall into one of the following categories:

Which of the following must be true?

All of the following must be true EXCEPT

Which of the following could be true?

Which of the following CANNOT be true?

The logical status of each choice dictates whether it is correct or incorrect:

- The correct answer to a question asking "Which must be true?" is a statement that is logically deducible from the information given.

- The wrong answers to such a question can be statements that are inconsistent with the given information or statements that are not deducible from the information given.

- The correct answer to a question asking "All must be true EXCEPT" is either a statement that is logically inconsistent with the information given or a statement that is not deducible from the information given.

- The wrong answers to this type of question are statements that can be logically deduced from the information given.

- The correct answer to a question asking "Which can be true?" is a statement that is neither deducible from nor inconsistent with the information given.

- The correct answer to a question asking "All can be true EXCEPT" is a statement that is logically inconsistent with the information given.

Although wording may differ from problem set to problem set, every question will fall into one of these four categories. For example, a question that asks this belongs in the first category:

> If the traveler visits Paris on Wednesday, on which day must she visit Rome?

It will be possible to deduce from the information given on which day she must visit Rome. But a question that asks this belongs in the fourth category:

> If the traveler visits Paris on Wednesday, then she could visit all of the following cities on Friday EXCEPT

The correct answer will generate a logical contradiction with the given information: It will be logically impossible to visit that city on Friday. And a question that asks this belongs in the third category:

> Which of the following is a complete and accurate listing of the cities that the traveler could visit on Thursday?

The correct choice will enumerate all of the logical possibilities.

WHAT THE SMARTEST TEST-TAKERS KNOW

Breaking News on "Puzzles"

As a rule, it is probably not a good idea to try to work out all of the possibilities for an Analytical Reasoning set in order to create a master list to answer questions—for two reasons.

One, you're likely to find that there are simply too many possibilities to keep track of. Consider a problem set that requires you to put individuals into an order:

> Seven people—J, K, L, M, N, O, and P—are each going to do a solo act. The acts will follow one behind the other, and each person will perform exactly once.

As you can guess, there will probably be some additional restrictions on the order, and the questions will ask about permissible or impermissible sequences.

Now it would be possible to take the time to sketch all of the possibilities, but there are a lot of them. How many? 7 x 6 x 5 x 4 x 3 x 2 x 1=5,040—too many given the time limit.

In addition, most of the possible sequences will not be relevant to the questions asked. Only a handful will actually, play a role in problem solving.

So, as a rule, it's better to let the question stems be your guide. They will provide information to be used for answering questions about particular cases and guide you to the relevant possibilities.

As with every rule, however, there is an exception. And this exception has appeared on some recent test forms. If a sequencing problem has six or fewer constants to fill six or fewer positions, it may be more efficient to work out all possibilities before trying the questions.

The basis for this recommendation is mathematical and is illustrated by the following:

> Five dogs—Farley, Gunther, Hans, Jerry, and Kato—will appear in a dog show. During the show, each dog will be shown exactly once, one dog at a time.

In this situation, you have 5 x 4 x 3 x 2 x 1 or 120 possibilities. That is still too many to work out comfortably within the time given; but if we add another condition:

> Farley will be shown fourth.

Then we're left with only 24 possibilities, and those can be written out as follows:

	1st	2nd	3rd	4th	5th
1	G	H	J	F	K
2	G	H	K	F	J
3	G	J	H	F	K
4	G	K	H	F	J
5	G	J	K	F	H
6	G	K	J	F	H
7	H	G	J	F	K
8	H	G	K	F	J
9	J	G	H	F	K
10	K	G	H	F	J
11	J	G	K	F	H
12	K	G	J	F	H
13	H	J	G	F	K
14	H	K	G	F	J
15	J	H	G	F	K
16	K	H	G	F	J
17	J	K	G	F	H
18	K	J	G	F	H
19	H	J	K	F	G
20	H	K	J	F	G
21	J	H	K	F	G
22	K	H	J	F	G
23	J	K	H	F	G
24	K	J	H	F	G

You should be able to see how this table systematically works out all of the variations on the theme, and it does contain the answer to every possible question that could be asked about the dog show.

Of course, even 24 possibilities is a lot, but investing 3 to 4 minutes in creating the table is worthwhile because the questions can be answered very quickly:

> If Gunter is shown third, which of the following is a complete and accurate list of the positions in which Jerry could be shown if Jerry is shown after Kato?
> **(A)** 2
> **(B)** 2,3
> **(C)** 2,5
> **(D)** 2,6
> **(E)** 2,3,6

The correct answer is (D), as lines 14, 16, and 18 show.

And the number of possibilities is likely to be even smaller because there will probably be additional conditions such as "Hans cannot be shown first."

In light of this development, you might consider using the following strategy:

STEP ONE: Look at all four or five sets to determine whether there is a simple linear sequencing problem.

STEP TWO: If there is a simple linear sequencing set, ask:

> Does it have six or fewer positions?
> Does it have six or fewer individuals?
> Does each individual occupy exactly one position?

If the answers to these questions are "yes," then it is a simple sequencing set:

STEP THREE: Work out all of the possibilities before trying the questions.

Here's how the strategy would work:

Questions 1–4

Six athletes—two from Joplin High School, two from Kline High School, and two from Lorentz High School—run a series of races in which they finish first through last with no ties.

> No runner finishes either directly in front of or directly behind the other runner from the same high school.
> A runner from Joplin always finishes either first or second.
> Neither of the runners from Kline ever finishes last.
> Neither of the runners from Lorentz ever finishes third.

1. If the second and fourth place finishers in a race are from the same high school, then which of the following statements must be true?

    (A) A runner from Lorentz finishes first.

    (B) A runner from Joplin finishes second.

    (C) A runner from Lorentz finishes fourth.

    (D) A runner from Kline finishes fifth.

    (E) A runner from Joplin finishes sixth.

2. Both runners from the same high school CANNOT finish

    (A) first and third.

    (B) first and fourth.

    (C) second and fourth.

    (D) second and sixth.

    (E) third and sixth.

3. If a runner from Joplin finishes third, which of the following must be true?

    (A) A runner from Joplin finishes first.

    (B) A runner from Lorentz finishes second.

    (C) A runner from Kline finishes fourth.

    (D) A runner from Lorentz finishes fifth.

    (E) A runner from Kline finishes sixth.

4. Which of the following statements must be false?

    (A) A runner from Lorentz finishes first.

    (B) A runner from Kline finishes first.

    (C) A runner from Joplin finishes second.

    (D) A runner from Kline finishes third.

    (E) A runner from Lorentz finishes fifth.

Here we have six runners, six positions, and no ties. So let's try systematically working out all of the possibilities:

A runner from Joplin always finishes first or second, and the two Joplin runners do not finish consecutively:

1st	2nd	3rd	4th	5th	6th
J		J			
J			J		
J				J	
J					J
	J		J		
	J			J	
	J				J

Neither runner from Kline finishes last, and neither runner from Lorentz finishes third:

1st	2nd	3rd	4th	5th	6th
J		J			-K
J		-L	J		-K
J		-L		J	-K
J		-L			J
	J	-L	J		-K
	J	-L		J	-K
	J	-L			J

So:

1st	2nd	3rd	4th	5th	6th
J		J			L
J	L	K	J		L
J		K		J	L
J		K			J
	J	K	J		L
	J	K		J	L
	J	K			J

Further:

1st	2nd	3rd	4th	5th	6th
J	K	J	L	K	L
J	L	K	J	K	L
J		K		J	L*
J	L	K	L	K	J
L	J	K	J	K	L
K	J	K	L	J	L
L	J	K	L	K	J

*Not possible.

Now we can turn to the answers to the questions.

1. **The correct answer is (D).** Lines 4 and 5 show orders in which runners from the same high school finish second and fourth, and in both a K appears in position 5.

2. **The correct answer is (E).** As the table shows, there is no sequence in which the third and sixth positions have the same designation.

3. **The correct answer is (A).** This is the sequence described by line 1, and position 1 is designated J.

4. **The correct answer is (E).** As the diagram shows, position 5 cannot be filled by an L.

EXERCISES: ANALYTICAL REASONING

Exercise 1

20 Questions • 30 Minutes

Directions: Each group of questions is based on a set of propositions or conditions. Drawing a rough picture or diagram may help in answering some of the questions. Choose the best answer for each question and circle the letter of your choice.

Questions 1–7

A candidate for public office plans to visit each of six cities—J, K, L, M, N, and O—exactly once during her campaign. Her aides are setting up the candidate's schedule according to the following restrictions:

The candidate can visit M only after she has visited both L and N.

The candidate cannot visit N before J.

The second city visited by the candidate must be K.

1. Which of the following could be the order in which the candidate visits the six cities?
   (A) J, K, N, L, O, M
   (B) K, J, L, N, M, O
   (C) O, K, M, L, J, N
   (D) M, K, N, J, L, O
   (E) J, K, L, M, N, O

2. Which of the following must be true of the candidate's campaign schedule?
   (A) She visits J before L.
   (B) She visits K before M.
   (C) She visits K before J.
   (D) She visits M before J.
   (E) She visits N before L.

3. If the candidate visits O first, which of the following is a complete and accurate listing of the cities that she could visit third?
   (A) J
   (B) L
   (C) J, L
   (D) J, M
   (E) M, L

4. If the candidate visits J immediately after O and immediately before N, then she must visit L
   (A) first.
   (B) third.
   (C) fourth.
   (D) fifth.
   (E) sixth.

5. Which of the following could be true of the candidate's schedule?
   (A) She visits J first.
   (B) She visits K first.
   (C) She visits L sixth.
   (D) She visits M fourth.
   (E) She visits N sixth.

6. The candidate could visit any of the following immediately after K EXCEPT

(A) J.

(B) L.

(C) M.

(D) N.

(E) O.

7. If the candidate visits O last, which of the following could be the first and third cities on her schedule, respectively?

(A) J and L

(B) J and O

(C) L and N

(D) L and O

(E) N and J

Questions 8–13

At a certain restaurant, above the kitchen door there are four small lights, arranged side by side, and numbered consecutively, left to right, from one to four. The lights are used to signal waiters when orders are ready. On a certain shift, there are exactly five waiters—David, Ed, Flint, Guy, and Hank.

To signal David, all four lights are illuminated.

To signal Ed, only lights one and two are illuminated.

To signal Flint, only light one is illuminated.

To signal Guy, only lights two, three, and four are illuminated.

To signal Hank, only lights three and four are illuminated.

8. If lights two and three are both off, then the waiter signaled is

(A) David.

(B) Ed.

(C) Flint.

(D) Guy.

(E) Hank.

9. If lights three and four are illuminated, then which of the following is a complete and accurate listing of the waiters whose signals might be displayed?

(A) David

(B) Guy

(C) David and Guy

(D) Guy and Hank

(E) David, Guy, and Hank

10. If light one is not illuminated, then which of the following is a complete and accurate listing of the waiters whose signals might be displayed?

(A) Ed

(B) Guy

(C) Hank

(D) Guy and Hank

(E) Hank, Guy, and Ed

11. If light three is on and light two is off, then the waiter signaled is

(A) David.

(B) Ed.

(C) Flint.

(D) Guy.

(E) Hank.

12. If one of the five waiters is being signaled, the lights in which of the following pairs could NOT both be off?

(A) One and two

(B) One and three

(C) Two and three

(D) Two and four

(E) Three and four

13. If light four is on, then which of the following must be true?

(A) Light one is on.

(B) Light two is not on.

(C) If light one is on, David is signaled.

(D) If light two is not on, Flint is signaled.

(E) If light three is not on, Ed is signaled.

Questions 14–20

A lawyer must schedule appointments with eight clients—F, G, H, I, J, K, L, and M—during one week, Monday through Friday. She must schedule two appointments for Monday, Tuesday, and Wednesday and one each for Thursday and Friday.

She must see H on Thursday.

She must see G on a day before the day on which she sees I.

She must see J on a day before the day on which she sees L.

She must see F on a day before the day on which she sees L.

She must see K and F on the same day.

14. Which of the following is an acceptable schedule for the week's appointments?

	Mon.	Tues.	Wed.	Thurs.	Fri.
(A)	G,M	I,L	K,F	H	J
(B)	G,M	I,J	K,F	H	L
(C)	G,I	M,L	J	H	K,F
(D)	L,G	I,J	K,M	H	F
(E)	G,L	M,K	F	H,J	I

15. Which of the following CANNOT be true?

(A) She sees M on Monday.

(B) She sees K on Tuesday.

(C) She sees L on Tuesday.

(D) She sees I on Wednesday.

(E) She sees M on Friday.

16. Which of the following is a complete and accurate listing of the clients the lawyer could see on Friday?

(A) I, J

(B) I, M

(C) L, M

(D) I, L, M

(E) M, L, G

17. If the lawyer sees I on Tuesday, then which of the following must be true?

(A) She sees J on Monday.

(B) She sees M on Tuesday.

(C) She sees K on Tuesday.

(D) She sees M on Friday.

(E) She sees L on Friday.

18. If the lawyer sees K on Wednesday, all of the following must be true EXCEPT

(A) she sees I on Tuesday.

(B) she sees L on Friday.

(C) she sees M on Monday.

(D) she sees G on Monday.

(E) she sees F on Wednesday.

19. If the lawyer sees I and L on the same day, which of the following is a complete and accurate listing of the days on which she could see them?

(A) Monday

(B) Tuesday

(C) Wednesday

(D) Monday and Wednesday

(E) Tuesday and Wednesday

20. Which of the following, if true, provides sufficient additional information to determine on which day each client will have his appointment?

(A) M's appointment is scheduled for Monday.

(B) G's appointment is scheduled for Monday.

(C) G's appointment is scheduled for Tuesday.

(D) K's appointment is two days before G's.

(E) G's appointment is two days before I's.

Exercise 2

13 Questions • 20 Minutes

> **Directions:** Each group of questions is based on a set of propositions or conditions. Drawing a rough picture or diagram may help in answering some of the questions. Choose the best answer for each question and circle the letter of your choice.

Questions 1–7

A student planning his curriculum for the upcoming semester must enroll in three courses. The available courses fall into one of five general areas: math, English, social studies, science, and fine arts.

The student must take courses from at least two different areas.

If he takes a fine arts course, he cannot take an English course.

If he takes a science course, he must take a math course; and if he takes a math course, he must take a science course.

He can take a social studies course only if he takes a fine arts course.

1. Which of the following is an acceptable schedule of courses?
   - **(A)** One science course, one English course, and one fine arts course
   - **(B)** One math course, one science course, and one social studies course
   - **(C)** One math course, one social studies course, and one fine arts course
   - **(D)** One English course, one social studies course, and one fine arts course
   - **(E)** One math course, one science course, and one fine arts course

2. Which of the following is NOT an acceptable schedule?
   - **(A)** Two math courses and one science course
   - **(B)** Two science courses and one math course
   - **(C)** Two fine arts courses and one math course
   - **(D)** Two social studies courses and one fine arts course
   - **(E)** One social studies course and two fine arts courses

3. Which of the following courses, when taken with one course in social studies, is an acceptable schedule?
   - **(A)** One course in math and one in science
   - **(B)** One course in fine arts and one course in English
   - **(C)** Two courses in fine arts
   - **(D)** Two courses in math
   - **(E)** Two courses in English

4. If the student wishes to take a course in math and a course in English, then he must select his third course in the area of
   - **(A)** English.
   - **(B)** fine arts.
   - **(C)** math.
   - **(D)** science.
   - **(E)** social studies.

5. Which of the following pairs of courses CANNOT be combined in an acceptable schedule?

   (A) A course in math and a course in fine arts

   (B) A course in science and a course in fine arts

   (C) A course in math and a course in English

   (D) A course in social studies and a course in science

   (E) A course in science and a course in English

6. If the student wishes to take a course in science, then which of the following pairs of courses would complete an acceptable schedule?

   (A) Two math courses

   (B) Two science courses

   (C) Two English courses

   (D) One science course and one English course

   (E) One math course and one social studies course

7. An acceptable schedule CANNOT include two courses in

   (A) English.

   (B) fine arts.

   (C) math.

   (D) science.

   (E) social studies.

Questions 8–13

A certain musical scale consists of exactly six notes: F, G, H, I, J, and K. The notes are arranged from lowest (the first note of the scale) to highest (the sixth note of the scale). Each note appears once and only once in the scale, and the intervals between the notes are all equal.

   J is lower than K.

   G is higher than F.

   I is somewhere between F and G.

   H is the highest note of the scale.

8. Which of the following CANNOT be true of the scale?

   (A) G is the second note.

   (B) G is the third note.

   (C) I is the second note.

   (D) I is the third note.

   (E) I is the fourth note.

9. If J is the fourth note of the scale, which of the following must be true?

   (A) F is the third note.

   (B) F is the fifth note.

   (C) I is the fourth note.

   (D) I is the second note.

   (E) G is the first note.

10. If exactly two notes separate F and I, then which of the following must be true?

   (A) F is the lowest note.

   (B) K is the fifth note.

   (C) K is higher than I.

   (D) J is somewhere between G and I.

   (E) K and J are separated by exactly one note.

11. If J is the second note, then which of the following is a complete and accurate listing of the notes that G and I, respectively, could be?

    (A) 4 and 3
    (B) 5 and 3
    (C) 5 and 4
    (D) 5 and 3 or 4 and 5
    (E) 4 and 3, 5 and 3, or 5 and 4

12. If F and I are separated by exactly one note, which of the following must be true?

    (A) G is note 4.
    (B) K is note 5.
    (C) J is lower than I.
    (D) I is lower than K.
    (E) J is between F and I.

13. If J is lower than F, then the total number of different possible orderings of the six notes, from lowest to highest, is

    (A) 1
    (B) 2
    (C) 3
    (D) 4
    (E) 5

EXERCISE 1: ANSWER KEY AND EXPLANATIONS

1.	A	5.	A	9.	E	13.	C	17.	E
2.	B	6.	C	10.	D	14.	B	18.	C
3.	C	7.	A	11.	E	15.	C	19.	C
4.	A	8.	C	12.	B	16.	D	20.	D

Questions 1–7

Here we have a common ordering set. Begin by summarizing the information:

$$(L + N) < M$$
$$J < N$$
$$K = 2$$

> **Note:** Since the candidate cannot visit two cities simultaneously, the condition "The candidate cannot visit N before J" is equivalent to "She must visit J before N."

1. **The correct answer is (A).** This question supplies no additional information, so just take each condition and apply it to the answer choices, eliminating those that fail to comply with any condition. The first condition requires that L and N come before M. Using this condition, we eliminate choices (C) and (E). The second condition states that J must come before N, and we eliminate choice (D). The third condition requires that K be the second city, so we eliminate choice (B). This leaves us with choice (A); and choice (A), which respects all three conditions, is a possible order.

2. **The correct answer is (B)**. M must be visited after both L and N, so given that K is visited second, M could not possibly be visited earlier than fourth, which means that K comes before M. So choice (B) is correct. In fact, given that J comes before N, and N comes before M, M must also come later than J. So M cannot be visited until L, N, J, and K have been visited, which means M is either fifth or sixth. As just noted, J must come before M, so choice (D) is necessarily false. The other three responses describe possible schedules only,

1	2	3	4	5	6
J	K	N	L	M	O

which shows that choices (A), (C), and (E) are possible. But

1	2	3	4	5	6
O	K	L	J	N	M

shows that choices (A), (C), and (E) are not necessarily true.

3. **The correct answer is (C).** Begin by entering the additional information on a diagram:

1	2	3	4	5	6
O	K				

Next, we reason that J, N, and L must all come before M, which means that M comes last:

1	2	3	4	5	6
O	K	J	N	L	M
O	K	J	L	N	M
O	K	L	J	N	M

So either J or L could be third.

4. **The correct answer is (A).** This question stipulates an order for three of the cities: O, J, and N. Given that J and N must come before M, this means that the order must be

1	2	3	4	5	6
	K	O	J	N	M

That means that L must be visited first:

1	2	3	4	5	6
L	K	O	J	N	M

5. **The correct answer is (A).** This question is a good occasion to talk about test-taking strategy. A question of this form has this peculiarity: A choice like choice (A) may not contradict any single initial condition and may still be wrong because of the way the initial conditions work together. The only way to exclude this possibility is to devise a complete order, part of which is the segment you want to test—a time-consuming process. What should you do?

The solution to the dilemma is this: Make a first run through the choices, testing them by each single initial statement. If you can eliminate all but one, then you have your correct answer. If more than one choice remains, then the key to the question is some interaction among the initial conditions, e.g., a further inference that you have overlooked. Then, and only then, try working up an entire order to test the remaining choices.

Here we are fortunate because we can find the correct choice quickly:

(A) Doesn't contradict any single condition, so go to the next choice.

(B) No. (K must be second.)

(C) No. (L must come before M.)

(D) No. (M must come after J, L, and N and therefore K as well. So M cannot be visited earlier than fifth.)

(E) No. (N must come before M, so N cannot be last.)

Thus, choice (A) must be the correct choice, so we don't have to try to construct the entire order using choice (A).

Just for reasons of completeness of explanation, however, here is a schedule in which J is the first city:

1	2	3	4	5	6
J	K	L	N	M	O

6. **The correct answer is (C).** As just noted, M cannot be earlier than fifth, so M could not immediately follow K. That the others could follow K is shown by the following schedules:

	1	2	3	4	5	6
(A)	O	L	J	J	N	M
(B)	J	K	L	N	M	O
(D)	J	K	N	L	M	O
(E)	J	K	O	N	L	M

7. **The correct answer is (A).** Start by entering the additional information on a diagram:

1	2	3	4	5	6
	K				O

Next, we have already determined that M cannot be earlier than fifth:

1	2	3	4	5	6
J	K	N	L	M	O
J	K	L	N	M	O
L	K	J	N	M	O

(A) describes the second of these possibilities. The other choices do not describe one of the three possible schedules.

Questions 8–13

This is a "characteristics" set; each waiter has a characteristic signal. Summarize the information using a table:

Lights	1	2	3	4
David	ON	ON	ON	ON
Ed	ON	ON		
Flint	ON			
Guy		ON	ON	ON
Hank			ON	ON

Whatever further conclusions you might need are already implicitly contained in the table, so go directly to the questions.

8. **The correct answer is (C).** Flint is the only waiter whose signal lights two and three are both off. For every other waiter, either two or three or both are on.

9. **The correct answer is (E).** As the table shows, if lights three and four are both on, the signal might be for David (all four on), Guy (two, three, and four on), or Hank (three and four on).

10. **The correct answer is (D).** As the table shows, if light one is off, then the signal might be for either Guy or Hank. It could not be for David, Ed, or Flint, since their signals include an illuminated light one.

11. **The correct answer is (E).** As the table shows, there are three waiters whose signals include light three: David, Guy, and Hank. For David and Guy, however, light two must be on; for Guy, it must be off. Therefore, if light three is on and light two is off, then Guy is the waiter signaled.

12. **The correct answer is (B).** Consult the table:

    (A) Lights one and two will be off if Hank is signaled.

    (B) There is no signal for which both one and three are off.

(C) Lights two and three will be off if Flint is signaled.

(D) Lights two and four will be off if Flint is signaled.

(E) Lights three and four will be off if either Ed or Flint is signaled.

13. **The correct answer is (C).** As the table clearly shows, neither choice (A) nor choice (B) is necessarily true. Choice (C), however, is necessarily true, as the table shows. If four is on, then the signal might be for David, Guy, or Hank; but if one is also on, then the signal can only be for David. As for choice (D), if four is on and two is not, then it is Hank who is signaled—not Flint. As for choice (E), none of the five signals includes light four on and light three off.

Questions 14–20

This is a distributed order set, as opposed to a linear ordering set. Here, more than one individual can be placed in a given position (more than one appointment can be scheduled for certain days).

Start by summarizing the information:

$$H = Th.$$
$$G < I$$
$$(J + F) < L$$
$$K = F$$

You might notice that there is one further conclusion to be drawn. Since K and F must be scheduled for the same day and since F must come before L, we can infer that K also comes before L. Aside from that, there do not appear to be any further important inferences to be drawn, so we go to the questions.

14. **The correct answer is (B).** Since the question supplies no additional information, we just apply each condition to the answer choices, eliminating those that fail to respect one or more conditions.

The first condition states that there are two appointments for Monday, Tuesday, and Wednesday and one appointment on the other two days. On this basis, we eliminate choices (C) and (E) because it is not possible to schedule two appointments on Thursday or Friday. The second condition states that H must be seen on Thursday, and our remaining choices reflect that. Then, the next condition states that G must come on a day before that on which I has his appointment, and our remaining choices respect this condition. Next, the fourth condition states that J and F must both come before L, so we eliminate choices (A) and (D). This leaves us with choice (B) as the correct choice, and you might want quickly to confirm that choice (B) does respect that final condition: K and F are both scheduled for the same day.

15. **The correct answer is (C).** This question allows us to talk about strategy. One way of proving that a particular partial order is possible is to construct an example of a permissible order using that part. Thus, the following example proves that choice (A) is a possible order (and therefore not the correct answer to this question):

M	TU	W	TH	F
M	K	L	H	I
J	F	G		

The difficulty with this approach is that constructing an example for each choice is time-consuming. Instead of trying to construct an entire order for each choice, a better strategy is to look for an answer choice that is not possible for a specific reason, e.g., because X cannot follow Y or because Z must come before W. Here is how this strategy would apply to this question.

(A) is not likely to be correct because M is not under any specific restriction; thus, M could go almost anywhere. As for choice (B), though K is under a certain restriction, the import of that restriction is that K come earlier in the week—as choice (B) suggests. So choice (B) is probably not the correct choice. Now look at choice (C). L is under the restriction that he be scheduled later than both J and F and (as we learned above) later than K as well. This "pushes" L toward the latter part of the week. This choice, however, has L early in the week. So this choice merits some study.

The way to determine whether it is possible for L to have an appointment on Tuesday is to assume that he can and see whether that assumption is consistent with the initial conditions. If L is scheduled for Tuesday, then both J and F must be scheduled for Monday. But that can't be, as K would also have to be scheduled for Monday. This demonstrates that choice (C) cannot be true.

As for choices (D) and (E), you can construct schedules that show that they are all possible.

16. **The correct answer is (D).** One way of attacking this question would be to try to construct all of the possibilities for Friday. For example, you would reason that K cannot be seen on Friday because K must be seen on the same day as F (and only one appointment is available on Friday). The difficulty with this "direct" approach is that you must do a lot of "grinding." Here it is better to use an "indirect" approach. Look at the choices.

Since one of the choices is correct, the test writer has already done the "grinding" to find all of the possibilities for Friday. You just need to find the one choice that contains all the ones that are workable schedules.

Eliminate choice (A) because J cannot be seen on Friday. As for choice (B), I and M could be seen on Friday, because they are very "flexible." (M is under no restriction, and I is under a restriction that forces him to a day later in the week.) As for choice (C), L is under a restriction, but that restriction pushes L to a later day, so L too seems a possibility for Friday. As for choice (D), this contains I, L, and M, so it begins to look like a correct choice. As for choice (E), G cannot be scheduled for Friday, because G comes before I.

At this point, you must make a decision. Perhaps intuition tells you that choice (D) is the correct choice. You can either mark choice (D) as correct and move on to another item, or you can work out examples that prove that I, L, and M can be scheduled for Friday. Which you choose to do will depend on how much time you have left.

17. **The correct answer is (E).** Start by entering the additional information on a diagram:

M	TU	W	TH	F
	I		H	

G must come before I:

M	TU	W	TH	F
G	I		H	

K and F must be scheduled for the same day, which must now be Wednesday:

M	TU	W	TH	F
G	I	K,F	H	

L must be later in the week than F, however:

M	TU	W	TH	F
G	I	K,F	H	L

So J and M must have appointments on Monday and Tuesday, though not necessarily in that order. The diagram shows that choice (E) is necessarily true; that choices (A) and (B) are possibly, though not necessarily true; and that choices (C) and (D) are false.

18. **The correct answer is (C).** Enter the additional information on a diagram:

M	TU	W	TH	F
		K	H	

This means that F is also scheduled for Wednesday:

M	TU	W	TH	F
		K,F	H	

L must be seen sometime after F:

M	TU	W	TH	F
		K,F	H	L

Then, G must be seen before I:

M	TU	W	TH	F
G	I	K,F	H	L

M and J will be seen on Monday and Tuesday, though not necessarily in that order:

M	TU	W	TH	F
G,J	I,M	K,F	H	L	OR
G,M	I,J	K,F	H	L

19. **The correct answer is (C).** There are two ways of approaching this question. You can use a direct approach, in which you work with the initial conditions to track down all of the possibilities. The problem with the direct approach is that you will always worry that you haven't

gotten all the possibilities. The alternative approach is to work backward from the answer choices. Here's how this second approach works.

Does choice (A) contain all and only the possible days? No. I must follow G; therefore, I cannot be seen on Monday, and we eliminate choice (A). What about choice (B)? As for Tuesday, L must follow later in the week than J, F, and K, so L cannot be seen on Tuesday—and we eliminate choice (B). At this point, we should eliminate both choices (D) and (E), for choice (D) contains "Monday" and choice (E) contains "Tuesday." The only day on which both I and L could have appointments is Wednesday. For example:

M	TU	W	TH	F
J,G	K,F	I,L	H	M

20. **The correct answer is (D).** Here, one way or another, you are going to have to test each choice. That makes this a difficult question, but that is to be expected since it is the last one. To make the question manageable, you have to think abstractly about the individuals who are most likely to determine a certain order. As for choice (A), as we have noted, M is not under any particular restriction, so he is not likely to precipitate a fixed order. As for choices (B) and (C), G and I are under a certain restriction, but this works primarily only between the two of

them. Choice (E) is a bit better than either choices (B) or (C), because it establishes that G and I are scheduled for either Monday and Wednesday, or Wednesday and Friday.

Choice (D), however, offers even more promise. It affects not only G and I but also K and therefore F and L as well. Start with choice (D). If K has his appointment two days before G, then (given that H is already scheduled for Thursday) they must be scheduled for Monday and Wednesday or Wednesday and Friday. Here, since G must come before I, K and G must be scheduled for Monday and Wednesday:

M	TU	W	TH	F
K		G	H	

This means that F is scheduled for Monday and I for Friday:

M	TU	W	TH	F
K,F		G,L	H	I

However, L cannot be scheduled before Wednesday:

M	TU	W	TH	F
K,F		G,L	H	I

That means that J and M must be scheduled for Tuesday:

M	TU	W	TH	F
K,F	J,M	G,L	H	I

EXERCISE 2: ANSWER KEY AND EXPLANATIONS

1.	E	4.	D	7.	A	10.	A	13.	D
2.	C	5.	D	8.	A	11.	E		
3.	C	6.	A	9.	D	12.	C		

Questions 1–7

This is a selection set. Begin by summarizing the information:

Two different areas

(E ⊃ ~ FA) + (FA ⊃ ~ E)

(S ⊃ M) + (M ⊃ S)

SS ⊃ FA

There are no further obvious conclusions to draw, so go to the questions.

1. **The correct answer is (E).** Just test each choice by the initial conditions. First, the student must select from at least two different areas, and all of the choices pass muster on this score. Next, he cannot take courses in both English and fine arts, so we eliminate choices (A) and (D). Next, if he takes a science course, he must take a math course, and vice versa, so we eliminate choice (C). Finally, if he takes a social studies course, he must take a course in fine arts, so we eliminate choice (B). By the process of elimination, choice (E) is the correct choice.

> **Note:** Don't misread that last condition. It states only that a course in social studies must be accompanied by a course in fine arts. It is possible to take a fine arts course without taking a social studies course.

2. **The correct answer is (C).** This question is the mirror image of the first. Just test each choice by the initial conditions.

All are acceptable on the basis of the first condition (that he take courses in at least two different areas) and the second condition (English and fine arts cannot be taken together). Choice (C), however, runs afoul of the third condition, for there we have a math course without an accompanying science course. (You can check the other choices and see that they do respect the final condition.)

3. **The correct answer is (C).** If the student takes social studies, then he must take a course in fine arts. With a course in fine arts, he cannot take a course in English; and with two courses already scheduled (social studies and fine arts), he cannot take either math or science (for those must go together). His only choice, therefore, is to take another fine arts course—as choice (C) suggests—or another social studies course.

4. **The correct answer is (D).** If the student takes a course in math, he must also take a course in science, so his third course must be science.

5. **The correct answer is (D).** If you simply screen choices here by the initial conditions, it seems that all of the pairs taken in isolation are acceptable. This means that the trick to the question must be what happens to the third course. As for choices (A) and (B), math requires science and vice versa, and a schedule of math, science, and fine arts is acceptable. As for choices (C) and (E), math requires science, and a schedule of math, science, and English is acceptable. Choice

(D), however, is not acceptable; social studies requires fine arts, and science requires math, but there is not room on the schedule for both fine arts and science.

6. **The correct answer is (A).** Test each of the choices:

   (A) Science, two math (OK.)

   (B) Three science (No. Must schedule two different areas.)

   (C) Science, two English (No. Math must accompany science.)

   (D) Two science, one English (No. Math must accompany science.)

   (E) Science, math, social studies (No. Fine arts must accompany social studies.)

7. **The correct answer is (A).** Test each choice. As for choice (A), it is not possible to take two English courses. With two English courses, the student can neither take math or science (each requires the other), nor social studies (because social studies requires fine arts). It is possible to take two courses in the other areas:

   (B) Two fine arts plus one social studies

   (C) Two math plus one science

   (D) Two science plus one math

   (E) Two social studies plus one fine arts

Questions 8–13

This is a linear ordering problem. Begin by summarizing the information:

J < K

F < G (G is higher than F = F is lower than G.)

F – I – G or G – I – F

H = 6

There is one further conclusion you should probably note. Since G is higher than F and

since I is between F and G, the order for those three notes is F < I < G.

8. **The correct answer is (A).** Test each choice to learn which is possible and which is not. As for choice (A), G cannot be the second note on the scale because G must be higher than both F and I. You can grasp that the other choices are possible if you think in the following way. Imagine that F, I, and G are consecutive notes (they may be, though they don't have to be). If they are, then they could be 1, 2, and 3; or 2, 3, and 4; or even 3, 4, and 5. This will not affect the placement of J and K since in each of those arrangements, there will be two spaces left on the scale and K can be higher than J.

9. **The correct answer is (D).** Enter the additional information on a diagram:

   6   H
   5
   4   J
   3
   2
   1

   Since J is lower than K:

   6   H
   5   K
   4   J
   3
   2
   1

   Further, G, I, and F must be notes 3, 2, and 1:

   6   H
   5   K
   4   J
   3   G
   2   I
   1   F

10. **The correct answer is (A).** If exactly two notes separate F and I, then they must be placed as follows:

```
6    H
5    G
4    I
3
2
1    F
```

J and K are entered as follows:

```
6    H
5    G
4    I
3    K
2    J
1    F
```

The diagram shows that choice (A) is necessarily true, while the other choices are necessarily false.

11. **The correct answer is (E).** Enter the new information:

```
6    H
5
4
3
2    J
1
```

If J is second, then K must be either third, fourth, or fifth:

```
6    H    H    H
5    K
4         K
3              K
2    J    J    J
1
```

For G to be higher than I, and I higher than F, they must be entered as follows:

```
6    H    H    H
5    K    G    G
4    G    K    I
3    I    I    K
2    J    J    J
1    F    F    F
```

There are three possibilities: G and I are 4 and 3, 5 and 3, or 5 and 4.

12. **The correct answer is (C).** Start by assuming that F is the lowest note on the scale and that I is therefore the third. On that assumption, there are two positions for G:

```
6    H    H
5    G
4         G
3    I    I
2
1    F    F
```

J and K must be placed in the other two positions, with K higher than J:

```
6    H    H
5    G    K
4    K    G
3    I    I
2    J    J
1    F    F
```

Now assume that F is the second note on the scale and that I is therefore the fourth:

```
6    H
5
4    I
3
2    F
1
```

G must be higher than I:

6	H
5	G
4	I
3	
2	F
1	

K and J must be entered as follows:

6	H
5	G
4	I
3	K
2	F
1	J

Now try assuming that F is the third note on the scale, which would mean that I is the fifth. That is not possible, however, for G would then have to be higher than the fifth. Thus, we have accounted for all the possibilities:

6	H	H	H
5	G	G	K
4	I	K	G
3	K	I	I
2	F	J	J
1	J	F	F

Only choice (C) is necessarily true. The other choices are only possibly true.

13. **The correct answer is (D).** Again, we need to approach the question systematically. First, let us assume that J is the lowest note and that F is the second lowest. The possibilities are as follows:

6	H	H	H
5	G	G	K
4	I	K	G
3	K	I	I
2	F	F	F
1	J	J	J

That makes three possibilities. Now let's try J as the lowest note and F as the third lowest note. On this assumption, there is only one possibility:

6	H
5	G
4	I
3	F
2	K
1	J

This exhausts the possibilities. It is not possible (given the additional stipulation that J is lower than F) for J or F to be any higher on the scale. So there are exactly four possibilities.

The Writing Sample

OVERVIEW
- **What is the LSAT Writing Sample?**
- **How do you handle the Writing Sample?**
- **What smart test-takers know**

WHAT IS THE LSAT WRITING SAMPLE?

In addition to the three types of standardized multiple-choice questions that appear on the LSAT, the test also includes a Writing Sample. The Writing Sample is a short essay on a selected topic to be written in 30 minutes while you are in the examination room.

Writing Sample topics describe a decision that one person or a group of people must make, and you must write an argument for one of the two courses of action. The questions will not cover any topic requiring special knowledge. Paper and pens will be provided at the test center.

How Law Schools Use the Writing Sample

The Writing Sample will not be graded, but a copy of the essay will be forwarded with your score report to each school receiving your LSAT score. The point of requiring you to write an essay while in the examination room is to give a law school admissions committee a piece of writing definitely done by you and you alone. The essay gives the committee another perspective on your ability—specifically, on how well you write. The idea is that this can mitigate to some extent the severity of the artificial, multiple-choice format of the rest of the test.

Exactly what role the Writing Sample plays in the admissions process is decided by each law school. Many schools use the sample to help choose between otherwise equally qualified candidates. Very few law schools rely heavily upon the Writing Sample. Most law schools have adopted a middle-of-the-road approach. The Writing Sample will not figure heavily in the initial screening of applications, but it may be used to make decisions in difficult cases. For example, a student with marginal qualifications for a particular law school might be accepted if he or she writes a really good essay, and a student of similar background could be rejected on grounds that the Writing Sample is just not acceptable. Since no one is assured of a seat at a top law school, applicants to those schools who write a very poor essay will likely suffer.

chapter 8

LSAT Writing Sample Format

Here is a typical LSAT Writing Sample topic, along with directions for writing your essay.

Anatomy of the Writing Sample

Directions: Read the following proposals of Johnson and Smith, which were submitted to the city of Athens' Department of Urban Renewal, to renovate a decaying structure that is currently owned by the city and to operate a business in it. Then, in the space provided, write an argument in favor of the proposal that you think the Department of Urban Renewal should choose. The following considerations should guide your decision.

First come the directions. Read them now, and then you can forget about them. The point is to write an essay.

1. The Athens City Council eventually wants the ownership of the property to be transferred to the business as soon as the business is able to pay the property taxes that are in arrears.

2. The Department of Urban Renewal wants the building to be occupied by a business that will benefit the community.

Next comes the background for the situation. The criteria that should guide your decision will help you create an outline for an essay.

JOHNSON plans to operate a hardware store in the building. She will use the ground floor for retail displays and the second floor and basement for storing inventory. Johnson has $100,000 to commit to the project for purchasing inventory and for other start-up costs, plus a letter of credit from a local bank that will

Next comes a possible answer, though not necessarily the right answer. Use the details about Johnson's plan to fill in an argument patterned along the specified criteria—if this is the side that you choose.

allow her to borrow up to $150,000 for renovation. Johnson is willing to open this new business in the neighborhood because she believes that the neighborhood is about to experience a renaissance. Johnson worked for ten years as the manager of a hardware store that is part of a large chain.

SMITH plans to operate a personal financial consulting firm in the building. The firm will offer budget counseling, tax preparation, advice on completing loan applications, and help with legal documents—all for a fee. The fee will depend on the service rendered and the ability of the client to pay. Smith has $50,000 to cover the cost of renovating the building and has received a grant of $75,000 from the state's Human Resources Center to purchase computers and to cover other start-up costs. Smith's plan is initially just to renovate the ground floor and to open for business. The second floor would be renovated once the business has generated sufficient income. Smith worked for three years as a legal aid attorney and is familiar with the problems of the people in the neighborhood.

Next comes another possible answer, though again, not necessarily the right answer. Use the details about Smith's plan to fill in an argument patterned along the specified criteria—if this is the side that you choose.

HOW DO YOU HANDLE THE WRITING SAMPLE?

Here is a simple, four-step plan to help you succeed on the LSAT Writing Sample.

WRITING SAMPLE: GETTING IT RIGHT

1 Pick one side or the other—there is no right or wrong answer.
2 Make an outline.
3 Write your essay.
4 Proofread your essay.

NOTE

Organization is very important. Perhaps the most important thing that the readers will be looking for is organization. If you create an outline and follow it, you are already halfway home.

Now let's look at each of these steps in more detail.

1 Pick one side or the other—there is no right or wrong answer. Pick a side—any side. There are no right or wrong answers for the Writing Sample. The technical term for the topic is "prompt." It is just an excuse for you to write an essay. You can even toss a coin to choose a side.

2 Make an outline. After you have selected the side of the topic you are more comfortable with, construct an outline of your position. The outline will not be very detailed. It will just be some notes to guide you as you write. In fact, since the entire exercise takes only 30 minutes, you probably cannot write more than four or five short paragraphs.

The background information always provides criteria as guidelines for making the decision. Let these criteria form the basis for the contentions in your essay. Summarize them in your own words, then build your essay around them.

3 Write your essay. Your essay should consist of four or five short paragraphs: introduction, first main reason, second main reason, and third main reason (if you have one), and conclusion. Each paragraph will be only two or three sentences long.

If you think that this is not "grand" enough, remember that this essay is not going to get you into law school. The objective here is to avoid writing something that is totally unacceptable.

4 Proofread your essay. Law school admissions officers will understand that your essay is really just a rough draft. Still, it would be better not to leave any glaring mistakes. So spend the last 3 or 4 minutes of the 30-minute session proofreading. Make any needed corrections as neatly as possible.

Now let's use the four-step process to create an essay on the following typical Writing Sample topic:

Margaret Stone will receive her Ph.D. in comparative literature in six months and wants a job teaching on the university level. After several interviews, she receives job offers from two institutions, Middleburg College and Central State University. Write an essay arguing that Margaret should choose one of the two job offers. Two considerations should guide your decision:

1. Margaret wants a position that will allow her to maintain a decent standard of living. After eight years as a student, she has virtually no assets and has incurred several thousand dollars in student loans.

2. Margaret wants a position that will allow her to teach higher level courses in literature rather than the introductory course or courses designed to teach students a foreign language. In addition, she wants to earn a reputation as a scholar.

MIDDLEBURG COLLEGE is a small, liberal arts college with a student body of approximately 2,000. Although the college has a limited enrollment, its academic reputation is equal to that of many of the nation's best universities. There is no separate Comparative Literature Department at Middleburg. All literature courses are taught in various language departments. Margaret would be hired by the French Department and would be expected to teach three courses per semester: one basic French grammar course, one introduction to French literature course, and one upper-level literature course. The starting salary at Middleburg is $33,000 per year. The position is a tenure-track position, and Margaret could expect to receive tenure and a raise to $45,000 within three years.

CENTRAL STATE UNIVERSITY is a large public institution with a student body of 35,000. Margaret has been offered a position on the graduate faculty at a salary of $40,000 per year. As a member of the graduate faculty, she would offer courses of her own choosing, subject only to the approval of the Chief Executive Officer of the department. The Chief Executive Officer is a leading authority on literary criticism, and each year, the University sponsors one major and several minor conferences at which scholars from the University and other institutions present papers. The position at Central State is not considered a tenure-track position, but Margaret could hope to achieve a permanent appointment in seven or eight years if she earns a substantial academic reputation.

❶ Pick one side or the other—there is no right or wrong answer. It doesn't matter which job offer you think Margaret should choose.

❷ Make an outline. Based on the information given, you could argue that Margaret is concerned about (1) financial security and (2) professional satisfaction. Thus, your two main contentions would be as follows:

I. This job offers Margaret the financial security she wants.

II. This job offers Margaret the professional satisfaction she seeks.

Then find two or three specific points in the topic to prove each contention. Let the description of each option provide you with the subpoints needed to support your main points. For example, if you decide to argue in favor of Central State, your outline might look like this:

I. This job offers Margaret the financial security she wants.

    A. The starting salary is a generous $40,000 per year.

    B. There is the possibility of tenure if she succeeds.

II. This job offers Margaret the professional satisfaction she seeks.

   A. She will be able to teach courses she likes.

   B. She will work with leading figures in her field.

   C. She will participate in conferences.

   (You can also find equally good reasons for selecting the other job.)

❸ **Write your essay.** Now put the substance of the argument together with the formal outline given above. First, you need an introduction. An opening paragraph might be as follows:

> Margaret should accept the job offer from Central State for two reasons. First, it will give her the financial security she needs. Second, it will offer her the professional satisfaction that she seeks.

The second paragraph is the development of the first major contention. Begin the paragraph with a restatement of your first main point. Then supply the supporting details:

> First, the position at Central State provides Margaret with the income she needs to maintain a certain standard of living. The starting salary at Central State is a generous $40,000 per year. In addition, if Margaret is successful, she can expect to receive promotions after a few years, and such promotions usually carry corresponding salary increases.

The third paragraph is the development of the second major contention. Begin this paragraph with a restatement of your second main point. Then supply the supporting details:

> Second, Central State will allow Margaret to achieve her professional goals. In the first place, she will teach higher level courses and won't be required to teach the introductory courses she might find less interesting. In addition, she will be able to work with her Chief Executive Officer, who is one of the leading authorities in Margaret's field. Finally, the University itself is the center for conferences at which Margaret would meet others in her field and have an opportunity to exchange ideas.

The final paragraph should be a brief summary of the argument only a sentence or two long:

> Thus, because Central State offers better financial terms and the possibility of professional advancement, Margaret should accept its job offer.

The primary function of this paragraph is just to signal the reader that you have reached the end of your essay.

Now put all the paragraphs together. Here is how the essay would read:

> Margaret should accept the job offer from Central State for two reasons. First, it will give her the financial security she needs. Second, it will offer her the professional satisfaction that she seeks.

First, the position at Central State provides Margaret with the income she needs to maintain a certain standard of living. The starting salary at Central State is a generous $40,000 per year. In addition, if Margaret is successful, she can expect to receive promotions after a few years, and such promotions usually carry corresponding salary increases.

Second, Central State will allow Margaret to achieve her professional goals. In the first place, she will teach higher level courses and won't be required to teach the introductory courses she might find less interesting. In addition, she will be able to work with her Chief Executive Officer, who is one of the leading authorities in Margaret's field. Finally, the University itself is the center for conferences at which Margaret would meet others in her field and have an opportunity to exchange ideas.

Thus, because Central State offers better financial terms and the possibility of professional advancement, Margaret should accept its job offer.

4 **Proofread your essay.** Read over your work to make sure that there are no glaring errors of grammar or punctuation. Incidentally, if you still doubt that this sample essay is lengthy enough, see how much time it takes you to copy it over in your own hand.

WHAT SMART TEST–TAKERS KNOW

The Writing Sample Is Not Very Important.

The Writing Sample is not as important as the other sections of the LSAT. It is important to keep in mind that law schools use the LSAT as a screening device (coupled with the grade point average). This means that the LSAT is a threshold requirement that must be met before the Writing Sample even enters the picture. Moreover, the length of the sample is such that you are not really writing a "term paper." In 30 minutes, no one is going to be able to write the definitive essay on the topic given and no one is expected to do so. This Writing Sample is just a check to see if you can write clearly and grammatically; it is not to determine whether or not you would be a great novelist.

Thinking It Through First Is the Way to Avoid Mistakes.

Many errors in writing are the result of an attempt to change structures in midsentence. Verb tenses shift, points of view get mixed up, verbs get left out, pronouns get confused, and many other things happen if the sentence is not already formed when the writing begins. For example:

> Wrong: Even if a student is somewhat distracted, they may be even better able to concentrate when their attention returns to the teacher.

This sentence contains a grammatical error. The pronoun *they*, which begins the main clause of the sentence, is plural. But it refers to *student*, which is singular. This type of error usually occurs when writers do not have the complete thought or sentence in mind when they begin to write. They lose track of what they have said and shift from the singular to the plural. The best way for you to avoid such errors is to have a good idea of what the completed sentence will say before you begin to write it down.

Subjects and Verbs Must Agree.

Everyone remembers that a verb must agree with its subject, and by and large, we all observe this rule. We tend to get into trouble when prepositional phrases or other modifiers come between the subject and its verb.

> Wrong: This distraction, which occurs in students with more limited attention spans, are easily avoided by arranging desks so that the eyes of a student is directed away from the windows.

Two errors of subject-verb agreement occur here: "distraction . . . are" and "eyes . . . is." In this sentence, a clause that includes two prepositional phrases comes between the first subject and its verb, and it is therefore likely that one of the two nouns, "students" or "spans," was mistaken for the subject when the writer chose a verb. A prepositional phrase ("of a student") comes between the second subject and its verb, and the writer has mistaken "student" for the subject of the verb and written "is."

Pronouns Must Be in the Correct Number and Case.

Many people misuse pronouns. The two most common mistakes in pronoun reference are incorrect number and incorrect case. Sometimes students use a singular pronoun where a plural pronoun is needed and vice versa (incorrect number):

> Wrong: The easiest solution is to have the teacher order each student to keep their eyes directed toward the blackboard.

In this example, the choice of the pronoun "their" is incorrect. The pronoun must refer to "student," which is singular; but "their" is plural.

Consider the next example:

> Wrong: Under this seating arrangement, all of the people in the classroom, except the class monitor and she, will face the blackboard, not the windows.

In this sentence, the use of the pronoun "she" is incorrect because it is in the wrong case. The pronoun here functions as the object of a preposition ("except"), and it should therefore be in the objective case ("her"). One sure way of avoiding errors in the use of pronouns is to avoid unnecessary pronouns.

> Better: Under this seating arrangement, all of the people in the classroom, except the class monitor and the teacher, will . . .

Modifiers Must Stay Close to Home.

As a general rule, make sure that modifiers are close to the words they are intended to modify. Be especially wary of the introductory modifier.

> Wrong: While strolling through Central Park, a severe thunderstorm required my companion and me to take shelter in the band shell.

Given the construction of the sentence, it is made to appear that the severe thunderstorm was strolling through the park. When a modifying idea starts a sentence and is set off with a comma, the modifier must be taken to modify the first noun or noun phrase after the comma. A related error to be avoided is the squinting modifier, which is placed so that it may modify either one of two things, producing ambiguity in the sentence.

> Wrong: Paul told Mary that he would wed her down by the old mill.

Did Paul tell Mary down by the old mill that he would wed her, or did Paul tell Mary that he would wed her and the wedding would take place down by the old mill?

Each Sentence Should Express Just One Thought.

Rather than trying to tack on qualifications and exceptions to an already long sentence, break it down:

> Wrong: Although it might be argued that some students will be distracted by windows, but there is no proof of this presented, it is still the case that many students would benefit from the relaxing effect of open scenery, and that could even help them learn.

> Better: There is no proof presented that students are distracted by windows. Even assuming some students are distracted, many other students might find the view relaxing. A relaxed student should be a better learner than one who is tense, and learning is the goal of the classroom.

The Active Voice Is Generally Best.

As mentioned, it is important to write straightforward, declarative sentences in the active voice. These sentences are easy to compose, and they express thoughts clearly. But many students imagine that the more stilted the construction, the better the writing:

> Wrong: When the notice was received by me. . . .
>
> Correct: When I received the notice. . . .
>
> Wrong: The cake was baked by the chef to please. . . .
>
> Correct: The chef baked the cake to please. . . .

This is not an absolute prohibition against the passive voice, but a law school admissions committee is more likely to appreciate straightforward and direct composition than needlessly complicated and imprecise sentences.

Slang Is a Turn-off.

Whatever else you do, do not allow slang to slip into your writing.

> Wrong: Let the kids do their own thing. It's too heavy a trip to always have the teacher, the man, laying this guilt business on you. No windows would be a head trip. Some of the kids would wind up at the shrink's. So just lay off, and let them be themselves.

In conversation we often use expressions that are just not acceptable in formal writing. Can you dig that?

When in Doubt, It's Smart to Leave it Out.

You are in command of the Writing Sample. Unlike the other sections, in which you are forced to choose from among answers, the Writing Sample allows you to construct and write your own answer. It will be possible, to a certain extent, to "fake it": If you are not sure about the meaning or spelling of a word, find an alternative. There is absolutely no reason to expose yourself to the possibility of error when you could avoid that danger entirely by using another phrase.

Neatness Counts.

What we have tried to do in this section is reassure you that you will not be caught without anything to say. The questions will be drafted in such a way that you will be able to think of a point or two and probably more. The important thing is to express yourself clearly in order to impress upon the admissions officers that you can write, a skill every lawyer needs. Finally, although good penmanship is not a prerequisite to being a good lawyer, your writing will be read by some fairly important people. Present yourself in a way of which you can be proud. Some people have naturally beautiful handwriting, others do not. But everyone is capable of legible handwriting. It is only courteous to write clearly, so that the people who have to read your essay can do so easily. So write slowly (without sacrificing coverage), and try to use your best handwriting. Print if necessary.

Trying to Do Too Much Is a Mistake.

After you have practiced a few topics, you will have a pretty good idea of what you can hope to accomplish in the time allotted. The biggest problem for students is not going to be having too little to say but rather trying to say too much. Your little essay must be structurally complete. That is, it must have a beginning, a middle, and an end. You do not want to run out of time before you have completed your thought. Far better to write a nicely balanced and self-contained essay on the short side than a longer piece that stops in the middle of the next-to-last paragraph. Make sure you can chew what you bite off.

Legal Terminology Is Out of Place.

The LSAT is not a test of what you already know about the law, and law school admissions officers are not going to be impressed with your essay just because you flavor it with *henceforth, heretofore mentioned, above cited*, or similar terms. Such terms have no place in your essay. Your best bet is to try to write naturally, as though you were speaking to someone sitting across the table (though you should avoid slang expressions you might use in conversation).

**SUMMING
IT UP:**

What You Must Know about LSAT Question Types

Review these pages the night before you take the LSAT. They will help you do well on your test.

- The LSAT has three question types: Logical Reasoning, Reading Comprehension, and Analytical Reasoning.

- The scored portion of the LSAT contains two 35-minute Logical Reasoning sections of 24 to 26 questions each. It also contains one Reading Comprehension section of 26 to 28 questions and one Analytical Reasoning section of 22 to 24 questions.

- In addition, each LSAT includes a 30-minute Writing Sample that is sent directly to the law schools you designate for scoring.

Logical Reasoning

- These steps will help you solve Logical Reasoning problems:
  1. Preview the question stem.
  2. Read the stimulus material.
  3. Prephrase your answer.
  4. Identify the correct answer.

- There are six common types of Logical Reasoning questions:
  1. Identify the conclusion.
  2. Point out a premise.
  3. Identify strengths or weaknesses.
  4. Recognize parallel reasoning.
  5. Evaluate evidence.
  6. Draw a conclusion.

- Locating the conclusion is the first step in evaluating an argument.

- Key words often signal the conclusion or an important premise.

- In Logical Reasoning questions, watch out for the seven most common logical fallacies:
  1. Wrong cause
  2. False analogy
  3. Weak generalization

4 Ambiguous terms

5 Irrelevant evidence

6 Circular argument

7 Ad hominem attack

Reading Comprehension

- These steps will help you solve Reading Comprehension questions:

    1 Preview key sentences.

    2 Read for structure; ignore details.

    3 Do a mental wrap-up.

    4 Start with the main idea question.

    5 Next tackle specific detail and attitude/tone questions.

    6 Then do logical structure questions.

    7 Save inference and application questions for last.

- The LSAT uses six Reading Comprehension question types:

    1 Main idea

    2 Specific detail

    3 Inference

    4 Logical structure

    5 Application

    6 Author's attitude or tone

Analytical Reasoning

- These steps will help you solve Analytical Reasoning questions:

    1 Summarize the initial conditions in a "bookkeeping" system.

    2 Look for further conclusions.

    3 Treat each question separately.

    4 Use the answer choices to create a "feedback loop."

- The three most common types of Analytical Reasoning puzzles:

    1 Linear ordering

    2 Distributed order

    3 Selection sets

Writing Sample

- These steps will help you with the Writing Sample:

  1 Pick one side or the other—there is no right or wrong answer.

  2 Make an outline.

  3 Write your essay.

  4 Proofread your essay.

- The Writing Sample is not as important as the other sections of the LSAT.

- Watch your grammar.

- Don't try to do too much.

PART IV
THREE PRACTICE TESTS

Practice Test 1

Practice Test 2

Practice Test 3

Practice Test 1

SECTION 1

24 Questions • 35 Minutes

> **Directions:** In this section, the questions ask you to analyze and evaluate the reasoning in short paragraphs or passages. For some questions, all of the answer choices may conceivably be answers to the question asked. You should select the *best* answer to the question; that is, an answer that does not require you to make assumptions that violate common sense standards by being implausible, redundant, irrelevant, or inconsistent. After you have chosen the *best* answer, blacken the corresponding space on the answer sheet.

1. There are no lower bus fares from Washington, D.C., to New York City than those of Flash Bus Line.

   Which of the following is logically inconsistent with the above advertising claim?

   (A) Long Lines Airways has a Washington, D.C., to New York City airfare that is only half of that charged by Flash.

   (B) Rapid Transit Bus Company charges the same fare for a trip from Washington, D.C., to New York City as Flash charges.

   (C) Cherokee Bus Corporation has a lower fare from New York City to Boston than Flash does.

   (D) Linea Rapida Bus Company has a New York City to Washington, D.C., fare that is less than the corresponding fare of Flash Bus Lines.

   (E) Birch Bus Lines offers a late-night fare from Washington, D.C., to New York City that is two thirds the price of the corresponding fare of Flash Bus Line.

Questions 2 and 3

Roberts is accused of a crime, and Edwards is the prosecution's key witness.

   (1) Roberts can be convicted on the basis of Edwards' testimony.

   (2) Edwards' testimony would show that Edwards participated in Roberts' wrongdoing.

   (3) The crime of which Roberts is accused can be committed only by a person acting alone.

   (4) If the jury learns that Edwards committed some wrong, they will refuse to believe any part of Edwards' testimony.

2. If propositions (1), (2), and (3) are assumed to be true and (4) false, which of the following best describes the outcome of the trial?

 (A) Both Edwards and Roberts will be convicted of the crime of which Roberts is accused.

 (B) Both Edwards and Roberts will be convicted of some crime other than the one with which Roberts is already charged.

 (C) Roberts will be convicted, while Edwards will not be convicted.

 (D) Roberts will not be convicted.

 (E) Roberts will testify against Edwards.

3. If all four propositions are taken as a group, it can be pointed out that the scenario they describe is

 (A) a typical situation for a prosecutor.

 (B) impossible because the propositions are logically inconsistent.

 (C) unfair to Edwards, whose testimony may be self-incriminatory.

 (D) unfair to Roberts, who may be convicted of the crime.

 (E) one that Roberts' attorney has created.

Questions 4 and 5

There is a curious, though nonetheless obvious, contradiction in the suggestion that one person ought to give up his life to save the life of the one other person who is not a more valuable member of the community. It is true that we glorify the sacrifice of the individual who throws herself in front of the attacker's bullets, saving the life of her lover at the cost of her own. But here is the _____(4): Her life is as important as his. Nothing is gained in the transaction; not from the community's viewpoint, for one life was exchanged for another equally as important; not from the heroine's viewpoint, for she is _____(5); and not from the rescued lover's perspective, for he would willingly have exchanged places.

4. (A) beauty of human love

 (B) tragedy of life

 (C) inevitability of death

 (D) defining characteristic of human existence

 (E) paradox of self-sacrifice

5. (A) dying

 (B) in love

 (C) dead

 (D) a heroine

 (E) a faithful companion

6. It is a well-documented fact that for all teenaged couples who marry, the marriages of those who do not have children in the first year of their marriage survive more than twice as long as the marriages of those teenaged couples in which the wife does give birth within the first twelve months of marriage. Therefore, many divorces could be avoided if teenagers who marry were encouraged to seek counseling on birth control as soon after marriage as possible.

 The evidence regarding teenaged marriages supports the author's <u>conclusion</u> only if

 (A) in those couples to which a child was born within the first 12 months, there is not a significant number in which the wife was pregnant at the time of marriage.

 (B) the children born during the first year of marriage to those divorcing couples lived with the teenaged couple.

 (C) the child born into such a marriage did not die at birth.

 (D) society actually has an interest in determining whether or not people should be divorced if there are not children involved.

 (E) encouraging people to stay married when they do not plan to have any children is a good idea.

7. CLARENCE: Mary is one of the most important executives at the Trendy Cola Company.

   PETER: How can that be? I know for a fact that Mary drinks only Hobart Cola.

Peter's statement <u>implies</u> that

(A) Hobart Cola is a subsidiary of Trendy Cola.

(B) Mary is an unimportant employee of Hobart Cola.

(C) all cola drinks taste pretty much alike.

(D) an executive uses only that company's products.

(E) Hobart is a better-tasting cola than Trendy.

8. ERIKA: Participation in intramural competitive sports teaches students the importance of teamwork, for no one wants to let his teammates down.

   NICHOL: That is not correct. The real reason students play hard is that such programs place a premium on winning and that no one wants to be a member of a losing team.

Which of the following comments can most reasonably be made about the exchange between Erika and Nichol?

(A) If fewer and fewer schools are sponsoring intramural sports programs now than a decade ago, Erika's position is undermined.

(B) If high schools and universities provide financial assistance for the purchase of sports equipment, Nichol's assertion about the importance of winning is weakened.

(C) If teamwork is essential to success in intramural competitive sports, Erika's position and Nichol's position are not necessarily incompatible.

(D) Since the argument is one about motivation, it should be possible to resolve the issue by taking a survey of deans at schools that have intramural sports programs.

(E) Since the question raised is about hidden psychological states, it is impossible to answer it.

9. Clark must have known that his sister Janet and not the governess pulled the trigger, but he silently stood by while the jury convicted the governess. Any person of clear conscience would have felt terrible for not having come forward with the information about his sister, and Clark lived with that information until his death thirty years later. Since he was an extremely happy man, however, I conclude that he must have helped Janet commit the crime.

Which of the following assumptions must underlie the author's conclusion of the last sentence?

(A) Loyalty to members of one's family is conducive to contentment.

(B) Servants are not to be treated with the same respect as members of the peerage.

(C) Clark never had a bad conscience over his silence because he was also guilty of the crime.

(D) It is better to be virtuous than happy.

(E) It is actually better to be content in life than to behave morally toward one's fellow humans.

10. Current motion pictures give children a distorted view of the world. Animated features depict animals as loyal friends, compassionate creatures, and tender souls, while "spaghetti Westerns" portray men and women as deceitful and treacherous, cruel and wanton, and hard and uncaring. Thus, children are taught to value animals more highly than other human beings.

Which of the following, if true, would weaken the author's conclusion?

(A) Children are not allowed to watch "spaghetti Westerns."

(B) The producers of animated features do not want children to regard animals as higher than human beings.

(C) Ancient fables, such as *Androcles and the Lion,* tell stories of the cooperation between humans and animals, and they usually end with a moral about human virtue.

(D) Children are more likely to choose to watch animated presentations with characters such as animals than ones with people as actors.

(E) Animals often exhibit affection, loyalty, protectiveness, and other traits that are considered desirable characteristics in humans.

11. There is something irrational about our system of laws. The criminal law punishes a person more severely for having successfully committed a crime than it does a person who fails in an attempt to commit the same crime—even though the same evil intention is present in both cases. But under the civil law, a person who attempts to defraud a potential victim but is unsuccessful is not required to pay damages.

Which of the following, if true, would most weaken the author's argument?

(A) Most persons who are imprisoned for crimes will commit another crime if they are ever released from prison.

(B) A person is morally culpable for evil thoughts as well as for evil deeds.

(C) There are more criminal laws on the books than there are civil laws on the books.

(D) A criminal trial is considerably more costly to the state than a civil trial.

(E) The goal of the criminal law is to punish the criminal, but the goal of the civil law is to compensate the victim.

12. In his most recent speech, my opponent, Governor Smith, accused me of having distorted the facts, misrepresenting his own position, suppressing information, and deliberately lying to the people.

Which of the following possible responses by this speaker would be LEAST relevant to his dispute with Governor Smith?

(A) Governor Smith would not have begun to smear me if he did not sense that his own campaign was in serious trouble.

(B) Governor Smith apparently misunderstood my characterization of his position, so I will attempt to state more clearly my understanding of it.

(C) At the time I made those remarks, certain key facts were not available, but new information uncovered by my staff does support the position I took at that time.

(D) I can only wish Governor Smith had specified those points he considered to be lies so that I could have responded to them now.

(E) With regard to the allegedly distorted facts, the source of my information is a Department of Transportation publication entitled "Safe Driving."

13. Politicians are primarily concerned with their own survival; artists are concerned with revealing truth. Of course, the difference in their reactions is readily predictable. For example, while the governmental leaders wrote laws to ensure the triumph of industrialization in Western Europe, artists painted, wrote about, and composed music in response to the horrible conditions created by the Industrial Revolution. Only later did political leaders come to see what the artists had immediately perceived and then only through a glass darkly. Experience teaches us that _____.

Which of the following represents the most logical continuation of the passage?

(A) artistic vision perceives in advance of political practice

(B) artists are utopian by nature, while governmental leaders are practical

(C) throughout history, political leaders have not been very responsive to the needs of their people

(D) the world would be a much better place to live if only artists would become kings

(E) history is the best judge of the progress of civilization

14. A parent must be constant and even-handed in the imposition of burdens and punishments and the distribution of liberties and rewards. In good times, a parent who too quickly bestows rewards creates an expectation of future rewards that it may be impossible to fulfill during bad times. In bad times, a parent who waits too long to impose the punishment gives the impression that the response was forced, and the child may interpret this as _____.

Which of the following represents the most logical continuation of the passage?

(A) a signal from the parent that the parent is no longer interested in the child's welfare

(B) a sign of weakness in the parent that can be exploited

(C) indicating a willingness on the part of the parent to bargain away liberties in exchange for the child's assuming some new responsibilities

(D) an open invitation to retaliate

(E) a symbol of the transition to adulthood

15. As dietitian for this 300-person school, I am concerned about the sudden shortage of beef. It seems that we will have to begin to serve fish as our main source of protein. Even though beef costs more per pound than fish, I expect that the price I pay for protein will rise if I continue to serve the same amount of protein using fish as I did with beef.

The speaker makes which of the following assumptions?

(A) Fish is more expensive per pound than beef.

(B) Students will soon be paying more for their meals.

(C) Cattle ranchers make greater profits than commercial fishers.

(D) Per measure of protein, fish is more expensive than beef.

(E) Cattle are more costly to raise than fish.

Questions 16 and 17

New Weight Loss Salons invites all of you who are dissatisfied with your present build to join our Exercise for Lunch Bunch. Instead of putting on even more weight by eating lunch, you actually cut down on your daily caloric intake by exercising rather than eating. Every single one of us has the potential to be slim and fit, so take the initiative and begin losing excess pounds today. Don't eat! Exercise! You'll lose weight and feel stronger, happier, and more attractive.

16. Which of the following, if true, would weaken the logic of the argument made by the advertisement?

(A) Nutritionists agree that it is permissible to skip lunch but not a good idea to skip breakfast.

(B) Most people will experience increased desire for food as a result of the exercise and will lose little weight as a result of enrolling in the program.

(C) In our society, obesity is regarded as unattractive.

(D) A person who is too thin is probably not in good health.

(E) Not everyone is dissatisfied with his or her present build or body weight.

17. A person hearing this advertisement countered, "I know some people who are not overweight and are still unhappy and unattractive." The author of the advertisement could logically and consistently reply to this objection by pointing out that he never claimed that

(A) being overweight is always caused by unhappiness.

(B) being overweight is the only cause of unhappiness and unattractiveness.

(C) unhappiness and unattractiveness can cause someone to be overweight.

(D) unhappiness necessarily leads to being overweight.

(E) unhappiness and unattractiveness are always found together.

18. Since all swans that I have encountered have been white, it follows that the swans I will see when I visit the Bronx Zoo will also be white.

Which of the following most closely parallels the reasoning of the preceding argument?

(A) Some birds are incapable of flight; therefore, swans are probably incapable of flight.

(B) Every ballet I have attended has failed to interest me; so a theatrical production that fails to interest me must be a ballet.

(C) Since all cases of severe depression I have encountered were susceptible to treatment by chlorpromazine, there must be something in the chlorpromazine that adjusts the patient's brain chemistry.

(D) Because every society has a word for justice, the concept of fair play must be inherent in the biological makeup of the human species.

(E) Since no medicine I have tried for my allergy has ever helped, this new product will probably not work either.

Questions 19–21

The blanks in the following paragraph mark deletions from the text. For each question, select the phrase that most appropriately completes the text.

Libertarians argue that laws making suicide a criminal act are both foolish and an unwarranted intrusion on individual conscience. With regard to the first, they point out that there is no penalty that the law can assess that inflicts greater injury than the crime itself. As for the second, they argue that it is no business of the state to prevent suicide, for whether it is right to take one's own life is a matter to be addressed to one's own God—the state, by the terms of the Constitution, may not interfere. Such arguments, however, seem to me to be ill-conceived. In the first place, the libertarian makes the mistaken assumption that deterrence is the only goal of the law. I maintain that the laws we have proscribing suicide are _____ (19).

By making it a crime to take any life—even one's own—we make a public announcement of our shared conviction that each person is unique and valuable. In the second place, while it must be conceded that the doctrine of the separation of church and state is a useful one, it need not be admitted that suicide is a crime _____(20). And here we need not have recourse to the possibility that a potential suicide might, if given the opportunity, repent of the decision. Suicide inflicts a cost upon us all: the emotional cost on those close to the suicide; an economic cost in the form of the loss of production of a mature and trained member of the society that falls on us all; and a cost to humanity at large for the loss of a member of our human community. The difficulty with the libertarian position is that it is an oversimplification. It assesses the evil of_____(21).

19. **(A)** drafted to make it more difficult to commit suicide

(B) passed by legislators in response to pressures by religious lobbying groups

(C) written in an effort to protect our democratic liberties, not undermine them

(D) important because they educate all to the value of human life

(E) outdated because they belong to a time when church and state were not so clearly divided

20. **(A)** that does not necessarily lead to more serious crimes

(B) without victim

(C) as well as a sin

(D) that cannot be prevented

(E) without motive

21. **(A)** crimes only in economic terms

(B) suicide only from the perspective of the person who commits suicide

(C) laws by weighing them against the evil of the liberty lost by their enforcement

(D) the mingling of church and state without sufficient regard to the constitutional protections

(E) suicide in monetary units without proper regard to the importance of life

22. All high-powered racing engines have stochastic fuel injection. Stochastic fuel injection is not a feature that is normally included in the engines of production-line vehicles. Passenger sedans are production-line vehicles.

Which of the following conclusions can be drawn from these statements?

(A) Passenger sedans do not usually have stochastic fuel injection.

(B) Stochastic fuel injection is found only in high-powered racing cars.

(C) Car manufacturers do not include stochastic fuel injection in passenger cars because they fear accidents.

(D) Purchasers of passenger cars do not normally purchase stochastic fuel injection because it is expensive.

(E) Some passenger sedans are high-powered racing vehicles.

23. During New York City's fiscal crisis of the late 1970s, governmental leaders debated whether to offer federal assistance to New York City. One economist who opposed the suggestion asked, "Are we supposed to help out New York City every time it gets into financial problems?"

The economist's question can be criticized because it

(A) uses ambiguous terms.

(B) assumes everyone else agrees New York City should be helped.

(C) appeals to emotions rather than using logic.

(D) relies upon second-hand reports rather than first-hand accounts.

(E) completely ignores the issue at hand.

24. Some philosophers have argued that there exist certain human or natural rights that belong to all human beings by virtue of their humanity. But a review of the laws of different societies shows that the rights accorded a person vary from society to society and even within a society over time. Since there is no right that is universally protected, there are no natural rights.

A defender of the theory that natural rights do exist might respond to this objection by arguing that

(A) some human beings do not have any natural rights.

(B) some human rights are natural while others derive from a source such as a constitution.

(C) people in one society may have natural rights that people in another society lack.

(D) all societies have some institution that protects the rights of an individual in that society.

(E) natural rights may exist even though they are not protected by some societies.

STOP

END OF SECTION 1. IF YOU HAVE ANY TIME LEFT, GO OVER YOUR WORK IN THIS SECTION ONLY. DO NOT WORK IN ANY OTHER SECTION OF THE TEST.

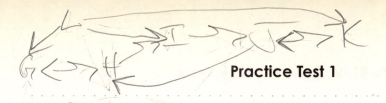

SECTION 2

24 Questions • 35 Minutes

> **Directions:** Each group of questions is based on a set of propositions or conditions. Drawing a rough picture or diagram may help in answering some of the questions. After you have chosen the *best* answer for each question, blacken the corresponding space on your answer sheet.

Questions 1–6

A railway system consists of six stations, G, H, I, J, K, and L. Trains run only according to the following conditions:

From	G to H
From	H to G and from H to I
From	I to J
From	J to H and from J to K
From	L to G; from L to K, and from L to I
From	K to J

It is possible to transfer at a station for another train.

1. How is it possible to get from H to J?
   - **(A)** A direct train from H to J
   - **(B)** A train to G and transfer for a train to J
   - **(C)** A train to L and transfer for a train to J
   - **(D)** A train to I and transfer for a train to J
   - **(E)** It is impossible to reach J from H.

2. Which of the following stations CANNOT be reached by a train from any of the other stations?
   - **(A)** G
   - **(B)** H
   - **(C)** I
   - **(D)** K
   - **(E)** L

3. Which of the following is a complete and accurate listing of the stations from that it is possible to reach I with exactly one transfer?
   - **(A)** G and H
   - **(B)** G and J
   - **(C)** J and K
   - **(D)** J and L
   - **(E)** J, G, and L

4. What is the greatest number of stations that can be visited without visiting any station more than once?
   - **(A)** 2
   - **(B)** 3
   - **(C)** 4
   - **(D)** 5
   - **(E)** 6

5. Which of the following trips requires the greatest number of transfers?
   - **(A)** G to I
   - **(B)** H to K
   - **(C)** L to H
   - **(D)** L to I
   - **(E)** L to K

6. If station I is closed, which of the following trips is impossible?
   - **(A)** G to J
   - **(B)** J to K
   - **(C)** L to K
   - **(D)** L to J
   - **(E)** L to G

Questions 7–12

A travel agent is arranging tours that visit various cities: L, M, N, O, P, Q, R, S, T. Each tour must be arranged in accordance with the following restrictions:

If M is included in a tour, both Q and R must also be included.

P can be included in a tour only if O is also included.

If Q is included in a tour, M must be included along with N or T or both.

P and Q cannot both be included in a tour.

A tour cannot include O, R, and T.

A tour cannot include N, S, and R.

A tour cannot include L and R.

7. If M is included in a tour, what is the minimum number of other cities that must be included in the tour?
   - (A) 2
   - (B) 3
   - (C) 4
   - (D) 5
   - (E) 6

8. Which of the following cities cannot be included in a tour that includes P?
   - (A) M
   - (B) N
   - (C) O
   - (D) S
   - (E) R

9. Which of the following is an acceptable group of cities for a tour?
   - (A) M, N, O, P
   - (B) M, N, Q, R
   - (C) M, N, Q, S
   - (D) L, M, Q, R
   - (E) N, S, R, T

10. Which one city would have to be deleted from the group M, Q, O, R, T to form an acceptable tour?
    - (A) M
    - (B) Q
    - (C) O
    - (D) R
    - (E) T

11. Which of the following could be made into an acceptable tour by adding exactly one more city?
    - (A) L, O, R
    - (B) M, P, Q
    - (C) M, Q, R
    - (D) N, S, R
    - (E) R, T, P

12. Exactly how many of the cities could be used for a tour consisting of only one city?
    - (A) 2
    - (B) 3
    - (C) 4
    - (D) 5
    - (E) 6

Questions 13–18

A child is stringing 11 different colored beads on a string.

Of the 11, four are yellow, three are red, two are blue, and two are green.

The red beads are adjacent to one another.

The blue beads are adjacent to one another.

The green beads are not adjacent to one another.

A red bead is at one end of the string, and a green bead is at the other end.

13. If the sixth and seventh beads are blue and the tenth bead is red, which of the following must be true?

  (A) The second bead is green.

  (B) The fifth bead is yellow.

  (C) The eighth bead is green.

  (D) A green bead is next to a yellow bead.

  (E) A blue bead is next to a green bead.

14. If the four yellow beads are next to each other and if the tenth bead is yellow, which of the following beads must be blue?

  (A) Fourth

  (B) Fifth

  (C) Sixth

  (D) Seventh

  (E) Eighth

15. If each blue bead is next to a green bead and if the four yellow beads are next to each other, then which of the following is a complete and accurate listing of the beads that must be yellow?

  (A) Fourth and fifth

  (B) Fifth and sixth

  (C) Sixth and seventh

  (D) Fourth, fifth, and sixth

  (E) Fifth, sixth, and seventh

16. If the fifth and sixth beads are blue and the ninth bead is red, which of the following must be true?

  (A) One of the green beads is next to a blue bead.

  (B) One of the red beads is next to a green bead.

  (C) Each yellow bead is next to at least one other yellow bead.

  (D) The second bead is yellow.

  (E) The eighth bead is yellow.

17. If the fifth, eighth, ninth, and tenth beads are yellow, then all of the following must be true EXCEPT

  (A) the fourth bead is green.

  (B) the sixth bead is blue.

  (C) exactly one red bead is next to a green bead.

  (D) both blue beads are next to yellow beads.

  (E) the second bead is yellow.

18. If one green bead is next to a red bead and the other green bead is next to a blue bead, which of the following must be true?

  (A) The second bead is blue.

  (B) The fourth bead is green.

  (C) The fourth bead is yellow.

  (D) The seventh bead is yellow.

  (E) The eighth bead is green.

Questions 19–24

The Executive Officer of a college English department is hiring adjunct faculty members for her evening courses. She must offer exactly eight courses during the academic year, four in the fall semester and four in the spring semester. The candidates are J, K, L, M, N, and O. Each person, if hired, must teach the following:

  J must teach one course on Marlowe and one course on Joyce.

  K must teach one course on Shakespeare and one course on Keats.

  L must teach one course on Marlowe and one course on Chaucer.

  M must teach one course on Shakespeare, one course on Marlowe, and one course on Keats.

  N must teach one course on Joyce, one course on Keats, and one course on Chaucer.

  O must teach one course on Shakespeare, one course on Marlowe, and one course on Joyce.

Only one course on an author can be offered in a single semester.

19. Which of the following combinations of teachers can be hired?
    (A) J, K, and N
    (B) K, M, and N
    (C) K, M, and O
    (D) L, M, and O
    (E) L, N, and O

20. If L and N are hired and if N is assigned to teach only in the spring semester, which of the following could be true?
    (A) Neither M nor O will be hired.
    (B) L will teach only in the spring semester.
    (C) L will teach only in the fall semester.
    (D) Courses on Keats and Joyce will be offered in the fall semester.
    (E) Courses on Shakespeare and Marlowe will be offered in the spring semester.

21. If M and N are hired and if M will teach only one of the two semesters and N the other, which of the following must be true?
    (A) J is hired.
    (B) K is hired.
    (C) L is hired.
    (D) A course on Shakespeare will be offered in the fall semester.
    (E) A course on Marlowe will be offered in the spring semester.

22. If K and N are hired, which of the following must be true?
    (A) A course on Joyce is offered in one semester or the other but not both.
    (B) A course on Keats is offered in one semester or the other but not both.
    (C) A course on Marlowe is offered both semesters.
    (D) A course on Shakespeare is offered both semesters.
    (E) A course on Chaucer is offered both semeseters.

23. If L is hired and will teach both her courses in the fall semester, which of the following must be true?
    (A) M and N are hired.
    (B) M and O are hired.
    (C) N and O are hired.
    (D) A course on Joyce will be offered in the spring semester.
    (E) A course on Chaucer will be offered in the spring semester.

24. If K, N, and O are hired and if N will teach all three of her courses in the fall semester, all of the following must be true EXCEPT
    (A) a course on Keats will be taught in the spring semester.
    (B) a course on Marlowe will be taught in the spring semester.
    (C) courses on Keats and Joyce will be taught in both semesters.
    (D) a course on Marlowe and a course on Shakespeare will be taught in the spring semester.
    (E) a course on Shakespeare and a course on Chaucer will be taught in the spring semester.

STOP

END OF SECTION 2. IF YOU HAVE ANY TIME LEFT, GO OVER YOUR WORK IN THIS SECTION ONLY. DO NOT WORK IN ANY OTHER SECTION OF THE TEST.

SECTION 3

28 Questions • 35 Minutes

> **Directions:** Below each of the following passages, you will find questions or incomplete statements about the passage. Each statement or question is followed by lettered words or expressions. Select the word or expression that most satisfactorily completes each statement or answers each question in accordance with the meaning of the passage. After you have chosen the *best* answer, blacken the corresponding space on the answer sheet.

War has escaped the battlefield and now can, with modern guidance systems on missiles, touch virtually every square yard of the earth's surface. It no longer
(5) involves only the military profession but also engulfs entire civilian populations. Nuclear weapons have made major war unthinkable. We are forced, however, to think about the unthinkable because a
(10) thermonuclear war could come by accident or miscalculation. We must accept the paradox of maintaining a capacity to fight such a war so that we will never have to do so.

(15) War has also lost most of its utility in achieving the traditional goals of conflict. Control of territory carries with it the obligation to provide subject peoples certain administrative, health, educa-
(20) tion, and other social services; such obligations far out-weigh the benefits of control. If the ruled population is ethnically or racially different from the rulers, tensions and chronic unrest often
(25) exist that further reduce the benefits and increase the costs of domination. Large populations no longer necessarily enhance state power and, in the absence of high levels of economic development,
(30) can impose severe burdens on food supply, jobs, and the broad range of services expected of modern governments. The noneconomic security reasons for the control of territory have been progres-
(35) sively undermined by the advances of modern technology. The benefits of forcing another nation to surrender its wealth are vastly outweighed by the benefits of persuading that nation to
(40) produce and exchange goods and services. In brief, imperialism no longer pays.

Making war has been one of the most persistent of human activities in
(45) the 80 centuries since men and women settled in cities and became thereby "civilized," but the modernization of the past 80 years has fundamentally changed the role and function of war. In pre-
(50) modernized societies, successful warfare brought significant material rewards, the most obvious of which were the stored wealth of the defeated. Equally important was human labor—control over
(55) people as slaves or levies for the victor's army—and the productive capacity of agricultural lands and mines. Successful warfare also produced psychic benefits. The removal or destruction of a
(60) threat brought a sense of security, and power gained over others created pride and national self-esteem.

Warfare was also the most complex, broad-scale, and demanding activ-
(65) ity of pre-modernized people. The challenges of leading men into battle—organizing, moving, and supporting armies—attracted the talents of the most vigorous, enterprising, intelligent, and
(70) imaginative men in the society. "Warrior" and "statesman" were usually synonymous, and the military was one of the few professions in which an able, ambitious boy of humble origin could
(75) rise to the top. In the broader cultural context, war was accepted in the

pre-modernized society as a part of the human condition, a mechanism of change, and an unavoidable, even noble,
(80) aspect of life. The excitement and drama of war made it a vital part of literature and legends.

1. The primary purpose of the passage is to

   (A) theorize about the role of the warrior-statesman in pre-modernized society.

   (B) explain the effects of war on both modernized and pre-modernized societies.

   (C) contrast the value of war in a modernized society with its value in pre-modernized society.

   (D) discuss the political and economic circumstances that lead to war in pre-modernized societies.

   (E) examine the influence of the development of nuclear weapons on the possibility of war.

2. According to the passage, leaders of pre-modernized society considered war to be

   (A) a valid tool of national policy.

   (B) an immoral act of aggression.

   (C) economically wasteful and socially unfeasible.

   (D) restricted in scope to military participants.

   (E) necessary to spur development of unoccupied lands.

3. The author most likely places the word "civilized" in quotation marks (line 46) in order to

   (A) show dissatisfaction at not having found a better word.

   (B) acknowledge that the word was borrowed from another source.

   (C) express irony that war should be a part of civilization.

   (D) impress upon the reader the tragedy of war.

   (E) raise a question about the value of war in modernized society.

4. The author mentions all of the following as possible reasons for going to war in a pre-modernized society EXCEPT

   (A) possibility of material gain.

   (B) promoting deserving young men to higher positions.

   (C) potential for increasing the security of the nation.

   (D) desire to capture productive farming lands.

   (E) need for workers to fill certain jobs.

5. The author is primarily concerned with discussing how

   (A) political decisions are reached.

   (B) economic and social conditions have changed.

   (C) technology for making war has improved.

   (D) armed conflict has changed.

   (E) war lost its value as a policy tool.

6. Which of the following best describes the tone of the passage?

   (A) Outraged and indignant

   (B) Scientific and detached

   (C) Humorous and wry

   (D) Fearful and alarmed

   (E) Concerned and optimistic

7. With which of the following statements
    about a successfully completed program
    of nuclear disarmament would the author
    most likely agree?

    (A) Without nuclear weapons, war in mod-
    ernized society would have the same
    value it had in pre-modernized society.

    (B) In the absence of the danger of nuclear
    war, national leaders could use pow-
    erful conventional weapons to make
    great gains from war.

    (C) Eliminating nuclear weapons is likely
    to increase the danger of an all-out,
    worldwide military engagement.

    (D) Even without the danger of a nuclear
    disaster, the costs of winning a war
    have made armed conflict on a large
    scale virtually obsolete.

    (E) War is caused by aggressive instincts,
    so if nuclear weapons were no longer
    available, national leaders would use
    conventional weapons to reach the
    same end.

Although it is now possible to bring most
high blood pressure under control, the
causes of essential hypertension remain
elusive. Understanding how hyperten-
(5) sion begins is at least partly a problem of
understanding when in life it begins;
and this may be very early—perhaps
within the first few months. Since the
beginning of the century, physicians have
(10) been aware that hypertension may run
in families, but before the 1970s, studies
of the familial aggregation of blood pressure treated only populations 15 years
of age or older. Few studies were at-
(15) tempted in younger persons because of a
prevailing notion that blood pressures
in this age group were difficult to measure or unreliable and because essential
hypertension was widely regarded as a
(20) disease of adults.

In 1971, a study of 700 children,
ages two to fourteen, used a special blood
pressure recorder that minimizes observer error and allows for standardiza-
(25) tion of blood pressure readings. Before
then, it had been well established that
the blood pressure of adults aggregates
familially, that is, the similarities between the blood pressure of an indi-
(30) vidual and his siblings are generally too
great to be explained by chance. The
1971 study showed that familial cluster-
ing was measurable in children as well,
suggesting that factors responsible for
(35) essential hypertension are acquired in
childhood. Additional epidemiological
studies demonstrated a clear tendency
for the children to retain the same blood
pressure patterns, relative to their peers,
(40) four years later. Thus a child with blood
pressure higher or lower than the norm
would tend to remain higher or lower
with increasing age.

Meanwhile, other investigators un-
(45) covered a complex of physiologic roles—
including blood pressure—for a vasoactive system called the kallikrein-kinin
system. Kallikreins are enzymes in the
kidney and blood plasma that act on
(50) precursors called kininogens to produce
vasoactive peptides called kinins. Several different kinins are produced,
at least three of which are powerful
blood vessel dilators. Apparently, the
(55) kallikrein-kinin system normally tends
to offset the elevations in arterial pressure that result from the secretion of
salt-conserving hormones such as aldosterone on the one hand and from activa-
(60) tion of the sympathetic nervous system
(which tends to constrict blood vessels)
on the other hand.

It is also known that urinary kallikrein excretion is abnormally low in
(65) subjects with essential hypertension.
Levels of urinary kallikrein in children
are inversely related to the diastolic
blood pressures of both children and
their mothers. Children with the lowest
(70) kallikrein levels are found in the families with the highest blood pressures. In
addition, black children tend to show
somewhat lower urinary kallikrein levels than white children, and blacks are
(75) more likely to have high blood pressure.
There is a great deal to be learned about

the biochemistry and physiologic roles of the kallikrein-kinin system. But there is the possibility that essential hypertension will prove to have biochemical precursors.

(80)

8. The author is primarily concerned with

   (A) questioning the assumption behind certain experiments involving children under the age of 15.

   (B) describing new scientific findings about high blood pressure and suggesting some implications.

   (C) describing two different methods for studying the causes of high blood pressure.

   (D) revealing a discrepancy between the findings of epidemiological studies and laboratory studies on essential hypertension.

   (E) arguing that high blood pressure may be influenced by familial factors.

9. Which of the following is mentioned as a factor that initially discouraged the study of hypertension in children?

   (A) An expectation that high blood pressure in children was untreatable

   (B) Repeated unsuccessful attempts to treat hypertension in adults

   (C) The belief that blood pressure in adults aggregates familially

   (D) The belief that it was difficult or impossible to measure accurately blood pressure in children

   (E) Ignorance of important differences in the physical constitution of ethnic subgroups

10. The argument in the passage leads most naturally to which of the following conclusions?

    (A) A low output of urinary kallikrein is a likely cause of high blood pressure in children.

    (B) The kallikrein-kinin system plays an important role in the regulation of blood pressure.

    (C) Essential hypertension may have biochemical precursors that may be useful predictors even in children.

    (D) The failure of the body to produce sufficient amounts of kinins is the cause of essential hypertension.

    (E) It is now possible to predict high blood pressure by using familial aggregations and urinary kallikrein measurement.

11. The author refers to the somewhat lower urinary kallikrein levels in black children (lines 71–75) in order to

    (A) support the thesis that kallikrein levels are inversely related to blood pressure.

    (B) highlight the special health problems involved in treating populations with high concentrations of black children.

    (C) offer a causal explanation for the difference in urinary kallikrein levels between black and white children.

    (D) suggest that further study needs to be done on the problem of high blood pressure among black adults.

    (E) prove that hypertension can be treated if those persons likely to have high blood pressure can be found.

12. The author states that the kallikrein-kinin system may affect blood pressure by

    (A) directly opposing the tendency of the sympathetic nervous system to constrict blood vessels.

    (B) producing kinins that tend to dilate blood vessels.

    (C) suppressing the production of hormones such as aldosterone.

    (D) controlling the levels of kallikrein in the urine.

    (E) compensating for cross-subgroup differentials.

13. The evidence that a child with blood pressure higher or lower than the norm would tend to remain so with increasing age (lines 40–43) is introduced by the author in order to

    (A) suggest that essential hypertension may have biochemical causes.

    (B) show that high blood pressure can be detected in children under the age of 15.

    (C) provide evidence that factors affecting blood pressure are already present in children.

    (D) propose that screening of children for high blood pressure should be increased.

    (E) refute arguments that blood pressure in children cannot be measured reliably.

14. The author presents the argument primarily by

    (A) contrasting two methods of doing scientific research.

    (B) providing experimental evidence against a conclusion.

    (C) presenting new scientific findings for a conclusion.

    (D) analyzing a new theory and showing its defects.

    (E) criticizing scientific research on blood pressure done before 1971.

Many critics of the current welfare system argue that existing welfare regulations foster family instability. They maintain that those regulations, which
(5) exclude most poor husband-and-wife families from Aid to Families with Dependent Children assistance grants, contribute to the problem of family dissolution. Thus, they conclude that
(10) expanding the set of families eligible for family assistance plans or guaranteed income measures would result in a marked strengthening of the low-income family structure.
(15)   If all poor families could receive welfare, would the incidence of instability change markedly? The answer to this question depends on the relative importance of three categories of potential
(20) welfare recipients. The first is the "cheater"—the husband who is reported to have abandoned his family but in fact disappears only when the social caseworker is in the neighborhood. The sec-
(25) ond consists of a loving husband and devoted father who, sensing his own inadequacy as a provider, leaves so that his wife and children may enjoy the relative benefit provided by public assis-
(30) tance. There is very little evidence that these categories are significant.
        The third category is the unhappily married couple, who remain together out of a sense of economic responsibility for their children, because of the high
(35) costs of separation, or because of the consumption benefits of marriage. This

group is large. The formation, maintenance, and dissolution of the family is in
(40) large part a function of the relative balance between the benefits and costs of
marriage as seen by the individual members of the marriage. The major benefit
generated by the creation of a family is
(45) the expansion of the set of consumption
possibilities. The benefits from such a
partnership depend largely on the relative dissimilarity of the resources or
basic endowments each partner brings
(50) to the marriage. Persons with similar
productive capacities have less economic
"cement" holding their marriage together. Since the family performs certain functions society regards as vital, a
(55) complex network of social and legal but-
tresses has evolved to reinforce marriage. Much of the variation in marital
stability across income classes can be
explained by the variation in costs of
(60) dissolution imposed by society, such as
division of property, alimony, child support, and the social stigma attached to
divorce.
　　　Marital stability is related to the
(65) costs of achieving an acceptable agreement on family consumption and production and to the prevailing social price
of instability in the marriage partners'
social-economic group. Expected AFDC
(70) income exerts pressures on family instability by reducing the cost of dissolution.
To the extent that welfare is a form of
government-subsidized alimony payments, it reduces the institutional costs
(75) of separation and guarantees a minimal
standard of living for wife and children.
So welfare opportunities are a significant determinant of family instability in
poor neighborhoods, but this is not the
(80) result of AFDC regulations that exclude
most intact families from coverage.
Rather, welfare-related instability occurs because public assistance lowers
both the benefits of marriage and the
(85) costs of its disruption by providing a
system of government-subsidized alimony payments.

15. The author is primarily concerned with
    (A) interpreting the results of a survey.
    (B) discussing the role of the father in low-income families.
    (C) analyzing the causes of a phenom-enon.
    (D) recommending reforms to the welfare system.
    (E) changing public attitudes toward welfare recipients.

16. Which of the following would provide the most logical continuation of the final para-graph?
    (A) Paradoxically, any liberalization of AFDC eligibility restrictions is likely to intensify rather than mitigate pres-sures on family stability.
    (B) Actually, concern for the individual recipients should not be allowed to override considerations of sound fis-cal policy.
    (C) In reality, there is virtually no evi-dence that AFDC payments have any relationship at all to problems of fam-ily instability in low-income mar-riages.
    (D) In the final analysis, it appears that government welfare payments, to the extent that the cost of marriage is lowered, encourage the formation of low-income families.
    (E) Ultimately, the problem of low-income family instability can be eliminated by reducing welfare benefits to the point where the cost of dissolution equals the cost of staying married.

17. All of the following are mentioned by the author as factors tending to perpetuate a marriage EXCEPT

(A) the stigma attached to divorce.

(B) the social class of the partners.

(C) the cost of alimony and child support.

(D) the loss of property upon divorce.

(E) the greater consumption possibilities of married people.

18. Which of the following best summarizes the main idea of the passage?

(A) Welfare restrictions limiting the eligibility of families for benefits do not contribute to low-income family instability.

(B) Contrary to popular opinion, the most significant category of welfare recipients is not the "cheating" father.

(C) The incidence of family dissolution among low-income families is directly related to the inability of families with fathers to get welfare benefits.

(D) Very little of the divorce rate among low-income families can be attributed to fathers deserting their families so that they can qualify for welfare.

(E) Government welfare payments are at present excessively high and must be reduced in order to slow the growing divorce rate among low-income families.

19. The tone of the passage can best be described as

(A) confident and optimistic.

(B) scientific and detached.

(C) discouraged and alarmed.

(D) polite and sensitive.

(E) calloused and indifferent.

20. With which of the following statements about marriage would the author most likely agree?

(A) Marriage is an institution that is largely shaped by powerful but impersonal economic and social forces.

(B) Marriage has a greater value to persons in higher income brackets than to persons in lower income brackets.

(C) Society has no legitimate interest in encouraging people to remain married to one another.

(D) Marriage as an institution is no longer economically viable and will gradually give way to other forms of social organization.

(E) The rising divorce rate across all income brackets indicates that people are more self-centered and less concerned about others than before.

21. The passage would most likely be found in a

(A) pamphlet on civil rights.

(B) basic economics text.

(C) book on the history of welfare.

(D) religious tract on the importance of marriage.

(E) scholarly journal devoted to public policy questions

An assumption that underlies most discussions of electric facility siting is that the initial selection of a site is the responsibility of the utility concerned—

(5) subject to governmental review and approval only after the site has been chosen. This assumption must be changed so that site selection becomes a joint responsibility of the utilities and

(10) the appropriate governmental authorities from the outset. Siting decisions would be made in accordance with either of two strategies. The metropolitan strategy takes the existing distribution

(15) of population and supporting facilities as given. An attempt is then made to

choose between dispersed or concentrated siting and to locate generating facilities in accordance with some eco-
(20) nomic principle. For example, the economic objectives of least-cost construction and rapid start-up may be achieved, in part, by a metropolitan strategy that takes advantage of exist-
(25) ing elements of social and physical infrastructure in the big cities. Under the frontier strategy, the energy park may be taken as an independent variable, subject to manipulation by policy-
(30) makers as a means of achieving desired demographic or social goals, such as rural-town-city mix. Thus, population distribution is taken as a goal of national social policy, not as a given of a
(35) national energy policy. In the frontier strategy, the option of dispersed siting is irrelevant from the standpoint of community impact because there is no pre-existing community of any size.
(40)   Traditionally, the resource-endowment of a location—and especially its situation relative to the primary industry of the hinterland—has had a special importance in American history.
(45) In the early agricultural period, the most valued natural endowment was arable land with good climate and available water. America's oldest cities were mercantile outposts of such agricultural
(50) areas. Deepwater ports developed to serve the agricultural hinterlands, which produced staple commodities in demand on the world market. From the 1840s onward, the juxtaposition of coal,
(55) iron ore, and markets afforded the impetus for manufacturing growth in the northeastern United States. The American manufacturing heartland developed westwards to encompass Lake Superior
(60) iron ores, the Pennsylvania coalfields, and the Northeast's financial, entrepreneurial, and manufacturing roles. Subsequent metropolitan growth has been organized around this national core.
(65)   Against the theory of urban development, it is essential to bear in mind the unprecedented dimensions of an energy park. The existing electric power

plant at Four Corners in the southwest
(70) United States—the only human artifact visible to orbiting astronauts—generates only 4 thousand megawatts electric. The smallest energy parks will concentrate five times the thermal en-
(75) ergy represented by the Four Corners plant. An energy park, then, would seem every bit as formidable as the natural harbor conditions or coal deposits that underwrote the growth of the great cit-
(80) ies of the past—with a crucial difference. The founders of past settlements could not choose the geographic locations of their natural advantages.
     The frontier strategy implements
(85) the principle of created opportunity; and this helps explain why some environmentalists perceive the energy park idea as a threat to nature. But the problems of modern society, with or without en-
(90) ergy parks, require ever more comprehensive planning. And energy parks are a means of advancing American social history rather than merely responding to power needs in an unplanned, *ad hoc*
(95) manner.

22. Which of the following statements best describes the main point of the passage?

(A) Government regulatory authorities should participate in electric facility site selection to further social goals.

(B) Energy parks will have a significant influence on the demographic features of the American population.

(C) Urban growth in the United States was largely the result of economic forces rather than conscientious planning.

(D) Under the frontier siting strategy for energy parks, siting decisions are influenced by the natural features of the land.

(E) America needs larger power-production facilities in urban and rural areas to meet the increased demand for energy.

23. All of the following are mentioned in the passage as characteristics of energy parks EXCEPT

(A) energy parks will be built upon previously undeveloped sites.

(B) energy parks will be built in areas remote from major population centers.

(C) energy parks will produce considerably more thermal energy than existing facilities.

(D) energy parks will be built at sites that are near fuel sources such as coal.

(E) energy parks may have considerable effects on population distribution.

24. According to the passage, which of the following is the most important feature of the traditional process of siting decisions for electric facilities?

(A) Sites were selected for the ability to advance social history.

(B) Siting was viewed as a tool for achieving economic goals.

(C) The primary responsibility for siting resided with the utility.

(D) Decisions were made jointly by utilities and government.

(E) Groups of affected citizens participated on advisory panels.

25. Which of the following, if true, would most seriously WEAKEN the author's position?

(A) The first settlements in America were established in order to provide trading posts with Native Americans.

(B) The cost of constructing an electric power plant in an urban area is not significantly greater than that for a rural area.

(C) An energy park will be so large that it will be impossible to predict the demographic consequences of its construction.

(D) Cities in European countries grew up in response to political pressures during the feudal period rather than economic pressures.

(E) The United States is presently in a period of population migration that will change the rural-town-city mix.

26. With which one of the following statements would the author most likely agree?

(A) Decisions about the locations for power plants should be left to the utilities.

(B) Government leaders in the nineteenth century were irresponsible in not supervising urban growth more closely.

(C) Natural features of a region such as cultivatable land and water supply are no longer important to urban growth.

(D) Modern society is so complex that governments must take greater responsibility for decisions such as power plant siting.

(E) The Four Corners plant should not have been built because of its mammoth size.

27. According to the passage, the most important difference between the natural advantages of early cities and the features of an energy park is

   (A) the features of an energy park will be located where the builders choose.

   (B) natural advantages are no longer as important as they once were.

   (C) natural features cannot be observed from outer space, but energy parks can.

   (D) early cities grew up close to agricultural areas, while energy parks will be located in mountains.

   (E) policy planners have learned to minimize the effects of energy parks on nature.

28. The author's attitude toward energy parks can best be described as

   (A) cautious uncertainty.

   (B) circumspect skepticism.

   (C) studied indifference.

   (D) qualified endorsement.

   (E) unrestrained enthusiasm.

STOP

END OF SECTION 3. IF YOU HAVE ANY TIME LEFT, GO OVER YOUR WORK IN THIS SECTION ONLY. DO NOT WORK IN ANY OTHER SECTION OF THE TEST.

SECTION 4

24 Questions • 35 Minutes

> **Directions:** Each group of questions is based on a set of propositions or conditions. Drawing a rough picture or diagram may help in answering some of the questions. After you have chosen the *best* answer for each question, blacken the corresponding space on your answer sheet.

Questions 1–6

Six contestants, F, G, H, I, J, and K, are to be ranked first (highest) through sixth (lowest), though not necessarily in that order, at the start of a singles Ping-Pong challenge tournament.

F is ranked above G.

J is ranked above both H and I.

K is ranked two places above H.

F is ranked either third or fourth.

During the tournament, a player may challenge only the player ranked immediately above him or the player ranked two places above him.

1. Which of the following is a possible initial ranking from highest to lowest?
   - **(A)** J, H, K, F, I, G
   - **(B)** K, I, H, J, F, G
   - **(C)** K, G, H, F, J, I
   - **(D)** J, K, F, H, I, G
   - **(E)** J, K, H, F, I, G

2. If K is initially ranked first, which of the following must also be true of the initial ranking?
   - **(A)** J is ranked second.
   - **(B)** H is ranked second.
   - **(C)** F is ranked third.
   - **(D)** G is ranked fifth.
   - **(E)** I is ranked sixth.

3. If F is initially ranked third, which of the following must also be true of the initial ranking?
   - **(A)** J is ranked first.
   - **(B)** K is ranked second.
   - **(C)** G is ranked fourth.
   - **(D)** I is ranked fourth.
   - **(E)** I is ranked sixth.

4. If K is initially ranked third and if K makes the first challenge, which of the following is a complete and accurate listing of the contestants K could play in the first match?
   - **(A)** I
   - **(B)** J
   - **(C)** J and F
   - **(D)** J and I
   - **(E)** J, F, and I

5. If the first challenge of the tournament is made by F against H, all of the following must be true of the initial ranking EXCEPT
   - **(A)** K is ranked first.
   - **(B)** J is ranked second.
   - **(C)** H is ranked third.
   - **(D)** F is ranked fourth.
   - **(E)** I is ranked fifth.

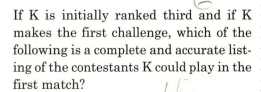

6. If J makes the first challenge of the tournament against K, then which of the following must be true of the initial rankings?

(A) K is ranked first.

(B) J is ranked third.

(C) F is ranked third.

(D) H is ranked fourth.

(E) G is ranked fifth.

Questions 7–10

The supervisor of a commuter airline is scheduling pilots to fly the round trip from City X to City Y. The trip takes only two hours, and the airline has one round-trip flight in the morning and one round-trip flight in the afternoon, each day, Monday through Friday. Pilots must be scheduled in accordance with the following rules:

Only W, X, and Y can fly the morning flight.

Only V, X, and Z can fly the afternoon flight.

No pilot may fly twice on the same day.

No pilot may fly on two consecutive days.

X must fly the Wednesday morning flight.

Z must fly the Tuesday afternoon flight.

7. Which of the following must be true?

(A) W flies the Monday morning flight.

(B) X flies the Monday afternoon flight.

(C) Y flies the Tuesday morning flight.

(D) W flies the Thursday morning flight.

(E) Z flies the Thursday afternoon flight.

8. If X flies on Friday morning, which of the following must be true?

(A) X does not fly on Monday afternoon.

(B) V flies on Friday afternoon.

(C) W flies Thursday morning.

(D) Y flies Thursday morning.

(E) Neither W nor Y flies Thursday morning.

9. If X flies only one morning flight during the week, which of the following must be true?

(A) W flies exactly two days during the week.

(B) X flies exactly three days during the week.

(C) Y flies only one day during the week.

(D) Z flies Monday afternoon and Friday afternoon.

(E) X flies more times during the week than V.

10. If W is not scheduled to fly at all during the week, all of the following must be true EXCEPT

(A) X flies on Monday morning.

(B) V flies on Monday afternoon.

(C) Y flies on Thursday morning.

(D) Z flies on Friday afternoon.

(E) X flies on Friday morning.

Questions 11–15

A restaurant offers three daily specials each day of the week. The daily specials are selected from a list of dishes: P, Q, R, S, T, and U. The daily specials for the menu are selected in accordance with the following restrictions:

On any day that S is on the menu, Q must also be on the menu.

If R is on the menu one day, it cannot be included on the menu the following day.

U can be on the menu only on a day following a day on which T is on the menu.

Only one of the three specials from a given day can be offered the following day.

11. Which of the following could be the list of daily specials offered two days in a row?

    (A) S, R, and T; R, P, and Q

    (B) Q, S, and R; Q, S, and T

    (C) P, Q, and S; S, R, and T

    (D) Q, S, and P; T, U, and Q

    (E) S, Q, and R; Q, T, and P

12. If P and S are on the menu one day, which of the following must be true of the menu the following day?

    (A) U is on the menu.

    (B) S is on the menu.

    (C) T and R are on the menu.

    (D) U and T are on the menu.

    (E) U and R are on the menu.

13. If P, R, and Q are on the menu one day and P, T, and R are on the menu two days later, which daily specials must have appeared on the menu for the intervening day?

    (A) P, R, and T

    (B) P, S, and T

    (C) Q, S, and T

    (D) Q, S, and U

    (E) S, T, and U

14. If on a certain day neither Q nor T is on the menu, how many different combinations of daily specials are possible for that day?

    (A) 1

    (B) 2

    (C) 3

    (D) 4

    (E) 5

15. If Q, R, and S are on the menu one day, which specials must be offered the following day?

    (A) P, Q, and T

    (B) P, R, and T

    (C) P, R, and U

    (D) R, S, and Q

    (E) T, S, and U

Questions 16–20

The personnel director of a company is scheduling interviews for eight people—J, K, L, M, N, O, P, and Q. Each person will have one interview, and all interviews are to be held on Monday through Friday of the same week.

> At least one person will be interviewed each day.
>
> More than one interview will be scheduled on exactly two of the days.
>
> O is the only person who will be interviewed on Wednesday.
>
> M and N must be scheduled for interviews exactly three days after Q.
>
> P must be interviewed later in the week than K.

16. Which of the following CANNOT be true?

    (A) O's interview is later in the week than K's interview.

    (B) L's interview is later in the week than J's interview.

    (C) K's interview is later in the week than N's interview.

    (D) L's interview is on the same day as N's interview.

    (E) J's interview is on the same day as K's interview.

17. Which of the following must be true?

    (A) A third interview is scheduled on the same day with M and N.

    (B) Exactly three interviews will be held on one of the days.

    (C) Exactly one person will be interviewed on Monday.

    (D) Exactly two persons will be interviewed on Friday.

    (E) Q will have the only interview on Tuesday.

18. If Q and J are the only persons interviewed on Tuesday, which of the following must be true?

    (A) K's is the only interview on one of the days.

    (B) L's is the only interview on one of the days.

    (C) P's is the only interview on one of the days.

    (D) P's interview is earlier in the week than N's interview.

    (E) L's interview is earlier in the week than O's interview.

19. If M, N, and K are interviewed on the same day, which of the following must be true?

    (A) J is interviewed on Monday.

    (B) Q is interviewed on Monday.

    (C) L is interviewed on Tuesday.

    (D) J and L are interviewed on the same day.

    (E) J and Q are interviewed on the same day.

20. If L is interviewed later in the week than P, which of the following CANNOT be true?

    (A) P is the only person interviewed on one of the days.

    (B) K is the only person interviewed on one of the days.

    (C) L and Q are interviewed on the same day.

    (D) L and J are interviewed on the same day.

    (E) M and P are interviewed on the same day.

Questions 21–24

A university acting class is presenting a series of five skits using six performers, M, N, O, P, Q, and R. Each performer must perform in exactly three of the skits.

Only O and P will perform in the first skit.

R and three others will perform in the second skit.

Only N will perform in the third skit.

More people will perform in the fourth skit than in the fifth skit.

21. Which of the following must be true?

    (A) N and Q perform in the second skit.

    (B) N and R perform in the fifth skit.

    (C) Q does not perform in the fifth skit.

    (D) Exactly four people perform in the fourth skit.

    (E) Exactly five people perform in the fifth skit.

22. For which of the following pairs of performers is it true that if one appears in a skit, the other must also appear?

    (A) M and N

    (B) M and R

    (C) P and O

    (D) P and R

    (E) Q and O

23. Which of the following CANNOT be true?

(A) Neither O nor P appears in the second skit.

(B) Neither O nor P appears in the fifth skit.

(C) N and Q appear in the second skit.

(D) N appears in the second skit.

(E) O, P, and Q appear in the fifth skit.

24. If N does not appear in the fifth skit, all of the following must be true EXCEPT

(A) P appears in the second skit.

(B) N appears in the second skit.

(C) O appears in the fifth skit.

(D) P appears in the fifth skit.

(E) Q appears in the fifth skit.

STOP

END OF SECTION 4. IF YOU HAVE ANY TIME LEFT, GO OVER YOUR WORK IN THIS SECTION ONLY. DO NOT WORK IN ANY OTHER SECTION OF THE TEST.

SECTION 5

25 Questions • 35 Minutes

> **Directions:** Below each of the following passages, you will find questions or incomplete statements about the passage. Each statement or question is followed by lettered words or expressions. Select the word or expression that most satisfactorily completes each statement or answers each question in accordance with the meaning of the passage. After you have chosen the *best* answer, blacken the corresponding space on the answer sheet.

1. There has been speculation that the Chairman of Global Enterprises will replace the company's CEO next week, but it would be risky for the Chairman to make such a change without first consulting formally with the Board of Directors. There have been no Board meetings recently, and no such meeting has been scheduled for the next few weeks. Therefore, the speculation regarding the change in management is probably wrong.

    Which of the following principles best describes the reasoning of the speaker above?

    (A) If two statements are logically inconsistent and it is known that one is false, the other statement is necessarily true.

    (B) A theory may turn out to be true even though all of the available data initially suggests that the theory is false.

    (C) It cannot be assumed from the fact that event E_2 follows event E_1 in time that event E_1 was therefore the cause of event E_2.

    (D) A hypothesis is weakened when conditions that are normally necessary for an expected result do not exist.

    (E) A cause necessary to ensure a certain outcome may not, in and of itself, be sufficient to guarantee that outcome.

2. Office supply stores and other retailers offer computer programs that will help anyone to prepare a will for themselves. The Bar Association warns that wills produced using these do-it-yourself kits might not be valid, but lawyers are simply afraid that the kits will cut into the fees that they charge. So there is no reason that a person should not create a will using a do-it-yourself kit.

    The reasoning above is flawed because the speaker

    (A) fails to consider the possibility that many people will still prefer to have a lawyer write their wills.

    (B) assumes that many lawyers do not use the same do-it-yourself programs offered by retailers to the public.

    (C) presents a false dichotomy in which a person must choose a lawyer or a do-it-yourself kit.

    (D) attempts to gain acceptance of a claim by creating apprehension about the alternative.

    (E) rejects a conclusion by attacking the source of the claim rather than its merits.

3.   CHARPENTIER: Research has demonstrated that the United States, which has the most extensive health-care industry in the world, has only the 17th lowest infant mortality rate in the world. This forces me to conclude that medical technology causes babies to die.

        ADAMANTE: That is ludicrous. We know that medical care is not equally available to all. Infant mortality is more likely a function of low income than of medical technology.

Adamante attacks Charpentier's reasoning in which way?

(A) By questioning the validity of the supporting data

(B) By offering an alternative explanation of the data

(C) By suggesting that the argument is circular

(D) By defining an intermediate cause

(E) By implying that the data lead to the opposite conclusion

4.   When this proposal to reduce welfare benefits is brought up for debate, we are sure to hear claims by the liberal politicians that the bill will be detrimental to poor people. These politicians fail to understand, however, that budget reductions are accompanied by tax cuts—so everyone will have more money to spend, not less.

Which of the following, if true, would undermine the author's position?

(A) Poor people tend to vote for liberal politicians who promise to raise welfare benefits.

(B) Politicians often make campaign promises that they do not fulfill.

(C) Poor people pay little or not taxes, so a tax cut would be of little advantage to them.

(D) Any tax advantage enjoyed by the poor will not be offset by cuts in services.

(E) Budget reductions when accompanied by tax cuts often stimulate economic growth.

5. Many people ask, "How effective is Painaway?" So to find out we have been checking the medicine cabinets of the apartments in this typical building. As it turns out, eight out of ten contain a bottle of Painaway. Doesn't it stand to reason that you, too, should have the most effective pain-reliever on the market?

The appeal of this advertisement would be most WEAKENED by which of the following pieces of evidence?

(A) Painaway distributed complimentary bottles of medicine to most apartments in the building two days before the advertisement was made.

(B) The actor who made the advertisement takes a pain-reliever manufactured by a competitor of Painaway.

(C) Most people want a fast, effective pain-reliever.

(D) Many people take the advice of their neighborhood druggists about pain-relievers.

(E) A government survey shows that many people take a pain-reliever before it is really needed.

Questions 6 and 7

An artist must suffer for the sake of art, say these successful entrepreneurs who attempt to pass themselves off as artists. They auction off to the highest bidder, usually a fool, the most mediocre of drawings; and then, from their well-laid tables, they have the unmitigated gall to imply that they themselves _____(6).

6. Choose the answer that best completes the paragraph.

(A) are connoisseurs of art

(B) suffer deprivation for the sake of their work

(C) are artists

(D) know art better than the art critics do

(E) do not enjoy a good meal

7. Which of the following must underlie the author's position?

(A) One must actually suffer to do great art.

(B) Financial deprivation is the only suffering an artist undergoes.

(C) Art critics have little real expertise and are consequently easily deceived.

(D) Most mediocre artists are fools.

(E) All successful entrepreneurs are fools.

Questions 8 and 9

Stock market analysts always attribute a sudden drop in the market to some domestic or international political crisis. I maintain, however, that these declines are attributable to the phases of the moon, which also cause periodic political upheavals and increases in tension in world affairs.

8. Which of the following best describes the author's method of questioning the claim of market analysts?

(A) Presenting a counterexample

(B) Presenting statistical evidence

(C) Suggesting an alternative causal linkage

(D) Appealing to generally accepted beliefs

(E) Demonstrating that market analysts' reports are unreliable

9. It can be inferred that the author is critical of the stock analysts because the author

(A) believes that they have oversimplified the connection between political crisis and fluctuations of the market.

(B) knows that the stock market generally shows more gains than losses.

(C) suspects that stock analysts have a vested interest in the stock market and are therefore likely to distort their explanations.

(D) anticipates making large profits in the market as an investor.

(E) is worried that if the connection between political events and stock market prices becomes well known, unscrupulous investors will take advantage of the information.

10. This piece of pottery must surely date from the late Minoan period. The dress of the female figures, particularly the bare and emphasized breasts, and the activities of the people depicted, note especially the importance of the bull, are both highly suggestive of this period. These factors, when coupled with the black, semi-gloss glaze that results from firing the pot in a sealed kiln at a low temperature, make the conclusion a virtual certainty.

Which of the following is a basic assumption made by the author of this explanation?

(A) Black, semi-gloss glazed pottery was made only during the late Minoan period.

(B) The bull is an animal that was important to most ancient cultures.

(C) Throughout the long history of the Minoan people, their artisans decorated pottery with semi-nude women and bulls.

(D) By analyzing the style and materials of any work of art, an expert can pinpoint the date of its creation.

(E) There are key characteristics of works of art that can be shown to be typical of a particular period.

11. Most radicals who argue for violent revolution and complete overthrow of our existing society have no clear idea what will emerge from the destruction. They just assert that things are so bad now that any change would have to be a change for the better. But surely this is mistaken, for things might actually turn out to be worse.

The most effective point that can be raised against this argument is that the author says nothing about

   (A) the manner in which the radicals might foment their revolution.

   (B) the specific results of the revolution that would be changes for the worse.

   (C) the economic arguments the radicals use to persuade people to join in their cause.

   (D) the fact that most people are really satisfied with the present system so that the chance of total revolution is very small.

   (E) the loss of life and property that is likely to accompany total destruction of a society.

12. At Clapboard Design, the average annual compensation, including bonuses, was $73,000 for graphic artists last year, while the average annual compensation, including bonuses, for copywriters was $48,000. Last year, the average annual compensation, including bonuses, for all employees at Clapboard Design was $40,000.

If the information provided is accurate, which of the following conclusions can be most reliably drawn?

   (A) There were more graphic artists at Clapboard Design last year than copywriters.

   (B) There was no graphic artist at Clapboard Design last year whose total compensation was less than the average for copywriters.

   (C) At least one graphic artist at Clapboard Design received less in total compensation last year than the highest paid copywriter.

   (D) The average bonus awarded to graphic artists at Clapboard Design last year was greater than the average bonus for copywriters.

   (E) The total compensation for at least one employee at Clapboard Design last year was less than the average of all copywriters.

Questions 13 and 14

Having just completed Introductory Logic 9, I feel competent to instruct others in the intricacies of this wonderful discipline. Logic is concerned with correct reasoning in the form of syllogisms. A syllogism consists of three statements, of which two are premises and the third is the conclusion. Here is an example:

MAJOR PREMISE:	The American buffalo is disappearing.
MINOR PREMISE:	This animal is an American buffalo.
CONCLUSION:	Therefore, this animal is disappearing.

Once one has been indoctrinated into the mysteries of this arcane science, there is no statement he may not assert with complete confidence.

13. The reasoning of the author's example is most similar to that contained in which of the following arguments?

   (A) Any endangered species must be protected; this species is endangered; therefore, it should be protected.

   (B) All whales are mammals; this animal is a whale; therefore, this animal is a mammal.

   (C) Engaging in sexual intercourse with a person to whom one is not married is a sin; and since premarital intercourse is, by definition, without the institution of marriage, it is, therefore, a sin.

   (D) There are 60 seconds in a minute; there are 60 minutes in an hour; therefore, there are 3,600 seconds in an hour.

   (E) Wealthy people pay most of the taxes; this man is wealthy; therefore, this man pays most of the taxes.

14. The main purpose of the author's argument is to

   (A) provide instruction in logic.

   (B) supply a definition.

   (C) cast doubt on the value of formal logic.

   (D) present an argument for the protection of the American buffalo.

   (E) show the precise relationship between the premises and conclusion of his example.

Questions 15 and 16

On a recent trip to the Mediterranean, I made the acquaintance of a young man who warned me against trusting Cretans. "Everything they say is a lie," he told me, "and I should know because I come from Crete myself." I thanked the fellow for his advice but told him in light of what he had said, I had no intention of believing it.

15. Which of the following best describes the author's behavior?

   (A) It was unwarranted because the young man was merely trying to be helpful to a stranger.

   (B) It was paradoxical for in discounting the advice he implicitly relied on it.

   (C) It was understandable inasmuch as the young man, by his own admission, could not possibly be telling the truth.

   (D) It was high-handed and just the sort of thing that gives American tourists a bad name.

   (E) It was overly cautious since not everyone in a foreign country will try to take advantage of a tourist.

16. Which of the following is most nearly analogous to the warning issued by the young man?

   (A) An admission by a witness under cross-examination that he has lied

   (B) A sign put up by the Chamber of Commerce of a large city alerting visitors to the danger of pickpockets

   (C) The command of a military leader to his marching troops to do an about-face

   (D) A sentence written in chalk on a blackboard that says, "This sentence is false."

   (E) The advice of a veteran worker to a newly hired person: "You don't actually have to work hard so long as you look like you're working hard."

17. Doctors, in seeking a cure for *aphroditis melancholias,* are guided by their research into the causes of *metaeritocas polymanias* because the symptoms of the two diseases occur in populations of similar ages, manifesting symptoms in both cases of high fever, swollen glands, and lack of appetite. Moreover, the incubation period for both diseases is virtually identical. So these medical researchers are convinced that the virus responsible for *aphroditis melancholias* is very similar to that responsible for *metaeritocas polymanias.*

The conclusion of the author rests on the presupposition that

(A) *metaeritocas polymanias* is a more serious public health hazard than *aphroditis melancholias.*

(B) for every disease, modern medical science will eventually find a cure.

(C) saving human life is the single most important goal of modern technology.

(D) *aphroditis melancholias* is a disease that occurs only in human beings.

(E) diseases with similar symptoms will have similar causes.

18. Concerned about the rough waters in the harbor caused by increasing reliance on commuter ferries, the Port Authority imposed a speed limit on boat traffic because it is well known that modern ferries running at very slow speeds produce little or no wake. Paradoxically, however, during the weeks following the enactment of the speed limit, sensors installed at key monitoring points in the harbor showed that water turbulence actually increased.

Which of the following, if true, best explains the paradox described above?

(A) The sensors showed that the harbor's water is the calmest from midnight to 4:00 am when very few ferries operate.

(B) Waves produced by ferries propagate outward to the shorelines where they are reflected off bulkheads and other hard surfaces.

(C) A boat that produces less wake is operating more efficiently than one that is producing a great deal of wake.

(D) The number of ferry trips made during the period immediately following the imposition of the speed limit did not increase appreciably.

(E) At faster speeds, modern ferries ride higher, displacing less water and producing less wake than at moderate speeds.

19. A dog's nose has roughly 200 million olfactory receptors, making it an instrument of remarkable sensitivity theoretically well suited to detective work, but dogs also return a very high rate of false positives when asked to identify people or substances. Subtle but misleading signals that a trainer can unknowingly communicate to the animal include a glance or step in a certain direction or allowing the dog to spend too much or too little time in a particular spot. A dog that works out of sight of the handler, however, cannot be influenced in these ways, so permitting it to work off-leash would eliminate the problem of false positives.

Which of the following, if true, would most weaken the reasoning above?

(A) Dogs are trained using positive reinforcements such as food treats for finding scents and so exhibit behavior calculated to earn rewards.

(B) Dogs are trained to identify basic chemicals but find it difficult to recognize these chemicals when they are included in a mixture.

(C) Handlers keep logs of all training exercises and review these records periodically for evidence that suggests they are influencing the dog.

(D) Handlers are reluctant to admit that their dogs return false positives and so usually claim that the animal reacted to a "trace" of a substance.

(E) Miniature cameras can be attached to a dog's collar to permit a handler to monitor how the dog is working even when out of sight.

20. There are over 400 species of ladybugs in North America, but more and more, the multicolored Asian lady beetle predominates. The Asian lady beetle is slightly larger than many native species, about one third of an inch long; and it characteristically has 19 spots on its wing covers, though there may be no spots at all. A black "W" is usually found on the thorax. So if you find a ladybug without spots and with no black "W" on its thorax, it is definitely a member of a native species.

The reasoning in the argument is flawed because the argument

(A) presupposes what it is intended to prove.

(B) mistakes a cause of an event for its effect.

(C) fails to consider the possibility that the Asian lady beetle was introduced accidentally.

(D) makes a general claim based upon examples that are not fairly representative of the larger population.

(E) interprets evidence that a claim is probably true as establishing the certainty of the conclusion.

21. In Entonia where the Parliament chooses the Prime Minister, anyone who supports the majority party in Parliament should also support the Prime Minister because the Prime Minister is chosen by the majority party.

The pattern of reasoning that characterizes the argument above is most closely paralleled by that which characterizes which of the following?

(A) People who enjoy watching rugby should also enjoy watching American football because American football, in its patterns of play, its rules, and its structure, derives from rugby.

(B) People who go to bed before 10:00 pm should eat dinner before 6:00 pm to ensure that the food that they've eaten is thoroughly digested before they retire for the night.

(C) People who appreciate paintings by Monet should also appreciate paintings by Renoir since both were members of the Impressionist school of painting in late nineteenth-century France.

(D) A person who is able to operate a crane can probably also operate a dredge since the mechanisms and the controls of the two machines are very similar.

(E) A person who reads a daily newspaper will have no reason to read a weekly news magazine since the magazine is just a compilation of the week's news.

22. Personal video recorders that allow viewers to skip commercials have television network executives worried that the public will stop watching commercials. However, I have noticed that people with such devices watch truly entertaining commercials two or three times because just as it is easy to fastforward past commercials, it is easy to rewind and view them again.

The statements above best support which of the following conclusions?

(A) Television executives need not be concerned that personal video recorders will result in a loss of ad revenue.

(B) People using personal video recorders may watch entertaining commercials more than once.

(C) Entertaining television commercials are more effective at promoting a product than ads that are not entertaining.

(D) Personal video recorders will someday replace traditional television sets as the primary means of viewing telecasts.

(E) Television advertising will become less effective as a means of promoting products than it has been in the past.

Questions 23 and 24

DEBORAH: The policy of legacy admissions, by which elite universities give preference to the children of the university's graduates, is unfair and should be discontinued. The policy gives an unfair advantage to exactly those applicants who don't need one: students who have one or perhaps two parents who themselves were the beneficiaries of a superb education.

ANNA: But these universities see the policy of legacy admissions as an important tool for securing alumni donations. A wealthy graduate is more likely to contribute and to contribute more generously if his or her child is a student or graduate of the university.

23. Anna's response to Deborah can best be described as

(A) denying that legacy admissions give the children of graduates any advantage.

(B) noting that the policy, whatever its disadvantages, serves a useful purpose.

(C) suggesting that fairness is not a consideration in university admissions procedures.

(D) outlining some minor changes in the policy of legacy admissions to make it fair.

(E) challenging Deborah to define more precisely the key terms used in her argument.

24. Which of the following pieces of information would be most useful in assessing the validity of Deborah's claim?

(A) A comparison of the overall acceptance rates at schools with legacy policy with those for schools with no such policy

(B) A comparison of the rates of acceptance for legacy applicants at schools with such a policy with overall acceptance rates at those schools

(C) A comparison of the number of applicants who apply as legacy students at schools with such a policy with the number of applicants who claim no such affiliation

(D) A comparison of the number of legacy applicants to schools with such policies over the last five years with the number who applied 25 years ago

(E) A comparison of the number of legacy applicants rejected at schools with such a policy with the number of legacy applicants at those same schools

25. Every passenger who flew to St. Louis purchased an e-ticket. Therefore, some passengers who flew first class did not fly to St. Louis.

The conclusion of the argument follows logically if it is assumed that

(A) some passengers who flew first class purchased e-tickets.

(B) every passenger who purchased an e-ticket flew to St. Louis.

(C) some passengers who did not purchase e-tickets flew first class.

(D) every passenger who purchased an e-ticket flew first class.

(E) every passenger who flew first class purchased an e-ticket.

STOP

> END OF SECTION 5. IF YOU HAVE ANY TIME LEFT, GO OVER YOUR WORK IN THIS SECTION ONLY. DO NOT WORK IN ANY OTHER SECTION OF THE TEST.

WRITING SAMPLE

Time—30 Minutes

The Marietta Township School Board must decide which of two candidates, Paul Sellers or Francine Goode, should receive its annual Outstanding Teacher Award. Write an essay in favor of one of the two candidates. Two considerations should guide your thinking:

1. The Outstanding Teacher Award honors teaching excellence and contribution to the community and school system.

2. The Award carries with it a one-year leave of absence with pay. The Board hopes that the recipient will use this time to pursue a course of study or a project that will eventually benefit the school system and community.

PAUL SELLERS, age 55, is a social studies teacher with more than thirty years of classroom teaching experience in the school system at the junior high and high school level. For the past fifteen years, he has been coach of his school's debating team and faculty adviser to a number of clubs; and for ten consecutive years, students have voted him the outstanding teacher at their school. Last year, Sellers worked 4 hours per week without compensation tutoring disadvantaged students. Sellers says that if he receives the award, he will spend the year finishing a book about the early history of the Marietta Township.

FRANCINE GOODE, age 35, is a high school foreign languages teacher who has taught for twelve years, ten of them in the Marietta school system. She consistently receives top evaluations from her district supervisor and last year was voted Outstanding Foreign Language Teacher by the statewide conference of teachers of foreign languages. Recently, on her own time, she conducted a series of district-wide Parent Participation Seminars for parents who do not speak English. Because she speaks French, Spanish, and Italian, Francine is able to converse with parents about helping their children in school. Francine has stated that if she receives the award, she will spend the year in Europe improving her language skills. During that time, she will also compile a photographic "tour" of various cities, which she then plans to use in teaching.

ANSWER KEY AND EXPLANATIONS

Section 1

1.	E	6.	A	11.	E	16.	B	21.	B
2.	D	7.	D	12.	A	17.	B	22.	A
3.	B	8.	C	13.	A	18.	E	23.	E
4.	E	9.	C	14.	B	19.	D	24.	E
5.	C	10.	A	15.	D	20.	B		

Section 2

1.	D	6.	A	11.	C	16.	D	21.	E
2.	E	7.	B	12.	E	17.	E	22.	D
3.	B	8.	A	13.	D	18.	D	23.	E
4.	E	9.	B	14.	B	19.	E	24.	E
5.	B	10.	C	15.	E	20.	C		

Section 3

1.	C	7.	D	13.	C	19.	B	25.	C
2.	A	8.	B	14.	C	20.	A	26.	D
3.	C	9.	D	15.	C	21.	E	27.	A
4.	B	10.	C	16.	A	22.	A	28.	E
5.	E	11.	A	17.	B	23.	D		
6.	B	12.	B	18.	A	24.	C		

Section 4

1.	D	6.	A	11.	E	16.	C	21.	E
2.	A	7.	E	12.	C	17.	B	22.	B
3.	A	8.	B	13.	C	18.	A	23.	B
4.	D	9.	A	14.	A	19.	B	24.	A
5.	E	10.	D	15.	A	20.	C		

Section 5

1.	D	6.	B	11.	B	16.	D	21.	A
2.	E	7.	B	12.	E	17.	E	22.	B
3.	B	8.	C	13.	E	18.	E	23.	B
4.	C	9.	A	14.	C	19.	A	24.	B
5.	A	10.	E	15.	B	20.	E	25.	C

Section I

1. **The correct answer is (E).** This question is primarily a matter of careful reading. The phrase "no lower bus fares" must not be read to mean that Flash uniquely has the lowest fare; it means only that no one else has a fare lower than that of Flash. It is conceivable that several companies share the lowest fare. So choice (B) is not inconsistent with the claim made in the advertisement. Choice (C) is not inconsistent since it mentions the New York City to Boston route, and it is the Washington, D.C., to New York City route that is the subject of the ad's claim. Choice (A) is not inconsistent since it speaks of an air fare, and the ad's language carefully restricts the claim to bus fares. Choice (D) is a bit tricky, but the ad cites only the D.C. to New York trip—choice (D) talks about the New York to D.C. trip. So there is no contradiction. Choice (E) is fairly clearly a contradiction, and this is a good time to remind you to read all of the choices before selecting one. You might have bitten on choice (D), but when you see choice (E), you know that it is a better answer.

2. **The correct answer is (D).** We take the first three propositions together and ignore the fourth since we are to assume it is false. Roberts cannot be convicted without Edwards' testimony (1), but that testimony will show that Edwards participated in the crime (2). But if Edwards participated in the crime, Roberts cannot be convicted of it because Roberts is accused of a crime that can be committed only by a person acting alone (3). Either Edwards will testify or Edwards will not testify—that is a tautology (logically true). If Edwards testifies, according to our reasoning, Roberts cannot be convicted. If Edwards does not testify, Roberts cannot be convicted (1). Either way, Roberts will not be convicted. Choice (E) cannot be correct since we have no way of knowing, as a matter of logic, whether Edwards will or will not testify. We know only that *if* Edwards does, certain consequences will follow, and *if* Edwards does not, other consequences will follow. Choice (A) can be disregarded since the crime is one that only a solo actor can commit (3). Choice (C) is incorrect because we have proven that, regardless of Edwards' course of action, Roberts cannot be convicted. Finally, choice (B) is a logical *possibility*, that is not precluded by the given information, but we cannot logically deduce it from the information given.

3. **The correct answer is (B).** Examine carefully the connection between (2) and (4). Suppose Edwards testifies. The testimony will show Edwards, too, has committed some wrong (2); but when the jury learns this, they will not believe any part of that testimony (4), that means that they will not believe Edwards committed the wrong—a contradiction. Since (2) and (4) cannot both be true at the same time, the scenario they describe is an impossible one—like saying a circle is a square. The remaining answers are all distractions. There is nothing in the information to suggest that the situation was created by Roberts' attorney, so choice (E) is incorrect. Choices (C) and (D) are value judgments that cannot be inferred from the information given and so are wrong—even if the situation is *difficult* for them, what reason is there for concluding that it is unfair? In any event, the situation is not even difficult for Roberts, who will be acquitted (see our analysis of the preceding question). Choice (A) is

wrong, and remember that the LSAT does not presuppose you have any information about the law or its workings.

4. **The correct answer is (E).** In the very first sentence, the author remarks that this is "curious" and a "contradiction," so the only correct answer choice will be one that follows up on this idea, as choice (E) does when it speaks of *paradox*. Nothing that precedes the blank suggests that the author is speaking of "beauty" or "tragedy," so choices (A) and (B) can be disregarded. As for choice (C), the passage does speak about death but not of death's inevitability; rather it dwells on death under certain circumstances that may not be inevitable. As for choice (D), while death may characterize human existence, the kind of death mentioned—self-sacrifice—is not indicated to be an inherent part of all human life.

5. **The correct answer is (C).** The author is explaining why the sacrifice is meaningless. From three different perspectives, the argument shows that it can have no value. The community does not win, because both lives were equally important. The lover who is saved does not profit, and that is shown by the fact that he would be perfectly willing to do the transaction the other way. If he has no preference (or even prefers the alternative outcome, his death), it cannot be said that he benefited from the exchange of lives. Finally, the need to prove that the action has no value to the heroine: He says she does not benefit, because she is not in a position to enjoy or savor, or whatever, her heroism. The reason for that is that she is *dead*, choice (C), not dying, choice (A), for dying would leave open the possibility that her sacrifice would bring her joy in her last minutes, and then the author's contention that the transaction has *no* value would be weakened. Choice (D) is wrong, for it is specifically stated that she is a heroine, so it is an inappropriate *completion* of the sentence. Choices (B) and (E) may both be true, but they do not explain why the action has no value to anyone.

6. **The correct answer is (A).** The main point of the passage is that pregnancy and a child put strain on a young marriage, and so such marriages would have a higher survival rate without the strain of children. It would seem, then, that encouraging such couples not to have children would help them stay married; but that will be possible only if they have not already committed themselves, so to speak, to having a child. If the wife is already pregnant at the time of marriage, the commitment has already been made, so the advice is too late. Choices (B) and (C) are wrong for similar reasons. It is not only the continued presence of the child in the marriage that causes the stress but also the very pregnancy and birth. So choices (B) and (C) do not address themselves to the *birth* of the child, and that is the factor to which the author attributes the dissolution of the marriage. Choice (D) is wide of the mark. Whether society does or does not have such an interest, the author has shown us a causal linkage; that is, a mere fact of the matter. The author states: If this, then fewer divorces. The author may or may not believe there should be fewer divorces. Choice (E) is wrong for this reason also and for the further reason that it says "do not *plan*" to have children. The author's concern is with children during the early part of the marriage. The author does not suggest that couples should never have children.

7. **The correct answer is (D).** Peter's surprise is over the fact that an important executive of a company would use a competitor's product, hence choice (D). Choice (B) is wrong because Peter's surprise is not that Mary is unimportant; rather, he knows Mary is important, and that is the reason for surprise. Choice (E) is irrelevant to the exchange, for Peter imagines that regardless of taste, Mary ought to consume the product she is responsible in part for producing. The same reasoning can be applied to choice (C). Finally, choice (A) is a distraction. It has legal overtones, but it is important to always keep in mind that this section, like all sections of the LSAT, tests reasoning and reading abilities—not knowledge of business or law.

8. **The correct answer is (C).** The dispute here is over the motivation to compete seriously in intramural sports. Erika claims it is a sense of responsibility to one's fellows; Nichol argues it is a desire to win. But the two may actually support one another. In what way could one possibly let one's fellows down? If the sport was not competitive, it would seem there would be no opportunity to disappoint them. So the desire to win contributes to the desire to be an effective member of the team. Nothing in the exchange presupposes anything about the structure of such programs beyond the fact that they are competitive; that is, that they have winners and losers. How many such programs exist, how they are funded, and similar questions are irrelevant, so both choices (A) and (B) are incorrect. Choice (D) is close to being correct, but it calls for a survey of *deans*. The dean is probably not in a position to describe the motivation of the *participants*. Had choice (D) specified participants, it too would have

been a correct answer. Of course, only one answer can be correct on the LSAT. Finally, choice (E) must be wrong for the reason cited in explaining choice (D); it should be possible to find out about the motivation.

9. **The correct answer is (C).** Clark was unhappy if he had a clear conscience but knew, or Clark was happy if he knew but had an unclear conscience. It is not the case that Clark was unhappy, so he must have been happy. Since he knew, however, his happiness must stem from an unclear conscience. Choices (A), (D), and (E) are incorrect because they make irrelevant value judgments. As was just shown, the author's point can be analyzed as a purely logical one. Choice (B) is just distraction, playing on the connection between "governess" and "servant," which, of course, are not the same thing.

10. **The correct answer is (A).** The author's point depends upon the *assumption* that children see both animated features and "spaghetti Westerns." Obviously, if that assumption is untrue, the conclusion does not follow. It may be true that children get a distorted picture of the world from other causes, but the author has not claimed that. The author claims only that it comes from their seeing animated features and "spaghetti Westerns." Presumably the two different treatments cause the inversion of values. The intention of the producers in making the films is irrelevant since an action may have an effect not intended by the actor. Hence, choice (B) would not touch the author's point. Further, that there are other sources of information that present a proper view of the world does not prove that the problem cited by the author does not produce an inverted view of the world. So choice (C) would not weaken his point.

Choice (D) reminds us of the importance of careful reading. You might want to interpret choice (D) to say the same thing as choice (A), but then you'd have to choose choice (A) because it tells the point more forcefully and directly. Finally, choice (E) is irrelevant to the author's conclusion: children learn to value animals more than people. Of course, as an exercise in debate, you might argue that this is a good thing, but that is not what choice (E) says.

11. **The correct answer is (E).** The point of the passage is that there is a seeming contradiction in our body of laws. Sometimes a person pays for attempted misdeeds and other times does not pay for them. If there could be found a good reason for this difference, then the contradiction could be explained away. This is just what choice (E) does. It points out that the law treats the situations differently because it has different goals: Sometimes, we drive fast because we are in a hurry; other times, we drive slowly because we want to enjoy the scenery. Choice (B) would not weaken the argument, for it only intensifies the contradiction. Choice (D) makes an attempt to reconcile the seemingly conflicting positions by hinting at a possible goal of one action that is not a goal of the other. But, if anything, it intensifies the contradiction because one might infer that we should not try persons for attempted crimes because criminal trials are expensive, yet we should allow compensation for attempted frauds because civil trials are less expensive. Choices (C) and (A) are just distractions. Whether there are more of one kind of law than another on the books has nothing to do with the seeming contradiction. And whether persons are more likely to commit a second crime

after they are released from prison does not speak to the issue of whether an unsuccessful attempt to commit a crime should be a crime in the first place.

12. **The correct answer is (A).** The question stem asks us to focus on the "dispute" between the two opponents. What will be relevant to it will be those items that affect the merits of the issues or perhaps those that affect the credibility of the parties. Choices (C) and (E) both mention items—facts and their source—that would be relevant to the substantive issues. Choices (B) and (D) are legitimate attempts to clarify the issues and so are relevant. Choice (A) is neither relevant to the issues nor to the credibility (e.g., where did the facts come from) of the debaters. Choice (A) is the least relevant because it is an *ad hominem* attack of the illegitimate sort.

13. **The correct answer is (A).** The point of the passage is that artists see things as they really are, while politicians see things as they want them to be. Choice (B) is wrong, for if anything, it is the politicians who see things through rose-colored glasses, while the artists see the truth of a stark reality. Choice (C) can be overruled, for the passage implies that political leaders are responsive to the needs of people—it is just that they are a little late. Moreover, the point of the passage is to draw a contrast between artists and politicians; and even if the conclusion expressed in choice (C) is arguably correct, it is not as good as choice (A), which *completes* the comparison. Choice (D) has no ground in the passage. Be careful not to move from an analysis of facts—artists saw the problems earlier than the politicians did—to a conclusion of value or policy: therefore, we should turn out the politicians. The

author may very well believe that as sad as these circumstances are, nothing can be done about them; for example, things are bad enough with the politicians in charge, but they would be much worse with artists running things. Choice (E) also finds no ground in the passage.

14. **The correct answer is (B).** The argument for consistency is that it avoids the danger that actions will be misinterpreted. If a parent is overly generous, a child will think the parent will always be generous, even when generosity is inappropriate. By the same token, if a parent does not draw the line until pushed to do so, the child will believe that the parent's response was forced. A parent, so goes the argument, should play it safe and leave a cushion. Choice (D) makes an attempt to capture this thought but overstates the case. The author implies only that this may show weakness, not that the child will necessarily exploit that weakness and certainly not that the child will exploit it violently. And were that thought intended, the author surely would not have used the word "retaliate," which implies a *quid pro quo.* Both choices (A) and (E) have no basis in the passage, and neither is relevant to the idea of rewards and punishments. Choice (C) does treat the general idea of the passage, but it confuses the idea of weakness with the more specific notion of willingness to bargain.

15. **The correct answer is (D).** The key phrase in this paragraph is "beef costs more per pound than fish." A careful reading would show that choice (A) is in direct contradiction to the explicit wording of the passage. Choice (B) cannot be inferred since the dietitian merely says, "I pay." Perhaps the dietician intends to keep the price of a meal stable by cutting

back in other areas. In any event, this is another example of not going beyond a mere factual analysis to generate policy recommendations (see #13) unless the question stem specifically invites such an extension; for example, which of the following courses of action would the author recommend? Choice (C) makes an unwarranted inference. From the fact that beef is more costly, one would not want to conclude that it is more profitable. Choice (E) is wrong for this reason also. Choice (D) is correct because it focuses upon the "per measure of protein" that explains why a fish meal will cost the dietitian more than a beef meal, even though fish is less expensive per pound.

16. **The correct answer is (B).** One of the most common patterns to look for with this type of question is the "surprise result," that is, an unanticipated factor that defeats the expected outcome. Choice (B) fits this pattern: you'll be so hungry from the workout that you'll eat more. (Remember that you are told to accept the soundness of each of the answer choices.) The other choices just don't have the same logical "zip." Anyway, choice (A) seems to strengthen the argument: it's okay to do what the ad suggests. And choice (C) doesn't focus on the logic of the ad—even though it probably helps to explain why the ad might be effective. Choices (D) and (E) are wrong because they address issues that are not really on the table (so to speak): the ad is addressing neither those who are already happy nor those who are overly thin.

17. **The correct answer is (B).** This question is like one of those simple conversation questions: "X: All bats are mammals. Y: Not true, whales are mammals too." In this little exchange, Y misunderstands X to have said that "all mammals are bats."

In the question, the objection must be based on a misunderstanding. The objector must think that the ad has claimed that the only cause of unhappiness, etc., is being overweight, otherwise the objector would not have offered the counterexample. Choice (A) is wrong because the ad never takes a stand on the *causes* of overweight conditions—only on a possible cure. This reasoning invalidates choices (C) and (D) as well. Choice (E) makes a similar error but about effects, not about causes. The ad does not say everyone who is unhappy is unattractive, or vice versa.

18. **The correct answer is (E).** The sample argument is a straightforward generalization: All observed S are P. X is an S. Therefore, X is P. Only choice (E) replicates this form. The reasoning in choice (A) is "Some S are P. All M are S. (All swans are birds, which is a suppressed assumption.) Therefore, all M are P." That is like saying: "Some children are not well behaved. All little girls are children. Therefore, all little girls are not well behaved." Choice (B), too, contains a suppressed premise. Its structure is "All S are P. All S are M. (All ballets are theatrical productions, which is suppressed.) Therefore, all M are P." That is like saying "All little girls are children. All little girls are human. Therefore, all humans are little girls." Choice (C) is not a generalization at all. It takes a generalization and attempts to explain it by uncovering a causal linkage. Choice (D) is simply a *non sequitur*. It moves from the universality of the *concept* of justice to the conclusion that justice is a *physical* trait of humans.

19. **The correct answer is (D).** The author is attempting to argue that laws against suicide are legitimate. The author argues against a simplistic libertarian position that says suicide hurts only the victim. The goal of the law, he argues, is not just to protect the victim from himself. A society passes such a law because it wants to underscore the importance of human life. Reading beyond the blank in the second paragraph makes clear the author's views on the value of human life. Choice (A) flies in the face of the explicit language of the passage. The author does not defend the law as being a deterrent to suicide. Choice (B) might be something the author believes, but it is not something developed in the passage. The author is not concerned here with explaining how the laws came to be on the books but is concerned only with defending them. If anything, choice (B) would be more appropriate in the context of an argument against such laws. Choice (C) also is something the author may believe, but the defense of the suicide law is not that it protects liberties—only that it serves a function and does not interfere with constitutional liberties any more than laws that prohibit doing violence to others. Choice (E) is wrong for the same reasons that choice (B) is wrong. It seems to belong more in the context of an argument against suicide laws.

20. **The correct answer is (B).** With the comments in #19 in mind, it is clear that choice (B) must be correct. The author wants to make the point that suicide is not a victimless crime; it affects a great many people—even, it is claimed, some who were never personally acquainted with the suicide. Again, reading the whole passage is helpful. Choice (A) is a joke—obviously suicide does not lead to more serious crimes. That is like saying the death penalty is designed to rehabilitate the criminal. Choice (C) simply focuses

on the superficial content of the sentence: One, it's talking about church and state, so choice (C), which mentions sin, must be correct. Choice (D) is wrong because the author is not concerned to defend the laws as deterrents to suicide, as we discussed in #19. Finally, choice (E) is irrelevant to the point that the entire community is affected by the death of any one of its members.

21. **The correct answer is (B).** This third question, too, can be answered once the comments of #19 are understood. The key word here is "oversimplification." The libertarian oversimplifies matters by imagining that the only function of the law is to protect a person from self-harm. This is oversimplified because it overlooks the fact that such laws also serve the functions of (1) underscoring the value of life and (2) protecting the community as a whole from the loss of any of its members. Choice (A) is incorrect because the libertarian does not make this error but the related one of evaluating the function of the law only from the perspective of the suicide. Choice (C) is wrong, for the author apparently shares with the libertarian the assumption that a law must not illegitimately interfere with individual liberty. The whole defense of the laws against suicide is that they have a legitimate function. Choice (D) is wrong for the same reasons that choice (C) of #20 is wrong. Finally, choice (E) is very much like choice (A).

22. **The correct answer is (A).** Choices (C) and (D) are wrong because they extrapolate without sufficient information. These are very much like choices (C) and (E) in #15. Choice (E) contradicts the last given statement and so cannot be a conclusion of it. That would be like trying to infer

"all men are mortal" from the premise that "no men are mortal." Choice (B) commits an error by moving from "all S are P" to "all P are S." Just because all racing engines have SFI does not mean that all SFIs are in racing engines. Some may be found in tractors and heavy-duty machinery.

23. **The correct answer is (E).** This is a very sticky question, but it is similar to ones that have been on the LSAT. The key here is to keep in mind that you are to pick the BEST answer, and sometimes you will not be very satisfied with any of them. Here, choice (E) is correct by default of the others. Choice (A) has some merit. After all, the economist really isn't very careful in stating the claim. The author says "here we go again" when there is no evidence that we have ever been there before. But there is no particular term the author uses that we could call ambiguous. Choice (B) is wrong because, although the economist assumes some people take that position (otherwise, against whom would the argument be directed?), the statement does not imply that the economist alone thinks differently. Choice (C) is like choice (A), a possible answer, but this interpretation requires additional information. You would have to have said to yourself, "Oh, I see that the economist is against it. He is probably saying this in an exasperated tone and in the context of a diatribe." If there were such additional information, you would be right, and choice (C) would be a good answer. But there isn't. Choice (E) does not require this additional speculation and so is truer to the given information. Choice (D) would also require speculation. Choice (E) is not perfect, just BEST by comparison.

24. **The correct answer is (E).** The argument assumes that a right cannot exist unless it is recognized by the positive law of a society. Against this assumption, it can be argued that a right may exist even though there is no mechanism for protecting or enforcing it. That this is at least plausible has been illustrated by our own history, e.g., minority groups have often been denied rights. These rights, however, existed all the while—they were just not protected by the government. Choice (A) is incorrect, for the proponent of the theory of natural rights cannot deny that some human beings do not have them. That would contradict the very definition of natural right on which the claim is based. Choice (B) is incorrect because it is not responsive to the argument. Even if choice (B) is true, the attacker of natural rights still has the argument that there are no universally recognized rights, so there are no universal (natural) rights at all. Choice (C), like choice (A), is inconsistent with the very idea of a "natural" right. Choice (D) is incorrect because it does not respond to the attacker's claim that no one right is protected universally. Consistency or universality within one society does not amount to consistency or universality across all societies.

Section 2

Questions 1–6

This is a fairly simple "connective" set. A "connective" set is a problem set in which one event is somehow connected with another event; for example, X causes Y, or Y leads to Z. The connection can be expressed by an arrow. We begin with the first condition:

$$G \longrightarrow H$$

Adding the second condition:

$$G \rightleftarrows H \longrightarrow I$$

And the third:

$$G \rightleftarrows H \longrightarrow I \longrightarrow J$$

And the fourth:

$$G \rightleftarrows H \longrightarrow I \longrightarrow J \longrightarrow K$$

And the fifth:

$$L \longrightarrow G \rightleftarrows H \longrightarrow I \longrightarrow J \longrightarrow K$$

And the sixth:

$$L \longrightarrow G \rightleftarrows H \longrightarrow I \longrightarrow J \rightleftarrows K$$

Of course, there is no necessity that the stations be oriented in exactly this way on the page, so long as the relative connections are specified. An equivalent diagram is as follows:

Once the diagram is drawn, answering the questions is merely a matter of using the picture.

1. **The correct answer is (D).** The diagram shows that it is possible to get from H to J only via I. Choice (A) is incorrect since the direct connection between J and H runs only from J to H, not vice versa. As for choice (B), while it is possible to get from H to G, there is no connecting train between G and J. Choice (C) is incorrect because there is no train from H to L. Finally, choice (E) is incorrect for there is a route from H to J, via I.

2. **The correct answer is (E).** Notice that there are no arrows in the diagram that point toward L. This means that it is

possible only to leave L. It is not possible to arrive at L. As for choice (A), one can arrive at G from L or H. Choice (B) is incorrect since one can arrive at H from either G or J. Choice (C) is incorrect since there is a connection between H and I and between L and I. Finally, choice (D) is incorrect since K can be reached from either L or J.

3. **The correct answer is (B).** Consulting the diagram, we see that I can be reached from either H or L. H, however, can be reached from either G or J. Thus, one can go from G and J via H and reach I with only one transfer.

4. **The correct answer is (E).** All six stations can be visited, without revisiting any station, if we begin at L. The trip then proceeds L to G to H to I to J to K.

5. **The correct answer is (B).** To get to H from K, we must go via I and J, and that is a total of two transfers. As for choice (A), the trip from G to I is accomplished by transferring only at H. As for choice (C), the trip from L to H is accomplished by going via G, again requiring only one transfer. As for choice (D), though the trip from L to I would require two transfers if the L, G, H, I route is selected, note that the trip can be made directly from L to I without *any* transfers. Choice (E) is incorrect because a direct route is available from L to K.

6. **The correct answer is (A).** If I is closed, the only transfer point from H to J is closed, and that means that it is not possible to get from G to J. Choice (B) is incorrect since there is a direct link between J and K. Choice (C) is incorrect since there is a direct link between L and K. Choice (D) is incorrect since the L to K to J route remains unimpaired. Choice (E) is incorrect since there is a direct link from L to G.

Questions 7–12

This is a "selection" set; that is, we must select cities for the tours according to the restrictions set forth in the problem set. There are many different ways of summarizing the information, and each of us has our own idiosyncratic system of notational devices. There are, however, some fairly standard symbols used by logicians, and we will employ them here. We summarize the information in the following way:

1. $M \to (Q \& R)$
2. $P \to O$
3. $Q \to (M \& N) \lor (M \& T) \lor (M \& N \& T)$
4. $P \neq Q$
5. $\sim (O \& R \& T)$
6. $\sim (N \& S \& R)$
7. $L \neq R$

Some clarifying remarks about this system are in order. We are using the capital-letter designation of each city to make the statement that the city will be included on the tour, e.g., "M" means "M will be included on the tour." The $\to$ stands for "if . . . then . . ."; the "&" stands for "and"; the "v" stands for "or"; the ~ stands for "not." We use parentheses as punctuation devices to avoid possible confusion. So the first condition is to be read, "If M, then both Q and R"; that is, "If M is included on the trip, then both Q and R must be included on the trip." Notice that the parentheses were necessary, for the statement

$M \to Q \& R$

might be misinterpreted to mean "If M is included on the tour, then Q must also be included. In addition, R must be included on the trip." That would be punctuated with parentheses as follows:

$(M \to Q) \& R$

As for the second condition, we note simply that if P is included, O must also be included.

As for the third condition, some students will find it easier to write this condition out rather than use the notational system. That is fine.

Statement 3 is to be read, "If Q, then M and N, or M and T, or all three," which is, of course, equivalent to the statement included in the initial conditions of the problem.

The fourth condition is similar to the second in that we use a non-standard symbol, "≠." The same information could be written as ~(P & Q) or P→~Q. This last notation is equivalent to Q→~P, for logically P→~Q is the same as Q→~P.

The fifth and sixth conditions are to be read, respectively, "It is not the case that O and R and T are included" and "It is not the case that N and S and R are included." And finally, condition seven is summarized using the "≠," which we have already discussed.

We now have the information ready for easy reference, and we turn to the individual questions.

7. **The correct answer is (B).** If M is included on the trip, we know that we must also include Q and R. And if Q is included on the trip, we must include N or T (or both, but we are looking for the minimum number of other cities). No other cities need be included. So, including M requires both Q and R plus one of the pair N and T. So a total of three *additional* cities are needed.

8. **The correct answer is (A).** By condition 4, Q cannot be included with P. Unfortunately, that is not an available answer choice, so we will have to dig a little deeper. If Q cannot be included on the tour, then we conclude that M cannot be included, for condition 1 requires that Q be included on any tour on which M is a stop.

9. **The correct answer is (B).** This question requires only that we check each of the choices against the summary of conditions. Choice (A) is not acceptable because we have M without Q. Choice (C) is not acceptable because we have M without R. Choice (D) is not acceptable because we have L with R (in violation of condition 7) and because we have Q without either N or T. Choice (E) is not acceptable because we have N, S, and R together, in violation of condition 6. The group in choice (B), however, meets all of the requirements for an acceptable tour.

10. **The correct answer is (C).** By deleting O, we have the tour M, Q, R, and T. This satisfies condition 1, since Q and R are included with M. And this satisfies condition 3 since we have M and T. No other condition is violated, so the group M, Q, R, T is acceptable. Choice (A) is incorrect, for eliminating M leaves Q in the group (without M), in violation of condition 3. Similarly, eliminating Q leaves M on the tour without Q, violating condition 1. Choice (D) is incorrect because it also violates condition 1. Choice (E) is incorrect for this would leave Q on the tour without the (M & N) or (M & T) combination required by condition 3.

11. **The correct answer is (C).** To make the group M, Q, R into an acceptable tour, we need only to add N or T. This will finally satisfy both conditions 1 and 3 without violating any other requirement. Choice (A) is incorrect, for adding another city will not remedy the violation of condition 7 (L ≠ R). Choice (B) is incorrect, because satisfying the conditions requires the addition of O (condition 2), R (condition 1), and either N or T (condition 3). Choice (D) is incorrect since the addition of another city will not correct the violation of condition 6. Finally, choice (E) is incorrect because the addition of O to satisfy condition 2 would then violate

condition 5 (O, R, and T on the same tour).

12. **The correct answer is (E).** Here we must test each lettered city. M cannot constitute a tour in and of itself, for condition 1 requires that Q and R be included on any tour that includes M. P, by condition 2, cannot constitute a tour of a single city. Finally, by condition 3, Q's inclusion requires more cities. The remaining cities, L, N, O, R, S, and T, however, can be used as single-city tours.

Questions 13–18

This set is a linear ordering set. At first glance, the set appears to be very complex, involving as it does the positioning of 11 items. But a closer examination shows the questions are not that difficult, since the particular restrictions considerably simplify the problem. For example, we know that a red bead is on one end, and we know further that all three red beads are together. So there are only two possible arrangements for the red beads:

```
1  2  3  4  5  6  7  8  9  10 11
R  R  R
```
or
```
                  R  R  R
```

In fact, each additional condition on the placement of the beads tends to simplify matters for us because it eliminates possible arrangements. With a linear ordering set, we begin by summarizing the information:

Color	Number	
Blue	2	B = B
Red	3	G ≠ G
Green	2	R = R = R
Yellow	4	G or R = ends
	11	

We have made a note of the number of beads of each color, and we have summarized the particular conditions: Blue is next to blue (B = B), green is not next to green (G ≠ G), red is always next to red (R = R = R), and green or red is on each end (G or R = ends). Now we turn to the questions.

13. **The correct answer is (D)** From the given information and our own deductions based on the restrictions that all red be together and that one end be red and the other green, we set up the following diagram:

```
1  2  3  4  5  6  7  8  9  10 11
               B  B        R
G              B  B        R  R  R
```

This leaves the four yellow beads and the one remaining green bead to be positioned. The only restriction on the placement of these five beads is that the green bead may not be next to the other green bead; that is, the remaining green bead cannot be in position 2. This eliminates choice (C), since the green bead might be in position 8, though it could also be in positions 3, 4, and 5. This also eliminates choice (B), since position 5 might be filled by a green bead. Choice (A) is clearly incorrect since that is the one remaining position that cannot be occupied by the other green bead. Choice (E) is incorrect since the green bead could be placed in position 3 or 4, separated from the blue beads by one or more yellow beads. We do know, however, that at least one green bead, the one in position 1, will be next to a yellow bead, for a yellow bead is needed to separate the green beads. Of course, the other green bead may also be next to a yellow bead, but that is not necessary. In any event, the fact that the green bead must be separated from the other green bead is sufficient to show the correctness of choice (D).

14. The correct answer is (B). The question stem stipulates

1	2	3	4	5	6	7	8	9	10	11
							Y			

$$Y = Y = Y = Y$$

and we fill in YYYY

since the last position cannot be yellow. This then allows us to deduce

1	2	3	4	5	6	7	8	9	10	11
						Y	Y	Y	Y	G

since the three red beads are together and one of them must be on the end of the string. Then, since the two blue beads must be together, we know that only two different arrangements are possible:

1	2	3	4	5	6	7	8	9	10	11
R	R	R	G	B	B	Y	Y	Y	Y	G

or:

1	2	3	4	5	6	7	8	9	10	11
R	R	R	B	B	G	Y	Y	Y	Y	G

Under either arrangement, the fifth bead must be blue.

15. The correct answer is (E). The question stem stipulates that each blue bead be next to a green bead. Because the blue beads are next to each other, this means the blue and green beads are arranged as a bloc: GBBG. According to the stipulation in the question stem, the four yellow beads are also arranged as a bloc: YYYY. And we know from the initial presentation of restrictions that the three red beads are a bloc: RRR. The only open question is which end of the string is green and which is red. So there are only two possible arrangements:

1	2	3	4	5	6	7	8	9	10	11
G	B	B	G	Y	Y	Y	Y	R	R	R

or:

1	2	3	4	5	6	7	8	9	10	11
R	R	R	Y	Y	Y	Y	G	B	B	G

Under either arrangement, positions 5, 6, and 7 are occupied by yellow beads.

16. The correct answer is (D). The question stem stipulates

1	2	3	4	5	6	7	8	9	10	11
			B	B				R		

and, given the restriction on the reds and the further restriction on the end beads, we can deduce

1	2	3	4	5	6	7	8	9	10	11
G			B	B				R	R	R

The only restriction that remains to be observed is the separation of the green beads. This means that the remaining one can occupy positions 3, 4, 7, or 8—though not 2. What is established, however, is that 2 must be yellow, not green.

17. The correct answer is (E). The question stem stipulates

1	2	3	4	5	6	7	8	9	10	11
			Y				Y	Y	Y	

and we deduce

1	2	3	4	5	6	7	8	9	10	11
R	R	R		Y			Y	Y	Y	G

on the basis of the restrictions regarding the placement of the red beads and the colors of the end beads. Further, there is only one open pair left for the blue beads, 6 and 7, which means bead 4 will be green:

1	2	3	4	5	6	7	8	9	10	11
R	R	R	G	Y	B	B	Y	Y	Y	G

18. The correct answer is (D). Since we do not know on which end to place the red beads (nor the green bead), we have the possibility

1	2	3	4	5	6	7	8	9	10	11
R	R	R	G						B	G

and its mirror image

1	2	3	4	5	6	7	8	9	10	11
G	B						G	R	R	

We know also that the two blue beads are together, and this means the yellow beads must form a bloc:

1	2	3	4	5	6	7	8	9	10	11
R	R	R	G	Y	Y	Y	Y	B	B	G

or:

G B B Y Y Y Y G R R R

In either case, the seventh bead must be yellow.

Questions 19–24

The key to this set is organizing the information in such a way that it is usable. We recommend a table:

	Marlowe	Joyce	Shakespeare	Keats	Chaucer
J	YES	YES			
K			YES	YES	
L	YES				YES
M	YES		YES	YES	
N		YES		YES	YES
O	YES	YES	YES		

If you study the table, you will see that only one teacher can be chosen from the group J, K, and L. Two teachers must be chosen from the group M, N, and O. The reason for this is that the only distribution that will give the Executive Officer exactly eight assignments is to have three courses taught by each of two faculty members and two courses by a third, $3 + 3 + 2 = 8$. This is an important insight that should have occurred to you.

Further study would also show that there is a limited number of permissible combinations. Theoretically, there are nine possibilities:

M & N & →J (OK)
         →K (No, three Keatses)
         →L (OK)

M & O & →J (No, three Marlowes)
         →K (No, three Shakespeares)
         →L (No, three Marlowes)

N & O & →J (No, three Joyces)
         →K (OK)
         →L (OK)

To see this without careful study, however, requires not only powerful insight but considerable luck as well. In any event, it is not necessary to perceive this to answer the questions, for the questions will guide you to the conclusion that some groupings are not permissible.

Having done this preliminary work, we can use our chart of possibilities in explaining the answers to the individual questions.

19. **The correct answer is (E).** Choice (A) is incorrect because it generates a total of only seven courses. Choices (B), (C), and (D) are shown to be incorrect by our chart. Choice (E) is the only acceptable combination listed.

20. **The correct answer is (C).** Using the information provided in the question stem, we know

Spring

Joyce
Keats   } (by N)
Chaucer

and that L will teach Marlowe and Chaucer. Then our chart informs us that there are two teachers who can teach with L and N, O or M. Thus, the additional courses will be Marlowe, Joyce, and Shakespeare (by O) or Marlowe, Keats, and Shakespeare (by M). We know, therefore, that both Marlowe and

Shakespeare will be offered during the year since both O and M offer those courses. This means Marlowe must be offered in both the fall and the spring and further that L will teach Chaucer in the fall.

Fall	Spring	
Marlowe (by ?)	Joyce	
Chaucer (by L)	Keats	(by N)
Shakes. (by ?)	Chaucer	
Joyce or Keats (by ?)	Marlowe (by ?)	

From this we can see that choice (C) is correct. It is possible that L will teach Marlowe in the fall, so L *could* teach only in the fall semester. Choice (A) is incorrect as shown by our chart—either M or O must be hired with L and N. Choice (B) is incorrect since the question stipulates that N will teach only in the spring and that accounts for three of the four courses that semester. Choice (D) is incorrect since either Joyce or Keats, though not both, will be offered in the fall. Finally, choice (E) is incorrect since Shakespeare can be offered only in the fall.

21. **The correct answer is (E).** Our chart shows that if M and N are hired, either J or L can be hired. Choices (A) and (C), therefore, are possibly, though not necessarily, true. Hence, they are both incorrect answers. Choice (B) must also be incorrect, as shown by the chart. Hiring M and N, and separating their courses by semester, we have

Semester—M	Semester—N
Marlowe	Joyce
Shakes.	Keats
Keats	Chaucer

The remaining two courses will be Marlowe and Joyce (by J) or Marlowe

and Chaucer (by L). Since both J and L teach Marlowe, that will give a total of two Marlowe courses, so one of them must be offered in the spring. Choice (D) is possibly true, provided that M teaches that course in the fall, but it is not necessarily true.

22. **The correct answer is (D).** If K and N are hired, O must also be hired. This gives us a course mix of Shakespeare and Keats (by K); Joyce, Keats, and Chaucer (by N); and Marlowe, Joyce, and Shakespeare (by O). We have two courses on Shakespeare, two on Keats, and two on Joyce. So those three courses must be offered both semesters, plus a course on Marlowe one semester and one on Chaucer the other.

23. **The correct answer is (E).** If L is hired to teach only in the fall, this means Marlowe and Chaucer will be offered then. With L, it is possible to hire either M and N or N and O. We must hire N, and this means Joyce, Keats, and Chaucer will be taught. Since both L and N offer Chaucer, N must teach Chaucer in the spring. As for choice (D), this is possible but is necessarily true only if O, rather than M, is hired. Since that is not a logically necessary choice, choice (D) is merely possible.

24. **The correct answer is (E).** For this question we are told which teachers will be hired. So the course mix will be

Fall

Joyce	
Keats	(by N)
Chaucer	

with courses on Marlowe, Joyce, and Shakespeare (by O) and on Shakespeare and Keats (by K). Observing the restriction that the same courses may not be offered in a single semester, we have

Fall	Spring
Joyce	Joyce (by O)
Keats ⎫ (by N)	Shakes. (by ?)
Chaucer ⎬	Marlowe (by O)
Shakes. (by ?)	Keats (by K)

We can see that choices (A), (B), (C), and (D) are all logically necessary. Choice (E) is our exception since Chaucer is taught only in the fall.

Section 3

1. **The correct answer is (C).** This is a main idea question, and the task is to find a choice that expresses the main thesis of the passage without being too narrow and without being overly broad and going beyond the scope of the argument. Choice (A) is too narrow since this is but a minor feature of the discussion. Choice (E) can be eliminated on the same grounds, since the possibility of nuclear destruction is but one important difference between war in a modernized society and war in a pre-modernized society. Choice (B) is an attractive choice, but it is not the main thesis of the passage. The author does indeed discuss some of the effects of war on both modernized and pre-modernized societies, but this discussion is subordinate to a larger goal: to show that because of changing circumstance (effects are different), the value of war has changed. Choice (D) is incorrect because it misses this main point, and it is incorrect for the further reason that the author discusses more than just pre-modernized societies.

2. **The correct answer is (A).** The second paragraph describes the attitude of pre-modernized society toward war: accepted, even noble, necessary. Coupled with the goals of war in pre-modernized societies, described in the first paragraph, we can infer that leaders of pre-modernized society regarded war as a valid policy tool. On this ground, we select choice (A), eliminating choices (B) and (C). As for choice (D), although this can be inferred to have been a feature of war in pre-modernized society, choice (D) is not responsive to the question: What did the leaders think of war, that is, what was their attitude? Choice (E) can be eliminated on the same ground and on the further ground that "necessity" for war was not that described in choice (E).

3. **The correct answer is (C).** The author is discussing war, a seemingly uncivilized activity. Yet, the author argues that war, at least in pre-modernized times, was the necessary result of certain economic and social forces. The use of the term "civilized" is ironic. Under other circumstances, the explanations offered by choices (A) and (B) might be plausible, but there is nothing in this text to support either of those. Choice (D), too, might under other circumstances be a reason for placing the word in quotation marks, but it does not appear that this author is attempting to affect the reader's emotions: the passage is too detached and scientific for that. Finally, choice (E) does articulate one of the author's objectives, but this is not the reason for putting the one word in quotations. The explanation for that is something more specific than an overall idea of the passage.

4. **The correct answer is (B).** This is an explicit idea question, and choices (A), (C), (D), and (E) are all mentioned at various points in the passage as reasons for going to war. Choice (B), too, is mentioned, but it is mentioned as a feature of the military establishment in pre-modernized society—not as a reason for going to war.

5. **The correct answer is (E).** This is another main idea question, and choices (B), (C), and (D) can be eliminated as too narrow. It is true the author mentions that economic and social conditions, technology, and armed conflict have all changed, but this is not the ultimate point to be proved. The author's main point is that *because* of such changes, the value of war has changed. Choice (A) is only tangentially related to the text. Though we may learn a bit about how decisions are made, in part, this is not the main burden of the argument.

6. **The correct answer is (B).** We have already mentioned that the tone of the passage is neutral—scientific and detached. Choices (A) and (D) can be eliminated as overstatements. To be sure, the author seems to deplore the destruction that might result from a nuclear war, but that concern does not rise to the status of outrage, indignation, fear, or alarm. Choice (E) is a closer call. While it is true that the author expresses concern about the ability of modernized society to survive war and while there is arguably a hint of optimism or hope, it cannot be said that these are the *defining* features of the passage. A better description of the prevailing tone is offered by choice (B). As for choice (C), the one ironic reference ("civilized") does not make the entire passage humorous.

7. **The correct answer is (D).** This is an application question, and we must take the information from the passage and apply it to a new situation. The author offers two reasons for the conclusion that war is no longer a viable policy tool: (1) the danger of worldwide destruction and (2) the costs after victory outweigh the benefits to be won. We can conclude that even in the absence of nuclear weapons,

war will still lack its traditional value, as argued by the author in the fourth paragraph. Thus, we can eliminate choices (A) and (B) on the grounds that they are contradicted by the author's thinking. Choice (E) can be eliminated for the same reason and because no such "instincts" are discussed in the text. A close look at choice (C) shows that it is not in agreement with the author's view, since the author believes that though nuclear weapons deter nuclear war, war is obsolete for other reasons as well.

8. **The correct answer is (B).** This is a main idea question. As correctly described by choice (B), the author explains the results of some studies and suggests some implications of these findings for detecting high blood pressure. Choice (E) is incorrect since it is but a minor aspect of the passage. The author notes that there is such a correlation but is not primarily concerned to prove the existence of such a relationship. Choice (C) can be eliminated because the main point is not to describe the epidemiological and clinical studies from a methodological point of view. Rather, the author is concerned with the findings of these studies. Choice (D) can be eliminated on similar grounds, for the author indicates that the two methods of study both point to the existence of a familial connection. Choice (A) can be eliminated since the author does not criticize but rather relies on these experiments.

9. **The correct answer is (D).** This is a specific detail (explicit idea) question, so the main task is to find the right part of the passage. In the last sentence of the first paragraph, the author explicitly states that a factor that initially discouraged the study of hypertension in children was the unfounded belief that it was

difficult to measure blood pressure in children. Choices (A), (B), and (E) are just not mentioned anywhere. The idea suggested by choice (C) is mentioned but in the second paragraph, so you know it can't be an answer to this question.

10. **The correct answer is (C).** This is a question that asks us to make a further application of the arguments given in the passage, and the greatest danger may be the temptation to overstate the case. This is the difficulty with choice (E). The author remarks in the closing sentences, "It may be possible." It is never asserted that it is now possible to do this. Choice (D) also overstates the case. The author states that these chemical deficiencies are associated with high blood pressure, not that such deficiencies *cause* high blood pressure. And to the extent that one wants to argue that such deficiencies *contribute* to high blood pressure (based on paragraph three), that is not sufficient to support the causal statement expressed in choice (D). As for choice (A), the author notes that the low output of urinary kallikrein is associated with high blood pressure; that is, it may be another symptom of whatever physiological disorder causes high blood pressure. But that means it is an effect of the underlying cause and not the cause itself. Finally, choice (B) can be eliminated because it is not a further conclusion of the passage. To the extent that choice (B) reiterates what is stated already (and note that it states the kallikrein-kinin system is important in determining blood pressure, not that the system *causes* high blood pressure), it is not appropriate as a further statement based on arguments presented. Choice (C) is, however, a natural extension of the argument. Remember, the author begins by noting that it is

important to determine when high blood pressure begins and suggests that it may begin as early as infancy.

11. **The correct answer is (A).** This is a logical detail question. In essence, the question stipulates that the author does introduce such evidence and then asks for what reason. In the final paragraph, the author is discussing the connection between low urinary kallikrein excretion and high blood pressure. By noting that black children often show this and noting further that blacks often have high blood pressure, the author hopes to provide further evidence in the connection. As for choice (B), though this may be an incidental effect of the reference, it cannot be said that this is the logical function of the argument in the overall development of the passage. Choice (C) is incorrect since the author is not asserting a causal connection but only a correlation. Choice (D) is incorrect for a reason similar to that which eliminates choice (B). Though this might be a further application for the point, it is not the reason the author incorporates the data into the argument of this passage. Finally, choice (E) is one of the main themes of the passage, but it does not explain why the author introduced the particular point at the particular juncture in the argument.

12. **The correct answer is (B).** This is an explicit detail question. In the third paragraph, the author discusses the operation of the kallikrein-kinin system. There it is stated that it produces chemicals that operate to dilate blood vessels. As for choices (A) and (C), the author does not state that the kallikrein-kinin system interferes directly with either the sympathetic nervous system or the production of aldosterone—only that it *offsets* the effects of those actions. As for

choice (D), the reference to kallikrein levels in urine comes in the last paragraph, the wrong place for an answer to this question. And whatever choice (E) is saying, it just doesn't answer the question.

13. **The correct answer is (C).** This is a logical detail question: Why does the author introduce this information? In the second paragraph, the author is describing new research done on children, research that suggests that the factors related to high blood pressure are already detectable in children. Choice (A) is incorrect since the author has not yet begun to discuss the biochemical research—only epidemiological surveys. Choice (B) is incorrect since it is not a correct response to the question. The author does state that such research is actually possible but does not cite the results of the study in order to prove the study was possible. Rather, the author cites the results to prove the further conclusion outlined in answer choice (C). Choice (D) is incorrect, for it is not a response to the question. To be sure, one might use the results of the study cited to support the recommendation articulated in choice (D), but that is not the author's motivation for introducing them in the argument. As for choice (E), this fails for the same reason that choice (B) fails.

14. **The correct answer is (C).** This is a logical structure question. The author develops the argument primarily by describing findings and supporting a conclusion. As for choice (A), though the author does mention two types of research, epidemiological studies and clinical studies, the author does not contrast these. Choice (B) is incorrect since the main purpose is to support a conclusion, and whatever refutation is offered in the passage (e.g., against the position that blood pressure in children cannot be measured accurately) is offered in the service of a greater point. Choice (E) must fail for a similar reason. And choice (D) fails for this reason as well: the author is supporting a position, not refuting it.

15. **The correct answer is (C).** This is a main idea question. The main point of the passage is that those who believe AFDC restrictions contribute to family dissolution are in error. It is not the restrictions on aid but the aid itself, according to the author, that contributes to low-income family dissolution. So the primary purpose of the passage is to analyze the causes of a phenomenon. Choice (A) is incorrect, for any such results are mentioned only obliquely and are only incidental to the main development. Choice (B) describes something that is integral to, but is not the main point of, the argument. As for choice (D), the author himself offers no such recommendation. While an argument for reform might use the argument in the passage for such recommendations, we cannot attribute any proposal for reform to the author. Finally, choice (E) describes what may be a result of the argument, but changing the attitude of the public, as opposed to engaging in scholarly debate, does not appear to be the objective of the text.

16. **The correct answer is (A).** As we noted above, the author argues that it is not restrictions on aid that create pressures on low-income families; it is the aid itself. We can apply this reasoning to answer this question. The analysis in the text can be used to predict that an increase in the availability of aid would tend to increase pressures on the family unit. Thus, reducing restrictions, because it would

result in an increase in aid availability, would actually tend to create more pressure for divorce. This would have the exact opposite effect predicted by those who call for welfare reforms such as eliminating restrictions. Choice (A) is nice also because of the word *paradoxically* that opens the statement, for the result would be paradoxical from the standpoint of the reformer. Choices (C) and (D) can be eliminated because they are contradicted by the analysis given in the passage. Choice (B) is eliminated because the author never addresses questions of fiscal policy. Finally, choice (E) goes too far in two respects. First, it overstates the author's case. The author does not suggest that the only factor operating in the dissolution of low-income families is welfare and therefore would not likely suggest that the problem could be entirely controlled by manipulating benefit levels. Further, it is not clear that the author advocates any particular policy. The scholarly tone of the article suggests that the author may or may not believe public policy on welfare should take into account the problem of divorce.

17. **The correct answer is (B).** This is an explicit idea question. In discussing the costs of divorce in the third paragraph (costs meaning both economic and social costs), the author mentions choices (B), (C), and (D) as encouraging people to stay married. Earlier in that same paragraph, the author mentions consumption possibilities as a factor tending to hold a marriage together. Choice (B) is never mentioned in this respect. Although the author is primarily interested in low-income family stability, it is never stated that social or economic class is a factor in perpetuating a marriage. And to the extent that one mounts an argument

to the effect that the pressures described in paragraph three (costs of divorce and greater consumption possibilities) would naturally tend to operate more powerfully for lower-income families, one is applying that reasoning to a new situation. So that argument, since it is new, cannot be a factor mentioned by the author in this passage and cannot, therefore, be an answer to the question asked.

18. **The correct answer is (A).** This is obviously a main idea question, and we have already analyzed the main point of the passage. It is nicely stated by choice (A). Choice (B) is not the main idea but only an incidental feature of the argument. Choice (C) is incorrect since this is in direct contradiction to the main point of the passage. Choice (D) fails for the same reason that choice (B) fails. Finally, choice (E) is incorrect because there is no warrant in the passage to support the conclusion that the author would make such a recommendation. The author argues in a very scholarly and neutral fashion. Given that, we cannot attribute any attitude to the author about the wisdom of welfare policy.

19. **The correct answer is (B).** As we have just noted, the scholarly treatment of the passage is best described as scientific and detached. As for choice (A), though the author may be confident in the presentation, there is no hint of optimism. Choice (C) can be eliminated for a similar reason: there is no hint of alarm or discouragement. As for choice (D), to the extent that it can be argued that the author's treatment is scholarly and therefore polite and sensitive, choice (B) is a better description of the overall tone. The defining elements of a scholarly treatment are those set forth in choice (B). Those elements suggested by choice (D)

would be merely incidental to and parasitic upon the main features of scientific neutrality and detachment. Finally, though the author's treatment is detached, it would be wrong to say that the author is callous and indifferent—any more than we would want to say that a doctor who analyzes the causes of a disease in clinical terms is therefore callous and indifferent.

20. **The correct answer is (A).** With an application question of this sort, we must be careful not to overstate the strength of the author's case. This is the reason choice (D) is incorrect. Though the author points out that there are economic pressures on families that tend to encourage divorce, it would go beyond that analysis to attribute to the author the statement in choice (D). Choice (E), too, overstates the case. Though the author prefers to analyze family stability primarily in economic terms, the text will not support the judgment that people are getting more self-centered. If anything, a rising divorce rate would be analyzed by the author in broad social and economic terms, rather than in personal terms as suggested by choice (E). Choice (B) is incorrect because it takes us too far beyond the analysis given in paragraph three. While it is conceivable that further analysis would generate the conclusion in choice (B), choice (A) is much closer to the actual text. This is not to say that choice (B) is necessarily a false statement; rather, this is to accept the structure of the question: Would the author *most likely* agree? Finally, choice (C) attributes to the author a value judgment that has no support in the text.

21. **The correct answer is (E).** This, too, is an application question and, as was just pointed out, we are looking for the most

likely source. It is not impossible that the passage was taken from a basic economics text or a book on the history of welfare. It could, conceivably, be one of several readings included in such books, but on balance, it seems more likely, given the scholarly tone and the particular subject, that choice (E) is the correct answer. It seems unlikely that this would have appeared in choices (A) or (D).

22. **The correct answer is (A).** Here we have a main idea question. The structure of the passage is first to explain that previous siting decisions have been made by regulatory agencies with only a review function exercised by government. The author then explains that in the past, the most important features affecting the demographic characteristics of the population were natural ones. Then the author argues that, given the effect siting decisions will have in the future, the government ought to take an active role in making those decisions and that the government ought to take social considerations into account in making such decisions. Given this brief synopsis of the argument, we can see that choice (A) neatly restates this thesis. Further, we can see that choice (B) constitutes only a part, not the entirety, of the argument. Choice (C), too, forms only one subpart of the whole analysis. Choice (D) can be eliminated since the author believes that future siting decisions need not be governed by only natural features. Finally, choice (E) may very well be true, but it surely is not the main point of the argument presented.

23. **The correct answer is (D).** This is an explicit idea question. Choice (A) is mentioned in the final sentence of the first paragraph along with choice (B). Choice (E) is a theme that runs generally through

that paragraph, and choice (C) is specifically mentioned in the third paragraph. Nowhere does the author suggest that proximity to fuel sources needs to be taken into the siting decision.

24. **The correct answer is (C).** This is a specific detail question, so the answer will be explicitly provided by the text. Your main task is to find the right part of the passage. The answer is given in the first paragraph where the author explains that, traditionally, siting decisions were made by the utilities with government relegated to a review function. Choices (A) and (B) are mentioned in the passage but as advantages of a different process, or, if you prefer, they're mentioned but in the wrong place to answer this question. Choice (D), of course, contradicts the selection; and choice (E) just is not mentioned by the author.

25. **The correct answer is (C).** This is a logical structure question. The author's analysis and recommendation depend on the assumption that it will be possible to predict the demographic consequences of an energy park. Without this assumption, the recommendation that the government use electric facility siting decisions to effect social goals loses much of its persuasiveness. As for choices (A) and (D), the historical explanation is in large part expository only; that is, background information that is not, strictly speaking, essential to the argument supporting the recommendation. To the extent, then, that either choices (A) or (D) does weaken the historical analysis, and that is doubtful, the damage to the overall argument would not be great. As for choices (B) and (E), these are both irrelevant, and the proof is that whether choices (B) and (E) are true or false does not affect the argument.

26. **The correct answer is (D).** The correct answer to this application question, is clearly supported by the concluding remarks of the passage. Choice (A) is contradicted by these remarks and must be incorrect. Choice (B) goes beyond the scope of the passage. We cannot attribute such a critical judgment (". . . were irresponsible") to the author. In fact, the passage at least implies that decisions during the nineteenth century were made in a natural (no pun intended) way. Choice (C) overstates the case. Though the author believes that siting decisions for power plants need not depend on natural features, there is no support in the text for such a broad conclusion as that given in choice (C). Finally, as for choice (E), there is no evidence that the author would make such a judgment.

27. **The correct answer is (A).** This is an explicit idea question, the answer to which is found at the end of the third paragraph. The most important feature of an energy park is that the place in which the massive effects will be manifested can be chosen. So, unlike the harbor, a natural feature located without regard to human desires, the energy park can be located where it will serve goals other than the production of energy. As for choice (B), even to the extent that it makes an accurate statement, the statement is not responsive to the question. This is not an important difference between the natural advantages of an early city and the created features of the energy park. A similar argument invalidates choice (D). As for choice (C), this is obviously irrelevant to the question asked. Finally, choice (E) is incorrect for two reasons. First, such a conclusion is not supported by the pas-

sage. Second, it is not a response to the question asked.

28. **The correct answer is (E).** There can be little doubt that the author is an advocate of energy parks. The criticism noted in passing in the final paragraph is simply dismissed. Thus, we can conclude that his attitude is one of wholehearted support, as indicated by choice (E). We can eliminate choice (D) because the author in no way qualifies his recommendation. Choices (A), (B), and (C) can be eliminated because of the author's positive attitude.

Section 4

Questions 1–6

This problem set is a linear ordering set with the additional complication of the challenge provision. You would probably want to summarize the information:

F > G (F above G)

J > (H & I) (J above both H and I)

K = H + 2 (K is two above H)

F = 3 or 4 (F is 3rd or 4th)

1. **The correct answer is (D).** For this question, we need check only each of the choices against the conditions. Choice (A) can be eliminated since K is not ranked two places above H. Choice (B) can be eliminated since J is not ranked above H and I and for the further reason that F is out of place. Choice (C) is not acceptable since G is ranked above F. Choice (E) is incorrect since K and H are together, not separated by another person. Only choice (D) meets all of the requirements for the initial ranking.

2. **The correct answer is (A).** For this question, we are given additional information. On the assumption that K is ranked first, we know that H must be

ranked third, which in turn places F fourth. Since J must be ranked above H, J must be ranked second. No further conclusion can be definitely drawn about the positions of G and I, so our order is:

1 2 3 4 5 6

K J H F G I

At this juncture, we check our deductions against the answer choices. Choices (B) and (C) are contradicted by the diagram. Choices (D) and (E) are possible—not necessary. Choice (A), however, makes a statement that is confirmed by the diagram.

3. **The correct answer is (A).** For this question, we assume that F is ranked third. On that assumption, there are only two positions available for K: 2 (with H in 4) and 4 (with H in 6).

1 2 3 4 5 6   1 2 3 4 5 6

  K F H   F K   H

As for the first possibility, G must be in position 5 with I in 6, or vice versa, for J must be above H, and that means J must be in first position. As for the second possibility, G must be in position 5, which forces J and I to occupy positions 1 and 2, respectively:

1 2 3 4 5 6   1 2 3 4 5 6

J K F H I G   J I F K G H

So there are a total of three possible arrangements. We are looking, however, for a statement that is necessarily true. That is choice (A), since J is ranked first in all three possibilities. Choice (B) is incorrect since it is only possible, not necessary, that K be second. Choice (C) is incorrect, for it makes a false statement. Choice (D) is incorrect for the same reason. Finally, choice (E) makes a statement that could be true, but it is not necessarily true.

4. **The correct answer is (D).** For this question, we assume that K is ranked third. This means F is fourth, H is fifth, and G must be sixth. Finally, since J must be above I, J is first, with I second.

```
1 2 3 4 5 6
J I K F H G
```

K can challenge only the players one or two ranks above him, and those players are J and I.

5. **The correct answer is (E).** If F is able to issue a challenge to H, this can only be because F is ranked fourth with H third. It is not possible for F to be in the third position with H in the first or second. With H and F in third and fourth, respectively, we are able to deduce the following:

```
1 2 3 4 5 6
K J H F G I
```

K must be in the first position since that is two positions above H, who is in third. Since J must be above H, this means J must be second. Now we check our answer choices. Choices (A), (B), (C), and (D) are all necessarily true, as shown by the diagram. Choice (E) is possible but is not necessary, so choice (E) is the exception and therefore our correct answer.

6. **The correct answer is (A).** We assume that J challenges K, so K must be ranked above J. But J can be ranked no lower than second, so K must be first with H in third and F in fourth:

```
1 2 3 4 5 6
K J H F G I
```

Checking the answer choices, we see that choice (A) is necessarily true, while choices (B), (C), and (D) are necessarily false and choice (E) only possibly true.

Questions 7–10

Although this problem set involves a temporal ordering, we render that ordering spatially:

	M	Tu	Wed	Th	F
W,Y A.M.			X		
X					
V, Z P.M.		Z	(V)	(Z)	

With X flying on Wednesday morning, X cannot fly Tuesday or Thursday morning, nor on Wednesday or Thursday afternoon. Further, with Z flying on Tuesday, Z is not available for Wednesday afternoon. This means V must fly Wednesday afternoon and Z Thursday afternoon.

7. **The correct answer is (E).** We were able to draw only two further conclusions from the initial conditions: V flies Wednesday afternoon and Z flies Thursday afternoon. Choices (A), (B), (C), and (D) are all possibly true; only choice (E) is necessarily true.

8. **The correct answer is (B).** We begin by processing the additional information. Since X is flying Friday morning, X cannot fly either Thursday morning or Friday afternoon. This means that either W or Y will fly on Thursday morning and that V will fly on Friday afternoon.

	M	Tu	Wed	Th	F
A.M.			X		X
P.M.		Z	V	Z	V

The diagram shows that choices (A), (C), and (D) are possibly true and that choice (E) is necessarily false. Only choice (B) is necessarily true.

9. **The correct answer is (A).** We assume that X flies only one morning flight. This does not allow us to draw any specific conclusion about a particular flight, so we are forced to look to the answer choices;

that is, we must test each choice and arrive at the correct answer by the process of elimination. Choice (A) is correct. W and Y must cover Monday, Tuesday, Thursday, and Friday. And since a pilot cannot fly on consecutive days, W must do either Monday or Tuesday and either Thursday or Friday. Choice (B) is incorrect since V could do both Monday and Friday afternoons, and then X would make only the one flight each week. Choice (C) is incorrect as shown by our analysis of choice (A)—Y also must fly two days each week. Choice (D) is incorrect, for Z cannot fly either Monday or Friday. Choice (E) is possibly, though not necessarily, true. We do not know whether Monday and Friday afternoons will go to X or V.

10. **The correct answer is (D).** We begin by processing the additional information:

	M	Tu	Wed	Th	F
A.M.	X	Y	X	Y	X
P.M.	V	Z	V	Z	V

If W does not fly at all during the week, then Y must fly on Tuesday and Thursday. This means that X must fly on Monday morning and Friday morning. Further, we must assign V to Monday and Friday afternoons. The diagram shows that choices (A), (B), (C), and (E) are all necessarily true and that choice (D) is necessarily false.

Questions 11–15

This is a selection set, and we begin by summarizing the restrictions on our selections:

$S \rightarrow Q$ (S requires Q)

$R \rightarrow \sim R$ (Not two consecutive days)

$T \leftarrow U$ (U can only follow T)

Only one carryover

11. **The correct answer is (E).** For a question such as this, which does not supply any additional information, we simply check each answer choice against the restrictions we have summarized. Choice (A) is not acceptable because R is used on two consecutive days and, further, because S appears the first day without Q. Choice (B) can be eliminated because two selections carry over from day 1 to day 2 (S and Q). Choice (C) can be eliminated because S appears on day 2 unaccompanied by Q. Choice (D) can be eliminated because U appears on day 2, but T did not appear on day 1. Only choice (E) is consistent with all of the restrictions.

12. **The correct answer is (C).** If P and S are on the menu, then Q is also on the menu for that day. As for the next day, U cannot be used since T was not offered the day before. Further, S cannot be used since S requires Q and we cannot carry over both S and Q. This leaves us with R and T to be offered along with one dish from the first day (either P or Q).

13. **The correct answer is (C).** We know that neither R nor U can be offered on the intervening day. R cannot be used on two consecutive days, and U must follow T. So we must use S and T. With S offered, we must also offer Q. So the three specials for the intervening day are S, Q, and T.

14. **The correct answer is (A).** If neither Q nor T is on the menu, this leaves us with P, R, S, and U. But S cannot be used without Q, so this leaves only P, R, and U. Hence, there is only one possible combination of specials, given the assumption that Q and T are not offered.

15. **The correct answer is (A).** On the assumption that Q, R, and S are offered on one day, R cannot be offered the following day. Nor can U be offered since T

did not appear on the preceding day. This means that both P and T will have to be included since only one of the original three can be carried over. S cannot be carried over because that would also require the carrying over of Q. Q, however, can appear without S (Q is not "dependent" on S). So the second day, the specials must be P, Q, and T.

Questions 16–20

Here we have an ordering set, but the ordering is not strictly linear. That is, rather than having a single file of items (e.g., books on a shelf), several people here could occupy the same position simultaneously, for example, three people interviewed on Thursday. We begin by summarizing the information:

M   Tu   Wed   Th   F
O

(M & N) = Q + 3 (M and N interviewed
3 days after Q)

P later than K

It does not appear possible to draw any definite conclusions about what individual will be interviewed on which day (other than O). But there are some general conclusions that are available. First, we know that Q must be interviewed on either Monday or Tuesday, with M and N coming on Thursday or Friday, respectively, for those are the only ways of observing the restriction that M and N be interviewed exactly three days after Q. Second, we can also deduce that on one day, three persons will be interviewed; on one day, two persons will be interviewed; and on the remaining three days, only one person will be interviewed. Given that Wednesday is used for only one interview and that only two days have more than one interview, a 1-1-1-2-3 arrangement (though not necessarily in that order) is the only possible distribution.

16. **The correct answer is (C).** This problem does not supply us with additional information, so we must find the correct choice using only the initial conditions. You will observe that the answer choices all make relative statements (e.g., O's interview is later in the week than K's interview) and not specific statements (e.g., K is interviewed on Thursday). The incorrect answers can all be shown to be possible by constructing examples:

M   Tu   Wed   Th   F
Q   K   O   M   P
    J   N
            L

This, of course, is not the only possible schedule, but the diagram shows that choices (A), (B), (D), and (E) are possible. Choice (C), however, is not possible. At the latest, K could be interviewed on Thursday, since K must be followed by P. At the earliest, M and N could be interviewed on Thursday, since they are interviewed on the third day following Q's interview. So it is impossible to interview K on a day *later* in the week than that set aside for N.

17. **The correct answer is (B).** Again, we have a question that does not supply us with any more information. Our analysis regarding the distribution of interviews proves that choice (B) is necessarily true. As for the incorrect answers, using our diagram from the preceding explanation, we can prove that they are not necessarily true. As for choice (A), L can be interviewed on Tuesday with K and J, which proves that the M-N day need not be the day with three interviews. As for choice (C), we can change the diagram to have K and J on Monday and Q on Tuesday. As for choices (D) and (E), the diagram

already proves these statements are not necessarily true.

18. **The correct answer is (A).** Here we have additional information:

M	Tu	Wed	Th	F
		Q		M
		J		N

We know that M and N must be scheduled for Friday, and we know further that a third person must be scheduled for Friday in order to meet the 1-1-1-2-3 distributional requirement. Beyond that, no further conclusions are evident, and we must turn for guidance to the choices. Choice (A) is the correct answer since P must follow K. This means that K cannot be interviewed on Friday, and we know that K cannot be interviewed on Tuesday. This means that K must be interviewed on either Monday or Thursday, days reserved for only one interview. Choices (B), (C), (D), and (E) are all possible but not necessarily true.

19. **The correct answer is (B).** Since P must follow K and since M and N can be interviewed only on Thursday or Friday, the stipulation that K is interviewed with M and N forces us to schedule M and N for Thursday. This requires that we schedule Q for Monday. The remaining statements are all possible, but none of them is necessarily true.

20. **The correct answer is (C).** If L is interviewed later in the week than P, then Thursday is the earliest available date for L (P must follow K). However, the latest date by which Q can be interviewed is Tuesday. So L and Q cannot be scheduled for the same day.

Questions 21–24

For this set we will use an information matrix:

	M	N	O	P	Q	R
1						
2						
3						
4						
5						

This allows us to keep track of which performers are used in which skits. We enter the information:

	M	N	O	P	Q	R
1	NO	NO	YES	YES	NO	NO
2						YES
3	NO	YES	NO	NO	NO	NO
4						
5						

Is there anything more to be learned? Yes. If each of the 6 performers is to appear 3 times, we need a total of 6×3, or 18, appearances. Thus far, we have 2 for the first performance, 4 for the second, and 1 for the third, for a total of 7. We need 11 more appearances. Skits 4 and 5 have spaces for 12 performers (6 for each performance), but we are told that fewer people are used in the fifth than in the fourth skit. So skit 5 can use a maximum of 5 people, and 4 can use a maximum of 6 people. But that is exactly the number we need, 11. So all 6 performers must appear in skit 4, and 5 out of 6 in skit 5. Thus, the distribution is 2, 4, 1, 6, and 5, for a total of 18. Now, we can enter further information on our matrix:

	M	N	O	P	Q	R	
1	NO	NO	YES	YES	NO	NO	2
2						YES	4
3	NO	YES	NO	NO	NO	NO	1
4	YES	YES	YES	YES	YES	YES	6
5							5

Total 18

But we also know that each performer must appear three times, so we deduce the following:

	M	N	O	P	Q	R	
1	NO	NO	YES	YES	NO	NO	2
2	YES				YES	YES	4
3	NO	YES	NO	NO	NO	NO	1
4	YES	YES	YES	YES	YES	YES	6
5	YES				YES	YES	5
	3	3	3	3	3	3	18

Totals

For example, if M does not appear in skits 1 and 3, we know M must appear in 2, 4, and 5.

21. **The correct answer is (E).** We were able to deduce this by reflecting on the overall distributional requirements. Our chart shows that choices (A) and (B) are possibly, though not necessarily, true. Choices (C) and (D) are shown to be false by our chart.

22. **The correct answer is (B).** The chart confirms that choice (B) is the correct answer, for M and R both appear in skits 2, 4, and 5. Choice (C) is perhaps, though not necessarily, true, as shown by the chart. Choices (A), (D), and (E) are shown by the chart to be false.

23. **The correct answer is (B).** Since we need a total of five performers in the fifth skit (two in addition to M, Q, and R), at least one member of the pair, P and O, must be used. As for choice (A), it is possible that N will be used and therefore neither P nor O. As for choices (C) and (D), the same reasoning shows that they are possible. Finally, choice (E) is possible if N appears in the second skit rather than in the fifth.

24. **The correct answer is (A).** For this question, we add the additional information to our matrix:

	M	N	O	P	Q	R
1	NO	NO	YES	YES	NO	NO
2	YES	(YES)	(NO)	(NO)	YES	YES
3	NO	YES	NO	NO	NO	NO
4	YES	YES	YES	YES	YES	YES
5	YES	(NO)	(YES)	(YES)	YES	YES
	3	3	3	3		

Section 5

1. **The correct answer is (D).** According to the speaker, a Board meeting normally precedes a shakeup in management but no such meeting has or will take place, so the shakeup is not going to occur. The other choices, in various ways, just don't describe this development. As for choice (A), although there are two competing theories discussed (shakeup v. no shakeup), these are not logically inconsistent statements. As for choice (B), this would be an apt description only if it later turned out that there was a shakeup in management even though no meeting occurred—perhaps because of special circumstance or a new policy. Then it would be correct to say, "Well, the theory that there would be a change seemed to be wrong given what we knew at the time, but now we know differently." Choice (C) cautions against the fallacy of the false cause. Just because one event follows another does not mean that the one was the cause of the other.

Finally, choice (E) talks about necessary versus sufficient causes. This is a useful distinction with which to be familiar. A necessary cause is one that is required for an event to take place: the virus is necessary for the disease to develop. But a necessary cause is not always a sufficient cause: the virus may be present but yet not cause the disease.

2. **The correct answer is (E).** The speaker rejects the position of the Bar Association that a do-it-yourself will might turn out to be invalid by attacking lawyers—the source of the claim. Choice (A) is incorrect because even though the speaker fails to mention this possibility, it is not necessarily the case that the speaker has failed to consider it; and, in any event, the fact that a proponent of a claim doesn't discuss all possible objections to the claim is not a logical weakness. Choice (B) is wrong because the speaker need not take any position on this issue. As for choice (C), while the speaker only discusses two options, the speaker doesn't claim these are the only two available. (A person might just write a will without any help at all or copy one from some other source.) And choice (D) is wrong because the alternative would be to have no will at all, an option not urged by the speaker.

3. **The correct answer is (B).** The basic move by Adamante is to offer a competing explanation for the phenomenon: Yes, the U.S. has the 17th lowest infant mortality rate, but this is due to distributional factors rather than to medical technology itself. Choice (D) is the second most attractive answer. But Adamante does not introduce any intervening variables; for example, technology allows more pregnancies that would otherwise abort to go to term, which in turn means

that weaker infants are born, and so more die. Choice (A) is incorrect since Adamante seems to accept the validity of the data and to contest the explanation. Choice (E) is incorrect for the same reason. Finally, choice (C) is incorrect since Adamante does not suggest that the first speaker has made a logical error—only a factual one.

4. **The correct answer is (C).** The speaker is arguing that the budget cuts will not ultimately be detrimental to the poor. Choice (C) attacks this conclusion directly by pointing out that they will receive little or no advantage. Choices (A) and (B) are wrong because they are irrelevant: how or why politicians are elected is not a concern of the speaker. And choices (D) and (E) both seem to strengthen the speaker's position by suggesting ways in which the poor would benefit.

5. **The correct answer is (A).** The author reasons from the premise "there are bottles of this product in the apartments" to the conclusion "therefore, these people believe the product is effective." The ad obviously wants the hearer to infer that the residents of the apartments decided themselves to purchase the product because they believed it to be effective. Choice (A) directly attacks this linkage. If it were true that the company gave away bottles of the product, this would sever that link. Choice (B) does weaken the ad but only marginally. To be sure, we might say to ourselves, "Well, a person who touts a product but does not use it is not fully to be trusted." But choice (B) does not aim at the very structure of the argument as choice (A) does. Choice (C) can hardly weaken the argument, since it appears to be a premise on which the argument itself is built. Choice (C),

therefore, actually strengthens the appeal of the advertisement. It also does not link to Painaway's effectiveness. Choice (D) seems to be irrelevant to the *appeal* of the ad. The ad is designed to *change* the hearer's mind, so the fact that someone does not now accept the conclusion of the ad is not an argument against the ability of the ad to accomplish its stated objective. Finally, choice (E) is irrelevant to the purpose of the ad for reasons very similar to these cited for choice (D).

6. **The correct answer is (B).** The author is accusing the artists of being inconsistent: they give lip service to the idea that an artist must suffer, but that they then live in material comfort—so they do not themselves suffer. Only choice (B) completes the paragraph in a way so that this inconsistency comes out. Choices (A) and (D) can be dismissed because the author is concerned with those whom he attacks as *artists*, not as connoisseurs or purchasers of art, nor as critics of art. Choice (C) is inadequate, for it does not reveal the inconsistency. The author apparently allows that these people are, after a fashion, artists but objects to is their claiming that it is necessary to suffer while they do not themselves suffer. Choice (E) is the second-best answer, but it fails, too. The difficulty with choice (E) is that the author's point is that there is a contradiction between the actions and the words of those accused: They claim to suffer, but they do not. But the claimed suffering goes beyond matters of eating and has to do with deprivation generally.

7. **The correct answer is (B).** Choice (B) is an assumption of the author because the inconsistency would disappear if, though artists were not poor, they nonetheless endured great suffering, such as

emotional pain or poor health. Choice (A) is not an assumption of the author. The author is trying to show a contradiction in another's words and actions: It is the others who insist suffering is necessary. The author never says one way or the other whether suffering is necessary to produce art—only that these others claim it is and then eat well. Choice (C) incorrectly construes the author's reference to purchasers of art. The author never mentions the role of the critic. Choices (D) and (E) both make the mistake of applying the term "fools" to a category other than "bidders."

8. **The correct answer is (C).** Take careful note of the exact position the author ascribes to the analysts: They *always* attribute a sudden drop to a crisis. The author then attacks this simple causal explanation by explaining that, though a crisis is followed by a market drop, the reason is not that the crisis causes the drop but that both are the effects of some common cause, the changing of the moon. Of course, the argument seems implausible, but our task is not to grade the argument, only to describe its structure. Choice (A) is not a proper characterization of that structure since the author never provides a specific example. Choice (B), too, is inapplicable since no statistics are produced. Choice (D) can be rejected since the author is attacking generally accepted beliefs rather than appealing to them to support a position. Finally, though the author concedes the reliability of the reports in question, he wants to draw a different conclusion from the data, choice (E).

9. **The correct answer is (A).** Given the implausibility of the author's alternative explanation, the suggestion is probably spoken tongue-in-cheek—ridiculing the

analysts for *always* attributing a drop in the market to a political crisis. But whether you took the argument in this way or as a serious attempt to explain the fluctuations of the stock market, choice (A) will be the correct answer. Choice (E) surely goes beyond the mere factual description at which the author is aiming, as does choice (D) as well. The author is concerned with the *causes* of fluctuations; nothing suggests that he or anyone else is in a position to exploit those fluctuations. Choice (C) finds no support in the paragraph, for nothing suggests that he wishes to attack the credibility of the source rather than the argument itself. Finally, choice (B) is inappropriate to the main point of the passage. Whether the market ultimately evens itself out has nothing to do with the causes of the fluctuations.

10. **The correct answer is (E).** The assumption necessary to the author's reasoning is the fairly abstract or minimal one that there is a connection—between the characteristics of a work of art and the period during which it was produced. If there were no such connection—that is, if there were not styles of art that lasted for some time but only randomly produced works unrelated to one another by medium, content, or detail—the argument would fail. Every other choice, however, attributes too much to the author. Choice (D), for example, states that the expert can *pinpoint* the date of the work, but this goes far beyond the author's attempt to date generally the piece of pottery he is examining. Choice (C) says more than the author does. He mentions that the details of semi-nude women and bulls are characteristic of the *late* Minoan period, not that they generally characterize the entire history of that people.

Choice (B) also goes far beyond the details offered. The author connects the bull with a period of *Minoan* civilization—not ancient civilizations in general. Finally, choice (A) fails because, while the author apparently believes that Minoan pottery of this period was made in a certain way, it is not claimed that all such pottery came from this period. The author uses a group of characteristics in combination to date the pottery: It is the combination that is unique to the period, not each individual characteristic taken in isolation.

11. **The correct answer is (B).** The weakness in the argument is that it makes an assertion without any supporting argumentation. The author states that things might turn out to be worse but never mentions any specific way in which the result might be considered less desirable than what presently exists. As for choice (A), the author might have chosen to attack the radicals in this way, but that the author did not adopt a particular line of attack available is not nearly so severe a criticism as the one expressed by choice (B)—that the line of attack finally adopted is defective or at least incomplete. The same reasoning applies to both choices (C) and (E). It is true the author might have taken the attack proposed by choice (C), but the fact that it was not chosen is not nearly so serious a weakness as that pointed out by choice (B). Choice (E) comes perhaps the closest to expressing what choice (B) says more explicitly. Choice (E) hints at the specific consequences that might occur, but it is restricted to the *transition* period. It is not really detailing the bad results that might finally come out of a revolution, only the disadvantages of undertaking the change. Finally, choice (D) describes

existing conditions, but it does not treat the question of whether there *should* be a revolution; and, in any event, to defend against the question whether there *should* be a revolution by arguing there *will not be* one would itself be weak, had the author used the argument.

12. **The correct answer is (E).** Since the average compensation for all employees was less than that for copywriters, at least one employee must have earned less than the average for the copywriters. Choice (A) cannot be inferred because the speaker provides information only about compensation, not number employed. Choice (B) and (C) are wrong for essentially the same reason: although the average for the graphic artists was greater than that for copywriters, the salary range may or may not have included the extremes described in those choices. And choice (D) cannot be inferred since the speaker talks about total compensation, including the bonuses; that is, no information is given to let you draw a conclusion about the size of the bonuses alone.

13. **The correct answer is (E).** The sample syllogism uses its terms in an ambiguous way. In the first premise, the category "American buffalo" is used to refer to the group as a whole, but in the second premise, it is used to denote a particular member of that group. In the first premise, "disappearing" refers to extinction of a group, but in the second premise, "disappearing" apparently means fading from view. Choice (E) is fraught with similar ambiguities. The argument there moves from wealthy people as a group to a particular wealthy person, an illegitimate shifting of terminology. Choice (A) is a distraction. It mentions subject matter similar to that of the question stem,

but our task is to parallel the *form* of the argument, not to find an argument on a similar topic. Choice (A), incidentally, is an unambiguous and valid argument. So, too, is choice (B), and a moment's reflection will reveal that it is very similar to choice (A). Choice (C) is not similar to choices (A) and (B), but then again it is not parallel to the question stem. Choice (C) contains circular reasoning—the very thing to be proved had to be assumed in the first place—but while circular reasoning is incorrect reasoning, it does not parallel the error committed by the question stem: ambiguity. Choice (D) is clearly a correct argument, so it cannot be parallel to the question stem that contains a fallacious argument.

14. **The correct answer is (C).** The tone of the paragraph is tongue-in-cheek. The author uses phrases such as "mysteries of this arcane science" and "wonderful discipline" but then gives a silly example of the utility of logic. Obviously, he means to be ironic. The real point he wants to make is that formal logic has little utility and that it may even lead one to make foolish errors. Choice (A) cannot be correct because the example is clearly not an illustration of correct reasoning. Choice (B) can be rejected since the author does not attempt to define the term "logic"; he only gives an example of its use. Choice (D) is a distraction. The author's particular illustration does mention the American buffalo, but he could as easily have taken another species of animal or any other group term that would lend itself to the ambiguous treatment of his syllogism. Choice (E) is incorrect since the author never examines the relationship between the premises and the conclusion. He gives the example and lets it speak for itself.

15. **The correct answer is (B).** The author's behavior is paradoxical because he is going along with the young man's paradoxical statement. He concludes the young man is lying because the young man told him so, but that depends on believing what the young man told him is true. So he accepts the content of the young man's statement in order to reject the statement. Once it is seen that there is a logical twist to this problem, the other answer choices can easily be rejected. Choice (A), of course, overlooks the paradoxical nature of the tourist's behavior. The stranger may have been trying to be helpful, but what is curious about the tourist's behavior is not that he rejected the stranger's offer of advice *but rather* that he relied on that very advice at the moment he rejected it! Choice (C) also overlooks the paradox. It is true the tourist rejects the advice, but his rejection is not *understandable;* if anything, it is self-contradictory and therefore completely incomprehensible. Choice (D) is the poorest possible choice since it makes a value judgment totally unrelated to the point of the passage. Finally, choice (E) would have been correct only if the tourist were possibly being victimized.

16. **The correct answer is (D).** As we explained in the previous question, the tourist's behavior is self-contradictory. The sentence mentioned in choice (D) is also self-contradictory. For if the sentence is taken to be true, what it asserts must be the case, so the sentence turns out to be false. On the other hand, if the sentence is taken to be false, then what it says is correct, so the sentence must be true. In other words, the sentence is true only if it is false and false only if it is true: a paradox. Choice (A) is not paradoxical. The witness *later* admits that he lied in the first instance. Thus, though his later testimony contradicts his earlier testimony, the statements taken as a group are not paradoxical, since he is not claiming that the first and the second are true *at the same time.* Choices (B) and (C) do not have even the flavor of paradox. They are just straightforward statements. Do not be deceived by the fact that choice (C) refers to an about-face. To change directions, or even one's testimony, is not self-contradictory—see choice (A). Finally choice (E) is a straightforward, self-consistent statement. Although the worker is advised to dissemble, he does not claim that he is both telling the truth and presenting a false image at the same time.

17. **The correct answer is (E).** The author cites a series of similarities between the two diseases, and then in his last sentence, he writes, "So . . . ," indicating that the conclusion that the causes of the two diseases are similar rests upon the other similarities listed. Choice (E) correctly describes the basis of the argument. Choice (A) is incorrect, for nothing in the passage indicates that either disease is a public health hazard, much less that one disease is a greater hazard than the other. Choice (B) is unwarranted, for the author states only that the scientists are looking for a cure for *aphroditis melancholias.* The author does not state that they will be successful; and even if there is a hint of that in the argument, we surely would not want to conclude on that basis that scientists will eventually find a cure for *every* disease. Choice (C), like choice (A), is unrelated to the conclusion the author seeks to establish. All the author wants to maintain is that similarities in the symptoms suggest that scientists should look for similarities in

the causes of these diseases. The author offers no opinion of the ultimate goal of modern technology, nor does he need to do so. The argument is complete without any such addition. Choice (D) is probably the second-best answer, but it is still completely wrong. The author's argument based on the assumption that similarity of effect depends upon similarity of cause would neither gain nor lose persuasive force if choice (D) were true. After all, many diseases occur in both man and other animals, but at least choice (D) has the merit—which choices (A), (B), and (C) all lack—of trying to say something about the connection between the causes and effects of disease.

18. **The correct answer is (E).** This question asks you to explain the "paradox," and this is a fairly typical test question. Similar question stems ask for you to "account for the unexpected result" or to "explain the unusual outcome," but they are essentially asking for the same thing: Given the background, why did things turn out differently than expected? Applying that insight to this item, the stimulus material leads us to expect a decline in turbulence following the imposition of a speed limit because, after all, going slow produces less wake. Yet, the unexpected (opposite) occurred. Why? Choice (E) answers this question: the boats were operating too slowly to take advantage of the advanced designs and actually produced more, not less, wake. Now, one typical kind of wrong answer is one that mentions a fact related to the passage but that doesn't cut one way or the other, and choice (A) is such a choice. Fewer ferries operate late at night, but that doesn't explain why turbulence increased following the imposition of the speed limit. Choices (B) and (C) also fit this

pattern. Choice (D) illustrates another wrong-answer pattern: suppressing an alternative explanation. When you read the stimulus material, you might think "But maybe boat traffic increased and that accounts for the increase in turbulence." But choice (D) eliminates this possible explanation, so it does nothing to explain the "paradox."

19. **The correct answer is (A).** A question such as this, which asks you to weaken an argument that offers a proposal, usually is answered by a choice that highlights a hidden causal factor that will defeat the purpose. In this case, the speaker claims that working the dog off-leash will solve the problem of false positives by removing the influence of the handler, but choice (A) points out that the dog's previous training (treats for finding stuff) predisposes it to return positives in anticipation of rewards. Wrong answers tend to fall into one of three categories. Some are wrong because they simply miss the point, and these are usually fairly obviously wrong, as is choice (C) here. Others cite interesting facts, like choices (B) and (D), but the facts just don't go anywhere. For example, does the "mixture" problem make it more or less likely that the dog will return false positives? And perhaps most troublesome, some choices actually strengthen the argument. This type is vexing because there is a certain logical force to the choice—but it pushes in the wrong direction. This is illustrated by choice (E). This idea does bear on the issues raised in the stimulus material, but it actually strengthens the argument by pre-empting a possible objection: Don't worry about the fact that the dog is off-leash, because we can still keep tabs on it.

20. **The correct answer is (E).** Remember that you must pay careful attention to the way in which the speaker qualifies and quantifies the claims made. In this case, words such as "usually" and "characteristically" provide support for a certain view but do not establish it definitively. In other words, the speaker overstates the case or claims too much from the evidence. Choice (A) is a description of the logical fallacy of "begging the question." This is similar to saying that the Smith Almanac predicts a hard winter, and it can't be wrong since Smith himself says that he is the leading authority on weather in the world, and the world's leading authority must be accurate. Choice (B) is a description of the fallacy of the "false cause," for example, saying that shortly after the administration announced the release of oil reserves, OPEC said it would curtail production; so it seems that OPEC retaliated for the administration's decision. (Was the release in anticipation of OPEC's actions?) Choice (D) describes the "hasty generalization": "Hello from the Eyewitness-Action-on-the-Spot News Team; we've interviewed three people leaving the poll, and all three said they voted for Johnson, so we're projecting Johnson as the winner." Finally, choice (C) doesn't address the logic of the argument.

21. **The correct answer is (A).** The initial reasoning claims that support for one institution, the majority party, entails support for another, the Prime Minister, because of a connection between the two (the one gives rise to the other). So, too, choice (A) says that appreciation for one game entails appreciation for another because the one is derived from the other. If you can imagine a diagram in which the majority party is connected by an arrow to the Prime Minister, that might help you understand the reasoning of the stimulus material. And then you could use a similar diagram to capture the thinking of choice (A): rugby is connected by an arrow pointing to American football. Choice (C) would have two arrows leading from the Impressionist school to Monet and Renoir. Choice (D) has a similar structure: the controls might point to both machines. And choice (E) would show the week's news leading to both the newspaper and the magazine. Choice (B) simply doesn't have any similar structure.

22. **The correct answer is (B).** When you are asked to draw a conclusion from a set of statements, you want to make sure that your answer choice is the one most *strongly* supported by the information given. And that means reading critically and paying careful attention to exactly what is said. In this case, you have a speaker who says that some people using personal video recorders watch entertaining commercials a couple of times, so it's safe to conclude that such people use the machines to watch the commercials more than once. That's choice (B). Now notice how each of the other choices goes further—out on a limb, so to speak. As for choice (A), while it's a safe bet that some people will watch certain commercials extra times, if you were an executive, you would not want to conclude that your revenue stream would continue uninterrupted. After all, the people who buy the ads and pay the money might not agree. They could decide to put their money elsewhere. Or, as for choice (C), people may watch the ads but not buy the products. As for choice (D), while you're told that more and more people

are using these devices, it's a big jump to conclude that these devices will replace TV sets. And as for choice (E), you have no basis for such a conclusion.

23. **The correct answer is (B).** Anna doesn't deny the validity of Deborah's claims. Instead, she says that the legacy policy serves a useful function.

24. **The correct answer is (B).** The crux of Deborah's claim is that legacy candidates get favorable treatment. The proof of the claim would be found by comparing the acceptance rates of legacy candidates with those for all candidates. Choice (A) is interesting but wide of the mark. What is wanted is a measure of the advantage provided by the policy. A comparison between overall acceptance rates at legacy and non-legacy schools doesn't address that issue. And choice (C) is wrong because the raw number of applicants won't tell us anything about the admissions decisions—for that we need acceptance rates. Choice (D) is incorrect for the same reason: comparisons of raw numbers of any sort are just not going to be helpful, even a longitudinal study more precise than that hinted at by choice (D). And choice (E) is wrong because it provides only half the picture: the acceptance rate for legacy candidates. But we need the other part of the picture to complete the comparison: the acceptance rate for non-legacy candidates.

25. **The correct answer is (C).** Since this is a problem involving three overlapping categories, it seems a good candidate for the Venn diagram approach:

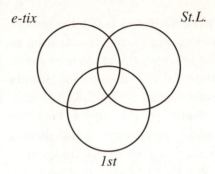

And since all of the passengers who flew to St. Louis purchased an e-ticket:

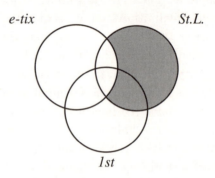

If it is assumed that some passengers who did not purchase e-tickets flew first class:

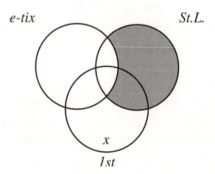

Then it follows that some passengers who flew first class did not go to St. Louis.

WRITING SAMPLE

Following are two responses to the Writing Sample prompt, one in favor of the first option and the other in favor of the second option. These responses are not necessarily Pulitzer

Prize winning essays, but remember they're not supposed to be. The objective, as developed in Chapter 8, is to write something that is serviceable. You'll notice how these responses fit the model developed in Chapter 8.

Sample Response for Option One

The Board should name Paul Sellers to receive the award. Mr. Sellers has demonstrated the teaching excellence and commitment to the community that the award is intended to honor, and he has a plan to make effective use of the sabbatical.

By any measure, Mr. Sellers is possessed of the qualities that the award is designed to honor. He has more than 30 years of teaching experience and has repeatedly been recognized for his effectiveness by the students whom he teaches. In addition, the award recognizes community service, and Mr. Sellers also qualifies on this measure. He has served as an adviser to a number of student organizations, and he has volunteered his time in other ways. These activities benefit not just the students but enrich the greater community.

Additionally, Mr. Sellers would make good use of the sabbatical that accompanies the award. He intends to finish a book about the history of the township. Importantly, this is already a work in progress and not just an idea or suggestion. A book about township history would be useful for students studying state and local history and as a way of acquainting the entire community with its local history.

While it cannot be denied that Ms. Goode also is worthy of recognition, Mr. Sellers' accomplishments simply seem weightier—he has more extensive service for more years. Also, Mr. Sellers' proposed use of the free time is more directly connected to the community of Marietta.

Sample Response for Option Two

Francine Goode should receive the Outstanding Teacher Award. She is certainly an "Outstanding" teacher who has shown the kind of commitment to students and community that the award honors, and she will make good use of the year off.

The Outstanding Teacher Award honors "teaching excellence" and "contribution to the community." Ms. Goode's teaching excellence is demonstrated by her exceptional evaluations and her selection as the Outstanding Foreign Language Teacher in the entire state. She also makes an important contribution to the community. Her unusual facility with languages gives her a unique opportunity to bring non-English speaking parents into the school and greater community. Importantly, she does this both as part of her regular teaching responsibilities and on "her own time" as a volunteer.

The award also carries with it a year off from teaching duties, a year that the Board hopes will be spent on study or some other project that will benefit the schools and community. Although Ms. Goode is already an excellent teacher, she will use her travels during the year to develop new teaching materials to engage students. Additionally, she can further improve her language skills and thereby become even more valuable in her community service.

The Outstanding Teacher Award honors excellence and service and is designed to encourage the recipient to return something to the community. Ms. Goode qualifies on both counts.

Answer Sheet

Use a No. 2 pencil only. Be sure each mark is dark and completely fills the intended oval. Completely erase any errors or stray marks. Start with number 1 for each new section. If a section has fewer than 30 questions, leave the extra answer spaces blank.

SECTION 1	SECTION 2	SECTION 3	SECTION 4	SECTION 5
1 Ⓐ Ⓑ Ⓒ Ⓓ Ⓔ	1 Ⓐ Ⓑ Ⓒ Ⓓ Ⓔ	1 Ⓐ Ⓑ Ⓒ Ⓓ Ⓔ	1 Ⓐ Ⓑ Ⓒ Ⓓ Ⓔ	1 Ⓐ Ⓑ Ⓒ Ⓓ Ⓔ
2 Ⓐ Ⓑ Ⓒ Ⓓ Ⓔ	2 Ⓐ Ⓑ Ⓒ Ⓓ Ⓔ	2 Ⓐ Ⓑ Ⓒ Ⓓ Ⓔ	2 Ⓐ Ⓑ Ⓒ Ⓓ Ⓔ	2 Ⓐ Ⓑ Ⓒ Ⓓ Ⓔ
3 Ⓐ Ⓑ Ⓒ Ⓓ Ⓔ	3 Ⓐ Ⓑ Ⓒ Ⓓ Ⓔ	3 Ⓐ Ⓑ Ⓒ Ⓓ Ⓔ	3 Ⓐ Ⓑ Ⓒ Ⓓ Ⓔ	3 Ⓐ Ⓑ Ⓒ Ⓓ Ⓔ
4 Ⓐ Ⓑ Ⓒ Ⓓ Ⓔ	4 Ⓐ Ⓑ Ⓒ Ⓓ Ⓔ	4 Ⓐ Ⓑ Ⓒ Ⓓ Ⓔ	4 Ⓐ Ⓑ Ⓒ Ⓓ Ⓔ	4 Ⓐ Ⓑ Ⓒ Ⓓ Ⓔ
5 Ⓐ Ⓑ Ⓒ Ⓓ Ⓔ	5 Ⓐ Ⓑ Ⓒ Ⓓ Ⓔ	5 Ⓐ Ⓑ Ⓒ Ⓓ Ⓔ	5 Ⓐ Ⓑ Ⓒ Ⓓ Ⓔ	5 Ⓐ Ⓑ Ⓒ Ⓓ Ⓔ
6 Ⓐ Ⓑ Ⓒ Ⓓ Ⓔ	6 Ⓐ Ⓑ Ⓒ Ⓓ Ⓔ	6 Ⓐ Ⓑ Ⓒ Ⓓ Ⓔ	6 Ⓐ Ⓑ Ⓒ Ⓓ Ⓔ	6 Ⓐ Ⓑ Ⓒ Ⓓ Ⓔ
7 Ⓐ Ⓑ Ⓒ Ⓓ Ⓔ	7 Ⓐ Ⓑ Ⓒ Ⓓ Ⓔ	7 Ⓐ Ⓑ Ⓒ Ⓓ Ⓔ	7 Ⓐ Ⓑ Ⓒ Ⓓ Ⓔ	7 Ⓐ Ⓑ Ⓒ Ⓓ Ⓔ
8 Ⓐ Ⓑ Ⓒ Ⓓ Ⓔ	8 Ⓐ Ⓑ Ⓒ Ⓓ Ⓔ	8 Ⓐ Ⓑ Ⓒ Ⓓ Ⓔ	8 Ⓐ Ⓑ Ⓒ Ⓓ Ⓔ	8 Ⓐ Ⓑ Ⓒ Ⓓ Ⓔ
9 Ⓐ Ⓑ Ⓒ Ⓓ Ⓔ	9 Ⓐ Ⓑ Ⓒ Ⓓ Ⓔ	9 Ⓐ Ⓑ Ⓒ Ⓓ Ⓔ	9 Ⓐ Ⓑ Ⓒ Ⓓ Ⓔ	9 Ⓐ Ⓑ Ⓒ Ⓓ Ⓔ
10 Ⓐ Ⓑ Ⓒ Ⓓ Ⓔ	10 Ⓐ Ⓑ Ⓒ Ⓓ Ⓔ	10 Ⓐ Ⓑ Ⓒ Ⓓ Ⓔ	10 Ⓐ Ⓑ Ⓒ Ⓓ Ⓔ	10 Ⓐ Ⓑ Ⓒ Ⓓ Ⓔ
11 Ⓐ Ⓑ Ⓒ Ⓓ Ⓔ	11 Ⓐ Ⓑ Ⓒ Ⓓ Ⓔ	11 Ⓐ Ⓑ Ⓒ Ⓓ Ⓔ	11 Ⓐ Ⓑ Ⓒ Ⓓ Ⓔ	11 Ⓐ Ⓑ Ⓒ Ⓓ Ⓔ
12 Ⓐ Ⓑ Ⓒ Ⓓ Ⓔ	12 Ⓐ Ⓑ Ⓒ Ⓓ Ⓔ	12 Ⓐ Ⓑ Ⓒ Ⓓ Ⓔ	12 Ⓐ Ⓑ Ⓒ Ⓓ Ⓔ	12 Ⓐ Ⓑ Ⓒ Ⓓ Ⓔ
13 Ⓐ Ⓑ Ⓒ Ⓓ Ⓔ	13 Ⓐ Ⓑ Ⓒ Ⓓ Ⓔ	13 Ⓐ Ⓑ Ⓒ Ⓓ Ⓔ	13 Ⓐ Ⓑ Ⓒ Ⓓ Ⓔ	13 Ⓐ Ⓑ Ⓒ Ⓓ Ⓔ
14 Ⓐ Ⓑ Ⓒ Ⓓ Ⓔ	14 Ⓐ Ⓑ Ⓒ Ⓓ Ⓔ	14 Ⓐ Ⓑ Ⓒ Ⓓ Ⓔ	14 Ⓐ Ⓑ Ⓒ Ⓓ Ⓔ	14 Ⓐ Ⓑ Ⓒ Ⓓ Ⓔ
15 Ⓐ Ⓑ Ⓒ Ⓓ Ⓔ	15 Ⓐ Ⓑ Ⓒ Ⓓ Ⓔ	15 Ⓐ Ⓑ Ⓒ Ⓓ Ⓔ	15 Ⓐ Ⓑ Ⓒ Ⓓ Ⓔ	15 Ⓐ Ⓑ Ⓒ Ⓓ Ⓔ
16 Ⓐ Ⓑ Ⓒ Ⓓ Ⓔ	16 Ⓐ Ⓑ Ⓒ Ⓓ Ⓔ	16 Ⓐ Ⓑ Ⓒ Ⓓ Ⓔ	16 Ⓐ Ⓑ Ⓒ Ⓓ Ⓔ	16 Ⓐ Ⓑ Ⓒ Ⓓ Ⓔ
17 Ⓐ Ⓑ Ⓒ Ⓓ Ⓔ	17 Ⓐ Ⓑ Ⓒ Ⓓ Ⓔ	17 Ⓐ Ⓑ Ⓒ Ⓓ Ⓔ	17 Ⓐ Ⓑ Ⓒ Ⓓ Ⓔ	17 Ⓐ Ⓑ Ⓒ Ⓓ Ⓔ
18 Ⓐ Ⓑ Ⓒ Ⓓ Ⓔ	18 Ⓐ Ⓑ Ⓒ Ⓓ Ⓔ	18 Ⓐ Ⓑ Ⓒ Ⓓ Ⓔ	18 Ⓐ Ⓑ Ⓒ Ⓓ Ⓔ	18 Ⓐ Ⓑ Ⓒ Ⓓ Ⓔ
19 Ⓐ Ⓑ Ⓒ Ⓓ Ⓔ	19 Ⓐ Ⓑ Ⓒ Ⓓ Ⓔ	19 Ⓐ Ⓑ Ⓒ Ⓓ Ⓔ	19 Ⓐ Ⓑ Ⓒ Ⓓ Ⓔ	19 Ⓐ Ⓑ Ⓒ Ⓓ Ⓔ
20 Ⓐ Ⓑ Ⓒ Ⓓ Ⓔ	20 Ⓐ Ⓑ Ⓒ Ⓓ Ⓔ	20 Ⓐ Ⓑ Ⓒ Ⓓ Ⓔ	20 Ⓐ Ⓑ Ⓒ Ⓓ Ⓔ	20 Ⓐ Ⓑ Ⓒ Ⓓ Ⓔ
21 Ⓐ Ⓑ Ⓒ Ⓓ Ⓔ	21 Ⓐ Ⓑ Ⓒ Ⓓ Ⓔ	21 Ⓐ Ⓑ Ⓒ Ⓓ Ⓔ	21 Ⓐ Ⓑ Ⓒ Ⓓ Ⓔ	21 Ⓐ Ⓑ Ⓒ Ⓓ Ⓔ
22 Ⓐ Ⓑ Ⓒ Ⓓ Ⓔ	22 Ⓐ Ⓑ Ⓒ Ⓓ Ⓔ	22 Ⓐ Ⓑ Ⓒ Ⓓ Ⓔ	22 Ⓐ Ⓑ Ⓒ Ⓓ Ⓔ	22 Ⓐ Ⓑ Ⓒ Ⓓ Ⓔ
23 Ⓐ Ⓑ Ⓒ Ⓓ Ⓔ	23 Ⓐ Ⓑ Ⓒ Ⓓ Ⓔ	23 Ⓐ Ⓑ Ⓒ Ⓓ Ⓔ	23 Ⓐ Ⓑ Ⓒ Ⓓ Ⓔ	23 Ⓐ Ⓑ Ⓒ Ⓓ Ⓔ
24 Ⓐ Ⓑ Ⓒ Ⓓ Ⓔ	24 Ⓐ Ⓑ Ⓒ Ⓓ Ⓔ	24 Ⓐ Ⓑ Ⓒ Ⓓ Ⓔ	24 Ⓐ Ⓑ Ⓒ Ⓓ Ⓔ	24 Ⓐ Ⓑ Ⓒ Ⓓ Ⓔ
25 Ⓐ Ⓑ Ⓒ Ⓓ Ⓔ	25 Ⓐ Ⓑ Ⓒ Ⓓ Ⓔ	25 Ⓐ Ⓑ Ⓒ Ⓓ Ⓔ	25 Ⓐ Ⓑ Ⓒ Ⓓ Ⓔ	25 Ⓐ Ⓑ Ⓒ Ⓓ Ⓔ
26 Ⓐ Ⓑ Ⓒ Ⓓ Ⓔ	26 Ⓐ Ⓑ Ⓒ Ⓓ Ⓔ	26 Ⓐ Ⓑ Ⓒ Ⓓ Ⓔ	26 Ⓐ Ⓑ Ⓒ Ⓓ Ⓔ	26 Ⓐ Ⓑ Ⓒ Ⓓ Ⓔ
27 Ⓐ Ⓑ Ⓒ Ⓓ Ⓔ	27 Ⓐ Ⓑ Ⓒ Ⓓ Ⓔ	27 Ⓐ Ⓑ Ⓒ Ⓓ Ⓔ	27 Ⓐ Ⓑ Ⓒ Ⓓ Ⓔ	27 Ⓐ Ⓑ Ⓒ Ⓓ Ⓔ
28 Ⓐ Ⓑ Ⓒ Ⓓ Ⓔ	28 Ⓐ Ⓑ Ⓒ Ⓓ Ⓔ	28 Ⓐ Ⓑ Ⓒ Ⓓ Ⓔ	28 Ⓐ Ⓑ Ⓒ Ⓓ Ⓔ	28 Ⓐ Ⓑ Ⓒ Ⓓ Ⓔ
29 Ⓐ Ⓑ Ⓒ Ⓓ Ⓔ	29 Ⓐ Ⓑ Ⓒ Ⓓ Ⓔ	29 Ⓐ Ⓑ Ⓒ Ⓓ Ⓔ	29 Ⓐ Ⓑ Ⓒ Ⓓ Ⓔ	29 Ⓐ Ⓑ Ⓒ Ⓓ Ⓔ
30 Ⓐ Ⓑ Ⓒ Ⓓ Ⓔ	30 Ⓐ Ⓑ Ⓒ Ⓓ Ⓔ	30 Ⓐ Ⓑ Ⓒ Ⓓ Ⓔ	30 Ⓐ Ⓑ Ⓒ Ⓓ Ⓔ	30 Ⓐ Ⓑ Ⓒ Ⓓ Ⓔ

Practice Test 2

SECTION 1

24 Questions • 35 Minutes

Directions: Each group of questions is based on a set of propositions or conditions. Drawing a rough picture or diagram may help in answering some of the questions. After you have chosen the *best* answer for each question, blacken the corresponding space on your answer sheet.

Questions 1–6

A genealogist has determined that M, N, P, Q, R, S, and T are the father, the mother, the aunt, the brother, the sister, the wife, and the daughter of X, but she has been unable to determine which person has which status. She does know the following:

P and Q are of the same gender.

M and N are not of the same gender.

S was born before M.

Q is not the mother of X.

1. How many of the seven people—M, N, P, Q, R, S, and T—are female?

    (A) 3
    (B) 4
    (C) 5
    (D) 6
    (E) 7

2. Which of the following must be true?

    (A) M is a female.
    (B) N is a female.
    (C) P is a female.
    (D) Q is a male.
    (E) S is a male.

3. If T is the daughter of X, which of the following must be true?

    (A) M and P are of the same gender.
    (B) M and Q are of the same gender.
    (C) P is not of the same gender as N.
    (D) R is not of the same gender as S.
    (E) S is not of the same gender as T.

4. If M and Q are sisters, all of the following must be true EXCEPT

    (A) N is a male.
    (B) M is X's mother.
    (C) Q is X's aunt.
    (D) T is X's daughter.
    (E) S is not X's brother.

5. If S is N's grandfather, then which of the following must be true?

    (A) R is N's aunt.
    (B) X is P's son.
    (C) M is X's brother.
    (D) Q is S's husband.
    (E) P is N's aunt.

6. If M is X's wife, all of the following could be true EXCEPT

(A) S is X's daughter.

(B) P is X's sister.

(C) Q is X's sister.

(D) R is X's father.

(E) N is X's brother.

Questions 7–12

Seven persons, J, K, L, M, N, O, and P, participate in a series of swimming races in which the following are always true of the results:

K finishes ahead of L.

N finishes directly behind M.

Either J finishes first and O last or O finishes first and J last.

There are no ties in any race, and everyone finishes each race.

7. If exactly two swimmers finish between J and L, which of the following must be true?

(A) J finishes first.

(B) O finishes first.

(C) K finishes second.

(D) M finishes fifth.

(E) N finishes fourth.

8. Which of the following CANNOT be true?

(A) K finishes third.

(B) K finishes sixth.

(C) M finishes second.

(D) N finishes fourth.

(E) P finishes third.

9. If O and K finish so that one is directly behind the other, which of the following must be true?

(A) K finishes sixth.

(B) O finishes seventh.

(C) J finishes seventh.

(D) L finishes third.

(E) M finishes fourth.

10. If K finishes fourth, which of the following must be true?

(A) J finishes first.

(B) N finishes third.

(C) P finishes third.

(D) P finishes fifth.

(E) L finishes fifth.

11. If J finishes first and if L finishes ahead of N, in how many different orders is it possible for the other swimmers to finish?

(A) 2

(B) 3

(C) 4

(D) 5

(E) 6

12. Which of the following additional conditions makes it certain that P finishes sixth?

(A) J finishes first.

(B) K finishes second.

(C) M finishes second.

(D) N finishes third.

(E) L finishes fifth.

Questions 13–18

A group of six players, P, Q, R, S, T, and U, are participating in a challenge tournament. All matches played are challenge matches and are governed by the following rules:

A player may challenge another player if and only if that player is ranked either one or two places above.

If a player successfully challenges the player ranked immediately above, the two players exchange ranks.

If a player successfully challenges the player two ranks above, the player who issued this challenge moves up two ranks, and both the loser of the match and the player ranked below the loser move down one rank.

If a player is unsuccessful in a challenge, that player and the player immediately below exchange ranks, unless the unsuccessful challenger was already ranked last, in which case the rankings remain unchanged.

The initial rankings from the highest (first) to the lowest (sixth) are P, Q, R, S, T, U.

Only one match is played at a time.

13. Which of the following is possible as the first match of the tournament?

    (A) P challenges Q.
    (B) Q challenges R.
    (C) R challenges P.
    (D) S challenges P.
    (E) T challenges Q.

14. If S reaches first place after the first two matches of the tournament, which of the following must be ranked fourth at that point in play?

    (A) P
    (B) Q
    (C) R
    (D) T
    (E) U

15. All of the following are possible rankings, from highest to lowest, after exactly two matches EXCEPT

    (A) P, R, Q, T, S, U
    (B) P, R, Q, S, U, T
    (C) R, P, Q, U, S, T
    (D) Q, P, S, R, T, U
    (E) Q, P, S, R, U, T

16. If exactly two matches have been played, what is the maximum number of players whose initial ranks could have been changed?

    (A) 2
    (B) 3
    (C) 4
    (D) 5
    (E) 6

17. If after a certain number of matches the players are ranked from highest to lowest in the order R, Q, P, U, S, T, what is the minimum number of matches that could have been played?

    (A) 2
    (B) 3
    (C) 4
    (D) 5
    (E) 6

18. If after the initial two matches two players have improved their rankings and four players have each dropped in rank, which of the following could be the third match of the tournament?

    (A) R challenges P.
    (B) R challenges Q.
    (C) Q challenges U.
    (D) U challenges P.
    (E) T challenges Q.

[handwritten notes in left margin: "F needs X", "G ≠ X", and a grid/table with columns "1 2 3" showing F, G, H, I, J with notations F(X) F(X), G G(-X) G(-X), H H H(=Y), (Z)—(-Z), I I, J(≠H in 2)]

Questions 19–24

A farmer has three fields, 1, 2, and 3, and is deciding which crops to plant. The crops are F, G, H, I, and J.

F will grow only in fields 1 and 3, but in order for F to grow, it must be fertilized with X.

G will grow in fields 1, 2, and 3, but in order for G to grow, fertilizer X must not be used.

H will grow in fields 1, 2, and 3, but in order for H to grow in field 3, it must be fertilized with Y.

I will grow only in fields 2 and 3, but in order for I to grow in field 2, it must be sprayed with pesticide Z, and in order for I to grow in field 3, it must not be sprayed with Z.

J will grow only in field 2, but in order for J to grow, H must not be planted in the same field.

All crops are planted and harvested at the same time. More than one crop may be planted in a field.

19. It is possible to grow which of the following pairs of crops together in field 1?

(A) F and G

(B) F and J

(C) G and H

(D) J and H

(E) J and G

20. It is possible for which of the following groups of crops to grow together in field 2?

(A) F, G, and H

(B) F, H, and I

(C) G, H, and J

(D) G, I, and J

(E) H, I, and J

21. Which of the following is a complete and accurate listing of all crops that will grow alone in field 2 if the only pesticide or fertilizer used is Y?

(A) F

(B) F and H

(C) G and H

(D) G, H, and J

(E) G, H, I, and J

22. Which of the following pairs of crops will grow together in field 3 if no other crops are planted in the field and no fertilizers or pesticides are applied?

(A) F and H

(B) F and I

(C) G and H

(D) G and I

(E) H and J

23. What is the maximum number of different crops that can be planted together in field 3?

(A) 1

(B) 2

(C) 3

(D) 4

(E) 5

24. Which of the following is a complete and accurate list of the crops that will grow alone in field 2 if X is the only pesticide or fertilizer applied?

(A) H, J

(B) I, G

(C) I, H

(D) I, J

(E) J, G

STOP

END OF SECTION 1. IF YOU HAVE ANY TIME LEFT, GO OVER YOUR WORK IN THIS SECTION ONLY. DO NOT WORK IN ANY OTHER SECTION OF THE TEST.

SECTION 2

25 Questions • 35 Minutes

Directions: In this section, the questions ask you to analyze and evaluate the reasoning in short paragraphs or passages. For some questions, all of the answer choices may conceivably be answers to the question asked. You should select the *best* answer to the question; that is, an answer that does not require you to make assumptions that violate commonsense standards by being implausible, redundant, irrelevant, or inconsistent. After you have chosen the best answer, blacken the corresponding space on the answer sheet.

1. Children in the first three grades who attend private schools spend time each day working with a computerized reading program. Public schools have very few such programs. Tests prove, however, that public-school children are much weaker in reading skills when compared to their private-school counterparts. We conclude, therefore, that public-school children can be good readers only if they participate in a computerized reading program.

   The author's initial statements logically support the conclusion only if which of the following is also true?

   (A) All children can learn to be good readers if they are taught by a computerized reading program.

   (B) All children can learn to read at the same rate if they participate in a computerized reading program.

   (C) Better reading skills produce better students.

   (D) Computerized reading programs are the critical factor in the better reading skills of private-school students.

   (E) Public-school children can be taught better math skills.

2. Is your company going to continue to discriminate against women in its hiring and promotion policies?

   The question above might be considered unfair because it

   (A) fails to mention that other companies might have similar practices.

   (B) assumes that the interviewee agrees with the policies of the company.

   (C) reveals a bias on the part of the questioner.

   (D) contains a hidden presupposition that the responder might wish to contest.

   (E) shifts the focus of attention from the person interviewed to the company.

Questions 3 and 4

Ms. Evangeline Rose argued that money and time invested in acquiring a professional degree are totally wasted. As evidence supporting her argument, she offered the case of a man who, at considerable expense of money and time, completed his law degree and then married and lived as a house-husband, taking care of their children and working part-time at a day-care center so his wife could pursue her career.

3. Ms. Rose makes the unsupported assumption that

   (A) an education in the law is useful only in pursuing law-related activities.

   (B) what was not acceptable twenty-five years ago may very well be acceptable today.

   (C) wealth is more important than learning.

   (D) professional success is a function of the quality of one's education.

   (E) only the study of law can be considered professional study.

4. The logical reasoning of Ms. Rose's argument is closely parallelled by which of the following?

   (A) A juvenile delinquent who insists that his behavior should be attributable to the fact that his parents did not love him

   (B) A senator who votes large sums of money for military equipment but who votes against programs designed to help the poor

   (C) A conscientious objector who bases his draft resistance on the premise that there can be no moral wars

   (D) When a policeman is found guilty of murdering his wife, an opponent of police brutality who says, "That's what these people mean by law and order"

   (E) A high school senior who decides that rather than going to college, he will enroll in a vocational training program to learn to be an electrician

5. A cryptographer has intercepted an enemy message that is in code. The code is a simple substitution of numbers for letters. Which of the following would be the least helpful in breaking the code?

   (A) Knowing the frequency with which the vowels of the language are used

   (B) Knowing the frequency with which two vowels appear together in the language

   (C) Knowing the frequency with which odd numbers appear relative to even numbers in the message

   (D) Knowing the conjugation of the verb "to be" in the language on which the code is based

   (E) Knowing every word in the language that begins with the letter R

6. One way of reducing commuting time for those who work in the cities is to increase the speed at which traffic moves in the heart of the city. This can be accomplished by raising the tolls on the tunnels and bridges connecting the city with other communities. This will discourage auto traffic into the city and will encourage people to use public transportation instead.

Which of the following, if true, would LEAST weaken the argument above?

(A) Nearly all of the traffic in the center of the city is commercial traffic that will continue despite toll increases.

(B) Some people now driving alone into the city would choose to car-pool with each other rather than use public transportation.

(C) Any temporary improvement in traffic flow would be lost because the improvement itself would attract more cars.

(D) The numbers of commuters who would be deterred by the toll increases would be insignificant.

(E) The public transportation system is not able to handle any significant increase in the number of commuters using the system.

7. An independent medical research team recently did a survey at a mountain retreat founded to help heavy smokers quit or cut down on their cigarette smoking. Eighty percent of those persons smoking three packs a day or more were able to cut down to one pack a day after they began to take End-Smoke with its patented desire suppressant. Try End-Smoke to help you cut down significantly on your smoking.

Which of the following, if true, offers the strongest criticism of the advertisement?

(A) Heavy smokers may be psychologically as well as physically addicted to tobacco smoking.

(B) Of the 20 percent who failed to achieve significant results, most were addicted to other substances as well.

(C) The independent medical research team included several members who were experts in the field of nicotine addiction.

(D) A survey conducted at a mountain retreat to aid smokers may yield different results than one would expect under other circumstances.

(E) The overall percentage of the general population who smoke regularly has not declined dramatically over the past twenty years.

8. JOCKEY: Horses are the most noble of all animals. They are both loyal and brave. I knew of a farm horse that died of a broken heart shortly after its owner died.

VETERINARIAN: You're wrong. Dogs can be just as loyal and brave. I had a dog who would wait every day on the front steps for me to come home, and if I did not arrive until midnight, it would still be there.

All of the following are true of the claims of the jockey and the veterinarian EXCEPT

(A) both claims assume that loyalty and bravery are characteristics that are desirable in animals.

(B) both claims assume that the two most loyal animals are the horse and the dog.

(C) both claims assume that human qualities can be attributed to animals.

(D) both claims are supported by only a single example of animal behavior.

(E) neither claim is supported by evidence other than the opinions and observations of the speakers.

9. Rousseau assumed that human beings in the state of nature are characterized by a feeling of sympathy toward their fellow humans and other living creatures. In order to explain the existence of social ills, such as the exploitation of humans by humans, Rousseau maintained that our natural feelings are crushed under the weight of unsympathetic social institutions.

Rousseau's argument described above would be most strengthened if it could be explained how

(A) creatures naturally characterized by feelings of sympathy for all living creatures could create unsympathetic social institutions.

(B) we can restructure our social institutions so that they will foster our natural sympathies for one another.

(C) modern reformers might lead the way to a life that is not inconsistent with the ideals of the state of nature.

(D) non-exploitative conduct could arise in conditions of the state of nature.

(E) a return to the state of nature from modern society might be accomplished.

10. Every element on the periodic chart is radioactive, though the most stable elements have half-lives that are thousands and thousands of years long. When an atom decays, it splits into two or more smaller atoms. Even considering the fusion taking place inside of stars, there is only a negligible tendency for smaller atoms to transmute into larger ones. Thus, the ratio of lighter to heavier atoms in the universe is increasing at a measurable rate.

Which of the following sentences provides the most logical continuation of this paragraph?

(A) Without radioactive decay of atoms, there could be no solar combustion and no life as we know it.

(B) Therefore, it is imperative that scientists begin developing ways to reverse the trend and restore the proper balance between the lighter and the heavier elements.

(C) Consequently, it is possible to use a shifting ratio of light to heavy atoms to calculate the age of the universe.

(D) Therefore, there are now more light elements in the universe than heavy ones.

(E) As a result, the fusion taking place inside stars has to produce enough atoms of the heavy elements to offset the radioactive decay of large atoms elsewhere in the universe.

Questions 11 and 12

SPEAKER: The great majority of people in the United States have access to the best medical care available anywhere in the world.

OBJECTOR: There are thousands of poor in this country who cannot afford to pay to see a doctor.

11. Which of the following is true of the objector's comment?

(A) It uses emotionally charged words.

(B) It constitutes a hasty generalization on few examples.

(C) It is not necessarily inconsistent with the speaker's remarks.

(D) It cites statistical evidence that tends to confirm the speaker's points.

(E) It overlooks the distinction the speaker draws between a cause and its effect.

12. A possible objection to the speaker's comments would be to point to the existence of

(A) a country that has more medical assistants than the United States.

(B) a nation where medical care is provided free of charge by the government.

(C) a country in which the people are given better medical care than Americans.

(D) government hearings in the United States on the problems poor people have getting medical care.

(E) a country that has a higher hospital bed per person ratio than the United States.

13. EVERT: The newly proposed amendments to the tax code will result in a fairer tax system that puts more of the burden on the wealthy. Almost all of the projected increase in taxes will be paid by households earning $100,000 a year or more.

SCOTT: The amendments will tax individuals without regard to their wealth. Income, for tax purposes, is defined as the amount earned in any given year without regard to the accumulated assets of the taxpayer or the prospects for the future. For example, a small business taxpayer who ordinarily nets $20,000 a year but who happens, because of a single large deal, to earn $100,000 in a single year is considered just as wealthy as a taxpayer who has earned $100,000 in each of the previous 30 years.

The second speaker takes issue with the first speaker by

(A) attempting to shift the burden of proof to the first speaker.

(B) accusing the first speaker of circular reasoning.

(C) questioning the definition of a key term of the debate.

(D) pointing out a logical contradiction in the first speaker's remarks.

(E) offering expert opinion to support a conclusion.

Questions 14–16

The blanks in the following paragraph indicate deletions from the text. For questions 14 and 15, select the completion that is most appropriate.

I often hear smokers insisting that they have a *right* to smoke whenever and wherever they choose, as though there are no conceivable circumstances in which the law might not legitimately prohibit smoking. This contention is obviously indefensible. Implicit in the development of the concept of a right is the notion that one person's freedom of action is circumscribed by the _____ (14). It requires nothing more than common sense to realize that there are situations in which smoking presents a clear and present danger: in a crowded theater, around flammable materials, during take-off in an airplane. No one would seriously deny that the potential harm of smoking in such circumstances more than outweighs the satisfaction a smoker would derive from smoking. Yet, this balancing is not unique to situations of potential catastrophe. It applies equally as well to situations where the potential injury is small, though in most cases, as for example a person's table manners, the injury of the offended person is so slight we automatically strike the balance in favor of the person acting. But once it is recognized that a balance of freedoms must be struck, it follows that a smoker has a *right* to smoke only when and where _____ (15).

14. (A) Constitution of our nation

(B) laws passed by Congress and interpreted by the Supreme Court

(C) interest of any other person to not be injured or inconvenienced by that action

(D) rights of other persons not to smoke

(E) rights of non-smoking persons not to have to be subjected to the noxious fumes of tobacco smoking

15. **(A)** the government chooses to allow smoking

    (B) the smoker finally decides to light up

    (C) the smoker's interest in smoking outweighs the interests of other persons having a smoke-free environment

    (D) the smoker can ensure that no other persons will be even slightly inconvenienced by the smoke

    (E) there are signs that explicitly state that smoking is allowed in that area

16. The author's strategy in questioning the claim that smokers have a right to smoke is to

    (A) cite facts that are not generally known.

    (B) clarify and fully define a key concept.

    (C) entertain arguments on a hypothetical case.

    (D) uncover a logical inconsistency.

    (E) probe the reliability of an empirical generalization.

17. The average selling price at auction of a painting by Renard Fox is directly proportional to the number of people who bid on the painting. Since 12 more people placed bids on Fox's "Afternoon of the Faun" than on "Teacups under Glass," the selling price of "Afternoon of the Faun" was greater than that for "Teacups under Glass."

    The reasoning of which of the following arguments is most similar to that of the argument above?

    (A) The average cost of the computers shipped by Altaric Electronics to students entering the State University is directly proportional to the conventional memory included and to the ratio of units with DVDs rather than CDs. Since the average cost of the computers shipped to entering students this year was higher than last year, more units had DVDs than CDs.

    (B) The number of computers shipped by Altaric Electronics in September is directly proportional to the number of students in the entering class at State University. Since the number of students entering State University this year was 250 more than the number last year, Altaric shipped more computers this September than last September.

    (C) The number of students in the entering class at State University is directly proportional to the number of students who have applied and to the acceptance-to-rejection ratio. For this year's entering class, the number of applicants was greater than for last year's, but the acceptance-to-rejection ratio was lower. Therefore, the number of students in this year's entering class was greater than last year's.

    (D) The average class size of courses at State University depends not only upon the number of students and the number of faculty members, but on the number of course offerings. Since the number of students and faculty this year is the same as last year but fewer courses are being offered, the average class size at State University is less this year than last.

    (E) The average salary of full professors at State University is directly proportional to the total budget of the University. Since the total budget of the University this year is 10 percent greater than the budget for last year, the total cost of salaries for full professors is higher this year than last year.

Questions 18 and 19

A study published by the Department of Education shows that children in the central cities lag far behind students in the suburbs and the rural areas in reading skills. The report blames this differential on the overcrowding in the classrooms of city schools. I maintain, however, that the real reason that city children are poorer readers than non-city children is that they do not get enough fresh air and sunshine.

18. Which of the following best describes the form of the above argument?

    (A) It attacks the credibility of the Department of Education.

    (B) It indicts the methodology of the study of the Department of Education.

    (C) It attempts to show that central city students read as well as non-city students.

    (D) It offers an alternative explanation for the differential.

    (E) It argues from analogy.

19. Which of the following would LEAST strengthen the author's point in the preceding argument?

    (A) Medical research that shows a correlation between air pollution and learning disabilities

    (B) A report by educational experts demonstrating that there is no relationship between the number of students in a classroom and a student's ability to read

    (C) A notice released by the Department of Education retracting that part of their report that mentions overcrowding as the reason for the differential

    (D) The results of a federal program that indicates that city students show significant improvement in reading skills when they spend the summer in the country

    (E) A proposal by the federal government to fund emergency programs to hire more teachers for central city schools in an attempt to reduce overcrowding in the classrooms

20. Some judges have allowed hospitals to disconnect life-support equipment of patients who have no prospects for recovery. But I say that is murder. Either we put a stop to this practice now, or we will soon have programs of euthanasia for the old and infirm as well as others who might be considered a burden. Rather than disconnecting life-support equipment, we should let nature take its course.

Which of the following objections is the LEAST effective criticism of the argument above?

    (A) It is internally inconsistent.

    (B) It employs emotionally charged terms.

    (C) It presents a false dilemma.

    (D) It oversimplifies a complex moral situation.

    (E) It fails to cite an authority for its conclusion.

21. If Paul comes to the party, Quentin leaves the party. If Quentin leaves the party, either Robert or Steve asks Alice to dance. If Alice is asked to dance by either Robert or Steve and Quentin leaves the party, Alice accepts. If Alice is asked to dance by either Robert or Steve and Quentin does not leave the party, Alice does not accept.

If Quentin does not leave the party, which of the following statements can be logically deduced from the information given?

    (A) Robert asks Alice to dance.

    (B) Steve asks Alice to dance.

    (C) Alice refuses to dance with either Robert or Steve.

    (D) Paul does not come to the party.

    (E) Alice leaves the party.

22. All students have submitted applications for admission. Some of the applications for admission have not been acted upon. Therefore, some more students will be accepted.

The logic of which of the following is most similar to that of the argument above?

(A) Some of the barrels have not yet been loaded on the truck, but all of the apples have been put into barrels. So, some more apples will be loaded onto the truck.

(B) All students who received passing marks were juniors. X received a passing mark. Therefore, X is a junior.

(C) Some chemicals will react with glass bottles but not with plastic bottles. Therefore, those chemicals should be kept in plastic bottles and not glass ones.

(D) All advertising must be approved by the Council before it is aired. This television spot for a new cola has not yet been approved by the Council. Therefore, it is not to be aired until the Council makes its decision.

(E) There are six blue marbles and three red marbles in this jar. Therefore, if I blindly pick out seven marbles, there should be two red marbles left to pick.

23. New Evergreen Gum has twice as much flavor for your money as Spring Mint Gum, and we can prove it. You see, a stick of Evergreen Gum is twice as large as a stick of Spring Mint Gum, and the more gum, the more flavor.

All but which of the following would tend to WEAKEN the argument above?

(A) A package of Spring Mint Gum contains twice as many sticks as a package of Evergreen Gum.

(B) Spring Mint Gum has more concentrated flavor than Evergreen Gum.

(C) A stick of Evergreen Gum weighs only 50 percent as much as a stick of Spring Mint Gum.

(D) A package of Evergreen Gum costs twice as much as a package of Spring Mint Gum.

(E) People surveyed indicated a preference for Evergreen Gum over Spring Mint Gum.

24. Judging from the tenor of the following statements and the apparent authoritativeness of their sources, which is the most reasonable and trustworthy?

(A) FILM CRITIC: Beethoven is really very much overrated as a composer. His music is not really that good; it's just very well known.

(B) SPOKESPERSON FOR A MANUFACTURER: The jury's verdict against us for $2 million is ridiculous, and we are sure that the Appeals Court will agree with us.

(C) SENIOR CABINET OFFICER: Our administration plans to cut inefficiency, and we have already begun to discuss plans that we calculate will save the federal government nearly $50 billion a year in waste.

(D) FRENCH WINE EXPERT: The best buy in wines in America today is the California chablis, which is comparable to the French chablis and is available at half the cost.

(E) UNION LEADER: We plan to stay out on strike until management meets each and every one of the demands we have submitted.

25. That it is impossible to foretell the future is easily demonstrated. For if a person should foresee being injured by a mill wheel on the next day, the person would cancel the trip to the mill and remain at home in bed. Since the injury the next day by the mill wheel would not occur, it cannot in any way be said that the future has been foretold.

Which of the following best explains the weakness in this argument?

(A) The author fails to explain how one could actually change the future.

(B) The author uses the word *future* in two different ways.

(C) The author does not explain how anyone could foresee the future.

(D) The argument is internally inconsistent.

(E) The argument is circular.

STOP

END OF SECTION 2. IF YOU HAVE ANY TIME LEFT, GO OVER YOUR WORK IN THIS SECTION ONLY. DO NOT WORK IN ANY OTHER SECTION OF THE TEST.

SECTION 3

24 Questions • 35 Minutes

> **Directions:** Each group of questions is based on a set of propositions or conditions. Drawing a rough picture or diagram may help in answering some of the questions. After you have chosen the *best* answer for each question and blacken the corresponding space on your answer sheet.

Questions 1–6

Six persons, J, K, L, M, N, and O, run a series of races with the following results.

O never finishes first or last.

L never finishes immediately behind either J or K.

L always finishes immediately ahead of M.

1. Which of the following, given in order from first to last, is an acceptable finishing sequence of the runners?
   - **(A)** J, L, M, O, N, K
   - **(B)** L, O, J, K, M, N
   - **(C)** L, M, J, K, N, O
   - **(D)** L, M, J, K, O, N
   - **(E)** N, K, L, M, O, J

2. If in an acceptable finishing sequence, J and K finish first and fifth, respectively, which of the following must be true?
   - **(A)** L finishes second.
   - **(B)** O finishes third.
   - **(C)** M finishes third.
   - **(D)** N finishes third.
   - **(E)** N finishes sixth.

3. If in an acceptable finishing sequence, L finishes second, which of the following must be true?
   - **(A)** O must finish fourth.
   - **(B)** N must finish fifth.
   - **(C)** Either J or K must finish sixth.
   - **(D)** K or O must finish fifth.
   - **(E)** O or J must finish fourth.

4. All of the following finishing sequences, given in order from 1 to 6, are acceptable EXCEPT
   - **(A)** J, N, L, M, O, K
   - **(B)** J, N, O, L, M, K
   - **(C)** L, M, J, K, O, N
   - **(D)** N, J, L, M, O, K
   - **(E)** N, K, O, L, M, J

5. Each of the following additional conditions determines the exact order of finish of a race for all six persons EXCEPT
   - **(A)** J and K finish second and third, respectively.
   - **(B)** J and K finish third and fourth, respectively.
   - **(C)** J and K finish fourth and fifth, respectively.
   - **(D)** L and K finish second and fourth, respectively.
   - **(E)** J and L finish third and fifth, respectively.

6. If in an acceptable finishing sequence, exactly three runners finish between J and K, which of the following CANNOT be true?
   - **(A)** O does not finish fourth.
   - **(B)** Either J, K, or N finishes first.
   - **(C)** L finishes either third or fourth.
   - **(D)** If O finishes second, either J or K finishes last.
   - **(E)** If O finishes third, either J or K finishes last.

Questions 7–12

Nine people, J, K, L, M, N, O, P, Q, and R, have rented a small hotel for a weekend. The hotel has five floors, numbered consecutively 1 (bottom) to 5 (top). The top floor has only one room, while floors 1 through 4 each have two rooms. Each person will occupy one and only one room for the weekend.

Q and R will occupy the rooms on the third floor.

P will stay on a lower floor than M.

K will stay on a lower floor than N.

K will stay on a lower floor than L.

J and L will occupy rooms on the same floor.

7. Which of the following CANNOT be true?

   (A) J stays on the first floor.

   (B) K stays on the first floor.

   (C) O stays on the second floor.

   (D) M stays on the fourth floor.

   (E) N stays on the fifth floor.

8. If M occupies a room on the second floor, which of the following must be true?

   (A) J stays on the fifth floor.

   (B) N stays on the fifth floor.

   (C) J stays on the fourth floor.

   (D) K stays on the second floor.

   (E) O stays on the first floor.

9. Which of the following is a complete and accurate list of the persons who could stay on the first floor?

   (A) K, O

   (B) M, N

   (C) M, O

   (D) K, M, O

   (E) K, O, P

10. If M occupies a room on the fourth floor, which of the following must be true?

    (A) J stays on the first floor.

    (B) K stays on the first floor.

    (C) O stays on the fourth floor.

    (D) O stays on the fifth floor.

    (E) N stays on the fifth floor.

11. If K and M stay in rooms on the same floor, which of the following is a complete and accurate list of the floors on which they could stay?

    (A) 1

    (B) 2

    (C) 4

    (D) 1 and 4

    (E) 2 and 4

12. Which of the following, if true, provides sufficient additional information to determine on which floor each person will stay?

    (A) P stays on the first floor.

    (B) M stays on the second floor.

    (C) K stays on the second floor.

    (D) M stays on the fourth floor.

    (E) N stays on the fifth floor.

Questions 13–18

The planning committee of an academic conference is planning a series of panels using eight professors, M, N, Q, R, S, T, U, and V. Each panel must be put together in accordance with the following conditions:

N, T, and U cannot all appear on the same panel.

M, N, and R cannot all appear on the same panel.

Q and V cannot appear on the same panel.

If V appears on a panel, at least two professors of the trio M, S, and U must also appear on the panel.

Neither R nor Q can appear on a panel unless the other also appears on the panel.

If S appears on a panel, both N and V must also appear on that panel.

13. Which of the following CANNOT appear on a panel with R?
    - (A) M
    - (B) N
    - (C) Q
    - (D) S
    - (E) T

14. Exactly how many of the professors can appear on a panel alone?
    - (A) 1
    - (B) 2
    - (C) 3
    - (D) 4
    - (E) 5

15. If S appears on a panel, that panel must consist of at least how many professors?
    - (A) 3
    - (B) 4
    - (C) 5
    - (D) 6
    - (E) 7

16. Which of the following is an acceptable group of professors for a panel?
    - (A) M, N, Q, R
    - (B) M, Q, R, T
    - (C) M, R, T, U
    - (D) M, S, U, V
    - (E) N, R, T, U

17. Which of the following groups of professors can form an acceptable panel by doing nothing more than adding one more professor to the group?
    - (A) M, R, T
    - (B) N, Q, M
    - (C) Q, R, S
    - (D) Q, R, V
    - (E) V, R, N

18. Of the group N, S, T, U, V, which professor will have to be removed to form an acceptable panel?
    - (A) N
    - (B) S
    - (C) T
    - (D) U
    - (E) V

Questions 19–24

On a certain railway route, five trains each day operate between City X and City Y: the Meteor, the Comet, the Flash, the Streak, and the Rocket. Each train consists of exactly five cars, and each car is either a deluxe-class car or a coach car.

On the Meteor, only the first, second, and fifth cars are coach.

On the Comet, only the second and third cars are coach.

On the Flash, only the second car is coach.

On the Streak, only the third and fourth cars are coach.

On the Rocket, all cars are coach.

19. On a typical day, which of the following must be true of the railway's trains operating between City X and City Y?

    (A) More deluxe cars than coach cars are used as first cars.

    (B) More deluxe cars than coach cars are used as second cars.

    (C) Every train uses a deluxe car for the fifth car.

    (D) More deluxe cars are used than coach cars.

    (E) More deluxe cars are used on the Rocket and the Streak combined than on the Flash and the Comet combined.

20. Which of the following cars cannot both be deluxe cars on the same train?

    (A) First and second

    (B) First and third

    (C) Second and third

    (D) Third and fourth

    (E) Fourth and fifth

21. To determine which train is the Streak, correct information on whether a car is deluxe or coach is needed for which car or cars?

    (A) First

    (B) Second

    (C) Third

    (D) First and fifth

    (E) Third and fifth

22. If a train has a coach car as the second car, then that train could be any train EXCEPT the

    (A) Meteor.

    (B) Comet.

    (C) Flash.

    (D) Streak.

    (E) Rocket.

23. If a train has deluxe cars as the first and third cars of the train, that train must be the

    (A) Meteor.

    (B) Comet.

    (C) Flash.

    (D) Streak.

    (E) Rocket.

24. If only one of the third, fourth, and fifth cars of a train is a deluxe car, then that train must be the

    (A) Meteor.

    (B) Comet.

    (C) Flash.

    (D) Streak.

    (E) Rocket.

STOP

END OF SECTION 3. IF YOU HAVE ANY TIME LEFT, GO OVER YOUR WORK IN THIS SECTION ONLY. DO NOT WORK IN ANY OTHER SECTION OF THE TEST.

SECTION 4

28 Questions • 35 Minutes

Directions: Below each of the following passages, you will find questions or incomplete statements about the passage. Each statement or question is followed by lettered words or expressions. Select the word or expression that most satisfactorily completes each statement or answers each question in accordance with the meaning of the passage. After you have chosen the *best* answer, blacken the corresponding space on the answer sheet.

Meteorite ALH84001 is a member of a family of meteorites, half of which were found in Antarctica, that are believed to have originated on Mars. Oxygen iso-
(5) topes as distinctive as fingerprints link these meteorites and clearly differentiate them from any earth rock or other kind of meteorite. Another family member, ETA79001, was discovered to con-
(10) tain gas trapped by the impact which ejected it from Mars. Analysis of the trapped gas shows that it is identical to atmosphere analyzed by the spacecraft which landed on Mars in 1976.

(15) The rock of ALH84001 was formed 4.5 billion years ago and 3.6 billion years ago was invaded by water containing mineral salts precipitated out to form small carbonate globules with intricate
(20) chemical zoning. These carbonates are between 1 and 2 billion years old. Sixteen million years ago an object from space, possibly a small asteroid, impacted Mars and blasted off rocks. One of these
(25) rocks traveled in space until it was captured by the earth's gravity and fell on Antarctica. Carbon-14 dating shows that this rock has been on earth about 13,000 years.

(30) The carbonate globules contain very small crystals of iron oxide (magnetite) and at least two kinds of iron sulfide (pyrrhotite and another mineral, possibly greigite). Small crystals of these min-
(35) erals are commonly formed on earth by bacteria, although they can also be formed by inorganic processes. In addition, manganese is concentrated in the

center of each carbonate globule, and
(40) most of the larger globules have rims of alternating iron-rich and magnesium-rich carbonates. The compositional variation of these carbonates is not what would be expected from high tempera-
(45) ture equilibrium crystallization but is more like low temperature crystallization. It is consistent with formation by non-equilibrium precipitation induced by microorganisms.

(50) There are also unusually high concentrations of PAH-type hydrocarbons. These PAHs are unusually simple compared to most PAHs, including PAHs from the burning of coal, oil, or gasoline
(55) or the decay of vegetation. Other meteorites contain PAHs, but the pattern and abundances are different. Of course, PAHs can be formed by strictly inorganic reactions, and abundant PAHs
(60) were produced in the early solar system and are preserved on some asteroids and comets. Meteorites from these objects fall to earth and enable us to analyze the PAHs contained within the
(65) parent bodies. While some of these are similar to the PAHs in the Martian meteorite, all show some major differences. One reasonable interpretation of the PAHs is that they are decay products
(70) from bacteria.

Also present are unusual, very small forms that could be the remains of microorganisms. These spherical, ovoid, and elongated objects closely resemble
(75) the morphology of known bacteria, but many of them are smaller than any

known bacteria on earth. Furthermore, microfossil forms from very old earth rocks are typically much larger than the
(80) forms that we see in the Mars meteorite. The microfossil-like forms may really be minerals and artifacts which superficially resemble small bacteria. Or perhaps lower gravity and more restricted
(85) pore space in rocks promoted the development of smaller forms of microorganisms. Or maybe such forms exist on earth in the fossil record but have not yet been found. If the small objects are
(90) microfossils, are they from Mars or from Antarctica? Studies so far of the abundant microorganisms found in the rocks, soils, and lakes near the coast of Antarctic do not show PAHs or microorganisms
(95) that closely resemble those found in the Martian meteorite.

There is considerable evidence in the Martian meteorite that must be explained by other means if we are to
(100) definitely rule out evidence of past Martian life in this meteorite. So far, we have not seen a reasonable explanation by others which can explain all of the data.

1. The main purpose of the passage is to

    (A) argue that the available data support the conclusion that life once existed on Mars.

    (B) examine various facts to determine what thesis about ALH84001 is most strongly supported.

    (C) answer objections to the contention that Martian meteorites contain evidence of primitive life.

    (D) pose challenges to scientists who hope to prove that ALH84001 proves that life exists on Mars.

    (E) explore different scientific theories as to the origin of life on earth.

2. According to the passage, what evidence most strongly establishes that meteorite ALH84001 originated on Mars?

    (A) Comparison of trapped gases and the Martian atmosphere

    (B) Presence of alternating iron and magnesium carbonates

    (C) Evidence of shapes that resemble known bacteria

    (D) Pattern of carbonate globules with unusual zoning

    (E) Discovery of unusual PAHs in unusual abundances

3. It can be inferred that discovery in Antarctica of fossils of tiny microorganisms the size of the objects noted in meteorite ALH84001 (line 15) would tend to show that the objects

    (A) are the remains of bacteria that lived on Mars.

    (B) were produced by inorganic processes.

    (C) are the remains of bacteria that lived in Antarctica.

    (D) were present in the rock when it broke from Mars' surface.

    (E) are the decay products from once living organisms.

4. The passage mentions all of the following as tending to prove that ALH84001 may once have contained primitive life EXCEPT

    (A) presence of objects resembling the morphology of known bacteria.

    (B) extraordinarily high concentrations of unusual PAHs.

    (C) presence of iron oxide and iron sulfide crystals.

    (D) unusual zonings of carbonate globules.

    (E) distinctive oxygen isotopes trapped in gasses.

5. According to the passage, the compositional variation of the carbonate deposits (line 30) and the PAH-type hydrocarbons (line 51) both

(A) result from chemical processes more likely to occur on Mars than on Earth.

(B) might be the product of an organic reaction or the product of an inorganic process.

(C) tend to occur at relatively cooler temperatures than other, similar reactions.

(D) are evidence of chemical processes that occurred during the formation of the Solar system.

(E) are bi-products of organic processes and cannot result from inorganic reactions.

6. The author mentions lower gravitation and restricted space (lines 83–86) in order to explain why

(A) bacteria on Mars might be smaller than ones found on Earth.

(B) no microfossil record of bacteria has yet been found in Antarctica.

(C) the spherical, ovoid, and elongated shapes in ALH84001 cannot be bacteria.

(D) restricted pore space in Martian rocks were a hindrance to bacterial growth.

(E) non-equilibrium precipitation is probably not the result of an organic reaction.

7. With which of the following conclusions about the possibility of life on Mars would the author most likely agree?

(A) The available evidence strongly suggests that conditions on Mars make it impossible for life to have developed there.

(B) The scientific evidence is ambiguous and supports no conclusion about the possibility of life on Mars.

(C) Scientific evidence cannot, in principle, ever demonstrate that life existed on Mars.

(D) Scientific data derived from ALH84001 is consistent with the proposition that life once existed on Mars.

(E) It is as likely that life developed in a hostile environment such as Antarctica as on Mars.

Behavior is one of two general responses available to endothermic (warm-blooded) species for the regulation of body temperature, the other being in-
(5) nate (reflexive) mechanisms of heat production and heat loss. Human beings rely primarily on the first to provide a hospitable thermal microclimate for themselves, in which the transfer of
(10) heat between the body and the environment is accomplished with minimal involvement of innate mechanisms of heat production and loss. Thermoregulatory behavior anticipates hyperthermia, and
(15) the organism adjusts its behavior to avoid becoming hyperthermic: it removes layers of clothing, it goes for a cool swim, etc. The organism can also respond to changes in the temperature
(20) of the body core, as is the case during exercise; but such responses result from the direct stimulation of thermoreceptors distributed widely within the central nervous system, and the ability of
(25) these mechanisms to help the organism adjust to gross changes in its environment is limited.

Until recently it was assumed that
organisms respond to microwave radia-
(30) tion in the same way that they respond
to temperature changes caused by other
forms of radiation. After all, the argument runs, microwaves are radiation
and heat body tissues. This theory ig-
(35) nores the fact that the stimulus to a
behavioral response is normally a
temperature change that occurs at the
surface of the organism. The thermoreceptors that prompt behavioral changes
(40) are located within the first millimeter of
the skin's surface, but the energy of a
microwave field may be selectively deposited in deep tissues, effectively by-
passing these thermoreceptors,
(45) particularly if the field is at near-reso-
nant frequencies. The resulting temperature profile may well be a kind of
reverse thermal gradient in which the
deep tissues are warmed more than
(50) those of the surface. Since the heat is
not conducted outward to the surface to
stimulate the appropriate receptors, the
organism does not "appreciate" this
stimulation in the same way that it
(55) "appreciates" heating and cooling of the
skin. In theory, the internal organs of a
human being or an animal could be
quite literally cooked well-done before
the animal even realizes that the bal-
(60) ance of its thermomicroclimate has been
disturbed.

Until a few years ago, microwave
irradiations at equivalent plane-wave
power densities of about 100 mW/cm^2
(65) were considered unequivocally to produce "thermal" effects; irradiations
within the range of 10 to 100 mW/cm^2
might or might not produce "thermal"
effects; while effects observed at power
(70) densities below 10 mW/cm^2 were assumed to be "nonthermal" in nature.
Experiments have shown this to be an
oversimplification, and a recent report
suggests that fields as weak as 1 mW/
(75) cm^2 can be thermogenic. When the heat
generated in the tissues by an imposed
radio frequency (plus the heat generated by metabolism) exceeds the heat-
loss capabilities of the organism, the

(80) thermoregulatory system has been com-
promised. Yet surprisingly, not long ago,
an increase in the internal body temperature was regarded merely as "evidence" of a thermal effect.

8. The author is primarily concerned with
   (A) showing that behavior is a more effective way of controlling bodily temperature than innate mechanisms.
   (B) criticizing researchers who will not
   discard their theories about the effects of microwave radiation on organisms.
   (C) demonstrating that effects of microwave radiation are different from
   those of other forms of radiation.
   (D) analyzing the mechanism by which
   an organism maintains its bodily temperature in a changing thermal environment.
   (E) discussing the importance of thermoreceptors in the control of the internal temperature of an organism.

9. Which of the following would be the most
   logical topic for the author to take up in
   the paragraph following the final paragraph of the selection?
   (A) A suggestion for new research to be
   done on the effects of microwaves on
   animals and human beings
   (B) An analysis of the differences between
   microwave radiation and other forms
   of radiation
   (C) A proposal that the use of microwave
   radiation be prohibited because it is
   dangerous
   (D) A survey of the literature on the effects of microwave radiation on human beings
   (E) A discussion of the strategies used
   by various species to control hyperthermia

10. The author's strategy in lines 56–61 is to

    (A) introduce a hypothetical example to dramatize a point.
    (B) propose an experiment to test a scientific hypothesis.
    (C) cite a case study to illustrate a general contention.
    (D) produce a counter-example to disprove an opponent's theory.
    (E) speculate about the probable consequences of a scientific phenomenon.

11. The author implies that the proponents of the theory that microwave radiation acts on organisms in the same way as other forms of radiation based their conclusions primarily on

    (A) laboratory research.
    (B) unfounded assumption.
    (C) control group surveys.
    (D) deductive reasoning.
    (E) causal investigation.

12. The tone of the passage can best be described as

    (A) genial and conversational.
    (B) alarmed and disparaging.
    (C) facetious and cynical.
    (D) scholarly and noncommittal.
    (E) analytical and concerned.

13. The author is primarily concerned with

    (A) pointing out weaknesses in a popular scientific theory.
    (B) developing a hypothesis to explain a scientific phenomenon.
    (C) reporting on new research on the effects of microwave radiation.
    (D) criticizing the research methods of earlier investigators.
    (E) clarifying ambiguities in the terminology used to describe a phenomenon.

14. In developing the argument, the author makes all the following points EXCEPT

    (A) behavior is the primary method by which humans regulate body temperature.
    (B) a report has shown that even microwave irradiations of a very weak power density can generate heat.
    (C) humans may remove clothing in anticipation of hyperthermia.
    (D) change of temperature at the body surface is the most common cause of thermoregulatory behavior.
    (E) new evidence supports the idea that microwave ovens are causing dangerous heat effects.

Under existing law, a new drug may be labeled, promoted, and advertised only for those conditions in that safety and effectiveness have been dem-
(5) onstrated and that the Food and Drug Administration (FDA) has approved, or so-called approved uses. Other uses have come to be called "unapproved uses" and cannot be legally promoted. In a real
(10) sense, the term "unapproved" is a misnomer because it includes in one phrase two categories of marketed drugs that are very different. It is common for new research and new insights to identify
(15) valid new uses for drugs already on the market. This is an important method of discovery in the field of therapeutics, and there are numerous examples of medical progress resulting from the ser-
(20) endipitous observations and therapeutic innovations of physicians. Before such advances can result in new indications for inclusion in drug labeling, however, the available data must meet the legal
(25) standard of substantial evidence derived from adequate and well-controlled clinical trials. Such evidence may require time to develop, and, without initiative on the part of the drug firm, it may not
(30) occur at all for certain uses. However, because medical literature on new uses exists, and these uses are medically beneficial, physicians often use these drugs

for such purposes prior to FDA review or
(35) changes in labeling. This is referred to
as "unlabeled uses" of drugs. A different
problem arises when a particular use for
a drug has been examined scientifically
and has been found to be ineffective or
(40) unsafe, and yet physicians who either
are uninformed or who refuse to accept
the available scientific evidence continue
their use. Such use may have been reviewed by FDA and rejected, or, in some
(45) cases, the use may actually be warned
against in the labeling. This subset of
uses may be properly termed "disapproved uses."
     Government policy should mini-
(50) mize the extent of unlabeled uses. If
such uses are valid—and many are—it
is important that scientifically sound
evidence supporting them be generated
and that the regulatory system accom-
(55) modate them into drug labeling. Continuing rapid advances in medical care
and the complexity of drug usage, however, make it impossible for government
to keep drug labeling up to date for every
(60) conceivable situation. Thus, when a particular use of this type appears, it is also
important, and in the interest of good
medical care, that no stigma be attached
to such use by practitioners while the
(65) formal evidence is assembled between
the time of discovery and the time the
new use is included in the labeling. In
the case of disapproved uses, however, it
is proper policy to warn against these in
(70) the package insert. Whether use of a
drug for these purposes by the uninformed or intransigent physician constitutes a violation of the current Federal
Food, Drug and Cosmetic Act is a matter
(75) of debate that involves a number of technical and legal issues. Regardless of that,
the inclusion of disapproved uses in the
form of contraindications, warnings, and
other precautionary statements in pack-
(80) age inserts is an important practical
deterrent to improper use. Except for
clearly disapproved uses, however, it is
in the best interests of patient care that
physicians not be constrained by regula-
(85) tory statutes from exercising their best

judgment in prescribing a drug for both
its approved uses and any unlabeled
uses it may have.

15. The author's primary concern is to
(A) refute a theory.
(B) draw a distinction.
(C) discredit an opponent.
(D) describe a new development.
(E) condemn an error.

16. According to the passage, an unlabeled use of a drug is any use that
(A) has been reviewed by the FDA and specifically rejected.
(B) is medically beneficial despite the fact that such use is prohibited by law.
(C) has medical value but has not yet been approved by FDA for inclusion as a labeled use.
(D) is authorized by the label approved by the FDA on the basis of scientific studies.
(E) is made in experiments designed to determine whether a drug is medically beneficial.

17. It can be inferred from the passage that the intransigent physician (line 72)
(A) continues to prescribe a drug even though he or she knows it is not in the best interest of the patient.
(B) refuses to use a drug for an unlabeled purpose out of fear that he or she may be stigmatized by its use.
(C) persists in using a drug for disapproved uses because he or she rejects the evidence of its ineffectiveness or dangers.
(D) experiments with new uses for tested drugs in an attempt to find medically beneficial uses for the drugs.
(E) is violating the Federal Food, Drug and Cosmetic Act in using drugs for disapproved uses.

18. All of the following are mentioned in the passage as reasons for allowing unlabeled uses of drugs EXCEPT

    (A) the increased cost to the patient of buying an FDA-approved drug.

    (B) the medical benefits that can accrue to the patient through unlabeled use.

    (C) the time lag between initial discovery of a medical use and FDA approval of that use.

    (D) the possibility that a medically beneficial use may never be clinically documented.

    (E) the availability of publications to inform physicians of the existence of such uses.

19. With which of the following statements about the distinction between approved and unlabeled uses would the author most likely agree?

    (A) Public policy statements have not adequately distinguished between uses already approved by the FDA and medically beneficial uses that have not yet been approved.

    (B) The distinction between approved and unlabeled uses has been obscured because government regulatory agencies approve only those uses that have been clinically tested.

    (C) Practicing physicians are in a better position than the FDA to distinguish between approved and unlabeled uses because they are involved in patient treatment on a regular basis.

    (D) The distinction between approved and unlabeled uses should be discarded so that the patient can receive the full benefits of any drug use.

    (E) The practice of unlabeled uses of drugs exists because of the time lag between the discovery of a beneficial use and the production of data needed for FDA approval.

20. The author regards the practice of using drugs for medically valid purposes before FDA approval as

    (A) a necessary compromise.

    (B) a dangerous policy.

    (C) an illegal activity.

    (D) an unqualified success.

    (E) a short-term phenomenon.

21. Which of the following statements best summarizes the point of the passage?

    (A) Patients have been exposed to needless medical risk because the FDA has not adequately regulated unlabeled uses as well as disapproved uses.

    (B) Physicians who engage in the practice of unlabeled use make valuable contributions to medical science and should be protected from legal repercussions of such activity.

    (C) Pharmaceutical firms develop and test new drugs that initially have little or no medical value but later are found to have value in unlabeled uses.

    (D) Doctors prescribe drugs for disapproved purposes primarily because they fail to read manufacturers' labels or because they disagree with the clinical data about the value of drugs.

    (E) The government should distinguish between unlabeled use and disapproved use of a drug, allowing the practice of unlabeled use and condemning disapproved use.

The existence of both racial and sexual discrimination in employment is well documented, and policy makers and responsible employers are particularly sen-
(5) sitive to the plight of the black female employee on the theory that she is doubly the victim of discrimination. That there exist differences in income between whites and blacks is clear, but it
(10) is not so clear that these differences are solely the result of racial discrimination

in employment. The two groups differ in productivity, so basic economics dictates that their incomes will differ.

(15)   To obtain a true measure of the effect of racial discrimination in employment, it is necessary to adjust the gross black/white income ratio for these productivity factors. White women in urban

(20) areas have a higher educational level than black women and can be expected to receive larger incomes. Moreover, state distribution of residence is important because blacks are overrepresented in

(25) the South, where wage rates are typically lower than elsewhere and where racial differentials in income are greater. Also, blacks are overrepresented in large cities, and incomes of blacks would be

(30) greater if blacks were distributed among cities of different sizes in the same manner as whites.

     After standardization for the productivity factors, the income of black

(35) urban women is estimated to be between 108 and 125 percent of the income of white women. This indicates that productivity factors more than account for the actual white/black income differen-

(40) tial for women. Despite their greater education, white women's *actual* median income is only 2 to 5 percent higher than that of black women in the North. Unlike the situation of men, the evi-

(45) dence indicates that the money income of black urban women was as great as, or greater than, that of whites of similar productivity in the North and probably in the United States as a whole. For

(50) men, however, the adjusted black/white income ratio is approximately 80 percent.

     At least two possible hypotheses may explain why the adjustment for

(55) productivity more than accounts for the observed income differential for women, whereas a differential persists for men. First, there may be more discrimination against black men than against black

(60) women. The different occupational structures for men and women give some indication why this could be the case, and institutionalized considerations—

for example, the effect of unionization in

(65) cutting competition—may also contribute. Second, the data are consistent with the hypothesis that the intensity of discrimination against women differs little between whites and blacks. Therefore,

(70) racial discrimination adds little to effects of existing sex discrimination.

     These findings suggest that a black woman does not necessarily suffer relatively more discrimination in the labor

(75) market than does a white woman. Rather, for women, the effects of sexual discrimination are so pervasive that the effects of racial discrimination are negligible. Of course, this is not to say that

(80) the more generalized racial discrimination of which black women, like men, are victims does not disadvantage black women in their search for work. After all, one important productivity factor is

(85) level of education, and the difference between white and black women on this scale is largely the result of racial discrimination.

22. The primary purpose of the passage is to

(A) explain the reasons for the existence of income differentials between men and women.

(B) show that racial discrimination against black women in employment is less important than sexual discrimination.

(C) explore the ways in which productivity factors such as level of education influence the earning power of black workers.

(D) sketch a history of racial and sexual discrimination against black and female workers in the labor market.

(E) offer some suggestions as to how public officials and private employers can act to solve the problem of discrimination against black women.

23. According to the passage, the gross black/ white income ratio is not an accurate measure of discrimination in employment because the gross ratio

    (A) fails to include large numbers of black workers who live in the large cities and in the South.

    (B) must be adjusted to reflect the longer number of hours and greater number of days worked by black employees.

    (C) represents a subjective interpretation by the statistician of the importance of factors such as educational achievement.

    (D) is not designed to take account of the effects of the long history of racial discrimination.

    (E) includes income differences attributable to real economic factors and not to discrimination.

24. Which of the following best describes the relationship between the income level for black women and that for black men?

    (A) In general, black men earn less money than black women.

    (B) On the average, black women in the South earn less money than black men in large Northern cities.

    (C) Productivity factors have a greater dollar value in the case of black women.

    (D) Black men have a higher income level than black women because black men have a higher level of education.

    (E) The difference between income levels for black and white women is less than that for black and white men.

25. Which of the following best describes the logical relationship between the two hypotheses presented in lines 58–69?

    (A) The two hypotheses may both be true since each phenomenon could contribute to the observed differential.

    (B) The two hypotheses are contradictory, and if one is proved to be correct, the other is proved incorrect.

    (C) The two hypotheses are dependent on each other, and empirical disconfirmation of the one is disconfirmation of the other.

    (D) The two hypotheses are logically connected so that proof of the first entails the truth of the second.

    (E) The two hypotheses are logically connected so that it is impossible to prove either one to be true without also proving the other to be true.

26. Which of the following best describes the tone of the passage?

    (A) Confident and overbearing

    (B) Ill-tempered and brash

    (C) Objective and critical

    (D) Tentative and inconclusive

    (E) Hopeful and optimistic

27. If the second hypothesis mentioned by the author (lines 66–69) is correct, a general lessening of discrimination against women should lead to a(n)

    (A) higher white/black income ratio for women.

    (B) lower white/black income ratio for women.

    (C) lower female/male income ratio.

    (D) increase in the productivity of women.

    (E) increase in the level of education of women.

28. The author's attitude toward racial and sexual discrimination in employment can best be described as one of

(A) apology.

(B) concern.

(C) indifference.

(D) indignation.

(E) anxiety.

STOP

END OF SECTION 4. IF YOU HAVE ANY TIME LEFT, GO OVER YOUR WORK IN THIS SECTION ONLY. DO NOT WORK IN ANY OTHER SECTION OF THE TEST.

SECTION 5

24 Questions • 35 Minutes

> **Directions:** Below each of the following passages, you will find questions or incomplete statements about the passage. Each statement or question is followed by lettered words or expressions. Select the word or expression that most satisfactorily completes each statement or answers each question in accordance with the meaning of the passage. After you have chosen the *best* answer, blacken the corresponding space on the answer sheet.

The following passage contains blanks that represent deleted material. For questions 1 and 2, select the most appropriate completion of the passage.

When we reflect on the structure of moral decisions, we come across cases in which we seem to be subject to mutually exclusive moral demands. But the conflict is just that, a seeming one. We must be careful to distinguish two levels of moral thinking: the *prima facie* and the critical. A *prima facie* moral principle is analogous to a workaday tool, say a(n) _____ (1). It is versatile, that is, useful in many situations, and at your fingertips, to wit, no special skill is needed to use it. Unfortunately, the value of a *prima facie* principle derives from its non-specific language, which means that in some situations, it will turn out to be an oversimplification. For example, two fairly straightforward moral rules such as "keep all promises" and "assist others in dire need," which work well enough in most cases, seem to clash in the following scenario: "I have promised a friend I will run a very important errand on his behalf (and he is relying on me); but while en route, I happen across a person in need of emergency medical assistance, which I can provide, but only at the cost of leaving my original purpose unaccomplished." The appearance of conflict arises from the choice of tools used in analyzing the situation—the two *prima facie* rules do not cut finely enough.

What is wanted, therefore, is a more refined analysis that will be applicable to the specific situation. At this, the second level of moral thinking, critical moral thinking employs a finer system of categories so that the end result is _____ (2).

1. **(A)** surgical scalpel
   (B) kitchen knife
   (C) electrical generator
   (D) tuning fork
   (E) library book

2. **(A)** not two conflicting moral judgments but rather a single consistent moral judgment
   (B) an advance for the human species over the savagery of our forebears
   (C) the improvement of medical care for the population in general
   (D) moral principles of higher levels of abstraction that are applicable to larger numbers of cases
   (E) that value judgments will no longer depend on the particulars of any given situation

3. All effective administrators are concerned about the welfare of their employees, and all administrators who are concerned about the welfare of their employees are liberal in granting time off for personal needs; therefore, all administrators who are not liberal in granting time off for their employees' personal needs are not effective administrators.

If the argument above is valid, then it must be true that

(A) no ineffective administrators are liberal in granting time off for their employees' personal needs.

(B) no ineffective administrators are concerned about the welfare of their employees.

(C) some effective administrators are not liberal in granting time off for their employees' personal needs.

(D) all effective administrators are liberal in granting time off for their employees' personal needs.

(E) all time off for personal needs is granted by effective administrators.

4. CLYDE: You shouldn't drink so much wine. Alcohol really isn't good for you.

GERRY: You're wrong about that. I have been drinking the same amount of white wine for fifteen years, and I never get drunk.

Which of the following responses would best strengthen and explain Clyde's argument?

(A) Many people who drink as much white wine as Gerry does get very drunk.

(B) Alcohol does not always make a person drunk.

(C) Getting drunk is not the only reason alcohol is not good for a person.

(D) If you keep drinking white wine, you may find in the future that you are drinking more and more.

(E) White wine is not the only drink that contains alcohol.

5. In considering the transportation needs of our sales personnel, the question of the relative cost of each of our options is very important. The initial purchase outlay required for a fleet of diesel autos is fairly high, though the operating costs for them will be low. This is the mirror image of the cost picture for a fleet of gasoline-powered cars. The only way, then, of making a valid cost comparison is on the basis of _____.

Which of the following best completes the above paragraph?

(A) projected operating costs for both diesel- and gasoline-powered autos

(B) the average costs of both fleets over the life of each fleet

(C) the purchase cost for both diesel- and gasoline-powered autos

(D) the present difference in the operating costs of the two fleets

(E) the relative amount of air pollution that would be created by the one type of car compared with the other

6. The Dormitory Canteen Committee decided that the prices of snacks in the Canteen vending machines were already high enough, so they told Vendo Inc., the company holding the vending machine concession for the Canteen, either to maintain prices at the then current levels or to forfeit the concession. Vendo, however, managed to thwart the intent of the Committee's instructions without actually violating the letter of those instructions.

Which of the following is probably the action taken by Vendo referred to in the above paragraph?

(A) The president of Vendo met with the University's administration, and they ordered the Committee to rescind its instructions.

(B) Vendo continued prices at the prescribed levels but reduced the size of the snacks vended in the machines.

(C) Vendo ignored the Committee's instructions and continued to raise prices.

(D) Vendo decided it could not make a fair return on its investment if it held the line on prices, so it removed its machines from the Dormitory Canteen.

(E) Representatives of Vendo met with members of the Dormitory Canteen Committee and offered them free snacks to influence other members to change the Committee's decision.

7. The president of the University tells us that a tuition increase is needed to offset rising costs. That is simply not true. Weston University is an institution approximately the same size as our own University, but the president of Weston University has announced that it will not impose a tuition increase on its students.

The author makes his point primarily by

(A) citing new evidence.

(B) proposing an alternative solution.

(C) pointing out a logical contradiction.

(D) drawing an analogy.

(E) clarifying an ambiguity.

8. Only White Bear gives you all-day deodorant protection and the unique White Bear scent.

If this advertising claim is true, which of the following CANNOT also be true?

(A) Red Flag deodorant gives you all-day deodorant protection.

(B) Open Sea deodorant is a more popular deodorant than White Bear.

(C) White Bear after-shave lotion uses the White Bear scent.

(D) All-day deodorant provides all-day protection and uses a scent with a similar chemical composition to that of White Bear.

(E) Lost Horizons deodorant contains a scent with the same chemical composition as that of White Bear and gives all-day deodorant protection.

9. Clara prefers English Literature to Introductory Physics. She likes English Literature, however, less than she likes Basic Economics. She actually finds Basic Economics preferable to any other college course, and she dislikes Physical Education more than she dislikes Introductory Physics.

All of the following statements can be inferred from the information given above EXCEPT

(A) Clara prefers Basic Economics to English Literature.

(B) Clara likes English Literature better than she likes Physical Education.

(C) Clara prefers Basic Economics to Advanced Calculus.

(D) Clara likes World History better than she likes Introductory Physics.

(E) Clara likes Physical Education less than she likes English Literature.

10. In *The Adventure of the Bruce-Partington Plans,* Sherlock Holmes explained to Dr. Watson that the body had been placed on the top of the train while the train paused at a signal.

"It seems most improbable," remarked Watson.

"We must fall back upon the old axiom," continued Holmes, "that when all other contingencies fail, whatever remains, however improbable, must be the truth."

Which of the following is the most effective criticism of the logic contained in Holmes' response to Watson?

(A) You will never be able to obtain a conviction in a court of law.

(B) You can never be sure you have accounted for all other contingencies.

(C) You will need further evidence to satisfy the police.

(D) The very idea of putting a dead body on top of a train seems preposterous.

(E) You still have to find the person responsible for putting the body on top of the train.

11. PROFESSOR: Under the rule of primogeniture, the first male child born to a man's first wife is always first in line to inherit the family estate.

    STUDENT: That can't be true; the Duchess of Warburton was her father's only child by his only wife, and she inherited his entire estate.

The student has misinterpreted the professor's remark to mean which of the following?

(A) Only men can father male children.

(B) A daughter cannot be a first-born child.

(C) Only sons can inherit the family estate.

(D) Illegitimate children cannot inherit their fathers' property.

(E) A woman cannot inherit her mother's property.

Questions 12 and 13

The blanks in the following passage indicate deletions from the text. Select the completion that is most appropriate to the context.

    Contemporary legal positivism depends upon the methodological assumption that a theory of law may be conceptual without, at the same time, being normative. In point of fact, this assumption is a composite principle. It makes the fairly obvious claim that a conceptual theory, which strives to be descriptive rather than normative, says what the law is—not what it ought to be. A conceptual theory must be supplemented by a normative theory, and the arguments in favor of a particular content for law are couched in terms of the results that are expected to flow from proposed legal acts. It is never a part of an argument for what the law ought to be, in the positivist's view, that to be a law it must have a certain content. While the normative argument refers ultimately to agreed-upon ends, it does not assert that these ends _____ (12). Rather, that they are accepted and acted upon is merely a contingent matter. The second part of the methodological premise is more subtle: A conceptual theory such as legal positivism does not claim that the particular description it offers is uniquely correct. Proponents of legal positivism regard their study of law as analogous to the physicists' study of the universe: They have one theory of legal institutions, _____ (13).

12. **(A)** must be pursued as a matter of logical necessity

    (B) are not the best ends for any modern legal system

    (C) would not be adopted by courts in a democratic society

    (D) could be undermined by dissident elements in the community

    (E) are shared by everyone

13. **(A)** and that is the only possible correct theory of law

    (B) and someday, with sufficient work, that theory will be able to generate societal goals for us to pursue

    (C) but that theory may, someday, be displaced by a better one

    (D) although no theory of the physical universe is as reliable as the positivistic theory of law

    (E) which is, however, strongly supported by the findings of modern science

14. The ad agency handling advertising accounts for the Super Bowl says that it expects about 120 million television viewers to tune in to the game in the United States and about 100 million more in Europe. Given that the United States is the country with the biggest interest in the game, the 220 million total seems to be considerably inflated.

All of the following, if true, would tend to strengthen the argument above EXCEPT

(A) outside of the United States the Super Bowl is available only on a pay subscription basis.

(B) the Super Bowl will be broadcast beginning at 6:00 pm when it is 11:00 pm in Britain and later in Europe.

(C) the football organization in charge of the Super Bowl operates an American-style football league in Europe.

(D) the World Cup soccer finals, a sporting event of major interest in Europe, attracted 12 million viewers in Britain and 90 million in Europe.

(E) most Europeans have very little understanding of the rules and procedures of American football.

15. Chukar partridge chicks can run straight up the side of a tree by flapping their wings. The beating wings do not raise the chicks off the ground but rather serve the same purposes as spoilers on race cars: providing better traction for their feet. Feathered dinosaurs may have done something similar. They flapped their primitive wings to better run up inclines, which helped them to catch prey. Thus, the proto-wing offered a survival benefit not related to flight per se and only later did the wing-beating behavior lead to the eventual discovery of the aerial possibilities of the wings. This evolutionary path to flight is different from the two previous models, the arboreal model in which proto-birds first launched themselves from trees and the cursorial model in which they took off from the ground.

In the reasoning above, the speaker

(A) offers a third alternative to an either-or challenge.

(B) provides a counter-example to refute a popular theory.

(C) points out a contradiction in a competing position.

(D) attacks the proponent of plan rather than its merits.

(E) shifts the burden of proof to an opponent of a plan.

16. As the debate on the roots of the so-called obesity epidemic among children rages, it is becoming increasingly clear that public school lunches are not one of the causes. Fully 86 percent of the school lunches prepared on any given day meet the federal nutritional guidelines.

All of the following, if true, weaken the argument EXCEPT

(A) children are permitted to choose their own food items from several offerings and rarely select the most nutritious items.

(B) lunchroom administrators find it easier and less costly to heat cans of bland-tasting prepared vegetables than cook good-tasting fresh vegetables from scratch.

(C) the number of high school students taking daily physical education classes has dropped to 29 percent from 46 percent in the last ten years.

(D) school lunches feature surplus commodities high in saturated fats purchased by the government as a means of supporting farm prices.

(E) most schools permit children to obtain lunch items from vending machines that dispense sodas and candy.

17. It is the central tenet of the ethical theory of the German Idealist thinker Immanuel Kant that a person must not be treated as a means to an end but as an end only unique unto herself or himself. Therefore, it is wrong to use animals for food or clothing, for in doing so, we reduce them to mere instrumentalities and fail to consider their uniqueness.

Which of the following, if true, is the best criticism of the speaker's use of Kant's ethical doctrine?

(A) Kant never considered the possibility that animals might be deserving of ethical treatment.

(B) The use of animals for food and clothing is offensive to many people who themselves consider animals ends and not means.

(C) Kant implies that rehabilitation is not a legitimate objective of the penal system because it treats the criminal as an end.

(D) In nature, every animal is a potential source of nourishment for other animals below it on the food chain.

(E) Kant's conclusion about treating humans as ends rests upon the assumption that humans have the ability for rational thought.

18. Recently, six Magellanic penguins taken from the wild arrived at the San Francisco Zoo. The 46 long-time resident Magellanic penguins, which had spent relatively sedentary lives of grooming and staying in burrows, began to simulate migratory behavior when they watched the new penguins swimming around the 130-by-40 foot pool. All 52 birds now swim almost all the time, resting on the artificial island in the middle of the pool only at night. Indeed, when the pool was drained for cleaning, the penguins refused to leave, walking around it instead of swimming.

Which of the following conclusions can be most reliably drawn from the information above?

(A) Migratory behavior in animals is acquired rather than innate.

(B) Animals in zoo environments rarely exhibit active behavior.

(C) Magellanic penguins in the wild spend most of their time swimming.

(D) The close quarters of a zoo environment suppresses animal migratory behavior.

(E) Animals sometimes mimic the behavior they see in other animals.

19. Cary: Last year, an outbreak of E.coli bacterial poisoning caused by contaminated drinking water at a county fair in rural, upstate New York sent hundreds of people to the hospital and caused nearly a dozen fatalities. This type of poisoning can be prevented by requiring that all sources of public drinking water be treated.

Phil: Your suggestion is unwarranted. The number of cases of E.coli poisoning attributable to contaminated drinking water is relatively small compared to the number of cases caused by eating improperly stored or undercooked food at restaurants and other public eating places.

Phil's response to Cary is inadequate because it

(A) fails to show that Cary's suggestion would not result in advantages that more than offset any associated costs.

(B) oversimplifies a complex policy issue by quantifying public health in terms of hospital visits.

(C) provides no plan for eliminating the health risks associated with eating contaminated food in restaurants.

(D) does not provide information about the relative incidence of food poisoning contracted at restaurants versus other sources.

(E) conflates the exposure to contaminated foods from eating at restaurants with that from eating food prepared in other locations.

20. At a management training seminar, the presenter asked the class "What would you do if you made a truly horrendous error?" A class member answered, "I'd learn from my mistake." To which the presenter responded, "So what did you just learn?"

The presenter is suggesting that

(A) class members should respond directly to questions.

(B) managers do not make errors very frequently.

(C) corporations reward managers who make errors.

(D) corporate training seminars are not very productive.

(E) the class member's answer to the question was a mistake.

21. CLIFFORD: Five years ago, the Dairy Project bought the Grieg property down in Cambridge to try to show that it's possible to operate a dairy farm without purchasing feed from an outside source just by carefully monitoring the effects of grazing on pasture and rotating fields as needed. In the second year, the farm showed a profit, and it has showed a profit ever since. So it is possible to run a profitable dairy farm using just the resources available on the farm.

GENEVA: But the Grieg property has a lot of natural advantages that other farms don't. In the first place, the soil is extremely rich, so the pastures regenerate at a faster rate. In addition, the farm is about twice as large as your ordinary dairy farm, making it possible to let fields remain ungrazed for longer periods.

Which of the following best describes the exchange above?

(A) Geneva fails to point out that dairy farming, as a business, is extremely vulnerable to the uncertainties of weather and to unexpected changes in the demand for milk.

(B) Clifford's argument does not anticipate the possibility that the Dairy Project's operation might not be profitable in the next year.

(C) Geneva assumes without proof that other dairy farmers would be able to achieve the same results if their farms were configured differently.

(D) Geneva's points are irrelevant since the Dairy Project wanted only to show that techniques are feasible, not that they can be applied universally.

(E) Both Clifford and Geneva fail to consider that most diary farmers are dependent upon government subsidies to make the operation sufficiently profitable to continue in the farming business.

22. Some aromatic candles are not ginger-scented.

All Evening Balm tapers are ginger-scented.

Which of the following conclusions can be deduced from the two statements above?

(A) Some aromatic candles are not Evening Balm tapers.

(B) No ginger-scented candles are aromatic.

(C) All ginger-scented candles are Evening Balm tapers.

(D) All aromatic candles are ginger-scented.

(E) Some aromatic candles are ginger-scented.

23. A new restaurant named Frederico's just opened that will serve Northern Italian cuisine in a renovated dining room with a jazz ensemble. But because the restaurant combines eating with entertainment, it won't be able to do either function particularly well. Those who come for the food will be disappointed in their dining experience; those who come for the music won't be treated to the kind of musical performance they expect. The owners would be better advised to make the establishment a restaurant or a jazz club.

The argument above makes which of the following assumptions?

(A) There are no similarities between food service and entertainment.

(B) Jazz music is not well matched to Northern Italian cuisine.

(C) The location of the new establishment is better suited to a restaurant than a jazz club.

(D) There are no economies of scale to be achieved by combining restaurant functions.

(E) In order to be successful, a restaurant or a club must please its customers.

24. For many years, a financial analyst for a prominent newspaper would call the company from which he bought his suits when he wanted to assess where the economy was headed. If suit sales were strong, he would conclude that the economy was on a sound footing. Conversely, if sales of suits were weak, he would write that the economy was headed downward.

Which of the following, if true, provides the most support for the rule of thumb articulated above?

(A) The casual trend of the 1990s produced the worst decade of sales ever for suit manufacturers.

(B) Men's suits are classic in design and manufactured to last and so need not be replaced when the owner feels financially insecure.

(C) Women's wear is usually not affected by economic conditions because having the latest fashion has traditionally been a priority for women.

(D) Most retailers make little profit on men's suits because of the cost of alterations but do make money on other items such as shirts and ties.

(E) Few companies that manufacture men's suits survive beyond the first generation following the establishment of the company.

STOP

END OF SECTION 5. IF YOU HAVE ANY TIME LEFT, GO OVER YOUR WORK IN THIS SECTION ONLY. DO NOT WORK IN ANY OTHER SECTION OF THE TEST.

WRITING SAMPLE

Time—30 Minutes

Joyce Peterson, a French major, is graduating from college at the end of the spring term. Beginning in the fall, she will start teaching French at a high school in the South. She wants to spend her summer studying in France. Write an essay in favor of one of two summer programs, one offered by the American Institute in Paris, the other by the University of Reims. Two considerations should guide your thinking:

1   Joyce wants to improve her French accent and learn the kind of informal speech used by ordinary French people. She also wants to become as familiar as possible with the routine of French life.

2   Joyce wants to visit some of the typical attractions in France, but she also wants to avoid spending too much money on her summer studies.

The AMERICAN INSTITUTE IN PARIS is an extension of an American university that offers French language and culture study programs in Paris. It offers a six-week program in the modern French language. Students from more than twenty different countries will be enrolled in the program. Students attend classes 5 hours each day, five days a week; and all classes are taught by native speakers. The cost of the six-week program is $500, but that sum does not include room and board.

The UNIVERSITY OF REIMS is a public institution located in the small town of Reims, about 60 minutes by train from Paris, in the heart of the champagne-producing region. The University offers a four-week program in French and French literature. The classes are all taught by the faculty at the University. In addition, University students attending summer school conduct small group tutorials. Students spend an average of 6 hours a day in formal classes and another 2 hours each day in their small group tutorials. Saturdays and Sundays are free days. The fee for the program is $1,400, which includes double occupancy housing in University dormitories and two meals a day in the University cafeteria.

ANSWER KEY AND EXPLANATIONS

Section 1

1.	C	6.	A	11.	C	16.	E	21.	D
2.	C	7.	D	12.	E	17.	B	22.	D
3.	D	8.	B	13.	C	18.	D	23.	C
4.	D	9.	C	14.	C	19.	C	24.	A
5.	C	10.	B	15.	E	20.	D		

Section 2

1.	D	6.	B	11.	C	16.	B	21.	D
2.	D	7.	D	12.	C	17.	B	22.	A
3.	A	8.	B	13.	C	18.	D	23.	E
4.	D	9.	A	14.	C	19.	E	24.	D
5.	C	10.	C	15.	C	20.	E	25.	B

Section 3

1.	D	6.	D	11.	B	16.	B	21.	B
2.	E	7.	A	12.	C	17.	A	22.	D
3.	C	8.	C	13.	D	18.	C	23.	C
4.	D	9.	E	14.	D	19.	A	24.	D
5.	E	10.	B	15.	B	20.	C		

Section 4

1.	B	7.	D	13.	A	19.	E	25.	A
2.	A	8.	C	14.	E	20.	A	26.	C
3.	C	9.	A	15.	B	21.	E	27.	A
4.	E	10.	A	16.	C	22.	B	28.	B
5.	B	11.	B	17.	C	23.	E		
6.	A	12.	E	18.	A	24.	E		

Section 5

1.	B	6.	B	11.	C	16.	C	21.	D
2.	A	7.	D	12.	A	17.	E	22.	A
3.	D	8.	E	13.	C	18.	E	23.	E
4.	C	9.	D	14.	C	19.	A	24.	B
5.	B	10.	B	15.	A	20.	E		

Section I

Questions 1–6

This set is based upon family relationships. At the outset we note that of the seven people related to *X,* two are males (father, brother) and five are females (mother, aunt, sister, wife, and daughter). And we summarize the additional information:

$P = Q$ (same gender)

$M \neq N$ (not same gender)

$S > M$ (born before)

$Q \neq$ mother (*Q* is not *X*'s mother.)

There is a further deduction to be drawn. There are only two male relatives. Of the four individuals, *P, Q, M,* and *N,* three are of the same sex and one is of the opposite gender. Since there are only two males in the scheme, this means that the three of the same gender are female. So *P, Q,* and either *M* or *N* are females; either *M* or *N* is male.

1. **The correct answer is (C).** The answer to this question is evident from the analysis above.

2. **The correct answer is (C).** This question is also answerable on the basis of our previous analysis. As for choices (A) and (B), though we know that of *M* and *N* one is male and the other is female, we have no information to justify a judgment as to who is the female. Nor is there any information to support the conclusions in choices (D) and (E).

3. **The correct answer is (D).** We have established that *P* and *Q* are females and that either *M* or *N* is female. So *M* or *N* is male, and of the remaining three relatives, *S, R,* and *T,* one is male as well. If *T* is the daughter of *X,* this establishes that she is female and, further, that either *R* or *S* is the remaining male. Choices (A), (B) and (C) are incorrect since the additional stipulation of this question does not add anything to the analysis of gender distribution above. Choice (E) is incorrect since it asserts that *S* is the male, but there is nothing to support that conclusion. Choice (D), however, is necessarily true. Of the pair *R* and *S,* one must be male and the other female, so they are not of the same gender.

4. **The correct answer is (D).** In the scheme of relations, there is only one possible pair of sisters: the mother and the aunt. It will not do to argue that *X* might have married his sister, especially when an ordinary sister relationship is available. In any event, if *M* and *Q* represent the mother and the aunt, since *Q* is not the mother, *M* must be *X*'s mother, so choices (B) and (C) are both true. Further, since *M* must be female, *N* must be male, and choice (A) is true. Then, since *M* is *X*'s mother and since *S* was born before *M, S* could not be *X*'s brother and choice (E) is true. As for choice (D), *M, Q,* and *N* (a male) are eliminated as daughters, but this still leaves several possibilities.

5. **The correct answer is (C).** There is only one available grandfather–grandchild relationship: *S* must be *X*'s father and *N* his daughter. If *N* is female, then *M* is male and must be *X*'s brother. So choice (C) is necessarily true. As for the remaining choices, choice (A) is possible though not necessary. Choice (B) is also possible since *P* might be *X*'s mother. Choice (D) is not possible since *Q* is female. Finally, choice (E) is possible since *P* is a female and might be *X*'s sister and so *N*'s aunt.

6. **The correct answer is (A).** Since *M* was born after *S,* if *M* is the mother of

X's daughter, S cannot be the daughter. (Again, it will not do to argue about step-daughters, for that is clearly outside the bounds of the problem.) The remaining choices, however, are possible. As for choices (B) and (C), no restriction is placed on P and Q. And as for choice (D), R is not further defined. As for choice (E), we do know that N is male if M is female, and N could therefore be X's brother.

Questions 7–12

This set is a fairly straightforward linear ordering set: Individuals are arranged in a single file from 1 to 7. We summarize the information for easy reference:

$K > L$ (L behind K)

$M \to N$ (N directly behind M)

$J/O = 1/7$ (J and O are first and last or vice versa.)

7. **The correct answer is (D).** We know that J finishes first or last, though we do not know which, so choices (A) and (B) are incorrect. The fourth position is the middle position of the seven. Regardless of whether J finishes first or last, if L is in position 4, L and J are separated by two swimmers. So M and N are 5 and 6. Choice (E) is not possible; choice (C) is only possible.

8. **The correct answer is (B).** We are given no additional information, so the question must be solvable by some general conclusions based on the initial information. We are looking for the one statement that cannot, under any circumstances, be true. Since K finishes ahead of L and since L cannot be in last place, L can finish at worst sixth, and K can finish at worst fifth. That the remaining statements are possible can be proved by examples.

9. **The correct answer is (C).** If O and K are to finish one after the other, it must be because O finishes first and K second. Since L finishes after K, K and O cannot finish one after the other if O is seventh. Further, if O is first, J must be seventh.

10. **The correct answer is (B).** If K is fourth, there is only one pair of adjacent finishing positions available for the M–N pairing: second and third. So M finishes second and N third. As for L, we know that L finishes after K, but it is not clear whether it is L or P who finishes in fifth versus sixth position, nor is it established who finishes first and who finishes last.

11. **The correct answer is (C).** If L finishes ahead of N, we know that K finishes somewhere ahead of M. So we have the bloc K … M–N … L. And it is stipulated that J finishes first, so O finishes last. We have the order J, K, L, M–N, O. The only unresolved issue is where P goes. There are four possibilities:

P(?) P(?) P(?) P(?)
J   K   L   M–N   O

12. **The correct answer is (E).** We must test each condition. As for choice (A), knowing the first and last finishers tells us nothing about the order between 2 and 6. As for choice (B), this establishes nothing about positions 3 through 6. As for choice (C), this establishes only that N is third and leaves open positions 4, 5, and 6. Choice (D) does tell us that M finishes second, but that is all. Choice (E), however, allows us to infer that M and N finish before L (they must be together); and we know that K finishes before L. This leaves only position 6 for P.

Questions 13–18

For this set, no diagram is needed since the relationships are inherent in the system of arithmetic; that is, five is one more than six, etc. You may find it useful to make a marginal note or two, for example, "challenge +1 or +2."

13. **The correct answer is (C).** The setup for this group of questions is fairly long, but once the rules of the game are understood, this question is easy. Choices (A) and (B) are incorrect, for a challenge must issue from a player of lower rank. Choices (D) and (E) are incorrect, for a challenge can be issued only to a player at most two ranks superior.

14. **The correct answer is (C).** Since *S* begins in fourth position, *S* can reach first in two plays by issuing and winning two challenges. This can be done in two ways. *S* can first challenge *Q* and then *P*, or *S* can first challenge *R* and then *P*. Either way, *R* must be in fourth position.

15. **The correct answer is (E).** This arrangement could come about only after a minimum of *three* matches: *P* versus *Q*, *S* versus *R*, and *U* versus *T*, with the challenger prevailing in each case. The other rankings are possible after only two matches:

    (A) *R* versus *Q* and *T* versus *S*
    (B) *R* versus *Q* and *U* versus *T*
    (C) *R* versus *P* and *U* versus *S*
    (D) *Q* versus *P* and *S* versus *R*

16. **The correct answer is (E).** If *U* challenges and defeats *S*, the bottom half of the ranking changes from *STU* to *UST*; and if *R* challenges and defeats *P*, the top half of the ranking changes from *PQR* to *RPQ*. So in just two matches, all 6 players could be displaced from their initial ranks.

17. **The correct answer is (B).** For *P* to be moved down to third place, at least two matches must have been played (*Q* challenging and defeating *P* and then *R* challenging and defeating *Q* or *R* challenging and defeating *P* with *Q* in turn challenging and defeating *P*). The *UST* ordering of the bottom half of the ranking could be obtained in one match, with *U* challenging and defeating *S*.

18. **The correct answer is (D).** For one player to improve and two to drop in a single match, a player must have challenged and defeated a player two ranks superior. For such challenges to have the stipulated results, it must have been player 3 challenging and defeating player 1 and player 6 challenging and defeating player 4. So the rankings at the end of two matches will be *RPQUST*. The third match could pit *U* against *P*.

Questions 19–24

The primary task here is to organize the information. And for that we will use a matrix:

	F	G	H	I	J
1	YES(X)	YES(~X)	YES	NO	NO
2	NO	YES(~X)	YES	YES(Z)	YES(~H)
3	YES(X)	YES(~X)	YES(Y)	YES(~Z)	NO

Once the information has been organized, the questions are readily answerable.

19. **The correct answer is (C).** With regard to choice (A), *F* and *G* cannot grow together (because of "X"). Choices (B), (D), and (E) are not possible because *J* does not grow in Field 1 at all.

20. **The correct answer is (D).** Since *F* does not grow at all in field 2, choices (A) and (B) can be eliminated. Then, since *J* will not grow with *H*, both choices (C) and

(E) can be eliminated. Combination *G, I,* and *J,* however, is consistent with all conditions.

21. **The correct answer is (D).** Notice that this question asks for a list of all crops that could grow *alone*. *F* cannot, since *F* simply does not grow in field 2. *G* grows in field 2 so long as *X* is not applied to the field, so *G* is part of the correct answer. *I* will not grow since it requires *Z*. Finally, *J* will grow since the question stipulates the crops will grow alone. So the correct answer consists of *G, H,* and *J.*

22. **The correct answer is (D).** Neither *F* nor *H* will grow in field 3 unless certain fertilizers or pesticides are added, so we can eliminate choices (A), (B), and (C). Choice (E) can be eliminated on the further ground that *J* simply does not grow in field 3.

23. **The correct answer is (C).** *J* does not grow in field 3, so that reduces the number of possible crops to four. But *F* and *G* cannot grow together, which further reduces the number to three. So the maximum number of crops that can be planted together is three—*F, H,* and *I* or *G, H,* and *I.*

24. **The correct answer is (A).** Consulting the chart, we see that *F* does not grow there at all. *G* will not grow in the presence of *X,* and *I* will only grow in the presence of *Z.* So only *H* and *J* will grow under the stipulated conditions.

Section 2

1. **The correct answer is (D).** The author's recommendation that public schools should have computerized reading programs depends upon the correctness of the explanation of the present deficiency in reading skills in the public schools. The contrast with private-school students shows that the author thinks the deficiency can be attributed to the lack of such a program in the public schools. So, one of the author's assumptions, and that is what the question stem is asking about, is that the differential in reading skills is a result of the availability of a computerized program in the private school system and the lack thereof in the public-school system. Choice (E) is, of course, irrelevant to the question of *reading* skills. Choice (C) tries to force the author to assume a greater burden than has been undertaken. The author claims that the reading skills of public-school children could be improved by a computerized reading program and is not concerned to argue the merits of having good reading skills. Choices (A) and (B) are wrong for the same reason. The author's claim must be interpreted to mean "of children who are able to learn, all would benefit from a computerized reading program." When the author claims that "public-school children can be good readers," this does not imply that all children can learn to be good readers nor that all can learn to read equally well.

2. **The correct answer is (D).** The question contains a hidden presupposition: that the company has discriminatory practices in the first place. This rhetorical strategy is also called a complex question or, pejoratively, a loaded question. Choice (B) is not a correct description of the question, and the questioner doesn't make such an assumption. The other choices describe features of the question but not ones that would be considered unfair, as the question stem asks.

3. **The correct answer is (A).** There are two weaknesses in Ms. Rose's argument. One will be treated in the explanation of the following question—she reaches a

very general conclusion on the basis of one example. We are concerned for the moment with the second weakness. Even if Ms. Rose had been able to cite numerous examples like the case she mentions, her argument would be weak because it overlooks the possibility that an education may be valuable even if it is not used to make a living. Importantly, Ms. Rose may be correct in her criticism of the man she mentions—we need make no judgment about that—but the assumption is nonetheless *unsupported* in that she gives no arguments to support it. Choice (B) plays on the superficial detail of the paragraph—the inversion of traditional role models. But that is not relevant to the structure of the argument; the form could have been as easily shown using a woman with a law degree who decided to become a sailor or a child who studied ballet but later decided to become a doctor. Choice (D) also is totally beside the point. Ms. Rose never commits herself to so specific a conclusion. She simply says professional education is a waste; she never claims success is related to quality of education. Choice (E) is wrong because Ms. Rose is making a general claim about professional education—the man with the law degree was used merely to illustrate her point. Choice (C) is perhaps the second-best answer, but it is still not nearly as good as choice (A). The author's objection is that the man she mentions did not use his law degree in a law-related field. She never suggests that such a degree should be used to make money. She might not have objected to his behavior if he had used the degree to work in a public interest capacity.

4. **The correct answer is (D)**. As we noted at the beginning of our discussion of question 3, there is another weakness in

Ms. Rose's argument: She takes a single example and from it draws a very general conclusion. Choice (D) exemplifies this weakness. Here, too, we have a person who rests a claim on a single example, and obviously this makes the claim very weak. Choice (E) mentions education, but here education is a detail of the argument. The form of the argument—a foolish generalization—is not restricted to education. Choices (A), (B), and (C) are all wrong because they do not reflect the form of the argument, a generalization on a single example.

5. **The correct answer is (C).** To break the code, the cryptographer needs information about the language that the code conceals. Choices (A), (B), (D), and (E) all provide such information. Choice (C), however, says nothing about the underlying language. The code could even use all even or all odd numbers for the symbol substitutions without affecting the information to be encoded.

6. **The correct answer is (B).** The question is one that tests the validity or strength of a causal inference. Often such arguments can be attacked by finding intervening causal linkages, that is, variables that might interfere with the predicted result. Choice (A) cites such a variable. If the traffic problem is created by commercial traffic that will not be reduced by toll increases, then the proposed increases will not solve the problem. Choice (C), too, is such a variable. It suggests that the proposal is essentially self-defeating. Choice (D) undermines the claim by arguing that the deterrent effect of a price increase is simply not significant, so the proposal will have little, if any, effect. Choice (E) attacks the argument on a different ground. The ultimate objective of the plan is to reduce commut-

ing time. Even assuming a drop in auto traffic because some commuters use public transportation, no advantage is gained if the public transportation system cannot handle the increase in traffic. Choice (B), however, does very little to the argument. In fact, it could be argued that choice (B) is one of the predicted results of the plan: a drop in the number of autos because commuters begin to car-pool.

7. **The correct answer is (D).** The exam frequently uses arguments based on analogy, and often one that points out that two situations are not necessarily similar. That's a good way of describing this item: maybe it was the mountain retreat location rather than the medicine that was the deciding factor. Choice (A) is wrong because even granting the point, there is still a physical addiction to be addressed. Choices (B) and (E) are typical wrong answers for an item like this: interesting, but which way does this idea cut? Since neither clearly weakens the ad, neither could be the correct answer. Finally, choice (C), if anything, seems to strengthen the ad by suggesting that the study was authoritative.

8. **The correct answer is (B).** Notice that there is much common ground between the jockey and the veterinarian. The question stem asks you to uncover the areas on which they are is agreement, by asking which of the answer choices is NOT a shared assumption. Note that the exception can be an area neither has as well as an area only one has. Examine the dialogue. Both apparently assume that human emotions can be attributed to animals since they talk about them being loyal and brave choice (C), and both take those characteristics as being noble— that is, admirable choice (A). Neither speaker offers scientific evidence: each

rests content with an anecdote, choices (E) and (D). As for choice (B), though each speaker defends a choice for the first (*most* loyal), neither speaker takes a position on the second-most loyal animal. For example, the jockey might believe that horses are the most loyal animals and that goldfish are the second-most loyal animals.

9. **The correct answer is (A).** Although we do not want to argue theology, perhaps a point taken from that discipline will make this question more accessible: "If God is only good, from where does evil come?" Rousseau, at least as far as the argument is characterized here, faced a similar problem. If humans are by their very nature sympathetic, what is the source of non-sympathetic social institutions? Choice (A) poses this critical question. The remaining choices each commit the same fundamental error. Rousseau *describes* a situation. The paragraph never suggests that Rousseau proposed a *solution*. Perhaps Rousseau considered the problem of modern society irremediable.

10. **The correct answer is (C).** The last sentence of the paragraph is very important. It tells us that the proportion of light atoms in the universe is increasing (because heavy ones decay into light ones, but the reverse process does not occur) and that this trend can be measured. By extrapolation back into time on the basis of present trends, scientists can find out when it all began. Choices (B) and (E) are incorrect for the same reason. The author describes a physical phenomenon occurring on a grand scale but never hints that it will be possible to reverse it. Further, choice (E) is in direct contradiction with information given in the paragraph: The ratio is not stable because the

stars do not produce enough heavy atoms to offset the decay. Choice (D) cannot be inferred from the passage. Although the *ratio* of light to heavy atoms is increasing, we should not conclude that the ratio is greater than 1:1. And, in any event, this would not be nearly so logical a conclusion to the passage as choice (C). Finally, choice (A) is a distraction. It picks up on a minor detail in the passage and inflates that into a conclusion. Moreover, the passage clearly states that the process that keeps the stars going is fusion, not decay.

11. **The correct answer is (C).** It is important to pay careful attention to the ways in which a speaker qualifies a claim. In this case, the speaker has said only that the *great majority* of people can get medical care—not that all can. Thus, built into the claim is the implicit concession that some people may not have access to medical care. Thus, the objector's response fails to score against the speaker. The speaker could just respond, "Yes, I realize that and that is the reason why I qualified my remarks." Choice (A) is incorrect, for the only word in the objector's statement that is the least bit emotional is "poor," and it seems rather free from emotional overtones here. It would have been a different case had the objector claimed, "There are thousands of poor and starving people who have no place to live…" Choice (D) is wrong for two reasons. First, the evidence is really not statistical; it is only numerical. Second, and more important, the evidence, if anything, cuts against the speaker's claim—not that it does any damage given the speaker's qualifications on the claim; but it surely does not strengthen the speaker's claim. Finally, inasmuch as the speaker

does not offer a cause-effect explanation, choice (E) must be wrong.

12. **The correct answer is (C).** There are really two parts to the speaker's claim. First, he maintains that the majority of Americans can get access to the medical care in this country; and, second, that the care they have access to is the best in the world. As for the second, good medical care is a function of many variables: number and location of facilities, availability of doctors, quality of education, etc. Choices (A) and (E) may both be consistent with the speaker's claim. Even though we have fewer assistants, choice (A), than some other country, we have more doctors, and that more than makes up for the fewer assistants. Or, perhaps, we have such good preventive medicine that people do not need to go into the hospital as frequently as the citizens of other nations, choice (E). Choice (B) is wrong for a similar reason. Although it suggests there is a country in which people have greater access to the available care, it does not come to grips with the second element of the speaker's claim: that the care we get is the best. Choice (C), however, does meet both because it cites the existence of a country in which people are *given* (that is the first element) *better* (the second element) care. Choice (D) hardly tells against the speaker's claim since he has implicitly conceded that some people do not have access to the care.

13. **The correct answer is (C).** The crux of the debate between the two speakers is what constitutes "wealthy." According to Evert, anyone who makes $100,000 per year is "wealthy." But Scott points out that annual earnings don't include accumulated assets, which are an important component of what most people would

consider "wealth." Choice (A) is incorrect. A speaker shifts the burden of proof by taking a position and challenging someone else to prove it wrong—in other words, no real argument is offered. Circular reasoning occurs when a speaker presupposes or relies upon the claim that must ultimately be proved in order to prove the claim: Fairies must exist because they are invisible creatures; and since no one has ever seen a fairy, they must exist because it is in their nature not to be observed. A logical contradiction is an inconsistency. For example, opponents of capital punishment sometimes suggest that defenders of the death penalty who argue that execution is justified for murder as a matter of respect for the sanctity of life have fallen into a contradiction because they call for the death of someone to protect the "sanctity of life." An expert opinion would be just what the phrase suggests.

14. **The correct answer is (C).** Note the word *right* is italicized in the first sentence of the paragraph. The author is saying that this idea of a right can be only understood as the outcome of a balancing of demands. The smoker has an interest in smoking; the non-smoker has an interest in being free from smoke; so the question of which one actually has a *right* to have that *interest* protected depends upon which of those interests is considered to be more important. In some cases, the balance is easily struck; in other cases, it is difficult; but in all cases, the weighing, implicitly or explicitly, occurs. Choice (C) captures the essence of this thought. In the case of smoking, the interests of both parties must be taken into account. Choice (A) is a distraction. It is true the passage treats "rights," and

it is also true that our Constitution protects our rights; but the connection suggested by choice (A) is a spurious one. It fails to address itself to the logic of the author's argument. The same objections can be leveled against choice (B). The wording of choice (D) makes it wrong. The passage is concerned with the demands of the nonsmoker *to be free from* the smoke of others, not with whether someone chooses to smoke. Choice (E) is premature. At this juncture, the author is laying the foundation for the argument and is speaking about rights in general. The author reaches the conclusion with regard to smoking only at the end of the paragraph. (See discussion of the following question.) Choice (E) is wrong also because it mentions the "rights" of nonsmoking persons. The whole question the author is addressing is whether the non-smoking person has a *right* as opposed to an interest or a mere claim.

15. **The correct answer is (C).** Here is where the author makes the general discussion of the balancing of interests to determine rights specifically applicable to the question of smoking. A smoker will have a *right* to smoke when and where that interest outweighs the interests of those who object, and choice (C) provides a pretty clear statement of this conclusion. Choice (A) overstates the author's case. While it may be true that ultimately it will be some branch of the government that strikes the balance of interests, the phrase "chooses to allow" does not do justice to the author's concept of the balancing. The government is not simply choosing; it is weighing. Of course, since the balance may or may not be struck in favor of the smoker, choice (B) is incorrect. Choice (E) confuses the problem of enforcement with the process of

balancing. The passage leads to the conclusion that the balance must be struck. How that decision is later enforced is a practical matter the author is not concerned to discuss in this passage. Finally, choice (D), like choice (A), overstates the case. The smoker has an interest in being allowed to smoke, just as much as the non-smoker has an interest in being free from the smoke. A balance must be struck by giving proper weight to both. The author never suggests that the interest of the smokers can be completely overridden. Thus, for example, a smoker may have a more powerful interest in smoking than a non-smoker has in being free from smoke, if the non-smoker can—at some smaller cost—be protected from the smoke.

16. **The correct answer is (B).** The whole passage is to clear up a misunderstanding about the concept of a *right*. The author explains that the term is misused since most people fail to realize that the right is not absolute, but is qualified by the interests and claims of other persons. While it is true that this is not generally known, choice (A) is incorrect because the author's *strategy* in argument is to clarify that term, not merely to bring up facts to support a contention that is already well defined. Choice (C) also fails to describe the author's strategy. It is true that the author mentions hypothetical cases, but that is a detail, not the principal strategy. As for choice (D), though the author argues that smokers who claim an unqualified right to smoke are wrong, the author does not argue that they have fallen into contradiction. Finally, although the author argues that the general claim of smokers is ill-founded, the general claim under attack (smokers have a right to smoke) is

not an induction based on *empirical* evidence. A person who makes such a claim is not generalizing on observed instances (All swans I have seen are white…) but rather is making a conceptual claim.

17. **The correct answer is (B).** The stimulus material describes a situation in which a certain event (selling price) is contingent upon a single factor (number of bidders) and then compares two outcomes (two paintings) by contrasting two factors (bidders on two paintings). Similarly, choice (B) describes a situation in which a certain event (number shipped) is contingent upon a single factor (number of students) and then compares two outcomes (sales this year and last) by contrasting two factors (students last year and students this year).

18. **The correct answer is (D).** The author's argument is admittedly not a very persuasive one, but the question stem does not ask us to comment on its relative strength. Rather, we are asked to identify the form of argumentation. Here the author suggests an alternative explanation, albeit a somewhat outlandish one. Thus, choice (D) is correct. Choice (E) is incorrect because the claim about fresh air and the country is introduced as a causal explanation, not an analogy to the city. Choice (C) is wrong, for the author accepts the differential described by the report and just tries to explain the existence of the differential in another way. By the same token, we can reject both choices (A) and (B) since the author takes the report's conclusion as a starting point. Although the argument attacks the explanation provided by the *report* published by the Department of Education, it does not attack the *credibility* of the *department* itself. Further, though it disagrees with the *conclusion* drawn by the

report, it does not attack the way in which the *study* itself was *conducted.* Rather, it disagrees with the interpretation of the data gathered.

19. **The correct answer is (E).** The question stem asks us to find the one item that will not strengthen the author's argument. That is choice (E). Remember, the author's argument is an attempt (to be sure, a weak one) to develop an alternative causal explanation. Choice (A) would provide some evidence that the author's claim—which at first glance seems a bit far-fetched—actually has some empirical foundation. While choice (B) does not add any strength to the author's own explanation of the phenomenon being studied, it does strengthen the author's overall position by undermining the explanation given in the report. Choice (C) strengthens the author's position for the same reason that choice (B) does: It weakens the position that is attacked. Choice (D) strengthens the argument in the same way that choice (A) does, by providing some empirical support for the otherwise seemingly far-fetched explanation.

20. **The correct answer is (E).** Perhaps the most obvious weakness in the argument is that it oversimplifies matters. It is like the domino theory arguments adduced to support the war in Vietnam: Either we fight Communism now, or it will take us over. The author argues, in effect: Either we put a stop to this now, or there will be no stopping it. Like the proponents of the domino theory, the author ignores the many intermediate positions one might take. Choice (C) is one way of describing this shortcoming: The dilemma posed by the author is a false one because it overlooks positions between the two extremes. Choice (B) is also a weakness of the argument: "Cold-blooded murder" is obviously a phrase calculated to excite negative feelings. Finally, the whole argument is also internally inconsistent. The conclusion is that we should allow nature to take its course. How? By prolonging life with artificial means. But the failure of an argument to cite an authority is not necessarily a weakness. To be sure, the argument is subject to criticism; but, in general, unless the argument is one that requires an authority (say, for some key detail), the failure to cite an authority is not a defect.

21. **The correct answer is (D).** We can summarize the information, using capital letters to represent each statement:

> If P, then Q.
>
> If Q, then R or S.
>
> If R or S and if Q, then A.
>
> If R or S and if not-Q, then not-A.

P represents "Paul comes to the party," Q represents "Quentin leaves the party," R represents "Robert asks Alice to dance," S represents "Steve asks Alice to dance," (and conversely R represents "Alice is asked by Robert to dance" and S represents "Alice is asked by Steve to dance"), and A represents Alice accepts. If we have not-Q, then we can deduce not-P from the first statement; thus, we have choice (D). Choices (A), (B), and (C) are incorrect since there is no necessity that Robert or Steve ask Alice to dance. Choice (E) is incorrect since this statement is different from our other statements and must be assigned a different letter, perhaps X. Notice that "Alice will accept …" tells us nothing about whether Alice leaves the party.

22. **The correct answer is (A).** The question stem has the following form:

> All *S* are *AP*. (All Students are Applicants.)
>
> Some AP are *AC*. (Some Applicants are Accepted.)
>
> Some *more S* are *AC*. (Some more Students are Accepted.)

Notice that choice (A) preserves very nicely the parallel in the conclusion because it uses the word "more." Thus, the error made in the stem argument (that some *more* students will be *accepted*) is preserved in choice (A): *more* apples will be *loaded*. Choice (B) has a valid argument form (All *S* are *J*; *X* is an *S*; therefore, *X* is a *J*), so it is not parallel to the sample argument. Choice (C) is not similar for at least two reasons. First, its conclusion is a recommendation ("should"), not a factual claim. Second, choice (C) uses one premise, not two premises as the sample argument does. Choice (D) would have been parallel to the sample argument only if the sample had the conclusion "some more applications must be acted upon." Finally, choice (E) contains an argument that is fallacious, but the fallacy is not similar to that of the question stem.

23. **The correct answer is (E).** The advertisement employs the term "more" in an ambiguous manner. In the context, one might expect the phrase "more flavor" to mean "more highly concentrated flavor," that is, "more flavor per unit weight." What the ad actually says, however, is that the sticks of Evergreen are *larger*, so if they are larger, there must be more *total* flavor. As for choice (A), it is possible to beat the ad at its own game: Want more flavor? Chew more sticks? As for choice (B), more highly concentrated favor means more flavor per stick, so

size is not important. As for choice (C), a bigger stick doesn't necessarily mean more flavor. And choice (D), of course, cuts to the heart of the claim: money or value. Choice (E), however, if anything, would add to the appeal of the ad: Do what most people do.

24. **The correct answer is (D).** Again, we remind ourselves that we are looking for the most reliable statement. Even the most reliable, however, will not necessarily be perfectly reliable. Here, choice (D) is fairly trustworthy. We note that the speaker is an expert and so is qualified to speak about wines. In choice (A), the speaker is making a judgment about something outside the expertise of a film critic. Also, in choice (D), there is no hint of self-interest—if anything, the speaker is admitting against a possible self-interest that American chablis is a better buy than French chablis. By comparison, choices (B) and (C), which smack of a self-serving bias, are not so trustworthy. Finally, choice (E) sounds like a statement made for dramatic effect and so is not to be taken at face value.

25. **The correct answer is (B).** The weakness in the argument is the fallacy of ambiguity. It uses the term "future" in two different ways. In the first instance, it uses the word "future" to mean that which is fixed and definite, that which must occur. But then comes the shift. The author subtly changes usage so that "future" denotes events that might, though not necessarily will, come to pass. As for choice (A), the author gives a good example of how one might very well be able to change the future. As for choice (C), the author is concerned to refute the idea of foreseeing future events, so it is not surprising that there is no attempt to explain the mechanism by which such

foresight is achieved. Choices (D) and (E) are incorrect because the fallacy is that of ambiguity, not of internal inconsistency (self-contradiction) nor circular reasoning (begging the question).

Section 3

Questions 1–6

This is a linear ordering set. We begin by summarizing the information for easy reference:

$O \neq$ 1st or 6th

$L \neq J$ ⎫

$L \neq K$ ⎬ (We know that $L > M$, so this means L cannot be

$L \rightarrow M$ ⎭ next to J or K in the line.)

1. **The correct answer is (D).** For this question, we simply check each choice against the initial conditions. On the ground that O does not finish first or last, we eliminate choice (C). On the ground that L cannot be next in line to either J or K, we eliminate choices (A) and (E). Finally, since L must finish immediately ahead of M, we eliminate choice (B). Only choice (D) satisfies all of the restrictions.

2. **The correct answer is (E).** We begin by processing the additional information:

    1 2 3 4 5 6
    J   K

    This places the L–M combination in positions 3 and 4, respectively (to avoid the J–L conflict). And O must be in position 2, with N in position 6:

    1 2 3 4 5 6
    J O L M K N

    This shows that only choice (E) is true.

3. **The correct answer is (C).** We begin by processing the additional information:

    1 2 3 4 5 6
    N L M

We put N in first because J, K, and O cannot be there. We know further that either J or K must be sixth, since O cannot finish last. But there are four possible arrangements using these restrictions:

1 2 3 4 5 6
N L M O J K
N L M O K J
N L M K O J
N L M J O K

4. **The correct answer is (D).** For this question, we test each arrangement against the initial conditions. We know that four of the five will be acceptable and that only one will not be acceptable. The exception is the correct choice. Choice (D) is not acceptable since we have the impermissible arrangement of J in second and L in third.

5. **The correct answer is (E).** For this question, we must treat each statement as providing additional information. As for choice (A), we get:

    1 2 3 4 5 6
    N J K O L M

    With J and K in 2 and 3, respectively, we must put L in 5 and therefore M in 6. But O must then be in 4, with N in 1. So there is only one possible arrangement using this information. As for choice (B), we have:

    1 2 3 4 5 6
    L M J K O N

    With K in 4, we must put the L–M combination in 1 and 2. This means that N finishes last with O in position 5. So, again, the statement guarantees only one arrangement. As for choice (C):

    1 2 3 4 5 6
    L M O J K N

With J and K in 4 and 5, L and M must be in 1 and 2 or 2 and 3. But they cannot be in 2 and 3, for this would require O to be first or last. So L and M must be in 1 and 2, N must be in 6, and O must be in 3.

As for choice (D):

1 2 3 4 5 6
  L   K

We can put M in fifth:

1 2 3 4 5 6
  L M   K

And O is neither first nor sixth:

1 2 3 4 5 6
  L M K O

And with J not next to L:

1 2 3 4 5 6
N L M K O J

Now for choice (E):

1 2 3 4 5 6
    J   L

And we can put M on the diagram:

1 2 3 4 5 6
    J   L M

But that's as far as we can go. O could be second or fourth, K first or second, with N in the remaining position.

6. **The correct answer is (D).** For J and K to be separated by exactly three runners, they must finish in 1 and 5 or 2 and 6, though not necessarily in that order. We test each:

1 2 3 4 5 6
J/K O L M J/K N

With either J or K in 1, L and M must be in 3 and 4, with O in 2 and N in 6.

1 2 3 4 5 6
N J/K O L M J/K

With J or K in 2, L and M must be in 4 and 5 with N in 1 and O in 3. Now we are

looking for the answer choice that *cannot* be true. Choice (A) is true since O does not finish fourth. Choice (B) is true since only J, K, or N can finish last. Choice (C) is true since L finishes either third or fourth. Choice (E) is true since O in third means that either J or K is last. Choice (D) is not true, however: When O is second, N is sixth.

Questions 7–12

Here we have an ordering set that is not strictly linear; that is, the individuals are not aligned in a single file. We begin by summarizing the information:

$(Q \& R) = 3$
$P < M$
$K < N$
$K < L$
$J = L$

A moment's study will lead us to one or two further conclusions. If K is lower than L, then, of course, K cannot occupy the top floor. Further, since J and L occupy the same floor and since the fifth floor has only one room, J and L cannot occupy a floor higher than the fourth floor, which means that K cannot occupy a floor higher than the second floor. (Remember that Q and R must occupy the third floor.) With these preliminary conclusions in mind, we can turn to the questions.

7. **The correct answer is (A).** Since K must stay below J, J cannot occupy the first floor. Choice (A), as the exception, must be the correct answer. The other choices could be true, as illustrated by the diagram:

5 M/N		5 O	
4 J L		4 M N	
3 Q R	or	3 Q R	
2 O		2 J L	
1 K P		1 K P	

8. **The correct answer is (C).** We begin by processing the additional information. With *M* entered on the second floor, we deduce:

5
4   *J L*
3   *Q R*
2   *M*
1   *P*

With *M* on the second floor, *P* must be on the first floor. Then, with floors 1, 2, and 3 occupied, *J* and *L* must occupy floor 4 because the fifth floor has only one room. This seems as far as we can go. We know that *K* must occupy either 2 or 1, but that is not very helpful. So we look to the choices. We see that choice (A) is definitely incorrect, since choice (C) is proved by the diagram. Choice (B) is possibly, though not necessarily, true. As we just noted, choice (D) is also only possible. Finally, choice (E) is also just a possibility, since *O* might also be on floor 5 or 2.

9. **The correct answer is (E).** We have the list of people, *J, K, L, M, N, O, P, Q, R,* and we eliminate people as first-floor occupants as follows. *Q* and *R* must occupy the third floor. *J* and *L* occupy a floor together above that of *K*. *M* occupies a floor above *P* and so cannot occupy floor 1. And the same reasoning applies to *N*. So we eliminate *J, L, M, N, Q,* and *R*, leaving *K, O,* and *P*.

10. **The correct answer is (B).** We begin by assimilating the additional information. With *M* on floor 4, we have:

5
4   *M*
3   *Q* and *R*
2   *J* and *L*
1   *K* and *P*

With *M* on 4, we must put *J* and *L* on 2, for that is the only floor above floor 1 that remains open and has two rooms. Then, *K* must be on 1 (below *L*) and *P* must be on 1 (to be below *M*). As for *N* and *O,* they must occupy floors 4 and 5, though not necessarily in that order.

11. **The correct answer is (B).** We know that *K* and *M,* if they are together, cannot occupy floor 3 (because of *Q* and *R*) nor floor 5 (which has only one room). Nor can *M* occupy floor 1. *K* must be below *J* and *L,* so it cannot occupy 4. The only floor for *K* and *M* together is 2.

12. **The correct answer is (C).** The additional information provided in choice (C) proves the following:

5   *N*
4   *J* and *L*
3   *Q* and *R*
2   *K* and *M*
1   *P* and *O*

With *K* on 2, *J* and *L* must be on 4 (since *L* must be above K). Then, since *K* is lower than *N, N* must occupy 5. Next, since *P < M, P* must occupy 1 and *M* must occupy 2. And this leaves only *O* to occupy the other room on 1. The other answers will not do the trick. As for choice (A), putting *P* on 1 does not force *J* and *L* onto a floor. They might occupy either 2 or 4. As for choice (B), putting *M* on 2 means that *J* and *L* will occupy 4 and that *P* will occupy 1, but this leaves several individuals unplaced. As for choice (D), see Question 10, above. Finally, placing *N* on the top floor does not place *J* and *K,* and that is critical to fixing a definite order.

Questions 13–18

Here we have a selection problem, and we begin by using a notational system to summarize the information:

(1) ~(N & T & U)

(2) ~(M & N & R)

(3) Q ≠ V

(4) V ⊃ [(M & S) v (M & U) v (S & U) v (M & S & U)]

(5) R = Q

(6) S ⊃ (N & V)

Perhaps (4) requires some clarification. The statement given in the problem structure is logically equivalent to the following: If V is selected, then either (a) M and S are selected or (b) M and U are selected, or (c) S and U are selected, or (d) all three are selected.

13. **The correct answer is (D).** If R appears, then Q must appear (5). And if Q appears, then V cannot appear (3). But if V does not appear, then S cannot appear (6). So choice (D) is the correct answer. As for the remaining choices, we could have:

(A) R, Q, and M

(B) R, Q, and N

(C) R and Q

(E) R, Q, and T

14. **The correct answer is (D).** There are four professors who must be accompanied by other professors: V (4), R and Q (5), and S (6). Every other professor, M, N, T, and U, can appear without the necessity of including any other professor.

15. **The correct answer is (B).** If S appears, then both N and V must also appear (6). And if V appears, then two of the three, M, S, and U, must appear. Since S is already included (by stipulation), we need choose only one of the pair M and U. Thus, at minimum, we have S, N, V, and either M or U, for a total of four.

16. **The correct answer is (B).** We handle this question by the process of elimination, checking each of the available choices against the restrictions established in the initial set of conditions. Choice (A) can be eliminated because it violates (2). Choice (C) violates (5) since Q is not there to accompany R. Choice (D) can be eliminated because we have S without N, in violation of (6). And choice (E) violates (5) because we have R without Q.

17. **The correct answer is (A).** This question, too, is solved in a manner similar to that used for the preceding question. But here we must check each choice against the initial conditions in an effort to add exactly one more professor to obtain a permissible grouping. Choice (A) can be turned into an acceptable grouping just by adding Q: M, R, T, and Q. Choice (B) can be eliminated since Q requires R (5), but N, M, and R cannot appear together (2). Choice (C) can be eliminated since S will require the addition of both N and V (6), two professors, not just one. Choice (D) can be eliminated since V requires the addition of two out of three from the trio M, S, and U (4). Finally, choice (E) is incorrect since R requires Q (5) and V requires other professors (4).

18. **The correct answer is (C).** Removing T from the group eliminates the violation of (1), without violating any other restriction. As for choice (A), removing N eliminates the violation of (1), but this places the group in violation of (6) (S without N). As for choice (D), removing U corrects the violation of (1), but the resulting group violates (4) because V is included without two out of three from the group M, S, or U. Finally, eliminating V runs afoul of (5).

Questions 19–24

With a set such as this, the main task is organizing the information. We will use a matrix:

Cars

	1	2	3	4	5
Meteor	C	C	D	D	C
Comet	D	C	C	D	D
Flash	D	C	D	D	D
Streak	D	D	C	C	D
Rocket	C	C	C	C	C

D = Deluxe   C = Coach

19. **The correct answer is (A).** This is seen to be true by our matrix. Three of the five trains use deluxe cars in the first position. The matrix shows that choice (B) is false since the ratio of deluxe to coach here is only one to four. Choice (C) is also seen to be false since the Meteor and the Rocket have coach cars in the fifth position. Choice (D) is proved false by a quick count. In a typical day, 12 deluxe cars and 13 coach cars are used. Finally, choice (E) is incorrect since the Rocket and the Streak together use only three deluxe cars, while the Flash and the Comet use seven deluxe cars.

20. **The correct answer is (C).** No train has deluxe cars in positions 2 and 3. As for choice (A), the Streak has deluxe cars first and second. As for choice (B), the Flash has deluxe cars first and third. As for choice (D), the Flash has deluxe cars third and fourth. And as for choice (E), the Flash also has deluxe cars fourth and fifth.

21. **The correct answer is (B).** If we know correctly that the second car of a train is a deluxe car, this establishes that train as the Streak—as shown by the matrix. As for choice (A), knowing the first car to be deluxe does not distinguish the Streak from the Comet or the Flash. As for choice (C), knowing the third car to be a coach car leaves open the possibility that the train might be the Comet, the Streak, or the Rocket. As for choice (D), although the Streak has deluxe as its first and fifth cars, this is also true of the Comet and the Flash. Finally, as for choice (E), the Streak has coach and deluxe in places 3 and 5, but this is also true of the Comet.

22. **The correct answer is (D).** As the matrix shows, the Meteor, the Comet, the Flash, and the Rocket all have coach cars as the second car. Only the Streak has a deluxe car in the second position.

23. **The correct answer is (C).** A quick look at the matrix shows that only one train, the Flash, has deluxe cars as the first and third cars of the train.

24. **The correct answer is (D).** Again, a quick glance at the matrix gives us the needed information. For the Streak, of the last three cars, only the fifth is a deluxe car. For the Meteor, two of the three last cars are deluxe cars. The same is true for the Comet. For the Flash, the last three cars are all deluxe cars, while for the Rocket, none of the last three cars is a deluxe car.

Section 4

1. **The correct answer is (B).** One of the striking features about the passage is that the author doesn't first produce a contention and then offer facts to support it. Rather, the author's method is to produce the facts and then ask what conclusions might be drawn. And that is the description offered by choice (B). Choice (A) is wrong for this reason, to wit, the author is not arguing for a single conclusion but rather working toward a conclusion by exploring data. Choice (C) is wrong for the same reason. To be sure, the

author does answer some objections along the way, but that is not the main purpose. As for choice (D), while the final paragraph does seem to be a sort of challenge, there is a lot more going on the passage than (D) suggests. And finally, choice (E) just misses the point entirely.

2. **The correct answer is (A).** This is an explicit idea question. How do we know the meteor is from Mars? Oxygen isotopes found in the group of meteorites match the analysis of the Martian atmosphere. The other choices all mention ideas from the passage but each proves something different. The other choices may be evidence of microorganisms, but not where they originated.

3. **The correct answer is (C).** In paragraph five, the author notes that odd shapes seems to be microfossils of bacteria but cannot rule out the possibility that the bacteria were introduced after the rock left Mars, that is, while it lay in Antarctica. Finding microfossils in Antarctica would tend to prove that the bacteria originated on Earth.

4. **The correct answer is (E).** This is an explicit idea question. All of the ideas given are mentioned in the passage, but choices (A), (B), (C), and (D) all provide evidence that ALH84001 may shows signs of life. As for choice (A), the shapes that resemble bacteria suggest that bacteria once lived in the rock. As for choice (B), the PAHs, while possibly produced by inorganic processes, might have been produced by living matter. As for choices (C) and (D), the odd deposits suggest chemical processes. Choice (E), however, suggests only that that the rock came from Mars, not that it contains signs of extinct life.

5. **The correct answer is (B).** This an explicit idea question, and the passage specifically states that the carbonate deposits might have come from inorganic processes but seem more likely to have been deposited by a microorganism. Similarly, the PAHs are different from the by-products of ordinary combustion but, admits the author, might conceivably be the result of inorganic reactions.

6. **The correct answer is (A).** This is a logical structure question that asks about the connection between the two ideas mentioned in the stem and the larger argument. Why does the author mention gravitation and space? Well, there are some shapes in the meteorite that seem to be bacteria or at least they have the right shape, but they're very, very small compared to any bacteria we actually know. So the author suggests that the unique conditions on Mars (weaker gravitational field) and the conditions in the rock (small spaces) might mean that the bacteria would be small.

7. **The correct answer is (D).** This is an application question. The author seems to incline toward the view that the scientific evidence is at least consistent with the possibility of life on Mars even if the passage does not affirmatively support the conclusion that life once existed on Mars. Of course, the author doesn't go so far as to say that the data prove the existence of life on Mars, but, on balance, that would seem to be the author's view.

8. **The correct answer is (C).** This is a main idea question. Choice (A) describes a point made in the selection (in the last sentence in the first paragraph), but that idea is not the overall or main point of the selection. The idea suggested by choice (B) is certainly one that is consistent with the overall tone of the passage, but again, the idea is not the main point of the selection. The author is not just con-

cerned with criticizing those who won't abandon their theories; he is more concerned with demonstrating that those theories are in fact wrong. And this is the idea mentioned by choice (C): the main point of the passage is that the popular theories are incorrect. Choices (D) and (E) are like choice (A). They mention ideas covered in the passage, but neither describes the main point of the passage.

9. **The correct answer is (A).** This is a further application question. Since the last paragraph deals with a recent report suggesting that previous assumptions about microwaves were incorrect, the author would probably go on to talk about the need for more research. Choice (B) is incorrect because the author is dealing with microwave radiation and there would be no reason at this point to compare it to other forms of radiation. Besides, the author made the comparison earlier in the passage. Choice (C) is incorrect because it overstates the case. There is no evidence to suggest that microwave radiation is so dangerous that it should be prohibited—just understood and regulated. Choice (D) is incorrect because clearly the author is concerned with new information about microwave radiation. He has already suggested that what we now believe is erroneous. Finally, choice (E) is incorrect because a discussion of the strategies used by various species to control hyperthermia would not follow logically from his remarks that microwave radiation has not been correctly understood. In any event, the discussion of such strategies early in the passage is intended to set the stage for the main point of the selection.

10. **The correct answer is (A).** In the lines indicated, the author states that it is possible that an organism could be cooked by microwave radiation (because the radiation penetrates into the core) before it even realizes its temperature is rising. The verb tense clearly indicates that the author is introducing a hypothetical possibility. Given the shocking nature of the example, we should conclude that he has introduced it to dramatize a point.

11. **The correct answer is (B).** In the first sentence of the second paragraph the author remarks that proponents of the generally accepted theory (which treats microwave radiation like other radiation) simply assumed that one type of radiation would have the same thermal effect as other types of radiation. Then the author goes on to demonstrate that this assumption is wrong. Thus, (B) is the best description of the error identified by the author. Certainly, there is no suggestion that the proponents of the accepted theory did special laboratory research, control group surveys, or causal investigation. As for choice (D), while the proponents of the accepted theory may have used deductive reasoning to reach their conclusion, this would not have been the main basis for their conclusions. (Note the wording of the question stem.)

12. **The correct answer is (E).** This is a tone question. The author gives facts and analyzes or discusses a problem, so the tone could be called scholarly or analytical. The author is clearly concerned that other scientists made an error in their assessment of the effects of microwave radiation. Choice (A) is incorrect because the tone is not conversational at all, but expository. Choice (B) is incorrect because although the author seems disturbed by the ignorance of the scientists, he is never disparaging. He is also never facetious or cynical, choice (C). Choice

(D) is close because the tone is scholarly, but (E) is the best choice because the author is more "concerned" than he is "noncommittal."

13. **The correct answer is (A).** This is a main idea question. The passage explains why microwave radiation is not like other radiation and why it is therefore dangerous to warm-blooded species. Since it was until recently assumed that microwave radiation was like other radiation, the author is concerned with pointing out the weaknesses of this theory.

14. **The correct answer is (E).** This is an explicit idea question. Choice (A) is mentioned in the first paragraph, choice (B) is mentioned in the third paragraph, choice (C) is mentioned in the first paragraph, and choice (D) is mentioned in the second paragraph. Nowhere, however, does the author mention the dangers of microwave ovens.

15. **The correct answer is (B).** This is a main idea question. In the very first paragraph, the author presents the distinction between unlabeled and prohibited uses and then proceeds to develop the important implications of the distinction. Choice (B) correctly describes this form of argument. Choice (A) must be incorrect since no theory is cited for refutation. Choice (C) is incorrect since no opponent is mentioned. Choice (D) can be eliminated since there is no evidence that the practice of unlabeled uses is a recent development. Choice (E) can be eliminated for either of two reasons. First, if one interprets "error" here to mean the practice of forbidden uses, then that is not the main point of the argument. Or if one interprets "error" to mean the conflating of unlabeled with prohibited uses, then choice (E) is eliminated because "condemn" is inappropriate. The

author may wish to correct a misconception, but that is not the wording of choice (E). Moreover, the method he uses to accomplish that end is drawing a distinction. Thus, choice (B) stands as correct.

16. **The correct answer is (C).** This is an explicit idea question. The reference we need is to be found in paragraph 1. There the author explains that he uses the term "unlabeled use" to refer to any medically valuable use of an already approved drug that has not yet been specifically recognized by the FDA. Choice (A) is incorrect because this is a prohibited use, as that term is used in the text. Choice (B) is incorrect because an unlabeled use is one that was not considered when the drug was originally labeled. It is one discovered later, not one proposed, tested, and rejected. Choice (D) is incorrect because the author would term this use a labeled use. Finally, choice (E) is incorrect since this refers to research designed to determine whether a drug has labeled uses because it meets the legal standard of substantial evidence of such uses.

17. **The correct answer is (C).** This is an inference question that requires that we collate information from two parts of the passage. In paragraph 2, the author refers to physicians who persist in prohibited uses for one of two reasons: ignorance or refusal to accept evidence. Then, in paragraph 3, the author refers to physicians who use drugs in violation of labeling instructions as either uninformed or intransigent. The parallelism here tells us that the intransigent physician is the one who rejects the evidence that the drug is ineffective. This is neatly captured by choice (C). Choice (A) is incorrect since the intransigent physician prescribes the drug in violation of the labeling provision because he or she

believes that the drug is effective. Choice (B) is incorrect, for this would be a physician who is anything but intransigent. As for choice (D), an intransigent physician might take such actions, but this is not the defining characteristic of an intransigent physician. Finally, choice (E) can be eliminated since the author specifically expresses reservations as to whether such behavior is illegal.

18. **The correct answer is (A).** This is an explicit idea question. The danger that a medical benefit might be otherwise denied a patient during the period between the discovery of a new use and its approval is mentioned in paragraph 3 as a reason for allowing unlabeled uses. So both choices (B) and (C) receive explicit mention. Choice (D) is mentioned in paragraph 1: The use may never be researched. Finally, choice (E) is also mentioned in that paragraph as a further justification for the practice. Choice (A) is incorrect since the author never relates cost to unlabeled uses.

19. **The correct answer is (E).** This is an application question, and we must find the statement that is most likely to be acceptable to the author. Choice (E) would likely be embraced by the author since he explains in the first paragraph that unlabeled uses are created by the time lag between the discovery of the use and the accumulation of data needed to prove that use. Choice (A) is an attractive answer, but it fails upon careful reading. The distinction referred to there is that between approved and unlabeled uses. The distinction that the author attempts to draw is between two types of unapproved uses: unlabeled and prohibited. This is the distinction that has been blurred, says the author, not the distinction between approved and unlabeled.

Choice (B) is incorrect for the same reason. The blurred distinction is between unlabeled and prohibited uses (both types of unapproved uses), not between approved and unlabeled uses. Choice (C) is incorrect since the distinction between unlabeled and approved uses is a matter of practice, not categorization. The unlabeled use exists because a physician uses the drug in a beneficial but not yet approved way, not because the physician or government decides that the use is unlabeled versus approved. Choice (D) is incorrect since the author calls for caution in unlabeled use in the final paragraph.

20. **The correct answer is (A).** This is an attitude question. In our discussion of Question 18, above, we mentioned several points in the passage that argue for the value of unlabeled uses. But the author's support for this practice is not unqualified. He does recognize the value of FDA regulation. His attitude toward the practice is one of acceptance, as suggested by choice (A). Choice (B) is incorrect because the author argues for the practice, given the strictness of the FDA regulations. Choice (C) is incorrect since the author does not imply that unlabeled use is illegal (as opposed to the disapproved use). Choice (D) is incorrect because it overstates the case. Though the author sees the value of unlabeled uses, the practice receives only a qualified endorsement. Finally, choice (E) must be incorrect because the author sees unlabeled use as a practice inherent in the regulatory framework.

21. **The correct answer is (E).** This is a main idea question, and the main idea of this passage, already discussed at some length, is neatly summarized by choice (E). Choice (B) is surely the second-best answer, but choice (B) must fail by com-

parison to choice (E) because choice (B) is too narrow. To be sure, one point the author makes is that the physician who prescribes unlabeled uses should not be subject to legal liability, but that is only part of the argument. That recommendation depends upon the distinction between the two types of unapproved uses. Choice (E) makes reference to this additional point. Notice also that in a way choice (B) is included in choice (E), so it is broad enough to describe the overall point of the author. Choice (A) is incorrect since the author is cautioning against overzealous enforcement of laws against unlabeled uses. Choice (C) is incorrect because it is never mentioned in the passage. Finally, choice (D) is incorrect, for this is at best a minor part of the argument.

22. **The correct answer is (B).** This is a main idea question. The author begins by acknowledging that there exists an actual differential between the earnings of whites and blacks, but then the author moves quickly to block the automatic presupposition that this is attributable to "racial discrimination in employment." The author then examines the effect of various productivity variables on the differentials between black and white men and between black and white women, with particular emphasis on the latter. The conclusion of the argument is that there is little difference in the adjusted earnings of black and white women, and the reason for this is the overpowering influence of *sexual* discrimination. Choice (B) captures this analysis. Choice (A) is incorrect since the author's primary focus is the black woman. He studies workers who are both black and female by comparing them with white female work-

ers. The differentials between men and women generally are only incidentally related to this analysis. Choice (C) fails because this is a subordinate level of argumentation. To be sure, the author does introduce productivity factors to adjust actual earnings, but that is so he can better evaluate the effects of discrimination. Choice (D) is incorrect since no history is offered aside from casual references to distribution of workers. Finally, choice (E) is incorrect since the author makes no such recommendations.

23. **The correct answer is (E).** This is an explicit idea question, the answer to which is found in paragraphs 1 and 2. There the author states that the actual ratio is not an accurate measure of discrimination in *employment* because it fails to take account of productivity factors. Choice (A) is incorrect because of the word "include"—the gross ratio fails to *adjust* for distribution. Choice (B) is not mentioned and so cannot be an answer to a question that begins with the phrase "According to the passage ..." Choice (C), too, is never mentioned in the passage, and so it fails for the same reason, as does choice (D).

24. **The correct answer is (E).** This is an explicit detail question, and our needed reference is the third paragraph. That paragraph gives us comparisons or ratios of earnings by black men to earnings by white men and of earnings by black women to earnings by white women. Notice that the comparisons are relative. We never get actual dollar amounts, nor do we get comparisons between women and men. Choice (E) recognizes that the only conclusion that can be drawn on that basis is that the differential between black and white women is less than the differential between black and

white men. The first is a difference of only 2 to 5 percent (before adjustment for productivity factors), while the second is about 20 percent (before adjustment). Choices (A), (C), and (D) can be eliminated on the ground that no such male/female comparison is possible. Choice (B) can be eliminated since no such information is supplied.

25. **The correct answer is (A).** This is a logical structure question. The author states that there are two explanations to be considered: (1) black men are found in jobs characterized by greater discrimination, and (2) sexual discrimination renders insignificant the racial discrimination against black women. But each of these could be true since both could contribute to the phenomenon being studied. There is only an empirical, not a logical, connection between the two; that is, the extent to which each does have explanatory power is a matter of fact. On this ground, we can eliminate every other answer choice.

26. **The correct answer is (C).** This is a tone question, and the best description of the treatment of the subject matter is provided by choice (C). Choice (A) can be eliminated, for the treatment, while confident, is not offensive. Choice (B) can be eliminated for the same reason. Choice (D) is incorrect since there is nothing tenative or inconclusive about the treatment. To acknowledge that one is unable to determine which of two competing theories is preferable is not to be inconclusive or tentative. Finally, though some readers may find in the author's discussion reason for hope or optimism, we cannot say that the author himself shows us these attitudes.

27. **The correct answer is (A).** This is an application question. What would happen if sexual discrimination against women were no longer a factor? On the assumption that the second hypothesis is correct, racial discrimination for women is not a significant factor because it is overpowered by sexual discrimination. The author acknowledges the existence of racial discrimination, so elimination of the sexual discrimination should result in the manifestation of increased racial discrimination against black women (on the assumption that the second theory is correct). The result should be a greater disparity between white and black female workers, with white female workers enjoying the higher end of the ratio. This is articulated by choice (A). Choice (B) is contradicted by this analysis and must be incorrect. Choice (C) is inconsistent with the stipulation in the question stem. Finally, there is nothing to suggest that choices (D) or (E) would occur.

28. **The correct answer is (B).** This is a tone question. Notice that this question asks not about the tone of the presentation but about the author's attitude toward a particular subject. We must take our cue from the first paragraph, where the author refers to the efforts of "responsible employers." This indicates that the author is sympathetic to the situation of workers who are victims of discrimination. Choice (B) is the best way of describing this attitude. Choice (E) is much too strong, for concern is not anxiety. Further, choice (C) is much too weak, for the reference to "responsible employers" indicates the author is not indifferent. Choice (D), like choice (E), overstates the case. Finally, choice (A) is incorrect since the author offers no apology.

Section 5

1. **The correct answer is (B).** This is essentially an analogy question. Argument from analogy is an important form of argument, and the LSAT has many different ways of determining whether or not a student can use that argumentative technique. In this question, we are looking for the tool that is most analogous to a rule-of-thumb moral principle. Our task is made easier by the string of adjectives that follows the blank. We need a tool that is useful in many situations, which rules out a tuning fork, choice (D), and an electrical generator, choice (C), both of which have highly specialized functions. Moreover, we need a tool that requires no special training, so we can eliminate choice (A). Finally, although a library book requires no special training, it has only one use—to be read. Though the knowledge it contains may be generally useful, the book itself, *qua* book, has only one use.

2. **The correct answer is (A).** The point of the passage is that a moral decision sometimes seems difficult because we are using moral principles that are too general. They work most of the time, but sometimes they are too abstract, and as a result, two or more of them give contradictory results. Choices (D) and (E) are wrong, then, for they confuse the value of abstract and particular principles. When a conflict arises, we need principles that are more specific, not more abstract, choice (D) and particularly choice (E). Choice (C) is a distraction; the medical character of the example was purely fortuitous and irrelevant to the author's point about moral reasoning. Choice (B) is edifying but hardly a logical completion of the paragraph. The author is not trying to explain advances in moral reasoning; he is explaining two different levels of moral reasoning available to us now.

3. **The correct answer is (D).** Let us use letters to represent the categories. "All effective administrators" will be *A*. "Concerned about welfare" will be *W*. "Are liberal" will be *L*. The three propositions can now be represented as follows:

   ❶ All *A* are *W*.

   ❷ All *W* are *L*.

   ❸ All non-*L* are not *A*.

   Proposition #3 is equivalent to "all A are not non-*L*," and that is in turn equivalent to "all A are L." Thus, choice (D) follows fairly directly as a matter of logic. Choice (A) is incorrect, for while we know that "all *A* are *L*," we would not want to conclude that "No *L* are *A*"—there might be some ineffective administrators who grant time off. They could be ineffective for other reasons. Choice (B) is incorrect for the same reason. Even though all effective administrators are concerned about their employees' welfare, this does not mean that an ineffective administrator could not be concerned. He might be concerned but ineffective for another reason. Choice (C) is clearly false given our propositions; we know that all effective administrators are liberal. Finally, choice (E) is not inferable. Just because all effective administrators grant time off does not mean that all the time granted off is granted by effective administrators.

4. **The correct answer is (C).** The weakness in Gerry's argument is that he assumes, incorrectly, that getting drunk is the only harm Clyde has in mind. Clyde could respond very effectively by pointing to some other harms of alcohol. Choice (A) would not be a good response for Clyde since he is concerned with Gerry's

welfare. The fact that other people get drunk when Gerry does not is hardly a reason for Gerry to stop drinking. Choice (B) is also incorrect. That other people do or do not get drunk is not going to strengthen Clyde's argument against Gerry. He needs an argument that will impress Clyde, who apparently does not get drunk. Choice (D) is perhaps the second-best answer, but the explicit wording of the paragraph makes it unacceptable. Gerry has been drinking the same quantity for fifteen years. Now, admittedly, it is possible he will begin to drink more heavily, but that *possibility* would not be nearly so strong a point in Clyde's favor as the *present* existence of harm (other than inebriation). Finally, choice (E) is irrelevant, since it is white wine that Gerry does drink.

5. **The correct answer is (B).** The point of the passage is that a meaningful comparison between the two systems is going to be difficult since the one is cheap in the short run but expensive in the long run, while the other is expensive in the short run and cheap in the long run. The only appropriate way of doing the cost comparison is by taking account of both costs—which is what choice (B) does. To take just the long-run costs would be to ignore the short-run costs involved, so choice (A) is wrong; and taking the short-run costs while ignoring the long-run costs is no better, so choice (C) is wrong. If choice (A) is wrong, then choice (D) also has to be wrong, and the more so because it is not even projecting operating costs. Finally, choice (E) is a distraction—the connection between diesel fuel and air pollution is irrelevant in a paragraph that is concerned with a cost comparison.

6. **The correct answer is (B).** One way of "making more money" other than raising the price of a product is to lower the size or quality of the product. This is what Vendo must have done. By doing so, they accomplished the equivalent of a price increase without actually raising the price. Choice (C) contradicts the paragraph that states that Vendo did not violate the letter of the instructions—that is, the literal meaning—though they did violate the intention. Choice (D) also contradicts the paragraph. Had Vendo forfeited the franchise, that would have been within the letter of the "either-or" wording of the instructions. Choices (A) and (E) require much speculation beyond the information given, and you should not indulge yourself in imaginative thinking when there is an obvious answer such as choice (B) available.

7. **The correct answer is (D).** The author's argument seems fairly weak. He introduces the example of the second university without explaining why we should consider that case similar to the one we are arguing about (except for size). This shows that the author is introducing an analogy—though not a very strong one. Choice (A) is perhaps the second-best answer. But it would be correct only if there were a *contention* that the author had introduced new evidence in support of the argument. He does not articulate a contention and then adduce evidence for it. Choice (B) is wrong because the author really has no solution to the problem—he wants to argue the problem does not exist. Finally, choices (C) and (E) must be wrong because the author never mentions a logical contradiction nor does he point to any ambiguity in his opponent's argument.

8. **The correct answer is (E).** Another deodorant might also give all-day protection. The ad claims that White Bear is the only deodorant that gives you *both* protection and scent—a vacuous enough claim since White Bear is probably the only deodorant with the White Bear scent. Of course, choice (C) is not affected by this point, since the White Bear Company may put its unique scent into many of its products. Choice (B) is also not inconsistent with the ad—that another product is more popular does not say that it has the features the ad claims for the White Bear deodorant. Choice (D) is not inconsistent because the chemical composition is merely "similar." But choice (E) is inconsistent: it's the same protection and the same scent.

9. **The correct answer is (D).** The easiest way to set this problem up is to draw a relational line:

PE   IP   EL   BE

Dislikes ————————→ Likes

We note that Clara likes Basic Economics better than anything else, which means she must like it better than Advanced Calculus. So even though Advanced Calculus does not appear on our line, since we know that Basic Economics is the maximum, Clara must like Advanced Calculus less than Basic Economics. So choice (C) can be inferred. But we do not know where World History ranks on the preference line, and since Introductory Physics is not a maximal or a minimal value, we can make no judgment regarding it and an unplaced course. Quick reference to the line will show that choices (A), (B), and (E) are inferable.

10. **The correct answer is (B).** We have seen examples before of the form of argument Holmes has in mind: "*P* or *Q*; not-*P*; therefore, *Q*." Here, however, the first premise of Holmes' argument is more complex: "*P* or *Q* or *R* ... *S*," with as many possibilities as he can conceive. He eliminates them one by one until no single possibility is left. The logic of the argument is perfect, but the weakness in the form is that it is impossible to guarantee that all contingencies have been taken into account. Maybe one was overlooked. Thus, choice (B) is the correct answer. Choices (A), (C), and (E) are wrong for the same reason. Holmes' method is designed to answer a particular question—in this case, "Where did the body come from?" Perhaps the next step is to apply the method to the question of the identity of the murderer, as choice (E) suggests, but at this juncture, he is concerned with the preliminary matter of how the murder was committed. In any event, it would be wrong to assail the logic of Holmes' deduction by complaining that it does not prove enough. Since choices (A) and (C) are even more removed from the particular question raised, they, too, must be wrong. Finally, choice (D) is nothing more than a reiteration of Watson's original comment, and Holmes has already responded to it.

11. **The correct answer is (C).** Notice that the student responds to the professor's comment by saying, "That can't be true," and then uses the Duchess of Warburton as a counterexample. The Duchess would only be a counterexample to the professor's statement had the professor said that women cannot inherit the estates of their families. Thus, choice (C) must capture the student's misinterpretation of the professor's statement. What has misled the student is that he has attributed too much to the professor. The professor has cited the general rule of

primogeniture—the eldest male child inherits—but he has not discussed the special problems that arise when no male child is born. In those cases, presumably a non-male child will have to inherit. Choice (E) incorrectly refers to inheriting from a mother in discussing a case in which the woman inherited her father's estate. Choice (D) is wrong, for the student specifically mentions the conditions that make a child legitimate: born to the wife of her father. Choice (A) was inserted as a bit of levity: Of course, only men can *father* children of either sex. Finally, firstborn or not, a daughter cannot inherit as long as there is any male child to inherit, so choice (B) must be incorrect.

12. **The correct answer is (A).** The ends of law, according to legal positivism, are to be agreed upon—"accepted as a contingent matter." They are values that the community adopts; they are not handed down by God, nor are they dictated by logic. Choice (B) actually reverses the point. The legal positivist probably would say he does not claim these ends are the best for all modern legal systems. He does not want to commit himself to anything beyond a mere factual description of things as they are. The normative theory ultimately reduces to a question of practical politics—whatever succeeds. Choice (C) can be rejected because the question raised by the normative theory is what values the law ought to generally embody, not just what values the courts ought to promote. Choice (D) is incorrect because while it is perhaps true, it does not address itself to the *status* of the normative values: Are they universally held and dictated by logic? Are they given by God? etc. Choice (E) is similar to choice (D) in that it may be true simply as

a matter of fact, but, again, choice (E) does not address itself to the status of the values. It is true that the values are those the community chooses, but that such status is *selected* rather than dictated is not undermined because there is not complete agreement on the values. Whatever values are selected will be chosen by more or less unanimous agreement.

13. **The correct answer is (C).** The analogy to physical theory is highly suggestive. The physicist advances a theory that represents an improvement on existing theories, but he is aware that tomorrow another theory may be proposed that is more correct than his. So the legal positivist advances a descriptive theory—that is, a description of existing legal institutions—but new information or advances in theory may displace that theory. Choice (A) is directly contrary to the legal positivist's position that no one theory is uniquely correct. Choice (B) ignores the radical and complete divorce of description and normative recommendation upon which the legal positivist insists. Choice (D) just confuses the point of the analogy to physics. The author introduces the analogy to explain how the legal positivist views his theory—in the same way the physicist views his—not to compare the reliability of physics with jurisprudence. Choice (E) makes a mistake similar to that committed by choice (D).

14. **The correct answer is (C).** Choices (A), (B), (D), and (E) all give reasons why people outside the U.S. wouldn't be watching the Super Bowl: it costs money; it comes on too late; even soccer doesn't attract that many; and people outside of the U.S. don't know the game. Choice (C), however, is a reason to expect some interest in the game.

15. **The correct answer is (A).** The speaker says that there are two established theories: the arboreal model and the cursorial model. The newly discovered evidence supports a third explanation. As for choice (B), though the speaker does provide evidence, it is not adduced as a counterexample to a claim. As for choice (C), there is a new theory, but the speaker does not suggest that the existing theories are self-contradictory. And choices (D) and (E) are surely the weakest responses because there is nothing in the paragraph to support such conclusions.

16. **The correct answer is (C).** The conclusion of the argument is, in essence, that school lunches are healthful or at least not harmful. Choices (A), (B), (D), and (E) all contradict this conclusion. Choice (C), however, does not, and that is why it is correct. In fact, like so many right answers to this type of question (weakening), choice (C) seems to strengthen the argument: the obesity epidemic is partly caused by a decline in physical activity. So be particularly alert for choices like choice (C) that are, in fact, relevant but cut in the wrong direction.

17. **The correct answer is (E).** The speaker relies on a key element of Kant's ethical theory to reach a conclusion about the ethical treatment of animals. But is the theory applicable to animals? Choice (E) answers that question by saying that the theory, taken on its own terms, applies only to people. Choice (A) is perhaps the third-best answer, for it can be read to suggest that Kant's failure to consider the possibility somehow vitiates the use made of the theory by the speaker. But the fact that the original proponent did not see all possible implications of a theory doesn't mean that the theory itself does not have those implications. Choice (B) is

a fairly weak answer, unless you try to read it as saying those who use animals for food and clothing are behaving unethically because they give offense to others, but that seems a fairly attenuated reading. Choice (C) is pretty obviously irrelevant to the question of whether the argument can be applied to animals. And choice (D) may be the second-best answer, because it suggests, at least, that animals don't think—they just eat. But to the extent that you want to use choice (D) to make that kind of argument (and there's nothing wrong with making a creative argument in school), in the testing environment, you should quickly see that choice (E) is the better, more direct route to the same conclusion.

18. **The correct answer is (E).** Remember that the correct answer to a question stem that asks for a further conclusion is likely to be the "safest" response available, that is, the answer that is most limited. And that is why choice (E) is correct. Choice (E) says only that animals sometimes mimic the behavior they see. By contrast, the other choices make very ambitious claims. Choice (A), for example, seems to use the limited evidence provided to build an entire theory of animal behavior, and choice (C) draws a conclusion about penguins in the wild based upon their behavior in a zoo.

19. **The correct answer is (A).** This item asks you to describe the exchange between the two speakers, and the most striking thing about Phil's response is that it is tantamount to saying, Well, you've solved one problem, but there are other problems that you haven't solved. Ordinarily, we require the opponent of a policy suggestion to show that the policy would cost too much to implement or result in other disadvantages that out-

weigh the benefits. As for choice (B), given the topic, it would seem fair to measure health in terms of the reported incidence of illness; and, in any event, Cary first proposes, at least implicitly, this as an appropriate measure. Choice (C) is perhaps the second-most attractive answer because it is true that Phil fails to offer a plan to solve his problem, but neither does Cary. So while in the real world, you would press Phil on this issue, in the testing environment, choice (A) is a better answer because it addresses the *exchange* between the two speakers. Choice (D) is an accurate description of Phil's response, but remember that the stem asks for a *weakness* in that response. And choice (E), like choice (D), is arguably true, but it is not clear that this is a weaknesses of the response.

20. **The correct answer is (E).** This is one of those test items that turns on a cute little twist of reasoning, and once you've found that insight, the answer is clear. The leader's response is meant to say that it is a mistake to admit a mistake— and that's choice (E).

21. **The correct answer is (D).** This item asks you to describe the exchange. Clifford reports on an experiment to test a proposition about dairy farming; Geneva argues that the result should be discounted because the conditions were unique. But Geneva's response is not really relevant because the project was an experiment designed to test the proposition. Choices (A), (B), and (E) contain suggestions that are probably true about dairy farming, but as statements, they don't describe the exchange. And choice (C) is wrong because Geneva does not necessarily believe that just any farmer (as opposed to the Dairy Project, whatever that might be) could achieve the same result given a similar setting.

22. **The correct answer is (A).** You might attack this item using a circle diagram. To show the possible relationships of three categories, use three overlapping circles:

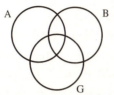

Now enter the information provided by the second statement:

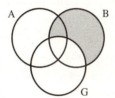

The area that is not logically possible given the second statement is shaded. Now enter the information provided by the first statement:

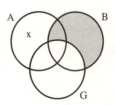

23. **The correct answer is (E).** This item asks you to identify a hidden assumption of the argument. The speaker says that neither set of customers will be entirely pleased and that the owners should reconsider their plans. The hidden assumption, perhaps obvious but nonetheless unstated, is that pleasing customers is good business. Choice (A) has some flavor of this idea but states the case too strongly. Choice (B) is pretty much a non-answer, since the particular type of cooking is not relevant. Choice (C) is a judgment not made by the speaker. And choice (D), like choice (A), overstates the case.

answers

24. The correct answer is (B). This is a somewhat unusual question in that the stimulus material involves a cute—and peculiar—twist of reasoning: Why would the analyst use sales of men's suits to assess the economy? Choice (B) provides the answer: sales of men's suits are correlated not so much with fashion trends as with underlying financial cycles. Choice (A), if anything, weakens the argument by suggesting the lack of such a correlation. Choice (C), because it talks about women's fashion, is irrelevant. Choice (D) is somewhat related to the general topic but nonetheless irrelevant since the issue is the tie between suits and the economy. And to make choice (E) directly relevant to the argument provided would require a lot of backing and filling—a sure sign that it is not the correct answer to a test question.

WRITING SAMPLE

Following are two responses to the Writing Sample prompt, one in favor of the first option and the other in favor of the second option. These responses are not necessarily Pulitzer Prize winning essays, but remember, they're not supposed to be. The objective, as developed in Chapter 8, is to write something that is serviceable. You'll notice how these responses fit the model developed in Chapter 8.

Sample Response for Option One

Given her objectives, Joyce should enroll in the program at the American Institute in Paris. The program will give her the chance to improve her French and to learn about the routine of French daily life. Additionally, it will leave her free to visit some of the important points of interest in the country at a reasonable cost.

First, the Institute of Paris provides a program based in Paris, the heart of French culture. There Joyce can refine her accent and converse with people who live in a typical urban environment, including students from around the world. Additionally, the curriculum emphasizes French culture as well as language skills, and all of the classes are taught by native speakers.

In addition, the cost of the program is reasonable—only $500 for a full six weeks. The difference between that figure and the $1,400 for the program at the University of Reims will leave her $150 per week for living expenses, and she can probably find a youth hostel or similar accommodation in that range.

To be sure, the total cost of the Paris-based program is likely to be greater, but then that is largely a function of the greater cost-of-living of an urban area. Moreover, since she will already be based in Paris, many museums, historical sites, and cultural activities will be accessible by walking or public transportation, inexpensive modes of travel.

Of course, there is much to be said for a program based at a French university in the countryside. In this case, however, it seems that the Paris-based American Institute better suits Joyce's needs.

Sample Response for Option Two

Joyce should choose the summer program offered by the University of Reims. The intense program of study will give her ample opportunity to improve her language skills, and the location and cost will make it possible to enrich her studies by visiting various sites of interest.

It should be noted first that the program at Reims is an intensive learning experience. It is four weeks of study of French and French literature, and all of the classes are taught by University faculty. These classes are then supplemented by small group sessions led by French university students. The total time devoted to study is 8 hours per day, five days a week for the four weeks.

Second, the location and cost of the program at Reims are attractive. The $1,400 tuition includes housing and meals. Perhaps the student dormitory and cafeteria do not provide deluxe accommodations, but they should be serviceable. Furthermore, Reims is just a short train ride from Paris, so Joyce will be able to see not only a portion of the French countryside but a lot of the capital as well. Weekends are left open for exactly this type of travel.

There is no doubt that a summer stay in Paris would be exciting, but the cost of the American Institute is substantially higher. By the time Joyce includes the cost of housing and meals, it could run to $4,000 or $5,000, triple the cost of the program at Reims. Aside from the convenience of being physically situated in Paris, there seems to be little that Joyce could not just as well obtain by staying at Reims.

Answer Sheet

Use a No. 2 pencil only. Be sure each mark is dark and completely fills the intended oval. Completely erase any errors or stray marks. Start with number 1 for each new section. If a section has fewer than 30 questions, leave the extra answer spaces blank.

SECTION 1	SECTION 2	SECTION 3	SECTION 4	SECTION 5
1 Ⓐ Ⓑ Ⓒ Ⓓ Ⓔ	1 Ⓐ Ⓑ Ⓒ Ⓓ Ⓔ	1 Ⓐ Ⓑ Ⓒ Ⓓ Ⓔ	1 Ⓐ Ⓑ Ⓒ Ⓓ Ⓔ	1 Ⓐ Ⓑ Ⓒ Ⓓ Ⓔ
2 Ⓐ Ⓑ Ⓒ Ⓓ Ⓔ	2 Ⓐ Ⓑ Ⓒ Ⓓ Ⓔ	2 Ⓐ Ⓑ Ⓒ Ⓓ Ⓔ	2 Ⓐ Ⓑ Ⓒ Ⓓ Ⓔ	2 Ⓐ Ⓑ Ⓒ Ⓓ Ⓔ
3 Ⓐ Ⓑ Ⓒ Ⓓ Ⓔ	3 Ⓐ Ⓑ Ⓒ Ⓓ Ⓔ	3 Ⓐ Ⓑ Ⓒ Ⓓ Ⓔ	3 Ⓐ Ⓑ Ⓒ Ⓓ Ⓔ	3 Ⓐ Ⓑ Ⓒ Ⓓ Ⓔ
4 Ⓐ Ⓑ Ⓒ Ⓓ Ⓔ	4 Ⓐ Ⓑ Ⓒ Ⓓ Ⓔ	4 Ⓐ Ⓑ Ⓒ Ⓓ Ⓔ	4 Ⓐ Ⓑ Ⓒ Ⓓ Ⓔ	4 Ⓐ Ⓑ Ⓒ Ⓓ Ⓔ
5 Ⓐ Ⓑ Ⓒ Ⓓ Ⓔ	5 Ⓐ Ⓑ Ⓒ Ⓓ Ⓔ	5 Ⓐ Ⓑ Ⓒ Ⓓ Ⓔ	5 Ⓐ Ⓑ Ⓒ Ⓓ Ⓔ	5 Ⓐ Ⓑ Ⓒ Ⓓ Ⓔ
6 Ⓐ Ⓑ Ⓒ Ⓓ Ⓔ	6 Ⓐ Ⓑ Ⓒ Ⓓ Ⓔ	6 Ⓐ Ⓑ Ⓒ Ⓓ Ⓔ	6 Ⓐ Ⓑ Ⓒ Ⓓ Ⓔ	6 Ⓐ Ⓑ Ⓒ Ⓓ Ⓔ
7 Ⓐ Ⓑ Ⓒ Ⓓ Ⓔ	7 Ⓐ Ⓑ Ⓒ Ⓓ Ⓔ	7 Ⓐ Ⓑ Ⓒ Ⓓ Ⓔ	7 Ⓐ Ⓑ Ⓒ Ⓓ Ⓔ	7 Ⓐ Ⓑ Ⓒ Ⓓ Ⓔ
8 Ⓐ Ⓑ Ⓒ Ⓓ Ⓔ	8 Ⓐ Ⓑ Ⓒ Ⓓ Ⓔ	8 Ⓐ Ⓑ Ⓒ Ⓓ Ⓔ	8 Ⓐ Ⓑ Ⓒ Ⓓ Ⓔ	8 Ⓐ Ⓑ Ⓒ Ⓓ Ⓔ
9 Ⓐ Ⓑ Ⓒ Ⓓ Ⓔ	9 Ⓐ Ⓑ Ⓒ Ⓓ Ⓔ	9 Ⓐ Ⓑ Ⓒ Ⓓ Ⓔ	9 Ⓐ Ⓑ Ⓒ Ⓓ Ⓔ	9 Ⓐ Ⓑ Ⓒ Ⓓ Ⓔ
10 Ⓐ Ⓑ Ⓒ Ⓓ Ⓔ	10 Ⓐ Ⓑ Ⓒ Ⓓ Ⓔ	10 Ⓐ Ⓑ Ⓒ Ⓓ Ⓔ	10 Ⓐ Ⓑ Ⓒ Ⓓ Ⓔ	10 Ⓐ Ⓑ Ⓒ Ⓓ Ⓔ
11 Ⓐ Ⓑ Ⓒ Ⓓ Ⓔ	11 Ⓐ Ⓑ Ⓒ Ⓓ Ⓔ	11 Ⓐ Ⓑ Ⓒ Ⓓ Ⓔ	11 Ⓐ Ⓑ Ⓒ Ⓓ Ⓔ	11 Ⓐ Ⓑ Ⓒ Ⓓ Ⓔ
12 Ⓐ Ⓑ Ⓒ Ⓓ Ⓔ	12 Ⓐ Ⓑ Ⓒ Ⓓ Ⓔ	12 Ⓐ Ⓑ Ⓒ Ⓓ Ⓔ	12 Ⓐ Ⓑ Ⓒ Ⓓ Ⓔ	12 Ⓐ Ⓑ Ⓒ Ⓓ Ⓔ
13 Ⓐ Ⓑ Ⓒ Ⓓ Ⓔ	13 Ⓐ Ⓑ Ⓒ Ⓓ Ⓔ	13 Ⓐ Ⓑ Ⓒ Ⓓ Ⓔ	13 Ⓐ Ⓑ Ⓒ Ⓓ Ⓔ	13 Ⓐ Ⓑ Ⓒ Ⓓ Ⓔ
14 Ⓐ Ⓑ Ⓒ Ⓓ Ⓔ	14 Ⓐ Ⓑ Ⓒ Ⓓ Ⓔ	14 Ⓐ Ⓑ Ⓒ Ⓓ Ⓔ	14 Ⓐ Ⓑ Ⓒ Ⓓ Ⓔ	14 Ⓐ Ⓑ Ⓒ Ⓓ Ⓔ
15 Ⓐ Ⓑ Ⓒ Ⓓ Ⓔ	15 Ⓐ Ⓑ Ⓒ Ⓓ Ⓔ	15 Ⓐ Ⓑ Ⓒ Ⓓ Ⓔ	15 Ⓐ Ⓑ Ⓒ Ⓓ Ⓔ	15 Ⓐ Ⓑ Ⓒ Ⓓ Ⓔ
16 Ⓐ Ⓑ Ⓒ Ⓓ Ⓔ	16 Ⓐ Ⓑ Ⓒ Ⓓ Ⓔ	16 Ⓐ Ⓑ Ⓒ Ⓓ Ⓔ	16 Ⓐ Ⓑ Ⓒ Ⓓ Ⓔ	16 Ⓐ Ⓑ Ⓒ Ⓓ Ⓔ
17 Ⓐ Ⓑ Ⓒ Ⓓ Ⓔ	17 Ⓐ Ⓑ Ⓒ Ⓓ Ⓔ	17 Ⓐ Ⓑ Ⓒ Ⓓ Ⓔ	17 Ⓐ Ⓑ Ⓒ Ⓓ Ⓔ	17 Ⓐ Ⓑ Ⓒ Ⓓ Ⓔ
18 Ⓐ Ⓑ Ⓒ Ⓓ Ⓔ	18 Ⓐ Ⓑ Ⓒ Ⓓ Ⓔ	18 Ⓐ Ⓑ Ⓒ Ⓓ Ⓔ	18 Ⓐ Ⓑ Ⓒ Ⓓ Ⓔ	18 Ⓐ Ⓑ Ⓒ Ⓓ Ⓔ
19 Ⓐ Ⓑ Ⓒ Ⓓ Ⓔ	19 Ⓐ Ⓑ Ⓒ Ⓓ Ⓔ	19 Ⓐ Ⓑ Ⓒ Ⓓ Ⓔ	19 Ⓐ Ⓑ Ⓒ Ⓓ Ⓔ	19 Ⓐ Ⓑ Ⓒ Ⓓ Ⓔ
20 Ⓐ Ⓑ Ⓒ Ⓓ Ⓔ	20 Ⓐ Ⓑ Ⓒ Ⓓ Ⓔ	20 Ⓐ Ⓑ Ⓒ Ⓓ Ⓔ	20 Ⓐ Ⓑ Ⓒ Ⓓ Ⓔ	20 Ⓐ Ⓑ Ⓒ Ⓓ Ⓔ
21 Ⓐ Ⓑ Ⓒ Ⓓ Ⓔ	21 Ⓐ Ⓑ Ⓒ Ⓓ Ⓔ	21 Ⓐ Ⓑ Ⓒ Ⓓ Ⓔ	21 Ⓐ Ⓑ Ⓒ Ⓓ Ⓔ	21 Ⓐ Ⓑ Ⓒ Ⓓ Ⓔ
22 Ⓐ Ⓑ Ⓒ Ⓓ Ⓔ	22 Ⓐ Ⓑ Ⓒ Ⓓ Ⓔ	22 Ⓐ Ⓑ Ⓒ Ⓓ Ⓔ	22 Ⓐ Ⓑ Ⓒ Ⓓ Ⓔ	22 Ⓐ Ⓑ Ⓒ Ⓓ Ⓔ
23 Ⓐ Ⓑ Ⓒ Ⓓ Ⓔ	23 Ⓐ Ⓑ Ⓒ Ⓓ Ⓔ	23 Ⓐ Ⓑ Ⓒ Ⓓ Ⓔ	23 Ⓐ Ⓑ Ⓒ Ⓓ Ⓔ	23 Ⓐ Ⓑ Ⓒ Ⓓ Ⓔ
24 Ⓐ Ⓑ Ⓒ Ⓓ Ⓔ	24 Ⓐ Ⓑ Ⓒ Ⓓ Ⓔ	24 Ⓐ Ⓑ Ⓒ Ⓓ Ⓔ	24 Ⓐ Ⓑ Ⓒ Ⓓ Ⓔ	24 Ⓐ Ⓑ Ⓒ Ⓓ Ⓔ
25 Ⓐ Ⓑ Ⓒ Ⓓ Ⓔ	25 Ⓐ Ⓑ Ⓒ Ⓓ Ⓔ	25 Ⓐ Ⓑ Ⓒ Ⓓ Ⓔ	25 Ⓐ Ⓑ Ⓒ Ⓓ Ⓔ	25 Ⓐ Ⓑ Ⓒ Ⓓ Ⓔ
26 Ⓐ Ⓑ Ⓒ Ⓓ Ⓔ	26 Ⓐ Ⓑ Ⓒ Ⓓ Ⓔ	26 Ⓐ Ⓑ Ⓒ Ⓓ Ⓔ	26 Ⓐ Ⓑ Ⓒ Ⓓ Ⓔ	26 Ⓐ Ⓑ Ⓒ Ⓓ Ⓔ
27 Ⓐ Ⓑ Ⓒ Ⓓ Ⓔ	27 Ⓐ Ⓑ Ⓒ Ⓓ Ⓔ	27 Ⓐ Ⓑ Ⓒ Ⓓ Ⓔ	27 Ⓐ Ⓑ Ⓒ Ⓓ Ⓔ	27 Ⓐ Ⓑ Ⓒ Ⓓ Ⓔ
28 Ⓐ Ⓑ Ⓒ Ⓓ Ⓔ	28 Ⓐ Ⓑ Ⓒ Ⓓ Ⓔ	28 Ⓐ Ⓑ Ⓒ Ⓓ Ⓔ	28 Ⓐ Ⓑ Ⓒ Ⓓ Ⓔ	28 Ⓐ Ⓑ Ⓒ Ⓓ Ⓔ
29 Ⓐ Ⓑ Ⓒ Ⓓ Ⓔ	29 Ⓐ Ⓑ Ⓒ Ⓓ Ⓔ	29 Ⓐ Ⓑ Ⓒ Ⓓ Ⓔ	29 Ⓐ Ⓑ Ⓒ Ⓓ Ⓔ	29 Ⓐ Ⓑ Ⓒ Ⓓ Ⓔ
30 Ⓐ Ⓑ Ⓒ Ⓓ Ⓔ	30 Ⓐ Ⓑ Ⓒ Ⓓ Ⓔ	30 Ⓐ Ⓑ Ⓒ Ⓓ Ⓔ	30 Ⓐ Ⓑ Ⓒ Ⓓ Ⓔ	30 Ⓐ Ⓑ Ⓒ Ⓓ Ⓔ

Practice Test 3

SECTION 1

28 Questions • 35 Minutes

Directions: Below each of the following passages, you will find questions or incomplete statements about the passage. Each statement or question is followed by lettered words or expressions. Select the word or expression that most satisfactorily completes each statement or answers each question in accordance with the meaning of the passage. After you have chosen the *best* answer, blacken the corresponding space on the answer sheet.

When we are speaking casually, we call *Nineteen Eighty-Four* a novel, but in a more exacting context we call it a political fable. This requirement is not re- *(5)* futed by the fact that the book is preoccupied with an individual, Winston Smith, who suffers from a varicose ulcer, nor by the fact that it takes account of other individuals, including Julia, Mr. *(10)* Charrington, Mrs. Parsons, Syme, and O'Brien. The figures claim our attention, but they exist mainly in their relation to the political system that determines them. It would indeed be possible *(15)* to think of them as figures in a novel, though in that case they would have to be imagined in a far more diverse set of relations. They would no longer inhabit or sustain a fable, because a fable is a *(20)* narrative relieved of much contingent detail so that it may stand forth in an unusual degree of clarity and simplicity. A fable is a structure of types, each of them deliberately simplified lest a sense *(25)* of difference and heterogeneity reduce the force of the typical. Let us say, then, that *Nineteen Eighty-Four* is a political fable, projected into a near future and incorporating historical references *(30)* mainly to document a canceled past.

Since a fable is predicated upon a typology, it must be written from a certain distance. The author cannot afford the sense of familiarity which is induced *(35)* by detail and differentiation. A fable, in this respect, asks to be compared to a caricature, not to a photograph. It follows that in a political fable there is bound to be some tension between a *(40)* political sense, which deals in the multiplicity of social and personal life, and a sense of fable, which is committed to simplicity of form and feature. If the political sense were to prevail, the nar- *(45)* rative would be drawn away from fable into the novel, at some cost to its simplicity. If the sense of fable were to prevail, the fabulist would station himself at such a distance from any imaginary con- *(50)* ditions in the case that his narrative would appear unmediated, free or bereft of conditions. The risk in that procedure would be considerable: a reader might feel that the fabulist has lost interest in *(55)* the variety of human life and fallen back upon an unconditioned sense of its types, that he has become less interested in lives than in a particular idea of life. The risk is greater still if the fabulist projects *(60)* his narrative into the future: the reader can't question by appealing to the conditions of life he already knows. He is asked to believe that the future is another country and that "they just do *(65)* things differently there."

In a powerful fable the reader's feeling is likely to be mostly fear: he is afraid that the fabulist's vision of any life that is likely to arise may be accu-
(70) rate and will be verified in the event. The fabulist's feeling may be more various. Such a fable as *Nineteen Eighty-Four* might arise from disgust, despair, or world-weariness induced by evidence
(75) that nothing, despite one's best efforts, has changed and that it is too late now to hope for the change one wants.

1. In drawing an analogy between a fable and a caricature (lines 35–37), the author would most likely regard which of the following pairs of ideas as also analogous?

   (A) The subject of a caricature and the topic of a fable

   (B) The subject of a caricature and the main character in *Nineteen Eighty-Four*

   (C) The subject of a fable and the artist who draws the caricature

   (D) The artist who draws the caricature and a novelist

   (E) The minor characters in a fable and a photographer

2. Which of the following would be the most appropriate title for the passage?

   (A) A Critical Study of the Use of Characters in *Nineteen Eighty-Four*

   (B) *Nineteen Eighty-Four*: Political Fable Rather Than Novel

   (C) *Nineteen Eighty-Four*: Reflections on the Relationship of the Individual to Society

   (D) The Use of Typology in the Literature of Political Fables

   (E) Distinguishing a Political Fable from a Novel

3. Which of the following best explains why the author mentions that Winston Smith suffers from a varicose ulcer?

   (A) To demonstrate that a political fable must emphasize type over detail

   (B) To show that Winston Smith has some characteristics that distinguish him as an individual

   (C) To argue that Winston Smith is no more important than any other character in *Nineteen Eighty-Four*

   (D) To illustrate one of the features of the political situation described in *Nineteen Eighty-Four*

   (E) To suggest that *Nineteen Eighty-Four* is too realistic to be considered a work of fiction

4. The "tension" that the author mentions in line 39 refers to the

   (A) necessity of striking a balance between the need to describe a political situation in simple terms and the need to make the description realistic

   (B) reaction the reader feels because he is drawn to the characters of the fable as individuals but repulsed by the political situation

   (C) delicate task faced by a literary critic who must interpret the text of a work while attempting to describe accurately the intentions of the author

   (D) danger that too realistic a description of a key character will make the reader feel that the fable is actually a description of his own situation

   (E) conflict of aspirations and interests between characters that an author creates to motivate the action of the narrative

5. The author's attitude toward *Nineteen Eighty-Four* can best be described as

(A) condescending.

(B) laudatory.

(C) disparaging.

(D) scholarly.

(E) ironic.

6. The author uses the phrase "another country" to describe a political fable in which

(A) political events described in a fable occur in a place other than the country of national origin of the author.

(B) a lack of detail makes it difficult for a reader to see the connection between his own situation and the one described in the book.

(C) too many minor characters create the impression of complete disorganization, leading the reader to believe he is in a foreign country.

(D) the author has allowed his personal political convictions to infect his description of the political situation.

(E) an overabundance of detail prevents the reader from appreciating the real possibility that such a political situation could develop.

7. The author's primary concern is to

(A) define and clarify a concept.

(B) point out a logical inconsistency.

(C) trace the connection between a cause and an effect.

(D) illustrate a general statement with examples.

(E) outline a proposal for future action.

In the art of the Middle Ages, we never encounter the personality of the artist as an individual; rather, it is diffused through the artistic genius of centuries
(5) embodied in the rules of religious art. Art of the Middle Ages is first a sacred script, the symbols and meanings of which were well settled. The circular halo placed vertically behind the head
(10) signifies sainthood, while the halo impressed with a cross signifies divinity. By bare feet, we recognize God, the angels, Jesus Christ, and the apostles, but for an artist to have depicted the Virgin
(15) Mary with bare feet would have been tantamount to heresy. Several concentric, wavy lines represent the sky, while parallel lines represent water or the sea. A tree, which is to say a single stalk with
(20) two or three stylized leaves, informs us that the scene is laid on earth. A tower with a window indicates a village; and should an angel be watching from the battlements, that city is thereby identi-
(25) fied as Jerusalem. Saint Peter is always depicted with curly hair, a short beard, and a tonsure, while Saint Paul has always a bald head and a long beard.

A second characteristic of this ico-
(30) nography is obedience to a sacred mathematics. "The Divine Wisdom," wrote Saint Augustine, "reveals itself everywhere in numbers," a doctrine attributable to the neo-Platonists who revived
(35) the genius of Pythagoras. Twelve is the master number of the Church and is the product of three, the number of the Trinity, and four, the number of material elements. The number seven, the most
(40) mysterious of all numbers, is the sum of four and three. There are the seven ages of man, seven virtues, seven planets. In the final analysis, the seven-tone scale of Gregorian music is the sensible em-
(45) bodiment of the order of the universe. Numbers require also a symmetry. At Chartres, a stained glass window shows the four prophets Isaac, Ezekiel, Daniel, and Jeremiah carrying on their shoul-
(50) ders the four evangelists Matthew, Mark, Luke, and John.

A third characteristic of this art is to be a symbolic language, showing us one thing and in inviting us to see an-
(55) other. In this respect, the artist was called upon to imitate God, who had hidden a profound meaning behind the literal, and who wished nature itself to be a moral lesson to man. Thus, every
(60) painting is an allegory. In a scene of the

final judgment, we see the foolish virgins at the left hand of Jesus and the wise at his right, and we understand that this symbolizes those who are lost
(65) and those who are saved. Even seemingly insignificant details carry hidden meaning: The lion in a stained glass window is the figure of the Resurrection.

These, then, are the defining char-
(70) acteristics of the art of the Middle Ages, a system within which even the most mediocre talent was elevated by the genius of the centuries. The artists of the early Renaissance broke with tradition
(75) at their own peril. When they are not outstanding, they are scarcely able to avoid insignificance and banality in their religious works; and even when they are great, they are no more than the equals
(80) of the old masters who passively followed the sacred rules.

8. The primary purpose of the passage is to

   (A) theorize about the immediate influences on art of the Middle Ages.

   (B) explain why artists of the Middle Ages followed the rules of a sacred script.

   (C) discuss some of the important features of art of the Middle Ages.

   (D) contrast the art of the Middle Ages with that of the Renaissance.

   (E) explain why the Middle Ages had a passion for order and numbers.

9. It can be inferred that a painting done in the Middle Ages is most likely to contain

   (A) elements representing the numbers 3 and 4.

   (B) a moral lesson hidden behind the literal figures.

   (C) highly stylized buildings and trees.

   (D) figures with halos and bare feet.

   (E) a signature of the artist and the date of execution.

10. Which of the following best describes the attitude of the author toward art of the Middle Ages?

    (A) The author understands it and admires it.

    (B) The author regards it as the greatest art of all time.

    (C) The author prefers music of the period to its painting.

    (D) The author realizes the constraints placed on the artist and is disappointed that individuality is never evident.

    (E) The author regards it generally as inferior to the works produced during the period preceding it.

11. The author refers to Saint Augustine in order to

    (A) refute a possible objection.

    (B) ridicule a position.

    (C) present a suggestive analogy.

    (D) avoid a contradiction.

    (E) provide proof by illustration.

12. All of the following are mentioned in the passage as elements of the sacred script EXCEPT

    (A) abstract symbols such as lines to represent physical features.

    (B) symbols such as halos and crosses.

    (C) clothing used to characterize individuals.

    (D) symmetrical juxtaposition of figures.

    (E) use of figures to identify locations.

13. The passage would most likely be found in a

   (A) sociological analysis of the Middle Ages.

   (B) treatise on the influence of the Church in the Middle Ages.

   (C) scholarly analysis of art in the Middle Ages.

   (D) preface to a biography of Saint Augustine.

   (E) pamphlet discussing religious beliefs.

14. By the phrase "diffused through the artistic genius of centuries," the author most likely means

   (A) the individual artists of the Middle Ages did not have serious talent.

   (B) great works of art from the Middle Ages have survived until now.

   (C) an artist who faithfully followed the rules of religious art was not recognized while still alive.

   (D) the rules of religious art, developed over time, left little freedom for the artist.

   (E) religious art has greater value than the secular art of the Renaissance.

The most damning thing that can be said about the world's best-endowed and richest country is that it is not only not the leader in health status, but that it is
(5) so low in the ranks of the nations. The United States ranks 18th among nations of the world in male life expectancy at birth, 9th in female life expectancy at birth, and 12th in infant mortality. More
(10) importantly, huge variations are evident in health status in the United States from one place to the next and from one group to the next.

The forces that affect health can be
(15) aggregated into four groupings that lend themselves to analysis of all health problems. Clearly the largest aggregate of forces resides in the person's environment. Behavior, in part derived from
(20) experiences with the environment, is

the next greatest force affecting health. Medical care services, treated as separate from other environmental factors because of the special interest we have
(25) in them, make a modest contribution to health status. Finally, the contributions of heredity to health are difficult to judge. We are templated at conception as to our basic weaknesses and strengths; but
(30) many hereditary attributes never become manifest because of environmental and behavioral forces that act before the genetic forces come to maturity, and other hereditary attributes are increas-
(35) ingly being palliated by medical care.

No other country spends what we do per capita for medical care. The care available is among the best technically, even if used too lavishly and thus dan-
(40) gerously, but none of the countries that stand above us in health status have such a high proportion of medically disenfranchised persons. Given the evidence that medical care is not that
(45) valuable and access to care not that bad, it seems most unlikely that our bad showing is caused by the significant proportion who are poorly served. Other hypotheses have greater explanatory
(50) power: excessive poverty, both actual and relative, and excessive affluence.

Excessive poverty is probably more prevalent in the U.S. than in any of the countries that have a better infant mor-
(55) tality rate and female life expectancy at birth. This is probably true also for all but four or five of the countries with a longer male life expectancy. In the notably poor countries that exceed us in male
(60) survival, difficult living conditions are a more accepted way of life and in several of them, a good basic diet, basic medical care and basic education, and lifelong employment opportunities are an every-
(65) day fact of life. In the U.S., a national unemployment level of 10 percent may be 40 percent in the ghetto while less than 4 percent elsewhere. The countries that have surpassed us in health do not
(70) have such severe or entrenched problems. Nor are such a high proportion of their people involved in them.

Excessive affluence is not so obvious a cause of ill health, but, at least
(75) until recently, few other nations could
afford such unhealthful ways of living.
Excessive intake of animal protein and
fats, dangerous imbibing of alcohol and
use of tobacco and drugs (prescribed and
(80) proscribed), and dangerous recreational
sports and driving habits are all possible
only because of affluence. Our heritage,
desires, opportunities, and our ma-
chismo, combined with the relatively
(85) low cost of bad foods and speedy vehicles, make us particularly vulnerable
to our affluence. And those who are not
affluent try harder. Our unacceptable
health status, then, will not be improved
(90) appreciably by expanded medical resources nor by their redistribution so
much as by a general attempt to improve
the quality of life for all.

15. Which of the following would be the most
logical continuation of the passage?

   (A) Suggestions for specific proposals to
   improve the quality of life in America

   (B) A listing of the most common causes
   of death among male and female
   adults

   (C) An explanation of the causes of poverty in America, both absolute and
   relative

   (D) A proposal to ensure that residents of
   central cities receive more and better
   medical care

   (E) A study of the overcrowding in urban
   hospitals serving primarily the poor

16. All of the following are mentioned in the
passage as factors affecting the health of
the population EXCEPT

   (A) the availability of medical care services.

   (B) the genetic endowment of individuals.

   (C) overall environmental factors.

   (D) the nation's relative position in health
   status.

   (E) an individual's own behavior.

17. The author is primarily concerned with

   (A) condemning the U.S. for its failure to
   provide better medical care to the
   poor.

   (B) evaluating the relative significance
   of factors contributing to the poor
   health status in the U.S.

   (C) providing information that the reader
   can use to improve his or her personal
   health.

   (D) comparing the general health of the
   U.S. population with world averages.

   (E) advocating specific measures designed to improve the health of the
   U.S. population.

18. The passage best supports which of the following conclusions about the relationship between per capita expenditures for medical care and the health of a population?

    (A) The per capita expenditure for medical care has relatively little effect on the total amount of medical care available to a population.

    (B) The genetic makeup of a population is a more powerful determinant of the health of a population than the per capita expenditure for medical care.

    (C) A population may have very high per capita expenditures for medical care and yet have a lower health status than other populations with lower per capita expenditures.

    (D) The higher the per capita expenditure on medical care, the more advanced is the medical technology; and the more advanced the technology, the better is the health of the population.

    (E) Per capita outlays for medical care devoted to adults are likely to have a greater effect on the status of the population than outlays devoted to infants.

19. The author refers to the excessive intake of alcohol, tobacco, and drug use in order to

    (A) show that some health problems cannot be attacked by better medical care.

    (B) demonstrate that use of tobacco and intoxicants is detrimental to health.

    (C) cite examples of individual behavior that have adverse consequences for health status.

    (D) refute the contention that poor health is related to access to medical care.

    (E) illustrate ways in which affluence may contribute to poor health status.

20. The passage provides information to answer which of the following questions?

    (A) What is the most powerful influence on the health status of a population?

    (B) Which nation in the world leads in health status?

    (C) Is the life expectancy of males in the U.S. longer than that of females?

    (D) What are the most important genetic factors influencing the health of an individual?

    (E) How can the U.S. reduce the incidence of unemployment in the ghetto?

21. In discussing the forces that influence health, the author implies that medical care services are

    (A) the least important of all.

    (B) a special aspect of an individual's environment.

    (C) a function of an individual's behavior pattern.

    (D) becoming less important as technology improves.

    (E) too expensive for most people.

Nitroglycerin has long been famous for its relief of angina attacks but ruled out for heart attacks on the theory that it harmfully lowers blood pressure and (5) increases heart rate. A heart attack, unlike an angina attack, always involves some localized, fairly rapid heart muscle death, or myocardial infarction. This acute emergency happens when the ar- (10) teriosclerotic occlusive process in one of the coronary arterial branches culminates so suddenly and completely that the local myocardium—the muscle area that was fed by the occluded coronary— (15) stops contracting and dies over a period of hours, to be replaced over a period of weeks by a scar, or "healed infarct."

In experiments with dogs, it was discovered that administration of nitro- (20) glycerin during the acute stage of myocardial infarction consistently reduced

the extent of myocardial injury, provided that the dogs' heart rate and blood pressure were maintained in the normal
(25) range. Soon after, scientists made a preliminary confirmation of the clinical applicability of nitroglycerin in acute heart attacks in human patients. Five of twelve human subjects developed some degree
(30) of congestive heart failure. Curiously, the nitroglycerin alone was enough to reduce the magnitude of injury in these five patients, but the other seven patients, whose heart attacks were not
(35) complicated by any congestive heart failure, were not consistently helped by the nitroglycerin until another drug, phenylephrine, was added to abolish the nitroglycerin-induced drop in blood pres-
(40) sure. One explanation for this is that the reflex responses in heart rate, mediated through the autonomic nervous system, are so blunted in congestive heart failure that a fall in blood pressure prompts
(45) less of the cardiac acceleration that otherwise worsens the damage of acute myocardial infarction.

It appears that the size of the infarct that would otherwise result from a
(50) coronary occlusion might be greatly reduced, and vitally needed heart muscle thus saved, by the actions of certain drugs and other measures taken during the acute phase of the heart attack. This
(55) is because the size of the myocardial infarct is not really determined at the moment of the coronary occlusion as previously thought. The fate of the stricken myocardial segment remains
(60) largely undetermined, hanging on the balance of myocardial oxygen supply and demand that can be favorably influenced for many hours after the coronary occlusion. So it is possible to reduce the
(65) myocardial injury during acute human heart attacks by means of nitroglycerin, either alone or in combination with phenylephrine.

Other drugs are also being tested
(70) to reduce myocardial infarct size, particularly drugs presumed to affect myocardial oxygen supply and demand, including not only vessel dilators such as

nitroglycerin but also antihypertensives
(75) that block the sympathetic nerve reflexes that increase heart rate and work in response to exertion and stress. Such measures are still experimental, and there is no proof of benefit with regard to
(80) the great complications of heart attack such as cardiogenic shock, angina, or mortality. But the drugs for reducing infarct size now hold center stage in experimental frameworks.

22. According to the passage, the primary difference between a heart attack and an angina attack is that a heart attack

(A) involves an acceleration of the heartbeat.
(B) cannot be treated with nitroglycerin.
(C) generally results in congestive heart failure.
(D) takes place within a relatively short period of time.
(E) always results in damage to muscle tissue of the heart.

23. In the study referred to in lines 25–28, the patients who developed congestive heart failure did not experience cardiac acceleration because

(A) the nitroglycerin was not administered soon enough after the onset of the heart attack.
(B) the severity of the heart attack blocked the autonomic response to the nitroglycerin-induced drop in blood pressure.
(C) administering phenylephrine mitigated the severity of the drop in blood pressure caused by nitroglycerin.
(D) doctors were able to maintain blood pressure, and thus indirectly pulse rate, in those patients.
(E) those patients did not experience a drop in blood pressure as a result of the heart attack.

24. The passage provides information to answer all of the following questions EXCEPT

    (A) What are some of the physiological manifestations of a heart attack?

    (B) What determines the size of a myocardial infarct following a heart attack?

    (C) What effect does nitroglycerin have when administered to a patient experiencing a heart attack?

    (D) What are the most important causes of heart attacks?

    (E) What is the physiological effect of phenylephrine?

25. It can be inferred from the passage that nitroglycerin is of value in treating heart attacks because it

    (A) lowers the blood pressure.

    (B) stimulates healing of an infarct.

    (C) causes cardiac acceleration.

    (D) dilates blood vessels.

    (E) counteracts hypertension.

26. The author's attitude toward the use of nitroglycerin and other drugs to treat heart attack can best be described as one of

    (A) concern.

    (B) resignation.

    (C) anxiety.

    (D) disinterest.

    (E) optimism.

27. It can be inferred that the phenylephrine is administered in conjunction with nitroglycerin during a heart attack in order to

    (A) prevent the cardiac acceleration caused by a drop in blood pressure.

    (B) block sympathetic nerve reflexes that increase the pulse rate.

    (C) blunt the autonomic nervous system, which accelerates the pulse rate.

    (D) reduce the size of a myocardial infarct by increasing oxygen supply.

    (E) prevent arteriosclerotic occlusion in the coronary arterial branches.

28. The author is primarily concerned with

    (A) explaining a predicament.

    (B) evaluating a study.

    (C) outlining a proposal.

    (D) countering an argument.

    (E) discussing a treatment.

STOP

END OF SECTION 1. IF YOU HAVE ANY TIME LEFT, GO OVER YOUR WORK IN THIS SECTION ONLY. DO NOT WORK IN ANY OTHER SECTION OF THE TEST.

SECTION 2

24 Questions • 35 Minutes

> **Directions:** Each group of questions is based on a set of propositions or conditions. Drawing a rough picture or diagram may help in answering some of the questions. After you have chosen the *best* answer for each question, blacken the corresponding space on your answer sheet.

Questions 1–6

Ten pennants are to be hung side by side on a rope that will then be stretched parallel to the ground between two poles. The positions are numbered consecutively 1 through 10, starting at the left.

There are two green, two blue, three red, and three yellow pennants.

The two green pennants are next to each other.

The two blue pennants are not next to each other.

The three red pennants are next to each other.

A blue pennant is at one end of the rope, and a red pennant is at the other.

1. If the fourth and fifth pennants are green and if the ninth pennant is red, which of the following must be true?

   (A) A blue pennant is next to a green pennant.
   (B) A blue pennant is next to a red pennant.
   (C) Each blue pennant is next to a yellow pennant.
   (D) The sixth pennant is a blue pennant.
   (E) The sixth pennant is a yellow pennant.

2. If a blue pennant is in position 7 and a yellow pennant in position 8, which of the following positions must be a green pennant?

   (A) 3
   (B) 4
   (C) 5
   (D) 6
   (E) 7

3. If each blue pennant is next to a green pennant, then which of the following pennants must be yellow?

   (A) Fifth and sixth
   (B) Fifth, sixth, and seventh
   (C) Fourth, fifth, and sixth
   (D) Fourth, sixth, and seventh
   (E) Fourth, fifth, sixth, and seventh

4. If a yellow pennant is in position 9 and the yellow pennants are next to each other, which of the following must be true?

   (A) A blue pennant is in position 1.
   (B) A green pennant is in position 3.
   (C) A green pennant is in position 4.
   (D) A yellow pennant is in position 5.
   (E) A green pennant is in position 5.

5. If yellow pennants are in positions 3 and 5, all of the following must be true EXCEPT

 (A) a yellow pennant is in position 4.

 (B) a green pennant is in position 6.

 (C) a green pennant is in position 7.

 (D) each blue pennant is next to at least one yellow pennant.

 (E) exactly one yellow pennant is not next to another yellow pennant.

6. If one green pennant is next to a blue pennant and the other green pennant is next to a red pennant, which of the following must be true?

 (A) The first pennant is a red pennant.

 (B) The first pennant is a blue pennant.

 (C) The third pennant is a red pennant.

 (D) A yellow pennant is flanked by blue pennants.

 (E) A yellow pennant is flanked by yellow pennants.

Questions 7–12

A winery is conducting a tasting of seven wines: $J, K, L, M, N, O,$ and P. Each wine will be tasted in succession according to the following conditions:

 J must be tasted either third or seventh.

 If J is tasted seventh, then N must be tasted fourth; otherwise, N is not tasted fourth.

 If J is tasted seventh, then L is tasted sixth.

 If J is tasted third, then O is tasted sixth.

 N must be the third wine tasted after K.

7. If L is tasted fourth, which wine must be tasted third?

 (A) J

 (B) K

 (C) M

 (D) N

 (E) O

8. If M is tasted immediately following L, which of the following must be true?

 (A) K is tasted first.

 (B) L is tasted second.

 (C) M is tasted third.

 (D) P is tasted fourth.

 (E) P is tasted fifth.

9. M CANNOT be which wine in the tasting sequence?

 (A) Second

 (B) Third

 (C) Fourth

 (D) Fifth

 (E) Sixth

10. Which of the following must be true?

 (A) J is tasted earlier than K.

 (B) J is tasted earlier than L.

 (C) K is tasted earlier than L.

 (D) K is tasted earlier than O.

 (E) M is tasted earlier than O.

11. If P is tasted earlier than N but later than O, which of the following must be true?

 (A) O is tasted first.

 (B) L is tasted third.

 (C) O is tasted third.

 (D) M is tasted fifth.

 (E) P is tasted fifth.

12. If M is the second wine tasted after P, in how many different orders can the wines be tasted?

 (A) 1

 (B) 2

 (C) 3

 (D) 4

 (E) 5

Questions 13–18

The principal of a high school is selecting a committee of students to attend an annual student leadership conference. The students eligible for selection are *P, Q, R, S, T, U,* and *V*. The committee must be selected in accordance with the following considerations:

If *V* is selected, *R* must be selected.

If both *R* and *Q* are selected, then *P* cannot be selected.

If both *Q* and *P* are selected, then *T* cannot be selected.

If *P* is selected, then either *S* or *U* must be selected; but *S* and *U* cannot both be selected.

Either *S* or *T* must be selected, but *S* and *T* cannot both be selected.

13. If neither *S* nor *U* is selected, what is the largest number of students who can be selected for the conference?

    (A) 2
    (B) 3
    (C) 4
    (D) 5
    (E) 6

14. If both *P* and *V* are selected, what is the smallest number of students who can be selected for the conference?

    (A) 3
    (B) 4
    (C) 5
    (D) 6
    (E) 7

15. If both *P* and *U* are selected, which of the following must be true?

    (A) *Q* must be selected.
    (B) *S* must be selected.
    (C) *T* must be selected.
    (D) *R* cannot be selected.
    (E) *V* cannot be selected.

16. Which of the following is an acceptable delegation to the conference if only three students are selected?

    (A) *P, Q,* and *S*
    (B) *P, Q,* and *T*
    (C) *P, R,* and *V*
    (D) *R, S,* and *T*
    (E) *R, S,* and *U*

17. If both *P* and *T* are chosen, which of the following CANNOT be true?

    (A) The committee consists of three students.
    (B) The committee consists of four students.
    (C) The committee consists of five students.
    (D) *U* is not chosen.
    (E) *V* is not chosen.

18. If *U* and three other students are selected, which of the following groups can accompany *U*?

    (A) *P, Q,* and *T*
    (B) *P, R,* and *T*
    (C) *P, Q,* and *V*
    (D) *P, V,* and *S*
    (E) *R, S,* and *V*

Questions 19–24

A musical scale contains seven notes—*J, K, L, M, N, O,* and *Q*—ranked from first (lowest) to seventh (highest), though not necessarily in that order.

The first note of the scale is *O*, and the last note of the scale is *Q*.

L is lower than *M*.

N is lower than *J*.

K is somewhere between *J* and *M* on the scale.

19. If *N* is the fifth note on the scale, which of the following must be true?

    (A) *J* is the sixth note, and *M* is the fourth note.

    (B) *K* is the fourth note, and *L* is the third note.

    (C) *M* is the third note, and *L* is the second note.

    (D) *M* is the fourth note, and *L* is the third note.

    (E) *L* is the fourth note, and *J* is the second note.

20. If *M* is the sixth note, then which of the following is a complete and accurate listing of the positions that could be occupied by *J* and *N*, respectively?

    (A) Fifth and third

    (B) Fourth and third

    (C) Third and second

    (D) Fourth and third or third and second

    (E) Third and second or fifth and third

21. If there are exactly two notes on the scale between *K* and *N*, which of the following must be true?

    (A) *K* is the fifth note on the scale.

    (B) *L* is between *J* and *K* on the scale.

    (C) *M* is the sixth note on the scale.

    (D) *M* is above *J* on the scale.

    (E) *L* and *M* are separated by exactly one note on the scale.

22. Which of the following CANNOT be true?

    (A) *J* is the fourth note on the scale.

    (B) *J* is the third note on the scale.

    (C) *K* is the third note on the scale.

    (D) *K* is the fourth note on the scale.

    (E) *K* is the fifth note on the scale.

23. If *N* and *O* are separated by exactly two notes, which of the following must be true?

    (A) *J* is the sixth note on the scale.

    (B) *L* is the fifth note on the scale.

    (C) *K* is below *M* on the scale.

    (D) *K* is between *N* and *O* on the scale.

    (E) *M* is above *N* on the scale.

24. If *N* is one note above *L* on the scale, what is the number of logically possible orderings of all seven notes from the bottom of the scale to the top of the scale?

    (A) 1

    (B) 2

    (C) 3

    (D) 4

    (E) 5

STOP

END OF SECTION 2. IF YOU HAVE ANY TIME LEFT, GO OVER YOUR WORK IN THIS SECTION ONLY. DO NOT WORK IN ANY OTHER SECTION OF THE TEST.

SECTION 3

24 Questions • 35 Minutes

> **Directions:** In this section, the questions ask you to analyze and evaluate the reasoning in short paragraphs or passages. For some questions, all of the answer choices may conceivably be answers to the question asked. You should select the *best* answer to the question; that is, an answer that does not require you to make assumptions that violate commonsense standards by being implausible, redundant, irrelevant, or inconsistent. After you have chosen the *best* answer, blacken the corresponding space on the answer sheet.

Questions 1 and 2

On his trip to the People's Republic of China, a young U.S. diplomat of very subordinate rank embarrassed himself by asking a Chinese official how it was that Orientals managed to be so inscrutable. The Chinese official smiled and then gently responded that he preferred to think of the inscrutability of his race in terms of a want of perspicacity in Occidentals.

1. Which of the following best describes the point of the comment made by the Chinese official?

    (A) It is not merely the Chinese but all Oriental people who are inscrutable.

    (B) Most Americans fail to understand Chinese culture.

    (C) What one fails to perceive may be attributable to carelessness in observation rather than obscurity inherent in the object.

    (D) Since the resumption of diplomatic relations between the United States and Communist China, many older Chinese civil servants have grown to distrust the Americans.

    (E) If the West and the East are ever to truly understand one another, there will have to be considerable cultural exchange between the two.

2. Which of the following best characterizes the attitude and response of the Chinese official?

    (A) Angry

    (B) Fearful

    (C) Emotional

    (D) Indifferent

    (E) Compassionate

3. People waste a surprising amount of money on gadgets and doodads that they hardly ever use. For example, my brother spent $25 on an electric ice-cream maker two years ago, but he has used it on only three occasions. Yet, he insists that regardless of the number of times he actually uses the ice-cream maker, the investment was a good one because _____.

Which of the following best completes the thought of the paragraph?

(A) the price of ice cream will go up in the future

(B) he has purchased the ice-cream maker for the convenience of having it available if and when he needs it

(C) in a society that is oriented toward consumer goods, one should take every opportunity to acquire things

(D) today $25 is not worth what it was two years ago on account of the inflation rate

(E) by using it so infrequently, he has conserved a considerable amount of electrical energy

4. A poet was once asked to interpret a particularly obscure passage in one of his poems. He responded, "When I wrote that verse, only God and I knew the meaning of that passage. Now, only God knows."

What is the point of the poet's response?

(A) God is infinitely wiser than humans.

(B) Most humans are unable to understand poetry.

(C) Poets rarely know the source of their own creative inspiration.

(D) A great poem is inspired by the muse.

(E) He has forgotten what he had originally meant by the verse.

5. A recent survey by the economics department of an Ivy League university revealed that increases in the salaries of preachers are accompanied by increases in the nationwide average of rum consumption. From 1965 to 1970, preachers' salaries increased on the average of 15 percent and rum sales grew by 14.5 percent. From 1970 to 1975, average preachers' salaries rose by 17 percent and rum sales by 17.5 percent. From 1975 to 1980, rum sales expanded by only 8 percent and average preachers' salaries also grew by only 8 percent.

Which of the following is the most likely explanation for the findings cited in the paragraph?

(A) When preachers have more disposable income, they tend to allocate that extra money to alcohol.

(B) When preachers are paid more, they preach longer; and longer sermons tend to drive people to drink.

(C) Since there were more preachers in the country, there were also more people; and a larger population will consume greater quantities of liquor.

(D) The general standard of living increased from 1965 to 1980, which accounts for both the increase in rum consumption and preachers' average salaries.

(E) A consortium of rum importers carefully limited the increases in imports of rum during the test period cited.

6. Since all four-door automobiles I have repaired have eight-cylinder engines, all four-door automobiles must have eight-cylinder engines.

The author argues on the basis of

(A) special training.

(B) generalization.

(C) syllogism.

(D) ambiguity.

(E) deduction.

7. Two people, one living in Los Angeles, the other living in New York City, carried on a lengthy correspondence by mail. The subject of the exchange was a dispute over certain personality traits of Winston Churchill. After some two dozen letters, the Los Angeles resident received the following note from the New York City correspondent: "It seems you were right all along. Yesterday I met someone who actually knew Sir Winston, and he confirmed your opinion."

The two people could have been arguing on the basis of all of the following EXCEPT

(A) published biographical information.

(B) old news film footage.

(C) direct personal acquaintance.

(D) assumption.

(E) third-party reports.

8. The protection of the right of property by the Constitution is tenuous at best. It is true that the Fifth Amendment states that the government may not take private property for public use without compensation, but it is the government that defines private property.

Which of the following is most likely the point the author is leading up to?

(A) Individual rights that are protected by the Supreme Court are secure against government encroachment.

(B) Private property is neither more nor less than that which the government says is private property.

(C) The government has no authority to deprive an individual of his liberty.

(D) No government that acts arbitrarily can be justified.

(E) The keystone of American democracy is the Constitution.

9. *Daily Post* newspaper reporter Roger Nightengale let it be known that Andrea Johnson, the key figure in his award-winning series of articles on prostitution and drug abuse, was a composite of many persons and not a single, real person, and so he was the subject of much criticism by fellow journalists for having failed to disclose that information when the articles were first published. But these were the same critics who voted Nightengale a prize for his magazine serial *General*, which was a much dramatized and fictionalized account of a Korean War military leader whose character was obviously patterned closely after that of Douglas MacArthur.

In which of the following ways might the critics mentioned in the paragraph argue that they were NOT inconsistent in their treatment of Nightengale's works?

(A) Fictionalization is an accepted journalistic technique for reporting on sensitive subject matter such as prostitution.

(B) Critic disapproval is one of the most important ways members of the writing community have for ensuring that reporting is accurate and to the point.

(C) Newspaper reporters usually promise confidentiality to their sources and have an obligation to protect their identities.

(D) There is a critical difference between dramatizing events in a piece of fiction and presenting distortions of the truth as actual fact.

(E) Well-known personalities are public figures whose personal lives are acceptable material for journalistic investigations.

10. Why pay outrageously high prices for imported sparkling water when there is now an inexpensive water carbonated and bottled here in the United States at its source—Cold Springs, Vermont. Neither you nor your guests will taste the difference, but if you would be embarrassed if it were learned that you were serving a domestic sparkling water, then serve Cold Springs Water—but serve it in a leaded crystal decanter.

The advertisement rests on which of the following assumptions?

(A) It is not difficult to distinguish Cold Springs Water from imported competitors on the basis of taste.

(B) Most sparkling waters are bottled at the source, but additional carbonation is added to make them more active.

(C) Import restriction and customs duties that are passed on to consumers artificially inflate the price of imported waters.

(D) Sparkling waters taste best when they are decanted from their bottles into another container for service.

(E) Some people may purchase an imported sparkling water over a domestic one as a status symbol.

11. Choose the best completion of the following paragraph.

Parochial education serves the dual functions of education and religious instruction, and church leaders are justifiably concerned to impart important religious values regarding relationships between the sexes. Thus, when the administrators of a parochial school system segregate boys and girls in separate institutions, they believe they are helping to keep the children pure by removing them from a source of temptation. If the administrators realized, however, that children would be more likely to develop the very attitudes they seek to engender in the company of the opposite sex, they would _____.

(A) put an end to all parochial education

(B) no longer insist upon separate schools for boys and girls

(C) abolish all racial discrimination in the religious schools

(D) stop teaching foolish religious tripe and concentrate instead on secular educational programs

(E) reinforce their policies of isolating the sexes in separate programs

12. Professor Branch, who is chair of the sociology department, claims she saw a flying saucer the other night. But since she is a sociologist instead of a physicist, she cannot possibly be acquainted with the most recent writings of our finest scientists that tend to discount such sightings, so we can conclude her report is unreliable.

Which of the following would be the most appropriate criticism of the author's analysis?

(A) The author makes an irrelevant attack on Professor Branch's credentials.

(B) The author may not be a physicist and therefore may not be familiar with the writings he cites.

(C) Even the U.S. Air Force cannot explain all of the sightings of UFOs that are reported to them each year.

(D) A sociologist is sufficiently well educated that she can probably read and understand scientific literature in a field other than her own.

(E) It is impossible to get complete agreement on matters such as the possibility of life on other planets.

13. INQUISITOR: Are you in league with the devil?

VICTIM: Yes.

INQUISITOR: Then you must be lying, for those in league with the "Evil One" never tell the truth. So you are not in league with the devil.

The inquisitor's behavior can be described as paradoxical because he

(A) charged the victim with being in league with the devil but later recanted.

(B) relies on the victim's answer to reject the victim's response.

(C) acts in accordance with religious law but accuses the victim of violating that law.

(D) questions the victim about possible ties with the devil but does not really believe there is a devil.

(E) asked the question in the first place but then refused to accept the answer that the victim gave.

14. "Whom did you pass on the road?" the King went on, holding his hand out to the messenger for some hay.

"Nobody," said the messenger.

"Quite right," said the King. "This young lady saw him, too. So, of course, Nobody walks slower than you."

The King's response shows that he believes

(A) the messenger is a very good messenger.

(B) "Nobody" is a person who might be seen.

(C) the young lady's eyesight is better than the messenger's.

(D) the messenger is not telling him the truth.

(E) there was no person actually seen by the messenger on the road.

15. An experienced attorney agreed to take on a law clerk and train her for admission to the bar. According to their agreement, the fee for the training would be due and payable at the time that the new attorney won her first case. After receiving the training, the new attorney decided not to practice law, and the experienced attorney, tired of waiting for payment, sued for the fee. The new attorney represented herself and claimed that the fee was not owed since she had not won her first case.

Which of the following conclusions can be logically inferred from the information above?

(A) If the younger attorney wins, the fee is then due.

(B) If the younger attorney wins, the fee is never payable.

(C) If the younger attorney wins, the fee was due before the suit was filed.

(D) If the suit is withdrawn, the fee is never payable.

(E) If the suit is withdrawn, the fee was due before the suit was filed.

16. In the new car market, purchasing decisions are often based on emotion rather than rationality. Consumers buy a bewildering array of packages that include secure child seats, antilock brakes, side airbags, and other safety features, while also choosing expensive options such as entertainment systems and extra-powerful engines. It is rare for consumers in similar circumstances to buy identical new car packages.

The reasoning above presupposes that

(A) automotive safety features are more important than other options

(B) consumers buy cars with options packages already on dealer lots

(C) different consumers cannot rationally reach different decisions

(D) safety features on cars are more expensive than other options

(E) reliability is not an important factor in the decision to buy a new car

17. BILL: The heating, ventilation and air conditioning (HVAC) controls in our office building are completely fake, intended to fool us into thinking that we are exercising control over office weather conditions. Remove the device from the wall, and you'll probably find that it doesn't even have a wire attached, or if it does have a wire attached, the other end dangles uselessly in the dead space behind the wall.

    RICHARD: But we did an experiment. We found that when we were uncomfortably warm and we adjusted the thermostat, a few minutes later, cooler air began to circulate. Or if we were uncomfortably cool and adjusted the thermostat accordingly, a few minutes later, warmer air began to circulate.

Which of the following, if true, best reconciles the conflicting opinions of Bill and Richard?

(A) People have different tolerances for temperature extremes, so conditions that some perceive as too warm or too cool will be regarded as comfortable by others.

(B) In order to conserve energy, temperature settings in office buildings are normally reduced during the night, and it takes about an hour's operation for the HVAC system to return the temperature to normal.

(C) The windows in modern office buildings are covered with a glaze that reflects sunlight, thereby reducing the penetration of the infrared rays that account for most of the heat buildup in offices.

(D) The working thermostat for the HVAC system is usually placed in a locked plastic or glass box to which only an office manager or other supervisory person has access.

(E) Real HVAC controls are set to conserve energy and so do not activate the heating or cooling system until conditions have become too warm or too cool for most occupants.

18. Copyright protection lasts for a fixed term of years following the death of the work's creator, after which anyone is free to reprint or otherwise copy a work without the permission of or the need to pay compensation to the heirs of the creator of the work. However, the protection of property rights is essential to a democracy. A copyrighted work such as a symphony or a novel has value, so it's property that should be protected by law. Therefore, copyright should be in perpetuity and not just for a limited time.

The reasoning above can be criticized because it

(A) fails to provide examples of named works that are protected by copyright

(B) presumes without argument that creative works are property

(C) attempts to discredit the source of an argument rather than address its merits

(D) reaches a general conclusion based upon an unrepresentative sampling

(E) ignores the possibility that some works are more valuable than others

19. If the artifacts include armaments, then the recently uncovered ruins are remnants of a fortress built by the Etonians. If the artifacts include writing utensils, then the ruins are remnants of a trading center built by the Heratians. The artifacts must include either armaments or writing utensils.

Which of the following can be deduced from the statements above?

(A) The Etonians built only fortresses while the Heratians built only trading centers.

(B) The remnants of any fortress built by the Etonians would include armaments among the artifacts.

(C) The remnants of any trading center built by the Heratians would not include armaments among the artifacts.

(D) If the artifacts do not include writing utensils, then the ruins are remnants of a fortress built by the Etonians.

(E) If the artifacts do not include armaments, then the ruins are remnants of a fortress built by someone other than the Etonians.

20. In determining what organisms may morally be used for food, vegetarians are often guided by the principle of "capacity for suffering." If the organism has the capacity for suffering, then it is not morally acceptable to use it for food. Given this rule of thumb, plants are acceptable because they lack even the rudiments of a central nervous system.

The reasoning above depends on which of the following assumptions?

(A) All animals, even the most primitive, have a central nervous system.

(B) Only organisms with a central nervous system have the capacity for suffering.

(C) Primitive animals such as mollusks lack a functioning central nervous system.

(D) Any organism with a central nervous system has the capacity for suffering.

(E) Only organisms that have the capacity for suffering should not be eaten.

21. In the earliest stages of the common law, a party could have a case heard by a judge only upon the payment of a fee to the court and then only if the case fit within one of the forms for which there existed a writ. At first, the number of such formalized cases of action was very small, but judges invented new forms that brought more cases and greater revenues.

Which of the following conclusions is most strongly suggested by the paragraph above?

(A) Early judges often decided cases in an arbitrary and haphazard manner.

(B) In most early cases, the plaintiff rather than the defendant prevailed.

(C) The judiciary at first had greater power than either the legislature or the executive.

(D) One of the motivating forces for the early expansion in judicial power was economic considerations.

(E) The first common law decisions were inconsistent with one another and did not form a coherent body of law.

22. If Martin introduces an amendment to Evans' bill, then Johnson and Lloyd will both vote the same way. If Evans speaks against Lloyd's position, Johnson will defend anyone voting with him. Martin will introduce an amendment to Evans' bill only if Evans speaks against Johnson's position.

If the above statements are true, each of the following can be true EXCEPT

(A) if Evans speaks against Johnson's position, Lloyd will not vote with Johnson.

(B) if Martin introduces an amendment to Evans' bill, then Evans has spoken against Johnson's position.

(C) if Evans speaks against Johnson's position, Martin will not introduce an amendment to Evans' bill.

(D) if Martin introduces an amendment to Evans' bill, then either Johnson will not vote with Lloyd or Evans did not speak against Johnson's position.

(E) if either Evans did not speak against Lloyd's position or Martin did not introduce an amendment to Evans' bill, then either Johnson did not defend Lloyd or Martin spoke against Johnson's position.

23. Once at a conference on the philosophy of language, a professor delivered a lengthy and tiresome address, the central thesis of which was that "yes" and related slang words such as "yeah" can be used only to show agreement with a proposition. At the end of the paper, a listener in the back of the auditorium stood up and shouted in a sarcastic voice, "Oh, yeah?" This constituted a complete refutation of the paper.

The listener argued against the paper by

(A) offering a counterexample.

(B) pointing out an inconsistency.

(C) presenting an analogy.

(D) attacking the speaker's character.

(E) citing additional evidence.

24. If military aid to Latin American countries is to be stopped because it creates instability in the region, then all foreign aid must be stopped.

Which of the following is most like the argument above in its logical structure?

(A) If a war in Central America is to be condemned because all killing is immoral, then all war must be condemned.

(B) If charitable donations are obligatory for those who are rich, then it is certain that the poor will be provided for.

(C) If the fascist government in Chile is to be overthrown because it violates the rights of the people, then all government must be overthrown.

(D) If a proposed weapons system is to be rejected because there are insufficient funds to pay for it, then the system must be purchased when the funds are available.

(E) If a sociological theory is widely accepted but later proven wrong by facts, then a new theory should be proposed that takes account of the additional data.

STOP

END OF SECTION 3. IF YOU HAVE ANY TIME LEFT, GO OVER YOUR WORK IN THIS SECTION ONLY. DO NOT WORK IN ANY OTHER SECTION OF THE TEST.

SECTION 4

28 Questions • 35 Minutes

Directions: Below each of the following passages, you will find questions or incomplete statements about the passage. Each statement or question is followed by lettered words or expressions. Select the word or expression that most satisfactorily completes each statement or answers each question in accordance with the meaning of the passage. After you have chosen the *best* answer, blacken the corresponding space on the answer sheet.

Desertification in the arid United States is flagrant. Groundwater supplies beneath vast stretches of land are dropping precipitously. Whole river systems
(5) have dried up; others are choked with sediment washed from denuded land. Hundreds of thousands of acres of previously irrigated cropland have been abandoned to wind or weeds. Several million
(10) acres of natural grassland are eroding at unnaturally high rates as a result of cultivation or overgrazing. All told, about 225 million acres of land are undergoing severe desertification.
(15)   Federal subsidies encourage the exploitation of arid land resources. Low-interest loans for irrigation and other water delivery systems encourage farmers, industry, and municipalities
(20) to mine groundwater. Federal disaster relief and commodity programs encourage arid-land farmers to plow up natural grassland to plant crops such as wheat and, especially, cotton. Federal
(25) grazing fees that are well below the free market price encourage overgrazing of the commons. The market, too, provides powerful incentives to exploit arid land resources beyond their carrying
(30) capacity. When commodity prices are high relative to the farmer's or rancher's operating costs, the return on a production-enhancing investment is invariably greater than the return on a
(35) conservation investment. And when commodity prices are relatively low, arid land ranchers and farmers often have to use all their available financial resources to stay solvent.
(40)   The incentives to exploit arid land resources are greater today than ever. The government is now offering huge new subsidies to produce synfuel from coal or oil shale as well as alcohol fuel
(45) from crops. Moreover, commodity prices are on the rise; and they will provide farmers and agribusiness with powerful incentives to overexploit arid land resources. The existing federal govern-
(50) ment cost-share programs designed to help finance the conservation of soil, water, and vegetation pale in comparison to such incentives.
    In the final analysis, when viewed
(55) in the national perspective, the effects on agriculture are the most troublesome aspect of desertification in the United States. For it comes at a time when we are losing over a million acres of
(60) rain-watered crop and pasture land per year to "higher uses"—shopping centers, industrial parks, housing developments, and waste dumps—heedless of the economic need of the United States
(65) to export agricultural products or of the world's need for U.S. food and fiber. Today the arid West accounts for 20 percent of the nation's total agricultural output. If the United States is, as it
(70) appears, well on its way toward overdrawing the arid land resources, then the policy choice is simply to pay now for the appropriate remedies or pay for more later, when productive benefits from arid
(75) land resources have been both realized and largely terminated.

1. The author is primarily concerned with

   (A) discussing a solution.

   (B) describing a problem.

   (C) replying to a detractor.

   (D) finding a contradiction.

   (E) defining a term.

2. The passage mentions all of the following as effects of desertification EXCEPT

   (A) increased sediment in rivers.

   (B) erosion of land.

   (C) overcultivation of arid land.

   (D) decreasing groundwater supplies.

   (E) loss of land to wind or weeds.

3. The author most likely encloses the phrase "higher uses" (line 61) in quotation marks in order to

   (A) alert the reader to the fact that the term is very important.

   (B) minimize the importance of desertification in non-arid land.

   (C) voice support for expansion of such programs.

   (D) express concern over the extent of desertification.

   (E) indicate disagreement that such uses are more important.

4. The passages mentions all of the following as economic factors tending to contribute to desertification EXCEPT

   (A) price incentives for farmers to use arid lands to produce certain commodities.

   (B) artifically low government fees for use of public grazing lands.

   (C) government subsidies for fuels that are manufactured from a variety of crops.

   (D) worldwide demand for the food and fiber produced in the United States.

   (E) lack of effective government financial incentives to conserve soil, water, and vegetation.

5. According to the passage, the most serious long-term effect of desertification would be the reduced ability of

   (A) the United States to continue to export agricultural products.

   (B) municipalities to supply water to meet the needs of residents.

   (C) farmers to cover their expenses.

   (D) the United States to meet the food needs of its own people.

   (E) the United States to produce sufficient fuel for energy from domestic sources.

6. The passage leads most logically to discussion of a proposal for

   (A) reduced agricultural output in the United States.

   (B) direct government aid to farmers affected by desertification.

   (C) curtailing the conversion of land to shopping centers and housing.

   (D) government assistance to develop improved farming methods to increase exploitation of arid land.

   (E) increased government assistance to finance the conservation of arid land.

7. The author's attitude toward desertification can best be described as one of

   (A) alarm.

   (B) optimism.

   (C) understanding.

   (D) conciliation.

   (E) concern.

The need for solar electricity is clear. It is safe, ecologically sound, efficient, continuously available, and it has no moving parts. The basic problem with the

(5) use of solar photovoltaic devices is economics, but until recently very little progress had been made toward the development of low-cost photovoltaic devices. The larger part of research funds

(10) has been devoted to the study of

single-crystal silicon solar cells, despite
the evidence, including that of the leading manufacturers of crystalline silicon,
that this technique holds little promise.
(15) The reason for this pattern is understandable and historical. Crystalline silicon is the active element in the very
successful semiconductor industry, and
virtually all of the solid state devices
(20) contain silicon transistors and diodes.
Crystalline silicon, however, is particularly unsuitable to terrestrial solar cells.
Crystalline silicon solar cells work
well and are successfully used in the
(25) space program, where cost is not an
issue. While single crystal silicon has
been proven in extraterrestrial use with
efficiencies as high as 18 percent, and
other more expensive and scarce mate-
(30) rials such as gallium arsenide can have
even higher efficiencies, costs must be
reduced by a factor of more than 100 to
make them practical for commercial uses.
Beside the fact that the starting crystal-
(35) line silicon is expensive, 95 percent of it
is wasted and does not appear in the
final device. Recently, there have been
some imaginative attempts to make polycrystalline and ribbon silicon that are
(40) lower in cost than high-quality single
crystals; but to date the efficiencies of
these apparently lower-cost arrays have
been unacceptably small. Moreover,
these materials are cheaper only be-
(45) cause of the introduction of disordering
in crystalline semiconductors, and disorder degrades the efficiency of crystalline solar cells.
This dilemma can be avoided by
(50) preparing completely disordered or
amorphous materials. Amorphous materials have disordered atomic structure as compared to crystalline materials: that is, they have only short-range
(55) order rather than the long-range period-
icity of crystals. The advantages of amorphous solar cells are impressive.
Whereas crystals can be grown as wafers about four inches in diameter, amor-
(60) phous materials can be grown over large
areas in a single process. Whereas crystalline silicon must be made 200 mi-

crons thick to absorb a sufficient amount
of sunlight for efficient energy conver-
(65) sion, only 1 micron of the proper amorphous materials is necessary. Crystalline silicon solar cells cost in excess of
$100 per square foot, but amorphous
films can be created at a cost of about
(70) 50¢ per square foot.
Although many scientists were
aware of the very low cost of amorphous
solar cells, they felt that they could never
be manufactured with the efficiencies
(75) necessary to contribute significantly to
the demand for electric power. This was
based on a misconception about the feature that determines efficiency. For example, it is not the conductivity of the
(80) material in the dark which is relevant,
but only the photoconductivity, that is,
the conductivity in the presence of sunlight. Already, solar cells with efficiencies well above 6 percent have been
(85) developed using amorphous materials,
and further research will doubtless find
even less costly amorphous materials
with higher efficiencies.

8. The author is primarily concerned with

(A) discussing the importance of solar energy.

(B) explaining the functioning of solar cells.

(C) presenting a history of research on energy sources.

(D) describing a possible solution to the problem of the cost of photovoltaic cells.

(E) advocating increased government funding for research on alternative energy sources.

9. According to the passage, which of the following encouraged use of silicon solar cells in the space program?

   (A) Plentiful supplies of materials such as gallium arsenide
   (B) Difficulties encountered in laboratory experiments with ribbon silicon
   (C) Low cost of silicon cells compared with ones made of other materials
   (D) Relatively high efficiency of extraterrestrial silicon solar cells
   (E) Highly disordered atomic structure of the materials used in the cells

10. The author mentions recent attempts to make polycrystalline and ribbon silicon (lines 38–43) primarily in order to

   (A) minimize the importance of recent improvements in silicon solar cells.
   (B) demonstrate the superiority of amorphous materials over crystalline silicon.
   (C) explain why silicon solar cells have been the center of research.
   (D) contrast crystalline silicon with polycrystalline and ribbon silicon.
   (E) inform the reader that an alternative type of solar cell exists.

11. Which of the following pairs of terms does the author regard as most nearly synonymous?

   (A) Solar and extraterrestrial
   (B) Photovoltaic devices and solar cells
   (C) Crystalline silicon and amorphous materials
   (D) Amorphous materials and higher efficiencies
   (E) Wafers and crystals

12. The material in the passage could best be used in an argument for

   (A) discontinuing the space program.
   (B) increased funding for research on amorphous materials.
   (C) further study of the history of silicon crystals.
   (D) increased reliance on solar energy.
   (E) training more scientists to study energy problems.

13. All of the following are mentioned in the passage as advantages of amorphous materials over silicon cells EXCEPT

   (A) the minimal trade-off required between cost of production and efficiency.
   (B) the relative thinness of amorphous materials needed for acceptable efficiency.
   (C) the cost per unit area of manufacturing amorphous materials.
   (D) the possibility of manufacturing large wafers in a single process.
   (E) the historical commitment of the semiconductor industry to a particular material.

14. The tone of the passage can best be described as

   (A) analytical and optimistic.
   (B) biased and unprofessional.
   (C) critical and discouraged.
   (D) tentative and inconclusive.
   (E) concerned and conciliatory.

According to legend, Aesculapius bore two daughters, Panacea and Hyegeia, who gave rise to dynasties of healers and hygienists. The schism remains today,
(5) in clinical training and in practice; and because of the imperative nature of medical care and the subtlety of health care, the former has tended to dominate. Preventive medicine has as its primary ob-
(10) jective the maintenance and promotion

of health. It accomplishes this by controlling or manipulating environmental factors that affect health and disease. For example, in some areas presently *(15)* there is serious suffering and substantial economic loss because of the failure to introduce controlled fluoridation of public water supplies. In addition, preventive medicine applies prophylactic *(20)* measures against disease by such actions as immunization and specific nutritional measures. Third, it attempts to motivate people to adopt healthful lifestyles through education.

(25) For the most part, curative medicine has as its primary objective the removal of disease from the patient. It provides diagnostic techniques to identify the presence and nature of the *(30)* disease process. While these may be applied on a mass basis in an attempt to "screen" out persons with preclinical disease, they are usually applied after the patient appears with a complaint. *(35)* Second, it applies treatment to the sick patient. In every case, this is, or should be, individualized according to the particular need of each patient. Third, it utilizes rehabilitation methodologies to *(40)* return the treated patient to the best possible level of functioning.

While it is true that both preventive medicine and curative medicine require cadres of similarly trained *(45)* personnel such as planners, administrators, and educators, the underlying delivery systems depend upon quite distinctive professional personnel. The requirements for curative medicine call *(50)* for clinically trained individuals who deal with patients on a one-to-one basis and whose training is based primarily on an understanding of the biological, pathological, and psychological processes *(55)* that determine an individual's health and disease status. The locus for this training is the laboratory and clinic. Preventive medicine, on the other hand, calls for a very broad spectrum of professional *(60)* sional personnel, few of whom require clinical expertise. Since their actions apply either to environmental situations

or to population groups, their training takes place in a different type of laboratory *(65)* tory or in a community not necessarily associated with the clinical locus.

The economic differences between preventive medicine and curative medicine have been extensively discussed, *(70)* perhaps most convincingly by Winslow in the monograph *The Cost of Sickness and the Price of Health*. Sickness is almost always a negative, nonproductive, and harmful state. All resources expended *(75)* pended to deal with sickness are, therefore, fundamentally economically unproductive. Health, on the other hand, has a very high value in our culture. To the extent that healthy members of the *(80)* population are replaced by sick members, the economy is doubly burdened. Nevertheless, the per capita cost of preventive measures for specific diseases is generally far lower than the per capita *(85)* cost of curative medicine applied to treatment of the same disease. Prominent examples are dental caries, poliomyelitis, and phenylketonuria.

There is an imperative need to provide *(90)* vide care for the sick person within a single medical care system, but there is no overriding reason why a linkage is necessary between the two components of a health-care system, prevention and *(95)* treatment. A national health and medical care program composed of semi-autonomous systems for personal health care and medical care would have the advantage of clarifying objectives and *(100)* strategies and of permitting a more equitable division of resources between prevention and cure.

15. The author is primarily concerned to

(A) refute a counterargument.

(B) draw a distinction.

(C) discuss a dilemma.

(D) isolate causes.

(E) describe new research.

16. Which of the following points about the nature of medical practice is NOT made by the author?

   (A) Curative medicine is aimed primarily at people who are already ill, while preventive medicine is aimed at healthy people.

   (B) Curative medicine is focused on an individual patient, while preventive medicine is applied to larger populations.

   (C) The per capita cost of curative medicine is generally much higher than the per capita cost of preventive medicine.

   (D) Both preventive care and curative care trace origins to classical legend and the dynasties of hygienists and healers.

   (E) Because of the urgency involved in treating disease, curative medicine is logically prior to preventive care.

17. It can be inferred that the author regards a program of controlled fluoridation of public water supplies as

   (A) an unnecessary government program that wastes economic resources.

   (B) a potentially valuable strategy of preventive medicine.

   (C) a government policy that has relatively little effect on the health of a population.

   (D) an important element of curative medicine.

   (E) an experimental program, the health value of which has not been proved.

18. Which of the following best explains the author's use of the phrase "doubly burdened" (line 81)?

   (A) A person who is ill not only does not contribute to production, but medical treatment consumes economic resources.

   (B) The per capita cost of preventive measures is only one half of the per capita cost of treatment.

   (C) The division between preventive medicine and curative medicine requires duplication of administrative expenses.

   (D) The individual who is ill must be rehabilitated after the cure has been successful.

   (E) The person who is ill uses economic resources that could be used to finance prevention rather than treatment programs.

19. It can be inferred that the author regards Winslow's monograph (lines 70–73) as

   (A) ill conceived.

   (B) incomplete.

   (C) authoritative.

   (D) well organized.

   (E) highly original.

20. The author cites dental caries, poliomyelitis, and phenylketonuria in order to prove that

   (A) some diseases can be treated by preventive medicine.

   (B) some diseases have serious consequences if not treated.

   (C) preventive medicine need not be linked to treatment.

   (D) the cost of preventing some diseases is less than the cost for treatment.

   (E) less money is allocated to prevention of some diseases than to treating them.

21. The main reason the author advocates separating authority for preventive medicine from that for curative medicine is

(A) the urgency of treatment encourages administrators to devote more resources to treatment than to prevention.

(B) the cost of treating a disease is often much greater than the cost of programs to prevent the disease.

(C) the professionals who administer preventive health-care programs must be more highly trained than ordinary doctors.

(D) curative medicine deals primarily with individuals who are ill, while preventive medicine is applied to healthy people.

(E) preventive medicine is a relatively recent development, while curative medicine has a long history.

From the time they were first proposed, the 1962 Amendments to the Food, Drug and Cosmetic Act have been the subject of controversy among some elements of
(5) the health community and the pharmaceutical industry. The Amendments added a new requirement for Food and Drug Administration approval of any new drug: The drug must be demon-
(10) strated to be effective by substantial evidence consisting of adequate and well-controlled investigations. To meet this effectiveness requirement, a pharmaceutical company must spend consid-
(15) erable time and effort in clinical research before it can market a new product in the United States. Only then can it begin to recoup its investment. Critics of the requirement argue that the added
(20) expense of the research to establish effectiveness is reflected in higher drug costs, decreased profits, or both, and that this has resulted in a "drug lag."

The term "drug lag" has been used
(25) in several different ways. It has been argued that the research required to prove effectiveness creates a lag between the time when a drug could theoretically

be marketed without proving effective-
(30) ness and the time when it is actually marketed. "Drug lag" has also been used to refer to the difference between the number of new drugs introduced annually before 1962 and the number of new
(35) drugs introduced each year after that date. It is also argued that the Amendments resulted in a lag between the time when the new drugs are available in other countries and the time when the
(40) same drugs are available in the United States. And "drug lag" has also been used to refer to a difference in the number of new drugs introduced per year in other advanced nations and the number
(45) introduced in the same year in the United States.

Some critics have used "drug lag" arguments in an attempt to prove that the 1962 Amendments have actually
(50) reduced the quality of health care in the United States and that, on balance, they have done more harm than good. These critics recommend that the effectiveness requirements be drastically modi-
(55) fied or even scrapped. Most of the specific claims of the "drug lag" theoreticians, however, have been refuted. The drop in new drugs approved annually, for example, began at least as early as
(60) 1959, perhaps five years before the new law was fully effective. In most instances, when a new drug was available in a foreign country but not in the United States, other effective drugs for the con-
(65) dition were available in the country and sometimes not available in the foreign country used for comparison. Further, although the number of new chemical entities introduced annually dropped
(70) from more than 50 in 1959 to about 12 to 18 in the 1960s and 1970s, the number of these that can be termed important— some of them of "breakthrough" caliber—has remained reasonably close
(75) to 5 or 6 per year. Few, if any, specific examples have actually been offered to show how the effectiveness requirements have done significant harm to the health of Americans. The require-
(80) ment does ensure that a patient ex-

posed to a drug has the likelihood of benefiting from it, an assessment that is most important, considering the possibility, always present, that adverse
(85) effects will be discovered later.

22. The author is primarily concerned with

  (A) outlining a proposal.

  (B) evaluating studies.

  (C) posing a question.

  (D) countering arguments.

  (E) discussing a law.

23. The passage states that the phrase "drug lag" has been used to refer to all of the following situations EXCEPT

  (A) a lag between the time when a new drug becomes available in a foreign country and its availability in the United States.

  (B) the time period between which a new drug would be marketed if no effectiveness research were required and the time it is actually marketed.

  (C) the increased cost of drugs to the consumer and the decreased profit margins of the pharmaceutical industry.

  (D) the difference between the number of drugs introduced annually before 1962 and the number introduced after 1962.

  (E) the difference between the number of new drugs introduced in a foreign country and the number introduced in the United States.

24. The author would most likely agree with which of the following statements?

  (A) Whatever "drug lag" may exist because of the 1962 Amendments is justified by the benefit of effectiveness studies.

  (B) The 1962 Amendments have been beneficial in detecting adverse effects of new drugs before they are released on the market.

  (C) Because of the requirement of effectiveness studies, drug consumers in the United States pay higher prices than consumers in foreign countries.

  (D) The United States should limit the number of new drugs that can be introduced into this country from foreign countries.

  (E) Effectiveness studies do not require a significant investment of time or money on the part of the pharmaceutical industry.

25. The author points out the drop in new drugs approved annually before 1959 in order to

  (A) draw an analogy between two situations.

  (B) suggest an alternative causal explanation.

  (C) attack the credibility of an opponent.

  (D) justify the introduction of statistics.

  (E) show an opponent misquoted statistics.

26. The author implies that the non-availability of a drug in the United States and its availability in a foreign country is not necessarily proof of a drug lag because this comparison fails to take into account

    (A) the number of new drugs introduced annually before 1959.

    (B) the amount of research done on the effectiveness of drugs in the United States.

    (C) the possible availability of another drug to treat the same condition.

    (D) the seriousness of possible unwanted side effects from untested drugs.

    (E) the length of time needed to accumulate effectiveness research.

27. The author attempts to respond to the claim that the number of new chemical entities introduced annually since the Amendments has dropped by

    (A) denying that the total number of new chemical entities has actually dropped.

    (B) analyzing the economic factors responsible for the drop.

    (C) refining terminology to distinguish important from non-important chemical entities.

    (D) proposing that further studies be done to determine the effectiveness of new chemical entities.

    (E) listing the myriad uses to which each new chemical entity can be put.

28. The comparisons made by proponents of the "drug lag" theory between the availability of drugs in foreign countries and their availability in the United States logically depend upon which of the following presuppositions?

    (A) The Food and Drug Administration is less efficient than its governmental counterparts in other countries around the world.

    (B) On balance, more important new drug therapies are developed in other countries than in the United States.

    (C) New drugs in foreign countries are subject to a more rigorous testing requirement than new drugs in the United States.

    (D) The pharmaceutical industry in the foreign country is roughly as sophisticated as that in the United States.

    (E) The pharmaceutical industry in the foreign country is more profitable than that of the United States.

STOP

END OF SECTION 4. IF YOU HAVE ANY TIME LEFT, GO OVER YOUR WORK IN THIS SECTION ONLY. DO NOT WORK IN ANY OTHER SECTION OF THE TEST.

SECTION 5

25 Questions • 35 Minutes

> **Directions.** Below each of the following passages, you will find questions or incomplete statements about the passage. Each statement or question is followed by lettered words or expressions. Select the word or expression that most satisfactorily completes each statement or answers each question in accordance with the meaning of the passage. After you have chosen the *best* answer, blacken the corresponding space on the answer sheet.

1. Senator Allen has admitted to having an illicit affair and lying to her husband about it. Although the affair ended several years ago and Allen and her husband are now reconciled, this episode should disqualify Allen from seeking higher office. How could world leaders be expected to negotiate with a president who has admitted lying to her spouse?

   Which of the following assumptions underlies the argument above?

   (A) A president who has committed adultery might be subject to blackmail or other pressures.

   (B) Many voters would not vote for Allen because she admitted to having an affair.

   (C) The personal life of a political leader may affect that leader's ability to make correct decisions.

   (D) A person who would tell an untruth in a personal situation is likely to tell a lie in public.

   (E) A public leader has an extraordinary obligation to set an example of high moral standards.

Questions 2 and 3

   (A) The safety of the new drug Zorapan has yet to be clearly demonstrated. Only one study of its effects has been conducted, and the results were inconclusive.

   (B) George is unlikely to make a good class president. He is hot-tempered and extremely critical of all those around him.

   (C) Mayor Warren favors the new zoning law for one reason only: Her husband is a building contractor who stands to profit from the increased construction the law will encourage.

   (D) It's almost impossible to get good repair service nowadays. I brought my camera to the local camera shop for repair, and it still doesn't work properly.

   (E) Helen probably got her interest in medicine from her family. Both of her parents, as well as two of her uncles, are physicians.

2. Which of the arguments above is a generalization that could be criticized because it is based upon a limited sampling?

3. Which of the arguments above attempts to discredit an opponent rather than attack the merits of a position?

4. Conservatives often boast of the freedoms that U.S. citizens enjoy, yet how much freedom do they really have? Housing, medical care, and other basic needs are increasingly costly, and no one is guaranteed a job. It is the people living in socialist nations who enjoy true freedom since they are free from the fear that the constant threat of poverty brings.

The persuasive force of the argument above depends largely upon the ambiguous use of which of the following pairs of terms?

(A) Basic needs and job

(B) Poverty and fear

(C) Free and freedom

(D) Guarantee and poverty

(E) Spokespeople and people

5. French painting during the first half of the nineteenth century was characterized by a lack of imagination. The Ecole des Beaux Arts, the quasi-governmental agency that controlled the dissemination of lucrative government scholarships and commissions, effectively stifled creativity. A student who hoped to achieve any fame or financial success was well advised to paint in the style of the Ecole. It is a small wonder then that the Impressionist painters initially earned only the scorn of their colleagues and empty bellies for their efforts.

The passage above implies that

(A) Impressionist painters did not paint in the style of the Ecole des Beaux Arts.

(B) the Impressionist painters eventually gained control of the Ecole des Beaux Arts.

(C) the Ecole des Beaux Arts promulgated rules defining the permissible subject matter of paintings.

(D) the Ecole des Beaux Arts determined licensing standards for those who wanted to become professional artists.

(E) French painting during the second half of the nineteenth century was less creative than during the first half of the nineteenth century.

6. TEACHER: Some students have received passing marks on the test, but you were not one of them.

STUDENT: I sure hate to tell my parents that I failed a test.

TEACHER: That is not yet necessary.

Which of the following, if true, best explains the teacher's second remark?

(A) The student should lie to the parents about the mark.

(B) One low test mark will not result in a failing mark for the course.

(C) The student should wait for an opportune time to tell the parents.

(D) The teacher has not finished grading the test papers.

(E) The student will have to take other exams before the course is over.

7. Most arguments in favor of legalizing marijuana focus attention on the lack of evidence of harmful effects of the drug. The purpose of such contentions is to neutralize the negative effect of arguments supporting prohibition because of a supposed correlation between the use of marijuana and violent antisocial behavior. Thus far, the burden of constructive argumentation has been borne by the doctrine of individual rights. "Liberty" has been the rallying cry of those who favor legalization. No serious proponent of legislative change has yet advanced the obvious proposition that the sale of marijuana should be legal because smoking marijuana is pleasurable.

The author of the paragraph implies that

(A) smoking marijuana can, in some cases, lead to criminal behavior.

(B) the sale of marijuana is illegal because the smoking of marijuana is pleasurable.

(C) the fact that an activity is pleasurable is a reason for allowing people to engage in it.

(D) advocates of the legalization of marijuana are not really concerned about individual liberty.

(E) opponents of the legalization of marijuana deny that smoking marijuana is a pleasurable activity.

8. DAVID: Every painting by Kissandra should be displayed in the National Art Museum.

   MARAT: I disagree. I have seen some very fine works by Electra and Bluesina that should be displayed in the Museum.

   Marat's response indicates that he has understood David to mean that

   (A) paintings by Electra and Bluesina should be displayed in the Museum.

   (B) only Kissandra's paintings should be displayed in the Museum.

   (C) every painting by Kissandra should be displayed in the Museum.

   (D) not every Kissandra painting should be displayed in the Museum.

   (E) Kissandra's paintings should only be displayed in the Museum.

Questions 9 and 10

Paul is older than Sally.

Sally is older than Fred.

Mike is older than Paul.

Ralph is younger than Mike but older than Fred.

9. If the statements above are true, which of the following must also be true?

   (A) Ralph is the oldest.

   (B) Paul is the second oldest.

   (C) Sally is the youngest.

   (D) Fred is the youngest.

   (E) Ralph is older than Paul.

10. If a sixth person, Chuck, is younger than Ralph, all of the following could be true EXCEPT

    (A) Chuck is younger than Sally.

    (B) Chuck is older than Sally.

    (C) Fred is younger than Chuck.

    (D) Chuck is younger than Fred.

    (E) Mike is younger than Chuck.

11. CHARLOTTE: I don't see any good reason for lending you the money you want.

    CATHY: By your own admission, there is a good reason for lending me the money—even though you can't see it. Therefore, you should lend me the money.

    The exchange above is characterized by

    (A) a hasty generalization.

    (B) the ambiguous use of language.

    (C) an attack on someone's character.

    (D) a reliance on authority.

    (E) circular reasoning.

12. The earliest vaccines used whole dead viruses or weakened live ones to stimulate the body's immune system. Unfortunately, in a small number of cases, the vaccines caused very serious allergic reactions and in some cases even the disease itself. Vaccines being developed today are much safer because they use only a specific subunit of the viral protein chain.

    Which of the following conclusions is best supported by the paragraph above?

    (A) The body's immune system responds to a particular part of a virus rather than the virus as a whole.

    (B) The body's immune system is more likely to react to a whole dead virus than a part of a live one.

    (C) Reactions to weakened live viruses are more predictable than reactions to whole dead viruses.

    (D) A vaccine manufactured from a subunit of a virus is more likely to trigger than to prevent a disease.

    (E) The body reacts to a subpart of a virus in the same way it reacts to the virus as a whole.

13. AURORA: Tony, who just bought a new Hugo Hatchback, test drove both the Hugo Hatchback and a Ouigo Hatchback. Standard equipment on the Hugo includes factory air conditioning. So Tony must have bought the Hugo because air conditioning comes as standard equipment on the Hugo.

ANTHONY: But Tony bought an entire car —not just an air conditioner. He might very well have bought the Hugo even if it were not equipped with air conditioning.

Which of the following, if true, would be the most effective attack on Anthony's conclusion?

(A) The Ouigo, which does not offer air conditioning as an option, is otherwise almost identical to the Hugo.

(B) The Ouigo, which does not offer air conditioning, is markedly inferior to the Hugo.

(C) The Ouigo, which does not offer air conditioning, is markedly superior to the Hugo.

(D) The Ouigo is imported from abroad, while the Hugo is manufactured by a foreign firm in this country.

(E) Both the Hugo and the Ouigo offer power steering and power brakes as standard equipment.

14. Ethical vegetarians argue that it is wrong to rank humans above other animal species. But what then is the rationale for ranking any animal species above plants? If a human being is on a par with a lobster, then perhaps a lobster is on a par with a spear of broccoli. So a spear of broccoli is really the equal of a human being. Why not try to protect vegetables against the animals that would eat them? Maybe we should stop eating altogether to protest the brutal rule of nature that requires living things to eat other living things in order to stay alive.

The speaker above argues primarily by

(A) accusing ethical vegetarians of being insincere in their convictions.

(B) suggesting that the argument for ethical vegetarianism leads to absurd conclusions.

(C) citing scientific evidence that contradicts the claim of the ethical vegetarian.

(D) calling on commonly accepted opinions regarding ethical vegetarianism.

(E) attempting to reconcile two seemingly inconsistent ethical positions.

15. Recently there has been a surge in the number of births per year in the United States, and many fear that a new baby boom is under way that will strain our social institutions just as the baby boom of the middle of this century did. These fears, however, are unfounded. The recent rise in births is attributable to the fact that the original baby boomers are now potential parents.

Which of the following is an unstated assumption of the argument above?

(A) Baby boomers who become parents begin their families at the same age as their parents did.

(B) The average number of children per family in the United States will decrease drastically.

(C) Baby boomers who are now becoming mothers are having babies at a much lower rate than their mothers.

(D) A third baby boom will occur thirty years after this one is over.

(E) Any increase in the population of the United States above current levels is undesirable.

16. U.S. chemical manufacturers currently export numerous chemicals used in agriculture that are banned here. Now Congress wants to prevent the companies from exporting chemicals. Yet, foreign governments are willing to allow the continued use of the chemicals and may have very good reasons for doing so. It seems to me wrong for the government of this country to substitute its judgment for that of another country about what is best for its citizenry. Therefore, the proposed ban should be voted down.

Which of the following, if true, would most WEAKEN the argument above?

(A) The chemicals that are the subject of the proposed ban greatly enhance agricultural productivity.

(B) The chemicals that are the subject of the proposed ban contaminate produce that is imported into the United States.

(C) The chemicals that are the subject of the proposed ban account for a very small part of the sales of the chemical companies that would be affected.

(D) The U.S. chemical companies that would be affected by the ban are the only ones with the technology to produce the chemicals that would be banned.

(E) Some foreign governments already prohibit the importation and the use of the chemicals that would be the subject of the ban.

17. Yes, it is true that a regular jar of Fulghum's Instant Coffee costs 50 percent more than a regular jar of the leading brand of instant coffee, but Fulghum's is still cheaper to use.

Which of the following, if true, best explains the seeming contradiction in the statement above?

(A) More than twice as many people use the leading brand of instant coffee as use Fulghum's.

(B) A regular jar of Fulghum's instant coffee will make twice as many cups as a regular jar of the leading brand.

(C) The regular jar of Fulghum's and the regular jar of the leading brand both contain 8 ounces of instant coffee.

(D) Both Fulghum's and the leading brand used to charge the same price for a regular jar, but the leading brand reduced its price by one third.

(E) In a taste survey using coffee prepared according to the instructions on the label of each brand's jar, coffee drinkers were unable to distinguish one brand from the other.

18. All employees who will be promoted by the company will receive higher salaries. Some of the employees who will be promoted by the company are highly skilled, others are merely competent, and still others are bunglers.

If the statements above are true, which of the following statements must also be true?

(A) Some of those who are promoted by the company do not receive higher salaries.

(B) Some of those who are not promoted by the company receive higher salaries.

(C) Both highly skilled employees and bunglers will receive higher salaries.

(D) All employees who receive higher salaries will be given promotions.

(E) No employee who receives a higher salary is a bungler.

19. It is often thought that crime in large metropolitan areas is much worse now than ever before. In fact, other periods of history have been far more violent. In his police history, James Richardson reports that in New York City between 1814 and 1834, the number of complaints at the police courts quadrupled while the population of the city little more than doubled. This increase in crime during a short period is simply unimaginable today.

The argument above depends upon all of the following assumptions EXCEPT

(A) a useful measure of the prevalence of violence in a society is the number of reported crimes.

(B) the experience of New York City with crime was representative of metropolitan areas of the time.

(C) the crimes that were committed between 1814 and 1834 were more serious than those committed today.

(D) the statistics used and reported by Richardson accurately describe the situation in New York City.

(E) the number of crimes that are reported can be expected to rise with an increase in population.

20. A country-western song tells of a man trying to impress a woman he has just met. After telling her a lot about himself, he finally says, "I want you so badly I would lie to you. And that's the truth."

Which of the following conclusions about the man in the song can be most reliably drawn?

(A) He is definitely lying.

(B) He is definitely telling the truth.

(C) He might or might not be telling the truth.

(D) He is contradicting himself.

(E) It is logically impossible to make such a statement.

21. There are at least three spies at a diplomatic reception. At least one spy knows the true identity of every other spy at the reception. At most, two spies know each other's true identities.

Which of the following is inconsistent with the information provided above?

(A) Four spies are at the reception.

(B) No spies at the reception know each other's true identities.

(C) Exactly one spy at the reception knows the true identities of every other spy at the reception.

(D) The true identity of one spy at the reception is known by every other spy at the reception.

(E) If a spy knows the true identity of another spy, that second spy in turn knows the true identity of the first.

22. A member of the University Council, who asked not to be identified, confirmed last week that without the support of the head of the faculty union, the proposed budget cuts would be defeated. Since the budget cuts were approved by the University Council, the head of the union must have supported the budget cut proposal.

The logic of which of the following is most similar to the logic of the argument above?

(A) The mechanic told us to replace the ignition module before we left for our vacation trip. Now the car won't start, so the ignition module must have gone bad.

(B) The medical book states that a high fever and chills are symptoms associated with severe sun poisoning. The patient, however, has not recently been exposed to the sun, so she cannot have a high fever or chills.

(C) The rules enacted by the Board of Bar Examiners state that a person cannot practice law in this state without first having passed the bar examination. Claudia is a licensed attorney in this state. Therefore, Claudia must have passed the bar examination.

(D) According to the rules of the American Kennel Club, a show dog cannot be declared a champion until it has accumulated 15 points at various shows. My 3-year-old Akita has already won 12 points, so he will probably become a champion.

(E) According to the company's work rules, a worker who is absent more than twelve days during a year can be terminated. Since Peter was fired last week, he must have been absent more than twelve days last year.

23. Chrysler Corporation's advertising campaigns often appeal to the chauvinism of American buyers. In the mid-1980s, it appealed explicitly to patriotic feelings with its "Born in the U.S.A." campaign. More recently, Chrysler calls its cars the "Americans that beat the Hondas." But when it came time for Chrysler to buy metal stamping presses, it bought Japanese models rather than American models. In addition, for years, Chrysler has sold under its own brand name a significant number of cars and trucks made in Japan by Mitsubishi.

The primary purpose of the speaker above is to

(A) prove that Chrysler cars are really not better than Japanese-made cars.

(B) suggest that Chrysler sever its ties with Japanese manufacturers.

(C) cast doubt on the credibility of the Chrysler corporation.

(D) encourage people to buy Japanese cars rather than Chrysler cars.

(E) discourage consumers from purchasing Japanese products in lieu of American products.

24. There is no theoretical objection to enforcing all verbal agreements. In practice, however, certain agreements—such as those for the conveyance of land and those for the sale of goods, the value of which exceeds a certain dollar amount—must be in writing to be enforceable. When a judge refuses to rule in favor of a plaintiff in a suit brought on a contract that must be in writing but is not, the judge does not deny the existence of a contract. Rather, the court refuses to recognize the agreement, if any, because it was not properly formalized.

The argument above is primarily concerned with the distinction between

(A) a court and a judge.

(B) plaintiffs and defendants.

(C) buyers and sellers.

(D) an agreement and the written record of the agreement.

(E) a contract for the sale of land and a contract for the sale of goods.

25. ALAN: The economy is definitely not entering a recession. Last month, according to the Bureau of Labor Statistics, the number of persons drawing unemployment benefits declined by 0.1 percent.

DICK: That just proves how bad the down turn really is. Virtually all of those who stopped drawing benefits did so because they had exhausted their benefits.

The speakers

(A) accept the accuracy of the government's report and reach similar conclusions.

(B) accept the accuracy of the government's report but interpret it differently.

(C) question the accuracy of the government's report and interpret it differently.

(D) question the accuracy of the government's report and reach different conclusions.

(E) disagree over the accuracy of the government's report and reach different conclusions.

STOP

END OF SECTION 5. IF YOU HAVE ANY TIME LEFT, GO OVER YOUR WORK IN THIS SECTION ONLY. DO NOT WORK IN ANY OTHER SECTION OF THE TEST.

WRITING SAMPLE

Time—30 Minutes

The Board of Trustees of State University has recently received an anonymous gift to the university in the amount of $100,000 for the construction of a memorial dedicated to students and graduates of the university who lost their lives in the service of their country. The board is considering proposals by Ann Gerson and Phil Maxwell. Write an argument in favor of one of the two proposals. The following criteria should be taken into consideration:

1 The $100,000 must be spent on a memorial, but the board would like the memorial to have some additional function.

2 The board wants a memorial that will assist students in understanding and appreciating the sacrifice made by others.

ANN GERSON is an artist with a substantial national reputation but no particular ties to the university. Many of her sculptures, such as the Plaza Fountain she designed for the Federal Government Center, combine function and art. Ann proposes to build an "oasis" in the center of the campus: a fountain surrounded by greenery and marble benches. The center of the fountain will be a shrouded figure sculpted from stone that is intended to symbolize death, and on the containing wall of the fountain will be engraved the names of university students and graduates who died and the dates and places of their deaths.

PHIL MAXWELL, a graduate of State University, is a local architect who paints and sculpts as a hobby. Several of Phil's paintings are on display in the university museum in the special wing devoted to student alumni work. In addition, Phil teaches a course in the History of Architecture in the university's continuing education division. Phil proposes a simple memorial, a wall on which will be inscribed the names of the students and graduates who died, the dates of their actual or intended graduation, and brief personal notes to be supplied by relatives such as major area of study, career plans, or outside interests. Phil has designed the wall so that it can be the outside wall of the main entrance of the new student union now being planned for the university.

ANSWER KEY AND EXPLANATIONS

Section 1

1.	A	7.	A	13.	C	19.	E	25.	D
2.	B	8.	C	14.	D	20.	A	26.	E
3.	B	9.	B	15.	A	21.	B	27.	A
4.	A	10.	A	16.	D	22.	E	28.	E
5.	D	11.	E	17.	B	23.	B		
6.	B	12.	D	18.	C	24.	D		

Section 2

1.	C	6.	E	11.	D	16.	A	21.	A
2.	C	7.	A	12.	A	17.	D	22.	C
3.	A	8.	E	13.	C	18.	B	23.	A
4.	E	9.	E	14.	B	19.	C	24.	B
5.	A	10.	D	15.	C	20.	D		

Section 3

1.	C	6.	B	11.	B	16.	C	21.	D
2.	E	7.	C	12.	A	17.	E	22.	D
3.	B	8.	B	13.	B	18.	B	23.	A
4.	E	9.	D	14.	B	19.	D	24.	C
5.	D	10.	E	15.	A	20.	B		

Section 4

1.	B	7.	E	13.	E	19.	C	25.	B
2.	C	8.	D	14.	A	20.	D	26.	C
3.	E	9.	D	15.	B	21.	A	27.	C
4.	D	10.	A	16.	E	22.	D	28.	D
5.	A	11.	B	17.	B	23.	C		
6.	E	12.	B	18.	A	24.	A		

Section 5

1.	D	6.	D	11.	B	16.	B	21.	E
2.	D	7.	C	12.	A	17.	B	22.	C
3.	C	8.	B	13.	A	18.	C	23.	C
4.	C	9.	D	14.	B	19.	C	24.	D
5.	A	10.	E	15.	C	20.	C	25.	B

Section 1

1. **The correct answer is (A).** This is an implied idea question. The author draws an analogy between a political fable and a caricature because the political fable emphasizes certain points over others; it paints with a very broad brush, dealing in types rather than characters. Similarly, a caricature emphasizes certain personal characteristics over others. Thus, this is the analogy: society:political fable::person:caricature.

2. **The correct answer is (B).** This is a main idea question of the variation "pick the best title." The author begins by announcing that *Nineteen Eighty-Four* is not a novel in the strict sense of that term but really a political fable. Choice (B) echoes the author's statement of his own purpose. Choice (A) is incorrect because it is too narrow. The author barely mentions in passing some of the characters in the book. Choice (C) also is too narrow. Although it is true that the author does state that one of the characteristics of a political fable is that characters are defined in relation to their society, that is but one of many points made in the selection. Choice (D) suffers from the same defect. There are several other points made by the author in the passage. In addition, choice (D) is in a sense too broad, for the author takes as the focus for his discussion the particular work *Nineteen Eighty-Four*—not political fables in general. Finally, choice (E) suffers from both of the ills that afflict choice (D). Choice (E) is both too narrow because the distinction between novel and political fable is but one part of the discussion and too broad because it fails to acknowledge that the author has chosen to focus on a particular work.

3. **The correct answer is (B).** This is a logical detail question. Why does the author mention this characteristic of Winston Smith? The answer to this question doesn't become clear until you have read the entire selection. One important feature of a political fable is that characters are reduced to mere types. They don't have the idiosyncrasies that they would have in a novel. The function of that part of the first sentence which begins, "a requirement not refuted. . . ." is to preempt an objection to this claim: Winston Smith is described in some detail. So the author mentions this to let the audience know that he is aware that Winston Smith is described in some detail and to insist that this makes no difference to his argument. Given this analysis, choice (A) must be incorrect. Small details like an ulcer would not be characteristic of a type but of an individual. Choice (C) simply represents a confused reading of that section of the passage. The author implies there that Winston Smith is the main character of the work. As for choices (D) and (E), though these echo some of the ideas developed in the selection, they are not responsive to the question.

4. **The correct answer is (A).** The tension the author describes is between the political sense of a political fable (the political element which must be conveyed by talking about individual people in their social situation) and the sense of fable (which must rely on type). The passage then states that the author faces a difficult task. If he errs on the side of the political sense, the value of the work as a fable is lost; if he errs on the side of the fable, the reader can't identify with the situation described. This dilemma is de-

scribed by choice (A). Choice (B) does refer to ideas mentioned in the text, but choice (B) is not responsive to the question. Choice (C) describes a "tension" that might exist in other situations, but this is not the situation the author describes. Choice (D) is contradicted by our analysis above, for the danger is that the reader won't find the situation realistic enough. Finally, though choice (E) does echo the idea of "tension," this is not the kind of tension the author is discussing.

5. **The correct answer is (D).** This is an author's attitude question. The tone of the passage is neutral. The author makes neither positive nor negative comments about the particular work, *Nineteen Eighty-Four.* So the best description is scholarly.

6. **The correct answer is (B).** This specific detail question asks that you show an understanding of the meaning of a particular part of the selection. Our analysis above will help us here. The dilemma faced by the political fabulist is the danger of too much versus too little detail. In discussing this dilemma, the author says that too little detail will leave the reader without a sense of connection to life. The author continues to say that this is particularly true if the writer projects his narrative into the future. Then the reader may conclude that the situation described by the fable is completely alien to him— just a foreign country with strange customs, meaning that he can't understand why anyone does anything so their actions are really not connected with his. Choice (B) summarizes this idea. Choice (A) is incorrect because the author does not mean that the action literally takes place in another country but that the reader feels no connection with the situation. As for choice (C), it is the lack of

detail (e.g., interacting characters) that creates the problem mentioned in this reference. Choice (D) finds no support in the passage; and, indeed, the political fabulist is actually presenting his own political vision. Finally, as for choice (E), it is the lack of detail, not the overabundance of detail, that creates the "foreign country" problem.

7. **The correct answer is (A).** This is a logical structure question that asks about the overall development of the selection. As we have seen, the author is concerned with discussing the elements of a political fable, and this development is described by choice (A). Choices (B) and (C) are incorrect because the author doesn't mention a logical inconsistency or a cause-and-effect connection. As for choice (D), to the extent that the author does introduce examples (the characters of the book), this is not the main concern of the selection. Finally, though the selection discusses a political fable that projects its situation into the future, the author doesn't introduce any proposals for future action himself.

8. **The correct answer is (C).** This is obviously a main idea question. The author discusses three important characteristics of art of the Middle Ages—the sacred script, the sacred mathematics, and sacred symbolic language. At the close of his remarks, the author mentions in passing the Renaissance, primarily as a way of praising the art of the Middle Ages. Choice (C) does a fair job of describing this development. Choice (A) can be eliminated because the discussion focuses upon the art of the Middle Ages, not upon the art preceding the Middle Ages. And to the extent that the author does mention what might be called influences, e.g., the revival of certain views of Pythagoras,

this is done in passing. They do not constitute the focus of the passage. Choice (D) is incorrect for the same sort of reason. The reference in closing to the art of the Renaissance cannot be considered the overall theme of the passage. Finally, choices (B) and (E) are incorrect because the author never takes on the "why."

9. **The correct answer is (B).** This is an inference question. In essence, the question is asking which of the five features listed was most likely to be found in a painting. Choice (E) can be eliminated since that is inconsistent with the concept of the artist who recedes into the background of the sacred rules. As for choice (A), the author's only example of numbers was their use in music. This does not lead us to conclude that numbers might not be important in painting as well, but we cannot conclude, on the other hand, that every painting was likely to use the numbers 3 and 4. Choices (C) and (D) are mentioned as characteristics of certain subjects. But the author does not imply that the subjects were treated in every painting. Choice (B), however, has the specific support of paragraph 3. There the author states that "Every painting is an allegory." So, though the specific content of paintings of the period would vary from work to work, the overarching idea of a literal and hidden meaning pervaded the work of the period.

10. **The correct answer is (A).** The tone of the passage is clearly one of appreciation—both in the sense that the author understands and in the sense that the author admires. This is further supported by the contrast between art of the Middle Ages and religious art of the Renaissance at the end of the passage. Choice (B) overstates the case. The author is only discussing the one period,

with only casual reference to the period following it. We cannot conclude from the fact that the author discusses art of the Middle Ages in this text that the author considers this art the greatest of all art. Choice (C) cannot be deduced from the passage: the reference to music will not support such a judgment. Choice (D) is inconsistent with the author's opening and closing remarks. Finally, choice (E) too must be incorrect given the general approving treatment of the passage.

11. **The correct answer is (E).** This is a question about a logical detail: Why does the author quote Saint Augustine? At that point, the author has just asserted that the art of the Middle Ages also is characterized by a passion for numbers. Then the author quotes a statement from Augustine that makes that very point. The reason for the quotation must be to give an example of the general attitude toward numbers. Choice (E) describes this move. Choice (A) is incorrect since no objection is mentioned. Choice (B) is incorrect for the same reason and for the further reason that "ridicule" is inconsistent with the tone of the passage. Choice (C) is incorrect because the author is not attempting to demonstrate the similarities between two things. Finally, choice (D) is incorrect since it does not appear that the author is in any danger of falling into a contradiction.

12. **The correct answer is (D).** This is an explicit idea question. Each of the incorrect answers is mentioned in paragraph 1 as an element of the sacred script. As for choice (A), lines may be used to represent water or the sky. As for choice (B), these indicate sainthood or divinity. As for choice (C), shoes are mentioned as an identifying characteristic. And choice (E) also is mentioned (a tree represents

earth). Choice (D), however, is not mentioned as an element of the sacred script. Symmetry is discussed in conjunction with numbers, and that has to do with another characteristic altogether.

13. **The correct answer is (C).** This is an application question. Of course, we do not know where the passage actually appeared, and the task is to pick the most likely source. We stress this because it is always possible to make an argument for any of the answer choices to a question of this sort. But the fact that a justification is possible does not make that choice correct; the strongest possible justification makes the choice correct. Choice (C) is the most likely source. The passage focuses on art and is scholarly in tone. Choice (A) can be eliminated, for the passage casts no light on social conditions of the period. Choice (B) can be eliminated for a similar reason. The author treats art in and of itself—not as a social force. And we certainly cannot conclude that by discussing religious art, the author wants to discuss the church. Choice (D) is incorrect because the reference to Saint Augustine is incidental and illustrative only. Choice (E) is incorrect because it is inconsistent with the scholarly and objective tone of the passage.

14. **The correct answer is (D).** This is an inferred idea question, one asking for an interpretation of a phrase. The idea of the first paragraph is that the rules of art in the Middle Ages placed constraints on the artist so that the artistic effort had to be made within certain conventions. As a result, painting was not individualistic. This is most clearly expressed by choice (D). Choice (A) is incorrect since the author is saying that the artist's talent just did not show as individual talent. Choice

(B) is incorrect, for though this is a true statement, it is not a response to the question. Choice (C) is perhaps the second-best answer because it at least hints at what choice (D) says more clearly. But the author does not mean to say the artist was not recognized while still alive. That may or may not have been the case. What the author means to say is that we do not now see the personality of the artist. Finally, choice (E) is just a confused reading of a part of the passage not relevant here.

15. **The correct answer is (A).** This is an application. As we have noted before, application questions tend to be difficult because the correct answer can be understood as correct only in context. With an explicit idea question, for example, an answer can be understood as right or wrong—either the author said it or did not. With a question such as this, the *most logical continuation* depends upon the choices available. Here the best answer is choice (A). The author concludes the discussion of the causes of our poor showing on the health status index by asserting that the best way to improve this showing is a general improvement in the quality of life. This is an intriguing suggestion and an appropriate follow-up would be a list of proposals that might accomplish this. As for choice (B), this could be part of such a discussion, but a listing of the most common causes of death would not, in and of itself, represent an extension of the development of the argument. Choice (C), too, has some merit. The author might want to talk about the causes of poverty as a way of learning how to improve the quality of life by eliminating the causes. But this argument actually cuts in favor of choice (A), for the justification for choice (C)

then depends on choice (A)—that is, it depends on the assumption that the author should discuss the idea raised in choice (A). Choice (D) is incorrect because the author specifically states in the closing remarks that redistribution of medical resources is not a high priority. Choice (E) can be eliminated on the same ground.

16. **The correct answer is (D).** This is an explicit idea question, and we find mention of choices (A), (B), (C), and (E) in the second paragraph. Choice (D), too, is mentioned, but it is not a factor "affecting the health of the population." It is a measure of, or an effect of, the health of the population, not a factor causing it.

17. **The correct answer is (B).** This is a main idea question. Choice (A) can be eliminated because the author actually minimizes the importance of medical care as a factor affecting the health of a population. Choice (C) can be eliminated because this is not the author's objective. To be sure, the information supplied in the passage might be used by a person to live more healthfully, but that is not why the author wrote the passage. Choice (D) is incorrect because this is a small part of the argument, a part that is used to advance the major objective outlined in choice (B). Finally, choice (E) is incorrect since the author leaves us with a pregnant suggestion but no specific recommendations. Choice (B), however, describes the development of the passage. The author wishes to explain the causes of the poor health status of the U.S. It is not, the author argues, lack of medical care or even poor distribution of medical care, hypotheses that, we can infer from the text, are often proposed. The author then goes on to give two alternative explanations: affluence and poverty.

18. **The correct answer is (C).** This is an application question. Choice (C) is strongly supported by the text. In paragraph 3, the author specifically states that we have the highest per capita expenditure for medical care in the world. Yet, as noted in the first paragraph, we rank rather low in terms of health. Choice (A) is not supported by the arguments given in the passage. Though medical care may not be the most important determinant of health, the author never suggests that expenditure is not correlated with overall availability. Choice (B) is incorrect and specifically contradicted by the second paragraph, where the author states that genetic problems may be covered over by medical care. Choice (D) is incorrect since the author minimizes the importance of technology in improving health. Finally, choice (E) is simply not supported by any data or argument given in the passage.

19. **The correct answer is (E).** This is a logical detail question. The author refers to excess consumption to illustrate the way in which affluence, one of his two hypotheses, could undermine an individual's health. As for choice (A), while it is true that such problems may not be susceptible to medical treatment, the author does not introduce them to prove that. They are introduced at the particular point in the argument to prove that affluence can undermine health. Choice (B) is incorrect for a similar reason. The author does not introduce the examples to prove that drinking and smoking are unhealthful activities. The passage presupposes readers know that already. Then, on the assumption that the reader already believes that, the author can say, "See, affluence causes smoking and drinking—which we all

know to be bad." Choice (C) must fail for the same reason. Finally, choice (D) is incorrect since this is not the reason for introducing the examples. Although it is argued that medical care and health are not as tightly linked as some people might think, this is not the point the author is working on when the examples of smoking and drinking are introduced. With a logical detail question of this sort, we must be careful to select an answer that explains why the author makes a certain move at the particular juncture in the argument. Neither general reference to the overall idea of the passage (e.g., to prove the main point) nor a reference to a collateral argument will do the trick.

20. **The correct answer is (A).** The answer to the question posed in choice (A) is explicitly provided in the second paragraph: environment. As for choice (B), though some information is given about the health status of the U.S., no other country is mentioned by name. As for choice (C), though some statistics are given about life expectancies in the U.S., no comparison of male and female life expectancies is given. As for choice (D), though genetic factors are mentioned generally in paragraph 2, no such factors are ever specified. Finally, the author offers no recommendations, so choice (E) must be incorrect.

21. **The correct answer is (B).** This is an inferred idea based on a specific reference. In the second paragraph, the author lists four groups of factors that influence health. In referring to medical services, the author says they are treated separately from environmental factors because of our special interest in them. This implies that the author would actually consider them to be just another,

although important, factor in the environment. As for choice (A), the least important group of factors is specifically stated to be genetic factors. As for choice (C), there is no support for such a conclusion in that paragraph. The same reason allows us to eliminate both choices (D) and (E).

22. **The correct answer is (E).** This is an explicit idea question. The answer can be found in the first paragraph, where the author notes that a heart attack is unlike an angina attack because the heart attack always involves the death of heart muscle. As for choice (A), although a heart attack may involve acceleration of the heartbeat, this is not what distinguishes it from angina. Choice (B) is incorrect since the author describes the way in which nitroglycerin may be used to treat heart attack. Choice (C) is incorrect both because this is not a statement that can be justified by the text (generally?) and because it is not the defining characteristic of a heart attack. Finally, choice (D) is incorrect, for though the heart attack involves rapid muscle death, it is the death of tissue and not the length of time of the attack that is the distinguishing feature.

23. **The correct answer is (B).** This, too, is an explicit idea question, but it is more difficult than the preceding question. The author cites the "curious" result that the nitroglycerin helped the most seriously stricken patients but did not help the less seriously stricken patients. The author explains that in the more seriously stricken patients, the ordinary autonomic response to a drop in blood pressure, which would be a faster heart rate, did not occur. Apparently, the congestive heart failure effectively blocked this reaction. Consequently, the drop in

blood pressure caused by the nitroglycerin did not invite the normal increase in heart rate. This explanation is presented by choice (B). Choice (A) is incorrect since no mention is made of any delay in administering drugs. Choice (C) is incorrect since phenylephrine was not available to the 12 patients at the time of the study. Phenylephrine was later used to counter the drop in blood pressure caused by nitroglycerin. Choice (D) is incorrect since the passage states that blood pressure did drop in those patients with congestive heart failure. The difference between those patients and the less seriously stricken ones was that the drop in blood pressure did not cause an increase in heart rate. For the same reason, choice (E) must also be eliminated.

24. **The correct answer is (D).** This is an explicit idea question. As for choice (A), several results of heart attack are mentioned at various points in the text. The answer to the question in choice (B) is explicitly provided in the third paragraph. As for choice (C), the author mentions the effect of nitroglycerin at various points; that is, it dilates blood vessels and reduces blood pressure. Finally, the question in choice (E) is answered in the second paragraph. Choice (D), however, is not answered in the passage. Though the author discusses the effects of heart attack, the passage does not discuss the causes of heart attack.

25. **The correct answer is (D).** The answer to this inference question can be found in the final paragraph. There the author states that research is being done on drugs that affect myocardial oxygen supply and demand "including . . . vessel dilators such as nitroglycerin . . ." From this, we can infer that nitroglycerin dilates blood vessels and this somehow

affects the oxygen balance in the heart muscle. This is the value of the drug. Choice (A) is incorrect because the lowering of blood pressure is an unwanted side effect of nitroglycerin, not its medical value. Choice (B) is incorrect since the value of nitroglycerin is to prevent damage, not to aid in healing. Choice (C) is incorrect for the same reason that choice (A) is incorrect. Finally, choice (E) is incorrect because nitroglycerin is mentioned as a vessel dilator in the final paragraph, not a drug that counters hypertension.

26. **The correct answer is (E).** This is a tone question. The author's attitude is best studied in the final paragraph. Having described the possibility of treating heart attack with nitroglycerin, the author adds the disclaimer that there is no proof yet of the value of the treatment in very serious cases. From this, we may infer, however, that the author believes it has some value in less serious cases. Moreover, since the passage refers to research being done, the author apparently believes that the treatment may prove to have value in other cases as well. This attitude is best described as one of optimism. Since the passage has, on balance, a positive tone, we can eliminate choices (B), (C), and (D). As for choice (A), though the author may be concerned about the treatment of heart attacks, the overall tone of the discussion is not concern or worry but rather hope or optimism.

27. **The correct answer is (A).** This is an inference question, the answer to which is found in the second paragraph. There it is stated that phenylephrine is used to maintain blood pressure: but that simple statement is not enough to answer the question. We must dig deeper. Why is it

important to maintain blood pressure? The final sentence of the paragraph states that a drop in blood pressure causes the heart to speed up. It is this increase in heart rate that "worsens the damage." So the value of phenylephrine is that it prevents cardiac acceleration by maintaining blood pressure. This is the explanation given in choice (A). As for choices (B) and (C), these answers make essentially the same statement using language drawn from different parts of the passage. But they describe something other than the effect of phenylephrine. Choice (D) is incorrect since the phenylephrine has a particular use that complements nitroglycerin. Although the effect of both drugs taken together may be something like that described in choice (D), this is not an answer to the question asked. Finally, choice (E) is just language taken from the first paragraph and is not an answer to the question asked.

28. **The correct answer is (E).** This is a main idea question. The best way of describing the development of the passage is given in choice (E). The author is discussing a treatment for heart attack. As for choice (A), the only suggestion of a predicament is contained in paragraph 1: Nitroglycerin has beneficial effects, but it also lowers blood pressure. But once that has been stated, the author proceeds to explain how the dilemma has been resolved. So the passage, if anything, explains not a predicament but how a predicament has been solved. As for choice (B), though the author does evaluate the results of a study, that evaluation is incidental to the larger goals of describing a treatment. As for choice (C), though we, the readers, may see implicit in the treatment some sort of

proposal, it cannot be said that the author's intention is to outline a proposal. Finally, choice (D) is the least effective choice since there is no argument presented.

Section 2

Questions 1–6

Here we have a linear ordering problem involving ten individuals. Since the number of individuals is so large, we will probably do better to sketch a diagram for each problem; after all, the diagram is nothing more than a series of positions numbered 1 through 10. We should also summarize the particular restrictions placed on each color pennant:

2 Green, 2 Blue, 3 Red, 3 Yellow

$G = G$ (Greens are next to each other.)

$B \neq B$ (Blues are not next to each other.)

$R = R = R$ (Reds are next to each other.)

B/R = ends (Blue at one end; red at the other.)

1. **The correct answer is (C).** We begin by entering the additional information:

1	2	3	4	5	6	7	8	9	10
				G	G			R	

And since the red pennants are together and one of the pennants on the end is red and the other blue, we know:

1	2	3	4	5	6	7	8	9	10
B			G	G			R	R	R

The only condition remaining to be observed is to separate the blue pennants. This means the remaining blue pennant can be placed in positions 3, 6, and 7 and that yellow pennants will fill the remaining places. Now we turn to the answer choices. Choices (A), (B), (D), and (E) are all incorrect since the other blue pennant can occupy positions 3 or 6 or 7 though precisely which is not determined. In any event, no matter which position the remaining blue pennant occupies, position 2 will be occupied by a yellow pennant, so both blue pennants will be next to yellow pennants.

2. **The correct answer is (C).** We enter the additional information on a diagram:

1	2	3	4	5	6	7	8	9	10
						B	Y		

Then, since the red pennants are together, with one on one end and a blue pennant on the other end, we deduce:

1	2	3	4	5	6	7	8	9	10
R	R	R				B	Y		B

We now must place two yellow and two green pennants; since the green pennants must go next to each other, they must occupy positions 4 and 5, or 5 and 6:

1	2	3	4	5	6	7	8	9	10
R	R	R	G	G	Y	B	Y		B

or

R	R	R	Y	G	G	B	Y		B

We can see from the diagram that position 5 is necessarily occupied by a green pennant.

3. **The correct answer is (A).** We begin by entering the additional information on a diagram:

1	2	3	4	5	6	7	8	9	10
B	G	G	B	Y	Y	Y	R	R	R

or

R	R	R	Y	Y	Y	B	G	G	B

There are only two possible arrangements given all of the restrictions. Since the question stem stipulates that the blue pennants are next to green pennants, we know those four pennants form a bloc, *BGGB*, at one end or the other. Further, at the opposite end will be the bloc *RRR*, which means that the yellow

pennants will be adjacent to each other. It is not determined from the information at which end the blue pennants will be and at which end the red pennants will be. But we can see that under either scenario, both the fifth and sixth positions are occupied by yellow pennants.

4. **The correct answer is (E).** We begin by entering the additional information on a diagram:

1	2	3	4	5	6	7	8	9	10
								Y	

So, we deduce

1	2	3	4	5	6	7	8	9	10
R	R	R				Y	Y	Y	B

for we know that the three red pennants are in a row at one end or the other and that a blue pennant occupies the other end. The only pennants left to place are the two green pennants, which must be next to each other, and the remaining blue pennant:

1	2	3	4	5	6	7	8	9	10
R	R	R	G	G	B	Y	Y	Y	B

or

R	R	R	B	G	G	Y	Y	Y	B

Then we look to the answer choices. We can see that choices (A), (B), and (D) are false. Further, choice (C) is only possibly true. Under either scenario, however, choice (E) is necessarily true.

5. **The correct answer is (A).** We enter the additional information on a diagram:

1	2	3	4	5	6	7	8	9	10
		Y		Y					

So we know:

1	2	3	4	5	6	7	8	9	10
B		Y		Y			R	R	R

given the restrictions on the red pennants and the end pennants. Now we may also deduce:

1	2	3	4	5	6	7	8	9	10
B	Y	Y	B	Y	G	G	R	R	R

because position 2 may not be blue and position 6 and 7 must be green. Now we can see that choices (B), (C), (D), and (E) are necessarily true and that choice (A) is necessarily false.

6. **The correct answer is (E).** Given the restriction that one end pennant is blue and that at the other end we have three red pennants, we can deduce the following since the question stem stipulates that one green pennant is next to a blue pennant and the other next to a red pennant:

	1	2	3	4	5	6	7	8	9	10
	R	R	R	G	G	B	Y	Y	Y	B
or	B	Y	Y	Y	B	G	G	R	R	R

So there are only two possible arrangements given the stipulation of the question stem. We can see that choices (A) and (B) are possibly, though not necessarily, true. Choice (D) is impossible. Choice (E) is, as the diagram proves, necessarily true.

Questions 7–12

This set is an ordering set with a twist: There are two main orders, depending on whether J is tasted third or seventh. We begin then with the following:

	1	2	3	4	5	6	7
			J				
or							J

Then we enter the second condition:

	1	2	3	4	5	6	7
			J	(~N)			
or			N				J

Then comes the third condition:

	1	2	3	4	5	6	7
			J	(~N)			
or		N				L	J

And the fourth condition:

	1	2	3	4	5	6	7
			J	(~N)			
					O		
or		N				L	J

and finally:

	1	2	3	4	5	6	7
	(~K)		J	(~N)	O		
or		K		N		L	J

7. **The correct answer is (A).** L can only be tasted fourth if we use the upper order. In that case, it will be J that is tasted third.

8. **The correct answer is (E).** For M to follow L, we cannot use the lower arrangement, for there L is already scheduled as the sixth wine followed immediately by J. We must therefore use the upper arrangement. The key to the solution is to see that there is a further conclusion to be drawn about the scheduling of K and N. Our original diagram shows positions 1 and 4, 2 and 5, and 4 and 7 as open and available for the K --- N schedule. A closer look shows that we can eliminate the 1–4 arrangement, because N cannot be the fourth wine tasted in that sequence. So K and N are either 2 and 5, or 4 and 7, respectively. If, however, M must be tasted immediately following the tasting of L, then K cannot be in position 2. Only if K and N are in positions 4 and 7 can we put L and M together in sequence. So the entire sequence is:

1	2	3	4	5	6	7
L	M	J	K	P	O	N

The only position left for *P* is fifth, and choice (E) is necessarily true. The other choices are necessarily false.

9. **The correct answer is (E).** *M* is under no particular restriction with regard to another wine, so *M* can be inserted in any open position. Positions 1, 2, and 4 are open under the first order. Positions 2, 3, and 5 are open under the second order. So depending on when *J* is tasted, *M* could be tasted second, third, fourth, or fifth. *M* cannot be tasted sixth, however, since either *O* or *L* is tasted sixth (depending on when *J* is tasted).

10. **The correct answer is (D).** This question must be answered on the basis of the information provided in the initial set of conditions. In spite of the fact that these conditions leave considerable flexibility in the scheduling of wines, it is necessarily true that *K* will be tasted earlier than *O*. In the second possible order, *K* is tasted first and necessarily ahead of every other wine. In the first order, *K* must be tasted either second or fourth (so that *N* can follow as the third wine after *K*). So choice (D) is the correct answer. Choice (A) is incorrect because *K* could be tasted second under the first arrangement. Choice (B) is incorrect since the second arrangement places *L* before *J*. Choice (C) is incorrect since *K* could follow *L* under the first arrangement. Finally, choice (E) is incorrect since *M* is under no restriction and could be tasted in every position except sixth (see explanation for question 9).

11. **The correct answer is (D).** In order for *P* to be tasted earlier than *N* and yet later than *O*, we must use the second possible sequence, placing *O* in the second tasting position and *P* in the third. This means that *M* will be tasted fifth:

1	2	3	4	5	6	7
K	O	P	N	M	L	J

Choice (D) is proved by the diagram to be true, while the other choices are shown by the diagram to be false.

12. **The correct answer is (A).** If *M* is to be the second wine after *P*, the first arrangement cannot be used. Under the first arrangement, *M* and *P* would have to be tasted second and fourth or fifth and seventh, but *K* must be second or fourth and *N* fifth or seventh. Under the second arrangement, one sequence is possible: *K, O, P, N, M, L, J*.

Questions 13–18

This is a selection set, and we begin by setting up the information in more usable form:

(1) $V \rightarrow R$

(2) $(R \& Q) \rightarrow \sim P$

(3) $(Q \& P) \rightarrow \sim T$

(4a) $P \rightarrow (S \vee U)$

(4b) $\sim (S \& U)$

(5a) $(S \vee T)$

(5b) $\sim (S \& T)$

The numbered statements (1) through (5b) correspond to the five conditions given in the set. We have broken the fourth and fifth conditions down into two statements because each of those conditions is actually two conditions. So (4a) corresponds to "If *P* is selected, then either *S* or *U* must be selected," and (4b) corresponds to "*S* and *U* cannot both be selected." (5) is treated in similar fashion.

13. **The correct answer is (C).** If neither *S* nor *U* is selected, then we know by (5a) that *T* is selected and by (4a) that *P* is not selected. Thus far we have eliminated *S* and *U* (by stipulation) and *P*, and we have selected *T*, which leaves *Q*, *R*, and *V* for consideration. Since *P* is not selected,

we may include both *R* and *Q* without violating (2). And having chosen *R*, we may include *V* without violating (1). So, on the assumption that neither *S* nor *U* is selected, the largest delegation would consist of *T*, *R*, *Q*, and *V*.

14. **The correct answer is (B).** If *V* is selected, then by (1), *R* must also be selected. Further, if *P* is selected, by (4a), either *S* or *U* must be selected. But we also have (5a), and either *S* or *T* must be selected. Since we have both (*S* or *U*) and (*S* or *T*), we will minimize the number selected if we choose *S* rather than *U* or *T*. So the smallest delegation that includes both *P* and *V* will also include *R* and *S*.

15. **The correct answer is (C).** If *P* is selected, then by (4a), either *S* or *U* must be selected. Since by (4b), we cannot choose both *S* and U, *S* cannot be selected. But we know by (5a) that either *S* or *T* must be chosen, so we must pick *T*. As for the incorrect answers, this reasoning eliminates choice (B) as definitely false. As for choice (A), we cannot choose *Q*, for to choose *Q* along with *P* would mean we could not select *T* [by (3)]. But we have already learned that we must choose *T* because *S* cannot be chosen. As for choices (D) and (E), it is possible to choose *R* or *V* and *R*: since *Q* cannot be selected [see rejection of choice (A)], this effectively isolates *R* and *V* from the other students by breaking the only connection with *R* and *V*, which is (2).

16. **The correct answer is (A).** *P*, *Q*, and *S* are a possible three-student delegation. Selecting *P* requires that we have either *S* or *U* (4a), and that condition is satisfied by including *S*. Having *P* and *Q* together means only that we may not have *T* (3), but that can be avoided if we choose *S* to satisfy (5a). As for choice (B), *P*, *Q*, and *T*

are not a possible delegation, since *Q* and *P* together require that *T* not be chosen, by (3). As for choice (C), *P*, *R*, and *V* are not acceptable because, by (5a), we must have either *S* or *T*. As for choice (D), *R*, *S*, and *T* are not permissible because this violates (5b). Finally, choice (E) is incorrect since the group *R*, *S*, and *U* violates (4b).

17. **The correct answer is (D).** If *P* is selected, then either *S* or *U* must also be selected, by (4a). But if *T* is chosen, then *S* cannot be chosen, by (5b), which means that *U* must be chosen. So it is not possible that *U* is not chosen. Then, since *T* and *P* are chosen, we cannot choose *Q*, by (3). *R* and/or *V* may be chosen, so the committee could consist of 3, 4, or 5 students.

18. **The correct answer is (B).** *P*, *R*, and *T* accompanied by *U* will satisfy all of the requirements. Choosing *T* satisfies (5a). Then, *P* and *U* together satisfy (4a). We do not have *S*, so both (4b) and (5b) are respected. And since we do not have *Q*, (2) and (3) are satisfied. Finally, without *V*, we have no problem with (1). As for choice (A), *P* and *Q* cannot accompany *T*; that is a violation of (3). As for choice (C), *V* must be accompanied by *R*, by (1); and choice (D) can be eliminated on the same ground. Finally, as for choice (E), *S* and *U* violates (4b).

Questions 19–24

For this ordering set, the order is so highly underdetermined that a single overall diagram is not likely to be of much assistance. Instead, for each problem, we will simply sketch the scale using dashes and numbers. To conserve space, we will render the scale horizontally

<u>1</u> <u>2</u> <u>3</u> <u>4</u> <u>5</u> <u>6</u> <u>7</u>

though a more intuitive approach would use a vertical arrangement

7

6

5

4

3

2

1

We know

$$L < M$$
$$N < J$$
$$J < K < M \text{ or } M < K < J$$

We can effectively ignore O and Q since they are placed in positions 1 and 7 and will not change.

19. **The correct answer is (C).** With N as the fifth note, we know that J, in order to be higher than N, must be the sixth note. Then, to keep M higher than L while keeping K between M and J, we must have the order

1	2	3	4	5	6	7
O	L	M	K	N	J	Q

which demonstrates that choice (C) is necessarily true, while each other choice is clearly false.

20. **The correct answer is (D).** If M is the sixth note, then J can be no higher than the fourth note, for K must come between J and M. Further, K could be no lower than the third since N must be below J. So we have the following:

1	2	3	4	5	6	7
O	N	J	K	L	M	Q

or

1	2	3	4	5	6	7
O	L	N	J	K	M	Q

These are not the only possible arrangements with M as note 6, but this does prove that J and N can be third and second, respectively, and fourth and third, respectively.

21. **The correct answer is (A).** For K and N to be separated by two notes, they must occupy positions 2 and 5 or 3 and 6. Ignoring the other restrictions we would have four possibilities:

1	2	3	4	5	6	7
O	N			K		Q
O		N			K	Q
O	K			N		Q
O		K			N	Q

The second and third possibilities are not permissible because K could not be between J and M. The fourth also can be eliminated since N must be lower than M. Only the first is possible, and this proves that K must be the fifth note on the scale. As for choice (B), though L might be between J and K:

1	2	3	4	5	6	7
O	N	J	L	K	M	Q

it is not necessarily true that L is between J and K:

1	2	3	4	5	6	7
O	N	L	J	K	M	Q

As for choice (C), we have just seen it is possible for M to be the sixth note, but that is not necessarily the case:

1	2	3	4	5	6	7
O	N	L	M	K	J	Q

As for choice (D), our diagrams show this is possibly, though not necessarily, the case. Similarly, choice (E) is incorrect since the diagrams show that L and M may or may not be separated by exactly one note.

22. **The correct answer is (C).** Since K must be between J and M, either J or M must be lower on the scale than K. In addition, some other note must be lower

than whichever note is lower than K; that is, if J is lower than K, then N is lower than K as well, and if M is lower than K, then L is lower than K as well. This means that K can be no lower than the fourth note. The other choices are possibilities:

Choices (A) and (E)	Choices (B) and (D)
1 2 3 4 5 6 7	1 2 3 4 5 6 7
O N L J K M Q	O N J K L M Q

23. **The correct answer is (A).** If N is separated by two notes from O, then N must be note 4; and we know J must be above N. Since K can be no lower than fourth, this means K must be note 5, and J note 6, leaving L and M as 2 and 3, respectively.

1 2 3 4 5 6 7
O L M N K J Q

The diagram confirms that choice (A) is necessarily true, while each of the other choices is necessarily false.

24. **The correct answer is (B).** If L and N are together, they must be notes 2 and 3, respectively, for both J and M must be higher than L and N, and K must be between J and M on the scale. This means that J, K, and M are notes 4, 5, and 6, though not necessarily in that order. So we have two possibilities:

1 2 3 4 5 6 7
O L N J K M Q
or O L N M K J Q

Section 3

1. **The correct answer is (C).** The point of the Chinese official's comment is that the Chinese may appear to some Westerners to be "inscrutable" because those Westerners simply do not pay very careful attention to what is directly before them. Thus, choice (C) is the best answer. Choice

(A) is misleading. The Chinese official refers to Occidentals in general, but he never mentions Orientals in general. Even so, choice (A) misses the main point of the anecdote. Choice (B) is better than choice (A) since it is at least generally related to the point of the Chinese official, but the precise point is not that Americans (rather than Occidentals) fail to understand Chinese culture but rather that they suffer from a more specific myopia: They find they are not able to penetrate the motivations of the Chinese. In any event, the point of the passage is not just that there is such a failure, but also that such failure is attributable to the lack of insight of Westerners—not any real inscrutability of the Chinese. Choice (E) mentions the problem of understanding, but the difficulty described in the passage is one way only. Nowhere is it suggested that the Chinese have difficulty in understanding Westerners. Finally, choice (D) would be correct only if the passage had contained some key word to qualify the official's response, such as *hesitatingly* or *cautiously*.

2. **The correct answer is (E).** Once it is seen that the passage is humorous, this question is fairly easy. The official "smiles," and he "gently" responds. Further, the scenario is set by the first sentence: a *junior* official *embarrassed* himself. This shows the situation is uncomfortable for the American, but it is not a serious international incident. And the Chinese official's response is kind—not angry, choice (A); not fearful, choice (B); and not indifferent, choice (D). Choice (C) requires an assumption of malice on the part of the Chinese official. By comparison, "compassion" better fits the description of the official's action—smiling and gentle.

3. **The correct answer is (B).** Here the problem is to make sense out of the brother's claim that a device he rarely used and may never use again is still a good investment. It is not land, a work of art, or some similar thing, so it does not appear as though it will appreciate in value. The advantage, then, of owning must come from merely being able to possess it. Thus, choice (B), which cites the convenience of having the item to use if and when he should decide to do so, is best. Choice (A) can be disregarded because the brother regards the investment as a good one *even if* he never again uses the device. To save money on ice cream, he would have to use it. Choice (C) is highly suggestive—is the brother saying that it is a good idea to have things around in case one needs them? If so, then choice (C) sounds a bit like choice (B). But choice (C) is not nearly so direct as choice (B), and it requires some work to make it into choice (B). Choice (D) is wrong because saving money by having purchased earlier would be worthwhile only if the item is actually needed. After all, a great deal you made by buying a ton of hay is not a great deal just because the price of hay is going up—you need an elephant (or a horse, or a plan to resell, or something) to make it worthwhile. Just buying hay because it's a "bargain" is no bargain at all. Choice (E) is fairly silly. It is like saying, "The bad news is you are to be executed tomorrow morning; the good news is you would have had liver for lunch." Or perhaps closer to this example would be, "The bad news is that someone stole your car; the good news is that the price of gasoline went up by 25¢ a gallon this morning." The point is that you will avoid some trivial injury or cost at the expense of something more serious.

4. **The correct answer is (E).** Again, the passage is somewhat lighthearted. The poet is saying that the poem is obscure: When he wrote it, only he and the Almighty could understand it, and now (it is so difficult) even he has forgotten the point of the verse. Choice (A) is somewhat attractive because the passage does state that God knows what people do not. Of course, once one understands the point of the passage, choice (A) can be discarded. Even so, there is something about choice (A) that lets you know it is wrong—"infinitely." One might infer from the poet's comments that people are not as wise as God, but it is not possible to conclude, on the basis of the one example, that God is infinitely wiser than people. Choice (B) is also attractive, for the poet is saying that it is difficult to understand this particular poem. But choice (B) is wrong because he is not saying that people cannot understand poetry in general. Choices (C) and (D) are distractions. They play on the term "God" in the paragraph. The poet cites God as the one who understands the verse—not the one who inspired it.

5. **The correct answer is (D).** Here we have one final humorous passage. Now this should not lead you to conclude that *many* LSAT paragraphs are amusing—to generalize to that conclusion on the basis of three examples would be a fallacy in and of itself—but taken individually, each is reflective of the LSAT. And even if the LSAT does not string together three or four in a row, we hope that you have found them diverting. After all, study for this test is not the most enjoyable pastime available to human beings. But back to the task at hand . . . . You must always be careful of naked correlations. Sufficient research would prob-

ably turn up some sort of correlation between the length of movies and the number of potatoes produced by Idaho, but such a correlation is obviously worthless. Here, too, the two numbers are completely unrelated to one another at any concrete cause-and-effect level. What joins them is the very general movement of the economy. The standard of living increases; so, too, does the average salary of a preacher, the number of vacations taken by factory workers, the consumption of beef, the number of color televisions, and the consumption of rum. Choice (D) correctly points out that these two are probably connected only this way. Choice (A) is incorrect for it is inconceivable that preachers, a small portion of the population, could account for so large an increase in rum consumption. Choice (B) is wildly implausible. Choice (C), however, is more likely. It strives for that level of generality of correlation achieved by choice (D). The difficulty with choice (C) is that it focuses upon *total* preachers, not the *average* preacher; and the passage correlated not *total* income for preachers with rum consumption but rather *average* income for preachers with consumption of rum. Choice (E) might be arguable if only one period had been used, but the paragraph cites three different times during which this correlation took place.

6. **The correct answer is (B).** This is a relatively easy question. The argument is similar to "All observed instances of S are P; therefore, all S must be P." (All swans I have seen are white; therefore, all swans must be white.) There is little to suggest the author is a mechanic or a factory worker in an automobile plant; therefore, choice (A) is incorrect—and would be so even if the author were an expert because the argument does not require expertise. A syllogism is a formal logical structure such as "All S are M; all M are P; therefore, all S are P," and the argument about automobiles does not fit this structure—so choice (C) is wrong. By the same token, choice (E) is wrong since the author generalizes. The author does not deduce, as by logic, anything. Finally, choice (D) is incorrect because the argument is not ambiguous, and one could hardly argue on the basis of ambiguity anyway, especially on the LSAT.

7. **The correct answer is (C).** The key phrase here—and the problem is really just a question of careful reading—is "who actually knew." This reveals that neither of the two knew the person whom they were discussing. There are many ways, however, of debating about the character of people with whom one is not directly acquainted. We often argue about the character of Napoleon or even fictional characters such as David Copperfield. When we do, we are arguing on the basis of indirect information. Perhaps we have read a biography of Napoleon, choice (A), or maybe we have seen a news film of Churchill, choice (B). We may have heard from a friend, or a friend of a friend, that so and so does such and such, choice (E). Finally, sometimes we just make more or less educated guesses, choice (D). At any event, the two people described in the paragraph could have done all of these things. What they could not have done—since they finally resolved the problem by finding someone who actually knew Churchill—was to have argued on the basis of their own personal knowledge.

8. **The correct answer is (B).** Here we have a question that asks us to draw a conclusion from a set of premises. The

author points out that the Constitution provides that the government may not take private property. The irony, according to the author, is that government itself defines what it will classify as private property. We might draw an analogy to a sharing practice among children: You divide the cake, and I will choose which piece I want. The idea behind this wisdom is that this ensures fairness to both parties. The author would say that the Constitution is set up so that the government not only divides (defines property), but it chooses (takes what and when it wants). Choice (A) is contradicted by this analysis. Choice (C) is wide of the mark since the author is discussing property rather than liberty. While the two notions are closely connected in the Constitution, this connection is beyond the scope of this argument. Choice (D) is also beyond the scope of the argument. It makes a broad and unqualified claim that is not supported by the text. Choice (E) is really vacuous and, to the extent that we try to give it content, it must fail for the same reason as choice (A).

9. **The correct answer is (D).** The insight required to solve this problem is that the apparent contradiction can be resolved by observing that the two cases are essentially different. The one is supposed to be a factual story; the other is a fictional account. Choice (B) misses the point of the problem: the task is to reconcile the seemingly conflicting positions of the critics, not to explain what role critics fill. Choices (A), (C), and (E) are possibilities. For example, you might argue any one of this points in defense of the journalist—but that's not what the question stem asks for. You're supposed to explain the seeming inconsistency in the position of the critics. And in the testing environment, to the extent that you want to argue that one or more of these choices might help to make an argument to support choice (D), then you'd have to choose choice (D) as the better answer just because it makes the point the most directly.

10. **The correct answer is (E).** The main point of the advertisement is that you should not hesitate to buy Cold Springs Water even though it is not imported. Choice (A) would weaken the appeal of the ad: if your guests can taste the difference, then the subterfuge (even though introduced only as a dramatic device) would not be effective. As for choice (B), while it may be true that even "naturally carbonated" waters are further carbonated at the time of bottling, this idea is not relevant. Choice (C) has some merit in the real world, but it is not an assumption of this speaker: why the imports are more costly is not relevant. And choice (D) is wrong because the subterfuge suggestion is not to be taken literally but only as a suggestion to make the point dramatically. Choice (E) is an assumption of the argument: status counts.

11. **The correct answer is (B).** Careful reading of the paragraph shows that the author's attitude toward parochial education is that insistence on instruction in religious values is *justifiable*; the author disagrees, however, on the question of how best to inculcate those values. The author believes that the proper attitude toward relations between the sexes could best be learned by children in the company of the other sex. Thus, choice (E) is diametrically opposite to the policy the author would recommend. Choices (A) and (D) must be wrong because the passage clearly indicates that the author

supports parochial schools and the religious instruction they provide. Choice (C) is a distraction. It plays on the association of segregation and racial discrimination. Racial segregation is not the only form of segregation. The word *segregation* means generally to separate or to keep separate.

12. **The correct answer is (A).** In this story, the identity of the person who reports the incident is irrelevant. So long as it is not someone with a special infirmity (very poor eyesight, for example) or poor credibility (an inveterate liar), the person is quite capable of reporting what she saw—or what she thought she saw. The most serious weakness of the analysis presented is that it attacks Professor Branch's credentials. To be sure, one might want to question the accuracy of the report: At what time did it occur? What were the lighting conditions? Had the observer been drinking? But these can be asked independently of attacking the qualifications of the source. Thus, choice (D) must be wrong, for special credentials are just not needed in this case, so the wrong way to defend Professor Branch is to defend those. By the same token, it makes no sense to defend Branch by launching a counter–*ad hominem* attack on her attacker, so choice (B) is incorrect. Choices (C) and (E) may or may not be true, but they are surely irrelevant to the question of whether or not this particular sighting is to be trusted.

13. **The correct answer is (B).** The inquisitor's behavior is paradoxical— that is, internally inconsistent or contradictory. The victim tells him that he is in league with the devil, so the inquisitor refuses to believe him because those in league with the devil never tell the truth. In other words, the inquisitor refuses to believe the victim because he accepts the testimony of the victim. Thus, choice (B) is correct. Choice (A) is incorrect because the inquisitor does not *withdraw* anything he has said; in fact, he lets everything he has said stand, and that is how he manages to contradict himself. Choice (E) is a bit more plausible, but it is incomplete. In a certain sense, the inquisitor does not accept the answer, but the real point of the passage is that his basis for *not* accepting the answer is that he *does* accept the answer: He believes the victim when he says he is in league with the devil. Choices (C) and (D) find no support in the paragraph. Nothing suggests that the inquisitor is violating any religious law, and nothing indicates that the inquisitor does not himself believe in the devil.

14. **The correct answer is (B).** The key here is that the word "nobody" is used in a cleverly ambiguous way; and, as many of you probably know, the "young lady" in the story is Lewis Carroll's Alice. This is fairly representative of his wordplay. Choice (E) must be incorrect since it misses completely the little play on words: "I saw Nobody," encouraging a response such as "Oh, is he a handsome man?" Choice (D) is beside the point, for the King is not interested in the messenger's veracity. He may be interested in his reliability, choice (A); but, if anything, we should conclude the King finds the messenger unreliable since "nobody walks slower" than the messenger. Choice (C) is wrong because the question is not a matter of eyesight. The King does not say, "If you had better eyes, you might have seen Nobody."

15. **The correct answer is (A).** This is an exercise in logic. The story told by the

stimulus material has the flavor of a paradox ("This sentence is false."), but in actuality, it does not present such a logical problem. Rather, the fee is not due until the younger attorney wins her first case, so the suit that is pending should be decided for the younger attorney. But once that judgment has been entered, then the younger attorney has won her first case and the fee does become due—but not before.

16. **The correct answer is (C).** Remember that it is important to find the conclusion of an argument. Sometimes the conclusion will be the last sentence of the paragraph, but that is not the case here. And sometimes you'll get help from a transitional word or phrase such as "therefore," "so," or "it follows." Again, no such luck here. Instead, you'll have to examine each idea in the paragraph to ask whether it is the main point the speaker hopes to prove, and the conclusion of this argument is found, unsignalled, in the very first sentence: consumers are not rational. And the proof of this conclusion is that consumers reach different decisions. But that presupposes that rationality would require consumers to reach substantially similar decisions—as choice (C) points out. If this item had been developed as a "weakening" question rather than a "presupposes" question, then the correct answer might have been worded: It is possible for rational consumers to weigh variables differently and arrive at different, though equally rational, decisions.

17. **The correct answer is (E).** The task here is to reconcile the two options expressed (like a "paradox" question). Richard's opinion that the experiment shows that manipulating controls is fol-

lowed by actual changes in climate conditions seems inconsistent with Bill's opinion that manipulating the thermostat is ineffective because the device is a fake. But Richard is really only reporting that event e^1 (adjusting the thermostat) is following by event e^2 (a change in climate). That could be true without a causal connection—as choice (E) suggests: people get uncomfortable and start to manipulate the fake thermostat just about the time that real control is going to kick in anyway.

18. **The correct answer is (B).** The problem with the argument is that it is circular. The speaker notes that a creative work has no value apart from that afforded by copyright protection and then concludes, based upon the fact that copyright protection gives the work value, that the work is valuable property that requires protection. As for choice (A), while the speaker doesn't provide examples, this is not a weakness of the argument. The listener can understand the argument as it is presented, and the persuasive force would not be greatly increased by mentioning a particular song or book. Choice (C) is wrong since the speaker does not attack another person. (That would be an *ad hominem* argument or attack.) Choice (D) is wrong because the argument is not a generalization. And choice (E) is wrong for the same reason that choice (A) is wrong. While it is true that this is not considered by the speaker, nothing seems to turn on this consideration.

19. **The correct answer is (D).** The argument has the structure:

    If A, then E.

    If WU, then H.

    Either A or WU.

So it can be deduced:

If not *WU*, then *A*.

A.

Therefore *E*.

The problem with the other choices is that they go beyond what is stated. Take choice (A) for example. The statements refer to a particular set of ruins. You cannot infer that these statements apply to all possible ruins. Thus, it is possible that the Etonians built trading centers, but, given the unique characteristics of this particular group of ruins, it is known that armaments would prove that Etonians built them as a fortress.

20. **The correct answer is (B).** The rule of thumb is based upon the assumption that a central nervous system is a necessary condition of the capacity for suffering: if the organism lacks a central nervous system, then it lacks the capacity for suffering. It's instructive to contrast choice (B) with choice (D). Choice (D) says that a central nervous system is a sufficient condition of the capacity for suffering but leaves open the logical possibility that other conditions may be the basis for a capacity for suffering.

21. **The correct answer is (D).** The author explains that the expansion of judicial power by increasing the number of causes of action had the effect of filling the judicial coffers. A natural conclusion to be drawn from this information is that the desire for economic gain fueled the expansion. Choice (A) is not supported by the text since the judges may have made good decisions—even though they were paid to make them. Choice (E) is incorrect for the same reason. Choice (C) is not supported by the text since no mention is made of the other two bodies (even assuming they existed at the time the au-

thor is describing). Choice (B) is also incorrect because there is nothing in the text to support such a conclusion.

22. **The correct answer is (D).** As we did in question 20, let us use letters to represent the form of the argument. The first sentence is our old friend: "If *P*, then *Q*." Now we must be careful not to use the same letter to stand for a different statement. No part of the second sentence is also a part of the first one, so we must use a new set of letters: "If *R*, then *S*." Do not be confused by the internal structure of the sentences. Though the second clause of the first sentence speaks about Johnson and Lloyd voting the same way, the second clause of the second sentence speaks about Johnson's defending someone. So the two statements are different ideas and require different letters. The first clause of the third sentence is the same idea as the first clause of the first sentence, so we use letter *P* again, but the second clause is different, *T*. The third sentence uses the phrase "only if," "*P* only if *T*," which can also be written "If *P*, then *T*." Our three sentences are translated as follows:

1 If *P*, then *Q*.

2 If *R*, then *S*.

3 If *P*, then *T*.

Now we can find which of the answers cannot be true.

Choice (A) "If *R*, then not *Q*." That is a possibility. While it cannot be deduced from our three assumptions, nothing in the three assumptions precludes it. So choice (A) could be true.

Choice (B) "If *P*, then *T*." This is true, a restatement of the final assumption.

Choice (C) "If *T*, then not-*P*." This is possibly true. Sentence 3 tells us, "If *P*, then *T,*" which is the same thing as "if not-*T,* then not-*P*"; but it does not dictate consequences when the antecedent clause (the if-clause) is *T.*

Choice (D) "If *P,* then either not-Q or not-T." This must be false, since sentences 1 and 3 together tell us that from *P* must follow both *Q* and *T.*

Choice (E) "If not-*T* or not-*P,* then either not-*S* or *U.*" We have to add a new letter: U. In any event, this is possible for the reasons mentioned in choice (C).

23. **The correct answer is (A).** The listener's comment constitutes a counterexample. It shows by sarcasm that "yeah" can be used to show disagreement. Obviously, the listener does not point out an inconsistency within the speaker's address (even though the listener's remark is inconsistent with the speaker's position). There is no analogy developed by the listener, whose remark is very brief, so choice (C) is incorrect. The argument is directed against the speaker's contention, not character, so choice (D) is incorrect. Finally, though the listener's comment is high evidence that the speaker is wrong, the comment itself does not cite evidence, so choice (E) is incorrect.

24. **The correct answer is (C).** The argument in the question stem commits the fallacy of hasty generalization in two respects. It reasons from *military* aid to *Latin America* (a particular type of aid to a certain region) to the general conclusion that *all* aid must be stopped, regardless of type or of recipient. Choice (C) parallels this. From a particular conclusion about one form of government in one country, it moves to a general conclusion about all government—regardless of form or of society. Although choices (A), (B), and (D) have superficial similarities of

content (war, donation, military), the logical structures of these arguments differ from that of the stem paragraph. Choice (A) is a valid argument: Given anything that is a war, if any war is to be condemned, then all wars are to be condemned. Choice (B) is not a valid argument but a nonsequitur. It does not follow that an obligation on one party guarantees a benefit to any other. For example, there may not be enough rich to provide for all the poor. Choice (D) is also a nonsequitur. That we reject a system now because we lack the money to buy it does not imply we should buy it when we have funds. Finally, choice (E) is not really an argument but only a statement. Not all "If . . . , then . . ." statements mean "*P,* therefore *Q.*" For example, "If you do not do the assignment, you will fail the course" is not an argument with a premise and a conclusion but a single statement that describes a causal relation.

Section 4

1. **The correct answer is (B).** This is a main idea question. The author's primary concern is to discuss the problem of desertification. So choice (B) is correct. A natural extension of the discussion would be a proposal to slow the process of desertification, but that is not included in the passage as written, so choice (A) must be incorrect. Choices (C), (D), and (E) are each incorrect because we find no elements in the passage to support those choices. Even admitting that the author intends to define, implicitly, the term "desertification," that is surely not the main point of the passage. The author also dwells at length on the causes of the problem.

2. **The correct answer is (C).** This is an explicit idea question. In the first para-

graph, the author mentions choices (A), (B), (D), and (E) as features of desertification. Choice (C), however, is one of the *causes* of desertification mentioned in the second paragraph.

3. **The correct answer is (E).** This is an inference question. The author places the phrase "higher uses" in quotation marks. In essence, this is similar to prefacing the phrase with the disclaimer "so-called." This impression is reinforced by the final entry in the list of examples of "higher uses": waste dumps. This is not to say that the author would argue that such uses are not important. Rather, this is to say that the author does not believe that those uses are more important than agricultural uses. Choice (A) is incorrect since this term is no more important than other terms used in the passage. Choice (B) is incorrect since the author is talking about the conversion of non-arid land to higher uses. Choice (C) is incorrect since the author is clearly opposed to such expansion. Finally, choice (D) is a sentiment expressed in the passage, but that is not the reason for placing this phrase in quotation marks.

4. **The correct answer is (D).** This is a specific detail (explicit idea) question with a thought-reverser. The author mentions world demand for U.S. products in the final paragraph, but "mention" alone does not make this a correct answer to the question. The right answer to a specific detail question must not only be mentioned; it must also answer the question asked. In this case, global need is mentioned as a reason to avoid desertification (feeding people is important) and not as a cause. The other choices are mentioned as causes: choices (A) and (B) in paragraph two; choices (C) and (E) in paragraph three.

5. **The correct answer is (A).** This is an explicit idea question, and the answer is found in the last paragraph. There the author states that the most serious long-term effect of desertification will be on the U.S.'s ability to export agricultural products. This will be harmful to the U.S. economically and to the rest of the world in terms of meeting the demand for food and fiber. As for choices (B) and (C), though these are plausible as effects of desertification, the author does not mention them specifically, and he certainly does not describe them as the most serious effects of desertification. Choice (D) is incorrect because the author's concern is over the ability of the U.S. to continue to export agricultural products, not the ability of the U.S. to meet domestic demand. Finally, choice (E) fails for the same reason that choices (B) and (C) are incorrect. Though it might arguably be one result of desertification (and that is an issue we need not address), the author never mentions it as a possible effect.

6. **The correct answer is (E).** This is an application question. In the passage, the author indicates that government programs that encourage exploitation of arid land are in large measure responsible for the rapid rate of desertification. A natural extension of the discussion would be a proposal for government spending to conserve arid lands. And this receives specific support in the third paragraph, where the author mentions that government conservation incentives are inadequate. With regard to choice (A), the author seems to believe that it is necessary for the U.S. to continue to export agricultural products to meet the world demand; the author favors conserving arid land while meeting this demand.

Choice (B) is surely incorrect, for the author argues that aid to farmers is one cause of the rapid rate of desertification. Choice (D) is incorrect for the same reason. As for choice (C), the conversion of land to "higher uses" is mentioned as a factor complicating the process of desertification. It is not a cause of desertification. The most natural extension of the passage would be a discussion of how to combat desertification.

7. **The correct answer is (E).** This is a tone question. We can surely eliminate choices (B), (C), and (D) as not expressing the appropriate element of worry. Then, between choices (A) and (E), choice (A) overstates the case. The author says we solve the problem now or we solve it later (at a higher cost). But that is an expression of concern, not alarm.

8. **The correct answer is (D).** This is a main idea question. The author begins by noting that solar energy is very important and, further, that the problem of the cost of solar cells, apparently an important part of solar energy technology, has not yet been solved. The author then discusses research on solar cells and the difficulties with silicon cells. In the third paragraph, the author states that there is a solution to this problem: amorphous materials. So the overall objective of the passage is to present amorphous material as a possible solution to the problem of cost. This is neatly summarized by choice (D). Choice (A) is incorrect since the author discusses the importance of solar energy only by way of introduction. Choice (B) is incorrect because the author never explains how solar cells work. Choice (C) is incorrect because the only reference to history is included to explain the bias in favor of silicon solar cells. Choice (E) is incorrect because the au-

thor never mentions such funding. To be sure, the arguments contained in the passage might be very useful in making the further point suggested by choice (E), but then that is to admit that choice (E) is not the main point of the passage as written.

9. **The correct answer is (D).** This is a specific detail (explicit idea) question. In paragraph two, the author specifically states that single crystal silicon is relatively efficient, even though expensive, and for that reason is used in the space program. Choices (A) and (C) are inconsistent with the passage, because gallium arsenide is said to be scarce and silicon cells are said to be expensive. Choice (B) is wrong because ribbon silicon can be produced, but it is not very efficient. And choice (E) is wrong because silicon is highly structured; the amorphous materials are not discussed until the next paragraph.

10. **The correct answer is (A).** This is a logical structure question: Why does the author mention polycrystalline and ribbon silicon? In a way, the mention of these techniques could undermine the case for amorphous materials, since these are recent developments in crystalline substances that improve silicon solar cells. The author surely does not intend to weaken the argument. The logical move is to acknowledge the existence of a possible objection and to attempt to demonstrate that it is not really a very important objection. This is described by choice (A). Choice (B) is incorrect, for though this is the general idea of the passage, choice (B) is not a proper response to the question asked. Choice (C) is a point raised in the passage, but this is not the reason for the reference to polycrystalline and ribbon silicon. Choice (D) is incorrect

because the author never elaborates on the distinction between crystalline silicon and other forms of silicon. The author only mentions that the latter are further developments on crystalline silicon. As for choice (E), though we infer from the mention of polycrystalline and ribbon silicon that other forms of solar cells exist, this is not the reason the author has introduced them into the discussion.

11. **The correct answer is (B).** This is an inference question. In the first paragraph, the author mentions that the basic problem with solar energy is the economics of solar photovoltaic devices. The rest of the passage discusses solar cells. We may infer from the juxtaposition of these terms that the author uses them synonymously. In any event, none of the other pairs are used interchangeably. As for choice (A), from the passage we may infer that "extraterrestrial" refers to space and that "solar" refers to the sun. As for choice (C), these terms are used as opposites. As for choice (D), though the author claims that amorphous materials are more efficient than silicon materials, the passage does not equate amorphous materials and efficiency. Finally, choice (E) is incorrect since a wafer is apparently a big crystal of silicon. But that means the terms are not used interchangeably.

12. **The correct answer is (B).** This is a further application question. We noted earlier, in question 8, that though the author does not specifically advocate greater funding for research on amorphous materials, the passage might be used in such an argument. Since there is a historical bias in favor of silicon cells and since such cells have been the focus of most research, and amorphous materials offer an alternative, the natural

conclusion is that further research should be done on amorphous materials. This is choice (B). Choice (A) must be incorrect since the author never condemns the space program. The author only notes that silicon cells were appropriate for the space program since cost was no object. Choice (C) must be incorrect since the author advocates amorphous materials as opposed to silicon crystals for solar cells. Choice (D) has some merit. To the extent that the entire passage advocates further research for solar energy, it could be used for the purpose suggested by choice (D). With an application question, however, the task is to find the answer choice most closely tied to the text, and that is choice (B). Logically, then, there is nothing "wrong" with choice (D); it is just that it is not so closely related to the passage as choice (B). Finally, choice (E) is incorrect for the same reason: One could conceivably use the passage in the service of this goal, but choice (B) is a more obvious choice.

13. **The correct answer is (E).** This is a specific detail question. Choices (A), (B), (C), and (D) are all mentioned in paragraph three. Choice (E) is mentioned in paragraph one but not as an advantage of amorphous materials. Rather, the commitment of the semiconductor industry to silicon-based technology was a historical factor, helping to explain the rather late development of other, better technologies.

14. **The correct answer is (A).** This is a tone question. The tone of the passage is clearly analytical. The final paragraph is the warrant for the "optimistic" part of choice (A). The author implies that the problem of the cost of solar cells can be solved by further research on amorphous materials. Choice (B) is incorrect since

though the passage advocates a position, it cannot be termed biased. Choice (C) is correct insofar as the passage is critical, but the author does not seem to be discouraged. Choice (D) is incorrect because the passage is argumentative and the author seems to be confident. Finally, choice (E) is correct in that it states that the author is concerned, but there is nothing mentioned in the passage about which the author could be conciliatory.

15. **The correct answer is (B).** This is a main idea question. The author draws a distinction between preventive health care and curative health care. Using this distinction, the text suggests that there should be established separate authorities for each. So the primary method of developing the argument is the drawing of a distinction, as correctly stated by choice (B). Choice (A) is incorrect since the author does not cite any counterarguments to the position. Choice (C) is incorrect, for a dilemma is a "damned if you do and damned if you don't" argument. To draw a distinction is not necessarily to set up a dilemma. Choice (D) is incorrect, for whatever causes of poor health are discussed in the passage are not the main focus of the discussion. Choice (E) is incorrect for a similar reason. Whatever new research we may try to read into the passage, such as the Winslow monograph, is surely not the main point of the passage.

16. **The correct answer is (E).** This is an explicit idea question. In the first sentence of the second paragraph, the author notes that treatment is aimed at a patient already ill, but we have been told in the first paragraph that preventive care is just that, aimed at people who are healthy in order to keep them that way. So choice (A) is mentioned in the pas-

sage. Choice (B) is supported by the first two paragraphs, particularly the sentence of the second paragraph that reads, "While these may be applied on a mass basis . . ., they are usually applied after the patient appears with a complaint," thus distinguishing preventive care from curative care. As for choice (C), per capita differences in cost are discussed in paragraph four. And as for choice (D), the historical roots of the distinction are discussed in the first paragraph. Choice (E), however, is not mentioned. In fact, choice (E) seems to be inconsistent with the author's point in that the author emphasizes the importance of and advantages to preventive care.

17. **The correct answer is (B).** This is an inference question. In the first paragraph, the author is discussing the basic strategy of preventive medicine. The text then states that in some areas, there is needless suffering and economic harm due to the failure of authorities to implement controlled fluoridation. The development of the argument leads us to conclude that the author regards the failure of the authorities to fluoridate water as a failure to implement a preventive health-care program. Choice (B) explains this reasoning. Choice (A) is incorrect since the author holds a positive attitude about fluoridation. Choice (C) is incorrect because the author cites the failure to fluoridate as an example of a failure to adopt a potentially valuable preventive strategy. Choice (D) is incorrect because fluoridation is a preventive, rather than a treatment, strategy. Finally, choice (E) is incorrect since the author recommends the fluoridation of water as a valuable preventive strategy.

18. **The correct answer is (A).** This is an inference question. In paragraph 4, the

author remarks that expenditure of resources on treatment is an expenditure that is lost, that is, produces nothing positive (eliminating the negative is not regarded as producing a positive result). Then, the sick person is also not contributing anything positive during the illness. So the economy is doubly disadvantaged because of the burden on or drain on resources to cure an ill person and because production is lost. Choice (A) neatly captures this idea. Choice (B) is incorrect because the author never quantifies the cost difference between the two types of care. The text says only that prevention is less costly than treatment. Choice (C) is incorrect because the author eventually will support such a division on the ground that the two activities are sufficiently dissimilar to warrant a division of authority. Choice (D) is incorrect since both rehabilitation and cure belong to curative medicine, so that will not explain why the economy is doubly burdened. Finally, choice (E) is attractive because it is at least consistent with the general theme of the passage. But choice (E) is not responsive to the question. It does not explain why the economy is doubly burdened by the person who requires treatment.

19. **The correct answer is (C).** This is an attitude, or tone, question. Two clues support choice (C). First, the author refers to the monograph and then continues to make points made by Winslow. This indicates the author agrees with Winslow. Second, the author refers to the analysis by Winslow as "convincing." Choices (A) and (B) can be eliminated because of the negative connotations associated with both terms. Choice (D) can be eliminated because style is not relevant to the point under discussion. Fi-

nally, choice (E) is the second-best answer. We eliminate choice (E) because the author states that the economics of prevention have been widely discussed, indicating that the uniqueness of Winslow's contribution is not necessarily originality. Further, the reference to the persuasiveness of Winslow's analysis makes choice (C) a better descriptive phrase to apply to the author's attitude than choice (E).

20. **The correct answer is (D).** This is a logical detail question. The author introduces these three diseases in the paragraph discussing the economics of prevention and following the statement that the cost of prevention is less than the cost of treatment when averaged out on a per capita basis. Choice (D) makes this point. Choice (A) is incorrect, for while this is a statement the author would surely accept, it is not the reason for introducing the examples. Choice (B) is incorrect for a similar reason. This may very well be true, but it is not an answer to the question. Choice (C) must be wrong, for though this is one of the main points of the discussion, it will not answer this particular question. Finally, choice (E) is also a statement that the author could accept, but it is not responsive to the question.

21. **The correct answer is (A).** This is a question about the logical structure of the argument. The author mentions several differences between preventive and curative medicines: cost, personnel, persons addressed. But these differences are not compelling reasons for creating a division of authority. The need to separate authority for the two strategies is discussed in the first and last paragraphs. The value of the division will be to clarify objectives and redress the inequitable

division of resources. These are problems, so says the first paragraph, because "the imperative nature of medical care" will allow it to dominate health care. In other words, the urgency of treatment attracts attention. This is the explanation provided in choice (A). And for this reason, it is not cost, choice (B); personnel, choice (C); or persons addressed, choice (D) that is the important difference. Finally, choice (E) is directly contradicted by the opening sentences of the passage.

22. **The correct answer is (D).** This is a main idea question. The author cites several arguments in favor of the "drug lag" theory, then offers refutations of at least some of them. The author concludes that the arguments for "drug lag" are not conclusive and that, contrary to the view of the "drug lag" theoreticians, the 1962 Amendments are not, on balance, harmful. The main technique of development is refutation of arguments cited. Choice (D) is therefore the best answer to this question. Choice (A) can be eliminated since the author does not outline a proposal. Discussing the effectiveness of some past action is not outlining a proposal. Choice (B) has some merit because the author does analyze the evidence presented by the "drug lag" theoreticians. This analysis, however, is not the final objective of the passage. It is presented in order to further the goal of refuting the general position of that group. Choice (C) is incorrect since the author poses no question and indeed seems to answer any question that might be implicit in the passage regarding the value of the Amendments. Choice (E) has some merit since the focus of the passage is a law. But the intent of the author is not to discuss the law per se. Rather, the intent of the passage is to refute objections to

the law. On balance, choice (D) more precisely describes the main idea than the other choices.

23. **The correct answer is (C).** Choices (A), (B), (D), and (E) are all mentioned as "drug lag" arguments in the second paragraph. As for choice (C), the argument that effectiveness studies cost money is mentioned in the first paragraph. But "drug lag" results from the time and cost of effectiveness studies. "Drug lag" is not the increased cost itself.

24. **The correct answer is (A).** This is an application question. Support for choice (A) is found in the closing sentences of the passage. In the final paragraph, the author insists that there are few, if any, examples of harm done by the requirements of effectiveness studies. Then the author says that we are at least assured that the drug, which might actually prove harmful, does have some benefit. The qualified nature of the claim suggests that the author would acknowledge that some "drug lag" does exist but that, on balance, it is justified. This thought is captured by choice (A). Choice (B) is incorrect because the author never states the effectiveness studies are designed to determine whether the drug has unwanted effects. Apparently, effectiveness studies, as the name implies, are designed to test the value of the drug. This is not to say that such studies may not, in fact, uncover unwanted side effects, but given the information in the passage, choice (B) is a more tenuous inference than choice (A). Choice (C) is incorrect for two reasons. First, the passage never states that the cost of drugs is higher in the United States than in other countries. The passage states only that the proponents of the "drug lag" theory argue that the effectiveness study require-

ment increases the cost of drugs here. That makes no comparison with a foreign country. Second, the author seems to discount the significance of the increased cost. Choice (D) is incorrect because there is no basis for such a recommendation in the passage. Finally, choice (E) is incorrect because the passage never states that the studies do not cost money or time. The author only doubts whether the cost or time create profit pressures serious enough to cause "drug lag."

25. **The correct answer is (B).** This is a logical structure question. In the final paragraph, the author states that the drop in new drugs introduced annually began before the Amendments took effect. The author does not deny that the drop occurred but rather points out that it predated the supposed cause. In other words, the author is suggesting that there must be some other reason for the drop. Choice (B) correctly describes the author's logical move. Choice (E) is directly contradicted by this analysis. The author does not deny that there was a drop in the number of new drugs introduced every year. As for choice (A), the author does not point to any similarity between two situations. The text says only that the situation being studied existed even before the Amendments took effect. Choice (C) is incorrect because the author never questions the credibility of an opponent, only the value of the opponent's arguments. Finally, choice (D) is incorrect because the author's use of statistics is not an attempt to justify the use of those statistics. The statistics are used to prove some further conclusion.

26. **The correct answer is (C).** This is a logical structure question. In the second paragraph, the author cites, as one argu-

ment for the existence of "drug lag," the non-availability in the U.S. of a drug that is available in a foreign country. In the third paragraph, the author offers a refutation of this argument. The simple availability–non-availability comparison is not valid because consumers may not suffer from the non-availability of that particular drug if another drug is available to treat the same condition. Choice (C) correctly describes the structure of this argument. The remaining answer choices are in various ways related to the overall argument of the passage, but they are not answers to this particular question.

27. **The correct answer is (C).** Again, we have a logical structure question. We have already noted that the author does not deny that fewer drugs were introduced each year after the Amendments than before the Amendments but does offer that the total number of new chemical entities is not necessarily a measure of the value of new drugs introduced. By redefining terms so that we speak not just of new chemical entities but of unimportant, important, and breakthrough chemical entities, the author minimizes the significance of the argument. The relevant comparison, the author claims, is between important and breakthrough chemical entities, not total new chemical entities introduced. Choice (C) correctly points out that the essence of this logical move is redefining terminology. Choice (A) is incorrect because the author does not deny that the total number had dropped. Choice (B) is incorrect because the author does not explain why that number has dropped. Choice (D) is incorrect because the author makes no such proposal. Finally, choice (E) is only remotely related to the correct answer. While it may be true that an important or

breakthrough chemical has many more uses than an unimportant chemical entity, the author does not list the uses of any chemical.

28. **The correct answer is (D).** This is an application question. What are the logical underpinnings of the comparison? Notice that the author's description of the arguments under attack includes reference to "advanced" nations. Apparently, the proponents of the "drug lag" theory realize that a comparison between the United States and a non-advanced country would not be relevant. They want a situation in which the only important difference is the strictness of the laws on new drugs. For this reason, choice (D) is a presupposition of the argument.

Section 5

1. **The correct answer is (D).** This item, too, asks you to identify a hidden assumption. First, find the conclusion of the argument. It is contained in the rhetorical question at the end of the paragraph, a question that should be read to assert affirmatively "World leaders would not trust someone who has admitted lying to her spouse." That conclusion rests upon the hidden assumption that a person who would lie to her or his spouse about an affair would also lie to world leaders.

2. **The correct answer is (D).** The only paragraph containing an argument that makes a generalization is choice (D). The speaker makes a claim about cameras in general based upon the one incident.

3. **The correct answer is (C).** The only paragraph containing an argument directed toward an opponent instead of the merits of the argument is choice (C). There the speaker attacks the Mayor by alleging that the Mayor is biased by a financial interest in the issue.

4. **The correct answer is (C).** The speaker uses the word "free" in two different ways. In the first occurrence of the word, it means "liberty"—a general term—meaning freedom from governmental or other constraint. The second occurrence is the use we reserve for being free of some particular problem, e.g., free or rid of a problem.

5. **The correct answer is (A).** The author states that the Ecole was a quasi-governmental agency that controlled the distribution of government money for artists. Since the Impressionist painters were scorned and received no money (only empty bellies) for their efforts, we can infer that they did not paint in the accepted style. Choice (B) goes beyond the scope of what is specifically stated in the initial paragraph. Although you can infer that the Impressionists rejected the standards of the Ecole and further that they were ultimately successful (note the word "initially," which qualifies their lack of success), you cannot infer that they gained control over the Ecole. Choices (C) and (D) also go beyond the scope of the initial paragraph. According to the author, the Ecole exercised its control by the ways in which it distributed money. The passage does not suggest that the Ecole exercised any direct control. Finally, choice (E) too goes beyond what can be legitimately inferred from the initial paragraph. In fact, if anything can be inferred from the selection about the state of painting in France in the second half of the nineteenth century, it is that it was more creative than the art of the first half of the century, for you might reasonably infer that the Impressionists constituted a new creative force.

6. **The correct answer is (D).** The task here is to explain why the teacher makes the second remark. Choice (D) provides the best explanation. The teacher's first remark says only that the student being addressed is not one of the students who has passed the test. You cannot infer from that remark that the student in the conversation has not passed the test. It is possible that his paper has not yet been graded. (Consider a similar situation: You look into a classroom through a door that is slightly ajar and see three students, all of whom are girls. You then say "Some of the students in this class are girls"—obviously a true statement. If you later open the door completely and see only female students in the classroom, you can say "All of the students in this class are girls"—also a true statement. But your first statement is not thereby rendered false. It remains true as well.) The other choices fail to explain why the teacher would say, "You don't yet need to tell your parents that you failed the test."

7. **The correct answer is (C).** The author notes that arguments in favor of legalizing marijuana have generally fallen into two categories: those that assert that there is no evidence that marijuana is dangerous and those that assert that laws proscribing the use of marijuana infringe on an individual's liberty. The arguments of the first sort are designed to show that there is no good reason to have laws against marijuana, while arguments of the second sort are intended to show that there is a reason to legalize marijuana. At this point, the author says that there is yet another reason to legalize marijuana: smoking marijuana is pleasurable. Thus, the author implies that the fact that an activity is pleasurable is a reason that might be given for allowing people to engage in it. Choice (A) is not inferable from the paragraph. In fact, the author states that there is no evidence to prove such a contention. Choice (B) represents a possible misreading of the paragraph. The author does not state that marijuana is illegal because it is pleasurable but that it should be legal because it is pleasurable. As for choice (D), the author states that arguments based on claims of individual liberty are not the only ones that could be advanced for the legalization of marijuana, not that those who use such arguments are insincere. Finally, as for choice (E), opponents of marijuana might not deny that the drug has a pleasurable effect, but they would insist that people are not entitled to that pleasurable effect because the use of marijuana leads to ill effects as well, such as antisocial behavior.

8. **The correct answer is (B).** A neat way to attack problems like this (in which a second speaker evidently misconstrues the remark of a first speaker) is to put each answer choice into the mouth of the first speaker. The correct choice will be the one that creates a meaningful exchange between the two speakers:

Choice (A)

DAVID:	Paintings by Electra and Bluesina should be displayed in the Museum.
MARAT:	I disagree. I have seen some very fine works by Electra and Bluesina that should be displayed in the Museum.

Choice (B)

DAVID:	Only Kissandra's paintings should be displayed in the Museum.
MARAT:	I disagree. I have seen some very fine works by Electra and Bluesina that should be displayed in the Museum.

Choice (C)

DAVID: Every painting by Kissandra should be displayed in the Museum.

MARAT: I disagree. I have seen some very fine works by Electra and Bluesina that should be displayed in the Museum.

Choice (D)

DAVID: Not every Kissandra painting should be displayed in the Museum.

MARAT: I disagree. I have seen some very fine works by Electra and Bluesina that should be displayed in the Museum.

Choice (E)

DAVID: Kissandra's paintings should be displayed only in the Museum.

MARAT: I disagree. I have seen some very fine works by Electra and Bluesina that should be displayed in the Museum.

Questions 9 and 10

9.   **The correct answer is (D).** A diagram makes it easy to keep track of the relationships:

Younger————————⟶ Older

Paul is older than Sally:

       S   P

————————⟶

Sally is older than Fred:

      F   S   P

————————⟶

Mike is older than Paul:

      F   S   P   M

————————⟶

Ralph is younger than Mike but older than Fred:

⟵————— R —————⟶
        F   S   P   M

————————————⟶

As the diagram shows, only choice (D) is necessarily true.

10.   **The correct answer is (E).** Since Chuck is younger than Ralph and Ralph is younger than Mike, Chuck must be younger than Mike.

11.   **The correct answer is (B).** Cathy's response exploits an ambiguity in the way that the word "see" is used in English. When Charlotte says that she doesn't "see" any good reason to lend Cathy money, she doesn't mean that there is such a reason but she cannot see it. Rather, she means that there is no reason to lend Cathy money.

12.   **The correct answer is (A).** This item asks you to draw a further conclusion. The speaker explains that older vaccines were more dangerous than newer ones because they used entire viruses, whereas newer vaccines use only part of the virus. Although the newer vaccines use only a part of the virus, they are still effective in stimulating the body's immune system. We are entitled to conclude, therefore, that it is a specific subunit of the virus that makes the vaccine effective. As for the wrong answers, choices (B) and (C) can be eliminated because the speaker contrasts old and new vaccines, not the two different older methods of creating vaccines using entire viruses. Choice (D) is contradicted by the passage, for the speaker notes that the newer vaccines are safer. Finally, choice (E) is perhaps the second-best response. But choice (E) overstates the speaker's position. The body does not react to a subpart of the

virus in exactly the same way as it reacts to the whole virus. Rather, the immune system reacts to the subpart (as though it were embedded in a whole virus), but the body as a whole is not at risk as it would be if the vaccine used whole viruses.

13. **The correct answer is (A).** Here we are asked to weaken the second speaker's position. Anthony maintains that air conditioning was not the feature that prompted Tony to buy his car. Choice (A) weakens this by stating that of two very similar vehicles, Tony chose the one with air conditioning. Choice (B) seems to strengthen rather than weaken Anthony's argument: the Ouigo is, on the whole, inferior to the Hugo. Choice (C) seems to strengthen the first speaker's position by implying that it was the air conditioning that made the difference in Tony's choice. As for choice (D), without further information, this idea does not bear on the debate. (Does Tony like or dislike imports?) Finally, as for choice (E), though this statement establishes that Tony did not make his decision based on these two items of equipment, it doesn't help us decide whether Tony made his decision based on air conditioning.

14. **The correct answer is (B).** The stem here asks that you describe the argument. The best description is provided by choice (B). The speaker argues that the logical extension of the ethical vegetarian's argument leads to conclusions such as a human being is equal to a spear of broccoli and we should stop eating altogether. I am not saying that the argument succeeds—only that choice (B) is the best description of the argument. As for choice (A), there simply is no such insinuation in the speaker's argument: the speaker does not say, for example,

that the vegetarians continue to wear leather clothing. As for choices (C) and (D), the speaker doesn't cite any scientific evidence and doesn't mention any commonly accepted opinions. As for choice (E), though the speaker's own position seems irreconcilable with that of the ethical vegetarians, the speaker is not attempting to reconcile the two positions.

15. **The correct answer is (C).** The hidden assumption in this argument is not that easy to spot, and it may become clear to you only after you have studied the answer choices. The speaker concludes that the recent surge in births is not a serious problem. But why shouldn't we expect an echo of the earlier baby boom? There must be a crucial difference between the recent surge in births and the true baby boom of the 50s. Choice (C) highlights that difference. As for choice (A), this idea suggests that the speaker might be wrong: there is no reason for concern since the new parents are in a position to have the same number of offspring as their parents. Choice (B) overstates the speaker's position. The speaker is saying only that there is no reason to fear a sudden population explosion, not that the population will decline. Choice (D) seems to be inconsistent with the speaker's position. The speaker is arguing that we should not expect a recurring cycle of baby booms. Finally, choice (E) imputes a value judgment to the speaker that has no support in the factual statements of the paragraph.

16. **The correct answer is (B).** The speaker's argument rests on a hidden assumption that the Congress is acting to protect citizens of other countries and not citizens of the United States. Choice (B) attacks this hidden premise. As for choice (A), this idea can only strengthen

the speaker's position: the ban is unfair because other countries may need these very effective chemicals. Choice (C) too seems to cut in the speaker's favor; and the chemical companies won't be harmed. And so too choice (D) seems to pre-empt a possible objection to the speaker's position: foreign companies will simply fill the void. About the best justification for choice (E) is that it shows that the Congress doesn't need to enact a ban. But that is too strong a conclusion to rest on a statement that clearly says "some" (not "all") foreign governments have already banned the chemicals.

17. **The correct answer is (B).** The explanation for the seeming contradiction, given by choice (B), is that Fulghum's instant coffee is more concentrated than the leading brand. For this reason, Fulghum's is actually cheaper to use. As for choice (A), the number of people who use one brand or the other doesn't bear on the issue of cost. As for choice (C), this reinforces the seeming contradiction by eliminating a possible explanation, namely, Fulgum's regular jar is larger. As for choice (D), this is irrelevant since the ad specifically states that Fulghum's costs more. And as for choice (E), the taste test is irrelevant to the issue of cost.

18. **The correct answer is (C).** This item asks for a further conclusion. Since some of the employees who will be promoted are highly skilled and others bunglers and since all will receive higher salaries, we can infer that both highly skilled employees and bunglers will receive higher salaries. Choice (A) is directly contradicted by the first statement of the paragraph. Choice (B) is not inconsistent with the statements of the stimulus paragraph, but choice (B) cannot be inferred from those statements. Choice (D) makes

the following mistake: All *S* are *P*, therefore all *P* are *S*. Finally, choice (E) is inconsistent with the initial paragraph, for we know that some bunglers will be promoted and will therefore receive higher salaries.

19. **The correct answer is (C).** This question asks you to identify assumptions of the argument. First, choice (C) is not an assumption. Perhaps the speaker thinks that the seriousness of the crimes was equivalent for the two periods, but nothing commits the speaker to the idea that things were worse in the "old days." Choice (A) is a presupposition: since the speaker makes a descriptive judgment about whether a society is more or less violent, the speaker evidently thinks that the number of reported crimes is a good indicator of that characteristic. And choice (B) is an assumption since the speaker reaches a general conclusion about "large metropolitan areas" based upon the New York City experience. And choice (D) is an assumption since the Richardson data are the basis for the argument. And choice (E), while a little harder to detect, is also an assumption, because the speaker regards the increase in New York City as out of line; therefore, the speaker believes there is a correlation between population and crime.

20. **The correct answer is (C).** What sort of judgment can you make about a statement coming from a person who is a self-confessed liar? You can't confidently accept the statement, yet you can't know for certain that it is a lie. Choice (C) describes the appropriate conclusion. Choices (A) and (B) are wrong for the reason just given. As for choice (D), the language quoted here is not the same as the well-known Liar Paradox: This sentence is false. That sentence is paradoxical be-

cause if what it says is true, then it is false, and conversely if what it says is false, then it is true. As for choice (E), we know that it is logically possible to make such a statement—it's right there on the page.

21. **The correct answer is (E).** This item is primarily a problem in careful reading. Since there are at least three spies at the reception, choice (E) cannot be true. Assume that there are exactly three spies at the reception, X, Y, and Z, and further that X knows the true identities of both Y and Z. If choice (E) is also true, then both Y and Z would know the true identity of X. But then three spies would know each other's true identities—in violation of the final statement of the initial paragraph. As for choice (A), the first statement of the initial paragraph says that there are "at least" three spies at the reception, so there could be more. As for choice (B), the final statement says that "at most" two spies know each other's true identities, so there could be fewer. As for choice (C), the second statement says "at least" one spy has this knowledge, so there could be exactly one. And as for choice (D), this statement could be true so long as the spy whose identity is known doesn't know the true identity of more than one other spy.

22. **The correct answer is (C).** One way of analyzing this item is to use capital letters to represent the logical form of the stimulus argument:

If S, then P.

Not P, therefore not S.

Where S = "no union support," and P = "defeated." Then the "not P" of the second line indicates "not not defeated" or "passed," and "not S" indicates "not no union support" or more directly "union

support." The argument of choice (C) also has this form:

If S, then P.

Not P, therefore not S.

Where S = "not having passed bar," and P = "cannot practice law". Then, the "not P" of the second line indicates "not cannot practice" or more directly "can practice," and "not S" means "not not having passed bar" or more directly "passed bar." Choices (A), (B), and (E) present invalid arguments, so they do not parallel the form of the stimulus material. As for choice (A), there may be many other reasons the car won't start. Similarly for choice (B), a person can have the symptoms described without ever having been in the sun. And as for choice (E), there are many other reasons that Peter might have been fired. As for choice (D), this is a probabilistic argument that looks toward the future.

23. **The correct answer is (C).** The speaker here is pointing out an inconsistency of the policies of the corporation: their ads say "Buy American," but they buy Japanese. Choice (C) correctly describes this fact. Every other answer choice overstates the speaker's case. It is not clear what lesson should be drawn from the paragraph—except that the Chrysler corporation is not consistent in its policies.

24. **The correct answer is (D).** The speaker draws a distinction between the underlying agreement between the parties and the written document that commemorates that agreement. According to the paragraph, there are times when an agreement may exist but be unenforceable because it has not been reduced to writing. This is the distinction highlighted by choice (D).

25. The correct answer is (B). Both parties to the debate here apparently agree that the government has correctly gathered the statistics mentioned, but Dick uses the data to reach a conclusion directly opposite to that reached by Alan. Choice (B) best describes this exchange. As for choice (A), the two reach different conclusions. As for the remaining choices, both speakers accept and use as evidence the data mentioned.

Writing Sample

Following are two responses to the Writing Sample prompt, one in favor of the first option and the other in favor of the second option. These responses are not necessarily Pulitzer Prize winning essays, but remember they're not supposed to be. The objective, as developed in Chapter 8, is to write something that is serviceable. You'll notice how these responses fit the model developed in Chapter 8.

Sample Response for Option One

The Board of Trustees should award the contract for the memorial to Ann Gerson for two important reasons. One, from an artistic standpoint, Ms. Gerson's proposal is better calculated to have the intended effect on viewers. Two, the "oasis" approach will give the sculpture additional functionality.

First, Ms. Gerson's shrouded figure, symbolizing death, will make a powerful, though not overly dramatic, statement about the sacrifice of the university's students and graduates. This statement will be enhanced by the containing wall, which will personalize the artistic message by providing information about individuals. Additionally, by positioning the grouping at the center of the campus, Ms. Gerson announces the central impor-

tance of sacrifice in human life and says, in effect, that these individuals remain forever at the "heart" of the school.

Second, Ms. Gerson's oasis provides the additional functionality that the Board wants. The benches and greenery are likely to attract students who want to study quietly or to think reflectively—critical university functions. Plus, the memorial will be located at the center of the campus where it will be convenient for students and faculty to stop for a few minutes or even longer.

It must be allowed that Ms. Gerson does not have the close connections to the University that Mr. Maxwell has, but that doesn't seem to be important to the Board's thinking. In any case, the task is to create a memorial, and death is a universal artistic theme, not one that is the exclusive province of a teacher at a particular school.

Sample Response for Option Two

Mr. Maxwell's proposed memorial wall better meets the criteria set down by the Board. First, the idea of a memorial wall is familiar and will serve the function of encouraging students to think about the sacrifices of those who died. Second, the memorial wall will literally merge form and function, substance and style.

In the first place, the idea of a memorial wall is not a new one. Perhaps the most famous exemplar is the Vietnam Veteran's Memorial on the National Mall. A memorial wall is a concept that is both familiar and effective. Additionally, Mr. Maxwell's intention to add personal information to the usual "data" will make this wall particularly appropriate for its university setting. What better way of reminding current students that these were actual living people who died in the prime of their lives than to mention their unfulfilled goals and aspirations?

Second, Mr. Maxwell's wall will quite literally unite form and function, as the Board hopes. The wall will be integrated structurally into the new student union. Moreover, that merger is highly symbolic because the student union is often seen as the focus of campus life. At the risk of sounding overly dramatic, the interplay between campus life and sacrifice of death has to challenge the imagination.

Finally, Mr. Maxwell is a member of the university community; Ms. Gerson is not. Though the Board does not raise this issue, it is not unreasonable to think that someone who lives and teaches at the university will have a better understanding as to how the unique physical and emotional spaces of the university can be brought together.

answers

PART V
APPENDICES

Creating Your Law School Application

In order to create the most effective application you can, you must understand and appreciate the goals of the process by which some applicants are selected for legal study (and others not) as a social and economic process. With this knowledge, you can intelligently craft an application that is consistent with the workings of these processes—one that has the maximum chance of success.

Application success is no accident. You must have a plan. Your completed application must hang together as a coherent whole. Your GPA, your LSAT score, and your application form the core of this whole. Your personal statement should incorporate some of the most important themes from the application itself and weave them into a story or an argument for why you should be accepted. Plus, your letters should come from people who know you well enough to echo some of the points contained in both the core and your personal statement.

UNDERSTANDING THE APPLICATION PROCESS

If you're like most candidates, at the outset, you think of the application process as taking a test, answering a few questions about your educational background and employment history, writing a personal statement, and arranging for a couple of recommendations. After which, you put everything into an envelope (with a check) and then wait for an answer. The application process is much, much more than this. The cost of the application process routinely exceeds $1,000. The fees that you pay to the Law School Admissions Services to take the Law School Admission Test and for score and grade reports could be as much as $200. Further, the application fees charged by schools run between $50 and $75. Assuming that you apply to ten schools, you could easily spend $750 on application fees. In addition, you will probably spend at least $100 on administrative details such as document preparation, copying, postage, and long distance telephone calls. Add another $300 or so for test preparation for the LSAT, and you have already committed more than $1,000.

The total cost of a legal education can be more than $150,000. Concerned? You'd be crazy not to be. For further guidance, you might want to consult *Looking at Law School: A Student Guide from the Society of American Law Teachers*, 4th Ed., Stephen Gillers, Ed. (Meridian Books, 1997). NYU Law School Professor

529

Stephen Gillers, whom you may have seen on television, wrote a chapter entitled "Making the Decision to Go to Law School." It is particularly helpful on this issue. The Preface is by the late William J. Brennan, Jr., a former Associate Justice of the United States Supreme Court.

Don't let those numbers frighten you. They are not intended to dissuade you from pursuing a legal education but rather to dramatize a point. The decision to apply to law school has significant financial implications for you as an individual (and probably for your family).

To create the most powerful application possible given your GPA, test score, and background, you need to be aware of the criteria the law school will use when it reviews your application. That way, you can craft an application that, in its every detail, answers to the concerns of the admission committee.

The Business of Education

A law school, like any educational institution, is a corporate individual, and its admissions decisions reflect financial and social policies adopted by the corporation. Consider first some of the financial implications for a law school to accept or reject an applicant. The law school has to be run as a business. It has employees, it owns or rents property, it operates a library, it buys furniture and office equipment, it pays utility bills, and so on. A large part of those expenses are paid using student tuition. A law school, therefore, is dependent on a steady flow of tuition money. So admissions decisions must be made in the context of budgetary constraints. A law school simply cannot afford to have large numbers of students dropping out of school.

So one concern of a law school admissions officer is to ensure that those applicants who are accepted are committed to completing the course of study. In addition—though this may not be an explicit concern—law schools rely heavily on alumni donations. So it would not be surprising to learn that an applicant who shows considerable professional promise would be considered favorably. And a school that graduates successful lawyers gets a reputation for being a good school and such a reputation in turn tends to attract highly qualified applicants.

Financial considerations are only one aspect of the admissions decision. Law schools also have a sense of the social responsibility they bear as educators of lawyers—one of the most influential groups of people in our society. They meet this responsibility in some fairly obvious ways, such as actively seeking applications from groups who are underrepresented in the practice of law and by establishing programs to train lawyers for positions of special need.

The Competition

About 100,000 people start the admission process each year, but there are fewer than 50,000 seats. The admissions process, then, is the interface between two perspectives. The process is designed to match individuals and institutions who can mutually satisfy each other's needs. This matching function, however, is somewhat skewed. For decades, there have been more people interested in pursuing law as a career than there are seats available at accredited law schools. In recent times, there have been about two applicants for each available seat. As a consequence, applicants are competing for law school seats. Given the mismatch between the number of seats and the number of applicants, the application process is turned into a competition. You will have to compete against others for a law school seat (or at least for a seat at the law school of your choice). To do this, you must make yourself attractive to a law school. You must persuade the admissions committee that you will help them satisfy their economic and social needs. And that thought must guide you as you create your application.

Finally, tell them what they want to hear. Law schools want students who have the ability to handle the curriculum and the motivation to study hard and who will be interesting additions to the law school. Everything that goes into your application should bear on one of these points.

The LSAT/GPA Factors and the "Admissions Index"

Despite the variety of formal structures, one generalization is possible: Every law school relies to some extent on the applicant's Grade Point Average (GPA) and LSAT score, but there are few (if any) law schools that rely only on these quantitative factors. What does this statement mean for you? First, it says that every law school uses the GPA and the LSAT score. The exact use of these numbers varies from school to school, but many use a formula that combines the two together into an index. The formula is designed to weight the two numbers approximately equally to give admissions officers some idea of how one applicant stacks up against other applicants.

You've heard it said before, but it really is true: the two most important factors in your application are your GPA and your LSAT score. While law school admissions officers often say that they prefer to minimize the importance of the objective measures (and won't say exactly how much each is worth), an application with numbers that are too low will be rejected—whether there is a formal or just an informal cutoff.

The LSAT is scored on a scale from 120 (the minimum) to 180 (the maximum). You may notice that the 20 and the 80 are reminiscent of the 200 and 800 scale of the SAT, and this is not accidental. Originally, the LSAT was scored on a scale ranging from 200 to 800. In 1991, the present scale was adopted so that it wouldn't look exactly like the SAT scale but could still be used in formulas combining test score with GPA.

The 20-to-80 point scale has a special relation to the 0-to-4 grading system used by most colleges: 80 is 20 times 4. This permits the use of a formula to combine the two measures. For example:

$$Index = (LSAT - 100) + (20 \times GPA)$$

This formula combines the two numbers to create an index. Let's use some numbers, say a GPA of 3.5 and an LSAT score of 170:

$$I = (LSAT - 100) + (20 \times GPA)$$
$$I = (170 - 100) + (20 \times 3.5) = 140$$

Thus, the Index for this particular applicant is a 140—an artificial number but one that will make sense to the admissions committee because all other applications at their school are classified in the same manner.

Another Index formula might generate a number with a more familiar look.

$$Index = \frac{(LSAT - \frac{100}{20}) + GPA}{2}$$

An LSAT score of 170 and a GPA of 3.5 would generate the value 3.5 using this formula, and the 3.5 is a fairly intuitive number: this applicant is a B+/A– student.

What does the Index do? That varies from school to school. Some schools have a fairly mechanical admissions process that emphasizes the Index. The school may set a minimum Index below which applications receive little or no attention because they are probably going to be rejected anyway. Such schools may also have a second, higher minimum that triggers an automatic acceptance (unless the application shows some glaring weakness, e.g., the applicant is a three-time felon). At the opposite extreme are schools that minimize the importance of the "numbers." These schools may not even calculate an Index. Such schools have a very flexible admissions process.

Most schools fall somewhere in between these extremes. Many schools use the Index as a screening device to determine how much attention will be given to an application. Applications with very low Indices will receive little attention. The schools reason that unless there is something obvious and compelling in the application to offset the low numbers, then the applicant will be rejected. Applications with very high Indices will also receive little attention. The reasoning is that unless there is something obvious and compelling in the application to reject it, it should be accepted. On this theory, the applications with Indices in the middle receive the greatest attention. These are applications from candidates who are at least competitive for the school but who do not command an automatic acceptance. It is in this pool that competition is the most severe.

Here is a table that illustrates what happens at most law schools. (Law schools are notoriously edgy about releasing this kind information, so the table is a composite based on data from several schools.):

ADMISSIONS CHANCES

	LSAT (Percentile Rankings)			
	61–70	71–80	81–90	90+
G 3.75+	2/19	40/101	102/116	72/79
P 3.50–3.74	6/112	75/275	301/361	120/129
A Below 3.50	10/160	90/601	375/666	201/250

(The number to the right of the slash shows the number of applicants; the number to the left of the slash shows the number of applicants accepted.)

In the category in the upper right hand corner are candidates with scores above the 90th percentile and GPAs above 3.75. The table shows that 72 of the 79 were accepted and 7 rejected.

Interestingly, the table also shows that some candidates with higher Indexes were rejected in favor of candidates with lower numbers. For example, of those candidates with scores between the 81st and 90th percentiles, 74 more candidates were accepted with a GPA below 3.50 than the higher GPA between 3.5 and 3.74. Why would a law school reject an applicant with higher numbers for one with lower numbers? Because of the unquantifiable factors such as motivation, commitment, leadership, experience, and so on. (More information on the role of these factors and how you can demonstrate that you have them is given later in this chapter.)

As you prepare your applications, you are, of course, saddled with your GPA and your LSAT score. There is nothing you can do to change those factors. This means that you have to work hard to craft an application that presents your credentials in the best light.

Want to know more about your chances for success at a particular law school? Consult the *Official American Bar Association Guide to Approved Law Schools*, American Bar Association (Macmillan General Reference, 1998). The American Bar Association is the professional association for lawyers in the United States. And their committee on legal education is responsible for deciding which law schools will receive accreditation. This book is filled with admissions data on every ABA-accredited law school, and it will give you a good idea of what your chances are at particular schools.

ROLLING AND EARLY ADMISSIONS

Rolling admissions is a device used by many law schools that regulates the release of acceptances. A typical law school application season opens in October and closes in February or perhaps March. Applications will be received throughout the application season, and decisions are made on an ongoing basis. Rather than saving all applications until the deadline for applications is past and then making decisions, rolling admissions allows law schools to notify applicants on an ongoing basis.

Law schools begin the rolling admission process by creating a target profile of the entering class. Based on its admissions history, a law school will estimate what it thinks will be the range of LSAT scores and the range of GPAs of the students it will accept for the upcoming year. Then, as it receives applications (say, month by month), the school will act on them. Students with very strong applications compared with the target group will receive acceptances, and students with weak applications receive rejections. Applications that are neither weak nor strong are carried over—though these applicants receive no notification that the application is still pending.

The rolling admissions process has advantages for both the law school and the applicant. From the applicant's point of view, the earlier the notification of the disposition of an application, the better. That is, you know whether you were accepted or rejected and can go on from there. From the law school's viewpoint, the entering class (and the stability of the budget) begin to take shape as early as possible.

The rolling admissions process is also a tool you can use to your advantage: Apply early. Obviously, schools have greater flexibility earlier in the admission season than later. There are more seats available earlier in the year. That is not to say that if you apply late in the season, you will be rejected. In fact, it is impossible to quantify exactly the advantage that applications received earlier rather than later enjoy. Still, if you want to maximize your chances of acceptance, apply early!

The same advice applies for schools that offer early admission. Early admission procedures require applications by a certain date early in the application season and guarantee you a decision by a certain date. Early admission procedures may be restrictive or non-restrictive. A restrictive procedure requires the applicant to agree that if an offer of admission is extended then the candidate will withdraw applications from all other schools and decline any other offers of admission. In other words, applying for the early decision commits you to attending that law school if you are accepted. Other early admission procedures do not require such a commitment.

For more information on early admissions and other special features, visit law school web sites. For example, check out www.law.nyu.edu/, home page of the New York University (NYU) Law School. The Law School's tax, corporate, and clinical programs are unsurpassed. Plus, the Root-Tilden-Snow Scholars is a premier program for public interest law. And the law school, which has students and faculty members from around the world, is noted for its global orientation.

DECIDING WHERE TO APPLY

Given the financial commitment that you will be making, one of the obvious questions on your mind will be "Where should I apply?"

Let's assume that you have the resources to apply to ten schools and that you have an above average GPA and LSAT score. Depending on the exact numbers, you may very well have a chance at one of the top law schools. But those are your long shot schools. You are almost a sure thing at many schools. And there is a long list of schools in the middle at which your application will almost surely receive serious consideration but is not guaranteed for acceptance. Given these considerations, you should select two or perhaps three long shot schools. As the term *long shot* implies, the odds of your being accepted at these schools are not very good, but the potential pay-off justifies the gamble.

On the other hand, you should also select one or two sure thing schools. To do this, you may have to apply to a school in your geographical area that doesn't enjoy a particularly good reputation or to a school that is located in another part of the country. The rest of your applications should go to your good bet schools—schools for which the chances for acceptance are 40 percent to 75 percent.

Hedge your application bets. Given your LSAT score and GPA, classify schools on your list as "sure things" (odds of acceptance are better than 4 out of 5), "long shots" (odds are worse than 1 out of 5), and "solid favorites" (odds are 2 out of 5 to 4 out of 5). Put most of your "money" on the solid favorites with lesser amounts on sure things and long shots. (The exact proportions will depend on your personal risk-taking preferences.)

This strategy of "stacking" your applications will maximize your chances of acceptance at a school you want while minimizing the chance that you won't get into any school. Of course, the way the strategy gets implemented will vary from person to person. For people who are lucky enough to have a high GPA and a top LSAT score, the middle- and bottom-tier schools collapse into a single tier. And at the other extreme, those who are unlucky enough to have a GPA and LSAT score that are below what most schools accept will have to work with the second and third tiers.

As you prepare to implement your strategy, make a realistic assessment of your chances. Candidates unfortunately tend to overestimate the importance of what they believe to be their own interesting or unique factors. It is not unusual to hear candidates make statements such as "Well sure my GPA is a little low, but I had to work part-time while I was in school" and "I know my LSAT score is not that good, but I was a member of the University Senate." These are valid points and are usually taken into consideration by admissions officers. But the question is how much weight they will be given, for they (or some similar point) are true of most of the people who are applying to law school.

Be realistic. If you are thinking of applying to Yale Law School and you have a 3.25 GPA and an LSAT score of 75th percentile, then there had better be something really special in your background (such as the Nobel Peace Prize) because in some years, Yale has a hundred-plus applicants with such numbers and accepts none.

CRAFTING YOUR APPLICATION

To maximize your chances of success, you must create an application that satisfies the needs of the school to which you are applying. This does not mean that you create an application out of whole cloth, but it does mean that you organize and present your experiences in a way that depicts you in the most favorable light.

Answering the "Short Answer" Application Questions

Most of the questions you will be asked need only short answers; for example, "Did you work while you were in school?", "What clubs did you join?", and "What honors or awards did you receive?" You don't have much room to maneuver here. But you should try to communicate as much information as possible in your short answers. Compare the following pairs of descriptions:

Good	Member of the College Orchestra
Better	Second Violinist of the College Orchestra
Good	Played Intramural Volleyball
Better	Co-captain of the Phi Kappa Volleyball Team
Good	Member of the AD's CSL
Better	One of three members on the Associate Dean's Committee on Student Life
Good	Worked at Billy's Burger Barn
Better	Assistant Manager at Billy's Burger Barn (25 hours/week)

In addition to the short answer questions, most applications invite you to make a personal statement. Some applications ask for very little; for example, "In a paragraph, explain to us why you want to go to law school." Other applications are open-ended: "On a separate sheet of paper, tell us anything else you think we ought to know about you." The point of the question is to give you the opportunity to give the admissions committee any information that might not be available from the LSAT score, GPA, and short-answer questions.

Before filling out any applications, sit down and make a list of all of your accomplishments. Include everything. Then prioritize the list. Keep only the ones that are likely to be meaningful to a law school admission committee.

Writing an Effective Personal Statement

For two reasons, you should consider the personal statement to be the most important part of your application. First, the personal statement should be your argument to the admissions committee for your acceptance. It should give the reasons to accept you. Second, the personal statement is the one aspect of the application over which you can exercise any real control. Your GPA is already settled. Your work experience was accumulated over years; your LSAT has been scored. Those are aspects of the application that cannot easily be manipulated. The personal statement, however, is under your control. For an in-depth review "before and after" versions of some sample personal statements, see Appendix B, *Workshop: The Personal Statement.*

What should go into a personal statement? Arguments that interpret your academic, employment, and personal history in such a way as to indicate that you have the ability to do law school studies and that you are committed to studying and later to practicing law. Importantly, the personal statement must not be a simple restatement of facts already in the application.

Imagine, for example, a "personal statement" that reads as follows:

> *I went to State University where I got a 3.5 GPA. I was a member of the Associate Dean's Committee on Student Life, and I worked as the assistant manager on the night shift at Billy's Burger Barn. Then I took the LSAT and got a 160. I know I will make a really good lawyer and will enjoy the job.*

Not very interesting. Furthermore, all of that information is already included in the answers to the standard questions on the application. There is no point in simply repeating it.

Instead, your personal statement should interpret the facts of your life to make them reasons why you should be accepted into law school. Let's start with the GPA. Try to bring out facts that suggest that the GPA is really better than it looks:

- Did you have one particularly bad semester during which you took Physics, Calculus, and Latin that pulled your average down?

- Was there a death in the family or some other difficult time that interfered with your studies?

- How many hours did you work in an average week?

- What extracurricular or family commitments took time away from your studies?

- Did you follow an unusual course of study such as an honors program or a double major?

- Was your major a particularly challenging one?

- Did you participate in any unusual courses such as field research?

These are the points that the admissions committee wants to hear. For example:

> *The committee will see that my final GPA is 3.5. I should point out that the average would have been higher had I not had to work 20 hours each week to finance my education. In addition, my grades in the first semester of my junior year were disappointing because my grandmother, who lived with my family and with whom I was very close, died. Finally, in order to fulfill the requirements for the honors program, I wrote a 50-page honors thesis on the economics of the Dutch fishing industry of the eighteenth century. I have included with this application a copy of the introduction to this paper.*

You should take the same approach to your work experience. For example:

> *During my junior and senior years in college, I worked an average of 20 hours per week at Billy's Burger Barn as the manager on the night shift. I reported to work at midnight and got off at four a.m. As night manager, I supervised eight other employees and was responsible for making emergency repairs on kitchen equipment. For example, once I was able to keep the deep fryer in operation by using a length of telephone cable to repair a faulty thermostat. The night manager was also responsible for maintaining order. It's no easy job to convince intoxicated students who become too rowdy to leave without calling the police. And we were robbed at gunpoint not once but twice.*

Of course, if you have considerable work experience, e.g., if you graduated from college several years ago, you will want to go into your experience in more detail than student work experience merits.

Can you say anything about the LSAT? Probably not much. The LSAT score is not usually open to interpretation, but there are some exceptions. One such exception is a history of poor scores on standardized exams. Consider the following:

> *I believe that my LSAT score of 160 understates my real ability, for I have never had much success on aptitude tests. My SAT score was only 925. Yet, I finished college with a 3.6 GPA.*

Or

> *The committee will see that I have two LSAT scores, 131 and 160. During the first test, I had the flu and a fever and simply could not concentrate.*

These are the two most common excuses for a disappointing LSAT score.

Finally, you must also persuade the admissions committee that you are serious about studying law. It won't do to write "I really like those old Matlock reruns." You must be able to show the committee something in your background that explains why you want to go to law school. Also, it will help your case if you can suggest what you might do with a law degree. For example:

> *As a chemistry major, I joined the Student Environmental Association. Working with private lawyers, we provided evidence in court that ultimately forced the University to stop polluting the Ten Mile Run Creek. From this experience, I learned how the law helps to protect our environment. I plan to make environmental law my area of study, and I hope to work for the government or a private agency to protect the environment.*

A word of warning. Your career objectives have to be believable. It won't do to write "I plan to fight for truth, justice, and the American way." That's much too abstract. Nor are law school admissions officers interested in a general discourse on the advantages of democracy or the hardship of poverty. And any statement about motivation must be credible. If you write "I want to defend the poor and help the needy," then there better be something in your experience that makes this believable. For example:

> *As a member of the Volunteers for the Needy, I work 5 hours each week cooking in our neighborhood soup kitchen. In addition, I telephone local businesses trying to find jobs for the people we help. I have learned that many people who need our help are victims of rigid government standards or unfair landlord or employer practices. As a lawyer, I would be able to help attack the causes of some poverty.*

With regard to motivation, don't imagine that there is a preferred political position that you should adopt. Law school admissions officers span the political spectrum. To be sure, some are political liberals, but there are also conservatives. You don't have to make up a " tear jerker" to get accepted.

Finally, you may also wish to include in your personal statement information that shows that you have something that will help the school create a diverse student body. This additional information can be something dramatic:

> *One morning, a patron choked on a burger and lost consciousness. I used the Heimlich maneuver to dislodge the food and performed CPR until a team of paramedics arrived. The patron recovered fully in large part, according to her doctors, because of my first aid.*

Or the information may not be dramatic:

> *My parents are Armenian immigrants, so I am fluent in Armenian as well as English. I would enjoy meeting others who share an interest in the politics, legal developments, and culture of that part of the world.*

Don't overestimate the value of this kind of information. It is, so to speak, the icing on the cake. It makes you a more interesting individual and might tip the scale in your favor when all other things are equal. It will not, however, get you an acceptance at a school for which you are not otherwise competitive in terms of LSAT and GPA.

Organizing Your Argument

Your personal statement represents your "case" in that it presents your arguments for why you should be accepted. When you marshal your arguments for acceptance, you need to present them in an organized fashion. There is no single preferred format, but you might start with the following outline:

I.   I have the ability.
  A. My college studies were good.
    i. I had one bad semester.
    ii. I was in the honors program.
    iii. I wrote a thesis.
  B. My work experience is good.
    i. I was promoted to VP of my firm.
    ii. I worked while in college.
II. I want to become a lawyer.
  A. I worked with lawyers on the pollution problem.
  B. I would become a specialist in environmental law.
III. There is something interesting about me.

You should create your outline, using all the arguments you can think of. Then you must begin to edit. For most people, the final document should not be more than a page to a page and a half—typed of course! During the editing process, you should strive for an economy of language so that you can convey as much information as possible. In addition, you will be forced to make considered judgments about the relative importance of various points. You will be forced to delete those ideas that aren't really that compelling. To obtain a really good personal statement, it may be necessary to reduce five or six pages to a single page, and the process may require more than 20 drafts.

If your numbers (LSAT and GPA) are in the ballpark, then your personal statement is likely to be the most important part of the application. It will never be perfect, but make it as much so as possible. Ask professors, friends, and co-workers to read it and to comment on it. You might even want to consult a professional adviser to help to construct the application.

Finally, the prose you use should be your own natural style of writing. Don't try something cute. Admissions officers detest essays that try to look like legal briefs and refer to the "evidence" and "reasonable doubt."

Letters of Recommendation

Perhaps the best advice about so-called letters of recommendation is to think of them as evaluations rather than recommendations. Indeed, many admissions officers refer to letter-writers as evaluators. These letters can be very important factors in an application, so you need to choose their authors carefully.

Too many applicants choose evaluators because they think they need character witnesses (the applicant is honest and trustworthy) or endorsements from powerful people (Judge So-and-So). But admissions officers are not really interested in either of those qualities in an evaluator. Instead, they want to hear from someone who knows you well and who can detail the characteristics that you have that would make you a good law student—to wit, the ability to do the curriculum and the motivation to work hard.

First of all, most schools require a letter from the dean of students (or some similar functionary) at your college. Even if you never met the dean, you have to get this letter if the law school to which you're applying requires it. But law schools don't really expect the dean to have much to say. The requirement is in essence an inquiry to the college about your behavior. It is intended to evoke any information about disciplinary problems that might not otherwise surface. So the best letter from a dean, and the one that most people get, is just a statement to the effect that there is nothing to say about you.

In addition to the dean's letter, most law schools require or at least permit you to submit two or three letters of evaluation from other sources. Who should write these? First, let's dispose of a common misunderstanding. A letter of evaluation does not have to come from a famous person. How effective is the following letter?

William Hardy, Chief Judge
State Superior Court

To the Admissions Committee:

I am recommending Paul Roberts for law school. His mother appears frequently in my court and is a very fine attorney. If Paul is anything like his mother, he too will be a fine lawyer.

Sincerely,

William Hardy

The letterhead holds out great promise, but then the letter itself is worthless. It is obvious that the letter-writer doesn't really have any basis for the conclusion that the candidate will make a good lawyer.

The best letters of evaluation will come from people who know you very well, e.g., a professor with whom you took several courses, your immediate supervisor at work, or a business associate with whom you have worked closely. A good evaluation will incorporate the personal knowledge into the letter and will make references to specific events and activities. For example:

Mary P. Weiss
White, Weiss, and Blanche

To the Admissions Committee:

White, Weiss, and Blanche is a consulting firm that advises businesses on environmental matters. Paul Roberts has worked for us for the past two summers. His work is outstanding, and he is an intelligent and genial person.

Last summer, as my assistant, Paul wrote a 25-page report that outlined a way of altering a client's exhaust stack to reduce sulfur emissions. The report was organized so that it was easy to follow and written in a style that was clear and easy to understand. In addition, Paul made the live presentation during a meeting with the client's board of directors, engineers, and lawyers. He was confident and handled some very difficult questions in an easy manner. I should note that we have used Paul's innovation in several other plants.

Finally, I would note that Paul made an important contribution to our company softball team. The team finished in last place, but Paul played in every game. His batting average wasn't anything to brag about, but his enthusiasm more than made up for it.

Sincerely,

Mary Weiss

To get a letter such as this, you will have to ask someone who knows you well. It may also help to provide them with some "suggestions" about what should go into the letter. So if you have not been in recent contact, send a resume with a cover letter reminding them of some of the important points that you might want them to mention.

SOME FINAL THOUGHTS ON THE LAW SCHOOL APPLICATION PROCESS

You are about to make a huge investment in your future. The cost of applying to law school is virtually nothing when compared to the cost of a legal education. And the cost of a legal education is minuscule when compared with your earnings potential over a lifetime—depending on where you get in. More importantly, it is your life—your time needed to complete applications, three years in law school, and a career. So explore all options and maximize your opportunities.

Workshop: The Personal Statement

This part gives you a look at the "before" and "after" of two personal statements. The case studies used are composites, suitably sanitized, that have been created from two or more actual files in order to illustrate a wider range of points. For each case study, there is a summary of the candidate's credentials, a first version of the personal statement, a critique of the first version, and an "improved version" of the personal statement. The "improved version" should not be taken as a final version. Even the "improved version" needs further work, but the work becomes a matter of careful attention to detail rather than a major reorganization.

CASE STUDY 1: J.V.

J.V. was 27 when she decided to apply to law school. At the time, she was a civil service worker for a government agency. She realized that while she enjoyed considerable job security, that job security also meant a fairly tedious day-to-day routine and a plodding career track. She took the LSAT and got a 174 and the GMAT and got a 510. She decided to apply to law school. Her undergraduate grade point average was 3.7. After considering her options, she selected six schools—three Ivy League schools, two "second tier" schools, and one local school at which admission was all but assured.

RESUME OF J. V.
PERSONAL INFORMATION

Address:	355 West Oak Street
	Anywhere, USA
Telephone:	555-1212 (Day); 555-2323 (Evening)

Educational Background

M.A., State University, French Literature, 1994

Thesis: Deconstructing the Sartre–de Beauvoir Correspondence
Activities: University Graduate Student Council
French Literature & Philosophy Forum

B.A., State College, Romance Languages, 1993 (Honors)

Activities: Junior Year Abroad, Paris
University Choral Society
Italian-American Caucus

Employment History

1994–Present: Social Security Administration

Supervise 25 claims agents; responsibility for reviewing claimant appeals for benefits.

1993–1994: State University, French Dept.

Adjunct Professor

Other Interests

Music (Opera and Piano)
Travel

Personal Statement

WHY I WANT TO GO TO LAW SCHOOL

The decision to apply to law school represents the third and final important reorientation in my life. I came to college certain that I would want to pursue a teaching career and entered the School of Education. After a semester, I realized that I did not want to teach on the elementary or even secondary level, so I transferred to the College of Arts and Sciences to study languages and become a college teacher. After graduation, I took a Masters in French while I taught on the college level. During that year, I realized that even college teaching was not for me. At the end of that time, I took a job with the Federal Government.

While with the Federal Government, I have received several promotions. In my present capacity, I am a Supervisor for the Social Security Administration. I have the responsibility for supervising 25 Claims Agents. This means that I supervise their day-to-day activities (assigning cases and monitoring progress) and handle crisis situations (such as labor union grievances). One of my most important duties is to review the appeals of people whose claims for benefits have been denied. In order to do this, I have to have a detailed knowledge of the regulations governing the eligibility of claimants. I believe that my experience with our procedures is good training for practicing law.

Finally, I would add that my outside interests include both travel and music. Over the past five years, I have visited Mexico, Peru, Spain, and Israel. I have studied piano since I was a small child, and I been involved with several opera workshops.

One of the most common mistakes made by applicants is to write a personal statement that "moves across the surface," and that is the main weakness of this statement. For example, paragraph one simply repeats a chronology that will be available to the reader elsewhere in the application. (Just as it is available in the resume.) It simply reiterates "what" happened without addressing the "why" of the events. What is the significance of the transfer from the School of Education to the College of Arts and Sciences? And if it doesn't have any significance (from the perspective of an admissions officer), then it doesn't belong in the personal statement.

Next, why explain the move from academia to government service? On its face, the move looks like the applicant taught for a year while doing an M.A. and then moved on to the "real world." Unless there is something more to the event than that, it speaks for itself and doesn't need to be addressed in the personal statement—particularly since it happened so long ago.

The second paragraph likewise "moves across the surface." Much of the information provided there will already have been included in the "Q and A" part of the application. As you can see, the second paragraph really does not add anything to this. The last part of the second paragraph attempts to explain the significance that the employment experience has in terms of a law school application. This part should be expanded, and more detail should be included.

The third paragraph is a good idea, but its treatment is too cursory. How much time did the applicant spend in the places mentioned? If just a week or two, then this travel probably won't mean much to a law school admissions officer. In addition, the effectiveness of the discussion about musical talent would be considerably enhanced with some more detail.

As it turns out, further discussion with this applicant revealed some important information that was not apparent from the resume (and likely would not have shown up in the "Q and A" part of the application). After reworking, the applicant's statement has much greater impact. Here's the revised version of J. V.'s personal statement:

WHY I WANT TO GO TO LAW SCHOOL

My decision to apply to law school was made after careful reflection. My present employment affords me a comfortable standard of living and considerable job security, but the position no longer offers the challenges and variety that it once did. To be sure, there are occasional surprises. A few months ago, for example, a male employee filed a grievance claiming that he was the victim of sexual harassment in the workplace. (He alleged that two female co-workers had made suggestive remarks about parts of his anatomy.) As it turns out, what really happened was that a male co-worker reported to the complainant that such remarks had been made. Since they were not made directly to the complainant, there was no ground under our rules for any action. (And the comments of the male co-worker were not, in and of themselves, sexual harassment.) By and large, however, the supervisory duties are fairly routine.

Sometimes appeals claims offer a surprise. Last year, for example, a claimant appeared at a hearing accompanied by an adviser/translator. The adviser/translator would translate my questions (stated in English) into Spanish. What the adviser/translator did not realize is that I am fluent in Spanish, and I knew that throughout the hearing that the adviser/translator was instructing the claimant on how to fabricate a claim. At the end of the hearing, both claimant and adviser/translator were flabbergasted when I told them in Spanish that they were both being charged with attempted fraud. By and large, however, even the appeals on denied claims are usually fairly routine.

What I would hope to find in law school and later in the practice of law is more of the very best moments of the position I currently have. Even though I know that every occupation has its tedium, I expect that the practice of law would offer greater variety and challenge. While I hear 30 to 40 cases each month, most of these are similar in their details. Even those that present unusual facts are resolved by reference to a fairly compact body of regulations. I look forward with anticipation to the opportunity to handle cases with variety and surprises and to the need to address a much wider range of legal concepts.

I am confident in my ability to handle the law school curriculum. My college transcript shows that I graduated with "General Honors" (top 15 percent), but it does not show that my studies made me fluent in French and Italian (as well as Spanish). I anticipate that studying law will be like learning yet another "foreign" language—vocabulary, syntax, logic, etc. While a graduate student, I was a member of the French Literature & Philosophy Forum. During that academic year, three of the featured speakers were law professors who discussed the application of literary analysis to legal texts. For one of my courses, I wrote a paper entitled "Con-text-ualizing the Law." (I have enclosed a copy for the Committee's review.)

Finally, in addition to my experience in a government agency and my academic perspective, I think that I can add something to the law school on a personal level. I have studied voice for nearly ten years. I am a Mezzo-Soprano, and I have participated in several opera workshops. Most recently, I sang the role of Dorabella in Mozart's **Cosi Fan Tutte** with the Northern State Regional Opera Company. This was a particularly satisfying experience because, unlike most workshop productions, this one was done with an orchestra instead of just piano, and the orchestra included several well-known members of the City Orchestra.

In addition to eliminating the weaknesses mentioned, the revised version contains a couple of very nice features. The additional details—the name of the paper, the role of Dorabella, the importance of the orchestra—all make the revised version more readable as well as more credible. Also, the anecdote that illustrates the use of Spanish is a nice touch. It's an interesting story, in and of itself. In fact, don't underestimate the importance of holding the reader's attention. Admissions officers may be reading a dozen or more personal statements an hour and hundreds in just a few weeks. You need something that will make yours stand out.

CASE STUDY 2: P.D.

P.D. was 20 and a junior in college when he decided on a career in law. He took the LSAT in the spring of his junior year and scored 148. He took the exam a second time in the fall of his senior year and scored 162. His GPA through the first six semesters was 3.4. In order to maximize his options, P.D. decided to apply to ten schools—only one top-tier school, two second-tier schools, and seven schools with various distinguishing features. (The following application document was completed in the fall of P.D.'s senior year, so some information was not yet available.)

APPLICATION FOR ADMISSION

Educational Background

List the official names of all colleges, universities, and other postsecondary institutions attended, including those for summer session or evening class. Complete an LSDAS (Law School Data Assembly Service) report. Send any transcripts not a part of that report directly to the law school.

Institution	Dates	Major	Degree	Date
Loyola U.	94–	History	A.B.	NA
Kramer CC	Sum '93	NA	NA	NA

List Academic Honors and Other Awards Received

Dean's List (2 Semesters)

Honorable Mention, Robertson Prize in History

APPLICATION FOR ADMISSION (PAGE 2)

Employment History

Loyola U., Public Relations, Summer '96, 40 hours per week

City News, Account Rep., Summer '95, 40 hours per week

TV Cable Co., Installer, Summer '94, 40 hours per week

City News, Carrier, Spring '96, 15 hours per week

City News, Carrier, Spring '95, 10 hours per week

Personal Statement

Staple to this page a typed, signed personal statement that tells us why you want to pursue a legal education. Please discuss personal and professional goals that are important to you. You should consider this an opportunity to introduce yourself to us.

PERSONAL STATEMENT

I want to take this opportunity to introduce myself to the Admissions Committee. I will graduate from Loyola University next spring with a major in history. I hope to become a lawyer. I want to become a lawyer because I am vitally concerned with the important problems that face us as a society. These include issues such as the environment, ethics in government, and social injustice. As a lawyer, I know that I will be in a position to address these important matters.

If the Committee reviews my record, they will see that I have a strong academic background. Through my first six semesters, I have a 3.4 GPA, and

I expect to do better during the next two semesters. I have taken the LSAT twice because I did not do very well the first time (scoring only 148), but the second time I got a 162. I have been on the Dean's List twice, and my paper on the Federalist Papers received "Honorable Mention" in the History Department's Robertson Competition. I would point out that I achieved these accomplishments while working part-time. I even took courses at the community college during the summer.

My employment also demonstrates that I have the ability to do well in law school. While it is true that my first summer in college I worked as a laborer for TV Cable installing cable, my second summer I was an Account Representative for the City News. In that capacity, I dealt with people on a daily basis and had to think on my feet. After that I worked for the University in its Public Relations Office.

As a member of the Student Government, I was exposed to the legislative process. I was able to observe first hand the give and take that goes into the formation of laws. Plus I was a member of the Demosthenes Club and a member of an intramural basketball team.

The problem that P.D. faces—and it is one faced by thousands of candidates who are applying for admission directly out of college—is that it may be difficult to articulate specific reasons why one wants to become a lawyer. To be sure, many undergraduates may have fairly settled career goals; and if you are one of them, you should not hesitate to state your goals. Other students, however, may have only the vaguest idea of why they want to become lawyers; and if you are one of them, you should not overstate your case. Instead, you should address the issue in general terms and let your record speak for you. Let's walk through some of the weaknesses in P.D.'s personal statement.

There is nothing particularly wrong with the first paragraph. There may be better ways of beginning this type of essay, but certainly it cannot be said that this style is completely inappropriate.

The second paragraph, however, is almost completely a waste of ink. P.D. expects the reader to believe that he wants to go to law school because he wants, in essence, to "reform the world." Is there any evidence in P.D.'s background to suggest that this is a real commitment? Is a member of student government necessarily a social reformer? Is a member of an intramural basketball league? An account representative for a newspaper? No. Without some further evidence of a real and long-standing commitment to social reform, this sort of language seems contrived and will likely fall on deaf ears.

The next paragraph is also pretty much useless. The explanation regarding the LSAT score is typical of many personal statements: "I didn't do well the first time I took the test, so I took it again." Since the LSAS reports multiple scores to the law schools, that much will be obvious! If you are going to address the fact that you have taken the LSAT more than once, then you must be prepared with an explanation: "The first time I took the LSAT I got a 148, but I was very ill with the flu that day. My second test, taken when I felt well, is a better indicator of my ability."

The last part of the essay has the merit of mentioning the title of the paper that earned P.D. the "Honorable Mention." This is something that is probably not covered elsewhere in the application and so should be expanded upon. It might even be a good idea to include a copy of the paper or at least the introduction. One would not expect that an Admissions Committee would read it as thoroughly as a professor would, but one might hope that an admissions officer might say "Mmmmm, I don't have time to read all of this, but it does look like a good piece of work." The third and fourth paragraphs also don't say very much beyond what is already evident in the rest of the application. It is important to explain to an admissions officer the significance of events and accomplishments.

As for the entry about intramural basketball, P.D. was twice a member of the Intramural Allstars; and at this college, each spring the Intramural Allstars play an exhibition game in the arena against members of the college's varsity basketball team. This experience obviously does not qualify P.D. to practice law, but it is an experience that few other law school applicants will have had—and it may count for something.

With these points in mind, P.D. can revise his personal statement to carry much more impact:

PERSONAL STATEMENT

I want to take this opportunity to introduce myself to the Admissions Committee and to provide you with some information that is not included in other parts of my application. I want to discuss further both the issue of my ability to succeed in law school and my reasons for wanting to become a lawyer.

First, my GPA alone does not describe the full extent of my academic ability. It is lower than it otherwise would have been because my performance in my freshman year was not particularly good. In addition, it was financially necessary for me to work the past two spring semesters, and you will observe that my grades during the spring semesters are lower than those of the fall semesters. Finally, I devoted considerable time to extracurricular activities.

As for the LSAT, the first time I took the exam, I was sick with the flu and obviously did not do as well as I could. My second score is a better measure of my real ability.

Setting aside the considerations above, if the Admissions Committee is looking for a good example of my ability, you should look at my paper "Implicit Religious Convictions in the Federalist Papers." I wrote this paper for

Professor M.V., a notoriously hard grader, who not only gave it an "A" but also encouraged me to enter it in the Robertson Competition. The Robertson Competition is sponsored by the History Department each year as part of its Colloquium on American History and is open to both graduate and undergraduate students. Twelve students read papers to a panel of distinguished historians from universities across the nation. One paper receives the "Robertson Award," and two others receive "Honorable Mention." I have enclosed a copy of this paper.

I have decided on a career in law because I enjoy doing those things that I have seen lawyers do. The Demosthenes Club is a debating society with 35 active members. We meet for 3 hours every other week to debate a topic such as "Capital Punishment" or "U.S. Military Commitments." The schedule allows members time to do some additional background research on announced topics. I particularly enjoy playing "Devil's Advocate" during the debates, offering counterexamples or pointing out inconsistencies in the arguments of others. In addition, I enjoy writing, and my work in the University's Public Relations Office has been particularly helpful in this regard. A press release has to be carefully crafted because it usually deals with a complex situation that must be described in terms that those not familiar with its details can grasp.

Finally, I noted in your Bulletin that the Law School sponsors an intramural basketball league. In high school, I dreamed of playing college basketball; and, in a way, I fulfilled this dream. Each year, the Intramural Allstars play members of the Varsity in an exhibition game in the Arena, and I was selected to play for the Allstars twice. Thus, I have had the privilege of being soundly defeated by some of the best in college basketball.

You'll notice that the revised statement answers all of the objections that were raised in response to the first version. Beyond that, the revised version is an improvement in a couple of other ways. First, the mention of the paper (as recommended) drives the point home: It's an impressive title suggesting critical analysis and research. The further detail about the debating society is also useful since it hints at skills a lawyer ought to have. Finally, the mention of the basketball game is good fun. And the self-deprecating tone of that paragraph, because it is in good humor, avoids the danger of sounding like a boast.

Ask the Experts

Here are 50 Frequently Asked Questions (FAQs) about applying to law school. The topics are arranged in a logical order so that the list, when read in its entirety, tells a more complete story.

JUST THE FAQS

1. Is it difficult to get into law school?

In a typical year, about 100,000 people start the law school application process, but there are fewer than 50,000 places for entering students in the 175+ law schools that are accredited by the American Bar Association. So the chance of getting into law school is less than one out of two. However, law school seats are not assigned by lottery, so the chance of getting into a certain law school depends on your qualifications, the level of competition for seats at that law school, the time you invest in preparing for the LSAT, and the effort you spend on your application.

Do you want to know more about your chances for success at a particular law school? Consult the *Official American Bar Association Guide to Approved Law Schools*, American Bar Association Law Schools (Macmillan General Reference, 1998). This book has admissions data on every ABA-accredited law school, and it will give you a pretty good idea of what your chances are at particular schools.

2. Who makes the admissions decisions?

Each law school has an admissions committee of one or more people who are responsible for reviewing and acting on applications for admission. At some schools, the authority is given to a group of faculty members; at others, it is given to a dean or to professional admissions officers; at still others, students are included in the deliberations. Of course, there are many variations on these practices.

3. How are admissions decisions made?

The mechanics of the decision-making process vary from school to school. For example, at one school, applications are assigned an index that is calculated by mathematical formula to produce a weighted average of the GPA and the LSAT score. The dean of admissions, acting alone, has the authority to accept applications with very high indexes and to reject those with very low indexes. All other applications must be referred to the admissions committee as a whole for debate and a vote. At another school, applications are distributed for reading to committee members, who must then make a recommendation to the committee as a whole for debate and a vote. At a third school, the dean of admissions acts as the committee. The dean reads each application in its entirety before looking at the LSAT score. The LSAT score is then used to confirm or disconfirm the dean's impression of the applicant based on all other factors. Ultimately, however, even though the mechanics are interesting, they are not terribly important because you cannot control them. The best you can do is submit a well-prepared application and hope for the best.

For more detailed information on the law school admissions process, you can consult *Getting Into Law School Today,* Thomas H. Martinson and David P. Waldherr (ARCO/Thomson Learning, 1998).

4. What factors do law schools take into consideration?

Typically, a law school will say that its admissions committee takes into account "all relevant factors," including the applicant's GPA (undergraduate Grade Point Average) and LSAT score. However, you should distinguish between what might be called "factors" and what might be called "indicators." By far, the two most important factors in the admissions process are ability and motivation. On the one hand, the committee has to be convinced that you have sufficient intellectual ability to handle the curriculum; on the other hand, the committee needs to know that you are seriously committed to completing the curriculum. Intellectual talent without proper discipline or dedication is not likely to ensure successful completion of the curriculum. Similarly, great aspirations without intellectual ability will get a student nowhere. The LSAT score and GPA are indicators of these factors. The LSAT score is designed to measure intellectual ability; the GPA provides information about both intellectual ability and motivation. Thus, the two most important factors in the admissions process are ability and motivation, and the two most important indicators of those factors are the GPA and the LSAT score.

5. Do law schools have formal LSAT and GPA cutoffs?

Although the LSAT score and the GPA are the two most important indicators, law schools are reluctant to say that they use a mechanical device, like a cutoff, to reject applications. And the school mentioned earlier that uses an index does so only to sort applications, not to make final decisions on them. Other schools, however, may specifically announce that applicants with numbers below certain minimal are "not likely" to be accepted.

6. Does every applicant have a chance at every school?

Not necessarily. At most law schools, it is possible to find students whose LSAT score or GPA or both are markedly below the medians of the student body, but such students are the exceptions. For most applicants, the probability of acceptance is largely a function of the GPA and LSAT score. Furthermore, even though a school does not have a formal cutoff for applications, it may have a *de facto* cutoff. One school, for example, states that applicants with an LSAT score below the 90th percentile or a GPA below 3.0 are rarely accepted, though there are exceptions. This statement implies that there is an informal minimum LSAT score and an informal minimum GPA, and applications with numbers below these minimums don't receive serious consideration. Be realistic, but don't underestimate your chances.

7. Why do law schools use GPAs and the LSAT scores?

The GPA plays an important part in the admissions process because virtually every applicant has one. The GPA is a readily available yardstick of intellectual ability and motivation by which most applicants can be compared. Law schools recognize, however, that grading practices vary from school to school, and that the variation can be significant. The LSAT was designed as another measure of ability, one that tests all applicants in a uniform way. Taken together, the GPA and the LSAT score are, statistically speaking, relatively accurate in predicting success in the first year of law school.

8. What about the quality of my undergraduate school?

Some admissions offices actually keep records on how students from different colleges and universities perform at the law school and use this information to judge the GPAs of applicants from schools for which they have records. Other admissions officers may make a subjective judgment about the quality of the GPA.

9. Are law schools interested in leadership ability?

To a certain extent, yes, because many lawyers wind up in positions of leadership. But you should not overestimate the importance of leadership ability as a factor in the admissions process. Law schools are primarily looking for evidence of academic ability and commitment.

10. Are other indicators considered?

Absolutely! Other indicators that might be considered relevant are graduate study, employment experience, extracurricular activities, community service work, family background, or interesting accomplishments of any kind, such as mastery of a second language, success in athletic competition, or musical talent.

11. Why are law schools interested in other indicators?

GPA and LSAT scores are not the only measures of ability. Law schools also want to know about other accomplishments. For example, an applicant who earned a mediocre GPA while working full-time as an undergraduate might have as much academic promise as an applicant with a very high GPA who had the luxury of devoting every waking hour to studying. Also, schools recognize that the LSAT is not a perfect measure. An applicant with a low-to-average LSAT score may have demonstrated considerable ability in business or in a profession. Motivation is important too. A law student with perhaps less ability but a greater measure of motivation might very well outperform a law student with more raw talent but less motivation. For this reason, law schools take commitment and motivation into consideration.

12. Should I say that I want to "serve justice" or "save the world"?

As a factor in the law school admissions process, motivation doesn't necessarily mean having a specific post-law school goal. To be sure, a few people enter law school with specific career objectives in mind, and these individuals often already have specialized training or experience (e.g., a social worker who wants to practice family law or an engineer who wants to practice patent law). The great majority of first-year law students have no idea what position they will fill after graduation. It is not necessary to express some lofty aspiration such as the desire to serve justice. In fact, unless you can point to specific experiences to show that such a claim is sincere (e.g., a community organizer who wants to use a law degree for social change), expressions of noble purpose are likely to seem contrived and unconvincing.

13. How do I demonstrate motivation?

Only a small percentage of candidates can demonstrate their motivation by showing that the study of law is the natural extension of the work they have been doing and leads to a particular type of practice. Most applicants indicate their motivation by previous success as a student or by success in a career. For such an applicant, a thoughtful explanation about the decision to become a lawyer may also show motivation.

14. Is it necessary to be a law major?

No. Law schools are interested in candidates who have studied a rigorous and broad-based liberal arts curriculum. It is not important whether an applicant's major was history, political science, economics, or chemistry, so long as the transcript shows a variety of challenging courses that would help to develop analytical skills and writing ability.

15. Does a law major have an advantage?

No. Undergraduate law courses teach about the law; they do not teach the practice of law. The law school curriculum is designed not just to familiarize students with important legal principles but also to teach them how to think like lawyers; that is, how to interpret legal principles and how to apply them in different situations. In fact, an undergraduate transcript that shows too many "criminal procedure" or "business law" courses may be viewed as weak. It may not exhibit the range of courses desired by the law school, and it may raise suspicion about the broadness and rigor of the undergraduate liberal arts curriculum.

16. How can I determine my chances of being accepted?

Admissions bulletins of law schools include information about the median or average GPA and LSAT score of the student body. Using that information, you can at least determine whether your numbers are above or below those that are typically accepted at that school. You should also consult the ABA publication mentioned above.

17. Can other indicators offset a low GPA or a low LSAT score?

In many cases, the answer is "yes," but the mitigating power of alternative indicators depends on the weakness of the GPA or LSAT score. For example, a law school admissions committee might be willing to forgive a business executive for a 2.9 GPA earned several years earlier but not for a 2.3 GPA. Or, in another example, a candidate who has earned a Ph.D. in economics might be forgiven for having an LSAT score in the 50th percentile but not in the 20th percentile.

18. What if I have a good LSAT score but a low GPA?

Law school admissions officers are aware that the GPA is an average or a summary of an applicant's college grades, and they are on the alert for anomalies or trends that would help them better to understand the significance of the average. For example, a single poor semester that depresses an otherwise respectable GPA may be forgiven, or a rising trend in grades from the first through the senior year might create a favorable impression.

19. What if I have a good GPA but a low LSAT?

If there is any reason for a poor LSAT score, you should make the admissions committee aware of it. If, for example, you took the LSAT when you were ill and did not do very well but later performed better, you should make sure the committee knows this. More generally, if you have a history of poor performances on standardized exams and yet have done very well in school, this too could be important and should be called to the committee's attention.

20. What if I have a low GPA and a low LSAT score?

In that case, you might want to consider very seriously the wisdom of investing money in an application fee for that school. Unless there is something extraordinary in the personal background to overcome those two disadvantages, you may simply be wasting money. The greater the difference between the median scores accepted and yours, the worse your chances are for acceptance.

21. How can I assess my non-numerical indicators?

The GPA and LSAT scores are the most important indicators in the law school admissions process. Other significant achievements are also important, but you have to interpret them not only in light of your own background but also in light of the backgrounds of those against whom you will be competing. Most of the people who are successful in applying to law school not only have good LSAT scores and GPAs, but they also have some additional dimension: extracurricular activities, employment experience, unusual personal history, special talent, or other achievements. This is the rule, not the exception. So as you measure your own numerical credentials against the standard published by a particular law school, keep in mind that most of the people who applied to that school had other significant achievements as well. Nevertheless, don't underestimate yourself. Be sure to include those factors that make you an individual.

22. Is it important to attend an ABA-accredited law school?

Each state and the District of Columbia regulate admission to the practice of law. One requirement for admission to the bar is a degree from an approved school. Most jurisdictions defer to the American Bar Association and accept degrees only from those schools that are accredited by its Section of Legal Education and Admissions to the Bar. In those jurisdictions, a degree from a school not on the list of accredited law schools will not qualify its holder to practice law.

23. What about new schools that have not yet been accredited?

A newly opened law school is not eligible to apply for full accreditation with the ABA. Instead, it can apply for provisional accreditation, which will mature into full accreditation if and when the school is fully operational and meets all ABA standards. At that time, its graduates, including those of earlier classes, receive the official ABA stamp of approval and are eligible to apply for admission to the bar in those jurisdictions that require degrees from ABA-accredited schools.

24. What about state-accredited schools?

A few states, notably California, accredit law schools that do not also have ABA accreditation and permit their graduates to apply for admission to the practice of law. Such schools offer an alternative route to the bar, but there are some serious drawbacks: first, the bar-pass rate of the graduates of state-accredited schools is not very encouraging; and second, jurisdictions that require a degree from an ABA-accredited law school do not recognize degrees from state-accredited schools.

25. Can I become a lawyer by clerking?

Not any longer. Although there may be an exception or two buried in the fine print of the regulations governing admission to the bar in some states, for all practical purposes, the clerkship route to the bar has been eliminated. Of course, many law students do clerkships with lawyers, government agencies, and judges; but the clerkship is in addition to their formal studies—not a substitute for it.

26. Are any other factors taken into consideration?

Yes. Law schools want to assemble student bodies that include individuals from many different backgrounds, so diversity becomes a factor in admissions decisions. Given applicants with very similar indicators, those whose backgrounds suggest they are in a position to make a unique contribution to the law school stand a better chance of acceptance.

27. Do law schools give special consideration to members of minority groups?

Yes. At some schools, special consideration may simply mean reading applications of members of minority groups with heightened sensitivity; at other schools, formal procedures have been established for handling applications of members of minority groups. At one school, for example, all applications are reviewed by at least one member of the admissions committee, and that reader must make a recommendation to the committee as a whole. Applications from individuals who claim an ethnic or minority group status are reviewed by two readers, each of whom must make an independent recommendation to the committee as a whole. As you probably are aware, however, courts have been asked to review the constitutionality of such procedures.

28. Why do law schools have special procedures?

These special procedures consider three facts: one, members of certain ethnic and minority groups have traditionally been underrepresented in law schools; two, the indicators of ability and motivation may be different for individuals who come from backgrounds that are not like those of members of the majority; and three, individuals who come from different backgrounds can make different contributions to the law school. Again, however, whether these justifications will survive scrutiny by the courts is an open issue.

29. What other characteristics might be important?

Virtually anything imaginable. At those law schools that receive many more applications from qualified candidates than there are positions available, the diversity factor takes on even more importance. Indeed, it is a source of pride for an admissions officer to be able to point to someone with an unusual background (e.g., a nightclub singer, a jet pilot, a forest ranger).

30. What are the top law schools?

There is no single authoritative ranking of law schools, and the American Bar Association specifically declines to attempt one. As you look at schools, you will probably want to consider several quantitative factors, such as the percent of applicants accepted, the median LSAT and GPA of the student body, or the average starting salary of graduates. Any list of the top 10 law schools would surely include the University of Chicago, Columbia, Harvard, New York University, Stanford, and Yale. In addition to those schools, you probably find the remaining positions in the top ten list filled by four of the following: University of California at Berkeley, Cornell, Duke, Georgetown, the University of Michigan, Northwestern, the University of Pennsylvania, and the University of Virginia. A list of the top 25 would probably also include several if not all of the following: Boston College, UCLA, the University of California at Davis, Fordham University, George Washington, the University of Minnesota, the University of North Carolina at Chapel Hill, Notre Dame, the University of Southern California, the University of Texas, William and Mary, and Vanderbilt.

31. Are there jobs for lawyers?

Yes. In fact, a lawyer is never really unemployed if you consider that as a member of the bar, a lawyer is licensed to do legal work and collect a fee for it. Seriously, the job market for lawyers seems to be cyclical. But if you really, really want to practice law, once you are admitted to the bar, you are an attorney and will always have a job (even if you have to "hustle" to pay the bills).

32. Do graduates of top law schools have better job prospects?

In general, yes. The average starting salary of graduates of top law schools tends to be higher than those of other schools, but it is important to keep in mind that an average is just that. A person's standing in a graduating class is also a very important determinant of employment possibilities.

33. Should I go to school in the state where I want to practice?

Not necessarily. A degree from any ABA-accredited school is good in every jurisdiction, so it is not necessary to attend school in the state in which you plan to practice. There may, however, be some practical advantages to doing so. First, professors at some law schools may be more familiar with the law of the jurisdiction in which they teach than professors elsewhere, and this may translate into an advantage on the bar exam. Second, access to part-time and summer employment may in part depend on where a person lives while in school, and this may affect your finding full-time employment after graduation.

34. Do law schools offer specialties in certain fields?

Not really, or at least not in the same way that graduate programs are organized departmentally (e.g., history, philosophy, economics, and English). In fact, the first-year law school curriculum is remarkably uniform across the country. It almost always includes a mix of contracts, civil procedure, criminal law, property, torts, and a seminar on legal research and writing, with perhaps an elective or two. And every law school offers standard upper-division courses such as taxation, constitutional law, accounting, business organizations, and so on. Some law schools offer additional courses in areas such as "entertainment law" or "sports law"; but those additional courses do not really create specialists. For most applicants, it would probably be a mistake to choose one school over another because it offers a "specialization." For more information about law school curriculum, you might want to consult *Looking at Law School: A Student Guide from the Society of Law School Teachers,* 4th Ed., Stephen Gillers, Ed. (Meridian Books, 1997). It is edited by Stephen Gillers, a professor at New York University (NYU) Law School, with a preface by the late Supreme Court Justice William J. Brennan, Jr. It includes Part One: Deciding to Go to Law School, Part Two: The Law School Experience, Part Three: First-year and Required Courses, and Part Four: Special Courses and Course Selection.

35. To how many law schools should I apply?

To apply to every law school that seems interesting would be prohibitively expensive for most people. Instead, you must decide how many schools you can afford to apply to, say 10. For a candidate with average indicators, this means selecting a mix of schools that will maximize the chances of acceptance while offering the richest variety of options. The mix should include one or two "safe" schools at which acceptance appears to be certain. And it can include two or three "reach" school—perhaps top schools at which the chance of admission is less than 15 percent. The rest of the applications should go to schools where the chance for admission is solid. Of course, the application of this strategy will vary from candidate to candidate. For those with super indicators, even top schools are safe. For those with relatively low indicators, there are no safe schools.

36. When should I take the LSAT?

At least fifteen months before you plan to enter law school. The LSAT is given four times each year, usually in October, December, February, and June. Law schools begin accepting applications in October for the class that will enter the following year. So if you take the LSAT in February or June, you will have your score and be ready to file a completed application early in the application season.

37. Can I take the LSAT for practice?

Yes, but don't! You can take the LSAT as many times as you care to, but multiple scores are reported to the law schools that you designate to receive your scores whether or not you want them reported. Obviously, you don't want a practice score reported along with a "real" score. You can easily find plenty of material for practice without registering to take an actual LSAT.

38. How do law schools treat multiple LSAT scores?

Many use the average of the scores. Others may discount a low score if the candidate can explain that it is not a true measure of his or her ability. And some will discount a previous, lower score if a later score is significantly better.

39. Is it wise to take the test a second time?

As noted above, when a law school receives your LSAT report, it receives all of your recent scores. So the decision to retake the LSAT must be viewed in that light. Each year, 20,000 or so candidates take a second LSAT. On average, the results are not very encouraging. Some candidates improve, some candidates lose ground, and many candidates simply repeat their previous performance. Unless you have reason to believe that your score will improve (you were sick or exceptionally unnerved the first time), then it might be better to stick with the first score. Or if you were not adequately prepared the first time, then there is reason to believe that you will improve on a second attempt. Our advice is "Do it once, do it right, and don't do it again." So be prepared the first time.

40. Do I have to say if I am applying for financial aid?

If the question is asked, then you should answer truthfully. In any event, most schools make it quite clear that the application process is "need blind," meaning that your need to apply for financial aid will not affect the admissions decision. Most students need some form of assistance to finance their legal education.

41. What should be included in the personal statement?

Basically, the personal statement is your opportunity to add any information to your application that is not already covered in your responses to the questions on the standardized application form. And it is a golden opportunity! You can explain why you got that failing grade in Russian, discuss what you accomplished as a member of the university senate, or describe your responsibilities in your position of employment. Do not, however, simply repeat what is already contained in your application form. Rather, present information that you believe will help the committee get to know you better.

42. Is the personal statement really important?

From the standpoint of the applicant, the answer is an unqualified "yes." Not only does the personal statement offer you the opportunity to contribute something to the admissions process, but it is also the only such opportunity you have, so you will want to make the most of it. Also, law school admissions officers frequently stress that a thoughtful and well-written personal statement can greatly improve a candidate's chance for admission. As you write your personal statement, keep in mind the three factors that were discussed above: ability, motivation, and diversity. Select content for the personal statement that bears on one or more of these issues.

43. What if a school does not require a personal statement?

Send one anyway. It may be that some law schools do not require a personal statement simply because most of the personal statements they receive are neither thoughtful nor well written and so contribute nothing to the decision-making process. A good personal statement, even though not required, might very well make a favorable impression. And, in any event, no law school is going to reject you because you made the extra effort.

44. Should I send other supporting information?

Yes, but be selective. The introductory chapter to a thesis or a major term paper would provide an admissions officer with information about the author's analytical ability and writing skills. A videotape of a news program would provide an admissions committee with the opportunity to see firsthand the quality of the work done by a candidate who is a broadcast journalist. A photograph taken by an amateur photographer might catch the committee's fancy as it attempts to create a diverse student body. As you try to decide what you should include in the application, keep three important points in mind. One, any exhibit must bear on one of the three important factors: ability, motivation, or diversity. Two, do not overwhelm the committee by submitting a little of this and a little of that. Submitting a lot of extra material, no matter how impressive you think it is, will have a negative rather than a positive effect. Three, make it very clear that the additional material is just that, additional, and that the committee is welcome to review it if they wish—or to ignore and discard it. "Stunts" are risky. Sometimes they work; sometimes they don't work. One candidate submitted the application by inserting it into the arms of a full-size cardboard cutout of a human being with a photograph of her own face carefully trimmed to fit the cutout and a dialogue bubble saying "I'm a real person." It worked. Another submitted a collage of newspaper headlines reporting various injustices with a note attached saying "I want to fix this." It didn't work. Still another candidate pitched a tent in a public park opposite the law school and called the dean of admission on a cell phone to say "Look out your window; I'm here, and I'm not leaving until you accept me" and waved to the dean. It worked.

45. Why do law schools ask for letters of recommendation?

Law schools hope that letters of recommendation will provide them with information about applicants that will help them to make better decisions. A written evaluation of an applicant's ability and motivation gives an admissions committee another perspective.

46. Should my recommendations come from judges and lawyers?

Probably not. In fact, most law school applications specify that letters of recommendation should come from college professors. You should solicit a letter of recommendation from a judge or a lawyer only if the person knows your work well and can make a meaningful evaluation of your qualifications to study law—not just because you happen to know someone who is in the legal profession. A letter of evaluation from a prominent member of the profession is not wrong per se; it's just that a "Star Search" approach is probably not going to yield the best results.

47. What if I have been out of school for some time?

Law schools recognize that it will be difficult if not impossible for some applicants to secure academic recommendations. In such cases, letters from colleagues or employers may be substituted.

48. What about a personal interview?

At most law schools, evaluative interviews are not a part of the review process. Most schools feel that the written application, including the personal statement and letters of recommendation, provides an accurate picture of a candidate. Further, granting evaluative interviews might unfairly disadvantage candidates who cannot afford to travel to them. A few schools do use evaluative interviews. One school, for example, invites candidates whose applications are bordering on acceptance to meet with the admissions committee in order to help the committee reach final decisions on those applications. Of course, most schools will welcome a visit from an applicant who wants to learn more about the school, but that visit does not usually include an evaluative interview. One dean who does grant interviews explains that most don't make any difference. In a very few cases, the dean concludes that the applicant should be accepted (and probably would have been, anyway); in a few more cases, the dean decides that the candidate is just not right for the law school; and in the great majority of cases, the dean just sends the file on to the committee with no comment.

49. What else can I do to maximize my chances of acceptance?

One, as you prepare the application, keep firmly in mind the three factors discussed above: ability, motivation, and diversity. Your responses to the application questionnaire, the content of your personal statement, your choice of recommenders—in short, every aspect of the application—should be guided by those three criteria. Too many applicants go astray because they don't understand or have forgotten what factors are important in the admissions process. Two, present a professional image in every respect. All parts of the application should be typed (preferably using a word processor) and, if need be, clearly identified. Make sure that you read carefully all of the directions and abide by them. Finally, pay careful attention to detail and follow up on every procedure (e.g., proofread the application several times and call to make sure that letters of recommendation have been sent). Also, be sure you follow through. We know of an undergraduate who wrongly assumed that the canceled check to the university in payment for the transmittal of a transcript to LSDAS meant that the transcript was actually sent only to receive a note from Harvard Law School to the effect "We wanted to accept you but can't because Law Services never received your grades and the deadline has passed." The story did have a happy ending because the student, acting in a most lawyerly manner, threatened to sue the Registrar and university unless a letter of apology was sent to Harvard Law School. Upon receipt of the letter and later the processed transcript from LSDAS, the student was accepted.

50. Where can I get more information?

For further information about the law school admissions process and for detailed instructions on how to get admitted to the law school of your choice, consult the publications mentioned above. Also, request catalogues from the schools you're interesting in and visit their Web sites.

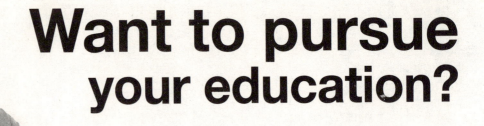